SPELLING RULES, REASONS AND REBELS AS YOU LEARN TO READ

Paquita Boston

Also available, from www.spellingexplained.com, as an EPUB book with an e-reader which can search for a word in upper case only, in order to find that word with its rule.

Thank you.
Thanks for asking and many thanks to all those who helped me find answers.

In 1978 I had no answer for "Why hasn't *his* got a zed?". I was scolded with, "Mum, you are making me learn stuff you do not understand." I promised I'd solve that, along with many more spelling puzzles. I felt sure that real teachers would know. I was just a supervisor of correspondence lessons. However the teachers I asked did not know. When we moved back to Australia I searched through the library of a teachers' college, but still no answers. Teachers told me that they are not trained to explain spelling. They are given some spelling rules, but they are not told the reasons behind the rules. My question to an English professor, "Why hasn't *his* got a zed?" drew a blank. So, to keep my promise, I had to find out on my own.

I began with the Oxford Paperback Dictionary and listed all the words like *cat* or *dog*, the simplest words to read, the ones in which single letters spell a single sound, according to the 'Ground Rules'. The next list built on that first list, after introducing the next rule, and so on, off down the 'road to reading'!

I called the first version *Reading with Rules* and revised it twice. I am very grateful for the personal support I received at a time when the internet was in its infancy, with particular thanks to the late Professor D. W. Cummings in USA. My local librarian Shirley Slatter sourced me books from 'elsewhere', the world beyond Carnarvon. My sister Ally Lynch mailed me relevant books, as gifts, as did other friends — noted in the bibliography.

Thanks for the encouragement from everyone who requested an e-book version. This stimulated further revision and a name change to *Spelling Rules, Reasons and Rebels as we Learn to Read*, which comes to you in print or as an e-book in EPUB so the reader can 'look up' any word, to find it under its spelling rule, rather than wait to meet it on the 'road to reading'.

This project has long been dedicated to the memory of Richard Steadman whose youthful enthusiasm for life continues to inspire me. Also, my thanks to his parents, Trish and Ainsley Steadman. Some years into researching, writing and improving the book, I wondered how much longer it would take. "It will take as long as you need to get it right," they advised. This calmed me, but alarmed my husband, Christopher. To Chris, my family, and my friends, thank you for all the comments and for surviving my code-busting obsession.

Author: Boston, Paquita
Title: *Spelling Rules, Reasons and Rebels as you Learn to Read*
ISBN 978-1-7641223-1-3
© 2025 Paquita Boston

Contact via website.
Sales of print and e-books on website.
Website URL is https://www.spellingexplained.com
By the same author: *The Inside Story on English Spelling*

Preface

This book explains how to read English, how to decode letters into words. It explains why letters spell different sounds in different situations. For instance, S spells four different sounds in *sit, his, sure* and *vision*. There are rules for reading words. Each rule is explained in the book. It is a huge resource because after each rule is explained, the book does not give mere examples, it lists every word a learner can now read. It lists any exceptions to each rule and explains them too. It answers all sorts of questions about English spelling. It does this in everyday language, adds in a few rhymes and fun terms to make the 'road to reading' enjoyable. It suggests dress-ups for events and characters met along the way, photos of which are on my website www.spellingexplained.com. The gallery was begun by professional photographer Rachael Steadman and Archer Steadman. Archer assisted me from the beginning, from a young age, willing to dress up and take on any role to help explain spelling. His enjoyment in, and serious application to, the challenge is evident throughout the Spelling Gallery. There are also many snaps taken by non-professionals, of children in dress-ups along the 'road to reading'.

This book is not just for children. English is easy to speak but hard to read and write, especially if you are dyslexic, autistically logical or used to your own, more readable language, like Italian.

I have tried to eliminate typing errors. Please send feedback. Let me know of any words I have not listed and I will list them, with their reading rules, and the reasons behind the rules, on my website.

Feedback and comments are welcome, via my website. Earlier versions prompted much comment. For example, in Carnarvon, Western Australia, the high school principal, Keith Chambers, said it was '*an extremely valuable reference book and will greatly assist the teaching of reading and spelling.*' The primary school principal, Judith Young, wrote, '*Every day I experience the need for such a text to support the teaching and learning of the English language in the classroom.*'

Dr Tom Burton, Adelaide University, South Australia, thought '*The book's very practical approach to apparent inconsistencies in English spelling and its accessible style will appeal both to learners and to their teachers and parents.*'

Professor Donald W. Cummings, Central Washington University, USA, declared '*Its emphasis on pattern, structure and order is what the teaching of reading and spelling needs. It is a wonderful job of making the rather drab stuff of orthography palatable to teachers and students.*'

Outline of the journey ahead.
The **Table of Contents** is a preview of our journey along the 'road to reading'.
The **Introduction** needs to be read before setting out on the 'road to reading'.
Part One is mainly about sounds spelt with single and twin letters. First rule takes us 300 words down the road.
Part Two is about consonants blended together. We meet some consonant digraphs too.
In **Part Three** we decode doublets, meet Fairy E and Bossy R and make paper planes to learn how to glide vowels onto vowels. We investigate consonant digraphs and Greek Y too.
Part Four takes us right to the end of the reading road with more letter codes — digraphs for vowels long and short and also for diphthongs (double songs or sounds).
The **Appendix** provides summaries of some of the information supplied along the 'road to reading'. It lists all the rebel words, with reference to the rules they break., Then comes a short list of the very unruly, the rascals. It presents 'Loose Lists' of words which share a decoding rule, but occur in a range of lists along the road.
The **Bibliography** lists books I have read about spelling. I refer to some by author's name and page number during the book. It also lists useful websites and high frequency word lists.

Abbreviations in this book include Ab'l for (Australian) Aboriginal; *abbrev.* for abbreviation; AD, after Christ was born and BC, before Christ was born; aka for 'also known as'; BTW for 'by the way'; ESL for English as a Second Language; *f* next to a Feather Word; GVS for Great Vowel Shift; Δ is after an Irregular Verb; § is after an Auxiliary Verb; OE for Old English; OED for Oxford English Dictionary; OPD for Oxford Paperback Dictionary; *PN* for Proper Noun; USA for United States of America, U.K. for United Kingdom; *VS* for normal vowel shift.

The slide show on the **Spelling Gallery,** at www.spellingexplained.com, indicates the fun to be had dressing up and acting out along the 'road to reading'.

Table of Contents

Introduction..6
   The Book is Big. 6
   Finding Your Way 7
   Listening to the Lists..7
   Five main points...8
   The Forty-three Sounds of English Speech 9
   Reading versus Writing..10
   The Rules 11
   The Rebels 11
   Frequently Used Words 12
   Getting Started 12
Part One..14
   Ground Rules, *ant* to *zip.* 14
   The Short Word Rule, *axe* not *ax.*..20
   Orm's Law and Terminal Twins 21
   Zed, 'Sez' and Said 23
   Affixes..24
   Feather Words — *love, son, blue, won* — aka Cursive Casualties....................26
   Shifty vowels — *fush 'n' chups*...27
   Tall Talk — *all, wall.*..27
   Don't Let W Muddle You — *quad, was*...29
   Double Gates and Stressed Starts — *abbot, wetted.* 30
   Terminal Vowels — *balsa, villa.* 34
   Silent letters — *where, there, thug.* 39
   Secret Agent Aitch or Helpful Handy Haitch. 40
   Semi-vowel Y — *by, rye.* 42
   Orm Again — *acne, zebra.* 43
   Plurals— *s, es, en.* 44
   Two syllables and Orm's Law — *apex, legal, zero.* 46
   The Curse of the Dagger — *nasal vs. bison.* 47
   Continental vs. English Sounds — vowels and yods...48
   Rebel Lemons — *alum, lemon, rebel, wagon.* 49
   Fairy E — *hope* vs. *hop* 51
   Soft in *City* but not in *Kitty.*..52
   Suffixes which shift stress and shorten vowels, — *acid, vomit.* 54
   Third Syllable from the End — *animal, holiday, veteran.* 56
   Unstressed starts— *banana, tuxedo.* 59

Terminal Semi-vowel Y — *baddy, any, very, baby.* 60
Dropping Yods —*ruby, sue.* 67

Part Two 71
The Bones of Speech — consonants...71
Clusters — adjacent consonants. 71
Blending Consonants — *scallop, zestful.* 72
Blending Unvoiced Consonants...73
    Two Types of Suffixes — Inflexional and Derivational...76
Bad Blenders — [b], [d], [g], [j], [v], [dh], [z] [zh]. 79
Zorro and Zed 80
Big Blenders...81
Idle E — *able, unstable.* 87
Double gate CK — *cackle, truckle.* 90
Big Blender R — *adracadabra, umbrella.* 90
The Can-do suffixes, Ible and Able 93
M and N, Nasal Consonants — *aplomb, zinc.* 95
Eng — *along, zing.* 98
On Going Verbs and Gerunds..100
King Canute and Silent K — *knack, knuckle.* 103
Silent T and C — *apostle, muscle.* 105
Triple Blends — *strut amongst.* 106
Singular terminal [s] — *dense, copse.* 110
Blending <ed> to Verbs — *boxed, bagged, batted.* 114
Old Fashioned and Worn Down Verbs aka Irregular. 117
Participles participate a lot. 118
Adding Ends to Blends — *acceptability, unpredictability* 122
Silent H. — *exhibit, vehicle.* 124
Secret Agent Aitch aka Helpful Haitch 126
    Digraph <th> — *this, thin*...127
    Ugh! Digraph <ugh> — *cough, laugh*..132
    Chat, chasm, chassis — busy Secret Agent H...133
    Ship Shape with Secret Agent H..137
    Secret Agent H — *alphabet, telegraph*..141
    Rhonda and Secret Agent H..142
    High and Mighty Secret Agent H..143
    Silent H in initial GH — *aghast, ghost*...144
Silent G with M and N — *phlegm, sign.* 145
Soothing Sonorants and Obstructive Obstruents 146

Part Three..150
Doublets — *baa, beet, boot, vacuum.* 150
    Doublet <aa>..151
    Doublet <ee>..151
    Doublet <ii>...155
    Doublet <oo>..155
    Looking Good, <oo> in Wool..159
    Doublet <uu>..161
Fossil E — *are, some.* 161

Terminal E speaks out — *abalone, vigilante*...163
Silent E in *adaptive, accomplice, advantage.* 163
French Fossils — *crevasse, rosette.* 165
Fairy E — *ape, hope, zone.* 166
Fairy E on Suffixes — *capsule, volume.* 172
No Magic Action in Baggage 177
No Magic Action in Alice...178
Ruts in the Road, <sive> and <tive>..181
Colourful R and Fairy E — *here, hire, cure.* 183
    Sure, Sugar..185
    Tulips mature..185
    Endure Duty..185
    Azure..186
Bossy R, as in *art, fern, bird, torn, urn.*..188
    Digraph <er> — *berg, verb* and *Motherly Other*...193
    Digraph <ir> — *affirm, zircon*..206
    Digraph <ur> — *accursed, urn*..207
    Subsets — *ensure, closure, future, endure* 210
    Digraph <or> — *abhor, vortex*...212
    Don't Let W Muddle You in <wor>!..218
    Digraph <ar> — *afar, yarn*..220
    Terminal <ary> — *binary, wary*..220
Collateral Damage — *award, war.* 225
Suffix <ory> — *accessory, valedictory.*...228
The Return of —*ible* and —*able* — *convertible, washable* 229
The Greek Suffix –itis — *tonsillitis.*...231
Vowels Glide over Syllable Boundaries 231
    Glide and Yap — *bias, violin*..233
    Little Imp, i, — *alias, venial* 235
    Glide and Yawn — *apnea, zamia* 239
    Glide and Roar — *acidifier, vilifier*...240
    Glide and Skate — *abbreviate, unevaluated*..245
Yod Fusions, [sh], ch], [zh] and [j]...246
    Yod Fusion [sh] — *action, vivisection*..249
    Yod Fusion [ch] — *actual, virtually*..257
    Yod Fusion [zh] — *abrasion, vision*..259
    Yod Fusion [j] — *contagion, soldier*...260
The Why's and Wherefores of Wye — *acrylic, acolyte.* 261
English Y — *crybaby, yucky, drying, typifying.* 267

Part Four..270
    Old and New Vowels — *wound* noun, *wound* verb...270
    Short and Long Vowels *A E I O U and Y* 270
    Vowel Best Friends, or Vowel Digraphs. 271
    A Digraphs 273
        Digraph <ay> — *may, always*..273
        Digraph <ai> — *abstain, wraith*...276
        Bossy R and <ai> — *affair, wheelchair*..278

- Digraph <ae>— *brae, Raeleen*..279
- Greek and Latin <ae> — *formulae, minutiae*...279
- French Aero Club — *aerate, aerospace*..280
- The Old Digraph <aw> — *awe, yawn*..281
- Digraph <au> spells [or] — *applaud, vaunt*...283
- An Aussie Assault on <au>...285
- Naughty Daughters are not French..285

E Digraphs..287
- The Pleasing Digraph <ea> — *please, zeal*..287
- Tear-a-way Rebels, — *tear, bear*..292
- Yea! The Great Steak Break Dancers...294
- Ready Redheads..294
- M' hearties! — *hearken, heart, hearth*...296
- Eleven Pearls — *pearl, yearn*...296
- Irregular Verbs with <ea> — *beaten, dreamt, meant*..297
- Continental Digraph <ei> — *abseil, weigh*..299
- German Digraph <ei> — *apartheid, stein*...300
- English Digraph <ei> — *ceiling, weird*...300
- Digraph <eu> — *neutral, pleurisy, therapeutic*...303
- Bossy R and <eu> — *amateur, secateurs*..305
- Digraph <ey> in Stem Words — *convey, they*..305
- Suffix <ey> — *blimey, valley*..306
- Digraph <ew> — *brew, crew*...306

I Digraphs...307
- Digraph <ie> — *achieve, yield*...311

O Digraphs,..312
- Digraph <oa> — *coast, toad*..312
- Bossy R Roars — *boar, soar*..313
- What does terminal <oe> spell? — *aloe, woe*...313
- Digraph <oe> and Ethel — *amoeba, subpoena*...315
- Old English Terminal <ow> — *arrow, yellow*..316
- Who put the [ow] in bow?..319
- Digraph <ou> inside words— *about, vouch*...322
- Cold Shoulder Words — *boulder, shoulder*..325
- Bossy R and <ou> — *arbour, court, your*...326
- Suffix <ous> — *amorous, wondrous*...327
- Suffix <uous> — *ambiguous, vacuous*..328
- Suffix <eous> — *crustaceous, herbaceous*..329
- Suffix <ious> — *amphibious, victorious*...330
- French digraph <ou> — *boulevard, group, you*...332
- R is not bossy Touring in Velour — *tour, velour*..333
- Mother's Country Cousins — *country, youngster*..333
- Gruff <ough> — *tough, enough*..334
- Silent <gh> — *plough, dough, through*..335
- Digraph <oy> — *annoy, tomboy*...339
- Digraph <oi> — *anoint, void*..340

U Digraphs...342

    Digraph <ui> — *bruise, suit*...344
    Penguin Words— *anguish, penguin, suede*..345
  Fossil U — *buoy, built, guard.* 347
Appendix..349
  Stress and the Rhythm of Speech..349
  Consonants — Yods, Obstruents and Sonorants 350
  Vowels and Great Vowel Shift. 353
  Punctuation and Grammar 355
  Affixes..359
  Rebels and Rascals..361
  Loose Lists...365
  Changes to English Over Time 372
  Some Dates and Developments in English and its spelling....................................373
Bibliography..378
  Books 378
  Websites...380

Introduction

The Book is Big.

It's big because it's a sequenced step-by-step road to reading. Words are not listed A to Z because it would take too long to explain how to decode twenty-six thousand words individually. This book groups words which use the same reading rule into alphabetical lists. The lists are sequential, simplest words to read, i.e., to decode, are in the first list. Then words which only need one more rule to decode, and so on. English is hard to read, compared to other languages. Its written words are cryptograms, messages in code, but not just one code. English letters operate, or 'play', according to many codes, under various sets of rules, because English is a mixture of many languages. Pure languages, by contrast, control their vocabulary and stick to their own spelling rules.

We start with *cat* and *dog* words but we cannot list *has* with them because it does not spell [has]. It spells [haz], and we find out why when it is listed in 1-3, the third list in Part One. *Was* is not listed with *has*. We learn why it spells [woz] at 1-15. We relish each list and roll along the road to the next list, learning to decode as we go. The lists are not just a few examples to illustrate how a rule works. If a word decodes using this rule, or this rule and other rules which have already been introduced, then I list it. Remember, these are sequenced lists. For example, *tack* is not listed with *tan* in 1-1 because <ck> has not been decoded. *Chick* is not listed with *tick* in 1-19 because <ch> had not been decoded. *Cherish* cannot be listed with *check* in 2-91 but is listed at 2-96 where <sh> is decoded.

Teachers, do not be daunted by the size of this book. It gives you the necessary detail to explain the spelling of every word. Many children are happy to learn spelling by rote, but for those children who like reasons, here they are. If the teacher wishes, the reasons behind well-known rules, like 'I before E except after C', can be taught, along with the rule — or at least explained if asked for. Sequenced lists provide a systematic way to teach the reading of English, to young or old, human or robot. The lists can be used to write 'listerature': my word for comic books, story books, essays etc. which only use words already listed, words which the reader already knows how to decode, how to read.

Finding Your Way
Start at the beginning and take time to enjoy the journey, one list at a time. Words are listed in upper-case, in capital letters, under the rule they obey. If a word is discussed in the text it is written in lower-case *italics*. Each list comes with a Rule, and the reason for the rule, and adds words which rebel against the rule. Their reasons for breaking the rule are discussed and the very few 'Rebels' without a valid excuse are labelled 'Rascals'.

The book unfolds on a 'need to know' basis. You will not be told anything until you need to know it. So, if you ask "But what about...?" wait and see if it comes later, maybe in a list of longer words or after a few more letters have been decoded. If I mention a word before it is listed, I put it in {curly brackets}. {These brackets show that it's coming later, maybe quite soon.} We need rules to decode and read the words in the lists. We shall get each rule as we need it. A 'need to know' approach makes learning to read easy. We might need to use two or even three rules to decode (read) a word. If you start at the beginning of the book you will be able to read every word you meet in a list.

If you wish to review what you have read about a word, to find it listed under its rule, or if you want to jump ahead and find a word prematurely, try the following.

Look at the examples given in the Table of Contents. Your word might match in some way, but remember, words often need more than one rule to fully decode. Your word might be amongst the Rebel Words listed alphabetically in the appendix, with the number of the rule they break. Use the number to find it in the book, e.g., ARE 3-37, 3-67 means that *are* is a rebel and is discussed twice, once after Rule 37 in Part Three and again after Rule 67 in Part Three. If your word is not a Rebel, it may be in the very short list of Rascals, after the Rebel List. (In tandem with the e-book, the e-reader will find your word.)

Even though each list comes with a rule, you need to start at the beginning of the book to get the full story behind a word's spelling. A full understanding relies on the accumulation of knowledge gained all along the way, along the 'road to reading'.

Sections beginning <u>Not needed but nice to know</u> and ending <u>Now back to things we need to know</u> can be missed. History is discussed, but only to explain spelling. The spelling of English words links them to past events. Therefore we enjoy glimpses of British and world history along the 'road to reading', but they come in no particular order. The appendix gives a time-line of changes to English and its spelling.

Listening to the Lists
We have a reading machine in our brain. It is a living machine, in three parts, all connected. The sounder, behind the left eye, matches letters to sounds and informs the word analyser (or working memory) behind it. We would be very slow readers if we had to analyse a word each time we read it. Luckily for us there is a third part to our reading machine, further on towards the back of the head, called the automatic detector. Each time we read a word it is loaded into the automatic detector, (Lynch p. 10), until one day it is automatically detected. This frees up the word analyser to analyse or decode more words and, in turn, load them into the auto detector. That is why the more we read the easier it gets. It's like playing the piano, when the fingers themselves seem to 'read' the notes. Reading lists of words out loud is like playing piano from sheet music, for the words, like the notes, become automatic. Current teaching methods insist on reading words in context (i.e. in sentences and stories). They also insist that practice makes perfect. Children are expected to practise reading at home and parents are expected to hear their children read stories. Some parents speak English but cannot read it. Some parents can read but do not 'hear the reading', do not have time to check each word as their children read a story. Hopefully they can 'listen to the lists' as they cook or drive. Each list comes with just one new rule and so the whole family can learn to read English together.

Five main points.

Linguists study everything about language. Some study phonetics and break the spoken word into tiny word-sounds, calling them phonemes. Most word-sounds make no sense on their own. Bigger chunks make sense, like *cat,* and other chunks add sense, like *ty* at the end of *catty.* These chunks are called morphemes. The complete set of these meaningful units, morphemes, are called the lexicon of a language. How these words and bits of words and word-sounds are represented by letters is called orthography. These terms belong to the vernacular or jargon of linguists.

All we need to know are the following five points.

First There are 26 letters **but** 43 word-sounds in English.

Second Letters are put inside pointy brackets like this: <a>, <b>, <c>, <ph>, which is easy to remember because pens are pointy and we write with pens. The sounds that letters spell are in square brackets like this: [a], [b], [k], [f].

Third When two letters in one syllable spell one word-sound, the letters form a **digraph,** like <ea> in *teach*, or like <th> in *those*. That's why <ea> in *idea* and <th> in *penthouse* are not digraphs — they are not side by side in the same syllable.

Fourth Word-sounds can be sorted in many ways but the simplest way to sort them is into two groups — **unvoiced,** the nine that are spoken without using the voice box, and **voiced,** the rest. The rest use the voice box. They make our fingers vibrate when placed on the voice box. The nine unvoiced word-sounds are all consonants, made with our breath and lips, teeth, palate and throat but not with voice box. They do not vibrate the voice box but they do blow out tissue paper hanging over the mouth. *Con-sonant* means 'with (vowel) sound'. Some vowel sounds, e.g., *I, a,* make words on their own. Consonants cannot, as they have to be with vowel sounds to form words, e.g., *me, the, am.* Archer feels his voice-box vibrate when saying a vowel or a voiced consonant. Then he shows how the nine unvoiced sounds, all consonants, blow out tissue paper.

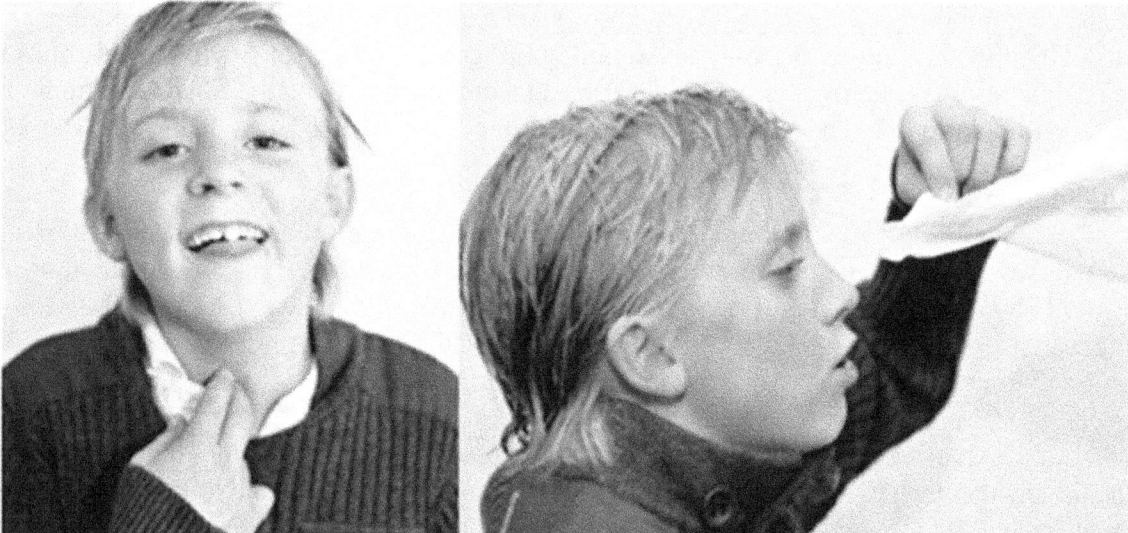

Fifth Stressed syllables are pronounced louder and/or longer than other syllables in a word. When we stress a syllable, we give it strength. A syllable is a vowel sound, with or without one or more consonants. Words are made of one or more syllables. We break words up into syllables so that we can read them and understand them, but at the same time we do not want to leave our words in pieces. Indeed, the word *syllable* means 'latch together' from Greek *syllabe* in which <syl> meant 'together' and <labe> meant 'latch' and it ends in <le> to match other grammar words like *particle* and *participle*. (There is more about stress in the appendix.)

Other languages have other word-sounds, some more than 43, some less. Young infants babble in most sounds of every known language and can recognize any consonant or vowel in any language. However, this ability to discriminate between word-sounds decreases if they do not hear them spoken and by twelve months a child acts as if deaf to non-native word-sounds. After that, most children can only repeat them as the most similar sound in their own language, (McGuinness p. 161).

The Forty-three Sounds of English Speech

Don't panic! Ony refer to this when you need to. You will meet all these word-sounds gradually. I have only added International Phonetic Alphabet (IPA) symbols (between slashes) for those who wish to cross-reference. As most parents and teachers do not know the IPA, I have used ordinary letters in square brackets, here and throughout the book, except for Eng and Schwa symbols.

The Nineteen Vowels are all voiced sounds.

Seven short vowel sounds
[a] is the sound <a> spells in *cat*. IPA /æ/
[e] is the sound <e> spells in *bed*. IPA /e/
[i] is the sound <i> spells in *pin*. IPA /ɪ/
[o] is the sound <o> spells in *top*. IPA /ɔ/, pronounced /ɒ/ in parts of USA.
[u] is the sound <u> spells in *cup*. IPA /ʌ/
[uu] is the vowel in *put* and *book*. IPA /ʊ/
[ə], IPA /ə/, is the small unstressed Schwa sound at the start of *ago*, and the last vowel in *taken*, *pencil*, *lemon*, and *circus*. It has no letter of its own and I rarely use its symbol, Schwa. It's best we pronounce our words as clearly as possible, even unstressed vowels, so that we learn to spell them at the same time as learning to read them.

Five long monophthong vowel sounds (straight vowels).
[ar] is the vowel in *far*, *path*, and *pa*. IPA /a:/
[ee] is the sound <ee> spells in *meet*. IPA /i:/
[or] is the vowel in *for*, *paw* and *talk*. IPA /ɔ:/
[oo] is the sound <oo> spells in *soon*. IPA /u:/
[er] is the sound <er> spells in *her*. IPA /ɜ:/

Note:- Some people pronounce the [r] in [ar] and [or]. They are called 'rhotic' speakers. It can only happen in words using <r>, as in *car* but not for the [ar] in *pa*. It can happen in *for* but not for the [or] in *paw* and *talk*.

Seven long diphthong vowel sounds (bent vowels).
[oi] is the sound <oi> spells in *join*. IPA /ɔɪ/
[ow] is the sound <ow> spells in *cow*. IPA /aʊ/
[ay] is the sound <ay> spells in *say*. IPA /eɪ/
[I] is the sound <i> spells in *idol*. IPA /aɪ/
[oh] is the sound <o> spells in *most*. IPA /əʊ/
[yoo] is the sound <u> spells in *unicorn*. IPA /ju:/
[air] is the sound <air> spells in *hair*. IPA /eɪə/

We shall all learn why AEIOU is pronounced [ay] [ee] [I] [oh] [yoo] in English but [ar] [ay] [ee] [or] [oo] in other languages. Here's a quick summary **for adult ESL students**. In English, these long vowels used to be extensions of the short vowel sounds spelt by those letters all over Europe. Between 1450 and 1650 they changed. The new way of pronouncing long vowels created a point of difference between French, the language which had been the official language of England since 1066, and English. Also, in English, <u> spells [yoo] rather than [oo], as in *use, unicorn* etc. This is because the English could not say the long sound that <eu> spelt in French, a high, shortish [oo]. They tried to copy French pronunciation by saying [ee-oo] but found it easier to say [yoo]. U is called [oo] in all but France and England. The French say [oo] in their own way and only the English say [yoo].

Another difference between English and other languages is with short vowels, the way <u> rarely spells the short [uu] in *put,* but, instead, the short [u]in *but, hut* etc. This is because <a> used to spell [u] but when the English letter spelling [a] was removed, letter <a> had to spell that too. Its old job of spelling [u] was mostly taken on by <u>.

Twenty-four Consonants

Fifteen consonants are voiced, of which three vibrate the nose as well as the voice box.
The Liquid consonants
    [l] is the sound <l> spells in *leg*. IPA /l/
    [r] is the sound <r> spells in *red*. IPA /r/
The Nasal consonants (Fingers vibrate on both nose and voice box.)
    [m] is the sound <m> spells in *man*. IPA /m/
    [n] is the sound <n> spells in *not*. IPA /n/
    [ŋ] is the sound <ng> spells in *sing*. IPA /ŋ/ called Eng.
The Semi-vowel consonants
    [w] is the sound <w> spells in *will*. IPA /w/
    [y] is the sound <y> spells in *yes*. IPA /j/
These consonants have unvoiced mates.
[z] is the sound <z> spells in *zebra*. IPA /z/
[d] is the sound <d> spells in *day*. IPA /d/
[g] is the sound <g> spells in *get*. IPA /g/
[v] is the sound <v> spells in *van*. IPA /v/
[b] is the sound <b> spells in *bat*. IPA /b/
[j] is the sound <j> spells in *jam*. IPA /dʒ/
[zh] is the sound <s> spells in *vision*. IPA /ʒ/ called Ezh.
[dh] is the sound <th> spells in *this*. IPA /ð/ called Edth.
(In think [dh] is better than [th], which I used in earlier books.)
Nine Consonants are Unvoiced, also called Voiceless.
[s] is the sound <s> spells in *sit*. IPA /s/ — Voiced Mate is [z]
[t] is the sound <t> spells in *top*. IPA /t/ — Voiced Mate is [d])
[k] is the sound <k> spells in *kit*. IPA /k/ — Voiced Mate is [g]
[f] is the sound in <f> spells in *fat*. IPA /f/— Voiced Mate is [v]
[p] is the sound <p> spells in *pen*. IPA /p/ — Voiced Mate is [b]
[h] is the sound <h> spells in *hat*. IPA /h/ — No Voiced Mate
[ch] is the sound <ch> spells in *chin*. IPA /tʃ/ — Voiced Mate is [j]
[sh] is the sound <sh> spells in *shop*. IPA /ʃ/ (Esh) — V.M. is [zh]
[th] is the sound <th> spells in *thin*. IPA /θ/ (Theta) — V.M. is [dh]

Reading versus Writing.
We decode letters into sounds to read. We encode words into letters to write. This book tells us how to decode, spell out, read words, using Reading Rules. <u>Relevant Writing Rules</u> will appear at times — of interest, but not needed for reading.

The Rules

Some say that English spelling has very few rules. Bill Bryson in his book "Mother Tongue" tells us that 85% of English words follow rules. However, he does not tell us the rules. Many books give us funny and interesting stories about English words, but this book explains them. By the end of this book, you will have met all the Reading Rules and you will find that the rebels to the rules are numbered in hundreds, not thousands. The rules are not there to punish our words. They are there to make it easier for us to read them. English spelling follows rules and just like footy rules they have to do a lot. Football rules have to keep the players safe, make the game flow, not interfere with other rules and some rules follow tradition to reflect the culture of the game, to set it apart from other games. Rules of any game can only change slowly, usually after much discussion. Rules are reassuring, even when a student is too young to fully understand them. Just knowing they exist is a comfort.

The first thing kids say when asked "Do you want to play?" is "Sure, what are the rules?" Reading should be as much fun as any game, taught with just enough rules to start playing and then the game can be developed with new rules along the way. To be able to give reasons for the rules, when teaching someone to read, shows respect for that person and also builds respect for the teacher.

The dictionary makers decided to use spelling as a code to the past, and they also saw that spelling links "cousin" words together and helps us get their meaning. For instance, *publisity* is easier to read than *publicity* but we would not see its link to *public* and we might think it meant "pub-loving" or "a lease on a pub", if written with an *s*. English is spoken all over the world and so if we wrote it down, as it sounded to us, people in another place may not understand what we have written at all. Noah Webster, the man who wrote America's first great dictionary, said spoken language is like a great river running freely under the rigid covering of winter ice — the icy, rigid, written word.

We play with our language, invent new words and pronunciations, speak in many accents, but in writing we make our message very clear. Rules which cover all situations are general rules, but reading needs a few special rules, too, as do all things. For instance, soccer players cannot touch the ball while in play, but the goal keeper can. Another special rule allows us to drive without a seat belt, if we are reversing. Most airlines have a special rule which lets children under the age of two fly free of charge. Section 51 xxvi of the Australian Constitution says when the Australian Government can make special rules for some people and not for others. Special rules always override general rules. Many complain that English has some really weird spelling rules, until they are explained. So does Aussie Rules football (AFL), e.g., if the ball hits a goal post on the way through the posts, it is not a goal, unlike every other ball game in the world. Explanation? To ensure that a goal is clean and direct, not just a lucky deflection. It rules out mistakes, just like the spelling of *love* and other Feather Words prevents mistakes when reading handwritten words. Reading rules, however outdated, are there to help us read.

The Rebels

Rebels, the words which disobey the rules, usually have good excuses. If not, we call them Rascals. Rebels and Rascals are listed in the appendix, with reference to their place in the book. Rappers are a small group of Rebels which obey their own little rule, a special rule, and we picture them dancing on the roadside in a pattern of their own. For instance, *should, could* and *would* are the only words which use <ould> to spell [uud], their own pattern.

The dictionary committee decided that we should spell our words in such a way that we can read them and get their meaning but **also** stay linked to our past, to all the stories of our culture. They wanted our words to 'carry our culture', which explains why *mystery* from Greek, uses <y> whilst *history*, from Latin, uses <i>, or why *Christmas*, from Greek via Latin, uses <ch> whilst *kilogram,* from Greek, *uses* <k>. Eponyms are one way that our words 'carry culture'. Some carry the names of great inventors, like *Pasteur* who invented what we call *pasteurization*. Words are derived from the names of both good and bad people, e.g., *sadism* after bad Marquis de Sade. Eponyms include verbs like *boycott*, adjectives like *petri* (dish), nouns like *sandwich*. Since personal names do not have to obey spelling rules, many eponyms are spelling rebels, but are rebels with a reason. Other rebels have excuses, too. Some have Diplomatic Immunity. Others have been adopted but not adapted. Many, like *choir*, have been re-spelt by the dictionary committee to reflect their origins. Rebels which are abbreviations of words or slang words are excused because, as such, they do not have to obey spelling rules. Nor do proper nouns and that includes personal names. Proper nouns and personal names which do obey rules have been added to the lists as an added resource. The word *repair* is not listed as a rebel, despite the fact it does not follow its mother *pare*, and siblings *compare*, *prepare*, and cousin word *reparations*. Why not? It is not a reading rebel because it follows another rule, along with *pair, chair, etc.*, which makes it easy to decode and read out loud. The rebel *colonel* is not an eponym and his excuses for breaking spelling rules are too weak to save him. He's a rascal!

Frequently Used Words

We use some words more than others. The words depend on who we are and where we live. The 20 most written words in London are, most to least, *the, of, to, in, and, a, for, was, is, that, on, at, he, with, by, be, it, an, as, his,* (Crystal, 1987, p. 86). Some 'High Frequency Word Lists' are given at the end of Bibliography. Children need to use common words early on, read and write them, so some words are introduced early, in Part One, and then again later, like the word *and* which really belongs in Part Two. *Said*, which is also required early, reappears in Part Four. *Her* and *for* appear early and then again in Part Three. Only about twenty words are introduced early, i.e. out of sequence.

Getting Started

To begin this book, I listed three very little words, see 1-0, and then all the words which are simplest to read, list 1-1. The next easiest became list 1-2 and so on. There are many rules and reasons to explain English spelling but you only need to know a rule at a time. Do not learn all the rules at once. Just learn them as you need them. I will tell you what you need to know as we go along. We go down one road, no branches. At times we have a little look ahead, so that we can read words we see a lot. The other early words, like *she*, come in early if they match simpler words — *she* matches *he*. We meet the rebel *shall* early, when we meet *ball*, because it is the only word in which <all> spells [al]. We meet all the other <sh> words later. When we want to talk about words which we have not yet met, we put them inside {} brackets, which is why, when I say, '*she* starts the same as {*shin*}', I put *shin* inside curly brackets to show we have not met *shin* yet. There are only three types of brackets to remember — the letters <sh> spell the sound [sh] in *she* and {*shin*}.

Part One sets the ground rules, tells us the sounds that the letters usually spell, taken one by one. We all agree that <c> spells [k] in cat. We all agree that <a> spells [a] in *cat*. However, we do not all agree that <a> spells [a] in *dance*. This is because we have one way to write English and many ways to speak it. My English is Australian, mid-way between British and American English. Australian speech has very little regional difference and Australians do not use a great variety of words in daily speech. We used to read some words which we never heard pronounced, and so we said them as we saw them. Radio changed that, and used to sound very British. Through TV and film, we learnt that people in England do not all speak English the same way and we've heard many American voices, e.g., some roll [r] in *car* and pronounce <o> in *sob* as the [ar] in *pa*. Australians do not pronounce [r] in *car*, so it rhymes with *pa*. Whilst we often sing like Americans, especially in *lost* [larst] *love* [larv] songs in which we *sob* [sarb] our hearts out, in Australian lingo, *sob* is still [sob] and *love* is still [luv].

<u>Not needed but nice to know.</u> The further north you go in England the more the vowels in *book* and *spook* rhyme. Also, *dance* and *ants* rhyme up north, but, down south, *dance* and *aunts* rhyme. "Why can't

the English teach their children how to speak? This verbal class distinction by now should be antique. An Englishman's way of speaking absolutely classifies him. The moment he talks he makes some other Englishman despise him. Hear a Yorkshireman, or worse, hear a Cornishman converse, the Scotch and the Irish leave you close to tears and there are parts where English is painful to the ears. There even are places where English completely disappears. In America, they haven't used it for years!" (Paraphrased from 'Why Can't the English' in the film *My Fair Lady.) It's true, "one common language I'm afraid we'll never get" because English is a living language. * The film was an adaptation of George Bernard Shaw's 1913 play Pygmalion. It concerns Eliza Doolittle, a Cockney flower girl who takes speech lessons from Professor Henry Higgins, a phonetician, so that she may pass as a lady. <u>Now back to things we need to know.</u>

Many children arrive at school able to sing the alphabet song to the tune of Twinkle, Twinkle, Little Star,
"A [ay], B [bee], C [see], D [dee], E [ee], F [ef], G [jee],
H [aych] or [haych], I [I], J [jay], K [kay], L [el], M [em], N [en], O [oh], P [pee],
Q [kyoo], R [ar], S [es], T [tee], U [yoo], V [vee],
W [dubel yoo], X [eks], Y [wI], Z [zed],
And now I'm off to bed."
or, if you call Z [zee], the song ends with
"Now I know my ABC, won't you come and play with me?"

Children learn the names of letters from the many beautifully illustrated alphabet books available. They will see that letters can be large capitals — upper-case or majuscules — and small, lower-case, minuscules. They might learn how printers kept the little letters close by, in a case on a lower shelf, closer than the big letters which they used less often. The big 'capital' letters were kept in an upper case, on a higher shelf. Maybe they will hear how the alphabet was invented, and why not every little lower-case letter is identical to its capital or upper-case letter, (see Davies, L in book list). With or without this information they can begin down the 'road to reading'.

Part One

Rule 1-0 No capital letters inside sentences unless they start names, i.e., proper nouns.
Reason. This is a writing rule rather than a spelling rule. Until the 1700's many ordinary nouns had a capital but then printers found it easier to get their metal letters from the nearest case, on the lower shelf, from the lower case. Then they only needed to reach up to the upper case for metal capital letters to start a specific name, of a person for instance. Wooden letters were used originally, then metal, painted with ink, pressed on paper. Ever since then, only proper nouns start with capital letters. *Proper* was French *propre,* from Latin *pro privus,* meaning 'for a private individual'. *Noun* means 'name'. Nouns for general use are called common nouns. *Boy* and *girl* are common nouns, but *Bob* and *Kate* are proper nouns. If you want to brush up on grammatical terms like *noun* and *verb,* see 'Punctuation and Grammar' in the appendix.
Rebels: I and I'M and O.
Reason The words *I* and *O* are written as capitals and so they break the 1-0 writing rule. At first, lower case letters were just miniatures of their capitals. Capitals when on their own spell their names, in this case, [I] and [oh]. The tiny rebel word *I* was hard to read in lower-case, especially back when it was a mini I with no dot on top, just <ɩ>. It was almost hidden by the words on either side. So, to make it more visible it was turned into a capital letter. In *I'm* we are looking at a little hook, <'>, which has hooked out the letter <a> of *I am.* We say *I am* so much that we have reduced it to *I'm.* Does it look like a hook to you? It is called an *apostrophe* [ap-ost-roh-fee] and in Greek it means turn away or hook out.

O is usually written as *oh* but, when on its own, is a capital to make it more visible and more important. O can only be used in prayers and poetry, e.g., 'O lord, hear us we pray,' or 'O rose thou art sick'. *O* is never followed by punctuation symbols, unlike *oh,* e.g., 'Oh, I think it was red," or "We waited for, oh, seven hours," or "Oh! You frightened me," (Bryson 2004, p. 149).

In the following 'ground rules', the vowel letters spell short sounds. We shall learn later how to know if they are spelling long sounds.

Ground Rules, *ant* to *zip*.

Rule 1-1 Twenty-five letters spell a single sound. Unless we are told otherwise, that is the sound they spell, as follows:

<a> spells [a] in *ant.*   <b> spells [b] in *bed.*   <c> spells [k] in *cat.*
<d> spells [d] in *dog.*   <e> spells [e] in *egg.*   <f> spells [f] in *fan.*
<g> spells [g] in *gate.*   <h> spells [h] in *hat.*   <i> spells [i] in *ink.*
<j> spells [j] in *jug.*   <k> spells [k] in *king.*   <l> spells [l] in *letter.*
<m> spells [m] in *mat.*   <n> spells [n] in *net.*   <o> spells [o] in *orange.*
<p> spells [p] in *pen.*   <q> spells [k] in *queen.*   <r> spells [r] in *rat.*
<s> spells [s] in *snake.*   <t> spells [t] in *tin.*   <u> spells [u] in *umbrella.*
<v> spells [v] in *van.*   <w> spells [w] in *web.*   <y> spells [y] in *yellow.*
<z> spells [z] in *zip.*

Reason Long, long ago people drew pictures to write stories. Then they began to draw word-sounds and join them up to make words. How did they write a sound? They drew just a bit of some thing and let it spell the first sound of that thing's name. A was a bit of an ox, just the head of Alph, which is what they called an ox. Then they turned it upside-down, so the horns pointed down. H was a bit of a fence or hedge, in those days called a Het. H is two posts and one rail of a Het. Each letter has a story. Lyn Davies tells each story in her book *A is for Ox*, listed in my bibliography. When people wanted to write with small letters some of the letters changed, like A, which became <a>, and H, which became <h>, but when O was written small, <o>, it did not change. If big, upper-case letters are used or small, lower-case letters are used, they still spell the same sounds.

In order to start reading we need simple decoding rules, ground rules. We can add more rules later for decoding more than just short vowel sounds, for reading additional consonants and for other ways to code word-sounds. If students make their own ground rules alphabet book, please ensure that illustrations show that <u> spells [u] as in *umbrella*. We do not want a picture of a unicorn, not yet!

Note: Two letters, <c> and <k> spell the same sound, [k].
Reason The Romans used <c> to spell [k] in their language which was Latin. They used <k> to spell [k] in the Greek words that they adopted into Latin.

A little driving lesson before we start off down the road of reading.
Readers start by sounding out each letter, like a gear change on each letter. Pretend you are in a car moving a gear stick as each letter spells a sound [a] [m]; [b] [a] [d]; [k] [a] [t]. As you become a better driver your gear changes will get smoother and smoother [a-m]; [b-a-d]; [k-a-t]. One day it will be like driving an automatic car. You will look at the word and your voice will be 'on automatic':– [am]; [bad]; [kat]; you will say. What fun! Then you'll start the next list!

List 1-1 in which letters spell their ground rule sounds.
AM, AN*, AND*, AT, BAD, BAG, BAN, BAT, BED, BEG, BET, BIB, BID, BIG, BIG TOP, BIN, BIT, BOB, BOG, BUB, BUD, BUG, BUM, BUN, BUT, CAB, CAD, CAM, CAN, CAP, CAT, COB, COD, COG, COP, COT, CUB, CUD, CUP, CUT, DAB, DAD, DAM, DEN, DIB, DID, DIG, DIM, DIN, DIP, DOC., DOG, DON, DOT, DUB, DUD, DUG, DUN, FAB, FAD, FAG, FAN, FAT, FED, FEN, FEZ, FIB, FIG, FIN, FIT, FOB, FOG, FOP, FUN, GAB, GAD, GAG, GAP, GET, GIG, GOT, GUM, GUN, GUT, HAD, HAG, HAM, HAT, HEM, HEN, HID, HIM, HIP, HIT, HOB, HOD, HOG, HOP, HOT, HUB, HUG, HUM, HUT, ID, IF IN, IT, JAB, JAG, JAM, JET, JIB, JIG, JOB, JOG, JOT, JUG, JUT, KEG, KEN, KID, KIN, KIP, KIT, LAB, LAD, LAG, LAM, LAP, LED, LEG, LET, LID, LIP, LIT, LOB, LOG, LOP, LOT, LUG, MAC, MAD, MAM, MAN, MAP, MAT, MEN*, MET, MET (office), MID, MOB, MOM (USA), MOP, MUD, MUG, MUM, NAB, NAG, NAN, NAP, NET, NIB, NIL, NIP, NIT, NOB, NOD, NOT, NUB, NUN, NUT, ON, OP*., PAD, PAL, PAN, PAP, PAT, PEG, PEN, PEP*, PET, PIG, PIN, PIP, PIT, POD, POP, POT, PUB, PUN, PUP, RAG, RAM, RAN, RAP, RAT, RED, REP. (representative), REV. (Reverend), RIB, RID, RIG, RIM, RIP, ROB, ROD, ROT, RUB, RUG, RUM, RUN, RUT, TAB, TAG, TAN, TAP, TAT, TEN, TIC, TIN, TIP, TIT, TOG, TOM, TOP, TOT, TUB, TUG, UNCUT, UNFIT, UNZIP, UP*, VAN, VAT, VET, VIM, VIZ.*, WAG, WEB, WED, WEN, WET, WIG, WIN, WIT, WOK, YAK, YAM, YAP, YEN, YET, ZED, ZIP.

You can read these words too.
AT IT, BIG TOP, CUT IN, CUT UP, DIG IN, FAT CAT, A FAT LOT, FED UP, FIT IN, GET AT, GET ON, GET IT, GET-UP, GET UP, GUN DOG, HET UP, HIP-HOP, HIT AND RUN, HIT MAN, HIT OFF, HIT ON, HOB-NOB, HOP IN, HOP IT, HOT DOG, HOT-POT, HOT ROD, HUB-CAP, JET LAG, A BAD JOB, JOB LOT, JOG ON, LAP-DOG, LEG UP, LEG IT, LET UP, LET IN, LET ON, BAD LOT, LOG IN, MID-ON, MOB-CAP, MOP UP, NON-U, PAL UP, PIT-A-PAT, POP-UP, PUG DOG, RAM-JET, RUB ON, ON TAP, TIN CAN, TIN GOD, TIN HAT, TIN POT, TIP TOP, TOG UP, TOM-CAT, TOM-TOM, ON TOP, TOP DOG, TOP HAT, TOP UP, ZIG ZAG, ZIP-BAG. <u>Slang</u> BIG GUN, BIGWIG, BOP, CON, CON MAN, DIM-WIT, FAT CAT, GAL, GOB, GUM UP, LAV, MAC (macintosh), MAG (magazine), MOG (cat), MUT (dog), NON-U, REV, TAD, TOP DOG, TUM, TUT-TUT, WOG (insect), YEP, YOB, YUM, YUP, ZAK, ZAP, ZIT. <u>Australian words</u> BOT, DAG, DAM, DOB, DOG, GIG, GUN (shearer), GUV, HUM, JOB *verb.*, KIP, LOB IN, MOB, MUD MAP, PAD,

POM, RUN, RUM, TAP (of work). <u>Proper Nouns</u>   BIG BEN, GOD, JAG (jaguar car), MED. (Mediterranean), ZEN. <u>Names</u> AL, BEN, BEV, BOB, CAL, DAN, DEL, DOM, DON, ED, HAL, JAN, JED, JEFF, JIM, JIM, KAT, KEN, KIM, LEN, LIZ, MAC, MAL, MAT, MEG, MEL, NAT, PAM, PAT, ROB, ROD, RON, ROZ, SAL, TED, TIM, TOM, VAL, VIN, ZAC.

When a word is shortened, e.g., from *operation* to *op.* the full stop shows that this has happened. Words which have been shortened are called *abbreviations*, or *abbrev.* for short.

*Pep is an example of a word which was once an abbreviation, of *pepper,* but is now written without a full stop, as in *He gave a pep talk, to pep up the team.*

Many abbreviations are treated as slang words. Some later become accepted as ordinary words, some fade away and some are slang forever. **Abbreviations do not have to obey rules.**

*Nowadays an always spells [an]. It used to spell [uun], and [un] too. We use it before a vowel sound and so we say **an** *egg in* **a** *box.* We use *an* before a vowel sound and so we say, '**An** *M.P.* [em-pee] *sent* **an** *S.O.S.*' but we say, '**A** *U.K.* [yoo-kay] *citizen.*' {Later we shall learn why we say **an** *umbrella* but **a** *useful tool* and also **an** *hour* and **an** *honest heir.*}

<u>Not needed but nice to know.</u> Long ago, when very few could read and write, King Sound ruled the land. People copied the sounds of words from each other. Words changed quite rapidly in those days. By the time Queen Quill came along and wrote them down some words had changed forever: *an ekename* had become *a nickname*, *an ewt* had become *a newt*, *a nadder* had become *an adder*. *An apron* has been *a napron* like a napkin, *an orange* was once *a narange* (from Arabic *nàranji*), *an auger* was *a nauger,* and *an umpire* used to be *a nonper*, as in "non-peer", impartial, not paired in any way with any of the players. <u>Now back to things we need to know.</u>

*And is the only word in this list which has two consonants together.

*Up is used a great deal. See {*awake*} for more about this very useful little word.

**Viz.* This is a word we read but do not say out loud, as you will soon see.

**Men.* Little children say *two mans.* Why do we say *men?* Why not *two mans?* New English speakers, big and little, are quick to learn this pattern: – *1 pan, 2 pans; 1 pin, 2 pins; 1 pen, 2 pens.* However long ago there was another pattern. That pattern has nearly faded out. It is only left in a few words – 1 *child,* 2 *children;* 1 *ox,* 2 *oxen;* 1 *brother,* some *brethren.* The word *man* used to belong to that pattern, 1 *man,* 2 *mannen.* However, if you say that often enough you get ready to say [e] and say it for [a] too! That is why *mannen* became *mennen* and then just *men.*

<u>Not needed but nice to know.</u> We say *man* "umlauts" to *men* because it changes its vowel sound. It umlauts to show it is plural. We shall see this again in *mice* and *lice, feet, teeth* and *geese. Umlaut* is German for "switch sound about" for *um* means *about* and *laut* means *sound.* Jakob Grimm, one of the Fairy Tale Brothers Grimm, began using *umlaut* for "vowel change" in words in 1819. He and Wilhelm noticed all the ways people said words as they travelled about collecting folk stories and fairy tales. <u>Now back to things we need to know.</u>

Three words in this list are very old but still in use, from Celtic days, before AD 1. Romans wrote about Celts and other tribes of ancient Britain. In some parts there are Celts still speaking Celtic languages. Look in list 1-1 for *cam* (crooked, as in camshaft), *dun* (a dingy -brown colour) and *tan* (a yellow-brown colour), all old Celt words.

A word which disobeys a rule is called a rebel or an exception to the rule. Some people go around saying "the exception proves the rule" without realizing that *prove* meant *test* when this saying began. Even today we test the yeast in dough by seeing if the bread will rise and we call this proving the bread or the yeast. So, when a word disobeys a rule, it tests the rule. If it has a good excuse for its rebellious behaviour then we cannot say the rule is wrong or useless.

Rebels I, I'M, O, A, OF.

Rebels' Reasons The words *I* and *O* are always capitals and spell the names of these capital letters.

Long ago they spelt long versions of [i] and [o], which were [ee] and [or], but these long vowels changed to their present sounds of [I] and [oh] in the Great Vowel Shift. During the GVS Modern English was born. Before that, A, E, I, O, U were called [ar], [ay], [ee], [or], [oo]. They are still called that in the rest of Europe but in England these long vowel sounds changed to [ay], [ee], [I], [oh], [yoo] and so the names of A,E,I,O,U changed too. The story of how, when and why this happened is an exciting one, as we shall see.

In the tiny rebel word *a*, <a> spells [u]. The little word *a* is used so much that it has become easier to say [u]. This sound, [u], uses fewer muscles than [a]. Try it for yourself. We just have to open our mouth to say [u], whereas we have to raise our cheeks to say [a]. Also, long ago, <a> spelt [u] and <u> spelt [uu] and a runic letter, Ash, spelt [a]. That runic letter was removed from the English ABC after the French conquered England in 1066. Letter <a> had to take over the job of spelling [a] as well as spelling [u] and so <u> helped out and now spells short [u] more often than it spells short [uu].

The rebel word *of* spells [ov]. Long ago the letter <f> spelt <v>. The word *of* is the only remaining word in which this still happens. *Off* and *of* spell [of] and [ov]. *Iff* long ago spelt [if] but, as there was no word [iv], (which would have been written <if>) the word *iff* shortened to *if*. So *of* is the only word left in which <f> spells [v].

Reasons for Rebels *I*, *I'm* and *O* were given earlier.

Slang words do not have to obey rules. We shall only add them to lists if they obey the rules. Their origins are usually very interesting. Some words, like *yob*, are 'Backslang', in this case *boy* backwards.

Words with <s> are missing from List 1-1. Why? The letter <s> spells [s] as in *snake*. However, it also spells [z], as in *has*. In fact, <s> is used more often than <z> to spell [z]. It depends where <s> is in a word. It never spells [z] if it starts a word. If <s> starts a word, it initiates it, and we say <s> is "initial". That is why we call the letters which start each of our names our "initials".

Rule 1-2 When <s> starts a word it spells [s], unless followed by <h>.

Reason Letter <s> obeys its ground rule, <s> spells [s] as in *snake*, at the start of words but not always inside words or at the end of words. There is a big group of words which start with <s> with the next letter <h>. All these words start with the sound [sh]. They are not rebels because they follow their own rule, the rule that <sh> spells [sh]. They are words like {*ship*} and {*shut*}, which you will meet later, when we meet Secret Agent H, aka Handy, Helpful H.

Rebels There are only two other words in which initial <s> does not spell [s]: {*sugar* and *sure*} and words made with these words. {} brackets indicate words which will be listed later, and so we shall hear more about these rebels later. Initial <s> does not spell [s] in *Sean* and *Seamus,* but **proper nouns do not have to obey rules.**

List 1-2 Initial <s> spells [s]
SAC, SAD, SAG, SAP, SAT, SET, SET IN, SET ON, SET-UP, JET SET, SIC, SIN, SIP, SIT, SIT ON, SIT UP, SIT-IN, SOB, SOD, SOP, SOT, SUB, SUP, SUM, SUN. <u>Names</u> SAL, SAM, SID, SOL.

Rule 1-3 Letter <s> spells [z] at the end of short words, words we can say in one short breath.

Reason Long ago people were afraid of the letter <z> because it was the Sign of the Dagger. So they used <s> to spell [z] and twin <ss> to spell [s]. This meant that *hiss* and *his* looked different and sounded different. Also, boys called *Les* were not called "Less" and girls called *Tess* were not called "Tez".

It is still the Sign of the Dagger, three zig-zag cuts made with Zag the Dagger. Old words like {*xylophone*} avoid it by using <x> but more recent words, like {*zebra*}, use it. So we do not always avoid it. We will not be afraid of it if we read stories about Zorro. He carved <z> on walls and doors with three quick cuts of his long thin sword. He was a good man, like Robin Hood, who lived in Spanish California. His Zed, or Zee, struck fear only into the wicked hearts of bullies. He only wrote Z to scare bad people. Dress up as Zorro — see website's Dress Up Gallery — and tell your class mates why we don't use <z> much.

<u>Not needed but nice to know.</u> The letter <z> was unpopular from earliest times, when it was the sign of the dagger and named "zag" or "zayin", meaning dagger. Long ago it crept into 7th place in the Roman alphabet to spell a few Greek words and was then thrown out and only let back in hundreds of years later at the very end of the Roman alphabet. For Greeks, the alphabet begins and ends with Alpha and Omega, but for Romans, with Alpha and the Zeta. It's said to have been the 14th letter of Ireland's Ogham tree alphabet, a letter named *straif* meaning *blackthorn.* Blackthorns traditionally stood for things getting out of control and beyond help and so the Ogham letter meant bad luck and strife.

The Romans ruled the Celts of Britain for four hundred years but their languages did not mix. The Celts only adopted a few Latin words. By contrast, the Gauls, in what is now France, mixed with Roman soldiers and shopkeepers and adopted many Latin words, during their five hundred years as a Roman colony, plus the Roman aversion to Zed. In Britain, when the Anglo Saxons replaced the Romans, they created a whole new language, English. It had no [z] sound until Norman French arrived in 1066. They changed some English [s] words into [z] words, e.g., *dysig* changed to *dizzy*. The Norman French descended from Vikings who, having never been under Roman rule, were not afraid of <z>. But other French speakers still had the Roman fear, or at least dislike, of <z>. They refused to write it and as they were in charge of written English there were no more words like *dizzy*. The sound [z] was written with <s>, as in *busy* and *cosy*. Hundreds of years later <z> was still unpopular. In 1606 Shakespeare uses <z> to insult a character in King Lear: "Thou whoreson zed! Thou unnecessary letter!" It had lots of names. *Zee*, from Greek *zeta*, was one of them and that name was taken to the American colonies but died out in England. Another name for Z was "*izzard*", meaning "*S hard*", for it was a hard sounding <s>. *Izzard* was shortened to *zed*. Zed is still the least used letter of written English. It is not just English which avoids using <z>. In Italian, <s> between vowels spells [z]. In French both <s> and <x> spell [z] between vowels. In German, <s> and <ts> can spell [z], and so <ss> spells [s], as in English, and the German letter <ß> is used in place of <ss> after long vowels. As we see, even today, we all go to a lot of trouble to avoid writing <z>. The names Z Force and Special Unit Z still evoke fear in the enemy. Russian tanks in the Ukraine display Z, even though there is no such letter in their alphabet. <u>Now back to things we need to know.</u>

Q. Weren't people afraid of S for Snake? After all, it looks like a snake!

Ans. No, because the letter S began as the sign of the Tooth! It was not a sharp tooth. It was a back tooth with two round bumps. The letter <s> first of all spelt [sh], because it started *shin*, which is still the Hebrew word for *tooth*. Later on, it was drawn sideways with only one bump, S, and then it spelt [s], (Davies p.98). The letter N began in Egypt as a drawing of a snake going up stairs, from right to left. The neighbouring Phoenicians called it a fish, which in their language was *nun* and, when the Greeks copied it, they called it *nu* and made the stairs very steep which turned it into N. So it is nothing like a snake anymore, (Davies p. 88).

List 1-3 Letter <s> spells [z].

AS spells [az], AS IF, AS YET, HAS spells [haz], HIS spells [hiz], IS spells [iz], 'TIS* spells [tiz]. <u>Names</u> LES [lez], ROS [roz], WES [wez.]

*'*Tis* is an old way of saying "it is".

Rebels BUS, GAS, PUS, US, YES, YES-MAN, SIS.

Rebels' Reasons Words which are abbreviations do not have to obey rules. *Bus* is short for *omnibus* which means "for all", Latin *omni* (all) followed by a suffix meaning *for,* (Cummings p. 83). *Sis* is short for sister, and is also a slang word, which is another reason it does not have to obey rules.

Words longer than one syllable can end in <s> spells [s] if they end 'weakly', like *tennis* in which we say <ten> louder than <is>. *Gas* comes from a word like that, *chaos*, [kay-os].

Pus is allowed to use a single <s> to spell [s] so that it does not look like *puss*, [puus], an old word for cat.

Us comes from Latin *nos* which in Latin spells [nos], not [noz].

Yes is a combination of *yea so,* 'Yea, let it be so', (Hewitt, p. 205). So the <s> in *yes* originally spelt [s] because it started a word.

Rebels? No, ITS, IT'S and LET'S are not rebels. They spell [its] and [lets], because <s> follows a consonant, not a vowel. That consonant is [t], which is a special sort of consonant. Say it with your fingers on your voice box. Do you feel a buzzing, a vibration? No. Now say [d] with your fingers on your voice box. You will feel your voice box vibrate. Look at Rule 1-3 again. It does not say what <s> spells after consonants. The truth is, it can spell [z] after a consonant if that consonant makes voice boxes vibrate. These consonants are called voiced consonants. There are only nine consonants which do not vibrate the voice box. Can you work out which they are by "listening" with your fingers when you speak? This is a good time to find out about Anne Sullivan, a wonderful teacher who taught little Helen Keller to communicate with her fingers because even though she was blind and deaf she could still feel – with her fingers, and with her heart too! There are many books and websites about Helen and Anne. We are lucky for we can hear the [z] in *dogs, pubs, fogs, dens,* and *hams* and we can hear the [s] in *dots, pups, docks* and *its* and *it's*. Now we know why <s> spells [z] at the end of some words and [s] at the end of others.

It's is short for *it is*. The old way to shorten *it is* was *'tis*. The newer way is *it's*. The little hook called an apostrophe pulls out a letter in both *'tis* and *it's*.

Its means "of it" and has no apostrophe because *its* has not had <i> hooked out of it, for *its* was never *itis* – just like *his* was never *hisis*.

Let's is short for *let us*. The apostrophe has hooked out the <u>.

Words with <q> are missing from List 1-1. That's because <q> never appears in English words without <u> after it and we need to know that when <u> follows <q> it spells [w].

Rule 1-4 The letter <q> is always followed by <u> and together they spell [kw].

Reason A very old word *gwen* meant 'woman' and in England it changed to *cwen* for 'queen', [kween]. However, when the French invaded, they said "You can't spell [kw] like that!" They used <u> to spell [w] and <q> to spell [k], because the French do not like <k>. The French ruled England for hundreds of years and imposed their way of spelling on to the English language. At first <u> spelt [w] in France and then it went silent. Words which arrived from France after that had silent <u> after <q>. So these are rebels to rule 1-4.

Rebels include {LIQUORICE, QUICHE and QUEUE; LIQUOR, BOUQUET and MOSQUITO and all words ending with QUE, like ANTIQUE}. We shall hear more about each of these words later.

List 1-4 <qu> spells [kw]
QUID, QUIN, QUIP, QUIT, QUIZ, QUOD.

All the words which use <u> to spell [w] are what I call Penguin Words. We shall meet them all on our 'road to reading'. You can see Penguin U in the website's Dress Up Gallery.

There is only one letter which spells more than one sound. That letter is <x>. It was not in the Ground Rules at 1-1 because what it spells depends where it is in a word. At the end of a word it spells [k] and [s], blended together, [ks]. When a letter ends a word, we call it terminal. Terminal <x> spells [ks], as in *ox* and *fox*.

Rule 1-5 Terminal <x> spells [ks].

Reason This is the sound that <x> spelt in the west of Greece, nearest to Rome. Maybe the Romans said "Let's use this letter from Greece. It is easy to carve and saves us carving two letters."

List 1-5
BOX, BOX IN, BOX UP, COX, FIX, FIX UP, FOX, FOX *verb.*, HEX, LAX, MAX *abbrev.*, MIX, NIX, OX, POX, SEX, SIX, TAX, TUX *abbrev.*, VEX, WAX. <u>Names</u> MAX, REX, SAX, TEX.

The Short Word Rule, *axe* not *ax*.

Over time, the nouns, adjectives, adverbs and verbs of a sentence have all become at least three letters long, except for *ox, do, go, be, am* and *is. Ox* is a noun which stayed short. The others are verbs which were longer but shrank right down to just two letters. Some words, like *axe*, added silent <e> in order to gain three letters, while others, like *egg*, repeat the last letter.

Other types of words can be as long or as short as they like. What are the other types? There are the articles *a, an* and *the*. Examples of prepositions are *in, on* and *at*, conjunctions include *as* and *if*, and there are pronouns like *I, me, my* and *mine*. Oh, and interjections like *Ah! Oh!* and *Wow!* As you can see, these sorts of words can be shorter than three letters, or longer.

Who made the rule that important words, the nouns and verbs, the adjectives and adverbs, have to have at least three letters? No one announced it. All the important words have just sorted themselves out this way. *Axe* was the last noun to join in. It used to be *ax* but after 1885 it gave in and conformed and added a silent <e> as you can see in dictionaries after that date. *Ox* still hasn't conformed. It can be traced back to the prehistoric language from which we think many languages spread, west across Europe, and also east across Asia, as far as India. We call it the Indo-European language. It's extinct now. Many languages started, but this one spread far and wide. *Ox* is a very old word, a 'living fossil', one of the first words to be written. *Axe* is just as old, but modernized by adding an <e>.

The verbs *to be* and *to do* and *to go* are used more than any other verbs. They have been shortened over time, from *beon, beom, beo, bist, be-eth*, to *be; eom, eam* to *am; est, ist* to *is; don, doth, doeth* to *do; gan* to *go.* All except *are* have shrunk down to two letters.

The Short Word Rule

Rule 1-6 All verbs, nouns, adjectives and adverbs have three or more letters except for the noun *ox* and the verbs *to be* and *to do* and *to go*.

Reason See above. Three letters or more ensures that nouns, adjectives, verbs and adverbs stand out on the page. The reason that *ox* has not conformed is maybe that it has two letters but three word-sounds—[oks]. *Axe* also has three word-sounds and it took a long time to obey the rule. We use the verb *to be* when we say *I am, you are, he is, she is, we are, you are, they are*. Also, when we say *I shall be, you will be, he will be* or *I was, he was, you were* and so on. We could write *are* with just two letters, *ar*, because as part of the verb *to be*, it does not have to obey the Short Word Rule. However, *are* hangs on to its silent <e>, (maybe to show it has shrunk down from the olden days words *aron* and *art*. Maybe, if it shrank anymore, it would look too much like *or.*) This is the first of many words in which <ar> spells [ar] and we shall meet them all later.

Please Note: Your teacher might decide to take you on a shortcut at this stage because now you know that <ar> spells [ar] you can read words like *ark, arm, bar, bark, etc* but you can't read *chart, sharp, large, quart, warm, arthritic, etc.* and many other words in which <ar> spells [ar]. If you take a shortcut, you still need to double back and go the long way or else you will miss out on how to decode <ch>, <ge>, <sh>, <th> and so on.

List 1-6

As we know, AM spells [am], IS spells [iz] and OX spells [oks].

Now we know that ARE spells [ar].

As we shall see {BE} spells [bee], {DO} spells [doo] and {GO} spells [goh].

Rebels? Are the words we sing for musical scales rebels? No, *do, re, mi, fa, so, la, ti*, do not disobey the Short Word Rule because they are all abbreviations, clipped from the words in a medieval hymn to which the notes were sung. Abbreviations do not need to obey rules. Babies are also allowed to break the rules it seems, in their own language, baby talk: *ma, pa. Jo* and *An* can break the Short Word Rule too because Proper Nouns need not conform to rules. The little word *id* does not break the Short Word Rule because it comes from "it" in Latin, a pronoun. Psychologists use it to describe the unconscious instinctual force in each of us, each individual's 'it' factor. The word game Scrabble quotes lots of two letter words from a 1998 Chambers dictionary but these words are either very foreign or Scottish or obsolete or misspelt names of the letters of the alphabet, e.g., *es* for the letter S, which we know would spell [ez], not [es], and *ef* for the letter F, which we know would spell [ev]. Whilst it is fun to try to spell the names of letters it is un-necessary.

Let's call repeated consonants **twins** and call repeated vowels **doublets**.
Vowels can be long or short, as in *hop* and *hope*. Long ago, when English was first written, the scribes put marks above vowel letters when they were long, marks like this ~ or this . Some dictionaries still use them. Sometimes they put marks on top of letters like this to show they were short vowels: ˆ ˇ ˘. Then the English began twinning consonants after short vowels, if they were stressed. Syllables in short words are all stressed, are all important. In longer words of two syllables, the English stressed the first one.
In about 1150, nearly a hundred years after England was conquered by Normans, from Normandy in France, a Norman scribe noticed this way the English followed short, strong vowels with twins. He made a note of it in his book and, on the cover, he wrote 'Ormulum', which meant 'Orm's' — in other words, 'This book belongs to Orm'. So we know his name and although he did not invent the rule, he did write it down. As far as we know, it is the first English spelling rule to be recorded, and we call it Orm's Law.

Orm's Law and Terminal Twins

Rule 1-7 Orm's Law: Twin consonants spell a single sound and follow a short, stressed vowel. They spell their ground rule sounds.
Reason As explained above, this meant vowel letters followed by twin consonants spelt short, stressed vowels. The consonant was said once, not repeated. We can think of the twin consonants as double gates, a strong barrier which blocks the vowel behind from spreading into a long sound. If the vowel in a stressed syllable was short, then scribes twinned the following consonant, as in *sitt, sett, annd, unnder*, (Crystal, p. 126). Although most twins have since been dropped, some remain. Although <s> can spell [z], terminal<ss> always spells just [s]. Scribes got tired of twinning terminal consonants after short vowels and only did so if necessary — necessary to obey the Short Word Rule, necessary to ensure <s> spells [s] and not [z], necessary to ensure that <f> spells [f] and not [v], because <f> used to spell [v] and only <ff> spelt [f]. Sometimes twins are necessary to differentiate words, like *set* and *sett*; *put* and *putt*.
Rebels BASS [bays]; PASS. For TALL, ALL, BALL, etc., see Rule 1-14 for explanation.
Rebels' Reasons When we talk about a *bass* singer, a singer who sings down low, at the base of musical pitch, we pronounce it exactly like *base* [bays] but write it *bass* in honour of the great Italian *basso* singers. There is a fish called a *bass* fish and this is not a rebel word. It spells [bas] and is in the next list. Some people say *pass* spells [pas] and some say it spells [pars]. Why? Generally the original sharp [a] vowel was softened to [ar] under French influence which was stronger in the south of England around London. Some even say the London cockneys were the first to exchange [a] for [ar].

<u>Not needed but nice to know</u>. Some twins are never terminal, some rarely and three often. Not all short vowels spelt with one letter are followed by twins because Orm's Law has been weakened. Scribes stopped twinning at the end of most words, but continued to twin inside words after short vowels, which is why we write, *peg* but *pegging*. Some words still obey Orm's Law entirely, especially words ending in <ll>, <ss>, and <ff>. You will meet rules for when to use <ll> and when to use <l> at the end of a word, because for <l> is still in the process of change. The change from <ll> to <l> is happening faster in USA than in U.K. and Australia. Although an English twin spells the same sound as its single letter, this is not always so in other languages. In Welsh <ll> spells an [l] without any vibration of the voice box, so it is light and unvoiced, said with lots of breath coming out both sides of the tongue curled up against the palate. Welsh <ff> spells [f] but <f> spells [v]. Words never end in <cc>, <hh>, <jj>, <kk>, <mm>, <pp>, <qq>, <vv>, <ww>, <xx> or <yy>. Also, very few end in <bb>, <dd>, <gg>, <nn>, <rr>, <tt> and <zz> — usually just

to make words obey the Short Word Rule, as in *add, ebb, odd, egg* and *inn*. We shall meet *err* later. <u>Now back to things we need to know when reading.</u>

Terminal twins come after short vowel sounds spelt with one letter, i.e. [a], [e], [i], [o], [u] and [uu], but not all short vowel sounds spelt with just one letter are followed by twins.

List 1-7 Terminal twins.
ADD, BASS, BELL, BELLE*, BILL, BOLL, BUFF, BUTT, BUTT IN, BUZZ, BUZZ OFF, CUFF, CULL, CUSS, CUT OFF, DELL, DILL, DOFF, DOLL, DOSS, DUFF, DULL, EBB, EFF, EGG, BAD EGG, EGG-CUP, EGG ON, FELL, FILL, FILL IN, FILL UP, FIZZ, FOB OFF, FUSS, FUSS-POT, FUZZ, GAFF, GAFF, GILL, GUFF, GULL, HELL, HILL, HISS*, HUFF, HULL, ILL, I'LL*, JAZ, JELL, JINN, JIZZ, KILL, KILL OFF, KISS, LASS, LESS, LET OFF, LOLL, LOSS, AT A LOSS, LUFF, LULL, MASS, MATT, MESS, MID-OFF, MILL, MISS, MITT, MOSS, MUFF, MULL, MASS, MUSS, MUSS UP, MUTT, NILL*, NULL, ODD, OFF, PELL MELL, PILL, PISS, PISS OFF, POLL, IF POSS., PUFF, PUTT, QUELL, QUILL, QUOLL*, RILL, RIP OFF, RIP-OFF, ROLL, ROLL ON, ROLL OFF, ROLL UP, RUB OFF, RUFF, SASS, SELL, SELL OFF, SETT, SILL, TELL, TIFF, TILL, TIP OFF, TIP-OFF, TOFF, TOLL, TOSS, UNLESS, WELL, WELL IN, AS WELL AS, WELL OFF, WILL, YELL.
<u>Names</u> ANN, BESS, BIFF, BILL, JEFF, JILL, KELL, NELL, RIPP, ROSS, RUSS, TESS, TODD.

Belle ends in a silent <e> to tell us it means a beautiful girl or woman, not the bell we ring for school. *Belle* is an adjective in French. The French adjective for a beautiful boy or man is "beau". They have both been turned into nouns (the *belle* and the *beau* of the ball). They are not adjectives in English. In fact the only adjective which is different for male and female in English is *blond* and *blonde*.

Hiss spells [his], meaning hiss like a snake, and *his* spells [hiz], as in 'his hat', as we already know.

I'll spells [Il] because it is short for *I will* or *I shall*. The little hook has hooked out <wi> or <sha>.

Quoll has become a general word for native cat but was adopted from the Guugu-Yimidhirr Ab'l language name for just one sort of spotted marsupial, (Blake, p. 103).

*We no longer use the Old English word *nill*, the opposite of *will*. "Will you, nill you, I will marry you," meant "Want to or not, I will marry you."

Rule 1-8 Terminal <ss> spells [s] and follows short stressed vowels spelt with one letter.

Reason These words obey Orm's rule for writing short vowels.

Rebels BASS (in music), GROSS

Rebels' Reasons Cummings p. 403 says that *bass* and *gross* are the only two words in which <ss> follows a long vowel sound. When *bass* spells [bas] it is a fish, but it can also spell [bays] and then it means 'low'. A *bass* singer sings down low, at the base of musical pitch, and so we pronounce it exactly like *base* [bays] but write it *bass* in honour of the great Italian *basso* singers. *Gross* spells [grohs] because it comes from the Old French word for large, *grosse*. It can be used to mean 144 items or 'a dozen dozen' based on the old French *grosse douzaine* or 'large dozen'. If spelt *grose* it would spell [grohz], rhyming with *hose* and *grows*. So the French spelling is used.

Where is *pull*? In the next list, because *pull* does not spell [pul].

Old Ways in Olden Days.

Rule 1-9 Long ago <u> spelt [uu], and still does in a few words.

Reason It was [v] said without using lips and teeth. The following word are always said the old way. Some people, especially up north in England, say many more words the old way. The vowel [uu] is a short vowel sound — <u> spells two short sounds, [u] and [uu].

List 1-9 <u> spells [uu]
BULL, FULL*, PULL, PUT, PUSS-CAT.

*Sometimes *full* is reduced to *ful* and added onto words, like *wilful, fitful,* but <ful> still spells [fuul].

Zed, 'Sez' and Said
Rule1-10 The Terminal Zed Rule: English words do not end in a vowel followed by <z>. Zed twins, <zz>, always follow a short one-letter vowel.
Reason When <z> is used, which is not often, it follows Orm's twinning rule.
Rebels FEZ, QUIZ and VIZ, {WHIZ, TOPAZ}
Rebels' Reasons *Fez, quiz* and *viz* are all foreign words which have been adopted into the English language but their spelling has not been adapted. In other words, their letters have not been changed to fit English spelling rules. These words are 'adopted but not adapted".
We call it 'diplomatic immunity' when foreign diplomats do not have to obey Australian laws inside their own embassies. We let some foreign letters disobey English spelling rules inside their own words.

Not needed but nice to know. *Viz.* is a faulty abbreviation of *videlicit*, Latin for *namely*. In fact we never read out "viz". Instead, we always say "namely". Someone copied a short hand squiggle thinking it was <z>, from a speech Cicero made around 60 BC. Marc Tiro was employed to write his speeches. He used his own shorthand — 4,000 symbols. One of these symbols was mistaken at a later date for a <z>. *Quiz* is made from Latin words, *quis quid*. We shall meet two more rebels which end in a single <z>, *whiz* and *topaz*. Some slang words are rebels too, e.g., *coz,* short for 'cousin' or 'because', *biz* for 'business', *schnoz* for 'nose'. Now back to things we need to know.

Eye Dialect Rebels
Have you ever seen SEZ in comic books? Maybe you have seen "FOO WOZ HERE" painted on a wall. In books, spellings like *sez* for *says* and *woz* for *was* are used when writing dialog to suggest that the speaker is talking carelessly, even though the pronunciation indicated by those respellings are the usual ones. Such use of unconventional spellings is called "eye dialect", because although we cannot hear the speaker, we can see he or she is speaking "funny", in a dialect. Due to the simple spelling, the words appear to come from an uncomplicated or uneducated or casual person.
So the word *sez,* which breaks the terminal <zz> rule, is only used when recording conversations.
We say it [sez] but we have to write it like this:- <says>, unless we are recording conversations such as "I sez to him I sez, if you don't watch out you'll be in big trouble. An' he sez, 'Sez hoo?' I wuz that mad I kooda shook him."

Now that we have learnt to read *sez* we had better learn to read *says,* which is the proper way to write [sez].
Rebel SAYS We know <s> spells [s] at the beginning of words. The sound [ay] is the same as the name of the letter A. So *say* spells [say]. However, *says* does not spell [sayz]. Instead, it spells [sez]. Because we use it a lot it shrank from long [sayz] to short [sez]. As we know, <s> spells [z] after a short, stressed vowel sound.
We say it many times a day: "Who says that?" "He says that." We also say the word *say* a lot but it did not shrink its long [ay] sound down to [e] because it is hard for our mouths to end a word in [e] and in fact there is no word in the English language which ends in the short [e] sound, (Cummings, p. 220). (We also say *plays* a lot, but not as often as we say *says.*)
So SAY spells [say] and SAYS spells [sez]. (*Says* is the only word in which <ay> spells [e].)
A related **Rebel**, SAID.
If you read <sed> you would know exactly how to say it: [sed], like its relation [sez]. However [sed] is spelt <said>. The simplest spelling, *sed*, was already in use, for the Latin word *but*. Normally we add <ed> to show past tense, which would produce <sayed>. Not only do we say this word a lot, we write it a lot and so the long vowel [ay] reduced to [e], as it did in *says,* and the written length of the vowel reduced from three letters, <aye>, to two, <ai>. The letter <i> is often used to replace <y> inside a word, as in *happiness* rather than *happyness,* and this would have produced <saied>. There is a strong English

aversion to using three vowels in a row, full vowels, not two vowels split by a semi-vowel, as in *played* and *owe*. This could be why <saied> reduced to <said>. Not only was the spoken vowel shortened but also the written vowel, which saved time.

The letters <ai> spell the sound [e] in only three words, *said, again, {against}*.

Rebels SAY, SAYS, SAID, AGAIN, {AGAINST}

Not needed but nice to know. The proper noun *Said* or *Sa'id* [sar-eed] is a popular Persian and Arabic name in many Australian families, meaning "Happy". Now back to things we need to know.

Maybe you are still wondering why *says* is not spelt <sez> and why *said* is not spelt <sed>. Letters show the links between words, especially the first letters of a word. So, if we look at *said* and *says* we can guess that they might be linked because they each start with <sa>. If we wrote *sed* and *sez* we would lose their link to *say* and to other related words like *saga*, which is when someone has a very long say, tells a long story. Words link up in this way to words in other languages, too. For instance, *say* in German is *sagen*. Naturally not every word starting <sa> is linked. However, words are linked to each other by their first letters, not their last. It is the opposite for people. As we know, just because we share a first name we are not related. However, if we share a last name, we might be related. Here are a few word pairs for you to investigate for links: *nephew* and *nepotism*; *vapid*, and *vapour*; *parade* and *apparent*.

Rule 1-11 Terminal <s> spells [s] after unstressed vowels.
Reason Such words are longer than one syllable. People got tired of obeying Orm's Laws. Also, they began saving ink and paper, as well as time. As we know, terminal <s> spells [z] because <z> was so unpopular. Terminal <ss> spelt [s], but to save time, paper and ink, scribes let just one <s> spell [s] at the end of words if the ends of the words were less important than the beginnings. English speakers give more importance to the beginning of most words. English words have strong, stressed, beginnings and weak endings, on the whole. Say *atlas* or *litmus*. Even a big word like *hippopotamus* has a weak ending. The vowel sound at the end of these words has shrunk to a short version of [uu]. Linguists have invented the letter called 'schwa' to write that little sound, [ə]. *Schwa* spells [shwar] and comes from a Hebrew word meaning 'emptiness'. So, they write [at-ləs] for *atlas* and [lit-məs] and [hip-o-pot-a-məs]. Words with shrivelled, unstressed endings use <s> to spell [s]. However, not all words with unstressed terminal syllables have reduced terminal <ss> to <s>, e.g., *cutlass, carcass, windlass*, and also nearly all words ending [es] have kept the twin <ss>, e.g., *abbess, actress, mattress*. These <ss> endings are not as weak as <s> endings: *actress* has a stronger ending than *tennis*. We shall meet terminal <s> spelling [s] in words like {*tennis* and *atlas* and *oasis*}, later.

Affixes
Affixes are bits which fix onto stem words to make longer words. Stem words, like *bat* or *do* or *red* or *sit*, grow by adding affixes, as in *batter, undo, redden, sitting.*
A **prefix** is fixed onto the beginning of a word, is **pre**vious to the word. Some words continue **on** by adding a **suffix** on, at the end. Suffix means "on-fix". A word without a prefix or a suffix is just a bare stem, a stem word. Some stems cannot stand alone anymore, are no longer **free stems.** They are called **bound stems,** e.g., *fy* in *defy* is a bound stem. Some words are made by joining up two separate words. They are 'compounded' or combined into one word and called **compound words**.
Two or more consonants side by side are called a **cluster** and they can cluster inside stem words, or where words and affixes join or where stem words join to make compound words.
All consonants, except for <s> and <f>, spell the same word-sounds whether single or twinned.
Relevant Writing Rules.
Writing Rule Twins are not welcome in clusters of three or more. This is only a weak rule.

Reason It is probably just to make words easy to read. Prof Cummings, on p. 77, shows that we avoid twins in clusters of three or more. We write *seven, seventh* but *eight, eighth* not *eightth, welcome* not *wellcome, also* not *allso, already* not *allready, fulsome* not *fullsome*.
Writing Rule Letter <l> is always twinned at the end of single-syllable words after a vowel spelt with one letter.
Rebels NIL and {GEL} are the only common single-syllable words which disobey this rule.
Rebels' Reasons They are both abbreviations, of *gelatine* and of *nihil* (Latin).
Writing Rule Suffixes cannot end in <ll>.
Reason The only time we see <ll> at the end of words of more than one syllable is if they are made of two separate whole words e.g., *blackball, standstill, install,* or a whole word and prefix e.g., *unwell*.
Rebels All words ending in <ful>, FITFUL, RUEFUL, WILFUL, {USEFUL, FEARFUL}.
Rebels' Reason *Full* is treated as a suffix when added to stem words. Note how *will* has dropped <l> to avoid twins in a cluster in *will full*. That is why we do not write *willful*.
Rebels? UNTIL, INSTIL and DISTIL? No, words ending in <til>, e.g., *until, instil* and *distil* are not rebels. These are whole English words, without prefixes. *Instil* and *distil* evolved from foreign words with prefixes, and were adopted into English as stem words. English never had a stem word *still* with its old foreign meaning of 'drip'. *Until* evolved from two Old English words and became one stem word. The two old words, *und* and *til*, are now obsolete, gone from the English language, extinct.
Is FULFIL a rebel? No. Due to the weak rule against twins in clusters, *full*, in *fulfil*, is written with a single <l> to avoid the cluster <llf>. Now that *fulfil* is no longer made of two whole words, it cannot end in <ll>.
Rebels THEREWITHAL, WHEREWITHAL and WITHAL
Rebels' Reasons The final word in the compounds *therewithal, wherewithal* and *withal* was originally *all*. No other compound words end in <all> or in <al>. Opinion is that by dropping the final <l> the compound is secure, cannot be mistaken for separate words, as in 'Where, with all that luggage, does she plan to go?" Contrast with "She has the wherewithal to hire a van and take it to her lovely new home, withal." Quite different meanings. Note:- In these words <al> spells [orl], whereas terminal <al> in other words spells unstressed [al] or [əl] as in *animal*, except for the British spelling of *appall*, which is APPAL, see 1-14.
Writing Rule Only twin <ff> spells [f] at the end of a word after a vowel spelt with one letter. So, it is *huff* but *leaf,* not *leaff*.
Rebels {CHEF, APERITIF, SERIF, CALIF, CLEF}; IF and OF.
Rebels' Reasons They have all been adopted from French but not adapted to English spelling rules except for *if* and *of*. *If* was once spelt *iff*. It was spelt *iff* in Orm's 1150 Ormulum and *iff* in other old books, because <ff> spelt [f] and <f> spelt [v]. There is no word [iv] and so about 300 years ago it was decided a single <f> was all that was needed to write [if], and was quicker than writing *iff*.
Off and *of* both began as one English word, *of,* back when <f> spelt [v]. This word meant *origin,* whether still there or away from that origin, just as Ally is still "Ally of the Glen" although she now lives elsewhere. Then when a thing was taken from its first place, as when it went away, folk started saying that it was 'of the ship' but it went 'off the ship', until there were two separate words. So we let *of* disobey the Terminal F rule so that we can tell it apart from *off*. We cannot write *ovv* for [ov] because, as we shall see, <v> cannot end a word, and also <vv> is not allowed because it looks like <w>.
Writing Rule Triplets are not used in English. This is a strong rule. Hyphens are used to keep some words within the law: e.g., "*The cat is bell-less.*" {Later we'll see *full* become *fully* not *fullly* to prevent triplets.}
Reason Three letters in a row are hard to distinguish, especially if they consist mainly of down strokes like <l> and <f>, handwritten in the old style, *lll, fff*. Return to Reading Rules.

The dot, on <i>, is called a tittle. It did not appear on English <i> until the fifteenth century. Irish writers did not use it and even today you can see Irish place names on Ireland's road signs without dots. It is thought that the phrase "to a T" derived from the word 'tittle". We "dot our *i's* and cross our *t's"* when we pay attention to every detail of a task.

Feather Words — *love, son, blue, won* — aka Cursive Casualties.

Rule 1-12 Old <u> before *n, m* or *v* is replaced by <o>.

Reason The scribes of Old England wrote with the rounded letters introduced by the Irish missionaries who brought Christianity back to England. This Insular Style is still used to write Irish Gaelic, (Pyles 1993 p. 49). Each pen was the shaft of a strong feather, sharpened and dipped in ink. Scribes after 1066 used the quicker, cursive style. William the Conqueror insisted they write faster and faster to complete the Domesday Books which held the records of his new English estates. They rounded angular letters, to make them easier to write. This meant that <v> got a round, hand-written bottom, like <u>. They joined the letters of each word. This made the letter *u* before *n, m* or *v* very hard to read. For instance, <wun> resembled <wm> in cursive. The scribes decided amongst themselves to write each <u> before *n, m* or *v* as <o> but still read it as a <u>, (Cummings 1988, p. 246). List words in which <o> should really be <u> will be marked like this: *f*, to show that it is a feather word, written by the scribes with their feather pens. (Latin for *feather* is "penna".)

Not many people could write and so a few scribes could make this decision for a nation — even kings could not write, (Crystal, 1987 p. 187). Scribes in various regions made additional decisions but this one has stuck. An <o> for <u> only occurs in old words. At this time <u> spelt [uu]. The letter <u> now spells [u] unless we are told otherwise, although in some parts it still spells its old sound [uu]. Australians who come from the north of England still say [hiz] [suun] [wuun] for *his son won,* [hiz] [sun] [wun]. The following are our first Feather Words. This is a gentle name for words which are damaged by cursive handwriting. So I also refer to them as Cursive Casualties. We shall meet many more Cursive Casualties along the 'road to reading'.

Try writing them without <o>, with <u> instead, in cursive 'running writing'. For instance, *wun*. Can you read it? Is it easier with <o> instead of <u> in *won*?

List 1-12

SON* *f* [sun], TON *f* [tun], WON *f* [wun].

**Son* [sun] meant a boy child, for in the olden days the *sun* was called *sol* or *sigel* or *the day star* or *suwen* which later became *sun. Sol* has been retained in *solar,* as in 'solar radiation'— sun shine.

There are some feather words which we use a lot and we shall meet them again.

They end with a silent <e> because they are very old. The words used to be longer but little silent <e> is all that remains. For instance, *come* was *cuman.* Then again *done* was *doen* and when it became *done* it was treated like a feather word, as if <o> had replaced <u>. Now we just read them all as feather words. The word *one,* is very, very old. Before it became a feather word it was *an* — and *un* when the Normans arrived. They said *un homme* (one man) but *une femme* (one woman). This French word for *an* was used for counting and was therefore important, an adjective, and needing at least three letters. So *une* was used. Then, to stop <u> followed by <n> looking like <m>, the scribes changed <u> to <o>, but kept pronouncing it as <une>. In those days <u> spelt both [uu] and [wuu]. So *one* spelt [wuun]. *One* shortened then to [wun], in most places. Maybe you have heard people who still say [wuun]. By the way, <u> in *penguin* still spells [w], and <u> in *queen* still spells [w]. Some people still say [kuum] for *come,* instead of [kum].

List 1-12 continued

SOME *f* [sum], COME *f* [kum], DONE *f* [dun], FULSOME*, NONE *f* [nun], ONE *f* [wun], SOMEONE *f* [sum-wun].

*_Fulsome praise_ used to be 'foul praise', which is why a single <l> is used. It was odiously overfull and offensively insincere praise, (Bryson 2004, p. 83) Now we use it for abundant praise but 'fulsome praise' from an ex-employer may not help you into the next job as it can sound insincere.

Rule 1-13 The letter <v> is never twinned nor terminal.
Reason Long ago, scribes saw that twin <v>, <vv>, looked like <w> and banned the use of <vv>, not just at the end of words but anywhere in a word. When scribes rounded the bottom of lower-case <v> in order to write faster in cursive, it became identical to <u>, except for the fact that <u> hooks on to the next letter down low and <v> hooks on to the next letter up high. However, when they joined to nothing at the end of a word the only way to tell them apart was to look at their little hooks. In order to make the hooks more visible a silent <e> was added. Silent <e> is still doing that job, even though printed <v> has a pointy bottom, for it is still hard to tell <v> and <u> apart when handwritten. This is why we do not write _hav_ or _blu_. So, in English, terminal <v> is always followed by <e>. We can say <e> insulates <v> from coming last. {The letter <u> is very, very rare at the end of English words as we shall see.}

List 1-13
ABOVE* ƒ [u-buv], DOVE ƒ [duv], GIVE [giv], HAVE [hav], LIVE [liv], LOVE ƒ [luv], MOVE ƒ <o> =[oo], I'VE* [Iv].

As you will remember our feather sign ƒ means that <o> in the preceding word spells [u]. You'll remember that <u> spelt [uu] before it spelt [u] and indeed in some places <u> still spells [uu]. So up north in England you will hear folk saying [luuv] for _love_ and [shuuv] for _shove_ and so on. However, words which came in from France had an [oo] sound for the original <u>, written as an <o>, e.g., _move_ and _prove_. In such cases the different sound is shown by <o>=[oo].

{There are 3 more feather words in which <e> insulates <v> from coming last. GLOVE ƒ comes later in a blend list; PROVE ƒ <o>=[oo] later in a blend list; SHOVE ƒ comes later with [sh] words.}

*_I've_. Having met _have_ we can guess, correctly, that _I've_ is short for _I have_.
*_Above_ is our second word of two syllables. We can say the 1st syllable as a quiet little [a] or [u]. We shall hear more about _above_ later.

Rebels REV, GUV, LAV, DIV, {SPIV}.
Rebels' Reasons As abbreviations of _revolution, governor, lavatory_ and _division,_ they do not have to obey rules — nor does the slang word _spiv_.

Shifty vowels — _fush 'n' chups_

We have already learnt that <u> used to spell [uu], like it still does in _put_ and _pull_. But then [uu] shifted to [u]. Vowels do that, change sound. In New Zealand the vowels in _fish and chips_ have changed. Why do I find myself saying 'fush und chups' when I am in N.Z.? For fun? Or to make myself understood? If we were not great mimics we'd never learn to speak. Maybe we mimic to mix with others, to gain acceptance..Some vowels take more energy to say than others — [ee] uses more muscles than [uu] and [uu] uses more muscles than [u]. This explains why some vowels have shifted.

Tall Talk — _all, wall._
Rule 1-14 Terminal <all> spells [orl].
Reason Long ago when a word ended in <ll> or <l> and another consonant, e.g., <k>, this pair showed that the preceding vowel spelt a long sound. In those times, the long sound that <a> spelt was [ar]. So back then <all> spelt [arl]. Then the vowel shifted, from [ar] to [or], after about 1550 but only after [w] or before [l]. Cummings p. 232 quotes Jespersen as saying it reached polite speech by the 1600's which means before that it was considered a lazy way of speaking, because [orl] takes less energy to say than

[arl]. In fact, one hardly has to move one's jaw at all, to say [orl] instead of [arl]. This change from <a> spelling [ar] to spelling [or] changed even further in some words in which <a> now spells [o], as in List 1-15.

Rebel word SHALL is the only rebel in which <all> spells [al]. Here's a 'preview': the letter pair <sh> spells [sh] as in {*shell, ship, wish, dish*}, coming soon.

Rebel's Reason *Shall* used to be *shal*, with a single <l> and the <al> ending was pronounced [al], like *pal*, (Hewitt, p. 186). *Shal* changed to *shall* to match the look of its working partner, *will.* "He will go soon. We shall go too." *Shall* still spells [shal]. The word did not change to [shorl]. Besides, another word spells [shorl]. Is there a *shawl* in your dress-up box?

Q. Are *ballot* and *mallot* rebels? No, because <all> is not terminal in these words.

List 1-14 Terminal <all> spells [orl].

ALL, APPALL (USA) BALL, CALL, FALL, GALL, HALL, MALL, ODD BALL, PALL, TALL, WALL.

ALSO, not *allso,* as twins are not welcome in clusters of three.

Q. What about OFFAL? It does not end <all> but we say [of-orl].

Ans. That is because *offal* comes from joining two words. It began as a compound noun of *off* and *fall,* the bits that *fall off* the carcass at the slaughterhouse. One <f> is removed to prevent a triplet. Now it is no longer two whole words joined up. The first syllable is stressed and the second one, being a weak terminal syllable, is treated like a suffix and given just a single <l>. Now *offal* spells just [of-əl].

Rebels APPAL, {THEREWITHAL, WHEREWITHAL and WITHAL} in which <al> spells [orl].

Rebels' Reasons We shall meet many more words in Part Two in which [a] spells [or], e.g., *bald* and *talk* — but the only time <a> spells a strong [or] before a single terminal <l> is in the British spelling *appal*, and in the three words *therewithal, wherewithal* and *withal.* In USA, *appall* sticks to the Latin origin, *pallere,* to be pale. In Britain, *appal* derives from French *palir,* to grow pale. Either is accepted, also *appalls* or *appals,* but only *appalled, appalling* is correct.

Why did *all* lose an <l> in these words? Look back at writing rules under Affixes, below 1-11.

In some words, [a] shifted to [ar], for instance before terminal <ss> and terminal <ff>. It only happens sometimes. {Later you will see this happen for *brass, class, glass* and *grass* but not *crass*, for *staff* and *chaff* but not *riffraff.*} The North of England shifted very few vowels, possibly because it was far away from the influence of softer French vowels in London. Up north when people say *pass* it rhymes with *mass*. Down south and elsewhere *pass* spells [pars].

PASS spells [pars] and is the first word we meet in which <ass> spells [ars].

In the website's Photo Gallery you can see Saxons arriving in Britain, slashing and bashing with axes. They moved in as the Romans left and introduced that sharp [a] sound in *Saxon, bash* and so on. The Angles arrived too. They brought the symbol Ash to spell the sharp [a] sound. It looked like the trunk of an ash tree with a few branches. Later it was added to the English alphabet as Æ because it spelt a sound between what A spelt back then and what E spelt.

The last time England was conquered by foreigners was in 1066. The French conquerors made their language the official language of England. They did not use the sharp [a] sound in *dad.* They used the soft [ar] sound in *father.* The French scribes used the English Æ and æ for the sharp English [a] vowel. However, it's gone now and we have to use <a> to spell both sounds. When there were two letters, <a> spelt [ar], which is why <a> spells [ar] in *father.* Its short vowel sound was [u] and we still say this when we say 'a man', [u] [man]. If letter Ash was still in the Anglo Alphabet we would write 'a mæn'. The conquered English changed their speech to gain acceptance from their French conquerors, especially in the south where the king and his court spoke only French — for hundreds of years!. Henry IV (1399-1413) was the first king to use English to rule his people and his son, Henry V, was the first king to write in English, but by then <a> and even <e> was preferred to Ash.

Don't Let W Muddle You — *quad, was.*

Back when <a> spelt [ar], the vowel in *was* and *wallet, want, wash* was [ar]. We still hear [ar] in these words in parts of America because some of the early settlers left England saying [warz] and [warlet], [warnt], [warsh] and some other words starting <wa>.] Then this vowel [ar] changed to [o], because it was easier to say after [w].

Rule 1-15 <wa> spells [wo] and <qua> spells [kwo], before a consonant.

Reason As we learnt in 1-14, <wa> changed from spelling [war] to [wor] in the sixteenth century because the latter is easier to say. This also happened before terminal <ll>, as in *fall*, also before <lk> as in *talk* and *walk*. Then, when [or] followed [w], it changed to short [o], unless a terminal <ll> kept it long as in *wall*, or before <lk> as in *walk*. This happened in lots of words, unless <wa> was followed by a consonant made at the back of the mouth. For instance, *wallet* began as [warlet], then [worlet] and lastly [wolet]. The vowel was able to shorten because <ll> was not terminal.

As we know, the old scribes wrote *son* to spell [sun], because <u> got muddled with <n>. We have already heard about *son* and other Feather Words. The <o> in *won* [wun] also stops <u> getting muddled with <w>, for <wu> in their old writing looked like a "Triple U". They all agreed that <wo> spells [wu], and it still does, except in a few new words which the old scribes did not write for us: *wombat, polliwog, golliwog, wog, wok*, and the re-spelt *wobble*.

Then *was, wallet, etc.* changed from spelling [warz] and [warlet] to spelling [woz] and [wolet] and a problem arose. "Why can't I write <woz>?" asked a young scribe. "Zed is bad luck," his old teacher warned, "Use <s>." So, the young man wrote <wos> but then the scribes said it spelt [wuz], just as *won* spells [wun]. "You can't use <o> for that is always used to spell [u] after <w>," they said. So he stuck to <a> to spell [o] after <w>. We still use <a> to spell [o] after <w>.

Then he learnt that <a> also spells [o] after <qu>. As we know, <u> spells [w] after <q>. But why *quad* instead of *quod*? Again, an old scribe said "If we write *quod* people will think it spells [kwud] and that we are using <o> to avoid the twin letters <uu> looking like <w>. So if we want *quod* to spell [kwod] we had better write *quad* and remember that it spells [kwod]." Then all the scribes probably chanted, "Don't let W muddle you." When you see <qua> or <wa>, don't let W muddle you! I say that these words have collateral damage, caused by Cursive Casualties. Do you agree?

Rebels WALL and {WALK} in which <wa> spells [wor] not short [wo]; WAG, WAX, {WAGGON/WAGON, {SWAG}, {SWAM, {SWANK}.

Rebels' Reasons Rebel *wall's* excuse is that <all> spells [orl], same as for <alk> which spells [ork] in *walk*. Terminal <ll> and terminal <lk> keep the vowel long. Historically, <a> began spelling [or] when followed by [l] after 1550, see Reason for Rule 1-14. It also began spelling [or] after [w] but then this went further until <a> spelt [o] after [w] but this only happened if <a> was followed by consonants made at the front of the mouth. The other rebel words use <wa> to spell [wa] not [wo] and have their reasons. *Wax* was written *weax* in Old English, so <a> did not follow <w>. *Wag* and *swag* are definitely northern expressions which came in from Norway quite late. The modern adjective *swanky* comes from *swank*, an old regional word from "walking with a swing".

List 1-15 <wa> spells [wo].
QUAD, QUAFF, WAD, WAN, WAS <s>=[z].

Rule 1-16 English words never start with twins.
Rebels LLAMA, LLANO
Rebels' Reasons These two, [lar-mar] and [lar-noh], are "adopted but not adapted" — adopted from Spanish but not adapted to obey English spelling rules.

Not needed but nice to know. The Welsh names *Lloyd* and *Llewelyn* can break the rule for they are proper nouns. In fact, in the Welsh language, <l> and <ll> spell two different sounds. In Welsh, these names start with [thl]. *Now back to things we need to know.*

Double Gates and Stressed Starts — *abbot, wetted.*
Rule 1-17 Orm's Law that twinned consonants come after short stressed vowels, still holds true.
Reason We saw that Orm's rule still holds true for single-syllable words ending in twins for they all have short vowels. The two matching consonants are like a double gate to keep a preceding vowel short. They do the same job in longer words, after the first vowel. Then just one consonant at the end is enough to keep the next vowel short. Orm's Law insists on "double gates" on vowels to keep them short, to stop them spreading, but only needed if the vowel is stressed. English words stress their beginnings not their endings and so a double gate is not needed to keep the second unstressed vowel short.
Rebels See words like *vixen* and *devil* at 1-21 and 1-22. They are all words which cannot obey this rule because <x> and <v> are never twinned — we never see <xx> or <vv>.
Not Rebels ABBESS and POSSESS each end with a strong, stressed syllable, because Orm's Law not only says that twins follow short vowels but that twins follow stressed vowels.

Rule 1-18 The first part of an English word is usually said with more strength than the rest, unless it is a prefix. This is called the Initial Stress Rule.
Reason English began as a German language and German languages stress the first part of a word. Prefixes are usually not as important as the main word, or stem word, and so they are not stressed. They are shorter and quieter than stressed syllables.
List 1-17/18 Use Orm's Law and Initial Stress Rule to read these words.
ABBESS*, ABBOT, AFFIX, ALLOT, ANNEX, ANNUL, ASSET, ATTIC, BALLAD, BALLOT, BARREL, BARREN, BILLET, BATTEN, BOBBIN, BOFFIN, BONNET, BOTTOM, BULLET <u> =[uu], BUTTON, CALLUS, CANNON, CANNOT, CARROT, CASSOCK, COFFIN, COMMIT, COMMON, COSSET, COTTON, CULLET, CUSSED, DERRIS, DOGGED, DOLLOP, DUBBIN, DUFFEL, FADDY, FAGGOT, FATTED, FATTEN, FERRET, FERRIC, FERRIS*, FILLET, FILLIP, FOSSIL, FUNNEL, GALLON, GALLOP, GAMMON, GANNET, GARRET, GIBBON, GOBBET, GODDESS, GOSSIP, GOTTEN, GULLET, GUNNEL, GUSSET, HAGGIS, HAPPEN, HELLISH, HICCUP, HIDDEN, HILLOCK, HOBBIT, HORRID, JAGGED, KENNEL, KITTEN, LESSON, LINNET, LISSOM, MADDEN, MAGGOT, MALLET, MAMMAL, MILLET, MISSAL, MISSUS*, MITTEN, MUFFIN, MULLET, MUSSEL, MUTTON, NOGGIN, NUGGET, OFFAL, OFFSET, OTTOMAN, PALLET, PALLID, PARROT, PELLET, PELL-MELL, PENNON, PITTED, POLLEN, POMMEL *f*, POPPET, POSSESS*, POSSUM, PUFFIN, PUPPET, PUMMEL, PUNNET, QUARREL*, RABBET, RABBIT, RAGGED, REDDEN*, RIBBON, RIDDEN, ROLLMOP, ROTTEN, RUSSET, RUTTED, SADDEN, SODDEN, SONNET, SORREL, {STANNIC}, SUDDEN, SUFFIX, SULLEN*, SUMMIT, SUMMON, TANNIC, TANNIN, TAPPET, TENNIS, TIFFIN, TORRID, TUNNEL, VASSAL *Celtic,* VELLUM, VESSEL, WAGGON, or {WAGON}, WARREN*, WEDDED, WETTED.
Proper Nouns/Adjectives ESSEX, GALLIC, JAFFA, LAMMAS, SUSSEX.
Names ALLEN, COLLIN, DALLAS, DARRELL, DENNIS, DONNA, ELLEN, GEMMA, HASSAN*, JEMMA, MORRIS, RUSSELL, SADDAM, WALLIS.
*Don't let W Muddle You. Remember the rule <a> spells [o] after [w] when reading *warren* [woren]; and *quarrel* [kworel].
Abbess is included in this list because it obeys Orm's Law.
Ferris, the adjective, as in 'ferris wheel' is an eponym. Google George W.G. Ferris.

*_Missus_ spells [mis-uz]. The final <s> spells [z] because <us> is not a weak unstressed ending and <s> spells [z] after short stressed vowels. In words with weak endings, as in _tennis_ and _callus,_ terminal <s> spells [s]. Some words have almost even stress, similar to _missus_. For instance, BALLET, [ba-lay] and BUFFET [boo-fay], both of which have short stressed vowels before twin consonants, as per Orm's Law, but French endings. The French do not follow the 'tum-te-tum' rhythm of English.

Not needed but nice to know. _Missus_ is shortened to _Mrs_ inn England where the short way of writing {_mister_} is _Mr_ without a full stop. Americans always add a full stop, which they call a period, to an abbreviation. The English only use a full stop if the word has been cut off, like _Capt._ for _Captain. Dr_ has kept the last letter of _Doctor_ and so, like _Mr, Mrs_ and _St_ there is no full stop in England, (Bryson, 2004, p.4.) In Australia it is up to the individual. Now back to things we need to know.

*_Possess_ spells [poz-es]. It is one of five words in which <ss> spells [z]. It's a rebel to the <ss> spells [s] rule. _Possess_ was formed from _possession_ (Etymonline) in which the middle syllable is stressed since the final syllable _-ion_ is unstressed. So when _possession_ became the verb _possess,_ it kept the stressed syllable _-ssess_, said with zest, the force of which might be why we let <ss> spell [z].

*_Redden_ is made up of _red_ plus the suffix —_en_. In order to keep [e] short, to stop it spreading into a long vowel sound, <d> is added to make a double gate. The same with _barren, batten, fatten, gotten, sodden_ and _rotten_.

Not needed but nice to know. Linguists have noticed that the suffix —_en_ only joins on to stem words of one syllable and only if that word ends with a consonant which significantly obstructs the airstream through the vocal tract. The consonants [l], [r], [m] and [n], {and [ng] and [ŋ]}, do not obstruct much air. So we see _redden_ but not _greenen, purplen_ nor even _orangen_ because, although [j] blocks air, _orange_ has two syllables. When we see <en> in _men_ and _women_ it is not a suffix. Later, you will read _tighten, loosen, stiffen, weaken, widen, deepen, lengthen,_ but you will not see _rowen_ or _blueen_ for they end in vowels, which do not block air at all. Nor will you see _greenen, groomen_ or _singen_, which end in consonants [n], [m] and [ŋ] in which air goes unblocked out the nose, nor _tallen_, nor _clearen_, for in [r] and [l] air flows freely over the sides of the tongue out through an open mouth. So, we _thicken_ cream, but we cannot say we _thinnen_ it. We just _thin_ it. Now back to things we need to know.

*_Sullen_ once meant a solitary type of person, "sole one", a loner, but then came to mean "unfriendly".

*_Hassan,_ the name, is also written _Hasan_ which still spells [ha-san] for, as we know, names do not have to obey rules. This name means "handsome", showing an English-Arabic language link.

Rule 1-19 The Double Equivalent <ck> is sounded [k] and by tradition occurs only after short vowel sounds spelt with just one letter. It is also a tradition that <c> does not end single-syllable words.

Reason When <cc> is written in cursive it can be mistaken for <u>. To avoid this, <ck> was used in place of <cc>, back when consonants were all twinned after short, single-letter vowels, as per Orm's Law. This has persisted, and the tradition is strongest with single-syllable words in which all but four use <ck> after short vowels spelt with one letter. The terminal <ck> tradition is dying out in longer words. We used to make _musick_ but we still sleep in a _hammock._ (The word _Muzak_ is for piped music in department stores, a registered brand name. Proper nouns do not have to obey spelling rules.

Not needed but nice to know.

A. The twin <cc> occurs in many non-stem words. The prefixes _ad-, ob-_ and _sub-_ change so they can join neatly on to stem words starting with <c>. They change to _ac-, oc-_ and _suc-,_ as in _accurate, occult, succumb_.

B. We shall meet all the rare occurrences of <cc> in stem words in which <cc> spells [k] later on, as we learn to decode them. Many of these <cc> words are recent adoptions. Others have kept <cc> to show their origins e.g., {_desiccate_} comes from Latin for dry, _siccus_. The English scientific term _sac_ was copied from French biologists using French _sac_ from Latin _saccus_. Italian _sacco_ became English {_saccule_}.

Look for the following unusual <cc> words in lists to come: {*broccoli, buccaneer, coccus, desiccate, gonococcus, impeccable, Malacca PN, moccasin, Morocco PN, peccadillo, peccary, piccolo, raccoon, recce, staccato, stucco, succour, succulent, tobacco, toccata, saccule, vaccine, yucca, zucchini*}. Also <cc> in *Rebecca*. Now back to things we need to know

Rebels SIC, SAC, TIC, TREK.

Rebels' Reasons *Sic* (means *thus*, in Latin), *sac* (as in *cul-de-sa*, is also a biological term) and *tic* (meaning spasmodic muscle twitch) all mean other things when ending <ck> and so we can excuse them. *Trek* has been **adopted** from Afrikaans but **not adapted** to our traditional <ck> ending.

List 1-19 <ck> spells [k].

ALMANACK*, BACK, BACK-PACK, BARRACK*, BECK *Celtic*, BUCK, BUCK UP, BUTTOCK, COCK, CUT-BACK, CUT BACK, DECK, DERRICK, DOCK, DUCK, DUCK IN, HADDOCK, FOSSICK, GIMMICK, HACK, HAMMOCK, HASSOCK, HECK, HICK, HOCK, HIT BACK, JACK, JOCK, KICK, KICK OFF, KICK-OFF, KICK UP, KICK-BACK, KNAPSACK*, LACK, LICK, LOCK, LOCK-UP, LUCK, IN LUCK, MATTOCK, MOCK, MOCK-UP, MUCK, MUCK UP, NECK, NICK, PACK, PACK A GUN, PACK IT IN, PACK OFF, PACK UP, PACKET, PADDOCK, PECK, PICK, PICK A BACK, PICK A LOCK, PICK OFF, PICK ON, PICK-UP, PICK POCKET, PICKET, PIN-TUCK, PICK, POCK, POCKET, PUCK, QUACK, QUICK, QUICK AS POSS., QUICK WITTED, QUICKEN, RACK, RACKET, RECKON, RECKLESS, RICK, RICKETS, RICKRACK, ROCK, ROCKET, RUCK, SACK, SET BACK, SET-BACK, SICK, SICK-BED, SICKEN, SICKNESS, SIT BACK, SOCK, SOCKET, SUCK, TACK, TICK, TICKET, TICK OFF, TICK-TACK, TICK-TOCK, TIN TACK, TUCK, TUCK IN, TUCK-IN, TUSSOCK, UNPACK, UNPICK, V-NECK, WACK, WICK, WICKED, WICKET, YUCK. Australian words ZACK, JACK OF IT, JUMBUCK* (a sheep), NICK OFF, RUCKSACK, QUACK, YACK, YAM-STICK, ZACK. Names BUCK, DICK, JACK, JOCK, MICK, NICK, RICK, TUCK, ZACK.

**Almanack* is the old spelling of a word we seldom use, modern spelling *almanac* [al-mə-nak].

**Barrack's* origins might be Irish and might be Aboriginal. Burton, p. 18, gives us seven paragraphs summarizing the evidence and decides the Irish and the Ab'l words are different. Blake, p. 88 says the Ab'l word *borak* from Victoria means 'to give cheek to' which is the English meaning of *barracking* someone. The Irish use *barrack* to mean *boast* or *brag*. It seems to me that Australians *barrack* with both meanings, abusing the opposition and cheering their own team.

**Jumbuck's* origin is a mystery, but not Aust. Ab'l, and may come from the way sheep jump up on each other when being herded along, (Moore, p. 15).

Rule 1-20 The double equivalent <ck> is used more often to spell [k] inside stem words than the twin <cc>. The letters <kk> to spell [k] are not welcome in English words.

Reason The French dislike <k> and so did not let their English subjects use <kk>. The French word for *sack* comes from Latin *saccus*, not Greek *sakkus*. In Hebrew it's *saq* and the French also use <q> to spell [k] rather than Greek <k>.

Rebels QUOKKA, PUKKA.

Rebels' Reasons These recent adoptions are not afraid to use <kk>. *Quokka* or *gwaga* is Nyungar for the large marsupial rat. Nyungar, or Noongar, is the Ab'l language spoken, in various dialects, in the South West corner of WA, from Geraldton to Esperance.

List 1-20

BACKUP, BECKON, BUCKET, COCCUS*, DOCKET, GECKO, HICCUP, JACKAL, JACKET, LOCKET, LOCKUP, MOCK-UP, PACKET, PICKET, PICKUP, POCKET, RACKER, RACKET, RECKON, ROCKET, RUCKUS, SICKEN, SOCKET, TICKET, TUCKET, WICKED, WICKET, YUCCA.

**Coccus* is the round, berry shape of some bacteria.

Rule 1-21 An exception to Orm's Law: stressed single letter vowels before <v> can be short.
Reason Twin <vv> is a "no-no" in English. So single letter vowels can never "get a double gate" to "keep them short". Cursive writing makes <vv> look like <w>.
List 1-21A in which stressed single letter vowels are short before a single <v>.
AVID, BEVEL, CAVIL, COVEN *f*, COVET *f*, DAVIT, DEVIL, DIVOT, GAVEL, GIVEN, HAVOC, HOVEL, LEVEL, LIVID, NOVEL, PIVOT, RAVEL, REVEL, RIVEN, RIVET, SEVEN, VIVID. Proper nouns DEVON. Names BEVAN, EVAN, KEVIN.
List 1-21B in which stressed single letter vowels are not short before a single <v>.
BOVID, HAVEN, LIVEN, NAVAL, NAVEL, RAVEN, RIVAL, WOVEN, which we shall meet again in list 1-39.
DUVET [doo-vay] and DIVAN [dee-van] also have long first vowels. They are both stressed on the second syllable, being French adoptions. They are in the Diplomatic Immunity word list, in the appendix, because, under English spelling rules, they should spell [joo-vet] and [dI-van], as we shall see.

Rule 1-22 Another exception to Orm's Law: all single letter vowels before <x> are short.
Reason Twin <xx> is a "no-no" — letter <x> is never twinned. Some say words with an <x> in the middle do not need a double gate. They say that *exam, exit, vixen, waxen etc.* do not really break Orm's "two gate" rule since *x* spells two consonant sounds. They say that <x> is already two letters, looking like ƆC in cursive, <c> and <c>, back-to-back, with the first spelling [k] and the second spelling [s], as if *exit* was written *eccit* [eksit], (like *accident* [aksident]).
We already know that <x> spells [ks], but <x> also spells the stronger sound [gz].

Rule 1-23A If <x> is between two vowels it spells [gz], (Fox, p. 69), but only if the second vowel is said stronger than the first, (Cummings, p. 351), as in *exam*, where the syllable "*am*" is stressed.
Reason The sound [gz] is a voiced sound and so it has more power than [ks] which is said without the voice box. It is as if [gz] is pushing or adding power to the following vowel, making that vowel stronger. Thus the rule that <x> spelling [gz] comes before a stressed vowel. However this only happens if <x> is between vowels.
English words are stressed on the first syllable, unless that syllable is a prefix. Prefixes are usually unstressed. So *exit* is unusual, having stress on the prefix. This is not so in *exam*, nor in its full version, {*examination*}. The others in the list are all said in the usual way, with stress on the first syllable. This means that *exam* is the only word in the list in which <x> spells [gz].
List 1-23A
AXIL, AXIS, BOXEN*, EXAM <x> = [gz], EXIT*, MAXIM, NEXUS, TAXI*, TOXIC, TOXIN, VIXEN*. Names ALEX, AXEL, SAXON.
Exam is short for *examination*, a long word which ends with a suffix. So it ends on a weak beat. The alternate weak and strong beats of English make *examination* start on a weak beat. This weak beat remains when it is shortened to *exam*, [əg-zam] in which the second syllable is stressed and strong, after a weak syllable. Do you hear the [z]? Letter <x> spells [gz] before a stressed vowel, when between vowels, see 1-23B.
Taxi is a rebel to the rule against terminal <i> with the reason that it is an abbreviation. It's short for *taxicab* which is short for *taximeter cabriolet* and *taximeter* is a compound of two stem words, *tax* and *meter* with <i> used as a linking particle, (Cummings, p. 85, Ayto p. 90).
*Prof. Lerer calls *vixen* a "shard", a piece of an old 'fossil' word. The female of *fox* was *fyxen* or *fixen*, all old Anglo-Saxon words. (If *en* was added to nouns it made them small, as in *kitten, maiden, chicken,* or female.) Then the Vikings invaded England and they said *vox* and *vixen* because the [f] sound was too soft

for them! They used the harder [v] sound. So the Vikings in England said *vox* and *vixen* and the Saxons in England said *fox* and *fixen*. The English people ended up using one of each: *fox* and *vixen*.

*Boxen is a brand-new word. One *window box* or just *box* is the name of a page on a computer using a Windows Program and the plural of *box* used in this way is *boxen*. The old suffix *–en* has been given a new lease of life!

Rule 1-23B At the beginning of words <x> spells [z].

Reason First syllables are usually stressed and so words starting with <x> would be followed by a stressed vowel and we would expect <x> to spell [gz]. However, when word-initial, <x> just spells [z] because [g] has been silenced, just as it has in *gnome*. The following word began as a trade name but has become an English verb. (We shall meet *xylophone* later.)

List 1-23B
XEROX [zee-roks]

Terminal Vowels — *balsa, villa*.
Rule 1-24 Terminal vowels spell long sounds.
Reason There is no consonant to block their flow. Unlike consonants, vowels can flow on and on for as long as breath remains. Opera singers excel at extending their vowels, especially in Italian which is full of words ending in vowels.

Rule 1-24 A Terminal <a> spells [ar].
Reason This is the Continental long sound spelt by <a>. The other long sound spelt by <a> is the Anglo long sound, [ay]. Even when [ar] lifted to [ay] in England's Great Vowel Shift, <a> still spelt [ar] at the end of words, not [ay]. This is because only stressed long vowels lifted in the GVS — ends of English words are not usually stressed. The abbreviations below have stressed endings which did not lift to [ay] because they were once long sounds inside words — *famuli, haha, labulii, mama, papa*. The last two are just nursery slang for *thanks* and *goodbye*.

List 1-24 A Terminal <a> spells [ar].
BALSA* [borl-sar], COMMA, CUPPA, FOSSA, GAMMA, GUTTA, , HA-HA (ditch fence), HAHA *expletive,* HENNA, MANNA, *NAMMA (water hole), *NULLA-NULLA, OKRA, PIZZA, SENNA, TERRA-COTTA, TOCCATA, *YAKKA, YUCCA, VILLA. Abbreviations FA, HA, LA, MA, PA, TA *slang,* TA-TA *slang.* Proper Nouns MALACCA. Names ABBA, DADDA, ELLA, EMMA, ILSA, HELGA, HILDA, MAMMA, MUMMA, *REBECCA, TESSA.

*Balsa spells [borl-sar], not [bal-sar], a Spanish word meaning "float", or "raft" on west coast of South America.

Musical notes are abbreviations and so can break the Short Word Rule: *fa* is short for Latin *famuli* and *la* is short for Latin *labii*.

*Namma was adopted from Ab'l languages and adapted to English pronunciation. It used to be *ngama*, (Blake, p. 100).

*Ab'l *ngala-ngala* was recorded in 1798 but early settlers adopted it as *nulla-nulla*, being easier to say, (Blake, p.101).

*Rebecca is stressed on the second <e> because the vowel before twinned consonants is always stressed. *Rebecca* and *Malacca* have the rare <cc>, instead of <ck>.

*Yakka means 'work' and was adopted into English from the Tharapal Ab'l language around Brisbane, usually used in the phrase 'hard yakka', (Blake p. 106).

Rule 1-24B Terminal <e> in one syllable words after a consonant spells [ee].
List 1-24B <e> spells [ee]
HE, ME, WE, BE, YE, RE *abbrev.* of *regarding*.

  Now that you can read *he*, you will want to read *she*. You know that <sh> spells [sh] in *shall*.

SHE spells [shee]. Long ago *she* was *heo*. *He* and *heo* were easily muddled up and so *heo* became *she*. The word *her* is used a lot and so we shall learn to read it now, the first of many words in which <er> spells [er]. HER spells [her], and [er] is the vowel sound in *fern*. *His* and *shis* would sound too similar so no wonder the old word *her* has remained.

Now you can read two [sh] words, SHE and SHALL and one [er] word, HER.

Rebel RE, as musical note, spells [ray] not [ree].

Rebel's Reason We sing the notes "do re me" [doh ray mee]. *Re* is an abbreviation of the Latin word *resonare,* [ray-son-air].

Rebels? No, *he, me, we* are just pronouns and do not have to obey the Short Word Rule, whereas nouns do. *Re* is short for *regarding* and abbreviations do not have to obey the Short Word Rule.

Rebels? *Dye* and *owe* have terminal <e> but are not rebels. In {*dye*} <y> is acting as a vowel, as we shall see. In {*owe*} <w> is acting as a vowel, as we shall see. So, terminal <e> does not follow a consonant in these one-syllable words. Letter <e> is only present to obey the Short Word Rule.

The reason that rule 1-24B applies to short one syllable words only is that terminal <e> in longer words is usually acting as a decider sign rather than a letter. When <e> is acting as a decider sign, we say it is doing a silent job, as we have seen when <e> insulates <v> from ending a word. In the following words <ee> seems to spell [ee], but the final <e> is silent. The first <e> stretches out into [ee] but a second <e> is required due to the Short Word Rule. The result is that <ee> spells [ee] at the end of these single-syllable words.

List 1-24B cont.
BEE, FEE, LEE, PEE, SEE, TEE, VEE.

Rebels RECCE [rekee] and POSSE [posee] and a few others look like single syllable words but have been adopted from languages which pronounce <e> at the end of their words, big words, bigger than one syllable. As for its <cc>, *recce* has begun to adapt to English ways, changing <cc> to <ck> in *reckon*. "*I took a recce and I reckon the coast is clear.*"

Rule 1-24C Terminal <i>, after a consonant, spells its long sound [ee], or its long sound [I]. Reason Most words which end with <i> have been adopted into English. English words as we shall soon see rarely end with <i>. Depending where they come from, the following few terminal <i> words end in [ee] or [I].

List 1-24C

<i> spells Continental long [ee] SKI, adopted from Norway; TI musical note short for "sancta"; MI musical note short for "mira"; PETRI an eponym.

<i> spells long [I] PI, used in maths, adopted from Greece; HI-FI, short for "high fidelity"; HI, slang for "hello" or "hail"; RABBI, Hebrew word.

Rule 1-24C cont. Terminal <ie> spells the long sound [ee], or the long sound [I].

Reason English words very rarely end in <i> because terminal <i> is usually insulated with a silent <e>. As we know, <i> used to be dotless and so at the end of a word it did not look like a letter, just a tail of a letter. The old scribes added <e> to show it was a letter, not just a final flourish. In very short words, this <e> does two jobs, insulating <i> and making sure these words obeyed the Short Word Rule. Names, like Di, do not have to obey rules, nor slang, like "*Hi!*" By the way, we can take it for granted that terminal <ie> comes after a consonant because three vowels in a row are very rare in English words. For instance, the French write *gaie* but the English write *gay,* although they both spell [gay].

Rule 1-24D Terminal <ie> in single-syllable words spells [I].

Reason We heard how that very small word *I* evolved from a little dotless <i> to an upper-case <I> and we heard how it changed from spelling a little [ee] sound which rhymed with *me* and *he* and *she* into a big loud [I] sound. In one syllable words with insulated <i> endings, <ie> spells [I], just like one syllable *I* spells [I]. We cannot add <i> to <di> to ensure the verb [dI] obeys the Short Word Rule because we never twin <i>. Why not? Because back when <i> had no dot on top, twin <i> in cursive looked like <u>. ιι without a gap between each dotless ı is ıı. So silent <e> was added instead, to achieve three letters. We can call all the following words Cursive Casualties.

List 1-24D

DIE, FIE, LIE, PIE, TIE, VIE.

(Later we shall see that this habit of <i> spelling [I] at the end of one syllable words continues when another syllable is added, e.g., *libel,* [lI-bel]. This does not happen in *kitten* because <i> does not come at the end of the first syllable in [kit-ten] Also, later on, we shall see that <ie> at the end of multi-syllable words spells [ee], as in *movie.*)

Rule 1-24E Terminal <o> spells [oh], and if followed by silent <e> then terminal <oe> spells [oh], and terminal <oh> spells [oh] too.

Reason It is free to spread from [o] into [oh] at the end of a word, even if it requires a silent <e> in order to obey the Short Word Rule.

Rebels LASSO, TO and DO.

Rebels' Reasons In *to* and *do* <o> spells [oo]. Between 1450 and 1650 many long English vowels lifted, rose higher in the mouth to a higher sound frequency. Before that, *to* and *do* sounded like *taw* and *daw* and then lifted to *toe* and *doe* and then lifted again from [oh] to [oo]. The long vowel [oh] is made lower in the mouth than [oo], try it. This period, when long vowels lifted, is called the Great Vowel Shift, see appendix. When vowels lifted from [oh] to [oo] in *to* and *do,* they lifted in *into* and *undo* and *to-do* as well. However, when "*Do not!*" is shortened to "*Don't!*" the vowel reverts to [oh], "D[oh]n't!" to ensure we can hear the difference between *do* and *don't* to avoid major accidents. We shall meet DON'T again in Part Two.

Lasso ends in [oo] not [oh]. The Spanish word *lazo* spells [lar-soh] which comes from a Latin word meaning *noose.* (Note how <z> spells Spanish [s] in this word!) Maybe in English [oh] became [oo] to match *noose.*

List 1-24E

AMMO (ammunition), BUFFALO, DITTO, DO*♫, DOE, DOGGO, EXPO *slang,* FOE*, GO, HALLO, HELLO, HIPPO, HO HO HO, HOE, HULLO, LO, LOTTO, MEZZO, MOTTO, NO*, NO GO, NOH*, OH! OH? PECCADILLO*, PICCOLO*, ROE, SO*♫, SO, SO AND SO, TOBACCO*, TOE, WOE, YOBBO, YO-YO. <u>Proper Nouns</u> ESKIMO, MOROCCO*. <u>Names</u> JO, JOE*, MONGO, OTTO, PEDRO, PABLO, ROLLO.

*Foe has a silent <e> in order to obey the Short Word Rule, for it is a noun.

*Musical notes *do* and *so* can break the Short Word Rule because they are shortenings. *Do* is short for Latin "Dominus" and *so* is short for Latin "solve".

**Morocco, piccolo, tobacco* and *peccadillo* have the rare <cc> instead of <ck>, all foreign adoptions.

*The name *Joe* does not have to obey the Short Word Rule because names do not have to obey rules but words 'like' rules and so when *Joseph* is shortened to *Jo* it often gains an <e>.

*Noh is English for a traditional Japanese play.

FOR could have just two letters, for it is not a noun or verb, adjective or adverb, but then it would spell [foh]. *For* spells [for] because Bossy R after <o> spells [or]. The word *for* is used a lot and so we learn to read it long before we meet all the other words in which <or> spells [or]. Now we can add OR to the words we know, too. We shall be properly introduced to Bossy R later on.

Rule 1-24F English words cannot end in <u> and so terminal <u> must be insulated with a silent <e>.

Reason This began when <u> was hard to tell from <v> at the end of a word written in cursive, i.e. running writing. By adding <e> the old scribes could see that <e> joined onto <u> down much lower than it joined on to <v>. Write *dove* and *due* in cursive and compare the low link between <u> and <e> with the high link between <v> and <e>. That was how they told <u> and <v> apart. Then adding <e> was kept on as a tradition, even when printing presses separated each letter! The letter <u> once spelt [yoo] for a long vowel sound at all times, but in most cases now spells [oo]. Later we shall get rules for choosing [yoo] or [oo].

In the next list, terminal <u> spells [yoo] unless marked otherwise. We shall learn later how to tell if <u> spells [yoo] or [oo], just by looking at a word. Meanwhile you will see that in most of them <u> spells [yoo], except for the rebels. In most of the rebels, <u> spells [oo] because they have mainly been adopted from the Continent, where <u> always spells [oo]. Only *emu* and *menu* end with <u> spelling [yoo], the English way. In the slang words *flu* and *lulu*, we do not hear [lyoo], just [loo], because, as we shall learn, the English eventually found it too hard to say [lyoo]. Same thing happened in *rue* — [ryoo] was too hard to say.

List 1-24F. CUE, DUE, HUE, RUE, <u>=[oo], SUE <u>=[oo], and the name SUE <u>=[oo].

Rebels EMU, FLU *abbrev.* of *influenza* <u>=[oo], FONDU,<u>=[oo], GNU <u>=[oo], GURU <u>=[oo], JUJU<u>=[oo], KURU<u>=[oo], LULU *slang,* <u>=[oo], MENU, MU, MUMU<u>=[oo], TABU<u>=[oo], TOFU<u>=[oo], TUTU,<u>=[oo], YOU [yoo], ZEBU<u>=[oo].

Rebels' Reasons Most of these terminal <u> words are adopted but not adapted and so they do not have terminal <e> to insulate <u> from coming last and being mistaken for round-bottomed cursive <v>. *Emu's* foreign ending reminds us it grew from a Portuguese word, not an Aboriginal word, whereas *kangaroo* is the English way of writing the Aboriginal word-sound [oo]. *Mu* breaks the Short Word Rule as well as the rule against terminal <u>. *Mu,* a Greek letter, is an example of adopting a word but not adapting its spelling because it needs to stand out as a technical word. (Many Greek words with unusual spellings, like <rh>, <ph> and <ch> are used in this way, to stand out, e.g., *rheostat, physics, chloride*. see Cummings, p. 20.)

The word *you* could be just *yu* because this little word does not have to obey the Short Word Rule because it is a pronoun, like *me*. It's spelt the French way, *you,* like the French coin, *sou* [soo]. If terminal <u> had then been insulated with a silent <e> the word would have had three vowels in a row, which is against tradition in an English word. By the way, verbs always treat *you* as plural. So we say 'you are hungry' to one person, not 'you is hungry' and 'you eat now,' not 'you eats now.'

Rule 1-25A The letters <ou> spell [ow] inside English words.

Reason French rulers controlled English spelling and in French <ou> spells [oo]. In the Great Vowel Shift long vowels lifted but [oo] was already a high sound said high in the mouth. It hit the roof of the mouth, bent over and became the bent sound [ow]. I call it a bent sound, but linguists call it a diphthong, which means 'double-sound'. An ordinary vowel does not move the lips from one shape. A diphthong bends the lips. Try saying straight and bent vowels looking in a mirror. The words below are frequently used and easy to decode. They will be listed again later with similar words.

Before the GVS, *mouse* rhymed with *moose*. Before the GVS the Old English word *mouse* was only used by the very poor. The rich, upper classes only spoke French. They called a *mouse* a *souris*. Tiny mice, and their cousins the rats, actually saved the English language, all because they carried even tinier fleas. After 1066, when England was conquered by the French, the official language of England was French. Only poor serfs and servants spoke English. Then a terrible plague broke out in Europe, called the Black Death. In June 1348 it spread to England in fleas which carried the deadly germs and passed them on to the humans they bit. The germs then travelled to other humans just on their breath. Over half of the people in England died before December 1349. Before the plague, travelling workmen got orders from the upper classes in French and they explained the job to the lowly serfs in English. After the plague there were very few travelling workmen to do the translating. So the upper classes had to learn to speak in English. They also let their serfs travel to jobs nearby and this spread the use of English. Soon everyone became proud of the English language and they added new words to it and changed the way it was pronounced. To see the effect of the plague, go to the Photo Gallery at www.spellingexplained.com.

List 1-25A
ABOUT, AROUND, FOUND, HOUSE [hows], MOUSE, OUR, OUT.
Rule 1-25B When <ou> spells [ow] at the end of a word it's written <ow>, as in *cow*.
Reason This is because <u> must not end an English word, so <u> was doubled and became <w>. Insulating <u> with a terminal<e> would have produced three vowels in a row, not welcome in English, a 'non-no'.
Rebel THOU
Rebel's Reason This old English word wasn't used by the French conquerors and their scribes, so it escaped being spelt *thow*. The French do not say [th] or [dh]. It nearly died out, but is still used in church and is seen in old books.

The following list is short and the words are short, nearly all single syllables. One advantage to ending in <w> was that <ing> and <ed> could be added without producing three vowels in a row, *bowing* not *bouing* and *mowed* not *moued*, (Cummings p. 304.)

List 1-25B
ALLOW, BOW (to the king), BOW-WOW, COW, ENDOW, HOW, NOW, POW-WOW, ROW (noisy fight), SOMEHOW *f*, SOW (lady pig), VOW, WOW.

Rebels? Is *window* a rebel? No, for the rule does not stop other words ending <ow> but spelling [oh]. Many words end in <ow> spells [oh]. Only a few end in <ow> spells [ow], which is why these few have been introduced first, in list 1-25B. You do not need to know the others yet. Learn to read these and file them in your brain's automatic detector. We do not proceed to words ending <ow> spells [oh] until Part Four. Try to connect the bent vowel [ow] with each word. For instance, in this list *bow* means *bend*. We *bow* to the king and queen. *Row* is a word for a noisy argumentative gathering, probably a shortening of *carousel*, a noisy drinking *bout*. *Sow* is a female pig. Pigs were called *swine* which is reflected in the <w> of *sow* but the sound of the word is said to match the *snout* [snowt] of a pig. *Allow* comes from the combination of two verbs, 'to place' (*allocate*) and 'to praise' (*laud*): *al-lau*. If you are praised for being in a place then you know you are allowed to be there. *Endow* began as *indowen* when first adopted into English, with <ow> inside the word.

The old scribes never wrote <ww> for they said that would be very muddly. The only time we see <ww> is when they meet at boundaries in compound nouns like *bowwow, powwow* but, even then, they are usually hyphenated, *bow-wow, pow-wow*. {*Glow-worm, slow-worm, screw-worm, willow-ware*} are further examples. We no longer write with feathers. Printers separate our letters now, but we stick to the tradition of the old scribes. However, we also follow our new masters of communication, our information technology experts of the 21st century, because we use the triplet <www> when writing website names and when otherwise referring to that modern invention, the world-wide-web. It's not the only rule broken by our modern I. T. scribes, for we see <ii> in the server 'iiNet', an eye-catching name. Advertising experts know that words which break spelling rules make us look twice, catch our attention, as in 'Weet-bix' and 'Kwik Kleen'.

Rebel Rappers
There are only three words in which <ould> spells [uud]: COULD, SHOULD AND WOULD.
Reason After 1066 the Norman conquerors changed the sound and the spelling of many Old English words including these three everyday words. The French scribes did all the writing so the new spelling remained but it was harder to control pronunciation. The long vowel in c*ould, should* and *would* shortened to [uu]. We do the same to [oo] in *you* when we say "What do you think?" Can you hear [yuu] for <you>? This only happens when *you* is used before a consonant, not in "Are you O. K?" for instance, or "You are lovely."

After short vowel [uu], [ld] was hard to say and [l] was dropped so that the words became [kuud], [shuud] and [wuud]. Try saying [l] in *cooled* and *cold* and *culled*. They are easier to say clearly and quickly than [kuuld]. Words that are said often need to be quick and easy to say. These rebels are dancing to a tune of their own. We can imagine them prancing along the 'road to reading', dancing to their own music. Street dancers are rap dancers. Let's call them our rappers and give them a list of their very own.

List 1-26 In these rappers <ould> spells [uud]
COULD, SHOULD, WOULD.
We can abbreviate them all to *could've, should've* and *would've*. After a consonant *'ve* spells [uuv]. Remember that *'ve* is short for *have,* not *of.* It's [kuud-uuv] not [kuud-ov].

Silent letters — *where, there, thug.*
Letters do not speak so they are all silent. However, some decode to silence and so we say they are silent. Rather than invent a symbol for silence we say <mb> in *lamb* spells [m], (Cummings, p. 54).
We can sort silent letters into boxes, imaginary boxes.
The smallest box has just a few silent letters which have been added long after the English word developed, either to link up to a newly discovered parent, like <b> in {*debt*} to link with Latin *debitus,* or to match their mates, e.g., {*could*} acquired <l> to look like {*would* and *should*}. The silent letters in this box have never spelt a word-sound in an English word.
Another box contains silent letters which protect other letters from breaking rules, like <e> in *axe* and *give*.
The biggest box is full of silent letters which are not acting as letters but as decider signs. They do not spell sounds, are not sound symbols, do not decode into word-sounds but instead direct how other letters are to be decoded. (Linguists call them diacritics, for they "discriminate"). For instance, <h> in *eh, ah, oh* tells us to decode these vowels as [ay], [ar], [oh] rather than their ground rule sounds [e], [a], [o]. By the way, these little words are pseudo words, informal words, not 'real words' and so they do not come under the Short Word Rule. We shall see <e> give many silent directions.
Some letters used to be decider signs but now they are ignored. The <h> in *whale* used to make <w> spell a breathy important [w] sound. Now <wh> just spells [w].

Rule 1-27 H is usually silent in Digraph WH
Reason A long time ago <wh> was written <hw> and [h] spelt a very clear [h]. *Whale* was written *hwale* by the Anglo Saxons — actually *hwæl,* but the old ash letter æ is gone now. Initial [hw] meant words began with an important "huff and a puff" and was used for really impressive things, like *whales*, and breathy things like *whispers* and *whistles,* (but not *windy,* which comes from the verb 'to wind or turn'). It was also used to express insistence, as in "<u>Wh</u>ere have you been?" "<u>Wh</u>at are you doing?" "<u>Wh</u>ich of you did this?" Other words adopted an <h> to sound more whip-like or whiffy or extreme. *Wham* sounded more extreme than *wam,* and *whit* sounded more extreme than *wit,* as in "Not a whit more!" and "*Whoa!*" more extreme than *"Woa!",* (Cummings, p. 388). As recently as the 1950's, Australian children were taught to pronounce <wh> as a very special [w] sound, said "higher" than [w] and with lots of breath. These days <wh> just spells [w], for <h>'s message is ignored. The digraph changed from <hw> to <wh> to match digraphs like <th> and <ch>.

List 1-27 <wh> spells [w]
SOMEWHAT <a>=[o], WHACK, WHAM, WHAT <a>=[o], WHATNOT <a>=[o], WHEN, WHET (to sharpen), WHIFF, WHIM, WHIP, WHIT, WHIZ (very rare single *z* ending).
Don't let W muddle you: <what> spells [wot] because it was originally written *hwat,* like *hwen* and *hwet.* It's quite easy to conclude that modern *whack* and *wham* have kept the harsh [a] sound because they were never *hwack* and *hwam*.

Rebels WHO spells [hoo], WHOSE spells [hooz] and WHOM spells [hoom]. We shall meet another rebel, *whole,* later.

Rebels' Reasons I t takes effort to say [w] before [oo] and so *who* is pronounced with the [h] sound still, as if it is still written *hwo*. In all three words <o> spells [oo], just like *to* and *do*.

Also TWO spells [too]. When Old English *twa* and *twegen* became *two* it became too hard to say [twoo]. Do you agree that [twoo] is harder to say than *twice* and *twin,* which kept the [w] sound? We still say [w] in *twain,* another word which means 'two'. We say [w] in *twist* too, two things around each other, a tasty twist loaf or twist your two legs and dance The Twist!

The slang word WHODUNIT spells [hoo-dun-it] and is now accepted to describe any book that solves who did a crime.

Rule 1-28 Letters <ere> used to spell [air] but now <ere> only spells [air] in just two stem words.
Reason Are *where,* and {*there*} rebels? No, they obey, they are "resistors" for they sat tight and did not change. To find out why <ere> stop spelling [air] we admire the sound and letter patterns in the following table from the Prof., (Cummings, p. 62). *Whither, hither, thither* all rhyme. So do *whence, hence, thence.* However, we do not use these words much now-a-days. *When, hen, then* used to rhyme but, *hen* kept getting mistaken for *then* and so *now* replaced it. *Where, here, there* rhymed once upon a time too, and that's the reason that *here* changed to [heer], to sound quite different to *there* and *where. Here* was a rebel but during the GVS words ending <ere> changed their sound to rhyme with *here,* except of course {*there*} and *where.*
WHERE? (What place?) {HERE} (This place.) {THERE} (That place.)
{WHITHER?} (To where?) {HITHER} (From here.) {THITHER} (To there.)
{WHENCE?} (From where?) {HENCE} (From here.) {THENCE} (From there.)
WHEN? (At what time?) HEN*/HENNE* (at this time.) {THEN} (At that time.)
*After 1450, *hen* and *henne* disappeared and *now* was used.
List 1-28
WHERE Compound Words SOMEWHERE *f*, WHEREIN, WHEREAS, WHEREBY.
Rule 1-29 *Were* **is the only word in which <ere> spells [er].**
Reason It should be written *wer* but that meant *man. Wer* and *wif* were *man* and *woman.* Note:- The syllable *were,* in imaginary {*werewolves*}, does not spell [wer] for *werewolves* spells [weer-woolvz].
List 1-29
WERE
Relevant Writing Rule, to be chanted. Never in the middle, nor at the end, <wh> is only at the beginning of a stem. *Where, when, why, which, while, who* and *what,* all begin with <wh>, but the following do not: *were, was, with, went, won't, wouldn't* and *will,* do not begin with <wh>, and never will. Return to Reading Rules.

Secret Agent Aitch or Helpful Handy Haitch.
A digraph is two letters which together spell a new sound. Digraph means a double-graphic, two graphics, two letters. They are called 'Best Friends' in some schools. The letter <h> is best friends to lots of letters. We call him Secret Agent Aitch or Helpful Handy Haitch when he is in a digraph because then he does not spell [h], but is very silent and just tells his best friend what to spell, instead of spelling a sound himself.
Long ago the English alphabet had extra letters. One of them spelt the sound starting *this.* Another letter spelt the sound starting *thin.* Now we only have the digraph <th> to spell them both.
So <th> spells two sounds. Put fingers on your voice box. Do you feel vibration for *this* but not for *thin?* Now hang a tissue in front of your mouth. It does not move when you say *this* but it puffs out when you

say *thin*. In some languages, the sound starting *this,* which vibrates the voice box, is written <dh> and the sound starting *this,* which puffs the tissue, is written <th>. But in English <th> is used for both sounds. When we discuss these sounds, we write [dh] for the sound which uses the voice box, the 'voiced' sound starting *this.* We write [th] when we are talking about the soft, unvoiced sound which starts *thin*. How do we know which is which when we write <th> in words? We shall look at words like *this* first, because [dh] is not in as many words as [th].

Rule 1-30 Hard or voiced [dh] usually starts 'pointer words' like *them, this,* and *that.*
(Pointer words are words we often say when pointing at something. It's just my way of describing these words.)
Reason Hard [dh] is more forceful and so is useful when pointing something out, *that thing, this thistle, thy thigh,* and when contrasting things, *bigger than, either ether or chloroform will do.*
List 1-30
THAN, THAT, THE*, THEM, THEN, THERE* [dhair], THIS*, THO/THÔ* *abbreviations,* THUS*, WITH, WITHIN, "WITH IT".

*The can be said in two ways. We can say *the* with a short vowel sound which sounds like the end of a grunt [ə] or a long one, [ee]. Usually we use a long ee sound before a vowel, e.g., [dhee] ant, but [dhə] dog.

Not needed but nice to know. *The* is more definite than *a.* Both little words are called 'articles' which means 'little joints' for they join nouns to the sentence and in doing so 'mark' them as nouns.
Here's a joke: The English definite article 'the' walks into a bar with his old friend, the English indefinite article 'a'. They sit down, order some drinks, and then 'a' asks "So, what're you up to now these days? Still marking nouns?" 'The' nods his head, sips his drink and then replies, "Definitely." Now back to things we need to know.
*This and *thus* both rebel against the rule that terminal [s] sound should be spelt <ss> after a single letter vowel. *This* is thought by some to have grown out of *that see,* which would explain the soft [s] ending. *Thus* is short for 'in this way' and has kept the soft [s] of *this.*
* *Tho/thô*. We know that <o> at the end of a word stretches out long and so <tho> spells [dhoh]. *Tho* is how the President of USA, Mr Roosevelt wanted everyone to spell *though.* *Thô* was written in England with a sign over the <o> to indicate missing letters. It was a popular way of writing *although* for a while but neither way was permitted in the OED.
*There is the other rebel which uses <ere> to spell [air]. You have already met its rebel mate *where.* These two words were the only ones to hold out against the change which occurred once *here* lifted its vowel from [hair] to [heer]. Only *there* and *where* were left looking and sounding French, like the French words *père* [pair], *mère* [mair] and *frère* [frair], (father, mother and brother).

Rule 1-31 Terminal <ey> in single-syllable words spells [ay], except *key*.
Reason There are many reasons that this happens. Some end <ey> because ending <ei> is a no-no. Some got terminal <ey> from French words, in which <ey> spells [ay] and some converted <eg> endings of Old English words into <ey>.
Terminal <ey> lists come later, but remember THEY spells [dhay].

Rule 1-32 Soft [th] is used in nouns and adjectives, adverbs and verbs unless a noun has been turned into a verb.
Reason English is made up of many languages. The soft [th] sound was used where the Anglo-Saxons came from. The Vikings arrived in England after the Anglo-Saxons. They used both [th] and [dh]. Maybe they were the ones who turned nouns into verbs by changing [th] to [dh], like we do in {*clothe*} from the noun *cloth.* The region the Anglo-Saxons came from stopped using [th]. In Dutch, for instance, *this* and

that, *thick* and *thin*, are now *dis* and *dat, dik* and *din*. Maybe we'd say that too if the Vikings hadn't added [dh] to English. The last to conquer England were the French. Their language is a Romance language, having a Roman language base. The Romans did not use [th] or [dh]. The Greeks never used [dh], but they did use [th]. When the Romans adopted Greek words with this sound, they wrote it as <th> but pronounced it as [t]. They did not want to use the Greek letter Theta for it, θ. So it was the Romans who invented the digraph <th>.

List 1-32
BATH <a>=[ar], BOTH* <o>=[oh], HATH, KITH, LATH, MATH, METHOD, MOTH, PATH <a>=[ar], PITH, QUOTH, SABBATH, THICK, THIN, THUD, THUG.

*Both used to be spelt *bothe,* which as we shall learn later, is why <o> spells [oh] in *bothe*. It lost its <e> maybe because if it kept the <e> then <th> would spell [dh] instead of nice soft [th]. When <th> is followed by a vowel it spells [dh]. Can you hear the difference between *cloth* and *clothe? Cloth* has a soft [th] and *clothe* has hard [dh]. We shall meet *clothe* when we meet Fairy E.

The old words *hath, quoth* and *kith* are not used today and are called "archaic".

The vowels in *bath* and *path* shifted from [a] to [ar] in the south of England and remain short up north.

Not needed but nice to know. After the Angles, Saxons and Jutes had lived in the country they called England for four hundred years, the Vikings arrived. They had lots of [th] and [dh] words. You may have heard of their god called Thor, the god of thunder. *Thursday* is named after Thor. The English said *he* for one man and *hei* for two men. The Vikings said *thei* instead of *hei*. This caught on, because it was easy to hear the difference between *he* and *thei*. However, as we know, English words cannot end in <i> and so *thei* became *they*. The Vikings also changed the word *hem* to *them*. Now back to things we need to know. We shall meet Secret Agent Aitch, and Helpful Handy Haitch again in Part Two. For a detailed history on <th>, wait until Part Two.

Semi-vowel Y — *by, rye.*
Rule 1-33 When <y> terminates a one syllable word it acts like the vowel <i> for it spells the sound [I]. Unlike <i> it does not need a silent <e> to insulate it at the end of a word.

Reason Y was a Greek letter which the Romans added rather late to their alphabet. By the time they quit Britain they had begun using it in place of I quite a lot. In fact, even today, the Spanish and the French refer to Y as 'Greek I'. After 1066, the English alphabet lost some of its letters. One was Yogh, which French scribes replaced with Y. So, in English, <y> spells a range of sounds, vowels and consonants. As we know, when <i> was dotless, it was hard to see at the end of words. One way to fix this was to add <e>. Another way to fix the problem was to replace <i> with <y>. Whatever <i> spells, so does its replacement, <y>. Originally, as is still the case in Continental Europe, <i> spelt the long sound [ee]. In the Great Vowel Shift [ee] became [I], but this only happened to stressed [ee]. Only vowels which were both long and stressed shifted in the GVS. Since all single syllable words are considered stressed, terminal <y> in these short words spells [I]. When <y> acts as a vowel it is acting as <i> and follows all rules for <i>. So, just as <ii> is not allowed, neither is <yy>.

List 1-33
BY spells [bI], BY AND BY; MY spells [mI], MY OH MY; WHY spells [wI], WHY OH WHY; THY spells [dhI].
BYE spells [bI], BYE BYE; BUY spells [bI], BUY IT *slang,* BUY OFF, BUY OUT, BUY UP; DYE spells [dI]; EYE* spells [I], EYE OFF, EYE FULL, PUT AN EYE ON, GET AN EYE IN; LYE spells [lI]; RYE spells [rI].

The last five, *bye* to *eye,* are nouns and need to obey the Short Word Rule. We cannot double the last letter because of the rule against <yy>. So, we usually use silent <e>, to make a word of three letters, not two. In this case <e> is not acting as a letter to spell a sound nor is it acting as a decider symbol. It is not insulating a letter from coming last either. It is merely making the words long enough to obey the short word rule.

When [bI] means "procuring a thing with exchange of money", in other words *buy,* it has three letters, to obey the short word rule. Terminal <e> is used for *bye* or *good-bye,* the abbreviation of "God be with you" and also the noun *bye,* a sporting term in cricket and play-off rosters. However *buy's* old Gothic ancestor word is *bugjan* and has retained <u> in *buy* to make three letters.

You will meet the other one syllable words ending in *y* later, like {*sty, try, fry, sly, cry, dry, wry, pry,* and *shy*}. As you can see, they do not require a terminal <e>.

Eye has changed a lot. At one stage it was spelt "egge" because if you boil an egg and cut it in half it looks like an eye. It's fun to read all the ways *eye* was said and written but to remember how to spell it today just think of a long-nosed face painted by a modern artist, ᵉyᵉ. Can you draw a smile under the tail of letter <y>? *Eye* has been spelt in forty-nine different ways (Cummings page 279. In Old English <g> spelt a similar sound to [y]. Later on, <g> was replaced by <y> and the first sound of the word changed from [ay] to [I]. (We still hear <e> spelling [ay] in *éclair.*) As for *egg,* it kept its <g> but dropped the final <e>.

Orm Again — *acne, zebra.*
Rule 1-34 Two syllables in a word, two consonants in the middle, means first vowel is short if it is written with one letter.
Reason This rule obeys Orm's Law. The two consonants in the middle act like a double gate and stop the first vowel from stretching out.
List 1-34
ACNE [ak-nee], ACME [ak-mee], ADMAN, ADMIT, AMBIT, ANTE, ANTIC, ANVIL, AQUA, ATLAS* [-əs], BANJO, BEDPAN, BIGWIG, BINGO, BONGO, BUNYA-BUNYA*, BUNYIP*, CACTUS [-əs], CANTO, CANVAS [kan-vəs] *n.,* CANVASS [kan-vas] *v.,* CATNAP, COBWEB, COMBAT, CONFESS, CONGA, CONVEX, CUSTOM, COSMIC, COSMOS [-əs], CUPRIC <u>=[uu], CUTLET, DAMSEL, DAMSON, DISPEL, DOGMA, EMBED, EMBOSS, ENROL, EQUIP, EXPAT *abbrev.,* EXPEL, EXTOL, FABRIC, FITFUL, FULFIL, FUNGAL, FUNGI*, FUNGUS, GAMBIT, GASKET, GIMLET, GOBLET, GODLESS, GONDOLA, GOSPEL, GUTLESS, HAMLET, HAPLESS, HUMBUG, IMPEL, INDEX, INDIGO, INGOT, INPUT <u>=[uu], INSET*, INSTIL, JACKAL, JACKASS, JACKET, JACKPOT, JETSAM, JOBLESS, JONQUIL, JUNTA*, KELVIN, KENDO, KIDNAP, KISMET, KITBAG, KUMQUAT <a>=[o], LIMBO, LEGLESS, LIMPET, LIMPID, LINDEN, LINGO, LIPSTICK, LIQUID, LITMUS, LOCKET, MADCAP, MADMAN, MAGNUM, MAMBA, MANGO, MANTEL, MANTIS, MAXIM, MENTAL, MISFIT, MUFTI*, MUMBO-JUMBO, MUSCAT, NAPKIN, NECKLET, NELSON, NETBALL, NICKEL, NITWIT, OBSESS, OCTET, ONSET, OPTIMISTIC, OPTIMUM, PADLOCK, PAMPAS, PANDA, PASTA, PASTEL, PATROL, PECTIN, PELMET, PELVIS [-əs], PENCIL, PEPLUM, PEPSIN, PEPTIC, PESSIMISTIC, PICNIC, PICRIC, PIDGIN, PIGLET, PINBALL, PISTOL, PISTON, PUNDIT, POLKA, POMPOM, POM-POM, POMPON, POPGUN, POPLIN, POTMAN, PUBLIC, QUANGO, QUICKSET, QUINTET, RAGLAN, RAMROD, RANCID, RANDOM, RANSACK, RANSOM, RASCAL*, RECTUM, REDCAP, RICRAC, RIFFRAFF, RIMLESS, ROLLICK, ROTTEN, RUEFUL, RUGGED, RUMPUS, RUSTIC, RUMBA, SACRUM, SAMPAN, SELDOM, SEPSIS [-əs], SEPTIC, SEPTET, SEXTON, SIGNAL, SIGNET, SISKIN, SITCOM, SUBLET, SUBMIT, SULTAN, SUN-GOD, SUN-HAT, SUN-LIT, SUNSET, SUN-TAN, SYNTAX, TABLET, TANDEM, TANGO, TEMPO, TENPIN, TICK-TACK, TID-BIT, TINPOT, TINSEL, TIPTOP, TIT-BIT, TOM-TOM *drum,* TONSIL, TOPLESS, TOXIC, TOXIN, TUT-TUT, UMBEL, UNCUT, UNFIT, UNLESS, UNLOCK, UNMAN, UNPACK, UNPICK, UNROLL, UNLESS, UNTIL, UNWELL, UNZIP, UPHILL, UPON, UPSET*, VANDAL, VELVET, VICTIM, VISTA,

VODKA, VULVA, WAXEN, WEDLOCK, WETTED, WHEREUPON, WHIZ-KID, WIGWAM <a>=[o], WILFUL, WISDOM, WITNESS, WITLESS, WOMBAT*, ZEBRA. Proper Nouns HINDI, HINDU, INCA, ISLAM, LISBON, MELBA, TALMUD, TONGA. Names ATLAS, DEBRA, DEVLIN, DUNCAN, DUSTIN, ELVIS, ENZO, EZRA, JACKSON, JASMIN, JUSTIN, KELVIN, MAGDA, PETRUS, SAMBO, SAMSON, SAXON, SIMBA, WILMA, YASMIN.

Atlas is an eponym. Does the mountain Atlas support the heavens or is it the Greek god Atlas who is doomed to uphold the pillars of heaven and earth? The first atlas, published in the 1500's, was named after Atlas, the god of astronomy and navigation.

Bunyip and *bunya-bunya tree* rebel against the rule that <y> is not allowed inside words, unless Greek. These are Ab'l words which have been adopted into English and if <i> replaced <y> in *bunyip* we would see <ii> which is a no-no. *Bunia* would sound like [bun-ee-ar] and so <y> is needed to spell [bun-yar], from Ab'l Kabi language, once spoken around Gympie in Queensland, (Blake, p. 90).

Fungi and other Latin words with plurals ending in <i> are rebels to the rule which forbids terminal <i>. Their excuse is that they have been borrowed from another language but their spelling has not been changed to suit English rules in order to show they are scientific words: adopted but not adapted. In ordinary English, *funguses* is acceptable.

Junta was adopted and adapted long ago, <j> spells [j], not Spanish [h] nor Portuguese [zh].
It has never been [yunta], [hunta] or [zhunta] in English. The English use a similar word usually, *union*, but when England and many other European countries formed a *junta* against Napoleon it became a well-known English word.

Mufti is a slang term based on the word *muphtie*, but spelt "funny" to show it is slang.

Rascal spells either [rar-scəl] or [ra-scəl] — do you say [darnce] or [dans]?

Upset can be used as a verb or as a noun. We can use stress to turn nouns into verbs and verbs into nouns. We say <u>up</u>set for the noun but up<u>set</u> for the verb. "What an <u>up</u>set! He up<u>set</u> me." It is easy to remember that verb stress comes later in a word than noun stress because *v* for *verb* comes later in the alphabet than *n* for *noun*. See Stress and the Rhythm of Speech, in the appendix, for a list of noun-verb pairs.

Wombat spells [wom-bat]. When Ab'l words are adopted into English they usually let W 'muddle' <a> to spell [o], as in *wandoo*. However Ab'l words with <wo> do not appear to be Feather Words, e.g., *wonga* spells [wong-ar], not [wung-ar]. *Wombat* is an Ab'l word adopted into English, recorded in 1798 as *wombat,* by a man who then noted that the Ab'l pronunciation was *womback,* (Blake, p. 105). However, some say it was closer in pronunciation to *numbat,* in which case *wombat* is a Feather Word, like *wonder*. Such words, in which <o> replaces <u> after <w> and/or before <m> or <n>, are also called Cursive Casualties. Their spelling was wounded, by cursive handwriting, which made <u> hard to read in such words.

Rule 1-35 The stress in verbs comes later in the verb word than the stress in an identical noun word.
Reason This helps separate identical nouns and verbs. Also, Prof. Cummings notes that verbs take suffixes, such as <ed> and <ing>, and suffixes are unstressed. So, to keep to the stress rhythm of English words, which alternates between weak and strong syllables, the stem of verbs needs to end on a strong beat, to which can be added a weak suffix.

Plurals— *s, es, en.*
Rule 1-36A The plural suffix <es>, on words ending [s] or [z], always spells [ez].
Reason This shows the word is plural, that it is not just an unstressed suffix on a singular stem word. This rule would not be needed if <z> was not so unpopular. It makes reading hard unless we know when <s> spells [s] and when it spells [z]. It is, however, a fairly simple reading rule, and follows the rule that terminal <s> spells [z] after a stressed vowel, as in *as, has, is etc*.

Rule 1-36B Words ending [s] or [z] add <es> to form plurals. {We shall see that words ending <sh> and <ch> also take <es> to form plurals.}
Reason As per Rule 1-36A, the plural suffix <es> always spells [ez]. Stressed [ez] shows they are plurals and not just nouns ending [es], nouns like *actress*. Most nouns take the suffix <s> to become plural, but not if they end in [s] or [z] because it's hard to say [s][s] or [z][s] and much easier with a vowel between. Also, if we add an <s> to words which end in a single <s> like *bus* and *pus* we change their meaning: *buss* and *puss*. And if we add an <s> to words ending in <ss> we will get <sss>: *kisss*. As we know, this would break the Triplet Rule, "English words never have three identical consonants in a row." We have already seen that <s> can spell [s] or [z]. So we treat words ending in <z> the same way: *fezzes, buzzes, quizzes*. Note: The little rebels *fez* and *quiz* get a double <z> in the plural form. We can say they are now **adapted,** not merely **adopted**.
Since <x> is always pronounced [ks] at the end of a word it also takes <es> to form plurals: *foxes* and *boxes*. Note, the rule says if the word ends in the sound [s], not just the letter <s>. *Axe* spells [aks] and so 2 *axes* spells 2 [aks-ez].
Old and New Rebels There is one old word ending in <x> which follows a much older rule. The very ancient word *ox* does not accept an <es> for we still say, 'One *ox*, but two OXEN'
We see new <en> plural endings on the world-wide-web where it is used on nouns with new computer related meanings like *vax,* VAXEN, *bix,* BIXEN, *box,* BOXEN.

Plurals by 'umlaut'. MEN and WOMEN and the new word WOMAN.
The plural of *man* is *men* and the plural of *woman* [wuu-man] is *women* [wi-men].
First we shall hear how these unusual plurals arose. Then we shall learn how to read them. Long ago <en> was a plural ending on words, as it still is in *oxen* and *children*. The plural of *man* was *manen*. Then it changed to *menen*. This is known as "umlauting". The mouth gets ready to say [en] too soon and turns the preceding [an] into [en] as well. This then shortened to *men*.
A *woman* was originally called a *wife-man*, which became *wifman* and then *wiman*. Now, in those days, <i> did not have a dot on top. Between <w> and <m> it was impossible to read. You guessed it! The scribes said let's write an <o> for dotless <i>, and we'll know it is standing in for <i>.
So now they wrote (singular) *woman* [wiman] and (plural) *women* [wimen]. However, as we know, the first syllable in English is stressed and so the second became reduced to [mən]. Then *woman* and *women* both spelt [wimən]. A single woman was written as *une woman* in those days and *une* spelt [wuun]. So, 'one woman' was [wuun] [wiman], and joined up to become just *wuman* [wuuman]. Singular and plural now sounded quite different: 1 [wuumən] and 2 [wimən]. Then the scribes said "Now <u> is hard to read after <w> and before <m>," and they changed <u> to <o>. So *wuman* became *woman*. And they changed the <u>in *une,* too, which is why we write *one* but say [wun]. (Some people still say [wuun]. We shall add the feather word symbol to remind us why *woman* spells [wuu-mən] and *women* spells [wi-mən]. Do you think *woman* should have three feathers? After all it changed thrice, from *wiman* to *woman,* then *woman* to *wuman,* then *wuman* to *woman.* WOMAN ƒ ƒ ƒ and WOMEN ƒ.
Surely *woman* has suffered more than any other word, as a Cursive Casualty!

Rule 1-37 After voiced consonants, <s> spells [z], as in *dogs* [dogz], and after unvoiced consonants, <s> spells [s], as in *docks* [doks].
Reason We shall learn all blending rules in Part Two but we have already tried this out for ourselves with fingers on the voice box after list 1-3. For instance, say *tunes*. We hear [tyoonz] for [n] is a voiced consonant.
Rule 1-38 When suffixes <s> or <es> are added to a long vowel sound, terminal <s> spells [z].

Reason The general rule is that <s> spells [z] after stressed vowels and long vowels are all stressed vowels. Why do some words add <es>? Without <e>, *tomatos* would rhyme with *rhinoceros*. However, the English also loved to collect European *curios* and they imported *pianos* and invited Italian *sopranos* to England and, when they wrote about them, they used the Continental spelling, without <e>. Now, in America, only a few words bother to add <e> before adding <s>.

Rebel DOES

Rebel's Reason When *do* takes the suffix <es> the rule holds, in that <s> spells [z] after the long vowel [oo] in *do*. However, the long vowel then shortens to [u]. Why? This is because [uz] is easier to say than [ooz] and also it ensures that three important words are clearly different: "That dog does bite." "Do as I say!" "Don't do that!" Also, bear in mind that little *does* was once longer, both *doeth* and *dost* and may have been pronounced in many ways.

List 1-38 Includes words like GOES and EGOS; TOES and TWOS; TAXIS and BABIES.

Relevant Writing Rule Use this later on, once you can read all the following words. ECHOES, EMBARGOES, GOES, HEROES, NEGROES, POTATOES, TOMATOES, VETOES always use <es>, even in USA, to make plurals. They are Prof. Cummings' most common <oes> words, from the "Basic Speller". Can you add to them? Not all plurals use <es> after vowels. *Negroes* did not always start with a capital. It was a common noun and then became a proper noun and then became offensive to some and is now considered 'dated'.   The following add just <s> to make plurals: ALTOS, BANJOS, CANTOS, CENTOS, CHROMOS, EGOS, ELECTROS, QUANTOS, PIANOS, RATIOS, SOLOS, SOPRANOS, TIROS, CURIOS, OCTAVOS, PROVISOS, DUODECIMOS, plus the plural of *Anglo*, which is ANGLOS. Dictionaries do not all agree on when to use <es> instead of just <s>. The OPD uses <es> in INNUENDOES, MOTTOES, ZEROES. Can you add to these? Some dictionaries list these plurals as INNUENDOS, MOTTOS, ZEROS. Return to Reading Rules.

Two syllables and Orm's Law — *apex, legal, zero.*

Rule 1-39. If consonants are not twinned after stressed vowels they are long vowels in words of two syllables.

Reason Orm's Law states that consonants are twinned after short stressed vowels The vowel is not kept short by Orm's "double gate" for there is only a single consonant, a single gate. We say that this is so for words of two syllables because when we meet longer words we shall see that Orm's Law has been modified, as in *animal* and *holiday*.

Rebels EQUAL, SEQUEL, SEQUIN.

Rebels' Reasons They spell [eek-wal], [seek-wal] and [seek-win], instead of [ekwal], [sekwal] and sekwin], because, although <qu> spells two consonants [kw], it often acts as if it spelt a single consonant, (Cummings p. 106), also in {*frequent*} and others. Compare *mental* and *sequel*. *Mental* obeys the rule, *sequel* does not. Soon we shall meet a very large group of rebels to Rule 1-39, but first we will learn to read all the words which obey Rule 1-39.

The first vowel letter in words which obey Rule I-39 spells a long vowel sound, as below.

<a> in *label* and *nasal* spells [ay] as in *say*.
<e> in *legal* and *ego* spells [ee] as in *meet*.
<i> in *bison* and *lino* spells [I] as in *eye*.
<o> in *omen* and *nova* spells [oh] as in *most*.
<u> in *tulip* and *tuba* spells [yoo] as in *unit*.

Where <u> also spells the long sound [oo] it will be shown.

The long sound that <u> spells is changing all the time. More and more people drop the [y] sound in [yoo]. It has changed the most in USA. Have you heard American movie stars pronounce *tulip* as [toolip]? We shall hear more soon on [oo] and [yoo].

Remember, they only stretch out because they are the first vowel in the word and are followed by a single consonant. The next vowel only gets to stretch if it is free at the end, without a consonant after it to hold it in. How do we read <s> in the middle of a word like *nasal?*

The Curse of the Dagger — *nasal vs. bison.*

As we know the Romans were afraid of <z> because it was the sign of the dagger. This is why even today <s> spells [z] much more often than <z> does. We have learnt that <s> spells [z] at the end of short words like *has,* and that it generally spells [z] after long vowels, as in *toes.* But what about in the middle of two syllable words? If it ends the first syllable it spells [z], as in *nasal,* but if it starts the second syllable it spells [s], as in *bison.* We know that <s> spells [z] after long vowels, as in *nasal,* but unless we know that this word relates to *nose* we might think <s> starts the second syllable, <sal>. We know that <s> always spells [s] at the beginning of words and now we hear that this goes for syllables too — <s> spells [s] at the beginning of syllables. But how do we know where the syllables begin and end? If only English had not fallen under the curse of the dagger! I will mark the lists to show you what <s> spells.

As we know, <a> spells [ar] at the end of words after consonants. Inside some 'Regal Words' <a> also spells its long Continental vowel sound, [ar], as in AMEN, GALA, LAVA, LLAMA, SAGA, if <a> ends the first syllable.

List 1-39 "Regal Words", including *amen* to *saga* above.
AGED [ay-jed], ANAL, ANUS, APEX, BASIN [bay-sin], BEFIT, BEGAN, BEGET, BESET [bee-set], BIFID, BIPED, BISON [bI-son], BOVID, CAPON, COLON, COMA, CUBIC, CUBIT <u> =[yoo], DADO, DEBUG, DEMOB, DEMON, DODO, EGO, EMIT, EMU*, ERA, EVEN, FATAL, FATED, FINAL, FOCAL, GIRO [jI-roh], GURU [goo-roo], HALO, HAVEN, HEBE, HELIX, HERO, HOBO *slang,* HOKUM, HOTEL, HUMAN, HUMID <u> =[yoo], JUDO, JUJU [joo-joo], IBEX, ICON, IDOL, IRON* [I-on], ITEM, JUDO [oo], KAPOK, KUDOS [yoo], KULAK [yoo], LABEL, LADEN, LATEX, LEGAL, LIBEL, LIKEN, LILAC, LI-LO, LINO, LIVEN, LOCAL, LOCUM, LOCO *slang,* LOGO, LUDO [oo], LUPIN [oo], LURID [oo], MODEM*, MOGUL, MOTEL, MURAL, MUSIC, NAKED, NASAL [nayz-al], NATAL, NAVAL, NAVEL, NOTED, NOVA, OMEN, OMIT, OPAL, OPEN, OVA, OVAL, OVEN *f,* OVUM, PAGAN, PENAL, PENIS, PESO [pee-soh], PILOT, POLO, PUBIC <u> =[yoo], PUMA <u> =[yoo], PUPA <u> =[yoo], PUPIL <u> =[yoo], QUOTA, RAVEN, REBUFF, REBUT*, REBUTTAL*, RECALL, RECAP, REDO, REFILL, REFIT, REGAL, REJIG, RELAX, REMIT, RENAL, REPEL, RESELL [ree-sel], RIPEN, RIVAL, ROBOT, ROLY-POLY, ROTA, RURAL [oo], SEMEN, SERUM, SILO, SINUS, SIREN, SISAL [sI-sal], SODA, SOFA, SOLO, *pl.* SOLOS [soh-lohz], TABU [tar-boo], TIDAL, TIRO, TOFU, TOPAZ, TOPI, TONAL, TOTAL, TOTEM, UNIT, UNI., VEGAN, VENAL, VETO, VIRAL, VISA* [veez-ar], VITAL, VIVA, VOCAL, WHITEN, WINO, WOKEN, WOVEN, YODEL, TOGA, XEROX*, YOKEL, ZEBU [oo], ZERO, ZONAL. <u>Proper Nouns</u>
ADEN, BIRO (pen brand), EDEN, FUJI* (apples), KIWI [kee-wee], LIDO [lee-doh], OMAN, QUITO [kee-toh], ROMAN, RUBIK [oo], SATAN, SUDAN [oo], YO-YO, YUKON [yoo-kon], ZULU [zoo-loo]. <u>Names</u> ABEL, ADEN, BADEN, CUPID <u> =[yoo], DAVID, DINA, EDEN, FAGAN, FELIX, FIDO, IDA, IVAN, JACOB, JASON [jay-son], JESUS [jeez-uz], JODY, LISA* [leez-ar], MABEL, MEGAN, MOSES [mohz-ez], NERO, NOLA, ODIN, RONAN, ROSA [rohz-ar], SARA, SIMON, SUSAN [sooz-an], TATUM, TINA* [tee-nar], TITO* [tee-toh], VERA, YOKO ONO, YOSEF, ZOLA.

*Emu is unusual, for, as we know, very few English words end with <u>. It's probably from Portuguese for ostrich, *ema.* It's not at all like *jarngurna* or *yalibirri,* two Ab'l names for the big bird.
*Fuji [fyoo-jee] or [foo-jee] apples are Japanese. Hence the unusual <i> ending.
*Iron [I-on] has a silent <r>. It is a very old Celtic word and is a cousin to Swedish *järn* [yarn].
*Kiwi [kee-wee] fruit or bird is adopted from a Maori language, which allows words to end in <i>.

*In *Lisa, Tina* and *Tito* <i> spells its Continental long sound, [ee]. Names vary, e.g. in *Fido,* <i> spells [I] on English-speaking lips but [feedor] elsewhere, soon to be explained.
Modem – this device modulates and then demodulates signals transmitted over phone lines, (Fleck 2007).
Rebut does not need <tt> to tell it from *but*. However it needs that double gate in *rebuttal*.
Xerox [zee-roks] was a trademark taken out in 1952 by Haloid Co. of Rochester, N.Y., for a copying device, from earlier *xerography* "photographic reduplication without liquid developers" (1948), from Gk. *xeros* "dry" *ography* as in photography. The verb grew from the noun, despite strenuous objection from the Xerox copyright department, (Etymonline).

Continental vs. English Sounds — vowels and yods.

Before the Great Vowel Shift began in 1450 the letters A, E, I, O and U spelt the same long vowels in England as on the Continent, i.e., in the rest of Europe. You can hear them in order if you say, **'Pa, may we all too?'** This makes good sense, because they were the long versions of the short vowels spelt by A, E, I, O, U. Back then, the English still had the letter Ash, Æ, which spelt [a], whereas the letter A spelt short [u] which lengthened to [ar]. E spelt short [e] which lengthened to [ay]. Try it. See what [i] lengthens to. You will find yourself saying [ee]. And [o] lengthens to [or]. Back then, <u> spelt short [uu], which lengthens to long [oo]. That's still how it works on the Continent, on mainland Europe.

When long vowels lifted in England in the Great Vowel Shift (see appendix), the letters of words did not necessarily change. For instance, <i> spelt long [ee] but, when it lifted, it hit the top of the mouth and bent a little, into long [I]. Many words adopted after the GVS have kept their long Continental vowels. That is why <i> spells Continental [ee] in *visa,* adopted 1831, and Anglo [I] in *virus,* adopted 1300's. Anglo is a way of saying English without confining the situation to England. Anglo long vowels can be heard when we say, **'Maybe I won't use glue.'** This gives the long vowels spelt by A, E, I, O and U in English. There are six vowels in 'Maybe I won't use glue,' because, in English, <u> spells two long sounds — [yoo] as in *use* and [oo] as in *glue.* Why?

The English Yod. When French was the official language of England, the English tried to copy the way French people spoke, in this case, the way they said [oo]. In French, <ou> spells the [oo] we hear in *you, maribou* and *toucan*. It's just like the [oo] in *kangaroo,* which we say with rounded lips pushed forward. The French have another [oo] sound which they spell with <eu>, or just <u>. If you hear a Frenchman say 'Dieu', 'lieu', or 'neveu' — *God, place* and *nephew* — you will hear a shorter, higher [oo] than in *maribou* and *kangaroo* or in French <ou> words, like *boutique.* To say this [oo], the French turn rounded lips into a pursed smile which raises and shortens [oo]. When the English tried to copy this sound all they could manage was [ee-oo] or [i-oo]. They found it easier to say [yoo]. So <u> spelt [yoo] and <eu> spelt [yoo], in English as well as French words, after that. That's why *use* begins with [yoo], not [oo], and *eucalypt* starts with [yoo], too. Other digraphs spelt [yoo] too, e.g. <ui> in *suit* [syoot] and <ew> in *few* [fyoo]. But the digraphs <ou> and <oo> never spell [yoo].

Letters are named after the long sounds they spell which is why <u> is called Yoo in English. The short consonant which starts 'Yoo', the sound I write as [y], has its own name. It is called Yod. Over time, Yod was dropped if it was awkward to say after some consonants.
Anglos still say the Yod in words like *due* and *tuna*. Listen for it: [dyoo] and [tyoona]. Many Americans have dropped Yod in those words and say [doo] and [toona]. One easy way to say such words is to fuse [d] or [t] with the Yod, which produces [j] or [ch].

Rule 1-40 If <u> spells a long sound after <d>, then <du> can spell [joo].
Reason This is because our mouths find [joo] easier to say than [dyoo]. It does not happen in *dully,* but it does happen in *duly* in which <u> spells a long sound. When we say "Did you really?" over and over again it sounds like "Dijoo reel-ee?" If <u> spells short [u] then <d> still spells [d], as in *dull*. We shall discuss this further when we meet [j] again in words like *soldier* and *duty*. We have met *due* spells [dyoo]

and now we can see that *due* usually spells [joo], because it is easier to say than [dyoo]. This rule only applies to words in which <u> spells a long vowel so it does not apply to *dully*.

List 1-40 DUCAL, DUE.

Rebel DUCAT rhymes with *bucket* even though it looks like it should start with the same syllable as *ducal*.

Rebel's Reason Apparently so called for the name or effigy of Roger II of Sicily, Duke of Apulia, which first issued the coins (c. 1140). A duke's land is a *duchy*, with short [u]. Maybe a duke's coin copied this short [u] in its name, *ducat*.

Rule 1-41 If <u> spells a long sound after <t>, then <tu> can spell [choo].

Reason We find it easier to say [choo] than [tyoo]. Try it and see. This does not happen when we say *tubby*. That is because in *tubby* <u> spells its short sound. It happens when <u> spells its long sound after [t], as in *tubal*, which spells [choobəl], and so *tuba* spells [choobu], *tuna* spells [choonu] and *tunic* spells [choonik]. Now we know another way to spell [ch]. By the way, we also hear <t> spelling [ch] if we say "Bet you" over and over, very quickly. Try it. Did you end up saying [bechoo]? We shall find out why this happens later when we hear more about [ch]. It is possible to say [tyoo-lip] but easier to say [choo-lip]. That's why we say, "If <u> spells a long sound after <t>, then <tu> <u>can</u> spell [choo]." Our pretty student with tulips from Stuart on the website's Photo Gallery reminds us that when <u> spells [yoo] after <t>, then <tu> spells [choo].

List 1-41
TUBA, TUBAL, TULIP, TUNA, TUNIC.

Rebel TUTU [too-too]

Rebel's Reason *Tutu* spells [too-too], never [tyoo-tyoo] or [choo-choo] because it has been adopted from the Continent where <u> spells [oo] not [yoo]. A lot of people in New York are from Continental Europe. So for them *tulip* spells [toolip]. , which is easy to say and does not need to change anymore. People who drop the [y] sound from <u> spells [yoo] are "Yod Droppers".

A very large group of rebels to Rule 1-39.
After 1066 England was flooded with French Normans and French words. The English knew when Frenchmen were coming because even if they were too far away to hear the French words they could hear **how** they spoke. The French like to stress the **end** of their words whereas the English think the **beginning** of a word is the most important. The English adopted lots of French words. They often changed the spelling to match the way they said them. They said them the English way, with a strong start, e.g., *mutton* [**mut**-ton] comes from French for sheep, *mouton* [moo-**ton**]. When the English changed [oo] in [moo-ton] to [u] in [muton] they doubled the <t> to keep the first vowel short, short [u], as in *cup*. Even if the scribes (often Norman scribes) did not alter the spelling, the English still said them the English way. They stressed and shortened the first vowel. This is why *lemon* has only one *m* when it should have two, *lemmon*.
Lemon looks like a 'Regal Word', with a long vowel in the first syllable. *Lemon* should spell [leemon]. Instead, it breaks Orm's Law which says short, stressed vowels should be followed by twin consonants, or at least two consonants. It's a Rebel. So is the word *rebel*. It should be written *rebbel*.
So is the name *Helen* a rebel. It should be *Hellen* but it is from France, *Hélène*, which in France is pronounced [el-**ayn**] like our *Elaine*. Let's call the rebels 'Rebel Lemon' words.

Rebel Lemons — *alum, lemon, rebel, wagon.*
No Rule for Rebel Lemons. We cannot use rules to decode Rebel Lemons. They are the words which give English spelling a bad name. We have to meet each one and learn to recognize it.
All such words are adopted, pronunciation adapted, but spelling not adapted.

The English took words from other languages too and changed them and often turned them into Rebel Lemons. For instance, *atom* is now a Rebel Lemon, but it used to be written in its full Latin form, *atomus*, which the English said with the sharp <a> and stressed at the beginning.

Here is a list of Rebel Lemons, words which break Orm's Law. They only have one consonant after the first vowel and yet the vowel remains short in our mouths. As we know, <v> is never twinned and so we never expect to read *devvil* even though <e> spells short [e]. *Riven, rivet, civic, Devon, devil, divot, hovel, cavil, avid, level, livid, vivid, seven, revel, Kevin, ravel, novel,* and *pivot* all appeared in an earlier list (1-21A) with short vowels in the first syllable. We now know that they belong to a large group of rebels called Rebel Lemons. Added to that list are words which should have <xx>, but as we know, <x> is never twinned. So, *axil, axis, boxen, exam, exit, maxim, nexus, taxi, toxic, toxin* and *vixen* from list 1-23A are all Rebel Lemons.

We shall meet more Rebel Lemons later. Maybe you'd like to make a separate list of Lemon Rebels for your own use, a "loose list".

Rebel Lemons never have <ss> inside them, just a single <s>, and so how do we know if it spells [s] or [z]?

Rule 1-42 Between vowels, <s> spells [z] if it follows a short, stressed vowel in a two-syllable word.
Reason As we know, <s> spells [z] in *as, has,* and *his,* and so we would expect this to continue after other short stressed vowels. That's why in the next list *basil* spells [bazil] and *resin* spells [rezin].

List of Rebel Lemons
ALUM, ARID, ATOM, BARON, BASIL, BATON, BERET*, BOSOM* ƒ, BUXOM, CABIN, CALIF, CAMEL, CANON, CARAT, CARET, COMET, CORAL, DENIM, DUCAT, FELON, FERAL, GAMUT, HARASS*, HERON, IMAM, LEMON, LINEN*, MADAM, MAMA, MEDAL, MEGA, MELON, MEMO*, METAL, MINIM*, MODEL, MONO- *prefix,* MORAL, NEMESIS*, ORAL, PANEL, PATEN, PEDAL, PERIL, PETAL, PICA, PITON, REBEL*, RESIN, RISEN, ROBIN, ROSIN, SALAD, SALON*, SATIN, SEDAN*, SERIF, SOLID, SOREL, TALON, TARIFF, TELEX, TENET, TENON, VALET*, VENOM, VIGIL, WAGON*. Proper Nouns/Adjectives ARAB, DEVON, IRAN, IRAQ, JAPAN, LATIN, PARIS, YEMEN, YETI*. Names ADAM, ALAN, BORIS, CECIL, CAROL, CORAL, DENIS, DEREK, DORIS, ERICA, ERIN, HABIB, HELEN, JANET, KEVIN, NICO, NIKI, PARIS, ROBIN, plus lists 1-21A and 1-23A.

Beret spells [be-ray], adopted but not fully adapted from French.

Bosom was spelt *bosm* in Old English, from an old word [bow-zm] or [boh-zm]. It changed to [buu-zuum] and became the feather word *bosom* to prevent <u> running into <m> and becoming hard to read.

Carol and *coral* and all the others with a single <r> in the middle have a good excuse for not using <rr>, because they obey a rule which we shall meet later, in Part Three.

Ducat spells [dukat] and is related to *duchy*. It was used for coins and tickets.

Harass spells [ha-ras], with stress on first syllable, (OPD p. 297) but due to the <ss> ending Americans stress the last syllable, [hə-ras]. *Harassment* spells Anglo [ha-ras-ment] and American [hə-ras-ment].

Linen [lin-en] comes from Latin for flax, which was called "linem" because the leaves lined up so regularly.

Memo spells [mem-oh], not [mee-moh]. It is short for *memorandum,* and now belongs with the Rebel Lemons.

Minim is an abbreviation of Latin *minimus* and as such can disobey spelling rules. We shall meet *minim* again with *minimum.*

Nemesis is an eponym, a word made from a Proper Noun — in this case the Greek goddess of vengeance, Nemesis.

*Many people stress the second syllable of *salon* but the Oxford Paperback Dictionary (OPD) Australian Version stresses the first syllable.

*_Rebel_ is stressed on the first syllable as a noun and the second syllable as a verb.

*_Sedan_ — Mr Johnson, the famous dictionary writer, believed that the first _sedan_ chairs were made in the town of Sedan, in France, and named after the town. So he spelt it like the town and pronounced it like the town. Others said it comes from Latin _sedere,_ meaning sit. Johnson's dictionary was a <u>describer</u>. It told how words were said and written in his day. This is different to the dictionary published 150 years later, the Oxford English Dictionary, because the OED is a <u>prescriber</u>, telling us how words <u>should</u> be written and pronounced.

*_Valet_ spells [val-ay], with an English stressed start but a French finish.

*_Wagon_ is only a Rebel Lemon when it is spelt like this. As we know, it is also written with 'double gates', _waggon._

*_Yeti,_ the Abominable Snowman, might not be very big. In Tibetan _yeh-teh_ is "a little animal which resembles a human", probably a spider monkey, (Fleck 2007).

Te-tum vs. tum-te-tum

Some English words do not sound English because they do not stress their first syllable. These words look as if they start with long syllable, a syllable with a long vowel, because Orm's Law states that long vowels are followed by single consonants. However, we know that words like _ago, again_ and _akin_ do not start with long vowels. They start with short vowels but we do not call them Rebel Lemons because their first syllable is not stressed, and Orm's Law refers to stressed vowels.

Some of these words begin with unstressed prefixes, words like _akin,_ "kin to". In such words initial <a> is a prefix and spells the short unstressed sound we call schwa, [ə]. Others are compounds of two words, like _upon,_ which would have lost meaning if written _uppon,_ with 'double gates' to keep [u] short, because then stress would have fallen on [up] and we'd say [upən], which is too close to _upend._ Instead, [pon] is stressed and [u] shrinks to [ə]. A third group of words have retained their French spelling and are still said like French words, like _canal,_ with stress on the last syllable. This reduces vowels in first syllables to swcha, [ə]. Although most English words follow the beat of 'tum-te', as in _legal,_ some follow the beat of 'te-tum', as in _ago._ The main thing to remember about an English accent is that syllables are stressed and unstressed alternately.

Here is a little list of some te-tum words.

ABET [ə-bet], ABOVE [ə-<u>buv</u>], AGO [ə--goh], AGOG [ə--gog], AKIN [ə--kin], ALAS [ə-las], AMASS [ə-mas], AMID [ə--mid], AMISS [ə-mis], AMOK ƒ [ə-muk], CADET [kə-det], CANAL [kə-nal], CARESS [kə-res], DIVAN [də-van], SEDAN [sə-dan], UPON [ə-pon].

Fairy E — _hope_ vs. _hop_

Long ago words were much longer. For instance, _hope_ and _hop_ were _hopian_ and _hoppian._ As we can see, they both obeyed Orm's Law. We know that <o> in _hopian_ spelt long [oh] because it was followed by just one consonant, <p>. We know that <o> in _hoppian_ spelt short [o] because it was followed by two consonants, <pp>. Then words shrank. All that was left of the second syllable of _hopian_ was a little <e> which spelt [ə], a little grunty sound, a short little [er] sound. Eventually everyone stopped saying this little second syllable but the silent <e> remained to show that <p> was never twinned. This ensured that <o> in _hope_ kept spelling its long sound, [oh].

When _hoppian_ shrank to _hoppe_ and then _hopp_ scribes got tired of writing <p> twice, in order to make <o> spell its short [o] sound. As we have already heard, they said amongst themselves, if the final vowel is short there is no need to write the following consonant twice. So to this day we write _hop_ but we twin <p> in _hopping_ because <o> is not the final vowel in _hopping._ _Henn_ became _hen_ and _penn_ became _pen_ but when we write "Henny Penny" twins return because words still obey Orm's Law, they just don't twin at the end of words anymore.

When little children are taught to read and write *hope*, they are told to add a silent <e>, to remind the vowel to remain long. This silent <e> is called Fairy E if we believe that it does not just remind the vowel to stay long but it spreads magic dust to keep it long! In Part Three we shall meet lots and lots of Fairy E words but for now we shall just list the five we use the most, for then you can read, "Name the time. I like to get home on time." "I hope he came home in time." and other such sentences which use these words.

List 1-43
CAME, HOME, HOPE, LIKE, NAME, TIME

Soft in *City* but not in *Kitty*.

Rule 1-44 Together, letters <ce> spells [s] and <ci> spells [s].

Reason The French speaking Norman invaders played havoc with English. After 1066, English was just used by the lower classes. English words were lost or lost their endings or were 'Frenchified' and, if they were written down, it was by scribes who used French spelling rules. For instance, before 1066, <s> spelt [s], not [z]. Back then, *is* [is] was frozen water, not today's verb *is* [iz]. After 1066, it was spelt *ice*. The French inherited the Roman fear of <z>. They used <s> for [z]. When they wanted to spell [s], they used <ce> or <ci>, as in *acid* and *France*. In this situation <e> and <i> are 'decider signs' because they tell <c> to spell [s]. When they don't follow right on after <c>, then the <c> still spells [k], as in [akrid], spelt <acrid>, (acid-like). This situation has remained, to avoid writing scary <z>. In *pens* [penz], <s> spells [z]. In *pence* [pens], <ce> spells [s]. The curse of the dagger, fear of <z>, continues to this very day. If you remember, Z was the sign of Zayin the Dagger, the zig-zag slash marks of a sword or a dagger.

List 1-44 A few examples of <ce> and <ci> spelling [s]. In this list all vowels before <v> are short.
ACCESS [ak-ses], ABSCESS [abs-ses], CELL, CENSUS, CEREBELLUM, CESSPIT, CINEMA, CIRRUS, CITADEL, CITRIC, CITRONELLA, CIVIC, CIVIL, CIVIT, DECIBEL*, EXCEL*, EXCESS*, NOTICE, NOVICE, OFFICE, ONCE* *f,* SUCCESS [suk-ses], RECIPE* [re-sip-ee]. <u>Names</u> ALICE [alis], CEDRIC, CECIL [ses-il], CICERO [sis-e-roh], EL CID, JANICE [janis], LETTUCE.

*ature**Decibel,* is an eponym. Google Alexander Graham Bell.

Excel and *excess* will always spell [ek-sel] and [ek-ses] because <ce> spell [s] and can never spell [z]. *Excel* is stressed on the second syllable, like *exam*. As we know, this means *exam* spells [eg-zam]. However, *excel* spells [ek-sel].

**Novice* is a Rebel Lemon.

**Once* grew from *one*. We met one *one* in list 1-12 and read why it's spelt like that. *Once* evolved when people said things happen in ones, twos, or threes, meaning one time only, *onece*, or two times (twice), and three times (thrice). The <s> at the end of *ones* was written <ce>, the new French way, *onece,* but this spelt [wun-es] and so an <e> was dropped and so now *once* spells [wuns]. We'll meet *once* again in Part Two, with other words with the [ns] terminal blend.

**Recipe* [res-ip-ee] belongs to a small group of words of more than one syllable in which terminal <e> spells [ee].

*In *success* and {*succeed*} a consonant twin spells two sounds, [ks]. If <cc> is followed by <i>, or <e>, or <y>, it no longer spells a single [k] sound for it spells [ks]. As we know, <ck> is used instead of <cc> in words like *bucket* and so this cannot happen. Also, we use <k> in *kitten* to prevent spelling [sit-ten]. {The French dislike <k> and so they use <qu> to spell [k] before <i> or <e>, in words like *quiche*.}

Rebels   RECCE, CELT, CELLO, {CELLIST, FASCIST, CRESCENDO, ARCED, ARCING and SOCCER}

Rebels' Reasons *Recce* is pronounced [rekee], not [rek-see], because it's a shortening of *reconnaissance* in which <c> spells [k] because it is followed by <o>. It belongs to a small group of words of more than one syllable in which terminal <e> spells [ee].

Cello spells [chel-oh] and {*cellist*} spells [chel-ist], adopted from Italy, where <ce> spells [ch].

In {*fascist* and *crescendo*} <sc> spells [sh], adopted from Italy where <sc> spells [sh]. We shall hear about *soccer* [sok-er] in Part Three.

Celt spells [kelt] and so some people write *Kelt*. However Proper Nouns can be written however the owner or owners of the name wish. *Celt* spelt [kelt] before the Norman Invasion and so we can continue to write it like that. However, before Celts reached Britain, they were called [chelts], because of the sharp stone chisels they made. The Celts spread out as they travelled westwards from the heart of Europe. (Some of them said Celt with the hard [k] sound of <ch> in *Christmas* and some of them said it with the soft [ch] of *chisel* which may also have become [s] in some places. People still argue over the "right" way to say Celt.)

Rule 1-45 <ge> and <gi> spell [j] in most words, but not if <g> is twinned to join a suffix, as in *ragged* [rag-ed] and *biggest* [big-est]}.

Reason This is another French spelling rule which was imposed on the English language. It began before the French used J. The letter <j> developed to make little <i> more visible, by giving it a tail. The tradition that <i> cannot end words in English — for legibility in cursive — has carried over to <j>. English words cannot end in <j>.

When <gg> is followed by <i> or <e> it is not softened to [j] when <g> occurs at the end of a stem word and has been twinned before adding a suffix. The suffix does not change the stem word. Compare *ragging* and *raging*. What about prefixes? Twin <gg> occurs in order to fit a prefix on smoothly — *suggest* is smoother than *subgest*. However, *suggest* does not spell [sug-jest]. That would not be a smooth fit and no better than *subgest*. This means that in {*suggest, suggestion* and *exaggerate*} <gg> spells [j], not [gj]. As the rule says, <gg> spells [g] before a suffix, not after a prefix.

Rebels Just a few old English words have kept their old spelling and their old pronunciation. Also, some **modern rebels,** with no French connections, insist that <g> always spells [g].

Old Rebels in which <g> is not softened by <e> to spell [j]. GET, {GELD, GELDING, GEESE, GEEK, GEWGAW, RENEGE, GEAR, TIGER}. Also names {GERTIE, GEBHARD}.

Old Rebels in which <g> is not softened by <i> to spell [j]. GIDDY, GIG, GILLS, GILLIE, GIMLET, GIVE, {GIFT, GILD, GILT, GIGGLE, GIDGEE, GIRL, GIRT, GIRTH, GIZZARD.} Also the names {GILBERT, GILROY, GIDEON}.

Modern Rebels GECKO, GEMSBOK, {GESTAPO, GEYSER, GEISHA}, slang {GEEZER} and GIMMICK, GIBBON, GILGIE* [jil-gee], {GINGHAM, GISMO *slang*}, and prefix GIGA*.

Gilgie [gil-jee] has been adopted from a WA Ab'l word for pond and freshwater crayfish, written with an insulator <e> to save <i> from ending the word. Another Ab'l word, *yabbie,* means the same thing in Eastern Australia, (Blake, p. 93).

Giga spells [gee-gar] and is a prefix which evolved from *gigantic*.

In lists, if <ge> or <gi> spell [g] it will be marked. Otherwise, <ge> and <gi> spell [j].

List 1-45 <ge> and <gi> spell [j].
GEL, GEM, GEN, GENUS [jeen-uus], GENERAL, {GENERIC}, GENET, {GENETIC, GENETICIST}, GENIE [jeen-ee], GENITAL, GENITIVE [jen-i-tiv], GIGOLO [jee-goh-loh], ANGEL* [ayn-jel], GIN*, GIN, GIPSY, GIRAFFE* [ji-rarf], GIRO, GIST. <u>Proper Nouns</u> GENEVA [jen-eev-ar]. <u>Names</u> ANGELA, ANGELO, GEMMA, GIGI [jee-jee], GINNY.

Gel [jel] is a rebel as it should end in twins, <ll>. As we know, *nil* and *gel* are the only words which rebel in this way.

Gin is an Ab'l word for *woman,* not used now as sadly, like most words for a female human, it has been used too often as an insult. It sounded more like *din* to the early settlers who wrote it *din, dyin* and *gin,* (Blake, p. 94).

Giraffe was once 'camelopard', a camel with spots like a leopard's spots, but then Italians learnt the Arabic word *zirafa*, (Fleck, 2007).

English words cannot end with <j> and so <ge> is used to spell terminal [j]. Letter <s> can spell [s] or [z] but <ce> always spells [s]. In the next list, *adage* to *visage* are Rebel Lemons. In this list all vowels before <v> are short.

List 1-45 continued.
ALLEGE, BAGGAGE, BANDAGE, BARRAGE* (barrier), CABBAGE, COLLEGE, COPPICE, COTTAGE, DOSAGE, DOTAGE, ENVISAGE, HOSPICE, INJUSTICE, JUSTICE, LATTICE, LETTUCE, LUGGAGE, LOVAGE ƒ, LUGGAGE, MESSAGE, PACKAGE, PASSAGE, PILLAGE, PINNACE, RAVAGE, RUMMAGE, SALVAGE, SAVAGE, SELVAGE, SILAGE, SULLAGE, TERRACE, TILLAGE, TONNAGE ƒ, USAGE, VANTAGE, VESTIGE, VILLAGE, WATTAGE* <a>=[o].
<u>Rebel Lemons</u> ADAGE, BODICE, BORAGE, CHALICE, DAMAGE, EDIFICE, FORAGE, HERITAGE, HOMAGE, IMAGE, MALICE, MANAGE, MENACE, PALACE, PUMICE, SOLACE, VISAGE.
*ced*Wattage. Don't let W muddle you in *wattage*.
*ced*Barrage* means "barrier" but if it is stressed on the second syllable it means "artillery fire" and uses the Continental long sound, [arj] not [ayj], [ba-<u>rarj</u>].

Rule 1-46 Terminal <s> spells [s] after unstressed vowels.
Reason In words of one syllable vowels are neither stressed nor unstressed, as they cannot be said to be any longer or stronger than another vowel in that word. So this rule only applies to [s] following unstressed vowels at the end of words of two or more syllables, as in *tennis* [ten-nis] and *office* [of-is]. Sometimes [s] is spelt <ce> and sometimes <s>. As we have seen, we can rely on <ce> to spell [s] at all times, even after stressed vowels, as in *police*.
List 1-46 unstressed terminal <s> spells [s].
ATLAS, AXIS*, BASIS, BOGUS, BONUS, CADDIS, CLEVIS*, DERRIS, FOCUS, HAGGIS, HOCUS-POCUS, HUMUS [hyoo-muus], IBIS, MINUS, LITMUS, LOCUS, LOTUS, MANTIS, MODUS, MUCUS, OPUS, ORRIS, PELVIS, PENIS, REBUS, RECESS, REMISS, SEPSIS, TENNIS, TESTIS, VIRUS. <u>Proper Noun</u> LAGOS. Names AMOS, JANUS, IRIS, MAVIS, MORRIS, OTIS, SILAS, TITUS.
Axis and *clevis* are Rebel Lemons.

Suffixes which shift stress and shorten vowels, — *acid, vomit.*

As we know, adding a suffix to a word makes a new word. Some suffixes not only change a word's meaning but also its rhythm and the length of its vowels. We shall now meet a few suffixes which do this. As we learn to read their stems, we shall meet more suffixes which do this.

The first syllable of English stem words is stressed, but this changes as new words are created with affixes. When prefixes are added, in front of words, the second syllable is stressed, not the prefix, e.g., *less, un<u>less</u>*. Usually the prefix *ex*— is stressed, as in *<u>exit</u>*, but this is not always so, as in *ex<u>am</u>*. Suffixes are usually unstressed syllables, unless they end verbs, as in *alternate*.

Since suffixes are unstressed, the syllable before a suffix is stressed to create a tum-te-tum-te rhythm, a pattern of alternating stress. So, words are not necessarily stressed on their first syllable. For example, the word *acid* is stressed on the first syllable, *<u>acid</u>*, but when the suffix —*ic* is added, the stress pattern changes to *a<u>cidic</u>*. Linguists say the syllable with the most stress has primary stress, and the next most stressed has secondary stress. So in a word like *<u>an-i-mal</u>*, the first syllable has primary stress and the third syllable has secondary stress.

Not needed but nice to know. Linguists call the final syllable the ultimate syllable and the one behind it, preceding it, they call the penultimate syllable. *Pen—* is a very old prefix meaning 'almost or nearly'. The *penultimate syllable* is 'almost the last syllable'. A *peninsula* is 'almost an island'. Now back to things we need to know.

Rule 1-47 Suffixes <id>, <it> and <ic> shorten and stress a one letter vowel in the preceding syllable if it is followed by a consonant, but cannot shorten <u> to [u].
Reason Look at *comic*. It spells [komik] but it is not written *commic*. The first vowel is short, but is not followed by twin consonants to stop it stretching out. Why? Is it just another Rebel Lemon, adopted from other languages but not adapted to English spelling rules? The Prof, Don Cummings, p. 112, gives a variety of historic reasons for the effect these tiny suffixes have on stem words. He concludes that the suffixes now follow firm spelling rules. To my mind, in these suffixes, <i> spells such an insignificant reduced [i] that the little sound barely separates the two consonants on either side of it, so it is as though the vowel is followed, if not by twins, by two consonants, which reduces it from a long to a short vowel sound.

As the rule states, these suffixes cannot reduce the vowel spelt by <u> as we see in *humid, lucid, lurid, cubic, Cupid, cubit, pubic, runic, tunic* and *music*. This is because <u> was long ago written <iu> and fell outside the rule, which is only for one letter vowels — and before that, before the Romans had the letter U, they carved IV for U, to tell it from V.
Note: words can have a twin before <id>, as in *pallid* and *horrid,* and a twin before <ic> in *classic*, but they do not need a twin because one letter vowels are always short before a consonant and <id>, <it> or <ic>, except if spelt with <u>.
Rebels? No. *bifid,* [bI-fid] meaning 'two forked' and *trifid* [trI-fid], 'three-forked', are not rebels because they end in <fid> not <id>. (Word-part *fid* means "made".)
Rebels ACETIC [u see-tik], ANEMIC [u-neem-ik].
Rebels' Reasons The Anglo spelling is *anaemic,* in which <ae> spells [ee], due to Greek origins. Suffix <ic> only shortens one letter vowels, and so its American spelling, *anemic,* made it a rebel. In *acetic* <e> spells [ee], probably to copy the sound of *anaemic/anemic*. It comes from French *acétique* in which <e> spelt its long Continental [ay].

The following rule answers the question "What does <s> spell before these suffixes?"
Rule 1-48 Before suffixes <id>, <it> and <ic>, a single <s> spells [s], unless the word is a verb or derives from a word which uses <s> to spell [z].
Reason These little suffixes shorten preceding vowels, so <ss> after the vowel is not required to keep it short. When <ss> reduces to <s> it still spells [s]. However, if the word is a verb, then <s> spells [z]. The noun *visit* developed from the verb *to visit,* (Etymonline) and so in both words <s> spells [z]. In *music,* <s> spells [z], because <s> spells [z] after vowel digraphs (Cummings p. 396) and as we know <u> is acting here as a vowel digraph which is why the suffix cannot shorten it to [u]. Therefore, because *—ic* does not shorten <u>to [u] in {*prussic*} (as in *prussic acid*), <s> requires twinning, to spell [prus-ik] with a short [u], which also ensures that [s], not [z] — as we know <ss> spells [s], (except for *hussar, scissors* and *hussy.*)
List 1-48
The *acid* group: ACID, AMID, ARID, AVID, FETID, LIPID, LIVID, RABID, RAPID, RIGID, SOLID, TEPID, TIMID, VALID, VAPID, VIVID.
The *magic* group: BASIC*, CIVIC, COLIC, COMIC, CONIC, EPIC, LOGIC, MAGIC, MANIC, MEDIC, MIMIC, PANIC, RELIC, RUNIC, SODIC, SONIC, TONIC, TOPIC, TOXIC. Name ERIC.

The *vomit* group: CIVIT, DAVIT, DEBIT, DIGIT, EDIT, HABIT, LICIT, LIMIT, MERIT, POSIT, TACIT, VISIT, VOMIT.

*Many people say [bay-sik] for *basic* but the correct pronunciation is [bas-ik].

Rebel? No. *Benefit* [ben-ee-fit] is not a rebel for it does not have a suffix, being a compound word made of *bene* and *fit*, 'good' and 'deed'.

Rebels ANNELID, HOMINID are not stressed on penultimate syllables, the syllable before —*id*. Primary stress is on the first syllable.

Rebels' Reason Cummings, p. 121, calls this suffix 'The Second —*id*.' *Annelid* and *hominid* have the —*id* ending because they are animals. Scientists end the names of animal families with —*idae* and then they say "hominids belong to the Hominidae Family and annelids to the Annelidae, just as Browns belong to the Brown Family." In these and some other scientific words the suffix —*id* does not cause the preceding syllable to be stressed.

What does <s> spell in the next words? We know that <s> spells [s] at the beginning of words, but prefixes can push an initial <s> inside a word. So, we need to remember that <s> spells [s] at the beginning of syllables as well as words, as in the third syllable of *parasitic*.

List 1-48 cont. The suffixes on these adjectives shorten and stress the preceding syllable.
ACIDIC, AGARIC, ANGELIC, AQUATIC, AQUAVIT, ARABIC, ASEPTIC, ATOMIC, BORACIC, BOTANIC, BUBONIC, BUCOLIC, BULIMIC, CAROTID, CERAMIC, CLIMACTIC, CLIMATIC, COLONIC, DEMONIC, DIDACTIC, DOGMATIC, DOMESTIC, ECONOMIC, ECONOMICAL, ELASTIC, ELICIT, EMETIC, EMPIRIC, ENDEMIC, EPIDEMIC, EROTIC, ERRATIC, ESOTERIC, EXOTIC, EXPLICIT, FANATIC, GENERIC, GENETIC, HEPATIC, HEPATIC, HERETIC*, ICONIC, ILLICIT, IMPLICIT, INHABIT, INHERIT, INHIBIT, INSIPID, INVALID, IRONIC, ITALIC, KINETIC, LACONIC, LUNATIC, MAGNETIC, MASONIC, MEDIC, MELODIC, METALLIC*, MONOPOLISTIC, NOMADIC, OPERATIC, OSMOTIC, OXALIC, PACIFIC, PALLID*, PANDEMIC, PARABOLIC, PARASITIC, PAROTID, PELAGIC, POLITIC, PROHIBIT, ROBOTIC, SATANIC, SATIRIC, SOMATIC, SOPORIFIC, SUBATOMIC, SUB-EDIT, SUB-SONIC, TITANIC, TOPIC, VOLCANIC, Proper Adjective GALLIC*.

**Heretic* is stressed on the first syllable as a noun, but obeys the rule for the adjective *heretic*.

**Metal* is a Rebel Lemon word. It was also spelt *mettle* until 1700. Then *mettle* came to mean the amount of 'steel' in a person's spine. *Metallic* retains the <ll> of its Greek parent, *metallikos*, in Anglo English but in USA it's just *metalic*.

*In *pallid* the unnecessary double gate <ll> is retained, from Latin *pallidus*, meaning 'pale'.

**Gallic*, originally 'like a Gaul', now means 'of France'. It is based on Latin *Gallicus* and retains <ll> to prevent a muddle with *Galic*, an old way of spelling *Gaelic*.

The rule that the suffix —*ic* makes the preceding one letter vowel short and stressed holds when another suffix is added.

List 1-48 continued
BOTANICAL, HERETICAL, MEDICAL, SATIRICAL, PARADOXICAL.

Third Syllable from the End — *animal, holiday, veteran.*

Old English is what we call the language of England before it was conquered in 1066, by Normans from Normandy in France. In Old English, short, stressed vowels were followed on paper by twin consonants, or two consonants, as in *catt* or *hand*. This rule was written in a book by a Norman scribe called Orm. It is known as the first recorded English spelling rule and rather misleadingly called Orm's Law. He did not invent it, but he did take note of it and use it. We shall learn, in Part Three, that future scribes got sick of twinning and so they stopped twinning at the end of words. This modification to Orm's Law also involved adding Silent E to words which did not end in twins, so that *hop* and *hope* did not look the same. We shall learn that scribes stopped twinning only at the end of words, not in the middle. So they kept twinning in words like *kitten* and *hopping.*

Right now we shall hear of another modification to Orm's Law.

Rule 1-50 The Third Syllable from the End Rule: When the stress is on the third (or fourth) syllable from the end of the word, its vowel is short, if it is spelt with one letter and if that letter is not <u>.

Reason This is a pattern observed by many linguists, Cummings on p. 131 lists Jespersen, Chomsky and Halle, all famous spellers. How did it happen? When *holy day* joined up to become *holiday,* the long [oh] of *holy* became the short vowel of *holiday.* Maybe people began speaking faster, shortened stressed vowels. Until then, a single <l> after <o> ensured it spelt a long vowel sound, as in *holy.* Twins after <o> ensured it spelt short [o], as in *holly.* Maybe scribes wanted to write faster. Did they tire of writing *annimal* in order to shorten and stress its first syllable? They must have decided that if the word is three syllables long and the first syllable is stressed then it has a short vowel, with no need of twins after it.

Scribes said, "Never mind writing twins to keep the vowel short if it is in a long word and near the beginning of the word. Let's stop writing twins to keep it short and save a bit of time. As long as it is stressed, we shall say that it does not need twin consonants to keep it short." They extended the rule to include syllables which were four syllables from the end of a word, as long as that syllable was stressed. Let's see how the rule works. If you did not know how to say *animal* you would say to yourself, "English words are usually stressed on their first syllable. *An* is the third syllable from the end of the word, and so the vowel <a> must be a short [a] sound, even though the <n> is not twinned. Let's call them 'Holiday Words', the words which obey the long Third Syllable from the End Rule.

Rebel? NUMERAL is not a rebel, because the long vowel written with <u> does not shorten, even though it is in a stressed syllable which is third from the end of the word.

Rascal COLONEL You will not find *colonel* in any list. Even though it looks like a 'Holiday Word', it does not spell [kol-on-el]. Long ago the English copied the French word *coronel* by saying [ker-nel], but then the French changed it. In order to sound more like the original Italian word, *colonnella,* the French said [kol-on-el] and wrote it as *colonel.* The English copied the French spelling, in 1583, but kept saying [ker-nel]. It would not matter how it was spelt, as few people could read and write in 1583, maybe 20% of men, and less than 10% of women. Maybe everyone just found [ker-nel] easier to say than three syllabled [kol-on-el] or stubbornly refused to use the modern French word. (The original Italian *colonnella* is short for "the commander of a small column of soldiers".)

Not needed but nice to know. Many Rebel Lemons gained their short first vowel due to the Third (or more) Syllable from the End Rule. They were long words which later shortened. For instance, the Rebel Lemon *manage* is thought to come from the Italian word for handling horses, *maneggiare.* Italian <a> spells [ar] but in English the fourth syllable from the end was stressed and became [man], without need of twins after <a>. Then the word shortened to *manage.* The Rebel Lemon *atom* was once much longer. In Latin it was *atomus* and the English shortened and stressed the third syllable from the end, [at-om-uus]. Then they pronounced it [at-om-əs] and then just [at-om] and [at-uum] and finally [at- əm]. Many long Latin words were shortened in this way, by converting a long vowel to a short, stressed vowel and then dropping the end of the word. I promise (*pro-mis-sum* in Latin) it is one reason the English language is full of Rebel Lemons, like *promise* and *atom* and many more. Now back to things we need to know.

List 1-50 'Holiday Words'
ALIBI*, ALKALI*, ANIMAL, AVENUE, BENEFICE, BENEFIT, CABINET, CAPITAL, CASANOVA*, DECIMAL, DOMINO, EDIFICE, ELEVEN*, HABITAT, HEXAGON, HIPPOPOTAMUS*, LANOLIN, LATERAL, LEXICON, MANIKIN, MARITAL, MEGATON, MELANIN, MINARET, MINERAL, MINIBUS, MINICAB, MINIMAL, MINIMUM*, MONUMENT,

<u> =[yoo], NOMINAL, OMNIBUS*, OPERA, ORIFICE, ORIGIN, ORIGINAL, PARADOX, PARAFFIN, PARAGON, PARALLAX, PARALLEL, PARAMEDICAL, PARAPET, PARASOL, PEDESTAL, PELICAN, PENINSULA*, PITIFUL, PIVOTAL, POPADAM, RAMADAN, SATIRIST, SEVERAL, TALISMAN, TETANUS, VIRULENT, VENISON, VETERAN, VIVIDNESS. Names ANABELLA, BENEDICT, CAROLINA, DOMENIC, FATIMA, HELENA, ISABELLA, JAPONICA, NICOLA, PARAQUAT*, PAMELA, ROXANA, ROXANNA, SOLOMON.

*Alibi [al-i-bI] and *alkali* [al-i-bI] are rebels to the rule forbidding terminal <i>. They are also very unusual in that terminal <i> spells [I] rather than [ee]. They are 'adopted not adapted'. *Alibi* is Latin for "elsewhere", *alkali* is Latin for "ashes" from Arabic: *al-galiy*.

*Eleven's <v> comes from the fact that it means 'one over ten'. In Old English it was *endleofan*, literally "one left" (a leftover after ten), (Etymonline).

*Minimum, 'the smallest thing', is Latin. The English reduced and stressed the first vowel, and then used *mini* in compound words, with the same pronunciation, e.g., *minicab, minibus, miniskirt*. Letter <i> usually spells [I] in the first syllable, but in these words <i> spells [i] due to the stress on this third syllable from the end. Note, *mini* is not a prefix but a stem used in a compound word, just as *hemi, semi* and *demi* are all stems in compound words, viz. *semicircle, demitasse* and *hemisphere*. The Rebel Lemon word *minim*, is an abbreviation of *minimus*, abbreviated after the English shortened the vowel in the third syllable from the end of Latin *minimus*. (*Minim* means a half note in music or a down stroke of letters like *m* or *n*. There is no such word as *minum* in English.)

*Casanova is a good example of a stressed vowel in the fourth syllable from the end of the word not needing twin gates to keep it short, and <s> not needing to be twinned in order to spell [s]. It is actually an eponym, ref. Giacomo Girolamo Casanova de Seignalt.

*The <s> of *omnibus* [om-nee-bus] continues to spell [s] when abbreviated to *bus*. Normally <s> after a short vowel in a single-syllable word spells [z], as we know, e.g., *has* spells [haz]. However, in *bus*, as the final, unstressed, syllable of *omnibus*, <s> spells [s] and continues to do so in the abbreviation *bus*.

*Peninsula is stressed on the third syllable from the end. The fourth syllable from the end is a prefix and prefixes are not stressed. *Pen—* means 'almost', almost an island in this case.

*Don't let W muddle you. In *Paraquat* <qua> spells [kwo]. Another bit of collateral damage, due to cursive casualties.

Rule 1-50 only says that twins are not needed, to keep the preceding vowel short. It does not say they cannot be used. Stress falls on the third syllable from the end of the following words which use twins to keep a vowel short in the following list:-

List 1-50 Short vowels before twins.
MILLIGRAM, MOCCASIN, PEMMICAN, PENNILESS, QUIZZICAL, TARRAGON, TERRAPIN, WITTINESS. Name WARRIGAL*.

*Don't let W muddle you. In *Warrigal* <wa> spells [wo], as in *what* and other such collaterally damaged words.

Since you are now able to read long words, words of more than two syllables, let's look at more long words. The first vowel in all the next words is short because it is followed by two consonants, but it is not necessarily stressed.

List 1-51 Short vowels before two consonants.
ALBUMEN, ALBUMIN, ASPARAGUS, COMMITTED, COMPARISON, ECZEMA*, HIPPOPOTAMUS*, IMPERIL, IMPETUS, INTERIM, MANDARIN, MANDOLIN, MUSCATEL, OCTAGONAL, OMBUDSMAN, OMNIBUS, PICKPOCKET, PUBLICAN, QUICK-WITTED,

TIMPANI, UNCOMMON, UNRAVEL, VERRUCA*, VOLCANIC. <u>Names</u> AFRICA, ANGELA, BENJAMIN, EDWINA, LANCELOT, SABRINA, SEPTIMUS.

*ractical**Eczema* spells [ek-zem-ar] but it is often shortened to [ek-zmar]. One American audio dictionary gives [ik-zee-mar].

**Hippopotamus* obeys four rules: [i] is short because it is spelt with one letter and is followed by twins; [ii] Orm's Law; the first <o> spells [oh] for it stretches out at the end of *hippo*; [iii] the second <o> spells [o] as it's the third syllable from the end of *potamus*; [iv] the <s> spells [s] after the unstressed vowel [u].

**Verruca* [ve-<u>roo</u>-kar] is straight Latin for *wart*, with no adaptations in spelling or pronunciation. In Latin words of two syllables, the stress is on the first syllable. In words of three or more syllables, the stress is on the penultimate syllable (second from the end) if this is 'heavy', otherwise on the antepenultimate syllable, (third from the end). A 'heavy syllable' either contains a long vowel or ends in a consonant, (Wikipedia, Latin).

Unstressed starts— *banana, tuxedo.*
Although most words begin with a stressed syllable and follow a tum-te-tum stress rhythm, some follow a te-tum-te rhythm, starting with an unstressed syllable. The following either start with a prefix or have been adopted from other languages and pronounced as if they have prefixes.

List 1-52 short, unstressed starts.
ABANDON, BANANA, BELOVED, BIKINI, GAZEBO, POTATO, TOBOGGAN, TOMATO, TUXEDO.

Abandon and *beloved* both start with an unstressed syllable, because suffixes *be—* in *beloved* and *a—* in *abandon* are never stressed.

Bikini [bi-kee-nee] is pronounced as if <bi> is a prefix which is not so. This swimming costume is named after Pikini Island, said with even stress by the locals, but not by English tongues. The island is said to look like the *pik* meaning 'surface', of a *ni*, meaning 'nut'.

Gazebo [ga-zee-boh]. In 1752 someone had a bit of fun and added a Latin ending to *gaze*. *Videbo* means 'I shall see' in Latin, hence *gazebo* for 'I shall gaze'. In Italy, a 'belvedere' is literally 'a fair sight' and applied to an open house top and this may have influenced the invention of *gazebo*. There is also the chance the word is an Asian name for an open-sided shelter. However it came about, the English pronounce it as though it has a prefix.

Toboggan [to-bog-gan] comes from *tobakun*, a Canadian Indian sled, but in English it is pronounced as if the first syllable is a prefix.

Tomato and *potato* sound as if they start with prefixes [tə] and [pə]. The rest of their pronunciation depends on personal preference, just like the pronunciation of {*either*} and {*neither*}. The Gershwins' lovers in "Let's Call the Whole Thing Off" agonize over how to say *potato* and *tomato*, "You say [pə-tay-toh] but I say [pə-tar-toh]. You say [tə-may-toh] and I say [tə-mar-toh]" etc. *Potato*, [pə-tay-toh] or [pə-tar-toh], is written *patata* in Spanish, from the Caribbean *batata,* a sweet potato. The name was then extended to a Peruvian potato. *Tomato,* [tə-mar-toh] or [tə-may-toh], has been written *tomato* since 1753 but before that it was *tomate* because it arrived in England with Spanish spelling and Etymonline thinks it changed to match *potato*. The Spanish pronunciation was probably [po-tar-tə], trying to copy the South American Nahuatl word *tomatl*.

Banana [bə-nar-nə] is also pronounced as though it begins with a prefix. Some say [bə-nar-nə] and some say [bə-nan-ə]. As we know, <a> spreads out and spells its long Continental sound at the end of words. It does the same at the end of syllables. So it all depends where *banana* is broken into syllables — does the middle syllable end in <a> or <n>?

The final syllable of *banana* ends in a vowel. Long words which end with a single vowel have usually been adopted into English — *banana, cicada, koala,* etc. In these long words, which end in a single vowel, <a> usually spells short [u] or long [ar], the Continental way, not the Anglo short [a] or long [ay].
Tuxedo [tuk-see-doh] or [tuk-say-doh] can be traced from the name for a rural resort in USA to the tribal name of a crooked river. Like *avocado, potato, soprano* and other English words ending in a single <o>, it ends in the long vowel [oh], its Anglo long sound.

Now we look at a special suffix. Spot the pattern — stressed syllables are underlined:-
Parent plus the suffix <al> becomes *parental*. Primary stress moves from one syllable to another.
Magic plus the suffix <al> becomes *magical*. Primary stress does not move.
Can you see why the suffix <al> changes stress in some words and not others?
You are right if you said that it only happens when <al> follows two consonants.
Monument plus the suffix <al> becomes *monumental*. Primary stress moves from one syllable to another.
Graphic plus the suffix <al> becomes *graphical*. Primary stress does not move.
This is more than a pattern. It is a strong rule which over-rides other stress rules.

Rule 1-53 The Con-con-al Rule: The little suffix -al after two consonants transfers the stress on to the syllable before it.

Reason The Con-con-al Rule says that if the syllable behind —al is short, because its vowel is followed by two consonants — 'con-con'— then it is stressed and what is more it has primary stress, is the most stressed syllable in the word. The syllable <ment> in *monument* has secondary stress, but in *monumental* it has primary stress. The tum-te-tum rhythm remains: *monument* tum-te-tum; *monumental* tum-te-tum-te. However, the stress pattern changes: from tum-te-tum to tum-te-tum-te.

So the suffix —al after two consonants stresses the preceding short vowel. Note, in *abdominal, octagonal, graphical* and q*uizzical* the short vowels preceding —al are not stressed because they are not followed by two consonant sounds. The two consonant letters <ph> and <zz> spell single consonant sounds.

The following list includes the <nt> blend, [nt]. Easy to say and we will meet it again in Part Two.

List 1-53 The suffix —al after two consonants changes the stress pattern.
ACCIDENTAL [ak-sid-en-tal], ACQUITTAL [ak-wit-al], BAPTISMAL [bap-tiz-mal], COMMITTAL [kom-mit-al], CONTINENTAL [kon-ti-nen-tal], DETRIMENTAL [det-ree-men-tal], DEVELOPMENTAL* [de-vel-op-men-tal], DOCUMENTAL [doc-yoo-men-tal], ELEMENTAL [el-e-men-tal], EXPERIMENTAL [eks-pe-ri-men-tal], FUNDAMENTAL [fun-du-men-tal], INCIDENTAL [in-si-den-tal], JUDGEMENTAL [juj-men-tal], MANAGEMENTAL [man-aj-men-tal], MONUMENTAL [mon-yoo-men-tal], PARENTAL [par-en–tal], OCCIDENTAL [ok-si-den-tal], REGIMENTAL [rej-i-men-tal], RUDIMENTAL [roo-di-men-tal], SACRAMENTAL [sak-ra-men-tal], SEGMENTAL [seg-men-tal], SENTIMENTAL [sen-ti-men-tal], SUBCONTINENTAL [sub-kon-ti-nen-tal], SUPPLEMENTAL [sup-le-men-tal], UNSENTIMENTAL [un-sen-ti-men-tal], HORIZONTAL* [ho-ri-zon-tal].

Horizon [ho-rI-zon] comes from French: *orizon* [o-ree-zon], but in order to prevent it sounding like *reason* [ree-zon] the <i> spells [I], the Anglo long sound, not the Continental long [ee] sound.

Terminal Semi-vowel Y — *baddy, any, very, baby.*
As we know, the semi-vowel <y> is a consonant which can act as a vowel.
We have seen <y> acting as a vowel at the end of short words, like *my* and *by,* spelling [I]. Y also acts as a vowel at the end of long words, but then it usually spells [ee].

Rule 1-54 In words of two syllables terminal <y> usually spells [ee].
Reason This is because <y> is usually a suffix in long words.

Rebels? No. What about *deny* and *satisfy*? In both words <y> is not a suffix, as we shall soon see.
List 1-54 Suffix <y> spells [ee]
BADDY, BAGGY, BATTY, BELLY, BERRY, BILLY, BILLY-O, BITTY, BOSSY, BUDDY, BUGGY, BULLY <u>=[uu], BUTTY, CADDY, CANNY, CARRY, CARROTY, CATTY, CUBBY, CURRY, DADDY, DALLY, DILLY BAG*, DITTY, DIVVY*, DIZZY, DOGGY, DOLLY, DOTTY, DULLY* <u>=[u], DUMMY, EDDY, FADDY, FATTY, FERRY, FILLY, FULLY* <u>=[uu], FOGGY, FOLLY, FOXY, FUNNY, FUSSY, FUZZY, GASSY, GIDDY <g>=[g], GOLLY, GULLY, GUMMY, GUNNY, HAPPY, HARRY, HILLY, HILL-BILLY, HOBBY, HOLLY, HUFFY, HURRY, HUSSY*, JAMMY, JAZZY, JELLY, JEMMY, JERRY-CAN, JETTY, JIFFY, KIDDY, KITTY, LASSY, LEGGY, LIPPY, LOBBY, LOLLY, LORRY, MAMMY, MARRY, MERRY, MESSY, MIDDY, MUMMY, MUDDY, MUGGY, MUZZY, NANNY, NAPPY, NATTY, NAVVY*, NIPPY, NITTY-GRITTY, PADDY, PALLY, PARRY, PATTY, PENNY, PERRY, PETTY, PICCANINNY, PIGGY, PINNY, POPPY, POPPYCOCK, POTTY, PUFFY, PUPPY, PUTTY, QUARRY <a>= [o], RALLY, RATTY, RUDDY, RUMMY, RUNNY, SALLY, SAVVY*, SCATTY, SEXY, SILLY, SISSY, SKIVVY*, SOGGY, SONNY ƒ, SOPPY, SORRY, SULLY, SUNNY, TABBY, TALLY, TALLY-HO, TARRY, TATTY, TEDDY, TELLY, TERRY, TINNY, TIZZY, TODDY, TOMMY-GUN, TOMMY-ROT, TUBBY, TUMMY, WADDY*, WAXY, WHINNY, WHIPPY, WILLY-NILLY, WILLY-WILLY, WITTY, WORRY* <o> =[u], YABBY*, ZIPPY. <u>Names</u> ALLY, BARRY, BIDDY, BILLY, BOBBY, BUDDY, BUFFY, BUZZY, CISSY, DOLLY, DONNY, DOTTY, EDDY, FANNY, GARRY, GINNY, HARRY, HOLLY, JENNY, JERRY, JIMMY, KELLY, KENNY, KERRY, KITTY, LARRY, LEXY, LIBBY, MATTY, MILLY, MOLLY, PADDY, PATTY, PEGGY, PENNY, PIGGY, POLLY, POLLYANNA, POPPY, ROBBY, RODDY, SALLY, SISSY, SOLLY, SONNY ƒ, SUNNY, TAFFY, TAMMY, TEDDY, TERRY, TILLY, TIMMY, TOMMY, TULLY, VINNY, WALLY, WIGGY, WILLY, ZIGGY.

Note: We know *foxy, sexy* and *waxy* only have one <x> because <xx> is a "no-no".
*Did you let W muddle you? *Quarry* spells [kworee].
**Fully* [fuul-lee] and **dully* [dul-lee] come from fullly and dullly but as <lll> would disobey the No Triplets Rule they have had to lose an <l>.
**Dilly* comes from the Ab'l word for a woven carrying bag, maybe from 'dhil'la' in Kabi, near Gympie, (Blake, p.92).
**Divvy* is slang, from *divide,* as in, "Let's divvy up the winnings." Slang words do not have to obey spelling rules, in this case the rule against <vv>.
**Hussy* is pronounced [huzee] by some people. A house-wife was called a *hus-wif* [huz-wif] and her spouse a *hus-bond* [huz-bond] ('house dweller'). These words became *hussy* [huzee] and *hubby.* Hussy is read more than said now and so we are led by the letters: *hussy* spells [husee] on most lips now. Also, *hussy* no longer means housewife but a brazen young woman. A *hussif* is another old term for a *house-wife.* Instead of a wife, a single man had a little sewing kit to mend his clothes which he called a HUSSIF. Sailors and soldiers still have them and so we can add that word to our rebels for, as we know, it should be <ff> after the short vowel [i].
**Navvy* is slang. See *divvy.*
**Savvy* is slang. See *divvy.*
**Skivvy* is slang. See *divvy.*
**Waddy* [wod-ee] was adopted from Ab'l languages around Sydney, for a club or whipping cane. Interestingly it was recorded as two words joined *'wad-dy'* for stick or tree.
**Worry* see 3-63.
**Yabby* or *yabbie* is adopted from an Ab'l word for freshwater crayfish. However, the Aborigines in Queensland used it for saltwater crayfish, (Blake, p. 106).
List 1-54 cont. terminal <y> spells [ee].

BABY, DULY* [jool-ee], DUTY* [joo-tee], FURY, HOLY, IRONY*, IVY, JURY, LADY, LAZY, PINY (of pine), PONY, PUNY, QUERY, ROLY-POLY, ROPY, ROSY, RUBY, TINY, WAVY. <u>Names</u> AMY, ROSY, RUBY, SUZY, TINY TIM, TONY.

*Irony is not related to *iron*. It is a cousin of *error* through Latin *ironia* which means 'deliberate error' which in turn came from a Greek word. Socrates made deliberate errors to get his pupils involved, as teachers still do.

*Duly and *duty* can spell [joo-lee] and [joo-tee], rather than [dyoo-tee] and [dyoo-lee], because if <u> spells [yoo] after <d>, then [y] fuses with [d] or [t] so that we hear [j]. This only happens when <u> is spelling the long sound [yoo], not when it is spelling the short sound [u], as in *dully* and *putty*. We met this new way to spell [j] at Rule 1-40 and we shall hear more about it in Part Three

List 1-54 cont. suffix <y> spells [ee] in **Rebel Lemons**
BODY, CITY, COPY, COPY-CAT, EMBODY, INFAMY*, LEVY, LILY, PITY, SOMEBODY ƒ, VERY*, EVERY*, EVERYBODY, EVERYONE, EVERYWHERE, ANY*, ANYBODY, ANYONE, MANY*, BURY*, BUSY*, BUSINESS.

*Any spells [en-ee] instead of [an-ee] because *any* began as "ænig" and was then spelt *eny* but *any* was chosen for the dictionary to show that it came from the Old English word with the old Ash letter, <æ>.

*Bury used to be spelt *byrgan*. In southern England the <y> was replaced with <u> and said [uu]. However, in one region, Kent, just south of London, it was pronounced [e]. Eventually it was said with the [e] sound everywhere but remained written with the <u> letter.' Both *bury* and *busy* are cases of "Mixed Convergence". Where there were earlier two separate pronunciations and spellings, we now have the convergence of one pronunciation with the other spelling", (Cummings, p. 229).

*Busy is the only stem word in which <u> spells [i]. It was *bysig* in Old English. When <y> was removed from the middle of words it was changed to <i>. However, it changed to <u> in the south of England due to the Norman pronunciation [buusy]. Eventually the southern <u> spelling was chosen by the printers in London, but the northern pronunciation prevailed, [biz-ee]. This is a case of "Mixed Convergence", see above, in *bury*. Now try reading BUSINESS. It no longer spells [biz-i-nis] and no longer means 'a state of being busy'. It now spells [biz-nəs] and means 'task, duty, trade, agenda, etc.

*Every [ev-ree] has nothing to do with *very*. It began as *ever each*, meaning that for ever, or always, each thing was to be counted or included. Nowadays if we want to say something stronger than *each* we say 'each and every one', or 'every last one'. It's easy to see how [ev-er eech] shortened to [ev-er-ee]. Since then we have shortened it to [ev-ree]. We shall meet *every* again. Meanwhile we can enjoy reading and writing it and its compounds.

*Infamy is not only a Rebel Lemon word but also rebels against the rule that prefixes are unstressed. This also happens in {*infamous*} which does not mean 'fameless' or 'without fame'. It means 'famous for badness', describes someone with a bad reputation, of ill repute. It was longer in Latin, *infamosus* which meant that since <us> spelt an unstressed syllable, the English stress pattern produced stress on first and third syllable. Then the noun *infamy* copied this stress in the first syllable and third too, but less so.

*Many spells [men-ee] instead of [man-ee]. *Many* and *manifold* are related and *many* used to sound like it: [man-ee], but it changed to sound like *any*. *Manifold* began as 'many folds' and in this word *many* is still pronounced [man-ee]. It now means more than just many folds.

*Very [ve-ree] did not begin as [və-ree]. It is a contraction of *verily* in which <e> spells [e] because it is stressed and in the third syllable from the end of the word.

Rebels? Are *terrify* and *horrify* rebels, because their <y> does not spell [ee]? No, because the ending is <ify> not just <y> and in this case <y> spells [I]. In words ending <efy>, <y> also spells [I]. There are only four words that end with —*efy*: *liquefy* and later {*putrefy, rarefy* and *stupefy*}.

Rule 1-55 The <y> in terminal <efy> and <ify> spells [I].
Reason Terminal <efy> and <ify> were once stem words, meaning 'to make or do', see 1-56.

List 1-55 <y> spells [I]
CODIFY, HORRIFY, HUMIDIFY, JOLLIFY, LIQUEFY*, MOLLIFY, MUMMIFY, NOTIFY, NULLIFY, PURIFY, TERRIFY, UNIFY.
Liquefy is [lik-wi-fI] — [kw] forms a double gate and so <i> spells [i].
The next list combines two rules: Suffixes <-ify> and <-efy> spell [I] and when the stress is on the third (or fourth) syllable from the end of the word, the vowel is short, even without a double gate, e.g., *modify* [mod-i-fI] not [moh-di-fI].

List 1-55 cont.
CALCIFY, DIGNIFY, DISQUALIFY*, EDIFY, FALSIFY*, INDEMNIFY, JUSTIFY, LIQUEFY, MAGNIFY, MODIFY, PACIFY, QUALIFY*, RATIFY, SAPONIFY, SIGNIFY, SOLIDIFY, TYPIFY <y> =[i], VERIFY, VILIFY.
Did you let W muddle you in *qualify* [kwol-i-fI] and *disqualify*?
Falsify spells [forl-si-fI] due to VS (Vowel Shift) in most of England but [fols-i-fI] in Australia.

Rule 1-56 Terminal <y> spells [I] in words in which <y> is part of a single-syllable stem word, not a suffix.
Reason Letter <y> is not welcome inside English words, but it is quite OK at the end of words. At the end of single-syllable words it is used to spell [I], which is handy, because <i> is not welcome at the end of words! (Words like {alkali} are very rare.) Some words are built onto old stems, old words which are no longer used on their own. They have become 'bound stems', unlike 'free stems' which can stand up on their own. They are all single-syllable words. The rule states that <y> spells <I> at the end of a stem word, but that can be a bound stem. Stem words ending <y> are, first the bound stems: *fy, ly, scry,* and then the free stems: *cry, dry, fly, try, pry, ply.* If you are wondering about *sy* at the end of *prophesy*, it changed from *fy* to *sy. Fy* means 'make or do'. Now we can see that suffixes <efy> snd <ify > are made from *fy* with a joiner, [i] or [e]. *Scry* means *scribe* or *write*. Some words are compound words, with the last word reduced to a single syllable ending in <y> spells [I], like *py* at the end of *occupy*, and *ny* ending *deny*.

List 1-56 <y> spells [I] as part of a stem word.
ALLY*, DEFY, DENY, {IMPLY}, {PLY}, OCCUPY*, RELY, {REPLY}, SATISFY, {DESCRY}.
<u>Proper Noun</u> JULY.
Rely [ree-lI] and *reply* [ree-plI] and *imply* [im-plI] have prefixes, before the old stem words *ly* and *ply. Ly* originally meant "bond" (it starts *ligament*) and *ply* is an old word for "fold" or "pleat". *Replicate* and *reply* both grew out of *ply. Rely*, meaning "retie or rebond", started out to mean "re-assemble, rejoin or rally with one's friends" and ended up meaning to "depend on one's friends."
Satisfy used to be *satisify* and was shortened to *satisfy* to match the noun *satisfaction* which entered the English language a hundred years before the verb. In Latin *satis* = "enough" and *facere* = "to make or do or perform", and so *satisfacere* meant "to do enough". It was an old church word, which meant doing enough penance to get your sins forgiven. Then *facere* was shortened in English to *ify, efy* or just *fy*. So satis *ify* = "make or do enough".
Defy and *deny* both have prefix *de—* (*away*). *Defy* originally meant "de-faith", denounce one's faith, *disfidare. Fidare* was reduced to *fi. Deny* was *de-negare* (refuse, say no). *Negare* was reduced to *nec* then *ne* and then *ny*, but it was never a suffix. When we "deny" something we are saying "Get away! No!"
In *descry* <de> is a prefix. Bound stem *scry* means *to scribe* or *write*. We'll see it again in *scribble a*nd *describe.*
*Ally [al-I], is now the odd word out, a complete word in itself, of two syllables, but long ago may have been a compound of two words. It is a cousin of the word *alloy,* and they both mean having a bond with someone or something. They are not related to *allay,* which is a prefix plus "lay" meaning "to lay aside, lighten the load.". The name Ally spells [al-lee].

Occupy comes from Latin 'take over', *ob* (over) plus the shortening of *capere* 'to seize.'

We know that terminal <y> spells [ee] unless part of a single-syllable stem word or in suffixes <ify> or <efy>. We know that 'con-con', two consonants, keeps vowels short. Now we can enjoy reading these words.

Rebel ONLY does not spell [on-lee].

Rebel's Reason *Only* spells [ohn-lee], not [on-lee], because it used to mean 'one-like', originally 'an-lic', [arn-lik], which became [arn-lee] and then [ohn-lee].

List 1-56 cont.
BILBY*, BINDY*/BINDI, CANDY, DANDY, DUMPY, DUSKY, ENVY, FILMY, FUSTY, GUTSY, HANDY, HANKY, HANKY PANKY, HEFTY, HONKY-TONK, HUMPY*, INKY, JUMPY, KINKY, MANLY, LANKY, LOFTY, LUMPY, LUSTY, MILKY, MISTY, MUSKY, PANSY, QUINSY, RANDY, RUGBY, RUSTY, SANDY, SIXTY, TANGY, TANSY, TESTY, TIPSY, UGLY, WINDY. <u>Names</u> ANDY, BETSY, CINDY, LINDY, MINDY, NANCY, PANSY, PATSY, POPSY, RANDY, RUSTY, SANDY, TANSY, TOPSY, WENDY.

Bilby is the Ab'l name for a 'rabbit bandicoot'. *Marcotis lagotis* and *Macotis leucra* were called [bil-bee] by the Wiradjurri of central and southern NSW.

Bindy is usually written *bindi,* which rebels against the rule against terminal <i>. It's an Ab'l word for the prickly seeds on *Calotis* plants, also known as *bindi-eye,* (Blake, p.87).

Humpy comes from an Ab'l word which sounded like [ump-ee], (Blake, p. 94). Ab'l words do not start with [h]. So why does this one? The mix up came because many of the English settlers, guards and convicts dropped their aitches and, although they accurately copied this Ab'l word for 'hut', saying it [umpy], it was written down by others as *humpy,* assuming the white speakers had dropped an aitch, as if saying [ut] for *hut,* and [ows] for *house*.

Rule 1-57 The letter <y> softens <c> to [s].
{We shall see later that <y> also softens <g> to [j] but not after <ng> nor after <gg>.}

Reason It is not just <i> and <e> which soften <c> to [s] but also semi-vowel <y> for it acts as the vowel <i>, spelling [ee] (in icy) or [I] in (*cycad* and *cycle*).

List 1-57
FANCY [fan-see], ICY [I-see], LACY [lay-see], LEGACY [leg-a-see], POLICY [pol-i-see], LEGITIMACY [le-jit-im-a-see].

Also <k> prevents <y> softening <c> to [s].
COCKY, COLICKY*, DICKY, DUCKY, FINICKY, FLECKY, GIMMICKY, HILLOCKY, ICKY, LUCKY, MUCKY, MULLOCKY, NITPICKY, PANICKY*, PECKY, PICKY, ROCKY, ROLLICKY, {STICKY}, TACKY, TUSSOCKY, UNLUCKY, WACKY, WHACKY, YUCKY. <u>Names</u> DICKY, MICKY, NICKY, RICKY, VICKY.

Colic and *panic* have added <k> to prevent <c> spelling [s], softening, with <y> after <c>.

<u>Relevant Writing Rule</u> When we add **any** suffix to a word ending consonant <y> we remove the <y> and replace it with <i> **unless** <y> ends a single-syllable stem word or the suffix starts with <i>. If the suffix is <s> we change it to <es>.

<u>Reasons</u> A. Although <y> is not allowed inside words the custom of leaving it when a suffix beginning with a consonant is added to a single-syllable stem word ending in <y> probably began because in this case <y> always spells [I] and if replaced by <i> long British [I] might be lost. E.g., *driness* could be decoded as [dree-nes], *shiness* as [shi-<u>nes</u>] or [shə-<u>nes</u>], like *finesse* spells [fə-<u>nes</u>].

We'll meet the rebels {*ladyship*} in Part 2, and {*babyhood, ladyhood* and *ladylike*} in Part 3.

B. Plurals. When we add <s> to nouns ending in consonant <y> we change the <y> to <i> and add <es>. If we just add <s> we'd get *bunnis* [bun-is] instead of *bunnies* [bun-eez]. Vowel terminal <y> comes later, e.g., {*monkey, monkeys*}.

C. Verbs. The same rule applies when we want to add <s> to change *I satisfy my empty tummy* to *He satisfies his empty tummy; I lobby the king* to *He lobbies the king.*

D. If the suffix begins <i> we do not change <y> to <i> for <ii> is a "no-no". So it is {*copyist* not *copyist*, also {*babyish, hurrying,* and *envying* but *funniest* and *happiest.*} Return to Reading Rules.

Rule 1-58 Suffix <ly> always spells [lee].
Most words ending —*ly* (abbreviation of *like*) tell how often something is done, e.g., *weekly,* or how it is done, e.g., man-like as in *manly.*
Most words ending —*ally* tell in what manner something is done.

List 1-58
BADLY, BASICALLY, BUSILY*, COMICALLY, DIMLY, DULY*, EPICALLY, FINALLY, FULLY, GODLY, LOGICALLY, MANICALLY, MEDICALLY, MADLY, MANLY, QUICKLY, SADLY, SUDDENLY, TOPICALLY, UNDULY.

*Busily, (busy-like) decodes like *busy,* explained after list 1-54.

*Duly is easy to decode, to read. The first vowel is long because there is no "double gate". *Dully* spells [dulee] but *duly* spells [dyoo-lee] which becomes [joo-lee] if [d] and [y] fuse to sound like [j].

Relevant Writing Rule. Suffix <ly> simply adds straight onto most stem words, e.g., *man, manly; game, gamely; love, lovely.*

Reason Most stem words keep <e> because adding suffixes can shorten preceding vowels and so the silent <e> shows us that it was once terminal and as a terminal vowel spells a long sound. However, in words like *festiveness* silent <e> is no longer needed, but words have fallen into ruts over the years. This is why we do not write *festivness,* s*helving,* or *shelvs.* A stem's final <e> which marks voiced <th> so that it spells [dh], and a final <e> which insulates <s>, <z>, <u>, and <v> from coming last, remains when the suffix starts with a consonant.

Rebels DULY and also TRULY in Part Two, belong to the 'DATA' Rebels. The others are {*Argument* and *Awful*}.

Rebels' Reasons *Due* and *true* are the only single-syllable words ending in a vowel sound which take <ly> as a suffix. If we wrote *duely* it would look like *cruely* and we might think that *duely* spelt [joo-el-ee] instead of [joo-lee] and if we wrote *truely* we might say it spelt [troo-el-ee]. We shall meet words in which vowels are split between syllables in Part Three. We'll hear the other 'DATA' rebels' excuses later — 'DATA' helps us remember their first letters.

American Rebels. Cummings, on p. 159 says that if final <e> marks a soft [j] that is spelt <dg> as in *judge,* it is removed when a suffix is added, as in *judgment,* in USA, but it can also remain. In Australia it remains, according to OPD 1983. So when we add the suffix <ly> it is usually just simple addition, except for *duly* and *truly,* and when adding <ment> to *judge etc.* we use our own judgement.

Rebels FULLY and BULLY.

Rebels' Reasons. Suffix <ly> simply adds straight onto most stem words, e.g., *man, manly; festive, festively.* However, we must remember that triplets are illegal, and so it is *fully* and *bully,* without writing <l> three times. We know that when a suffix is added to terminal <y> after a consonant, <y> changes to <i>, as in *funny, funnily; busy, busily.* When "growing" our own words with suffixes we need to know which words cannot add <ly> straight on. For instance, words ending <ic> do not add <ly> without first adding <al>, e.g., *magic, magical magically.* Lone Rebel:- PUBLICLY because *publical* is not a word. Other words add another suffix before adding <ly>, e.g., *cat, catty, cattily; nature, natural, naturally.*

List of examples follows — bossy bossily bossiness; canny cannily canniness; *copy copyist; cosy cosily cosiness; dizzy dizzily dizziness; *dry dryness drily/dryly; envy enviable [en-vee-ab-uul]; funny funnily funniness; fussy fussily fussiness; happy happily happiness; hazy hazily haziness; lazy lazily laziness; nosy nosiness; tidy tidily tidiness; tinny tinnily tinniness; uncanny uncannily uncanniness; witty wittily wittiness; zany zanily zaniness. **Note:** words ending –*ly* are adverbs, words ending –*ness* are nouns.

*In *dryness* and *dryly*, <y> remains before the suffix for it ends a single-syllable stem word, as in {s*hy, shyly, shyness*}. This does not occur in *laziness* or *tidily* which have two syllables. OPD gives us *drily*, but other dictionaries stick to the pattern with *dryly*. Lone Rebel: COPY is not a single syllable stem word but <y> remains in *copyist* to prevent the twinning of <i>. The letters <ii> do not appear in English words, unless Proper Nouns, as in *Iinet*.

Note. Suffixes <–ness> and <–ment> add straight on, as in *drunkenness, greenness, openness, thinness; embalmment*. Return to Reading Rules.

Rule 1-59 The suffix <ity> spells [itee], puts stress on the syllable before it and shortens the one letter vowel in that syllable, if that vowel is followed by a consonant, except for <u> which resists being shortened to spell [u].

Reason Suffix <ity>, like suffixes <it>, <id> <ic> and <ical>, shortens the preceding vowel and stresses it, but once again we see that <u> resists shortening to [uu] or [u]. We see suffix —*ity* ensuring a short, stressed vowel in the preceding syllable in *rigidity*, from *rigid ity*, *legality* from *legality* but in *community, obtusity, purity* and *unity*, the vowel spelt by <u> is stressed but is not shortened. This is because <u> used to be written <iu> and digraph vowels resist shortening in many situations, including before all the suffixes which usually shorten vowels before them. Hence in *tunic, lucid, unit,* and *unity*, <u> continues to spell long vowels. However, these suffixes do stress the syllable before them, even when the vowel is not shortened, so <ity> moves stress from first to second syllable in *lucidity,* and *humidity*. (A digraph vowel is one written with two letters.)

Rebel RARITY spells [rair-i-tee] due to its stem {*rare*} and so <ity> does not shorten <a> to spell [a].

Rascal SCARCITY This rascal of a word spells [skair-sitee]. Like *scare*, it rebels against the rule that <ar> spells [air] when and only when followed by a vowel. No good excuse for this behaviour makes it a rascal, like *scare* and *scarcely*.

List 1-59
ANIMOSITY, CAVITY, DENSITY, DIGNITY, ENMITY, ENTITY, EQUITY, FALSITY*, FEROCITY, FIDELITY, FIXITY, IMMENSITY, INTENSITY, LAXITY, LEGALITY, NECESSITY*, LEVITY, NUDITY, ODDITY, PRECOCITY, PURITY, QUALITY, RABBITY, REGULARITY, RIGIDITY, SANITY, UNANIMITY*, UNITY, VANITY, VERITY. Names UNITY, VANITY, VERITY, FIDELITY.

Necessity is the only word which uses <ss> before <ity>. It follows the original Latin *necesse*, 'no cesse' or 'no cease', 'no ceding', 'no backing away'.

**Falsity* spells [fol-sit-ee]

**Rickety, rackety* and *yackety* have been included because suffix <ety> works on the vowel before it the same way as <ity> does. Why <ety>? *Rackety* and *yackety* appear to copy *rickety* which follows the word *rickets,* a disease in which weak bones make one "rickety".

*In *unanimity* [yoo-nam-i-tee], <un> is not the prefix [un]. This word means 'of one mind', in Latin 'unus animus', i.e. one animation, one being.

Although <y> spells [ee] at the end of most English words, like *funny,* and spells another vowel, [I], at the end of a few, like *fly,* we should not assume that a terminal <y> spells [ee] or [I] in other languages. For instance, the Payungu Ab'l name for Lyons River in WA is *Mithirriny* in which <y> spells [y]. Languages which have been encoded quite recently for the first time make very clear use of letters. Aboriginal languages do not allow <y> to spell anything but the consonant sound [y]. Many English words start with [ny], as in *new, nubile, neuter, nuisance etc* but none end with [ny]. In fact, even words which start with [ny], have begun dropping [y] after [n]. Many Americans read *new* as [noo].

Dropping Yods —*ruby, sue.*

We learnt about the evolution of Yods before reading *due* and *tulip* in List 1-41&2. They are an English addition to the long [oo] sound, changing it to [yoo]. Yod is the name of the Hebrew letter which spells [y]. Leaving out the [y] sound is nick-named **"Yod Dropping"**, (Burbridge 2002, p. 30). Yods began dropping out of words a few hundred years ago. They have not all dropped yet and maybe never will. Yods only drop if they are pushed, which actually means if they are hard to say after a particular consonant. If there is nothing behind them, there is no risk of a shove. So when <u> spells its long sound at the beginning of a word it always spells [yoo], as in *unit* [yoo-nit].

First of all, English speakers began changing [yoo] to [oo] after [r], because it's quite hard to say [yoo] after [r], try it! Try saying [ryoo]. This change after [r] is complete in USA and Australia, e.g. *ruby* spells [roo-bee], not [ryoo-bee]. We never hear [yoo] after consonants spelt by <x> and <z>. There are no yods in *exude* and *Zulu* nor after <y>, — we only hear one [y] in *Yule*. The following rhyme reminds us that Yods have all dropped after [r] and [j] — Ruby and Judy — e.g. *rude, jujube*. And usually after [l] and [s] — Lucy and Sue.

If dropping yods does not come naturally to you, this may help you remember when to drop a yod.
How odd, the yod in Yoddy U.
Then U's yod was prodded,
By X, Y and Zed, and dropped.
In Ruby, Judy too, and usually Lucy Sue,
Lots of Yods dropped from Yoddy U.

Nearly every Yod has dropped after [l]. First of all, they dropped when another consonant added push to [l], as in *blue* and *glue*, [bloo] not [blyoo], [gloo] not [glyoo]. Then they dropped after a single [l], as in *dilute, salute*. However there are still some words with <u> after <l> without a consonant 'pushing behind it' in which the Yod has not dropped: *value* [val-yoo], *deluge* [del-yooj]. Even *lurid* has kept its Yod sound according to the OPD.

Nearly every Yod has dropped after [s], except in British English in complex words like *consume, assume, subsume* but there is no stem word *sume* which can stand alone. The verb *sue* once spelt [syoo] but now spells [soo]. The complex word *ensue* still has its Yod, but not in American English. Some very old Australians etc. still say *suitable* [syootabel]. Homework: watch the old BBC sitcom *Are You being Served* and listen for the yod when Mrs Slocombe and Mr Humphries say the word *suit*.

But many Yods are 'hanging on' to lips, teeth and the back of the tongue. So they remain
— after labial (lip) consonants [p] [b] [f] [v] [m]: *puny, butane, futile, ovule, commune*, but not everywhere in USA.
— after dental (teeth) consonants [t] [d] [n]: *tunic, duty, nudity*, but not everywhere in USA.
— after velar (throat) consonants [g], [k], [h]: *legume, kudos, Cupid, human*, but not everywhere in USA. Recent English adoptions arrived without a yod and stayed that way, like *hula* and the company name *Uber*.

Not needed but nice to know. There is no yod involved when <ou> spells [oo], as in *acoustic*, because, in French, <ou> spells [oo], not [yoo]. So <ou> never spells [yoo]. For instance, we do not hear [y] in *toucan* nor in the noun *wound*. In *you* and *youth* we hear [y] only because <y> spells [y]. We shall meet many ways to spell [yoo], as in *new, feud, nuisance, adieu, view*, and *Hugh*, but not <ou>. Digraph <ou>

either spells French [oo] or Anglo [ow], as in 'He wound the bandage around the wound.' Now back to things we need to know.

We have met words which end <ue> and rebels ending with <u>. We were told whether <u> spells [yoo] or [oo] in these words. Now we can see for ourselves, using Rule 1-60

Rule 1-60 When <u> spells a long sound it's [yoo], unless it follows <x>, <y>, <z>, <r>, <j>, <l> or <s>. Then it's [oo], having dropped the yod.

Reason As above, the yod was dropped when it was too hard to say after these four consonants.

Rebels FONDU, GNU, HULA, MUMU, TABU, TUTU, ZEBU. Proper Noun UBER

Rebels' Reasons These foreign adoptions do not fit the rule because they never had a yod to begin with, and so they are rebels with a reason.

List 1-60 Those in which <u> spells [yoo]: CUE, DUE, HUE, EMU, MENU, MU.
Those in which <u> spells [oo]: RUE, SUE and the name SUE, FLU *abbrev.* of *influenza*, GURU, JUJU, KURU, LULU *slang*.

Not only did the English drop yods after some consonants to make words easier to say, they fused yods with other preceding consonants to make words easier to say, as we shall discover further on down the 'road to reading'.

We can now read many long words. The list below uses the suffixes —*ity*, —*ety*, —*it*, —*id*, —*ic* and —*ical* which, as we know, all put stress on the previous syllable and shorten the one letter vowel in that syllable, even if it was a long vowel before adding a suffix, but <u> resists being shortened to [u]. Other suffixes are used too, —*ly*, —*y*, —*ness*. Since suffixes are not stressed, when —*ly* is added to —*ical*, we say [ik-lee] in order to retain the beat of English speech, e.g., *magically* [**mag**-ik-lee], *paradoxically* [pa-ra-**dox**-ik-lee], in which alternate syllables are stressed, either side of the syllable with primary stress.

Rebel OBESITY is said [oh-bee-si-tee], not [oh-bes-it-ee].

Rebel's Reason It is related to the word *over-eat*, [eet], in which [ee] is not a single letter vowel, (Ayto p. 192). Also, Latin *obesus* [oh-bee-suus] means 'very fat', (Readers Digest 2001 p. 664).

List 1-59 cont.
ABILITY, ACCESSIBILITY, ACIDITY, ADMISSIBILITY, ADVISABILITY, AFFABILITY, AFFINITY, AGILITY, AMENABILITY, AMENITY, AMICABILITY, ANGULARITY, ANIMOSITY, ANTIQUITY, ARIDITY, BANALITY, BANKABILITY, BIDDABILITY, BIPOLARITY, BOTANICALLY, CALAMITY, CAPABILITY, CAPACITY, CAPILLARITY, CELERITY, CIVILITY, COMMODITY, COMMUNITY, CUPIDITY, CURABILITY, DEBILITY, DISABILITY, DISPARITY, DISSIMILARITY, DISUNITY, DIVINITY, DIVISIBILITY, DOCILITY, DURABILITY, EDIBILITY, ELIGIBILITY, EQUALITY, EQUANIMITY, EXCITABILITY, FACILITY, FALLIBILITY, FATALITY, FELICITY, FEMININITY, FEROCITY, FIDELITY, FINALITY, FUTILITY, GARRULITY, GENERALITY, GENEROSITY, GENTILITY, GULLIBILITY, HEREDITY, HERITABILITY, HILARITY, HOSTILITY, HUMANITY, HUMIDITY, HUMILITY, ILLEGALITY, ILLEGIBILITY, IMMATURITY, IMMOBILITY, IMMORALITY, IMMUNITY, IMMUTABILITY, IMPASSIVITY, IMPECCABILITY, IMPOSSIBILITY, IMPUNITY, IMPURITY, INABILITY, INANITY, INCAPABILITY, INCAPACITY, INDEMNITY, INDIGNITY, INFIDELITY, INFINITY, INHUMANITY, INIQUITY, INSANITY, INSECURITY, INSINCERITY, INSOLUBILITY, INSULARITY, INVISIBILITY, IRASCIBILITY, IRREGULARITY, IRRITABILITY, JEJUNITY, JOCULARITY, <u>=[yoo], LEGALITY, LEGIBILITY, LIQUIDITY, LOCALITY, LONGEVITY*, LOQUACITY, LOVABILITY, LUMINOSITY, MAGICALLY, MAGNANIMITY, MAJORITY, MALIGNITY, MASCULINITY, MATURITY, MENDACITY, MENDICITY, MENTALITY, MINORITY, MISCIBILITY, MOBILITY, MODALITY, MOLARITY, MONOPOLISTIC,

MORALITY, MOTILITY, MOTIVITY, MUNICIPALITY, MUSCULARITY, MUSICALITY, NATIVITY, NAVIGABILITY, NEBULOSITY, NECESSITY, NEGATIVITY, NOBILITY, NONENTITY, NOTABILITY, OBSCENITY, OPACITY, ORIGINALITY, PALATABILITY, PARADOXICALLY, PASSIVITY, PLACIDITY, POLARITY, POMPOSITY, POPULARITY, POSITIVITY, POSSIBILITY, POSTERITY, POTABILITY, PUBLICITY, PUGNACITY, QUOTABILITY, RABBITY, RABIDITY, RACKETY, RANCIDITY, RAPIDITY, REGULARITY, RELATIVITY, RIGIDITY, RISIBILITY, ROTUNDITY, SAGACITY, SALINITY, SATIRICALLY, SECURITY, SENILITY, SENSIBILITY, SENSITIVITY, SENSUALITY, SEPARABILITY, SERENDIPITY, SERENITY, SEVERITY, SIMILARITY, SINCERITY, SOLIDARITY, SOLUBILITY, SORORITY, TEMERITY, TENACITY, TIMIDITY, TONALITY, TOTALITY, TOXICITY, UNANIMITY, UNIFORMITY, UNPOPULARITY, UNTENABILITY, UPPITY, UTILITY, VALIDITY, VANITY, VASCULARITY, VELOCITY, VENALITY, VENERABILITY, VERACITY, VERITY, VICINITY, VIRILITY, VISCOSITY, VISIBILITY, VITALITY, VIVACITY, VORACITY, VULGARITY, YACKETY-YACK *slang*.

*Longevity spells [lon-jev-i-tee], meaning 'long age-ity', except there is no such word *age-ity*. We'll meet {*long*}, later.

*Ma*gically, sat*ir*ically, para*dox*ically, *etc.* have grown long by adding more than one suffix.
For *monopolistic* we say [mon-**op**-o-**list**-ik]. Linguists talk about primary stress, secondary stress and speech rhythms. In the Dr Who TV series the Daleks use syllable-timed language, in which each syllable is given the same stress: "Ex-ter-mi-nate". English is not like that, for it is "stress-timed". "The main stresses fall roughly at regular intervals in the stream of speech. It is a 'tum-te-tum-te-tum' way of talking", (Crystal, p. 270). Suffixes never have primary stress and usually the suffix *–ically* spells shrunken unstressed [ik-lee].
In *accompany, unluckily* and *unhappily* we disregard the prefixes in these words and stress the next syllable [ak-**kum**-pa-nee]. Remember, prefixes aren't stressed. Let's sort them to show how we know if a vowel is short and stressed.

List 1-61
<u>Before 'double gates'</u> DOGGEDLY, FUNNILY, HAPPINESS, MERRILY, SICKLY, SICKLINESS (CK = CC), UNCANNY, UNGODLY, UNHAPPY, UNLUCKY.
<u>Before two consonants</u> COMPANY *f*, HORIZONTALLY*, SADLY, SADNESS.
<u>Before <ic> or <ical></u> BOTANICAL, MAGICAL, MEDICAL, MUSICAL, SATIRICAL.
<u>Before suffix —ic —al —ly,</u> in which <ically> spells [klee]: MAGICALLY, MEDICALLY, MUSICALLY, PARADOXICALLY, SATIRICALLY.
<u>Stressed and 3rd or more from end</u> ACCOMPANY *f*, AGONY, BOTANY, BODILY, COLONY, COMEDY, ECONOMY, ENEMY, FAMILY, HERESY, IGNOMINY, LITANY, MALADY, MELODY, MONOPOLY, MONOPOLISTIC, PANICKY, PARODY, SUBSIDY, TAXONOMY, UNHAPPILY, UNLUCKILY, VERILY.

**Horizontally.* Why does <i> spell [I] in *horizon* but [i] in *horizontal* and *horizontally?*
Ans. *Horizon* came from France with a silent <h> and sounded like *reason.* That might explain its long Anglo [I] sound in the second syllable, to stop it sounding like *reason.* However, when <al> puts stress on <ont> the letter <i> just spells [i] for it is unstressed, unimportant and no longer needed to stop the mix up with *reason.* It's the same in *horizontally* [ho-ri-**zont**-al-ee]. The introduction of <t> ensures <o> spells a short, stressed vowel, rather than [oh], as in *zonal.*
Rebels JALOPY, POLONY, ACADEMY.
Rebels' Reasons *Jalopy* [ja-**lop**-ee]. Webster records *jallopy* as well and Prof. Cummings says it has been recorded *jaloppy.* Etymonline gives variants *jaloupy, jaloppi, gillopy* and says it has been used since

1924 for a battered old automobile. The website adds that although of unknown origin it may derive from Jalapa in Mexcico where many used cars were sent from USA. In this case, like the region's jalapeno peppers, it is an Aztec word. *Polony* [pol-**oh**-nee] is an Italian word, stressed Italian fashion, second from end of word.

We shall end Part One with a Rebel word, ACADEMY. We pronounce *academy* as if it begins with an unstressed prefix, like *abandon.* But it has no prefix and if it did it would be spelt *accademy*. The word is an eponym. As you know, our well-educated elders, the people we call academics, decided that we should spell our words in such a way that we can read them and get their meaning but **also** stay linked to our past, to all the stories of our culture. They wanted our words to "carry our culture". The word *academy* has broken spelling rules in order to "carry culture".

This is the story behind the spelling of *academy*. The famous Greek philosopher Plato liked teaching outdoors in a park in a suburb of Athens. He had lots to pass on to the younger men, like Aristotle and his friends, for he had written down a lot of the wisdom he'd picked up from listening and debating with Socrates. This was around 400 BC. The park had been there for ages. About 1200 BC, at the time of the Trojan Wars, the land had been given to the people of Athens by a generous man called Akademos. This shady park with its grove of olive trees was called Akademeia which meant Grove of Akademos. So Plato's school in the park was also called Akademeia. Plato's school is often described at the first European university. Its curriculum offered subjects including astronomy, biology, mathematics, political theory, and philosophy. Plato hoped his Akademeia would provide a place where thinkers could work toward better government in the Grecian cities. The glory days of Greece and then of Rome faded away but then, during the Renaissance, many countries became very keen on education. The first English academy began in 1474. The elders copied the French word *académie* from the Latin way of spelling with <c> instead of <k>. Why didn't they double the <c> like the Italians have? The Italians doubled it to make reading the word easy. Their Accademia della Crusca 'winnowed' their language to refine it, rid it of rough spelling etc., like winnowing bran (crusca) from grain. By contrast, the crusty old English elders said if they doubled the <c>, the connection to the very first academy, set up by the great Greek philosopher Plato, thanks to Akademos, would be lost. So now that we know the story behind the spelling of *academy* we must pass it on and share it around, to young and old. That's part of our culture, the sharing of knowledge, the crusts and all!

Part Two

Now we shall decode lots of consonant combinations. We shall meet consonants side by side which blend their sounds, as in *strand,* and others side by side which spell new sounds, like <ph> and <th> in *philanthropy,* and others which can change the sound of vowels, like <nd> in *kind.* You need to remember everything we learnt in Part One in order to decode Part Two words.

The Bones of Speech — consonants
Consonants are often called the bones of speech, for they are more rigid than vowels. Vowels change within a language but consonants change between languages. Consonants changed as words travelled across Europe from language to language, or from one region to the next. Early Saxons said *vox* and took the word to Britain where it became part of the language. Later, some people found it easier to say the less energetic word *fox.* Some even changed *vixen* to *fixen.* Can you see why [f] was chosen to replace [v]? Yes, they are made in the same part of the mouth — [f] is as close as possible to [v]. Consonants do not change nearly as much as vowels. They are the 'stiff bones' of language, supporting the 'soft flesh' of vowels. Potter (on page 64) calls vowels the "flesh and blood" of language.

<u>Not needed but nice to know.</u> Want to know more? Skeletons and old bones are clues to the past. There is proof that a language arose in a region between Europe and Asia which spread both east and west and which is the ancestor of most of today's European languages and many Asian languages, (Swadesh, Lerer and others). As it spread it split every now and then. One big split occurred when it spread north, into today's Germany. The old way of speaking continued on into Italy etc. but the pronunciation changed as it headed north into Germany and beyond. The consonants changed! So, way before the Great Vowel Shift occurred in England, there was a Great Consonant Change, or Split, for voiced consonants split into voiced and unvoiced. In Europe, [b] split off to the north as [p], [d] split off as [t], and [g] went north as [k]. *Lip, tooth* and *knee* came into English from Germany and later on *labial, dental* and *genuflect* were adopted into English from Italy. The English used to pronounce the <g> in *genuflect* (= flex the knee) as [g], and the <k> in *knee* as [k]. Can you see how the Consonant Split produced different words for the same thing? *Lip* and *labial; tooth* and *dental; knee* and *genuflect.* Two more consonants, [p] and [k], split off to the north as [f] and [h]. So English got *pedal* and *cardiac* from Italy and *foot* and *heart* from Germany. <u>Now back to things we need to know.</u>

Clusters — adjacent consonants.
    When two or more consonants come together in a word, we say they **cluster**.
One place they cluster is where syllables join, like <bl> in *goblin* and <ckl> in *sickly*. Another place they cluster is when two words make one word, like <bg> in *hobgoblin* or <cks> in *quickset* or <tn> in *catnap*.
    In both cases the consonants do not require blending for they are pronounced separately, [gob-lin], [sik-lee], [hob-gob-lin], [kwik-set], [kat-nap].
However, when they cluster **in the same syllable** they **blend** with each other, as in *bled* where <bl> spells [bl], in *hand* where <nd> spells the blend [nd], and in *skin* where <sk> spells [sk] in *skin*. *Blend* has two blends, [bl] and [nd].
    Two adjacent consonants, e.g., <st> in *stop,* or three adjacent consonants, e.g., <str> in **strap**, in the same syllable **must** blend so that we can say the syllable in one breath. However there are some consonants which just **do not blend** with each other in English words. We shall read words which start [bl] or [gr] but never a word which starts [bs] or [jr]. We shall read words which end [kt] or [ft] but we shall never see a word which ends [zt] or [gt]. Meryl Thompson listed all the written ways English words start: *bl, cl, fl, gl, pl, sl, sc, sm, sp, sw, scr, spl, squ, br, cr, dr, fr, gr, pr, tr, sk, sn, st, tw, shr, spr, str, thr,* and finish: *ct, ft, ld, lk, lt, lp, lf, mf, nd, ng, nk, nt, nch, pt, sp, sk, st, xt, nce, nge, nch, nth, lse, lch, lsh, lth, tch, dth,*

71

pth, lves, (Thompson, 1980), but maybe you can add to that. However hard we search we will never find words beginning with every possible consonant combination, or ending with them, not in English. Many possible consonant blends are not used. English words follow well worn grooves.

<u>Not needed but nice to know</u>. Infants quickly learn to recognize the particular vowels and consonants of their native language and then they gradually develop a more acute sensitivity to complex combinations of sounds. The most difficult of all are the consonant clusters. Hence "poon" for *spoon* and as for hearing and repeating *street* and *splash,* "teet" then "steet" and "pash" then "plash" come first, for the most difficult to hear and reproduce are the triple clusters, (McGuinness, p. 162). <u>Now back to things we need to know</u>.

Blending Consonants — *scallop, zestful.*
Word-sounds need to join up inside syllables, because a syllable is said in one breath. As there are no stops and starts in a syllable, its word-sounds must blend. <u>All **consonants** can blend with all **vowels.**</u> As you know, the very word *consonant* means 'with vowel sound'. Consonants do not form words on their own. They are said with a vowel sound blended to them, before the consonant, after it or both before and after, as in *at, to,* or *bat.* Although we can express [p] or [b] on its own, such sounds are hard to tell apart outside a word. Although all consonants blend with all vowels, <u>not all consonants can blend with each other</u>.

We have already discussed **voiced** and **unvoiced** word-sounds. Only six voiced consonants blend with the unvoiced consonants. Voiced consonants split into these six Big Blenders and the rest, the Bad Blenders.

Big Blenders blend with all consonants, both voiced and unvoiced, with ease. They are the liquids [l] and [r]; the nasals [m], [n] and [ŋ]; and the semi-vowels [w] and [y].

Bad Blenders are very bad at blending. They are [b], [d], [v], [z], [g], [j], [dh], [z], and {[zh]}. They are all voiced consonants and do not blend with unvoiced consonants. Each Bad Blender has an unvoiced version. For instance, [b] is a voiced [p] - try saying [b] without using your voice box and what do you get? Yes, [p]. Try saying [p] with a noise from your voice box at the same time and you get [b]. Check out these voiced and unvoiced pairs: [t][d], [p][b], [f][v], [s][z], [k][g], [th] [dh]. Say them with your fingers on your voice box. Which ones make your fingers vibrate? Yes, the voiced consonants. Each partner in a pair is made the same way, by the same parts of the mouth, but one is voiced and the other unvoiced. Unvoiced [h] no longer has a voiced partner. We shall meet voiced [j]'s unvoiced partner, [ch], later on. We shall meet the partners [sh] and [zh] as well.

As an example, Bad Blender [b] will not blend with unvoiced [t], which is why, in *debt,* either B or T has to be silent. We shall learn later why B is silent. Bad Blenders do not even blend with each other, except that they all blend with [z], to make plurals, as in *dogs* [dogz] and all blend with [d] in past tense verbs, as in *mobbed* [mobd].

Big Blenders are voiced consonants and they blend with all consonants, both voiced, e.g., with [g] in (*glum*)*,* and unvoiced, e.g., with [k] in (clan). Big Blender [r] blends with voiced [b] in *bran* and unvoiced [p] in *pram*. Big Blender [m] blends with voiced [z] in [prizm], **prism,* and unvoiced [s] in [smak], *smack.* Big Blender [n] blends with voiced [g] in *ping* and unvoiced [n] in *tank.* Big Blender [w] blends with voiced [d] in *dwell* and unvoiced [t] in *twit.* Big Blender [y] blends with voiced [d] in *dune* [dyoon] and unvoiced [t] in *tunic* [tyoon-ik]. Actually, the blend becomes [joon] and [choon-ik] in Australia and wherever yods have fused, and is lost in American [doon] and [toon], and wherever yods have dropped.

*Prism, which spells [prizm], is not written *prizm* due to the unpopularity of <z>, because it is the sign of the dagger, an omen of trouble and strife.

Even when sounds can blend, there are traditional English blends, like [n] and [g] in *sing*, but the alternative blend, [g] with [n], does not occur in English, which is why <g> is silent in *sign*. In *signal* we hear [g] again, because [g] and [n] are now in separate syllables, with no need to blend. It is only when in the same syllable that word-sounds must blend with each other.

Rule 2-1 English Blending Rules
(1) Vowels and semi-vowels blend with all consonants.
(2) Unvoiced, also called voiceless, consonants blend with all word-sounds except with Bad Blenders.
(3) Big Blenders blend with everything but not much with themselves.
(4) Bad Blenders only blend with Big Blenders and with terminal [z] and [d].

Reason Partly the way our mouth and throat and nose and voice box works to make words and partly due to voice training. Each language has its own favourite blends of vowels with vowels, vowels with consonants and consonants with consonants. When we look in a Polish dictionary we see all sorts of letters side by side, e.g., "czytaj" meaning *read,* and "szóm" meaning *froth.*

Rebel SVELTE

Rebel's Reason *Svelte* [svelt] is a very rare word indeed, for it is the only word which breaks the blending rules. In it we hear unvoiced [s] blending with voiced [v]. It obeys the rule that <s> always spells [s] at the beginning of a word. It used to be two syllables, so that [s] and [v] did not blend, just met at syllable boundaries. It means 'slender, lithe, slim' but long ago it meant 'pulled out, lengthened'. In Latin the verb was *exvellere*, from e*x*- 'out' *vellere* 'to pluck, stretch'. So if something was stretched out it was [eks-velt-um]. The ordinary people who spoke Vulgar Latin just said [svelt-um] and this flowed into Italian and French and then into English, *svelte.*

Blending Unvoiced Consonants

Terminal <ask> in *ask, task* etc. spelt [ask] originally, just as *pass* spelt [pas]. They still spell [ask] and [task] in the north of England but spell [arsk] and [tarsk] in the south, and in Australia, New Zealand and Canada for instance, but not everywhere in USA. Early settlement in USA was by Pilgrim Mothers and Fathers, the first lot departing in *Mayflower* in 1620. They came from the English Midlands. So, some would have used the northern [ask] and some the southern [arsk]. American English has been a mixture of pronunciations from its earliest days.

The French use <a> to spell long [ar], as in *masque* [marsk]. The English were following French ways when they changed their vowels in words like *ask.* Since not everyone agrees that *ask* spells [arsk], preferring [ask], the letters *VS* for Vowel Shift after such words will give the reader a choice in the matter, [a] or [ar].

Rule 2-2 Terminal <que> spells [k].
Reason All such words have been adopted from French but not adapted to the English way of spelling [k]. French grew out of Latin which in turn developed from Greek and other languages. Early Latin speakers used <q> for soft Greek <k>, and <g> for harsh Greek [k]. They hardly used <k> and this is why we do not see it in French words. However <k> travelled from Greece into northern Europe, into Germanic languages. If you look in a German dictionary you will only see the letter <c> in digraphs (<sch>, <ch>, <ck>) never on its own. Letter <k> is used to spell German [k], never letter <c>. The letter <q> is very rarely used in languages like German and Swedish, but used much more often in French, Spanish and Italian which all grew out of Latin. As we'd expect, because English has two main ancestors, one German and one French, English uses <q> more than German but less than French, (Letter Frequency, Wikipedia).

Q. What about the 'ground rule' that <qu> spells [kw]?
Ans. When we speak of the ancestor words of the English language, we must remember that the first invasion of French words were not pure French for they were the French words used by Normans. The Normans were called that because they were North Men who invaded France from the north and they arrived in northern France speaking a Germanic language. They mixed their language with the local

French language and ended up speaking Norman French. They took this language to England and not only used it to rule over the English but also used their own letter codes, when they wrote English words. That is how *queen* got its <q>. Much later another invasion of French words entered England and the English language. They belonged to the sort of French spoken in Paris, not Normandy. This Parisian French produced English words which used terminal <que> to spell [k], and also started *quiche, queue etc.* in which <qu> spells just [k], not [kw].

Whenever <s> is followed by an unvoiced consonant it spells [s]. So *misty* spells [mis-tee], not [miz-tee] but <s> in *misery* spells [z] because it is not followed by an unvoiced consonant.

Rule 2-3 Inside a syllable, <s> spells [s] after any vowel if the vowel is followed by an unvoiced consonant.

Reason This rule explains why, although *has* spells [haz], the old word *hast* spells [hast], not [hazt]. We shall meet the word *haste* in Part Three. This spells [hayst], not [hayzt]. Remember, blending has to take place in syllables, or they would not be syllables. Try saying [hayzt] and you will hear [hayzd] because [z] and [t] cannot blend.

Part 2 of Rule 2-1 says that unvoiced, also called voiceless, consonants blend with all word-sounds, except with Bad Blenders. The unvoiced consonants [p], [t], [f], [s], [k], [h], [th] blend with each other in the next lists, and with vowels.

Rule 2-3A When adjacent in the same syllable, <s> and <k> or <c> spell the [sk] bend, unless <c> is followed by <i>, <e>, <y> or <h>.

Reason. See 2-3B and 2-3C.

List 2-3A word initial [sk] blend.
SCAB, SCALLOP, SCALLYWAG, SCAMPI*, SCAN, SCARAB, SCARIFY, SCAT, SCATTY, SCOFF, SCUBA*, SCUFF, SISKIN, SKELETAL, SKELETALLY, SKELETON, EXOSKELETON, SKI, SKID, SKIFF, SKILL, SKILLET, SKIM, SKIN, SKINNY, SKIP, SKIT, SKIVVY, SKULL, SKULL-CAP, SKY, SKYJACK, SKYROCKET, SQUALL [skworl], TELESCOPIC. <u>Name</u> SKYE.

*Scampi [skam-pee] has a rare terminal <i>, adopted from Italy but not adapted to English spelling.

*Scuba. When the first letter of each word in a phrase or clause makes a new word we call the new word an *acronym*. *Scuba,* which spells [scyoo-bar], is an acronym, from Self Contained Underwater Breathing Apparatus.

List 2-3A cont. [sk] blends
ASK* *VS,* BASILISK*, BASK *VS,* BASKET *VS,* BUSK, CASK *VS*, CASKET *VS,* DAMASK*, DESK, DESKTOP, DISC, DISCUS*, DISK, DUSK, DUSKY, ESKIMO, GASKET*, HUSK, HUSKILY, HUSKINESS, HUSKY DOG, MASK verb *VS,* MOLLUSC, MUSK, MUSKET, MUSKY, OBELISK, RISK, RISKINESS, RISKY, RUSK, TAMARISK, TASK *VS,* TASK-MISTRESS, TUSK, TUSKLESS, WHISK, WHISKY*. <u>Pseudoword</u> TSK! <u>Slang</u> PESKY, PESKILY.

*Ask is an old word. Cummings, on p. 98, shows how *ask* was once *asken.* With two consonants after it, <a> spelt [a], but, as noted, the vowel shifted to spell [ar] down south in England.

*Basilisk spells [baz-il-isk].

*Gasket is a new 1800's word, and is pronounced as it is written.

*Damask [dam-ask] sounds like the place that cloth came from, Damascus.

*Discus has the stem *disc*, whereas in *discuss* <s> and <c> are either side of a syllable break. The <ss> ending *discuss* ensures the final syllable is stressed, and shows that *dis* is an (unstressed) prefix, as in its cognate (cousin word) *discourse*.

*Whisky is spelt *whiskey* in Ireland and USA to reflect the old Irish *uisge beatha* (also *usquebaugh*), meaning "water of life", (Fleck 2007).

Rule 2-3B Letters <sc> spell [s] when followed by <e>, <i> or <y>.
Reason The French inherited the Roman fear of the letter <z> and replaced it with <s>. This meant they had to use another way of spelling <s>. They used <ce>, <ci> and <cy>. The English before 1066 did not use these ways to spell [s]. They just used <s>. We know that because they spelt *ice* with an <s>, not a <c>. After defeat in 1066 the French took control of English spelling and *is* became *ice*. Also *ist* became *is* and was then pronounced the French way, [iz].
Rebels SCEPTIC, spells [skeptik] {FASCISM} [fash-izm], FASCIST [fash-ist], CRESCENDO [kre-shen-doh].
Rebels' Reasons *Sceptic* now has an alternative spelling, *skeptic*, which not only ensures its correct pronunciation but matches the original Greek spelling of the [k] sound. The Romans changed the Greek <k> to <c> but it still spelt [k]. It was the French who adopted and changed Roman <c> spells [k] to <c> spells [s]. In English *sceptic* and *septic* would sound the same but no one wants to say [sep-tik] for the word *sceptic*. *Fascism* and *fascist* are recent adoptions from Italy where <sc> before a vowel spells [sh]. Italian musical terms are usually adopted but their spelling is not adapted, like *crescendo*.
List 2-3B
CONVALESCE, DEHISCE, REMINISCE, SCENT, {SCIENCE}, {SCION} [sI-on], SCYTHE, [sIth]
Rule 2-3C When <sc> is followed by <h> it spells either [sk] or [sh].
Reason We shall see why when we meet *schnapps* at 2-100 and *scholastic* at 2-101.

Rule 2-4 Terminal <sque> spells the blend [sk].
Reason See Rule 2-2.
Rebel RISQUÉ [ris-kay]
Rebel's Reason *Risqué* does not end in <sque>. The <e> is not silent, as indicated by the French diacritic or 'decider sign' above it. *Risk* and *risky* comes from German. This other version, *risqué*, is pure French and means 'risking decency'.
List 2-4
BISQUE [beesk], MASQUE [marsk], MOSQUE [mosk]. Proper Noun BASQUE [barsk].
In *bisque* and *masque* and *mosque* we see a very unusual thing.
For when ending words, the <que> of *queen* spells the [k] of king!

Rule 2-5 Word initial <st> always spells the blend [st].
Reason Word initial <s> never spells [z], so word initial <st> could never spell [zt].
List 2-5 initial [st] blend
NON-STICK, STAB, STABILITY, STACCATO, STACK, STAFF *VS*, STAG, STALL *VS*, STATIC, STEM, STEP, STEPPES* [steps], STET, STICK, STICKPIN, STIFF, STIFFEN, STIFFLY, STIFFNESS, STIGMA, STILL, STOCK, STOCK STILL, STOCK UP, STOCKINET, STOCKMAN, STOCKY, STODGE, STOLID, STOP, STOPCOCK, STOP-OFF, STOP-PRESS, STUB, STUBBY, STUCCO, STUCK, STUD, STUDY*, STUD-RAM, STUFF, STUFFILY, STUFFINESS, STUFFING, STUFFY, STUN, STY. Proper Nouns STAN, STELLA.
*Steppes has an old fossil ending and is a plural noun.
*Study should be *studdy* like *muddy* but then the link to *student* and *studious* would be lost. We can add *study* to our list of Lemon Rebels. I don't know why it doesn't rhyme with *Judy* or match its cousin words *studio* and *student* or sound like the car called *Studebaker*.
Rule 2-6 Terminal <st> spells the blend [st] but medial <st> must be in the same syllable to spell the [st] blend.

Reason Blends only occur inside syllables. *Distend's* syllable break comes between <s> and <t>. How do you say *atavistic, bombastic, destiny, hostel, justify,* and *Boston*? Where do you place the syllable break in each?

List 2-6

ATAVISTIC, BACKSTAB, BACKSTOP, BOMBASTIC, BOTANIST, BUSTED, CANASTA, CAPITALISTIC, CAPSTAN, COSTLESS, DESTINY, DIPSTICK, DISTEND, DOMESTIC, DISTIL, DUSTBIN, DUSTMAN, DUSTPAN, DUSTY, ECONOMIST, ECSTASY, FESTAL, FUSTY, GUSTO, HOSTEL, JUSTIFY, LIST, LISTLESS, LISTLESSNESS, LUSTY, MONASTIC, MUSTY, QUICKSTEP, TUNGSTEN*, ZESTFUL. <u>Proper Nouns</u> BOSTON, PAKISTAN, KAZAKISTAN.

*Tungsten In this word, [tung-sten], [sten] is not an unstressed suffix. It means 'stone' and *tung* means 'heavy'. If it was unstressed, short [t] would be swamped by long [s], as it is in {*listen*}.

Two Types of Suffixes — Inflexional and Derivational

Before blending <st> in *safest*, let's learn about its suffix, the suffix —*est*. The Prof explains that there are two types of suffixes.

A. Inflexional suffixes — 'flexible'.

English used to have plenty of suffixes which acted like dogs' tails, called inflexional suffixes, because they flexed or waved, like tails on words. The more common spelling of this word is *inflectional*. I myself call them 'flexible suffixes' because they flex and wag like a tail on a dog. A wagging or drooping or rigid tail tells us something about a dog. Inflexional suffixes tell us something about the word. English had many such 'flexible' word endings once upon a time but, as we have heard, most have shrunk or dropped off. Those that are left tell us **how many**, (plural suffixes <s>, <es>, <en>), **when**, (tense markers <s>, <es>, <ed>); verb participle suffixes <ed>, <ing>), **whose** (ownership suffixes <'s> <s'>) and **how much** (<er> <est>), (Cummings, p. 34). So there are very few flexible suffixes, and many do two or three jobs. These flexible suffixes make plurals, as in *dogs, foxes, oxen, toes;* mark tense, as in *runs, goes, hoped;* make verb particples, as in *hoping, hoped*; are possession markers, as in *cat's, fox's* and *cats', foxes' oxen's*; make comparisons, as in *bigger, biggest*. None of these flexible suffixes change the noun, adjective or verbs they are attached to. They tell us more about each word they are added to, but do not change its meaning.

<u>Not needed but nice to know</u>. Inflexional suffixes are used a lot in some languages. When added to Latin stems, they tell us many things. If added to a verb they tell us who did it or to whom it was done to, when, how many are/were/will be involved, and if it's a statement or a command, if it has not happened but it might and so on. If it is added to a noun we can learn a lot: if it is one or more things, if it is male or female or neither, if it owns something, if it is beside, with or from something, if it is to or for something, if it is doing something or if something is being done to it (or her or him). If it is added to an adjective, it links the adjective to a noun in the sentence so that it cannot be misunderstood. For instance, "*Big girls and boys*" in Latin cannot mean that the boys are big too. Aust. Aboriginal languages have even more suffixes like these. The suffix meaning 'with someone' is different to the suffix meaning 'with something'. Suffixes for *your* in 'your relation' differ from those which say 'your friend, boat or cat'. When giving something, Wajarri people add a suffix to it which says "You can have it but you owe me," or "You can have it for a while but give it back", or "You can have it and you can keep it". My favourite example is the suffix —*wily* which is added to show disapproval. Added to *dudu* (dog), the word *duduwily* means the dog is unwelcome. In English, this can only be said with body language when asking "Who brought that dog to the barbecue?" <u>Now back to things we need to know.</u>

B. Derivational suffixes — 'deriving'.

The other type of suffix actually changes the meaning of a word because it 'de-rails' a word from one path of meaning to another. Words belong to flowing rivers of language, so imagine that they are de-rivered rather than de-railed. By diverting a word from one river to another, derivational suffixes derive or create new words. When words add any other suffix than a flexible suffix, as described in type 1), they change course, are derivered, into a new stream of meaning, which is why we say a word is derived from another word, rather than created, by adding a derivational suffix. Let's call the two types of suffixes 'flexible suffixes' (flexing tails) and 'deriving suffixes' (deriving new words).

There are loads of deriving suffixes. For instance, the verb *to forgive* changes into an abstract noun when —ness diverts it to a new meaning, changes it into the noun *forgiveness.*

In the following list we shall read words with the flexible suffix <est>, like *biggest* and *finest* and also stem words which end in terminal <est>, like *rest* and *test*. Sometimes <est> is in stem words with prefixes, like *detest* and *digest*. *Rockfest* is an example of <st> in a compound word, (*fest* comes from *feast,* also used in *festival*). The list words follow the usual decoding rules. Only a few words with flexible suffix —est are listed. They are underlined.

List 2-7 terminal [st] As for Rule 2-6.

ADJUST, AGIST, ALMOST* <ost>=[ohst], ARREST, ASSIST, AVAST *VS,* BACKREST, BALLAST, BEST, BIGGEST, BUST, CAPITALIST, CAST *VS,* CELLIST*, COLUMNIST, COMPOST, CONGEST, CONQUEST, CONSIST, CONTEST, COST, DENTIST, DESIST, DETEST, DIGEST, DIMMEST, DISGUST, DISINFEST, DUST, EGOTIST, ELITIST, ENLIST, FASCIST* [fash-ist], FAST *VS,* FATALIST, FATTEST, FEMINIST, FINEST, FIST, FITTEST, FLUTIST, FOREST*, FULLEST, GABFEST, GAMEST, GHOST* [gohst], GHOSTLY*, GIST, GRUFFEST, GUST, HIST, HOST*, HOTTEST, HUGEST, INFEST, INQUEST, INVEST, JEST, JUST, LAMBAST, LAMEST, LAST *VS,* LEFTIST, LEST, LIST, LISTLESS, LOST, LUST, MANIFEST, MAST *VS,* MEDALLIST, MIST, MODEST, MOLEST, MORALIST, MOST* [mohst], MOSTLY*, MUST, NASTY *VS,* NEST, NICEST, REST, PACIFIST, PALEST, PANELLIST*, PAST *VS,* PASTY *VS,* PEST, POST* [pohst], PUREST, QUEST, REDDEST, RESIST, REST, ROCKFEST, RUDEST, RUMMEST *Oz. slang,* RUST, SAFEST, SANEST, SATIRIST, STALEST, STIFFEST, TALLEST, TEMPEST, TEST, UNREST, UNSTUCK, UTMOST* [utmohst], VAGUEST*, VAST *VS,* VEST, VILEST, WEST, WETTEST, WHIST*, WIDEST, WISEST, WISTFUL*, ZEST.

Cellist and *Fascist* use an Italian way to spell [sh], [fash-ist]. Long ago, before the Norman Invasion, it was the Englisc way too. Yes, that's how English was spelt before 1066.

*Most, *host, *ghost, *almost, *post* and *utmost* use an old technique to lengthen vowels. The best thing to do is to "memorize, don't analyse" these six <ost> words because they are historic 'left-overs' and we can not use a rule to decode them any differently to *lost, cost etc.* We'll meet some other old words which use <olk> and <old> to spell [ohk] and [ohd]. The silent <h> in *ghost* will be discussed later, meanwhile we can treat it as a reminder that <ghost> spells [gohst]. We hear the [sl] blend in *ghostly* and *mostly,* if we find the <stl> blend too difficult and let [s] flow over short [t] and silence it.

Whist spells [whist] because the old card game Whisk, named from *whisking* up cards after each trick, changed to Whist when silence was asked for — *whist* meant "keep quiet!" *Wistful,* however, is probably based on *wishful* according to Etymonline.

Words like *forest* don't use the twins <rr> to keep [o] short, which makes them Rebel Lemons. We shall hear their excuse for using only a single <r>.

Words like *panellist* are now written *panelist* in USA because 'double gate' <ll> is considered unnecessary.

Did you spot that *vaguest* needs <u> to insulate <g> from <e> so that <g> spells [g] and not [j]?

Rule 2-8 <ct> in the same syllable spells the blend [kt].
Rebel INDICT [indIt].

Rebel's Reason The <c> in *indict* is silent. It did not get its present spelling until the dictionary makers decided to add a silent <c> to show that it comes from Latin *indictare* and is related to *dictate* and *dictation,* because to *indict* someone is to write in about him, to the authorities, charging him with breaking the law. *Indict* translates as in-write. It came from the old French word *enditer,* (see Etymonline). Its long vowel changed from [deet] to [dIt] in the GVS, so since then it rhymes with *write*. Then <c> was added, but the new spelling did not stop the people saying [indIt] and [indItment] for *indictment*.

List 2-8 blend [kt]
ACT, AFFECT* *a verb only,* COMPACT, CONDUCT, CONTACT, CONTRADICT, CONVICT, CORRECT, DEPICT, DUCT, EFFECT* *noun/verb,* ELECT, ELECTRICAL, ELECTRONIC, ELECTRONICALLY, ENACT, ERECT, EVICT, FACT, IMPACT, INCORRECT, INDUCT, INFECT, INSECT, INTACT, NEGLECT, OBJECT, PACT, RECTIFY, RECTUM, SECT, SELECT, SUBJECT, SUSPECT, TACT, TACTFUL, TACTIC, TACTICAL, TACTICS, TACTLESS.

Affect,* **effect,* which is which? *Affect* is never a noun. *Effect* is rarely a verb for it is an old way of saying 'to bring about, to achieve or accomplish'. Here's a tip:- **Affect is the **A**ction, **E**ffect is the r**E**sult.

Not needed but nice to know. The influence Latin had on English spelling, e.g., on *indict,* is hard to understand now. In the sixties Latin was part of school life. My 1965 classmates had to matriculate in Latin to study Law, Medicine, Dentistry or Physiotherapy at Adelaide University. Universities like Cambridge and Oxford are in the country, outside London, but the Sorbonne is right in Paris. French university students were so immersed in Latin that they spoke it on the streets. A part of Paris which had cheap rooms for students and other penniless academics was called the Latin Quarter. It still is, but there is very little café chatter in Latin nowadays. British school yards no longer ring with Latin words like *ego, ipso facto, mater, pater* and *quiz*. The term '*dux* of the school' is becoming outmoded too. Now back to things we need to know.

Rule 2-9 If adjacent in the same syllable, <f> and <t> spell the blend [ft].
Rebels OFTEN, SOFTEN, in which <ft> spells [f], not [ft].
Rebels' Reasons See 2-59.
List 2-9 blend [ft]
AFT *VS,* ALOFT, DEFT, FITFUL, GIFT, GIFTED, GIFT-WRAP, HAFT *VS,* LEFT, LIFT, LOFT, OFT, RAFT *VS,* RIFT, SIFT, SOFT, SOFT SPOT, TUFT, UPLIFT, WAFT *VS*.

Rule 2-10 If adjacent in the same syllable, <p> and <t> spell the blend [pt].
Rebels? EXEMPT, EMPTY and some others when <mp> spells just [m] on some lips. See 2-64.
List 2-10 blend [pt]
ADAPT, ADOPT, APT, CORRUPT, DISRUPT, ERUPT, HEPTAGON, INEPT, KEPT, OPT, UNADOPTED, WEPT.

Rule 2-11 If adjacent in the same syllable, <s> and <p> spell the blend [sp].
Rebel RASPBERRY In *raspberry* <sp> does not always spell [sp].
Rebel's Reason *Raspberry* can spell many different sounding words. Due to Vowel Shift, it can spell **[rarsp-berry]** or **[rasp-berry]**. However, as we know, saying three adjacent consonants can be difficult. In this case, what does <spb> spell? Joining lips for [p] and again for [b] means one drops out. Which is it with you? If [b] drops out we hear **[rarsp-e-ree]**. It's usually [p] which drops out, in which case we hear **[rarzb-e-ree]** because then <s> spells [z] to blend with [b]. Why? Because [s] cannot blend with a voiced consonant and [b] is a voiced consonant. As we know, <s> can spell [s] or [z]. Also, if stressed hard at the beginning, it can spell **[rarz-bree]** or **[rars-pree]** — and, in some places, **[raz-bree]** or **[ras-pree]**. It is very unusual for one word to have seven or more alternative pronunciations!

List 2-11 blend [sp]
CLASP *VS*, CRISP, CUSP, GASP *VS*, GRASP *VS*, HASP *VS*, HOSPITAL, LISP, MISSPELL*, RASP *VS*, RASPBERRY* *VS*, SPAM*, SPAN, SPASTIC, SPAT, SPECK, SPED, SPELL, SPICK AND SPAN, SPIGOT, SPILL, SPIN, SPIN OFF, SPINET, SPIRIT, SPIT, SPIV, SPOT, SPOTLESS, SPOTTY, SPUD, SUN-SPOT, WASP, WISP.

*Misspell compounds *miss* and *spell* but, as triplets are outlawed in English, one <s> is dropped. They only appear in pseudo words like *brrr, shhh, zzz*. Some newer words have not compounded because of this, e.g., *cross-stitch* and *joss-stick* in which a dash is used to prevent a triplet. *Misspell* is now a fully compounded word and cannot return to *miss-spell*. As for past tense, in USA *misspelled* is preferred to *misspelt*. In Anglo English *misspelt* was more common until recently. Both are correct.

*Spam, unwanted e-mails, was so named due to the Monty Python skit in which a woman declares she does not want to eat Spam (tinned meat) and is then serenaded with "Spam, spam spam.....", (Fleck, 2007).

As we know, <x> spells the unvoiced blend [ks] after a stressed vowel but it spells voiced [gz] before a stressed vowel. When it comes before an unvoiced consonant it spells unvoiced [ks] and forms a blend of three consonants if in one syllable.

List 2-12
EXACT [eg-zakt], EXALT [eg-zolt], EXPECT [ek-spekt], EXIST [eg-zist], EXTOL [ek-stol], NEXT [nekst], TELETEXT [tel-ee-tekst], TEXT [tekst].

List 2-13
Names with S Blends
STACY, STEVEN, SKY, SKIP, SCOT, STAN, STEFAN.

Bad Blenders — [b], [d], [g], [j], [v], [dh], [z] [zh].

Rule 2-14A Bad Blenders never blend with unvoiced consonants.

Reason Linguists would be able to explain this rule by explaining the human anatomy of sound production. Let's just say that the 'proof is in the pudding'. This refers to the process of proving a loaf of bread or a yeast pudding. If the yeast works, the pudding will rise. Let's see if the rule works. Can you think of any word which breaks this rule?

Rebel? Although DEBT appears to have a blending of voiced and unvoiced sounds, [bt], in fact the <b> was always silent. *Debt* spells [det]. So voiced [b] does not blend with unvoiced [t]. The dictionary elders decided to add the silent <b> in order to show that long, long ago it came from a Latin word, *debitus*. Their aim was to capture history in the letters of a word. They did not aim to make the words easy to read.

Rebels? BATZ (a coin) spells just [bats] and WALTZ spells just [wols], BLITZ spells [blits] and The Ritz Hotel spells [dhə] [rits] [hoh-tel]. The words are not rebels. They are just German adoptions in which <z> spells [s] because in German it spells [ts].

Rule 2-14B Bad Blenders never blend with each other, except for [z] and [d].

Reason – Blending with [z] and [d] occurs when suffixes <s> and <ed> are added.

Rebels? What about *abdomen, abduct, bedbug, oddball, zigzag,* and *hobgoblin?* **Ans.** In these words Bad Blenders merely <u>cluster</u> at syllable boundaries, meet up but do not flow into each other. In *subgenus* [sub-jen-uus] Bad Blenders [b] and [j] merely cluster and in *exam* [eg-zam] the [g] and [z] of [gz] split at syllable boundaries, so the Bad Blenders [g] and [z] just cluster. Bad Blenders merely <u>cluster</u>. They only <u>blend</u> with terminal [z] and terminal [d], e.g., in *rags* [ragz] and in {*bagged*} [bagd].

A Very Rare Word ADZE [adz] is the only **stem** word in which Bad Blenders, [d] and [z], blend with each other. This word is not a rebel for the rule states that Bad Blenders do not blend with each other except with [z] and [d]. In USA it is spelt *adz*, for its fossil <e> was removed by President Theodore

Roosevelt. Nobody knows why the English changed the old word *adesa* to *adze* but I think it was to make the sharp little chopper seem more frightening. We are still so frightened of the letter <z> that although we say [adzez] when there is more than one adze, we still write the second [z] with an <s>. Adzes spells [adzez] in USA, but many Anglos say it spells just [adz] – 1 *adz* [wun] [adz], 2 *adzes* [too] [adz].) Are they too frightened to say another [z]?

Letter <x> can spell unvoiced [ks], as in *fox* and *exit*, or voiced [gz], as in *exam* and *exist.* It only spells [gz] before a stressed syllable. The <am> of *exam* is stressed because it is an abbreviation of *examination* in which <am> is stressed to ensure the word ends on an unstressed suffix:- ex-**am**-in-**a**-tion, [eg-zam-in-ay-shun]. Similarly, *exist* was derived from *existence*, in which the middle syllable is stressed, because it is followed by unstressed -*ence*.

Now we know why <x> spells [z] in *Xerox* and {*xylophone*} — it has to spell a voiced consonant to give oomph to the stressed vowel after it but it finds the blend [gz] too hard for [g] and [z] are both Bad Blenders and cannot flow together in the same syllable.

Wedge is not a rebel for it spells [wej], not [wedj], because Bad Blend [dj] is hard to say. The Ab'l language *Wajarri* used to be *Wadjarri* [war-dja-ree]. As English is now the first language of most Australian aborigines the [dj] blend has reduced to just [j] and the <d> of *Wadjarri* has been removed in many books. In the Aboriginal word *budgerigar* the blend [dj] has reduced to [j], but <d> remains to keep <u> spelling short [u]. *Didgeridoo* is not an Ab'l word, (Lonergan, p. 6), but, due to its [dj] blend and terminal [oo] written <oo>, it seems like one. The bad blend [dj] is avoided when abbreviated to *dij*. Even when in one syllable <dge> spells [j], not [dj], we continue to write <d> because this has two consonants to keep vowels short, e.g., *cadge* spells [kaj] but {*cage*} spells [kayj].

Rule 2-14C <dg>, when followed by <e>, <i> or <y>, spells just [j] and shortens the preceding vowel.
List 2-14C
BADGE, BUDGE BUDGIE*, BUDGET, CADGE, CUDGEL, DISLODGE, DODGE, DODGY*, {DREDGE}, {DRUDGE}, EDGE, EDGY*, FIDGET, FUDGE, GADGET, GUDGEON, HEDGE, LODGE, MIDGE, MIDGET, MISJUDGE*, MISLODGE*, NUDGE, PIDGEON, PIDGIN, PODGY, PORRIDGE, PUDGY*, RIDGE, SEDGE, SELVEDGE, WEDGE, WIDGET slang, WIDGEON. Australian Slang BODGY*, FRIDGE*, RIDGY-DIJ. WIDGY*. Names MADGE, GIDGET.

The Ab'l word *budgerigar* from the Kamilaroi language (Reader's Digest 2001) has been shortened to **budgie* [bujee] with terminal <i> spelling long Continental [ee] but followed by <e> to insulate it from coming last.

*We heard in Part One that <y> also softens <g> to [j] and now we see and hear that in *pudgy, dodgy, edgy, etc.* However, twin <gg> resists any softening by <y> and so *boggy* stays [bo-gee], unlike **bodgy* [bo-jee].

Since we cannot use <j> at the end of words, <ge> spells [j] is very useful. Adopted *raj* has diplomatic immunity, *dij* gets away with it as an abbreviation of a word which seems adopted, but *fridge,* short for *refrigerator,* does not dare!

**Fridge* needs <d> but *refrigerator* does not, because [i] is stressed and in fourth syllable from end.

**Misjudge* and **mislodge* use the prefix, *mis—*. They are not compounds of *miss* and *judge* or of *miss* and *lodge*.

Zorro and Zed
As we know, Zorro is not afraid to write the letter <z>. He slashes <z> on walls and doors to frighten bad people. In Part One we learnt that *dogs* spells [dogz] and *hums* spells [humz]. This is because our mouths naturally want to say [z] after a voiced consonant. We also know that *cats* spells [kats] because our mouths

naturally want to say [s] after unvoiced consonants. By now we can see that <s> spells [z] more often than <z> spells [z], all because of the curse of the dagger.

If we add [s] to *dog* it will sound like [doks]. Try it. It is just the way our mouths work. Now it sounds as if we are talking about *docks* instead of *dogs*. We write <s> to make plurals, or matched verbs and we also add <s> to show ownership. We cannot add [s] to *dad* in *dad's hat* without saying [dats] [hat] because [t] and [s] can blend, but [d] and [s] cannot blend. In order to ensure *dad* sounds like [dad], not [dat], our mouths change [s] to [z]. This happens to [s] after all voiced consonants. However, we only say [z], for we never write it. For example, we never write, "*It's Fred'z rev'z. He bogz Bob'z pop's car every time!*" Instead, we write, "*It's Fred's revs. He bogs Bob's pop's car every time!*"

If only we could write <z>! Then we would know whether to say [z] or [s]. Instead, we shall decode, read the words, knowing that <s> spells [s] after unvoiced consonants, and <s> spells [z] after voiced consonants.

Why do we say *mum's pins* spells [mumz] [pinz]? Why not say [mums] [pins]? **Ans.** We could say that. Some languages pronounce <ms> as [ms], but in English *mums* would sound like *mumps*. *Pins* would sound like *pince,* something which pinches like *pincers*.

In English <s> spells [z] after all voiced consonants.

Rule 2-15 Letter <s> spells [z] after all voiced consonants in the same syllable.

Reason — as above. This rule means that just by looking at a word ending with a consonant <s> we know if it spells [s] or [z].

List 2-15 Just a start – read these and add more words of your own choice.
BAGS [bagz], BATS [bats], BEDS [bedz], BETS [bets], BIBS [bibz], BITS [bits], BINS [binz], CABS [kabz], CATS [kats], DOGS [dogz], DOLLS [dolz], DUCKS [duks], EDGES [ej-ez], EGGS [egz], GAPS [gaps], GIVES [givz], HAMS [hamz], JETS [jets].

As we learnt in Part One, whenever <s> starts a word, it spells [s]. So initial <s> spells [s], even when it is followed by voiced consonants, including Bad Blender [v] in *svelte* and all Big Blenders.
SVELTE [svelt] *fossil e*, SLOT [slot], SMOG [smog], SNAG [snag], SWIM [swim].

Big Blenders

Rule 2-16 Big Blenders blend with every consonant except [z].

Reason The Big Blenders are like vowels in that they blend with every consonant, blending with both voiced and unvoiced consonants. This is because they are made like vowels are made. We learn in school how babies are made. This is sex education. However, we get no lex education. We do not learn how our lexicon is made. To us, our lexicon is all the words we speak, our vocabulary. To linguists, our lexicon is all the word-sounds we make in order to say these words. When we make vowels, we do not block air — each vowel is said with an open mouth and it is not blocked on the way from the lungs. When we make big blender consonants, air also flows from the lungs without being stopped on the way. It does not, however, have such an easy path on the way out. Two of the big blenders are [l] and [r], for which air flows up the upturned tongue and down over either side and then through the lips. These two are called 'liquids'. Air travels up and through the nose for the three 'nasals', [m] using only the nose. The mouth is partly open for [n] and [ŋ], but all three require an open nose — as you will discover if you try to say them with a blocked nose. The other big blenders are [w] and [y], in which air is a little constricted, by partially closing the lips for [w] and partially closing the throat for [y]. All of these five big blenders are Voiced Consonants for they vibrate the strings of our voice box, as they pass through it. These strings are two vocal cords, bands of muscle, inside the voice box, which is also called the larynx. This muscle tissue relaxes for the nine unvoiced consonants but tightens up for all the voiced sounds.

Repeat Rule At the beginning of a word <s> spells [s], not [z].

That is why [zl], [zm], [zn] nor [zw] never start a word. English words do not begin with <sr>. When <sy> starts a word, it is not a consonant blend because <y> always spells a vowel sound after <s>.

List 2-16
SLAB, SLACK, SLAM, SLAP, SLAT, SLED, SLEDGE, SLIP, SLIT, SLOB, SLOG, SLOP, SLOT, SLOVEN *f*, SLUDGE, SLUG, SLUM, SLACKEN, SLACKNESS, SLAP-HAPPY, SLY, SMACKS, SMALL* [smorl], SMALLEST, SMALLNESS, SMALLPOX, SMALLS, SMELL, SMELLS, SMELLY, SMELT, SMIDGEON, SMIDGIN, SMITTEN, SMOCK, SMOG, SMOKY, SMUDGE, SMUDGES, SMUDGY, SMUG, SMUT, SMUTTINESS, SMUTTY, SNACK, SNACKS, SNAG, SNAGGY, SNAKY, SNAP, SNAPBACK, SNAPDRAGON, SNAPPILY, SNAPPINESS, SNAPPY, SNAPS, SNAZZY, SNIB, SNIFF, SNIFFIEST, SNIFFILY, SNIFFINESS, SNIFFS, SNIFFY, SNIP, SNIPPET, SNIPPY, SNIPS, SNIVEL, SNIVELS, SNOB, SNOBBILY, SNOBBISM, SNOBBY, SNOBS, SNOG, SNOGS, SNOT, SNOTTINESS, SNOTTY, SNUB, SNUBBINESS, SNUBBY, SNUBNESS, SNUBS, SNUCK, SNUFF, SNUFFBOX, SNUFFBOXES, SNUFFILY, SNUFFING, SNUFFS, SNUFFY, SNUG, SNUGLY, SNUGNESS, SWAG, SWAGMAN, SWAM*, SWAMP, SWAN, SWANK*, SWAP, SWAT, SWELL, SWIG, SWILL, SWIM, SWIVEL, SWIZ, SWOP=SWAP, SWOT *slang*, SWUM.

*Note the terminal <all> always spells [orl], unchanged in compound words and before suffixes, *smallpox* [smorl-poks], *smallest* [smorl-est].

**Swam* [swam] and **swank* [swank] are two of the rare rebels to the rule that <wa> spells [wo].

Rule 2-17 When <s> precedes a voiced consonant in the same syllable it spells voiced [z].
Reason This is so the consonants can blend. That's why *egotist* spells [ee-goh-tist], but *egotism* spells [ee-goh-tizm]. Letter <z> could be used to spell [z]. In fact, <izm> should be used to spell [izm], but due to <z>'s continuing unpopularity <s> does the work of <z>. Note: *Excema* [eks-sem-ar] can reduce to [ek-smə] but it should not reduce to [eg-zma] because <ce> spells [s], as in *excel*, <ce> can never spell [z].

List 2-17
ANTAGONISM, BAPTISM, BOSM*/BOSOM, BOTULISM, CANNIBALISM, CAPITALISM, COMMUNISM, CUBISM, EGOTISM, EMBOLISM, EVANGELISM, FASCIM*, FEDERALISM, FEMINISM, MAGNETISM, METABOLISM, NUDISM, RACISM*, SEXISM, SOLECISM, SPASM, VANDALISM, WITTICISM.

**Bosm* is the original spelling of *bosom* [buuzuum]. The first vowel of *bosm* changed from [oh] to [uu] and then the second [uu] vowel heard in the [zm] blend was written in, not as <u>, which would have been muddled with <m> and so was written as <o>.

**Fascism* [fash-izm] See 2-3B.

**Racism* [ray-sizm]. As we know, <ci> spells [s].

Big Blender L
List 2-18 [bl]
BLAB, BLANKET, BLAST *VS*, BLESS, BLIP, BLITZ*, BLOB, BLOG*, BLOT, BLUB *slang*, BLUDGEON.

*In *blitz* [blits] <z> spells [s] because it is a German word and German <z> spells [ts].

**Blog* (coined 1999) combines *web* as in World Wide Web (from 1989) and *log*, such as one maintained by a pilot or mariner, but in cyberspace, *weblog*, (Fleck, 2007).

List 2-19 [kl]
CLACK, CLAD, CLAG, CLAM, CLAN, CLAP, CLARET, CLASS *VS*, CLASSIC, CLASSIFY, CLEF, CLERIC*, CLICK, CLIFF, CLINIC, CLIP, CLOCK, CLOD, CLOG, CLOT, CLOVEN [kloh-ven], CLINIC, CLUB, DECLASSIFY, MISCLASSIFY, O'CLOCK.
O'CLOCK.

Cleric spells [kle-rik], not [klee-rik]. As we know, <ic> shortens the preceding vowel.

List 2-20 [fl]
FLAB, FLABBY, FLAG, FLAGON, FLAK, FLAN, FLAP, FLAT, FLAX, FLIP, FLIT, FLOCK, FLOG, FLOP, FLOPPY, FLORIN, FLUFF, FLUFFY, FLURRY, FLUX, FLAGON, FLATTEN, FLORAL, FLORID, FLOTSAM, FLY.

List 2-21 [gl]
GLAD, GLADDEN, GLASS *VS,* GLEN, GLIB, GLOB, GLOBAL, GLOBALISM, GLOSS, GLOVE *f,* GLUE, GLUG, GLUM, GLUT, GLUTTON.
Note the silent <e> on *glove* to insulate <v>, and <o> in *glove* spells [u], as in most *f* (*feather*) words

List 2-22 [pl]
APPLY*, COMPLACENT, DUPLEX*, ECTOPLASM, ENDOPLASM, IMPLY* <y> =[I], PLAN, PLAQUE *VS,* PLEDGE, PLOD, PLOP, PLOT, PLUCK, PLUG, PLUM, PLURAL, PLUS*, PLACKET, PLACID, PLACENTAL , PLANET, PLASMA, PLASTIC, PLATINUM, PLATONIC, PLUCKY, PLUMMET, PLY [plI], REPLY* <y>=[I], SIMPLIFY* [ifI].
As we know **ply* with prefixes still spells [plI] and suffix <ify> spells [ifI], e.g., [sim-pli-fI].
**Duplex* spells [joo-pleks] because it is a compound, not <u> before double gates. Meaning 'two-plates', *duo* is short for *du* and *plex* is from 'flat plate'. *Duplex* is a 'duty' word, because <du> spells [joo], because <u> spells a long sound.
**Plus* spells [plus], not [pluz], even though <s> follows a stressed vowel. It's a Latin word which grew out of an older word, *pleos. Plenty* also grew out of *pleos. Pleos* changed to *plus* to match *minus,* (Etymonline).

Big Blenders blend with all consonants but they also blend really well with vowels, and [l] and [r], the "melting liquids", are the best at this. If they have a choice, if they are between a vowel and a consonant, they prefer to blend with the vowel if it is the main vowel in the word, i.e. a stressed vowel. In old words they sometimes blended so closely that they spelt a new sound, as in *folk* [fohk]. Sometimes we cannot hear <l> spell [l], if it melts into the vowel, e. g. in *calf* <alf> spells [arf], a new sound without [l]. It only happens when [l] follows <o> or <a> and then not always. It can happen when [m] follows <o> or <i> and when [n] follows <i>. Later we shall meet [r] blending, "melting", with **all** preceding vowels when followed by a consonant, as in *fork,* to form new sounds. The next lists have a few words in which [l] "melts" on to the vowel behind it rather than blending with the consonant in front of it.

Rule 2-23 Big Blenders blend with all other consonants but not much with themselves.
Rebels? When <yr> ends *satyr* and <ym> ends *gym,* the <y> is acting as a vowel, not as a consonant. The Proper Noun *Rwanda* is not an English word. The next list is not a long list because Big Blenders do not blend much with each other. Remember, when an L blend follows a vowel, it can change the vowel sound. This was an early, Old English, method of spelling long vowels.
List 2-23 Big Blenders blending with themselves.
ALMS [armz] plural noun, BALM* [barm], EMBALM, BULN BULN*, CALM [karm], CALMLY [karm], ELM, FILM [film], **not** [filim], FILMY, HELM, KILN, NAPALM [na-parm], PALM [parm], PSALM* [sarm], QUALM [kwarm], WHELM.
**Buln-buln* is another word for *lyre bird,* adopted from Ab'l Woiwuru and later recorded as *bulen-bulen* around Melbourne, (Blake, p. 89).

*_Embalm,_ not _enbalm,_ because suffix _en_ changes to _em_ before [b] and [p] because [m] ends with closed lips and [b] and [p] start with closed lips, as in _embody, embolden._ We shall see this in {_embrace, employ, empower_} later.

*The silent <p> in _psalm_ has been silent a long, long time, long before the Normans invaded in 1066. {_Psalter_} is also an old word, [sol-ter]. All the others, like _psychology,_ originally began [ps] as they do in Greek, but because <ps> had always spelt [s] in _psalm_ and {_psalter_} the others followed suit when they reached England! Now the only time we let <ps> spell [ps] is in "Pssst!" slang for "Be quiet and listen!" (The Greek [ps] word-sound is echoed in the name of the Greek god Poseidon, which we say [pəsIdən].)

Rule 2-24 Initial <mn> spells [n] and terminal <mn> spells [m].
Reason As we know, Big Blenders blend with everything else but not much with themselves. In fact, [m] and [n], like [l] and [r], prefer vowels to fellow consonants. In _damn_ we hear [m] because it is next to a vowel, and in _mnemonic_ we hear [n] because it is next to a vowel. This is why we no longer hear both consonants in the following list words but the silenced ones return when we add some suffixes, as in _indemnify_ [in-dem-ni-fI], {_damnable_} [dam-na-buul]. {We shall also meet _columnar, condemnation, solemnity, hymnal_ and _autumnal_ later}. The little suffix <ed>, as in _condemned,_ is not strong enough to split the syllables and blends on to the end of the terminal <mn> verbs. Strangely the longer suffix <ing> also fails to split [n] from [m] and Cummings, on p. 425, says <ing> might just be following the other verb suffix, <ed>.
List 2-24 Big Blenders silencing each other in blends.
{AUTUMN [ort-um]}, COLUMN, CONDEMN, DAMN, HYMN [him], MNEMONIC, SOLEMN.

Rule 2-25 Initial <wr> spells [r].
Reason As we know, Big Blenders blend with everything else but not much with themselves. The blend [wr] is so difficult that <wr> can be said to spell [r]. Lip readers are more likely to see lips forming [w] than others are likely to hear the [w] in such a blend. Words never end with terminal <wr>.
List 2-25 Big Blenders silencing each other in blends.
UNWRAP, UNWRITTEN, WRACK*, WRAP, WRAP UP, WRECK, WREN, WRIST, WRIT, WRITTEN, WRY.
*_Wrack_ is seldom seen nowadays. It's an old version of _wreck._ 'Wrack and ruin' but 'nerve-racking, rack one's brains', for _rack_ means put under strain, (Bryson 2004, p. 172).

Blends of [l]. If [l] has 'melted' onto a vowel and changed the vowel sound it is noted.
List 2-26 [lt]
ADULT, BELT, CULT, DIFFICULT* [uult], DOLT, BOLT, COLT, EXALT [exorlt], EXULT, FALSETTO*, FALSE* [forls], [fols], FELT, GILT <g>=[g], HALT [holt], HILT, INSULT, JILT, JOLT, KILT, LILT, MALT [holt], MELT, MOLTEN, OCCULT, PELT, QUILT, RESULT, REVOLT, SALT* [sorlt], [solt], SILT, STILT, TUMULT*, ULTRASONIC, VOLT*, WELT, WILT.
*_Salt_ has become [solt] in Australia, as has _false_ [fols], but in England they spell [sorlt] and [forls]. _Falsetto_ spells [for-set-oh] or [fol-set-oh]. Although _salt_ reads [salt], [solt] is easier to say and in all three words the Law of Ease takes over from King Sound, rather than Rex Text. If Rex Text and Queen Quill had their way, _salt_ would spell [salt].
*_Tumult_ obeys the Special Rule that if <u> spells [yoo] after <t>, the <tu> spells [choo].
*_Difficult_ can be difficult to spell, and _difficulty_ even harder, which is why my teacher taught is to chant, "Mrs. D, Mrs. I, Mrs. FFI, Mrs, C, Mrs. U, Mrs. LTY", bless her!
*_Volt_ is an eponym. Google Italian physicist Alessandro Volta.
List 2-27 [lp]

GULP, HELP, KELP, PULP, YELP, HELPFUL, HELPLESS.

List 2-28 [lf]
(on) BEHALF [bee-harf], CALF [karf], ELF, ELFIN, GOLF, GULF, HIMSELF, HALF [harf], ITSELF, SELF, WOLF* *f* [wuulf]
Alfalfa is not listed because it has no [lf] blend:- [al-fal-fa]
*Wolf was *wulf* in Old English but the Norman scribes replaced <u> with <o> so it would not muddle with <w> and look like "Triple W".

List 2-29 [ld]
BALD* [borld], BOLD, COLD, DOLDRUMS *pl. noun*, EMBOLDEN, FOLD, HOLD, GILD* <g>=[g], GOLD, GOLDEN, HOLD, HERALD* [-orld], HERALDIC*, MANIFOLD, MARIGOLD, MILD [mIld], OLD, OLDEN, SCALD* [skorld], SCOLD, SOLD, TENFOLD, TOLD, UPHOLD, UNTOLD, WILD [wIld], WELD.
WELD
*Gild must be an old, old word, for <i> does not soften <g> in *gild*.
*In *bald, herald* and *scald* <ald> spells [orld]. We have seen <all> spell [orl] in *hall, squall etc.* in Part One. Now we see that when Big Blender L blends with other consonants after vowels the vowel might lengthen. Some never did, some used to, and some still do lengthen. Some stopped doing it because King Sound and Queen Speech once ruled the land but when people learnt to read. Rex Text and Queen Quill took over. People began pronouncing words as they looked on paper, but only if it made words easier to say. Many things influence our speech. The Law of Ease is one but there is also Peer Pressure, which means we copy each other in order to be understood and accepted. Some people mimic strangers they admire, like film stars. Although <o> still spells [oh] in *folk, yolk,* and *wholly,* in Australia, when it precedes <ld> in *cold, old etc* it spells [o], just as the words are written.
Experiment: Ask an old Englishman how he says *cold, old, fold, hold.* He will probably say [kohld] and [ohld] and [fohld] and what's more you will hardly hear the [l]. *Cold* sounds like *code* and so on.
*Heraldic spells [he-ral-dik], not [he-rorl-dic] because as we know suffix <ic> shortens vowels.

List 2-30 [lk]
BALK [bork], CALK [kork], CALQUE, ELK, FOLK [fohk], HULK, ILK, MILK, SILK, MILKMAN, MILKY, POLKA, POLK INK [pohk][ink], SILKEN, TALC, TALK [tork], STALK [stork], WALK [work], YOLK [yohk].

List 2-31 [lv] — all with silent insulator <e>
ABSOLVE, BIVALVE, CALVE* [karv], EVOLVE, DELVE*, DEVOLVE, DISSOLVE*, EVOLVE, HALVE* [harv], INVOLVE, RESOLVE, REVOLVE, SALVE, SOLVE, TWELVE*, UNIVALVE, VALVE.
*Calve is a verb from the noun *calf.*
*Delve is a verb formed from the obsolete Old English word for a *quarry*, the noun *delf. Delve* is not used much. It's in the old homily: "When Adam delved and Eve span, who was then the gentleman?"
*Dissolve is a rare case of <ss> spelling [z]. Normally, when <s> follows a weak vowel, as in a prefix, e.g., in the verb *desert,* <s> spells [z]. However, in this case prefix *dis*, meaning 'apart', is added to *solve*, 'loosen, untie', creating <ss> after a weak vowel. Another word which has<ss> due to adding a prefix, *dessert,* also breaks the rule <ss> spells [s]. This does not happen in other words with prefixes ending <s>, e.g., <ss> spells [s] in *dissatisfied.*
*Halve is a verb formed from the noun *half.*

Twelve has <v> because 12 is 'two over ten'. In Old English it was *twelf*, literally 'two left' (over ten). The Goths said *twalif* for 12. The contraction *teen* means 'ten more than', so 16 is 'ten more than six', *sixteen,* (Etymonline).

List 2-32 [lb]
BULB, ALB.

What about the blend [lz]?
We hear [z] in plurals, like PALS, HOLS (slang for holidays), ILLS, BELLS, BULLS, HULLS. There are no singular words ending <ls>. We shall meet *else* [els] and *pulse* [puls] soon.

Big Blender L in Names.   DONALD, GERALD, GLEN, MALCOLM, PLACIDO, VLAD, WOLF, WOLFGANG.

Patterns. We see from these Big Blender lists that vowels [e] and [u] are not affected and <i> is only mildly affected when blended to Big Blender L and another consonant. One Loose List in the appendix gathers "most" of these "ghostly finds" into one spot. Only rarely we see <ild> can spell [Ild] but when [lld] is split across syllables in {*children* and *wilderness*} the vowel reverts to [i]. We never see <eld> spell [eeld]. We see that <old> and <ost> at times spell [ohld] and [ohst]. We see that <ald> always spells *[orld], and <alk> always spells *[orlk] or *[ork] and <alf> always spells [arlf] or [arf]. We find that when the vowel is lengthened, the <l> can "melt", fall silent, if it is followed by <f>, <k>, <m>. Saying [arlf] is not as difficult as [ohlk], and [arlm] seems the hardest of all, and [orld] the easiest to say.

Triple Blends occur in plural words in which <s> spells [s] after unvoiced consonants, e.g., *elks,* and <s> spells [z], after voiced consonants, e.g., *marigolds.* Most words ending <lf> do not form the triple blend [lfs] but instead spell [lvz] when plural. Why? Most of the old Viking [v] sound has been lost from English words, replaced by the softer [f] sound. However, some people still say [nevyoo] for *nephew* and we still use the [v] sound in some plurals. This is because in Old English <f> spelt [v] inside a word and [f] at the end of words. So, when <s> is added, <f> is pushed inside the word and spells [v]. Now we see why it's <es> instead of <s> which is added, for the old scribes still needed <e> to show up the difference between <u> and <v>. They wrote <s> quite differently to the <s> of a printing machine for it began down low. The letter <e> is best to show the high hook of <v> and the low hook of <u>, each joining <e>. Mind you, not all words remove terminal <f>, e.g., {*reef* & *reefs, serf* & *serfs, wharf* & *wharfs* or *wharves*}, (Cummings, p. 375). Noticeably, these words have long vowels spelt with digraphs and they do not involve [f] blends.

Rebel GULFS
Rebel's Reason The plural of *gulf* is *gulfs*. Translators into English use *gulves* but English speakers prefer to use the rebel word *gulfs* as *gulves* sounds like a verb.
List 2-33 Terminal [lf] singular, terminal [lvz] plural, in nouns.
ELF, ELVES; CALF, CALVES <al> =[ar]; GOLF, like *footy* and *rugby,* has no plural; HALF, HALVES <al> =[ar]; HIMSELF, THEMSELVES [dhem-selvz]; SELF, SELVES; WOLF*, WOLVES <o> =[uu].
**Wolf* is also a verb, but not *wolves*. We say, "He wolfs his food." Maybe we do not say, "I wolve, he wolves", because it could mean "to hunt wolves", or, as in the adjective *thieving*, to take on the entire persona of a wolf, not just its hunger and hasty eating habits. The rule to change [f] to [v] when inside a word, is very old but the verb *to wolf* (*one's food*) is new. Etymonline dates its first use in print as 1862.
<u>Relevant Writing Rule</u> Plurals of words ending <ff> are made by adding <s>, but a single <f> is replaced with <ves>, except for *chiefs, gulfs, oafs, reefs, roofs, serfs,* and *waifs*. It can be *dwarfs* or *dwarves* and *hoofs* or *hooves*, and the verbs *surfs* and *wolfs* are never otherwise. <u>Return to Reading Rules.</u>

Big Blender R. It takes time to learn to blend [r] with other consonants. Many little children say [w] instead of [r] in trying to blend [r]. We shall start blending [r] in just a few words whilst we continue on with Big Blender [l]. We shall blend [r] in *bridle* and *cradle* before meeting Big Blender R's main list.

Let's light a candle and put an apple on the slab for the next list.
They were *candel* and *æppel* in Old English, in the olden days before the French invaded. Very easy to read. As we know, <æ> spelt [a]. Old English words were easy to read. E.g., *isikel, idel, litel* and *sadel*. Now they are *icicle, idle, little* and *saddle*. In 1066, when the Norman French invaded England, everything changed. They called an English 'slab' a *table* [tar-bluu]. The English copied but said it the English way, with stress at the beginning and some one wrote *tabul*. "Non, non, non," said the French, and they made the English write it the French way, *table*. The French took over all the writing jobs for hundreds of years. By the time English was re-installed as the official language of England many French words had changed to match the way the English said them. English words, like *candle* and *apple* had been respelt, the French way. Words introduced by the French, like *table,* were written the French way. The French wrote *gentil* and said [jen-teel] but because the English said [jen-təl] they wrote *gentl*. The same with other words: *idl, candl, sadl, tabl* and *litl*. Sadly, all these words broke a rule, Rule 2-34.

Idle E — *able, unstable.*
Terminal Silent <e> blocks flow from liquid [r] and [l].
Rule 2-34 English words never end with consonant <r> or consonant <l> because a silent <e> is added.
Reason Consonants [r] and [l] are the Liquid Consonants, which flow from the mouth, unlike consonants [t], [p], [b] etc. Silent <e> blocks 'liquids' from flowing on and on when they follow a consonant. Some people say that all English syllables must contain a vowel and they say that silent terminal <e> provides that vowel for words like *acre* and *idle*. Well, the second syllable of *prism* does not have a vowel and so the best explanation for silent <e> is that it blocks the flow of the liquid consonants
Rebels AXOLOTL, CONEPATL and {DIRNDL}.
Rebels' Reasons *Axolotl* and *conepatl* foreign names for a salamander and a skunk. They have been adopted but not adapted. *Dirndl* is also a recent adoption, 1937. In Australia, *dirndl* used as an adjective, exclusively for a gathered skirt, a dirndl skirt. In Germany it means 'traditional dress'. See website's Photo Gallery.

Rule 2-35 The terminal cluster <le> after one consonant spells [uul] and lengthens the preceding stressed one letter vowel sound.
Reason Even when the English regained control of their language, they did not restore the easy spelling of Old English, such as *idel,* nor even went with *idl,* but stuck to the system of adding a silent <e> to such words. The vowel preceding a consonant plus <le> is long and stressed because such words were once written according to Orm's Law, with only one consonant after the vowel, e.g., *idle* was once *idel,* and therefore the first vowel was long, as in *idel,* and stressed, being English, because it was the first of two syllables.
List 2-35
ABLE, BIBLE, BRIDLE, BUGLE [yoo], CABLE, CRADLE, CYCLE, DEBACLE* <a>=[ar] , DISCIPLE, ENABLE, ENTITLE, FABLE, GABLE, IDLE, ISLE*, LADLE, LISLE*, MAPLE, MACLE* <a>=[ar], NOBLE, QUADRUPLE, QUINTUPLE, RECYCLE, RIFLE, RUBLE [oo], SABLE, SCRUPLE , SIDLE, STABLE, STAPLE, STIFLE, TABLE, TITLE, TRIFLE, UNABLE, UNBRIDLE, UNSTABLE.

*Debacle is related to the word *unbar* and describes the mess when a river was unbarrs and breaks free.
*Macles are dark spots in minerals, *marks*. That's why in these words <a> spells [ar] not [ay].
*Isle does not spell [Isuul] but instead rhymes with *I'll*. In *isle* and *lisle* <i> spells its long sound [I] as we'd expect in the first syllable of a word. However, <s> is silent in both. *Isle* and *island* used to be spelt without the silent <s> but scholars traced *island* back through France to Rome where long ago *island* was *insula* in Latin. Just to show off that they knew where it came from, they put in the silent <s>. The French popped an <s> into *isle,* their word for 'island', and the English adopted that word for 'island' too. Then the French took it out again but *isle* was in the English dictionary and words in English dictionaries are hard to change.
*Lisle [lll] is a fabric which is made with a thread that first came from spinners in a town called Lisle in France which later changed its name to Lille [leel]. The GVS changed the eponym to lll] but the original spelling remained, including the silent <s>. Thick brown lisle stockings and fine white lisle gloves were once in every lady's wardrobe.

Rule 2-36 One letter vowels spell short vowels if unstressed before a consonant plus <le> cluster, except if spelt with <u>, because [oo] and [yoo] resist shortening.
Reason In Orm's Law stressed vowels require 'double gates', two consonants, to stay short. That's why <a> spells long [ay] in *able* but short [a] in *apple*. We already know that [oo] and [yoo], spelt with <u>, resist shortening because long ago they were written with two letters, not just one — at times <iu> and other times <iv>. Vowels written with two letters, or digraphs, resist shortening, as in {*eagle* and *gargle*}.
List 2-36 in which the one letter vowels before <cle> and <ble> and <ple> are short because they are unstressed, except for those spelt <u>.
ARABLE, BICYCLE*, BINNACLE, CLAVICLE, CORACLE, CUBICLE, CURRICLE, CUTICLE, FOLLICLE, HORRIBLE, ICICLE, IMPLACABLE, MANACLE, MIRACLE, MONOCLE, MULTIPLE, OBSTACLE, ORACLE, PARABLE, PINNACLE, POPSICLE, PRINCIPLE, RADICLE, RECEPTACLE, SNOTSICLE*, SPECTACLE, SPIRACLE, STIPLE, TENTACLE, TESTICLE, TRIPLE, *TRICYCLE, VENTRICLE, VESICLE, VISIBLE, and ending <uble> and <uple> INSOLUBLE, SOLUBLE, QUADRUPLE, QUINTUPLE, VOLUBLE.
*Bicycle [bI-sik-uul] and *tricycle [trI-sik-uul] are stressed on the first syllable. Prefixes are not usually stressed, but this means that their second syllables are unstressed and therefore shortened before <cle>, unlike *cycle* in which <y> spells a stressed sound,[sI-kuul].
*Snotsicle is an Antarctic term, see Hince, B. . See bibliography for Hince. B. Antarctic Dictionary.

Rule 2-37 Stressed one letter vowels are kept short by two consonants (double gates) before <le>.
Reason They are following Orm's Law about short vowels before 'double gates'. *Axle* is not listed with *able* and *cable* for we do not say [ayk-suul]. The first syllable of *axle* is stressed but [a] is not lengthened to [ay] before <xle>. Why? *Axle* spells [aksel] in which [a] is kept short by the double gate [ks]. You can see double gates in *apple* and *ankle* too, which is why <a> spells [a] in *apple* and *ankle*. This matches Orm's Law for he said double gates are needed after stressed one letter vowels to keep them short.
Rebels TREBLE and TRIPLE, which have short stressed vowels but only one letter before <le>.
Rebels' Reasons Cummings, on p. 105, says that this is maybe because if <p> and <b> are added to the standard prefixes <tri> and <tre> for *thrice* the Latin link with *triplus* will be lost. Everyone knew that *tri* = 'three' and *plus* = 'more'. An extra <p> would link the word to *trip* instead of *tri* and *three* and *treble*.
List 2-37
ADDLE, AMPLE, ANGLE, ANKLE, APPLE, AXLE, BABBLE, BAFFLE, BANGLE, BATTLE, BATTLEMENTS, BEFUDDLE, BELITTLE, BOTTLE , BOTTLENECK, BRAMBLE, BRITTLE, BUBBLE, BUGLE*[yoo], BUMBLE, BUNDLE, CANDLE*, CANDLESTICK, CANDLEWICK,

CATTLE, COBBLE, CODDLE, CRIPPLE, CRUMBLE, CRUMPLE, CUDDLE, DABBLE, DANGLE, DAZZLE, DIDDLE, DINGLE*, DISENTANGLE, DISMANTLE, DISSEMBLE, DOTTLE, DRIBBLE, DRIZZLE, DWINDLE, ECCLES CAKE, EMBATTLED, ENTANGLE, EXAMPLE, FETTLE, FIDDLE, FIDDLESTICKS, FINAGLE, FIZZLE, FONDLE, FRAZZLE, FRIZZLE, FUDDLE, FUMBLE, GABBLE, GAGGLE, GAMBLE, GENTLE*, GENTLEFOLK [ohk], GENTLENESS, GENTLEMAN, GENTLEWOMAN, GIGGLE, GOBBLE, GOGGLE, GOGGLE, GOGGLE-BOX, GOGGLE-EYED, GOGGLES, GOMBLE*, GRAPPLE, GRIDDLE, HAGGLE, HANDLE, HANDLEBAR, HASSLE, GRIZZLE , GRIZZLED, HOBBLE, HUBBLE-BUBBLE, HUDDLE, BUCKLE, HUDDLE, INTERMINGLE, JANGLE, JIGGLE, JINGLE, JOGGLE, JUGGLE, JUMBLE, JUNGLE, KETTLE, KINDLE, LITTLE, MANGLE, MANGLE, MANHANDLE, MANTLE, MEDDLE, MEDDLESOME *f*, METTLE, METTLESOME *f*, MIDDLE, MISHANDLE, MOLLYCODDLE, MOTTLED, MUDDLE, MUFFLE, MULTIPLE, MUMBLE, MUZZLE, NETTLE, NIBBLE, NIPPLE, NOBBLE, NUZZLE, PACKSADDLE, PADDLE, PADDLE, PEBBLE, PEDDLE, PERIWINKLE, PIDDLE, PIMPLE, PINEAPPLE, PRATTLE, PRINCIPLE, PUDDLE, PUZZLE, QUADRUPLE <a>=[o], QUIBBLE, RADDLE, RAFFLE, RAMBLE, RANKLE, RATTLE, RATTLESNAKE, RAZZLE, RESEMBLE, RIDDLE, RIFFLE, RIPPLE, RUBBLE, RUFFLE, RUMBLE, RUMBLE, SADDLE, SADDLEBACK, SAMPLE *VS,* SCRABBLE, SCRAMBLE, SCRIBBLE, SCRUPLE, SCUFFLE, SCUTTLE, SELF-CENTRED, SIDE-SADDLE, SIMPLE, SINGLE, SIZZLE, SKEDADDLE *slang*, SKITTLE, SMUGGLE, SNIFFLE, SNUGGLE, SOLUBLE, SPINDLE, SPRINKLE, SQUABBLE, SQUIGGLE, STADDLE-STONE, STIPPLE, STRADDLE, STRAGGLE, STRANGLE, STRANGLEHOLD, STRUGGLE, STUMBLE, SUBTITLE, SUBTLE* *silent b*, SUSCEPTIBLE, SUPPLE, SWADDLE, SWINDLE, SWIZZLE, SWIZZLE-STICK, TANGLE, TARRADIDDLE, TATTLE, TANGLE, TEMPLE, TINGLE, TINKLE, TIPPLE, TITTLE-TATTLE, TODDLE, TOGGLE, TOPPLE, TREDDLE, TREMBLE, TRUFFLE, TRUNDLE, TUMBLE, TUSSLE, TWADDLE, TWIDDLE, TWINKLE, UNCLE, UNEXAMPLED, UNPRINCIPLED, UNSCRAMBLE, WADDLE, WAFFLE, WAGGLE, WANGLE, WATTLE <a>=[o], WHITTLE, WIDDLE *slang*, WIMPLE, WINKLE, WRANGLE, WRINKLE, WOBBLE* [wobuul]. <u>Slang</u> BOTTLE-OH. <u>Name</u> ARISTOTLE.

Candle is one of the few words adopted from the Romans when they ruled Britain. They spelt it *candela*. Most Latin words were adopted much later, when Latin had become a "dead language". Although it was no longer spoken much it provided good spare parts to make new words, just like we use old cars for their parts.

Cattle is a plural noun. *Cattle* cannot be singular.

Dingle and *gomble* are part of the Antarctic vernacular, see the 'coolantarctica' website.

Gentle arrived in England as *gentil* [jent-eel] from France meaning high-born, born into a noble family or clan, from Latin *gens, genis* for 'race or clan'. It changed to mean 'gracious, kind' and then 'mild', (Burton p. 75). Its end shrank to just <tl>, [təl], an <e> had to be added to insulate <l>. The old meaning of high-born is retained in *gentleman*.

Subtle was written *sutil* or *sotyle* until traced to *sub texla*, its Latin origin, depicting a faint pattern woven only into the cross threads of the weave of a cloth, the *texla*, later reduced to just *tela* — *subtela*.

Wobble [wob-uul] is a re-spelling of *wabble* [wob-uul]. *Wobble* is a rare case of <wo> spells [wo], not [wu] nor [wuu].

<u>Relevant Writing Rule</u>. We usually see <le> at the end of words after tall letters, like <b>, or tail letters — letters with tails — like <g>. For instance, *table, babble, angle* and *haggle*. We usually see <el> after small letters, as in *camel, panel, barrel*. However <t>, which is not very tall, breaks this rule in *hotel, mantel* and a few others. Words end in <le> far more often than in <el>. Many words were changed from <el> endings to the French <le> ending after 1066 but the English continued to say them the English way, [el]. <u>Return to Reading Rules.</u>

Double gate CK — *cackle, truckle.*

As we know, stressed one letter vowels are kept short by two consonants (double gates) before <le>. So <ckle> after a short one letter vowel keeps it short. The list continues, using <ck> as a double gate.

List 2-37 cont. **<ckle> is always preceded by a short, stressed vowel.**
CACKLE, COCKLE, CRACKLE, DECKLE , FICKLE, FRECKLE, HACKLES, HECKLE, HUCKLEBERRY, PICKLE, PICKLED, PRICKLE, STICKLEBACK, SUCKLE, TACKLE, TICKLE, TRICKLE, TRUCKLE.

<u>Not needed but nice to know</u>. In Old English (Saxon etc) and Middle English (Norman times) the suffix <le> was used for verbs which showed repeated action: e.g., *crumble, crumple, dazzle, dribble, giggle, joggle, sniffle, snuggle, twinkle,* (Cummings, p. 150). We have also seen this repetition in the plural noun *cattle*.

However not all <le> endings mean "repeated". Some words ending <le> are verbs which used to end <len>. Instead of *resemble* the English said *resemblen*. In the 14th century Londoners began dropping <n>. As all the printing was done in London, *resemble* and similar words were printed and spread. <u>Now back to things we need to know.</u>

Big Blender R — *adracadabra, umbrella.*

The liquid consonant [r] is often the last sound we learn to make (and [m] is usually the first).

Many Continental Europeans, and also the Welsh, trill the letter <r>. The tongue, forward and flat, vibrates as air passes between it and the roof of the mouth, called the palate. In Scotland, in the west of England, and in parts of USA, the tongue is curled back and kept still to produce a "darker" sound called a "burr". The Scottish burr is famous. Ab'l languages say both and now write:- <r> for flat British [r] and <rr> for burred Scottish [r]. Deep in the south of England some people lisp and say [w] instead of [r]. Once this lisp was considered prestigious, high class! Some folk still act like they cannot say [r], like cute babies. Until little children learn to curl the tongue they say [w] for [r].

Rule 2-38 Big Blender R blends with voiced and unvoiced consonants.

Word-sound [r] is hard to blend with [w]. Try saying *written, writing, wrap, wrestle* and *wrist*. Which sound dominates in the blend, [w] or [r]? Yes, [r] dominates, for we end up saying [rit-en], not [writ-en]. In a difficult blend, the long consonant flows over the short one, forwards or backwards! You can see which consonants are long in the appendix.

We have already met blends of [r] in *bramble, brittle, crumble, crumple, frazzle, frizzle, grapple, griddle, tremble, trestle, triple, truffle, trundle, wrestle, wrangle* and *wrinkle*

List 2-38 Big Blender R's main list.
ABRACADABRA, ABRIDGE, ACROSS, ACTRESS, ANGRY*, ARISTOCRAT, BEGRUDGE, BRA* *abbrev.,* BRAN, BRASS *VS*, BRAT, BREN GUN, BRICK, BRIDGE, BRIG, BRISKET, BROCCOLI, BROLGA*, BRUMBY*, BRUSQUE [uu], BUTTRESS, CAMBRIC, CONTRAST *VS*, CONTROL, CRAB, CRABBY, CRACK, CRAFT *VS*, CRASS, CRAVAT, CREDIT, CRESCENDO*, <sc> =[sh], CRETIN, CRESS, CRIB, CRIMINAL, CRISS-CROSS, CRITIC, CRITICAL, CRITICISM, CRONYISM, CROCK, CROCUS, CROQUET*, CROP, CROSS, CRUCIFY, CRY, DESCRY [des-krI], DISTRESS, DRAB, DRAFT *VS* DRAG, DRAGON, DRAM, DRAMATIC, DRAT, DREDGE, DRESS, DRILL, DRIP, DRIVEL, DRIVEN, DROLL, DROP, DROPLET, DRUDGE, DRUG, DRUM, DRY, ENGROSS* <o>=[oh], FRANTIC, FRET, FRIDGE* *abbrev.,* FRIGID, FRILL, FRIZZ, FROG, FROGMAN, FROLIC, FROM, FRY, GASTRIC, GENTRY, GENTRIFY [ifI], GRAB, GRAFFITI*, GRAFT *VS* , GRAM, GRAN, GRASS *VS* , GRATIFY [ifI], GRAVEL, GRAVELY, GRAVEN, GRAVITY, GRID, GRILL, GRIM, GRIMACE, GRIN, GRIP, GRISLY, GRIT, GROG, GROSS* <o>=[oh], GROTTO, GROTESQUE, GROVEL*, GRUDGE, GRUB, GRUBBY, GRUFF, GRUMMET, GUM DROP, HATRED* <a>=[ay], HINDRANCE, HUMDRUM, HUNGRY*, INTEGRAL, JOG

TROT, KINDRED*, KRILL, LUBRA*, MANTRA, MATRON* <a>=[ay], MATTRESS, METRIC, METRICAL, METROPOLIS, METROPOLITAN, MICROCOSM, MIDRIFF, MINESTRONE* [...ee], OPPRESS, PARALLELOGRAM, PATRON* <a>=[ay], PETREL, PETRI* , PETROL, PRAM, PREFACE [pref-əs], PREJUDGE, PREMISES *pl. noun,* PRESS, PRICK, PIN PRICK, PRETTY* [pritee], PRIG, PRIM, PRISON, PRISSY, PRIVET, PRIVY, PROD, PROP, PROFIT, PROPEL , PROVE *f* <o>=[oo], PRY, PUTREFY* [efI], RUBRIC, STRESS, SAFFRON, SUPPRESS, SUNDRY, ENTRY, EXTRA, CITRIC ACID, CITRUS, SUN-DRESS, SUN-TRAP, TELEGRAM, TENDRIL, TRACK, TRAFFIC , TRAMMEL, TRAGIC, TRUCK, TRUE, TRULY, TRAM, TRANSLUCENT, TRANSPARENT TRAP, TRAVEL, TREK, TRELLIS, TRESS, TRIBAL, TRICK, TRICKY, TRIFID, TRILL, TRIM, TRIP, TRIVET, TROD, TRODDEN, TROLL, TROLLOP, TROPIC, TROPICAL, TROT, TRUCK, TRUDGE, TRUSS, TRY*, UMBRELLA, UNABRIDGED. <u>Proper Nouns</u> APRIL, BRAZIL , BRITON, SRI LANKA. <u>Names</u> APRIL, BRENDAN, BRENDON, BRENNAN, BRENTON, BRET, BRIDGET, BRYCE, CASANDRA, FRANCESCA, FRANCIS, FRANK, FRANKLIN, FRED, FRITZ* <z>=[s], GRANT, GREG, GRETA, GRETEL, GRISELDA, KENDRA, KRISTY, LUCRENZA, MILDRED, PRISCILLA, PRUDY, PRUNELLA, TRAVIS, TRENT, TRINI, TRINITY, TRISTAM, TRUDY.

Angry and *hungry* are the only English words left containing the blend [gry]. *Hatred* and *kindred* are the only English words left ending in <red>. Once upon a time –gry and -red were popular suffixes, (Bryson, p. 75).

Bra is short for {*brassiere*}, a French adoption, in which <ss> sometimes spells [z], but not on my lips. How do you say this word, if at all? I use [s] in {*reconnaissance*} and {*renaissance*}, too, but some people let <ss> spell [z] in these words. Cummings p. 396 says that <s> spells [z] after digraphs, as in {raisin} but no one's sure what <ss> spells after digraphs and that this rarely occurs anyway.

Brolga is a wide-spread Ab'l word for the lovely crane which is also known 'Native Companion'.

Brumby may come from "baroomby" meaning 'wild' in the language of the Pitjara people on the Warrego and Nogoa Rivers in southern Queensland. Wikipedia says it may come from other sources.

*In *crescendo,* <sc> spells [sh], as in *cello.* See 2-96.

*The French word *croquet* spells [kroh-kay], with (silent <u>), also [kroh-kee] if it's said the English way, with initial word stress.

*In *fridge,* <dge> seems to spell the rare blend [dj], but we all know that it spells [frij]. However, no one is game to spell it that way, *frij,* even though it's short for {*refrigerator*} (which has no <d> because <i> spells [i] in the fourth stressed syllable from the end without need of help from <d>.)

Graffiti is adopted but not adapted and breaks the rule against a terminal <i>. A rebel word.

Graven [gray-ven] is the only word here obeying Orm's Law, with a single <v> after a long vowel. Other words, in list 2-38, which have a single <v> after a short vowel, e.g., *drivel, driven, gravel, grovel, trivet, privet* and *privy,* are Rebel Lemons, with an excuse. They cannot double <v>, because twin <vv> is a "no-no". Note *prove's* silent <e> to insulate <v>, plus its vowel shift [uu] to [oo]. In *gravity* <a> spells [a] due to suffix <ity>.

As we know, twins are not welcome in consonant clusters. Although this is a weak rule it eliminates <l> from *fulfil.* However, <t> remains in *mattress, buttress etc.* and even <p> in *suppress* and *oppress.* Why? To keep the preceding vowel short, safe from the lengthening affect of unstressed <re> which we shall see soon in {*acre*}. This is why *matron* and *patron* and*hatred* spell [may-tron] and [pay-tron] and [hay-tred]. It is an old-fashioned way of lengthening vowels.

Grovel is not a Cursive Casualty, not a Feather Word. It spells [grov-el]. As we'd expect, it was first used (by Shakespeare) well after the old scribes used <o> before <v> in place of <u>. See Etymonine.

Gross and *engross* spell [grohs] and [en-grohs], the only words in which <o> spells its long sound before <ss>, due to its Old French origin word *grosse.*

*Lubra [loo-brar] was first recorded as *loubra* by French explorers in Tasmania in 1834. The English usually use <oo> to spell [oo] in newly adopted words, e.g., *kookaburra. Lubra* is no longer used because this lovely word has in the past been used to give offence at times, as have all English nouns to do with women.

*Minestrone [min-est-roh-ne] means "big soup", an adopted word. The Italian suffix means "big" and spells [oh-nee].

*Petri is an adjective which describes a dish. It is an eponym and as such breaks the rule that <i> does not end words. Google the German bacteriologist Julius Petru for more information.

*Pretty long ago meant a 'pert prat'. Maybe, as the meaning changed, the vowel did too, but not its letter. Now it's the only common word in which <e> spells [i]. This also happens in the proper noun *England*, and adjective *English*.

*Putrefy is one of the four rare words with suffix <efy>, which spells [efI]. All the rest take <ify>, which spells [ifI].

*Truly like *duly* drops its insulator <e> after <u> in *due* and *true,* these two, plus *argument* and *awful*, are the only rebels to break the rule that when adding a suffix that starts with a consonant do not delete the final silent <e> of the stem word.

Letters <l> and <r> spell the Liquid Voiced Consonants [l] and [r], named' liquid' because they can both pour out of the mouth in continuous sounds and inside the mouth they both run out over the sides of the tongue.

*Try and do something is wrong. We *try to* do something. So, try to prevent saying 'try and prevent bad grammar'. Instead, try to prevent bad grammar.

We have seen [l] blends change vowel sounds, e.g., in *bib* <i> spells [i] but in *bible* it spells [I] and in *stab* <a> spells [a] but in *stable* it spells [ay]. In both words <e> is only added to stop <l> from coming last after a consonant.

The same thing happens when we blend [r] onto a terminal syllable: the <i> in *fib* spells [i] but in *fibre* it spells [I]. The <e> in *met* spells [e], but in *metre* <e> spells [ee]. As you can see, the letter <r> is followed by <e> in these words for, like <l>, the letter <r> cannot terminate a word if it follows a consonant.

Rule 2-39 English words never end with consonant <l> or consonant <r> and so a silent <e> is added.

Reason Consonants [l] and [r] are called Liquid Consonants because they flow with little obstruction, unlike other consonants which are blocked or restricted on their journey from lungs to atmosphere. The <e> shows us that they blend with the preceding consonant instead of starting a new syllable and flowing on and on (until the speaker runs out of breath).

Rebels We have already met AXOLOTL and CONEPATL, which are adopted but not adapted. {DIRNDL} is yet to come.

Other Rebels? No other words end in consonant <r>, except for words like *satyr* in which <y> is acting as a vowel.

Rule 2-40 Terminal <re> after one consonant spells [uu] and lengthens the preceding stressed one letter vowel.

Reason Adding <re> after a consonant to lengthen the preceding vowel is an old-fashioned way of turning short vowels into long ones. Only a few old words still do it and so the next list will be short. When the Spanish end their words in <re> they roll the [r], e.g., in *hombre* but the English do not roll the [r] and so at the end of words it shrank into a short grunt, [uu]. Sometimes the long vowel is Continental [ar] and [ee] instead of British [ay] and [I].

Remember, do not roll [r], <re> just grunts [uu]. Old English *æcer* would have spelt [ayk-er] (which is very like Latin *ager*) but as we know Ash, which spelt short [a] and long [ay] was discarded and now we can just say that termial <cre> and terminal <gre> lengthens preceding stressed vowels.
Rebels YOU'RE and WE'RE, in which *'re* is short for *are,* spell [yoor] and [weer].
List 2-40
ACRE [ay-kuu], LUCRE [loo-kuu], FIBRE [fI-buu], LITRE [lee-tuu], MACABRE* [mu-kar-buu], METRE [mee-tuu], MITRE [mI-tuu], NITRE [nI-tuu], SABRE [say-buu], OGRE [oh-guu].
In *macabre, the second <a> spells long Continental [ar].
Other words which use this old way of lengthening stressed vowels are *matron, patron* and *hatred,* which we have already met. In their case consonant <r> is followed by an unstressed syllable instead of an unstressed <e>.
Only stressed one-letter vowels are lengthened before a consonant plus <re>. That is why the botanical term INVOLUCRE [in-<u>voh</u>-loo-kuu] in which <u> does not spell a stressed vowel, is not in list 2-40. Unstressed one letter vowels remain short before consonant plus <re>, except if spelt with <u> which resists shortening. So, in *involucre*, <u> spells long [oo], because <u> resists shortening.

If <re> follows not one but two consonants the vowel is not lengthened, for it is behind 'double gates.'
List 2-40 cont.
CALIBRE, CENTRE, LUSTRE, MASSACRE, SEPTRE, SOMBRE, SPECTRE.
Initial stress on *calibre* and *massacre* means the next syllable is unstressed and unstressed one letter vowels remain short before consonant plus <re> cluster. We know that <a> spells [a] in *massacre* due to the twin <ss>, a double gate. We know that <a> spells [a] in *calibre* because it is stressed and third syllable from the end. In *macabre,* the first syllable is not stressed and so the next is and is lengthened by <bre> for the cluster consonant plus <re> lengthens the preceding stressed one letter vowel sound, in this case to its Continental long sound.

The Can-do suffixes, Ible and Able
Rule 2-41 The two suffixes —*ible* and —*able* spell [u-buul] and [u buul], not [Ibuul] and [aybuul]!
Reason Suffixes are unstressed. **Unstressed one letter vowels are short before the consonant plus <le> cluster (except if spelt with <u> for [oo] and [yoo] resist shortening).** Hence the long [yoo] in *soluble*. In a suffix, <ble> spells [buul] and receives secondary stress in order to match the alternate stress rhythm of English syllables. If <ble> is the second syllable of a stem word, as in *bible,* in which first syllable is always stressed, then, as the next syllable, <ble> spells an unstressed syllable, e.g., in [bI-buul]. Suffixes —*ible* and —*able* both come from Latin for *have,* "habere" or "abere" because ordinary Romans dropped their 'haitches'. They mean "having a hold" on a situation, having ability, (which is why, if someone is not coping, Australians say "Get a grip!")

We attach —*ible* and —*able* to verbs to make adjectives to describe someone who is, or something which is, capable of doing that verb. Words with suffix *ible* words are all old words modelled on Latin words. Newer words end in —*able*. The website Morewords lists 219 words ending <ible> and 1,478 ending <able>. The following writing rules explain which suffix to use, —*ible* or —*able*.
<u>Relevant Writing Rules</u> Enjoy these writing rules before the next word list. They will help you "grow your own" words.
A **-ible** is attached to stems that are not full words in their own right, e.g., *credible, indelible,* with **19 Exceptions**: *equitable, formidable, inexorable, inevitable, memorable, probable, unconscionable, portable, arable, ineffable, potable, inscrutable, insuperable, indomitable, malleable, vulnerable, affable, palpable, culpable.*

B **–ible** is attached to stems that **–ion** can attach to e.g., *access* becomes *accession*, and so it's *accessible*, not *accessable*. (We say *excitation* not *excition* and so it is *excitable*, not *excitible*.) There are **3 Exceptions**: *predictable, detectable* and *retractable*, regardless of *prediction, detection* and *retraction*.

C **–ible** is attached if the stem word ends in **–ns** or **–miss**, e.g., *defensible, expansible, admissible*, with **2 Exceptions** *indispensable* and *dispensable*

D **-ible** is added if the stem ends in <c> and <g> spelling [s] and [j], e.g., *negligible*.

E **-ible** is attached to words which are cognates with words ending *–ive*. Cognate*s*, like cousins, are the words which are related because they grow from a common stem. The (bound) stem *gest* is in *digestive* and *digestible*.

F **–able** is attached if the stem is a full word in its own right, a free stem, like *govern* in *governable*.

G **–able** is attached if the stem is a full word lacking only the final <e>, e.g., *blamable*.

H **–able** is attached if the preceding letter is <i> in order to avoid <ii>, e.g., *sociable*.

I **–able** is attached if the preceding letter is <y> which becomes <i>, *envy, enviable*.

J **–able** is attached if the stem has another suffix beginning with <a> as in *irritable* due to *irritate; demonstrable* due to *demonstrate; tenable* due to *tenacious; abominable* due to *abomination; capable* due to *capacious*.

K **–able** is attached if the preceding letter is <c> or <g> spelling [k] and [g], e.g., *applicable, navigable*. They use *-able* instead of *–ible* to ensure <c> spells [k] or <g> spells [g]. How indefatigable!

L **–able** is attached to words which do not fit these rules but have <a> in their Latin ancestor words. Some examples follow. *Amenable* from Latin *minare*, to drive cattle with shouts, and came to mean submit to influence (like cattle); *delectable* from Latin *delectabilis,* from *delectare*, to delight; *execrable* from Latin *cacare* " 'to excrete.' We still say "kak" for dung. The word for soft dung, *pappekak*, was adopted from Holland and hence 'poppycock' means 'rubbish'. *Probable* from Latin *probare*, to test or try; *hospitable*, from Latin *hospitari*, "be a guest"; *veritable* from Latin *veritatem* and *veritas*. Return to Reading Rules.

The writing rules above are very helpful if we are spelling words out on paper, i.e., writing them. If we are spelling words out loud we need to know how the letters decode and how the syllables fit the tum-te-tum rhythm of spoken English. Both suffixes, *—able* and *—ible* spell [u-buul], in which [uu] is destressed and [buul] has secondary stress. This means that in some words syllables are silenced in order to end on secondary stress, as in *abominable* [u-¹**bom** nu-²**buul**] and in other words prefixes are given tertiary stress, as in *indispensable* as in [³**in**-dis-¹**pen**-su-²**buul**]. Knowing that our "Can-do" suffixes *—able* and *—ible* end with secondary stress we can work out the rhythm of each word, always aiming to give the stem, bound or free stem, primary stress

List 2-41 <ible> spells [u-buul], with secondary stress on [buul].
ACCESSIBLE, ADMISSIBLE, COLLAPSIBLE, COMBUSTIBLE, COMESTIBLES, COMPATIBLE, COMPREHENSIBLE, COMPRESSIBLE, CONVINCIBLE, CORRUPTIBLE, CREDIBLE, CRUCIBLE , DEFENSIBLE, DEDUCIBLE, DESTRUCTIBLE, DIGESTIBLE, DIRIGIBLE, DIVISIBLE, EDIBLE, ELIGIBLE, EXPANSIBLE, EXPRESSIBLE, EXTENDIBLE, EXTENSIBLE, FALLIBLE, FLEXIBLE, GULLIBLE, HORRIBLE, ILLEGIBLE, IMPOSSIBLE, INACCESSIBLE, INADMISSIBLE, INCOMBUSTIBLE INCOMPATIBLE, INCOMPREHENSIBLE, INCORRIGIBLE, INCORRUPTIBLE, INDELIBLE, INFALLIBLE, INFRANGIBLE, INFLEXIBLE, INSENSIBLE, INSUSCEPTIBLE, INTANGIBLE, INTELLIGIBLE, INVINCIBLE, INVISIBLE, IRASCIBLE, IRREDUCIBLE, IRREPRESSIBLE, IRRESISTIBLE, IRRESPONSIBLE, LEGIBLE, MANDIBLE, MISCIBLE, NEGLIGIBLE, POSSIBLE, PRODUCIBLE, REDUCIBLE, REPREHENSIBLE, REPRODUCIBLE, RESPONSIBLE, SEDUCIBLE, SENSIBLE, TANGIBLE, TERRIBLE, UNINTELLIGIBLE.

Rule 2-42 Suffix <able> spells [u-buul], with secondary stress on [buul].

List 2-42 <able> spells [u-buul].
ABOMINABLE, ACCEPTABLE, ADAPTABLE, ADJUSTABLE, AFFABLE, AMENABLE, AMICABLE, APPLICABLE , ARABLE, ARRESTABLE, BIDDABLE, BRIDGEABLE, CAPABLE, COLLECTABLE, COMMENDABLE, COMMUNICABLE, CONSTABLE, CONTROLLABLE, CULPABLE, DAMNABLE, DELECTABLE, DEPENDABLE, DESPICABLE, DETACHABLE, DETECTABLE, DETESTABLE, DISCREDITABLE, DISPENSABLE, EQUITABLE, EXPANDABLE, EXPENDABLE, EXTRICABLE, HERITABLE, HOSPITABLE, IMPECCABLE, IMPLACABLE, IMPRACTICABLE, INCONTESTABLE, INDEFATIGABLE, INDISPENSABLE, INDICTABLE, INDOMITABLE, INEFFABLE, INEVITABLE, INHABITABLE, INSCRUTABLE, INEQUITABLE, INTRACTABLE, MANAGEABLE, MOVABLE, PALATABLE, PALPABLE, PASSABLE *vs,* PERISHABLE, PICKABLE, POTABLE, PROBABLE, PROGRAMMABLE, PREDICTABLE, PRESENTABLE, PREVENTABLE, PROFITABLE, PUNISHABLE, REGRETTABLE, RENTABLE, RESPECTABLE, RETRACTABLE, SELLABLE, SOLVABLE, TAXABLE, TENABLE, TRACTABLE, UN-GET-AT-ABLE, UNINHABITABLE, UNPREDICTABLE, UNSHOCKABLE, UNSHRINKABLE, UNTHINKABLE, UNWARRANTABLE, VERITABLE.

Relevant Writing Rules We know prefixes begin words and suffixes end them. We know suffixes can grow onto suffixes: *help, helpless, helplessly.* There are **4 suffixes** which change when another suffix is added to them. When this happens the suffixes **–ible, -able, {–ous}** change to **–ibil-, -abil-, {-os}-** as in *possibility, ability, {generosity.}* Return to Reading Rules.

Big Blender semi-consonant [w] blends with all consonants and vowels but, as we know, not much with other Big Blenders.

List 2-43 Big Blender [w] blends.
CWM* [kuum], DWELL, SQUAT, 'TWAS, TWIG, TWILIT, TWILL, 'TWILL, TWIN, TWIN BEDS, TWIN-SET, TWIST, TWIT. <squ> =[skw] SQUAT <a> = [o], SQUIB, SQUID, SQUIRREL, SQUITS *Oz. slang.* Proper Nouns GWENT, SWASTIKA. Name GWEN.

Did you let W Muddle you in *squat?* *Squat* spells [skwot] not [skwat], like <sw> spells [wo] in *swat, swan etc.* due to collateral damage from cursive casualties,

*The word *cwm* [kuum] only **looks** like a [kw] blend. It is so old that <w> is just a doublet of <u>, written <uu>, and that is why <w> and <u> shared the same sound long ago, [uu]. A cwm is a "bowl shaped hollow on a mountain" written *cwm* in Wales but *coomb* in England. However both spell [kuum].

M and N, Nasal Consonants — *aplomb, zinc.*
Hold your nose and only breathe through your mouth. Now try saying [m] and [n].
That is why they are called nasal. We say them through our nose!!! Let's call them the Nosey Nasals. Put your finger on your nose and say these two sounds. Can you feel your nose vibrating? Even more on the side of your nose? Now say [b] – did your nose vibrate? No, just your voice box.

Big Blender M Terminal <mb> is a fossil from the days of Old English when *mb* lengthened the preceding vowel, as marked below. Such words are very old, (Cummings, p. 102).

Rule 2-44 In all cases the [b] is silent when <mb> is terminal.

Reason Once, [m] and [b] were each pronounced, back when words had longer endings. "Olde Shoppe" signs remind us that words were longer once. When we enjoy eating "Bombe Alaska" we are reminded that once upon a time *bomb* was longer and used to spell [bom-buu]. All words ending <mb> sounded as if they ended [m-buu]. However, the [b] became a mumble and then fell silent, in the terminal blend <mb>. So now we do not say [b] but we still write <b>. We say [b] after [m] inside stem words, in words like *plumbago,* or {*chamber* and *number*} in Part Three, or {*rhomboid*} in Part Four. We shall see that <b> remains silent at the end of a stem word with a weak suffix, like {*number*}, meaning 'more numb,' or *numbs, numbly, numbing* or *numbingly*. Stronger suffixes pull <b> from its silent blend with [m] e.g., *crumble* and slang *dumbo*. *Plummet* (from *plumb*) *a*nd slang *dummy* (from *dumb*) have actually dropped the useless silent <b> from their 'letter codes'.

List 2-44 Terminal <mb> spells [m]. It lengthens preceding vowels in some old words but never lengthens <u> to spell [oo] or [yoo], because <u> resists change.
APLOMB, BOMB, CAMBRIC <a>=[ay], CATACOMBS* <o>=[oh], CLIMB <i>=[I], COMB <o>=[oh], COXCOMB 2nd <o>=[oh], CRUMB, DUMB, JAMB, LAMB, LAMBKIN, LIMB, NUMB, PLUMB, SUCCUMB, TOMB* *f* <o> = [oo], WOMB* *f* <o>=[oo].

Catacombs ends in <s>, being named after the Roman underground cemetery Coemeterium Catacumbas, (Ayto 1991 p. 100).

In two words <wo> spells [woo] and we can call them feather words.
Womb* [woom] in Old English was *wamb* or *womb* and Etymology On Line says it is "of unknown origin" **but adds that *child* in Old English was *umbor*. I think this means that *womb* was once *wumb* and replaced <u> with <o> to prevent <wu> looking like a Triple U, or <um> looking like Triple N.
**Tomb* [toom] comes from Anglo-French *tumbe*. It seems to me that *tumb* was treated like a feather word, <u> replaced with <o>. The <b> was silenced after 1400 according to Etymonline.

The blend [mt] occurs only in one word: {*dreamt*}.

Rule 2-45 Terminal <ms> spells the blend [mz], as in *sums* and other plurals. We'd expect this, after a voiced consonant. We'd also expect <s> to spell [z] between voiced word-sounds, in words like *clumsy*.
List 2-45 [mz] blends.
CLUMSY*, CRIMSON [krimzən], FLIMSY, WHIMSY, MUMSY *slang*. The HAM'S smelly. She HEMS her dress. The POMS are here. The GUMS are tall trees. HYMNS, COLUMNS, He DAMNS us to hell.

**Clumsy* originally meant "numb with cold" but never had a silent <b>.
There's no [mz] blend if *whimsy* spells [wim-see], because sounds only blend if in the same syllable, as in [whimz-ee].

No [md] blends, but it was once in *fremd*, an old obsolete word for *stranger*.
Rule 2-46 Big Blender [m] can blend with all consonants.
List 2-46 Big Blender M
BUMF, AMP, AMPLIFY*, BUMP, CAPITALISM*, CAMP*, COMPO *slang*, DAMP, DECAMP, TAMP, TEMP *secretary*, DUMP, ENCAMP, EXEMPLIFY, GAZUMP, HEMP, HUMP, HUMP BACK, IMP, JUMP, KEMP, LAMP, LIMP, LUMP, PIMP, POMP, PUMP, RAMP, REVAMP, ROMP, RUMP, SIMPLIFY, SUMP, SUNLAMP, UMP *umpire*, VAMP, WIMP.

**Amplify*. As we know, the suffix *–ify* spells [ifI].
**Camp* is one of the 4 or 5 words adopted directly from the Romans when they ruled Britain. To them *campus* meant an open field suitable for soldiers to practise their skills, a training ground, hence it is used in "university campus". Very few words were "left behind" when the Romans left Britain. One Latin word from the Roman Occupation is still all over Britain: *castra,* which means a "permanent military camp". It has changed a bit but we can still see and hear it in names like Lancaster, Chester, Gloucester and Manchester. Many English words with Latin connections came into English as French words. Many were built by the English because when they needed new descriptive words they used bits of Latin words, many of which began as Greek words, e.g. *platypus*.
**Capitalism* is just one example of —*ism* as a suffix, in which <sm> spells [zm], as expected, for <s> must spell voiced [z] to blend with voiced [m].

Big Blender N
Rule 2-47 Big Blender [n] can blend with any consonant.
We know that <ce> spells [s], that piece of French spelling which arrived in England with the French invasion from Normandy. This list includes a few words in which <ce> spells [s] more than once, e.g., *obsolescence*. Also, words followed by *VS*, for Vowel Shift, can be pronounced using either <a> spells [a] or <a> spells [ar]. The former is usual in the north of England and the latter in the south, where the French influence was greater. Once the French got rid of the English letter Ash, <a> had to spell two short sounds and two long ones, as in *ant, ago, father, later*. Sharp, short [a] was not a French word-sound. The English were influenced by the way French people spoke, around London etc., but the northerners stuck to English [a] which explains why {*laugh*} is [laf] up north and [larf] down south.

List 2-48 in which terminal <nc> spells the blend [nk] and terminal<nce> spells the blend [ns]
FRANC, ZINC. ADOLESCENCE, ASKANCE, CADENCE, CONDOLENCE, CONFIDENCE, CONTINENCE, CONVALESCENCE, CORRESPONDENCE, COVALENCE, DANCE *VS*, DEFENCE, DEPENDENCE, DELIQUESCENCE, DILIGENCE, DIFFIDENCE, ELOQUENCE, EMINENCE, ENHANCE *VS*, EVIDENCE, FENCE, GLANCE *VS*, HENCE, IMMINENCE, IMPOTENCE, IMPUDENCE, INCANDESCENCE, INCIDENCE, INCOMPETENCE, INCONSEQUENCE, INCONTINENCE, INDOLENCE, INNOCENCE, INSOLENCE, IRIDESCENCE, LANCE *VS*, LICENCE *noun*, LUMINESCENCE, MINCE, OBSOLESCENCE, OFFENCE, OPALESCENCE, PENANCE, PENCE, PENITENCE, PRANCE *VS*, PRESENCE, PRETENCE, PROVIDENCE, PRUDENCE, RECOMMENCE, RESIDENCE, SENESCENCE, SENTENCE, SEQUENCE, SILENCE, SINCE, SIXPENCE, STANCE *VS*, VALANCE, VALENCE, WHENCE. <u>Names</u> LANCE, TERRENCE, VINCE.

Terminal <nse> spells [ns] but we shall meet that blend later when we hear why some words end <nse>.

In the olden days a twin consonant, often followed by a silent <e>, kept the final vowel short. Now we only use twins inside words to keep vowels short — compare *red* and *redden*. In the olden days two consonants, not twins, did the opposite — lengthened vowels — if one was a nasal consonant. We have seen this in *folk* and *climb*, for instance, and in *acre* and *ogre*, *bible* and *able*, where the liquid terminal is blocked by a silent <e> to prevent it flowing on. This continues in other old words, for instance some with the terminal blend [nd]. As we do not know which words use this old method to lengthen [i] to [I] we shall mark where this occurs in a list word.

List 2-49 [nd] blend
AND, ALMOND, AMEND, APPEND, APPREHEND, ASCEND ATTEND, BACKBEND, BACKHAND, BALANDA*, BAND, BANDIT, BANDSTAND, BANDY-BANDY*, BARRAMUNDI*, BEHIND <i> =[I], BEND, BEYOND, BIND <i> =[I], BLAND, BLEND, BLIND <i> =[I], BLOND, BLONDE*, BOND, BRAND, BRIGAND, COMMAND, COMMEND, CONTEND, CONTRABAND, CORRESPOND, DECKHAND, DEFEND, DEMAND *VS*, DEPEND, DESCEND, DISBAND, DISTEND, DIVIDEND, DOCKHAND, DOCKLAND, ELAND, END, ENDEMIC, ERRAND, ERRANT, EXPAND, EXPEND, EXTEND, FECUND, FEND, FENLAND, FIND <i> =[I], FOND, FROND, FUND, GERUND*, GLAND, GOD-SEND, GRAND, GRANDSTAND, GRASSLAND, GRIND <i> =[I], HIND <i> =[I], HAND, HANDICAP*, HANDSTAND, HANDBAG, HANDCUFF, HANDY, HANDYMAN, HATBAND, HIND <i>=[I], HUSBAND, INLAND, INTEND, ISLAND* silent <s>, LAND, LEGEND, LEND, JOCUND, KIND <i> =[I], MIND <i> =[I], MORIBUND, MEND, OFFEND, OFFHAND, PEND, PRETEND, POND, QUICKSAND, RAND, RANDY, RED HANDED, REMAND, REMIND <i> =[I], REND, RESCIND, RESPOND, RIBAND, RIND <i> =[I], ROTUND,

RUBICUND, SAND, SAND BAG, SAND PIT, SANDAL, SANDY, SECOND, SEND, SPEND, STAND, STIPEND, STRAND, SUSPEND, TAMARIND, TEND, TENDON, TRANSCEND, TREND, UNATTENDED, UNBEND, UNBIND <i> =[I], UNHAN, UNKIND <i> =[I], UNWIND <i> =[I], UP-END, UPLAND, VAGABOND, VEND, WAND, WEND, WETLAND, WIND <i> =[I], WIND, WINDLASS, WINDLESS, WINDMILL, WIND-SOCK, WINDY. <u>Names</u> CANDY, EDMUND, GWENDOLYN, MANDY, RANDY, SANDY.

Blonde is used to describe females. *Blond* and *blonde* is the only English adjective to have a male and female form. Quite a few nouns in English have male and female form e.g., *fiancé* and *fiancée*, *actor* and *actress*, including *blond* and *blonde*. However, as an adjective, *blond* and *blonde* are the only adjectives left expressing different genders.

Balanda [bar-land-ar], or *belanda* [bee-land-ar] is used by English speaking Aborigines in Arnham Land to describe white people, adopted from Macassar where the word has Dutch origins, from Dutch colonial times. Not in general use elsewhere in Australia.

Bandy-bandy is a snake, *Vermicella annulata,* the Common Bandy-bandy. Australian Aborigines used *bandy-bandy* for all species of small snake.

Barramundi began as the Ab'l compound noun *burra-mundi*, "big meat", (34 Cockburn p. 34, Boston, p. 106). It changed to *barramundi* to copy another big fish, *barracouta,* (Blake, p. 86).

Handicap began as '*hand in cap*' and so it was never '*handy cap*'.

*The reason for silent <s> in *island* was explained with <s> in *isle* after List 2-35.

Gerunds are verbs ending <ing> which are used as nouns, e.g., "All the shouting woke me up." "Do you like cooking?" Gerunds are used in English and Welsh, and also in Aboriginal languages in Australia.

Very few words use <nz> to spell the blend [nz] because <z> is so unpopular. *Lens* is the only singular word to end in <ns>. *Hens* and all other plurals ending <ns> end in the blend [nz], except for words ending <mns>, which spells [mz].

List 2-50 [nz] blends
ANNALS*, BRONZE, LENS*, LENSES, ODDS*, <u>Plus plurals etc ending [n] in singular</u> e.g., PINS, MEN'S, "He PENS his name."

Odds (as in "long odds" [loŋ odz]) and *annals* [an-alz] (a history of events year by year, annually) are plural nouns, having no singular form. *Lens* [lenz] was adopted from a language which did not use <s> to make plurals. If it was adapted it would be spelt *lenz* but it remains adopted but not adapted. Scientists needed a word for a round, bi-convex piece of glass. As it looked just like a lentil they used the word *lens,* which is Latin for a single lentil, one lentil.

 Sounds only blend if in the same syllable, which is why we do not hear the [nz] blend in the following:-
BONANZA, BONZA slang, CADENZA, CREDENZA, EXTRAVAGANZA, FRENZY, STANZA.

Eng — *along, zing.*

The blend of [n] with [g] produces the word-sound we call Eng, written like this: [ŋ]. Its symbol is an <n> with the open tail of <g>. It is the third Nasal, with Nasals [n] and [m]. In English it's a medial word-sound and/or a terminal word sound, as in *singing*, but never an initial word-sound.

   Some languages start words with [ŋ], e.g., Ab'l Yinggarda words: *ngatha* — "I", *ngambu* — "tree" and your father's sister, your paternal aunt — your *ngabari*. Vietnamese family names frequently start with [ŋ], e.g., *Nguyen*. Just *Ng* is a short Chinese name. In New Zealand *ngaio* means 'competent' and is also the Maori name of a flowering bush and a name for girls. East Africa's 'sky' or 'rain god' *ngai*, and fish *ngege,* can be added to this parade of non-English words which start with [ŋ]. *Ngallo* and *Ngaloranna* are just two of many Ab'l place names in Australia. David Unaipon, the famous inventor on our $50 note, was a *Ngarrindjeri* man. Even inside Ab'l words <ng> always spells [ŋ], e.g., the Minga (Shady Ant) Bush is [miŋ-ar], not [min-gar].

Many languages use the tilde (~) above <n> to show it spells [ŋ], as in Spanish señorita. This particular diacritic, direction mark, is also called a 'swung dash' or a 'squiggly'. It is put to many uses in various languages. The English try to show that <n> spells [ŋ] in *senor* and *senorita* by using <g> in their adaptions:- *signor* and *signorita,* in which <g> never spells [g].

Although there are no English words which start with [ŋ], thousands of English words end with [ŋ], due to the popularity of the suffix <ing>. Many stem words also end in <ng>, like *sing,* and *song*. When we are moving about we say we are "to-ing and fro-ing". We seem to add *ing* to anything and everything. We go *logging,* even *frogging* and *googling*. English speakers have no trouble saying [ŋ] at the end of a word because it follows a vowel.

Rule 2-51 Terminal <ng> spells [ŋ] and terminal <nge> spells [nj].
Reason Terminal <nge> spells [nj], due to the softening action of silent <e> on [g]. For instance, in *orange* and *hinge*. In *longed,* we hear <ng> spelling [ŋ], because <nge> is not terminal in *longed,* and it is pronounced as one syllable, not as [lon-ged], unlike *longer* [lon-ger] and *longest* [lon-gest], both of which do not break rule 2-51 because in these words <n> and <g> are not in the same syllable. Wordsounds only blend if in the same syllable, which is why we are not surprised to hear [ŋ] in single syllable *longed* and *sings*. However, we also hear [ŋ] in *zingy* and *wrongly* and twice in *singing*. This is because suffixes do not pull [g] out of the [ŋ] blend unless they are the flexible suffixes —*er* and —*est*.
List 2-51A <ng> spells [ŋ]. See 2-52 for <nge> spells [nj].
ALONG, AMONG *f,* ANGST, BANG, BELONG, BILTONG, BILLABONG*, BONG, BRING, BUNG, BUNGARRA*, CLANG, CLING, CLUNG, CURRAWONG* *bird,* DEFANG, DING-DONG, DONG, DUCKLING, DUGONG [joo-goŋ], DUNG, FANDANGO [fan-dan-goh], FANG, GANG, GANG-GANG*, GINGHAM *silent h.* adopted word [giŋ-am], GINSENG , GONG, GOSLING, GONG, HANG, HUNG, BY JINGO! [jin-goh], KAMPONG, KING, KURRAJONG* *tree,* LINGO [lin-goh], LONG, LUNG, LUNGE, MAH-JONG, MUSTANG, OBLONG, ORANG-UTAN, PANG, PARANG, PING, PONG, PROLONG, QUANDONG* <a>=[o], REHANG, REHUNG, RANG, RING, RUNG, SANG, SARONG, SIBLING, SING, SING-SONG, SLING, SLUNG, SONG, STRING, STRUNG, SUNG, TAG ALONG, TANG, TING , TREPANG, TWANG, UNSUNG, WHANG, WING, WHIZ-BANG WINGLESS, WRING, WRONG, WRUNG, ZING, UNHUNG, UNSUNG, WEDDING, WING, ZING.
<u>Proper Nouns</u> BOGONG*, CONGO [kon-goh], HONG KONG, KING KONG, MING. <u>Slang</u> DANG, PONG.
**Billabong* is an Ab'l word, given to English by the Wiradjuri in central and southern NSW, (Blake, p. 86).
*Note that <h> in *dinghy* insulates <g> from being softened and that *dingy* spells [din-jee].
**Bogong* is now used in *bogong moth,* but was once the Ab'l name for some mountain ranges in NSW.
**Bungarra* [buŋ-a-ra] from the Ab'l Noongar word for a big edible lizard, well adopted into English in WA.
**Currawong* birds get their name from an adaption of their name in Awaba, an Ab'l language near today's Newcastle, NSW, (Blake, p. 92).
**Gang-gang* has been adopted from the Ab'l word for the grey red-crowned cockatoo.
**Kurrajong* has been adopted from an Ab'l word meaning 'fishing line' and trees that have fibrous bark which was used to make fishing lines. Nowadays it is only used for certain species of trees, (Blake, p. 97).
**Quandong* has been adopted from a Central NSW Ab'l language, (Blake, p. 102).

<u>Not needed but nice to know</u>. Swadesh, on page 134, says that *ping* and *bing* are used to imitate thin, high pitched impacts and *bang* and *bong* are used for loud, deep sounds. Imagine our prehistoric ancestors hearing the sound of a mosquito landing for a feed, "*ing ing sting!*" or a rock on a rock, "*bong!*" or metal

on metal, "*bang!*" Swadesh believes we use the [i] sound for little things or things very close to us and sounds made further back in the mouth for bigger things or things far away. He gives little bits of proof for this in many languages. In English, he points out, we say *this* for things close to us and *that* for things further away. It's fun to try to understand how language developed. He also says we say *sing, sink, sit* for now, at the present time, and *sang, sank, sat* for a time far away in the past.

If [i] is in *this little* thing, to show it is small and up close, I expect you will ask why is it in *big*? *Big* did not start off meaning large. It came in with the Vikings as *bug,* meaning "important man". Then it changed to "big man" meaning "powerful man", not necessarily due to size, and then just to "big". For "powerful and scary" there was *bugge*, a scarecrow in Old England, which is still with us as the imaginary *bogey-man.*

Some children say "ma-ma" and some say "da-da" as their first word. For instance, Holly Boston, when aged one, could only say "Da-da", but little Kaya Edwards said "Ma-ma" as her first word. Many races say "ma" for mother, and if not, they say it for father. Lingusits say that this is because, firstly, [m] is our first sound, and secondly, because the biggest thing in our lives at this stage is either mum or dad, we say [ar] in *ma* and *pa* because we are over-awed at our big mum or dad. In some countries it is the other way round, e.g., in Georgia it's *da-da* for mother and *ma-ma* for father.

We do not say *mi* for ma or pa, [mee] and [pee]. Swadesh says that later on, with self-awareness, a baby says [mee] for the closest thing to itself, *me*. Now back to things we need to know.

In the following words [n] and [g] are in different syllables and so they do not blend: BINGO [bin-goh], BONGO DRUM, DINGHY* [din-gee], DINGO* [din-goh], DINGY* [din-jee], FUNGUS [fun-guus], pl. FUNGI*, TANGO [tan-goh].

Dinghy [din-gee] uses <h> to insulate [g] from the softening effect of <y>. A *dingy dinghy* is a shabby, drab, small boat.

Dingo is adopted into English from Ab'l equivalents around Port Jackson, *tingo* and *dingo*.

Fungi is pronounced [fung-I], in OPD, but also [fun-gee] or [fun-jee].

We say [iŋ] a great deal in English, because of the suffix —*ing* on verbs, on adjectives and on nouns, as in, 'I was sleeping,' *verb*. 'Let sleeping dogs lie,' *adjective*. 'Sleeping is good for you, *noun*.' The following story behind —*ing* is not necessary. We can read —*ing* without knowing any of it, because when —*ing* is a suffix, an addition to a stem word, it always spells [iŋ]. Later, we shall learn what <ing> spells in *anger, finger, hunger*.

On Going Verbs and Gerunds

Adding –*ing* to verbs shows continuous action, as in, "I am *writing*" (Also, "I will be *writing*, I have been *writing*, I had been *writing*, I should have been *writing*, I will have been *writing*.") This happens in Welsh, too, but not in the rest of Europe's languages. The French just say "*I write*". They have no words to say "*I am writing.*"

How did it happen in English? To show an action, for instance *shout*, continued, the Old English said, '*on-shouting',* which meant shouting over and over, on and on, (Burton, p. 141), like today's word *ongoing*. 'On-shouting' shortened to '*a-shouting'*. Then, "I am *a-shouting* became I am *shouting*."

Sitting, however, is already a continuous activity and so why did Lewis Carol write 'an aged man, an aged man, a-sitting on the gate'? Why do we say 'Bye baby bunting, Daddy's gone a-hunting?' Is it because poets use the little prefix wrongly just to make 'te-tum-te-tum' rhythms, e.g., 'A-hunting we will go….',? David Crytsal (p. 20), thinks so.

However, John McWhorter (p. 27) traces it back to the Celts who did not just hunt, they went at it, went *at hunting*, turned a verb into a noun. This was shortened to went *a'hunting*, as in 'Bye baby bunting, daddy's gone a'hunting'. You guessed it, this was shortened again to just 'Gone *hunting*' — he's *hunting*'. Thus a verb, *hunt,* which became a noun, *hunting,* forms part of a verb again, *to be hunting.* 'McWhorter also says the Celts said they were 'in singing', when they sang. They did not do things by halves, it seems. And later, 'We are in singing' became 'We are singing.' Others, Germans and Dutch, for instance, say they are 'on singing', like being 'on' a job, but in English, the noun reverted back to a verb, dropped the 'at', the 'in' and the 'on' and produced an on-going verb.

Not needed but nice to know. McWhorter also tells us, on the very first page of his book *Our Magnificent Bastard Tongue,* that only the English and the Welsh say "I do love you," as well as "I love you". And other languages reverse the subject and the verb to ask a question — "Ran you?" — or say, "Is it that you ran?" Only the English and Welsh ask "Did you run?" McWhorter traces this use of *did* way back to the Celts, and so he shows us that the original language of the Britons did not totally disappear in England. Now back to things we need to know.

Personal observation: Etymonline explains that *thing* is a very old English word which originally meant a 'meeting or event', as in "We are going to a thing in the park". I think that the Celts went to a "hunt thing", or were at a "hunt thing" and ended up saying they went to a "hunting", or were at a "hunting". What do you think? The other original meaning of *thing* was 'action, deed to be done', which is maybe why we say, "He is doing his thing."

Nouns can become verbs. For example, we say 'Let's table that' and 'Let's google that'. Both *table* and *Google* were nouns before they became verbs. Verbs can become nouns. For example, *approval* and *commitment* began as the verbs *to approve* and *to commit.*

There is a special name for a noun which is formed by adding —*ing* to a verb. **It is called a gerund**. *Gerund* means a doing or a done thing. It comes from a Latin word, 'gerundium', which means an action which has been carried out or an action which is being carried on, because *to bear*, or *to carry*, in Latin, is 'gerere'. Examples of gerunds include *swimming, walking, writing, dancing, thinking, fishing, singing* and *driving.* Other nouns need articles, the little joints 'a' or 'the' which join them (articulate them) to the rest of the sentence. Gerunds do not need them, because *swimming*, for instance, just means swimming in general. However, if it does refer to a particular instance, we use the definite article *the,* as in 'The swimming today was spectacular." 'The singing of the choir was very melodious."

Relevant Writing Rule When adding <ing> remember to double the consonant to keep the vowel short: *beg, begging; sit, sitting.* However, we need to know when 'to twin' in more detail than that. Cummings calls them Twinning Rules. There is no need to double the g in *sting* for there are two consonants at the end of *sting*, <n> and <g>. It's the same for *sink,* <n> and <k> keep <i> short, [i], si**nk**. You will see here and later that the consonants <h>, <w>, <x> and <y> are never doubled before -*ing*. Also, instead of doubling a final <c> it becomes <ck> before a suffix: *trafficking, frolicking.* Verbs ending in <c> change in the continuous present to <ck> in order to keep the <c> hard.

Rebel: {*arc,* arcing} in which <c> remains hard, [ark-ing].

We do not double silent consonants found in words of foreign origin as in *crocheting, ricocheting.* Foreign words like these, which are said, as well as spelt, their foreign way, are words with "Diplomatic Immunity", see appendix. Return to Reading Rules.

List 2-51B Terminal <ing> spells [iŋ], examples only
ADDING, ADMITTING, BANGING, BACKING, BALDING, BATTING, BEGGING, BETTING, BIDDING, BIFFING, BUCKETING, BULLYING <u>=[uu], BUZZING, CARRYING, CLAPPING, CALLING <a>=[or], CARESSING, CAROLLING, COMING* ʃ, CUNNING, CUTTING, DURING [joo-r iŋ], ENROLLING, EQUIPPING, FATTENING, FALLING <a>=[or], FIBBING, FILLING,

LACKING, LIVING, MENDING, MIMICKING, KISSING, PANICKING, PICNICKING, SINGING, SOPPING, SUCKING, SUCKING-PIG, SWINGING, TRAFFICKING, UNWILLING, UNWITTING, WILLING, WINNING, YODELLING, ZAPPING, ZIGZAGGING, ZIPPING. <u>Slang</u> REVVING.
*Fossil <e> has been removed from *come.*

Q. Some people say "When ING comes to stay, E runs away." Does this always happen?
Ans. No, E does not always 'run away', because the saying "When ING comes to stay, E runs away" refers to Fairy E, the silent terminal <e> which turns *hop* into *hope* — from which, when <ing> is added, <e> 'runs away'.

List 2-51C adding suffix —i*ng*
BE, BEING [bee-ing], not *bing* which would spell [bing]
EYE, EYEING [I-ing], not *eying* which would spell [ee-ying]
DYE, DYEING [dI-ing] not *dying* because that would be the same as *dying* below.
DIE, DYING [dI-ing] to prevent a three vowel cluster, <iei>.
Also
TIE, TYING [tI-ing], but...
TIE, TIEING, when *tie* "means get an equal score", as in "Teams from Broome and Carnarvon keep tieing every time they play."
DIE, DYING [dI-ing]
VIE, VYING [vI-ing]
Also other terminal vowels do not "run away":
BAA, BAAING, as in 'The sheep were baaing.'
BOO, BOOING
SKI, SKI-ING [skee-ing]
ALIBI, ALIBI-ING [al-a-bI-ing]
DO, DOING [doo-ing]
LASSO, LASSOING [las-oo-ing]
GO, GOING [goh-ing], ONGOING INGOING
ZERO, ZEROING [zee-roh-ing] - 'zeroing in on it.'

Rule 2-52 Suffixes cannot remove or create the terminal [j] sound of a stem word.
Reason This retains the meaning of the stem word. Writing rules ensure [j] is not removed or created. Terminal <ge> spells [j]. As we know, both <i> and <e> soften [g] to [j]. If suffixes were allowed to create [j] then *singing* would spell [sinj-ing], *banged* would spell [banjd], *longest* would spell [lonjest]. This is a rule you already know, without knowing you know it. Well done!
To prevent a suffix removing [j], if the suffix does not start with <e> or <i>, the silent <e> after <g> remains, as in *singeable*, {*changeable*}. If the suffix starts with <e> then the silent <e> is removed, as in *hinged.* If it starts with <i>, then the silent <e> (after <g>) can remain or be removed, whatever you like, *hinging* or *hingeing*. However, because suffixes must not stop <ge> from spelling [j], terminal <e> must remain when adding suffixes <ed> and <ing> to *binge* and *singe*. Remove it and we get *bing, binged, binging, singing*, in which [j] is removed and replaced with [ŋ].
Q. Is [j] *longevity* [lon-jev-it-ee] created by a suffix?
Ans. No, because <evity> is not a suffix added on to *long*. The suffix is —*ity*, added onto a word made from joining *longus* and *aevum* to make *longaevitas,* Latin for 'long-age'. This reduced to *longevitas* and then became *longevity,* (like *gravitas* became *gravity*.)
List 2-52

AVENGE, BINGE, CRINGE, EXPUNGE, FLANGE, FRINGE, GRUNGE, HINGE, IMPINGE, INFRINGE, LOZENGE, LUNGE, ORANGE*, PLUNGE, REVENGE, SCAVENGE, SINGE, SPONGE ʃ [spunj], TINGE, TWINGE, UNHINGE, WHINGE. <u>Proper Nouns</u> HENGE in Stone Henge (*means "hanging stones"*).

Remember, only two words ending <nge> have to retain <e> when adding <ing>, The rest can lose it or choose it.

You can choose to keep <e> in AVENGEING, CRINGEING, EXPUNGEING and so on.

Or you may choose to lose <e> in AVENGING, CRINGING, EXPUNGING and so on.

But always use <e> in BINGEING and SINGEING.

Rule 2-53 When <ange> is in a stressed syllable it spells [aynj].
Reason This is the old way of lengthening vowel sounds, before nasal blends, as in *bind, climb, folk,* and *fork,* in which [n], [m], [l] and [r] are all 'nasals' and form nasal blends.
Rebel FLANGE
Rebel's Reason In *flange* <a> spells [a], instead of [ay], to show that *flange* is related to the word *flank*.
List 2-53 <ange> spells [aynj] in a stressed syllable.
ANGEL, ARRANGE, DERANGE, DISARRANGE, ESTRANGE, GRANGE, MANGE, MIDRANGE, PREARRANGE, RANGE, REARRANGE, STRANGE.
*Orange is not a rebel because it is stressed on the first syllable.

List 2-54 Blend [nk]
ANKLET, BANK, BUNKUM, BUNK, CONK, DANK, DUNK, FUNK, FUNKY, HANK, HANK PANKY, HONK, HONKY-TONK, HUNK, INK, INKY, JUNK, JUNKET, KINK, KINKY, LANK, LANKY, LINK, MINK, PINK, PUNK, RANK, RINK, SANK, SINK, SINK IN, SUNK, TANK, WINK, WONKY, YANK.

The blend [kn] no longer exists in English, but is still in use in Germany. To retain the blend [kn] in King Canute's name it was changed from King Knut.

King Canute and Silent K — *knack, knuckle.*
Rule 2-55 In the same syllable the letters <kn> spell [n].
Reason Although *knot* and *knit* and *knob* start [n] we still write <kn> to remind us that we used to say [kn], back when the Saxons (and Angles and Jutes) began English as a type of Low German – "low" because their land back in Europe was low, near sea level. A slightly different Low German came with the Vikings, carrying knapsacks on their backs. "Knappen" meant "eat". We no longer pronounce [k] when in words starting <kn>, but it reminds us of England's German and Viking ancestors, the most famous of which is the Viking who became king of all England, King Canute! His famous name has been retained by changing its spelling from King Knut to King Canute. There's no need to respell it in Norway, nor in Germany, where <kn> still spells [kn].

<u>Not needed but nice to know</u>. The French language was also influenced by the Vikings — the Norman French descended from Vikings — but the French (descended from Gauls, Romans and Franks) do not like writing <k>. The English write it but do not always say it, as in *knife,* which spells [nIf]. The French write *canif* and say [kə-neef], which in English means *knife*. The English write *know* and say [noh] but the French write *connais* and say [kə-nay]. Although the old Viking [k] was silenced in *know,* it re-entered England in French words, like *reconnaissance* (noun)*, reconnoitre* (verb), in which <con> has replaced <kn>. <u>Now back to things we need to know</u>.

List 2-55 <kn> spells [n]
KNACK, KNAPSACK, KNELT, KNIT, KNOB, KNOCK, KNOLL, KNOT, KNUCKLE*.
Knuckle is "Knöchel" in Low German, meaning "little bones". English began as a Germanic language, in which <k> is pronounced. *Knees* also have little bones and were called *knuckles*, hence the phrase "knuckle under", meaning give in, collapse at the knees.

Rule 2-56 The nasal blend [nt] can lengthen preceding [i] to [I].
List 2-56 If [nt] lengthens preceding vowels, it's indicated.
ABERRANT, ACCENT*, ACCIDENT, ACCOMPANIMENT ƒ, ADAMANT, ADJACENT, AGENT, ANT, ANTENNA, APPARENT, APPARENTLY, ASCENT*, ASTRINGENT, BELLIGERENT, BENT, BLATANT, BLUNT, CAN'T [karnt] VS, CEMENT, CENT, CLEMENT, ELEGANT, COMMENT, CONSENT, CONSONANT CONTENT, CONTINENT, CONTINENTAL, CONVENT, CORRESPONDENT, CURRANT, CURRENT, DENT, DENTIST, DEPENDENT, DESCANT, DESCENT*, DIDN'T, DISSENT, DISTANT, DON'T* [dohnt], DOMINANT, ELEGANT, ELEMENT, EMINENT, ENCAMPMENT, EQUIPMENT, EQUIVALENT, ERRANT, FONT, GANTLET, HINT, HUNT, IDENTIFY, IMMANENT, IMMINENT, INDENT, INDEPENDENT, INDIGNANT, INSOLENT, INTENT, INTOLERANT, INVENT, ISN'T, LAMENT, LENT, LENTIL, LIGAMENT, LINIMENT, LINT, LITIGANT, MALIGNANT, MISIDENTIFY, MEDICAMENT, MEDICAMENT, MERRIMENT, MILITANT, MINT, MOMENT, MOVEMENT ƒ, NON-EXISTENT, ODDMENT, OMNIPOTENT, PAGEANT*, PANT, PEDANT, PEDIMENT, PENITENT, PENNANT, PENT, PENTAGON, PENTAGONAL, PENT-UP, PERENTIE*, PETULANT, PIGMENT, PINT* <i>=[I], PIQUANT*, PUNT, QUANTIFY <a>=[o], RANT, RESENT, RENT, RENTAL, RUNT, SCENT*, SENT, SENTIMENT, SENTIMENTAL, SIBILANT, SPENT, SUCCULENT, TALENT, TALENTED, TENANT, TENT, TINT, TORRENT UNWONTED* ƒ, VENT, VISITANT, WANT <a> =[o], WANTON [wonton] *adj.*, WARRANT <a> =[o], WASN'T, WENT, WEREN'T [wernt], WONT* ƒ, WON'T* [wohnt]. Proper noun MONTEZUMA*. Names BUNTY, CLINT, GINTY, MONTY.
Don't let W muddle you! Remember, in *want, warrant* and *quantify* <a> spells [o], due to collateral damage.
*Do you see why *pageant* spells [paj-ant]?
Noun *accent* spells [<u>ak</u>-sent]. Verb *accent* spells [ak-<u>sent</u>].
**Accident* spells [ak-si-dent], a rare case of twins spelling two sounds, different sounds, too. Ditto *accent*. Nouns *ascent* [a-<u>sent</u>] and *descent* [de-<u>sent</u>] are both formed from verbs *ascend* and *descend*. They each begin with prefixes which are normally unstressed. The stem, *scend*, is from Latin *scandere* which came to mean 'to scan verse,' but in classical Latin, *adscendere* was 'to climb, rise or mount', hence the use of *scan* for the rising and falling rhythm of poetry. *Scand* can be traced back to the ancient ancestor it shares with India's Sanskrit language, in which *skandati* means 'hasten, leap or jump.' *Ascend* was 'stigan' in Old English and *descend* was 'sigan', but after 1066 the French words *ascendre* and *descendre*, from Latin, meant that <sce> no longer spelt [ske] but instead just [se], since <ce> spells [se] in French and they refused to use <k>.
**Perentie* is adopted from an Ab'l language in Southern Queensland and uses a silent terminal <e> to insulate final <i>.
**Piquant,* another rare time that <qu> spells [k], is an adopted not adapted word, [pee-karnt].
**Montezuma* is the English name of the famous Aztec emperor who was really *Moctezuma*. English speakers find the blend [nt] easier to say than [kt].
**Scent* has a silent <c>. It was probably added to distinguish it from *sent* and *cent*, Cummings p. 397.
**Won't* is a contraction of *will not*. In the 1400's it was written as *wynnot*, as *wonnot* in the late 1500's and then as *won't* after 1667, (Etymonline).

*_Wont_ (usual and customary) and _unwonted_ (unusual and uncustomary) are both read more than said and so are often said [wont] and [unwonted], in Bible readings for instance, instead of [wunt], [un-wunt-ed]. In old English _wunian_ meant "to dwell, be accustomed," from very old German in which _wun_ meant "to be content, to rejoice" which is also the ancestor word of _to win_, and _to wean,_ to accustom a child or a weaner to leaving the breast or udder. So the old word _wont_ is quite different to the word _want. Wont_ is a Feather Word, a Cursive Casualty and _want_ suffers consequent damage because if spelt as it now sounds, [wont], it would mean _wont._ This is an example of collateral damage.

*As we heard in Part One _do_ used to spell [doh], like _no_ spells [noh]. It reverts to that spelling in _don't_ maybe to make sure we can hear the difference between _do_ and _don't_

<u>Not needed but nice to know,</u> about _won't_. Ask a French infant or a young New Guinean, "You won't be naughty, will you?" and a child who intends to be good replies, "Yes," meaning, "Yes, I will not be naughty," but an English or an Aussie child has learnt the hard way that "no" is the required answer. "Yes, we have no bananas," in reply to "Haven't you got any bananas?" surprises someone who is expecting "No, we have no bananas," or "Yes, we have some bananas." In some languages a double negative yields an affirmative. In other languages, a double negative yields a more emphatic negative. This was explained by a famous philosopher at a philosophers' convention in New York. The British philosopher, JL Austin, ended, "I know of no language, either natural or artificial, in which a double affirmative yields a negative." However, from the back of the hall in a broad Brooklyn accent came the comment "Yeah, yeah", from Sidney Morgenbesser, a fellow philosopher. <u>Now back to things we need to know.</u>

List 2-57 <nx> blends spell [nks]
{LARYNX}, JINX, {LYNX}, MINX. <u>Proper Nouns</u> MANX CAT [manks], MANX MAN.

Silent T and C — _apostle, muscle._
Rule 2-58 The letters <st> and <sc> spell [s] before terminal <le>.
Reason The short version: In _apostle,_ [a-pos-uul] and other words ending <stle>, the <t> is silent, for, in this difficult cluster of three consonants, the long one, [s], flows over the short one, [t]. Also, <c> is silenced, does not spell [k], between <s> and <le>, e.g., _muscle_. This only happens in 4 words. The long consonant, [s], flows over short [k] in the difficult cluster [skl]. The letters <t> and <c> remain, even though silenced, to ensure that <s> continues to spell [s], not [z].
The long version: Which clusters are 'difficult'? Prof. Cummings says, on p. 400, that sometimes it is hard to fit some consonants in between [s] and certain vowels made at the back of the mouth. That is because [s] is said at the front of the mouth and, in moving the mouth action from front to the back of the mouth, sounds on the way get missed out. The long sound [s] flows over and covers up the short [t] sound. This does not happen when <st> is followed by a vowel made at the front of our mouth. It does not happen in _misty_ [mis-tee]. If we say [u] [e] [uu] and [ə] we feel them coming from the back of our mouth, almost the throat, compared to [ee] [oo] and [ay]. We call those made at the back of our mouth "back vowels". Marmeduke Hewitt says silent letters, e.g., <t>, <gh> and others were silenced to obey his Law of Ease, which is "All speech requires effort, uses muscular energy in lungs, throat and mouth. There is a permanent desire to make the utterance of a word as easy as possible", (Hewitt p. 657).
He explains that when [st] is terminal, it is easy to say, e.g., in _list_, and also [ft], when terminal in _soft_. However, when those blends are followed by unstressed back vowels like [e] it is not so easy. Because [f] and [s] are made with our lips at the front of our mouth and because [e] is made at the back of our mouth it takes energy to push the tongue forward for [s] or [f] position, further forward to say [t] and then pull it back to say [e]. So, the tongue takes a shortcut and misses out [t] altogether! By writing <t> in these words they remain linked to _soft,_ and the old word _list_ which means 'hear', as well as ensuring that <s> continues to spell [s] and not [z].

Note that <st> spells [st] in *misty* and <ft> spells [ft] in *lofty* because <y> spells [ee] which does not move the tongue far after saying [t] because [ee] is not a back vowel. When saying *sten gun,* the [st] blend is easy to say because [e] is stressed. Also, when we say *piston* the blend [st] is easy to say because, although followed by an unstressed syllable, [o] is not said as far back in the mouth as [e].

Words which drop sounds, due to the Law of Ease, flow gracefully. However, Marmeduke warns that sometimes consonants are dropped due to laziness, not because they are hard to pronounce after another consonant before a back vowel. He calls this false economy, for the word does not flow on smoothly at all, but requires a brief pause to separate vowels, as in [bo-əl] instead of [bot-əl], for *bottle*. It is good English and good economy that some words follow the Law of Ease. However it is bad English and false economy to drop sounds and then add pauses. Marmeduke urges us to avoid the Lapse into Laziness. For example, *mostly* can spell [mohs-lee], if long [s] silences short [t], unless carefully pronounced as [mohst-lee].

Not only does <stle> spell [suul] but <scle> spells [suul]. In other words, <c> is silenced, just as <t> is between <s> and <le>. This only happens in 4 words: *muscle* and *crepuscle* {*corpuscle* and *arbuscle*}. In all these words the <cle> means "a little": a little mouse, a little dark, a little body and a little tree. When these nouns become adjectives the <c> spells [k]: {*muscular, crepuscular, corpuscular, arbuscular*}, for <s> and <c> are split into separate syllables.

List 2-58 Terminal<stle> and <scle> spell [suul].
APOSTLE, CASTLE *VS*, CREPUSCLE, EPISTLE, HUSTLE, GRISTLE, GRISTLY, MISTLETOE, MUSCLE, NESTLE, RUSTLE, TRESTLE, WHISTLE, WHISTLE-STOP, WRESTLE.

Triple Blends — *strut amongst.*

Terminal <scle> and <stle> are actually triple blends, but they simplify to a blend of just two consonants. The weak second syllable [ən] in *listen* and *soften* and *often* means that these words, in effect, have triple blends, blends which simplify to [sn] and [fn].

List 2-59 Impossible Triplets
LISTEN, OFTEN, SOFTEN.

When [t] comes between two consonants, it is often dropped, because three consonants are harder to blend than two. In these three words, [t] is always dropped. It's true that [n] is in the next syllable in *listen, often* and *soften* but these final syllables are so unstressed that [ən] is all that is heard. Even when [n] starts the next syllable, as in *chestnut* and *mustn't* we drop [t] more often than not. It's always the short consonant which drops out, lets the long one flow over it, as in *handsome* [han-sum]. Many folk pronounce *acts* [aks] and *ducts* [duks] without [t], like *ax* and *dux*. Language changes all the time. *Ask* spells [arsk] or [ask] but once it only spelt [ask] and in some parts of England the word was *aks,* [aks], which is still preferred by little kids for it is easier to say.

Listen, often and *soften* always drop [t]. We say their<t> is silent but we always write it, to show their connections to *list, oft* and *soft*. The origin of each word was very important to the dictionary makers — more important than making words easy to read.

Blends of [s] with two more consonants.

List 2-60 [scr] blends We have already met *scramble, scrabble, scribble* and *scruple*.
DESCRY* <y> =[I], SCRAG, SCRAGGY, SCRAP, SCRAPPY, SCROLL, SCRUB, SCRUBBY, SCRUMPING.

*The <y> in *descry* is not a suffix. *Scry* is an old word for "cry" and to *descry* was to "cry out" or "proclaim". (*Scry* and *cry* means literally to call on the Quirites (Roman citizens) for help.) So *scry* is a stem word, with the prefix *de*. The <y> in *scry* obeys the rule that <y> ending single-syllable words spells

[I]. Ayto says that another, obsolete, *descry* is a shortening of *describe* when it meant a written description. The suffix *de* means "down" and the stem word *scry* is from *scribe*, "write", hence "write down".

List 2-61 [str] blends We met *straddle, straggle, strangle, stranglehold, struggle.*
AMONGST *f*, ANCESTRAL, ASTRAL, GASTRIC, GASTRONOMY, MISTRESS, MISTRUST, OSTRACISM, STRAND, STRANDED, STRAP, STRAPLESS, STRATA, STRATAGEM, STRATEGIC, STRATEGICAL, STRATEGICALLY, STRATEGIST, STRATEGY, STRATIFY, STRESS*, STRICKEN, STRICT, STRICTLY, STRICTNESS, STRING, STRING ALONG, STRING BAG, STRING UP, STRING VEST, STRINGY, STRIP, STROLL, STRONG, STRONGLY, STROP, STROPPY, STRUCK, STRUGGLING, STRUM, STRUNG, STRUT.

*Humans were not said to feel *stress* until Hans Seyle mistakenly used *stress* in place of the word *strain* in the 1930's. Prior to that it was a term used in engineering. Hans studied human stress, strain, pain and joy.

List 2-62 <squ> spells the blend [skw]
SQUAB, SQUAD, SQUALID, SQUALL*, SQUAT, SQUIB, SQUID, SQUILL, SQUINT, Slang SQUIDGY.
*In *squall,* the special rule that <all> spells [orl] over-rides <squa> spells [skwo].

List 2-63 (Word initial) [spl] and [spr] blends - at the beginning of words.
SPLAT, SPLENDID, SPLENDIDLY, SPLINT, SPLINTS, SPLIT, SPLITS, SPRANG, SPRAT, SPRIG, SPRIGGY, SPRING, SPRINGINESS, SPRINGING, SPRINGS, SPRINGY, SPRINT, SPRINTED, SPRINTS, SPRIT, SPROCKET, SPRUNG, SPRY, SPRYEST, SPRYLY, SPRYNESS.

Consonants blend depending on how we break a word into syllables. As we know blending can only happen inside a syllable. The next list has words which have three consonants which blend inside a syllable, and one blend of four.

List 2-64
AMIDST, AMONGST, ANGST*, CONTEMPT*, EXEMPT*, EXTINCT [eks-tinkt], HAMSTRING, HAMSTRUNG, INNINGS, INSTRUCT, LANDSMAN, LINCTUS, MIDST, MINSTREL, MINISTRY, MUMPS*, PANTS*, OFF-SPRING, PANIC STRUCK, PANIC-STRICKEN, *PRE-EMPT, SEMPSTRESS*, SPLODGE, TEMPT*, TEMPTING*, TEMPTRESS, TRAN-SCRIPT, UNKEMPT*, WALTZ* [wols], WHILST*.

Angst [angst], also written [aŋst] only arrived in English from German in 1944, (Etymonline), as a technical word translated from Freud's work. Maybe the novelty of a word with four consonants blended help it catch on whereas its Old English cousin *angsumnes* (anxiety), died out.

*In *tempt, sempstress, unkempt etc.* <p> is silent for in difficult blends a long consonant like [m] will flow over a short one like [p]. However, we say [p] again in *pre-emptive* [pree-emp-tiv] and *tempting* [temp-ting] for the difficult blend of three is split when the suffix is added. The words *sempstress* and *temptress* are rarely used nowadays, partly because of their particularly long consonant clusters.

**Mumps* and **pants* only occur as plurals. Many other plural words contain blends of three consonants — *banks, runts, bends, silks, belts, films, lumps, glands, wings etc.*

* In *waltz* [wols], < z> spells [ts] in this German word, because <z> spells [ts] in German. In the blend [lts] the longer consonant [l] flows over shorter [t] and silences it.

Whilst spells [wIlst] due to its stem *while*. Letters <s> and <t> were added in the same way they were added to *among* and *amid,* back when Old English words used many flexible suffixes, like Latin, Yingarrda and Wajarri.

In some words, three consonants cluster but do not all blend. The blends depend on which side of the syllable boundary they are pronounced.

List 2-65

BRISK-LY, CON-TRACT, CON-TRA-DICT, CRISP-LY, DIS-PROVE *f* <o>=[oo], E-LECT-RIC, E-LECT-RIFY, EM-BLEM, EN-TRANT, EN-TRUST, EX-TRA, EX-TRACT, EX-TRAVAGANT, EX-TRAVAGANZA, HANG-MAN, HUN-DRED, IM-PRESS, IM-PRINT, IN-BRED, IN-FLICT, IN-FLUX, IN-FRA DIG, IN-STINCT, IN-TREPID, IN-TRINSIC, IN-TRINSICALLY, KIN-DRED, LAMB-SKIN <b>=silence, KES-TREL, KIN-DRED <i> =[i], LIMP-NESS, LIST-LESS, LIST-LESS-NESS, MON-GREL, NUMBSKULL <b>=silence, PUMP-KIN, SING-LET, SQUAD-RON, SUB-CON-TRACT, SUL-TRY, TRANS-FIX, TRANS-GRESS, TRANS-MIT, TRANS-PLANT, 2nd <a>=[a],[ar], TREM-BLY, TUN-DRA, VEN-TRAL, VEN-TRIL-O-QUISM, VEN-TRIL-O-QUIST, VEST-RY, WIN-TRY, WIST-FUL, WRONG-FUL, WRONG-LY, WRONG-NESS, ZEST-FUL.

The fear of <z>, which I call the 'Curse of the Dagger', means <s> spells [z] a lot, but when? So far, we have learnt that **letter <s> spells [s] in prefixes and suffixes. In stem words <s> spells [s] at the beginning of syllables and <s> spells [z] at the end of syllables after stressed short vowels, unless they follow vowels which are short due to suffixes like** *ity,* e.g., *monstrosity,* **or in the third or more syllable from the end** e.g., *vesicle,* (Cummings, p. 402).

So, pronunciation of <s> depends on position of syllable boundaries, particularly where prefixes and stems join. In prefixes and suffixes only a single <s> is required because the vowels are weak in affixes, e.g., <s> spells [s] in the last syllable in *omnibus, hippopotamus,* and also in the first syllable of *disrupt, distant, disband.*

Few prefixes end in <s>, just *trans—, dis—,* and *mis—*. Two suffixes start with <s> spells [sh]: *—sion* and *—ship,* and only with <s> spells [s], *—some*. Suffixes which terminate in <s> spells [s] are: *—ics, —itis, —osis —ious, —ous,* and *—less.*

In others, like {*—wards* and *ways*}, <s> spells [z]. Also, the plural suffix *es* spells [ez] and plural suffix <s> spells [z] after voiced word-sounds, whether vowel or consonant.

Besides making plurals, the letter <s> as a suffix shows ownership, ends verbs and also forms abbreviations. In the following examples <s> spells [z] makes a plural in *dens*; shows ownership in *den's* and in *dens'*; ends a verb in (he) *wins*; and abbreviates in *3's*.

In the next examples, <s> spells [s]: plural *hats,* ownership *hat's* and *hats',* verbs, *he hits,* abbreviations *it's.*

In 2-66 syllable breaks are shown. Remember, [s] cannot blend onto a voiced consonant. Also, Bad Blenders do not blend with each other, except when blending with [z], as in singular *adze* and plural *dogs* — {also with [d] e.g., in *logged* [logd]}. To avoid gaps in words in which Bad Blenders block natural flow from syllable to syllable, as in *adjust,* the shortest of the Bad Blenders goes silent. This is why *adjust* spells [a-just] and *maladjusted* spells [mal-a-just-ed].

List 2-66

Examples of words with prefixes: ADJUST [a-just], ABSENT [ab-sent], ASTERISK [ast-e-risk] not [az-te-risk], DISRUPT [dis-rupt] not [diz-rupt], DISBAND [dis-band] not [diz-band], INSECT [in-sekt] not [inz-ekt], INSENSITIVITY [in-sen-si-tiv-i-tee], INSISTENT [in-sist-ent] not [inz-ist-ent], INSOLENT

[in-sol-lent] not [inz-ol-ent], INSPECT [in-spekt] not [inz-pekt], INSTANT [in-stant] not [inz-tant], INSTANTLY [in-stant-lee], INSTINCT [in-stinkt], INSULT [in-sult] not [inz-ult].
Examples of words without prefixes: HUSBAND [huz-band] not [hus-band], <s> follows short stressed vowel; OSMOSIS [oz-moh-sis] not [os-moz-is] <s> follows short stressed vowel; USURY [yooz –yoo-ree], based on the verb *use* [yooz]. We'll meet *use* in Part Three. The noun is *use* [yoos].

List 2-67 The following words contain a mixture of blends.
ABRUPT, ACTIVIST, AFFECT, ANTISKID, ASKING *VS*, BASKETRY *VS*, BLANK, BLEND, BLEST, BLIMP, BLINK, BLUNT, BRACT, BRACT, BRAND, BRING, BRINK, BRISK, BRISKET, CLAMP, CLANG, CLEFT, CLIMB, CLINK, CLOMP, CLUMP, COMPOST, CONSENT, CONTEND, CONTENT, CONTINENT, CONTINENTAL, CONVENT, CRAFT *VS*, CRAMP, CRAMPON, CRANK, CREPT, CREST, CRIMP, CRISP, CRISPY, CROFT, DENTIST, DEPENDENT, DISTANT, DISTINCT, DISTRACT, DRANK, DREGS, DRIBS AND DRABS, DRIFT, DRINK, DRUNK, DRUNKEN, DWELLING, ENCAMPMENT, EXACTING, EXCEPT, EXCREMENT, EXPERIMENT, EXPRESS, EXTANT, FLANK, FLASK *VS*, FLING, FLINT, FLIPPANT, FLUNG, FRANC, FRANK, FRANTIC, FRINGE, FRISK, FROND, FRONT *f*, FROSTY, FRUMP, GANG PLANK, GANGLING, GLAND, GLINT, GRAMPUS, GRAND, GRANDAD, GRANDSON, GRAND-STAND, GRIST, GRUMPY, GRUNT, HANDICRAFT *VS* HANDSTAND, HANDWRITTEN, IMMIGRANT, IMPENDING, IMPRINT, INCUMBENT, INDEPENDENT, INEPT, INFLICT, INFLUX, INFRINGE, INKLING, INQUEST, INSTRUMENT, INTEGRAL, INVESTMENT, JUNKETING, LANDING, LANDSLIP, MALADJUSTED, MALAPROPISM, MELTING-POT, MENDICANT , MISSPENT, MULTIPLEX, PENDANT, PENDING, PENTAGRAM, PICTOGRAM, PLANK, PLANKING, PLANKTON, PLANT, PLIMSOLL, PLONK, PLUMP, PLUMPNESS, PLUNK, PRAGMATIC, PRANG, PRANK, PREDICT, PREFIX, PRESENT, PRESIDENT, PRETEND, PRIMA BALLERINA, PRIMP, PRINCIPAL, PRISM, PROBLEM, PROBLEMATIC, PRODUCT, PROMINENT, PRONG , PRONTO, PROSPECT, PROSPECTUS, QUISLING, REPRESENT, RESTAMP, SACRAMENT, SANCTITY, SANCTUM, SAND BANK, SAPLING, SCALD <a>=[or], SCALP, SCAMP, SCANT, SCANTY, SCEPTIC, SCEPTICAL, SCEPTICISM, SCOLD, SCRIMP, SCULPT, SELF-CONTROL, SEXTANT, SINKING, SITTING, SKIMP, SKIMP, SKINFLINT, SKINT, SKUNK, SKUNK, SLACKS, SLANG, SLAP-STICK, SLEPT, SLING, SLINK, SLUMP, SLUNG, SLUNK, SMELT, SOLVENT, SONG, SPANK, SPANKING, SPASMODIC, SPASTIC, SPATTER, SPECS *abbrev.*, SPECTRAL, SPECTRUM, SPELT, SPEND, SPENT, SPILT, SPINNING, SPLINT, SPLITTING, SPRING, SPRINGBOK, SPRINT, SPRUNG, SQUINT, STAGNANT, STAMP, STAND, STANK, STILT, STING, STINK, STINT, STOCKING, STOCK-LIST, STOMP, STRING, STRING ALONG, STRING BAG, STRONG, STRUNG, *STUDENT, STUMP, STUNG, STUNT, STUNT MAN, SUBTENANT, SUBTRACT, SUPPLANT, SUPPLEMENT, SUSPECT, SUSPEND, SWAMP <a>=[o], SWALK, SWANK*, SWEPT, SWIFT , SWIMMING, SWING, SWING-WING, SWUNG, TEMPEST, TESTAMENT, TRACT, TRAMP, TRANSACT, TRANSOM, TREND, TRESPASS* *VS*, TRINKET, TRIPLET, TRUMP, TRUMPET, TRUNK, TRUST, TWANG, TWELVE, TWENTIES, TWIST, 'TWIXT, UNBENDING, UNCLAMP, UNWINKING, WELLINGTONS*, WIND-SWEPT, WRAPPING, WREST, WRING, WRIST, WRISTLET, WRITTEN, WRONG, WRONGFUL, WRONGNESS, WRUNG. <u>Proper Nouns</u> ENGLAND* [iŋ-land], FRANCE, JACK FROST , RWANDA , SRI LANKA.
Did you let W muddle you in *swamp*? *Swamp* spells [swomp]. However, the rebel word *swank* spells [swank], not [swonk] — once just a regional word and now, since 1913, used everywhere, but retaining the regional pronunciation.
*Croquet is read and written the French way but many people now say [kroh-kee].

*Some love letters have the acronym SWALK on the back of the envelop meaning, "Signed with a loving kiss".

*Vowel changes in words like *trespass*, in which <a> now spells [ar], did not happen all over England. This vowel stayed short in many regions of England, e.g., *basket* spells [bas-ket] in the north of England.

*Student If <u> spells [yoo] after <t>, then <tu> spells [choo]. See Rule 1-41.

*Wellingtons — a pair of rubber boots— or *wellington* (*boot*) as an adjective, is an eponym. Google Arthur, 1st Duke of Wellington.

England was named by the Engle. 1 Angle man, 2 Engle men. Their scribes did most of the writing, Saxons preferring the fighting and they all did lots of farming. Anglo-Saxons called their new home *England* in which <eng> spelt [ayng] until the GVS when it lifted to [eeng] and then shortened to [ing]. So Engle Land is now [ing-land] written *England*. Letter <e> spells [i] in three words: *England, English* and *pretty.* It is much harder to change the way a name is written than the way it is said. We can insist our names are said the way we like, but it takes a visit to the courthouse to change a name's spelling.

List 2-68 Now that you can blend consonants you can read all these too.
COSTLY, CRABBY, CRISPY, CURRENTLY, CUSTODY, EMPTY, ENTRY, EXTREMITY, FACTORY, FLIMSY, FREQUENT, [free-kwent], FRISKILY, FRENZY, FROSTY, GLADLY, GLOSSY, GRANNY, GRAVITY, GROGGY, GRUBBY, GRUMPY, HERALDRY, HUNGRY, INDUSTRY, INSENSITIVITY, INFANTRY, INSTABILITY, INSTANTLY, INTEGRITY, INTRINSICALLY, IRONY, KINGLY, LISTLESSLY, MISCOPY, NAMBY-PAMBY, NUBBLY, ODDLY, PANOPLY, PAGEANTRY*, PANTRY, PEBBLY, PENALTY, PLENTY, PLUCKY, PRICKLY, PUBLICLY, PULPY, QUICKLY, ROCKETRY, SANCTITY, SCEPTICALLY, SCRAGGY, SCRAPPY, SCRUBBY, SCURRY, SIMPLY, SKIMPY, SKINNY, SKIVVY, SLAP-HAPPY, SLINKY, SLURRY, SMELLY, SNAPPY, SNAZZY, SPIVVY, SPOTTY, SPRINGY, STABILITY, STICKY, STIFFLY, STRICTLY, STRINGY, STRONGLY, STROPPY, STUBBY, STUFFILY, STUFFY, STUMPY, SULKY*, SULTRY, SULTRY, SUNDRY, SUNDRY, SWIMMINGLY, TELEMETRY, TESTIMONY, TIDDLY, TIDDLY WINKS, TREMBLY, TRENDY, TRICKY, TRIGONOMETRY, TRILBY, TRUSTY, TWENTY, TWENTY-TWO, UNWITTINGLY, WARRANTY, WINTRY, WITTINGLY, WRONGLY.

Pageantry spells [paj-ant-ree].

Sulky, like *sullen,* once just referred to a loner, lacking friends, but came to mean "unfriendly" and also "a buggy for just one person, for a loner".

You can read all these —ing words and add many more of your own choice.

List 2-69 <ng> spells [ŋ]
ACTING, ASCENDING, ASKING, BRING, BOTTLING, BRIDGING, BUMPING, BUSTING, BUDGETING, CACKLING, CLASPING, CLINGING, CLINKING, CLIPPING, CLUCKING, CRABBING, CROSSING, CAMPING, CRACKLING, CRIPPLING, CRYING, DRYING, EMPTYING, ERUPTING, DAZZLING, DIBBLING, DIDDLING, DRESSING, DRIFTING, DRILLING, DRINKING, DRIPPING, DRYING, ENDING, EVICTING, EVOLVING, DEPICTING, ECLIPSING, FALTERING, FIDDLING, FLAPPING, FASTING, STOCKING, SPINNING, TRAPPINGS, DRIPPING, DWELLING, STUNNING, SNOGGING, SWIMMING, SWELLING, SWINGING, ZINGING.

Singular terminal [s] — *dense, copse.*
Rule 2-70 After a consonant, terminal <se> spells [s].
Reason If a word ends with [s] spelt by the single letter <s> after a consonant then it's followed by silent <e>, to show it is not a plural word. Two *laps* of the oval **sounds** like *lapse,* but we can **see the difference.** We see the difference between two policemen, two *cops* and a single *copse,* a small wood or forest on top

of a hill. We **hear and see** the difference between fox *dens* and a *dense* forest. These examples help us see why all stem words ending consonant [s] end in a silent <e>.

Rebels TSETSE, FLENSE.

Rebel's Reason Adopted not adapted, the *tsetse* fly is not listed with words ending <se> for terminal <e> is not silent. Swahili syllables usually end in vowels, and so *tsetse* spells [tsee-tsee], in Swahili – in English, [tet-see] with the first <s> silenced. *Flense*, [flenz], is a verb and so it has a stressed ending, and <se> spells [z].

List 2-70 Terminal <se> spells [s]. Note the "double gate" in the last syllable blocks the vowel behind it from spreading out. This keeps that vowel short.

COLLAPSE, CONDENSE, COMMONSENSE, CONVULSE, COPSE, DENSE, DISPENSE, ECLIPSE, ELAPSE, ELLIPSE, ELSE, EXPANSE, EXPENSE, EXPULSE, FALSE*, FRANKINCENSE, GLIMPSE, IMMENSE, IMPULSE, INCENSE, INTENSE, LAPSE, LICENSE *verb,* MANSE, NONSENSE, PROLAPSE, PULSE, RECOMPENSE, RELAPSE, REPULSE, RESPONSE, RINSE, SENSE, SUSPENSE, TENSE, ULTRA-DENSE, VALSE* <a>=[o], WALTZ*.

**False* spells [forls] like *talk* spells [torlk] but it has come to spell [fols] in Australia.

**Waltz* spells [wols], as we've heard, because it uses German <z> which spells [ts]. We also heard that the difficult blend [lts] is reduced to [ls] because short [t] is blotted out when [l] flows over it. In **Valse* In German <w> spells [v]. Hence *valse,* is an alternative spelling, (OPD), for this "riotous and indecent German dance", (1825 quote on Etymoline). *Valse* is not used much. After all, in German this would spell [fols], sound like *false,* because, in German, <v> spells [f]!

Relevant Writing Rule. Stem words ending <se> drop terminal <e> before a vowel when adding suffixes.

Reason If terminal <e> is not dropped before a vowel starting a suffix the resulting vowel pair will create codes for new sounds. We shall see how adjacent vowels spell sounds in Parts Three and Four. Return to Reading Rules.

Rule 2-71 If suffixes are added to words ending consonant <se> then <s> continues to spell [s].

Reason Same as reason for Rule 2-70.

List 2-71

COLLAPSIBLE ..seible, CONVULSING ..se ing, DENSENESS ..se ness, DENSITY ..se ity, FALSEHOOD ..se hood, IMMENSENESS ..se ness, IMMENSITY ..se ity, INTENSIFY ..se ify, NONSENSICAL ..se ical, PULSING ..seing, REPULSIVE ..se ive, RINSING ..se ing, SENSELESS ..se less, SENSIBLE ..se ible, SUSPENSEFUL ..seful.

Blend [ns]

The following words all end in the [ns] blend. Some, like *dance* and *pence,* are stem words. The rest are nouns which have been made from verbs, like *provide, providence; hinder* and *hindrance.* You guessed it – they end <ce> instead of <se> because they came into English via French in which <ce> spells [s].

King William of England was actually not English. He and his successors had strong links to France, for many generations, long after 1066. Strong enough to claim they controlled Normandy. When they lost Normandy, these English kings claimed land further south in France. Then they fought a long war to keep it. English soldiers were fighting on and off in France, from 1337 to 1453, in what we now call the Hundred Years' War. In those years, English was gaining re-acceptance as the official language of England, but, at the same time, soldiers were bringing home new (French) words to add to English. Later, the dictionary committee decided on whether some of the new words got <ance> or <ence> endings. They said it depends on the verb group of their Latin ancestor words. This does not help us write them correctly because we no longer learn Latin.

Not needed but nice to know. The Romans had four groups of verbs. If they grew out of Latin verbs in the first conjugation or group, the "love group", they took –*ance*, ("to love" was *amare*.) If they grew out of Latin verbs in the other three groups they took –*ence* because their *infinitives all ended –*ere*. "Pure" languages like Classical Latin and our local Ab'l language Yinggarda stay very well organized. Yinggarda also has groups of verbs, (five), with set endings, whereas English has lost its old Anglo-Saxon purity for the verbs in its seven old groups have mostly lost bits and joined the newer verbs from other languages. (These adoptions from many tongues are now so well adapted that they are called regular verbs and the dear old Anglo-Saxon ones have been named irregular!) *Infinitive will be explained soon. Now back to things we need to know.

List 2-72 of words ending <ence> spells [ens].
ABSENCE, ABSTINENCE, ADHERENCE, ADOLESCENCE, AMBIVALENCE, ANTECEDENCE, BELLIGERENCE, BENEFICENCE, BENEVOLENCE, CADENCE, CANDESCENCE, CO-DEPENDENCE, COHERENCE, COMMENCE, COMPETENCE, COMPLACENCE, CONCURRENCE, CONDESCENDENCE, CONDOLENCE, CONFERENCE, CONFIDENCE, CONSEQUENCE, CONSISTENCE, CONTINENCE, CONTINGENCE, CONVALESCENCE, CORRESPONDENCE, COVALENCE, CREDENCE, DEFENCE, DEFERENCE, DEHISCENCE, DELIQUESCENCE, DEPENDENCE, DESPONDENCE, DETERRENCE, DIFFERENCE, DIFFIDENCE, DILIGENCE, DISSIDENCE, DIVERGENCE, DIVULGENCE, ELOQUENCE, EMINENCE, ESSENCE, EVIDENCE, EXCELLENCE, EXCRESCENCE, EXISTENCE, FENCE, FLATULENCE, FLORESCENCE, GRANDILOQUENCE, HALFPENCE, HENCE, IMMINENCE, IMPOTENCE, IMPUDENCE, INCANDESCENCE, INCIDENCE, INCOHERENCE, INCOMPETENCE, INCONSEQUENCE, INCONSISTENCE, INCONTINENCE, INDEPENDENCE, INDIFFERENCE, INDOLENCE, INDULGENCE, INEXPERIENCE, INFERENCE, INFLORESCENCE, INNOCENCE, INSISTENCE, INSOLENCE, INTELLIGENCE, IRIDESCENCE, IRREVERENCE, JURISPRUDENCE, LICENCE, LUMINESCENCE, MAGNIFICENCE, MALEVOLENCE, MUNIFICENCE, NEGLIGENCE, OBSOLESCENCE, OCCURRENCE, OFFENCE, OMNIPOTENCE, ONCE*, OPALESCENCE, OPULENCE, PENCE, PENITENCE, PESTILENCE, PRECEDENCE, PREFERENCE, PRESENCE, PRETENCE, PREVALENCE, PROMINENCE, PROVIDENCE, PRUDENCE, RECOMMENCE, RECURRENCE, REDOLENCE, REFERENCE, REMINISCENCE, RESIDENCE, RESPLENDENCE, RETICENCE, SENESCENCE, SENTENCE, SEQUENCE, SILENCE, SIXPENCE, SOMNOLENCE, STRIDENCE, TELECONFERENCE, TENPENCE, TRANSCENDENCE, TRANSFERENCE, TRANSLUCENCE, TRUCULENCE, TUMESCENCE, TUPPENCE, TWOPENCE, VALENCE, VEHEMENCE, VIRULENCE, WHENCE.
Names FLORENCE, PRUDENCE.
*Once was introduced and explained in 1-44.

List 2-73 Words ending with <ance> spells [ans].
ABUNDANCE, ACCEPTANCE, ADMITTANCE, ADVANCE, AMBULANCE, ARROGANCE, ASCENDANCE, ASKANCE, ASSISTANCE, ATTENDANCE, BALANCE, CONCOMITANCE, CONDUCTANCE, CONNIVANCE, DANCE, DISINHERITANCE, DISSONANCE, DISTANCE, DOMINANCE, ELEGANCE, EMITTANCE, ENCUMBRANCE, ENHANCE, ENTRANCE, EXPECTANCE, EXTRAVAGANCE, EXULTANCE, FINANCE, FLAGRANCE, FRAGRANCE, GLANCE, HAPPENSTANCE, HESITANCE, HINDRANCE, IGNORANCE, IMBALANCE, IMPEDANCE, INHERITANCE, INSIGNIFICANCE, INSTANCE, JUBILANCE, LANCE, LUMINANCE, RESISTANCE, MALIGNANCE, MISBALANCE, PENANCE, PENETRANCE, PETULANCE, PITTANCE, PRANCE, PRECIPITANCE, PROVENANCE, RELEVANCE, REMEMBRANCE, REMITTANCE, REMONSTRANCE, REPENTANCE, RESEMBLANCE

RESISTANCE, RESONANCE, RIDDANCE, ROMANCE, SEMBLANCE, SIGNIFICANCE, STANCE, SUBSTANCE, TRANCE, TRANSMITTANCE, UTTERANCE, VALANCE, VENGEANCE, VIGILANCE*, Names NANCY, VANCE.

Vigilance. Vig was the Viking word for 'vengeance slaying', as opposed to murder. It changed from [vig] to [vij-a-lens] under French influence. It spread to Spain as VIGILANTE [vij-al-an-tee], which then spread into American English.

Relevant Writing Rule. It's hard to know when to use <ence> and when to use <ance> when writing. The dictionary makers knew Latin and if a word ending [əns] could be traced back to a Latin verb of the first conjugation they generally used <ance>. If they traced it back to Latin verbs of any other conjugation, they generally used <ence>. (*Conjugation* means "yoking together" — at the jugular, like two oxen yoked together at the neck). In Latin, verbs all have endings, to show if it's *I love* ('amo') or *you love* ('amas'), for instance. Verbs which yoke onto <o> and <as> etc. are the first yoking. Other groups of verbs yoke on to other endings. Aboriginal verbs do the same thing, yoke up to various endings.

As very few of us know Latin verb conjugations, we use the following tips. Thompson, 1980, says that words ending <ant> become <ance> words, *important, importance* and words ending <ent> become <ence> words, *independent, independence*. However, as suffixes are unstressed, just said [ənt], it's hard to hear if it's [ant] or [ent] unless we can add another suffix, <al> or <ial>, and then we can hear clearly: *existential, substantial*. {We'll hear suffix <ial> spelling [ee-al] in Part Three, and stressing the preceding syllable.}

Cummings says it's best to look for patterns.

Intelligent Patterns. I am sure you can see that <ence> and <ent> follow soft <g> and soft <c> *licence, innocence, intelligent, adolescent,* but two words break that pattern: {*allegiance*} and *vengeance*. The suffixes <ence> and <ent> follow <cid>, <fid>, <sid> and <vid>, as in *incidence, confidence, subsidence* and *evident*. The suffixes <ence> and <ent> also follow <flu> and <qu> as in *fluent, confluence* and *sequence*, and words ending <ist>, as in *existence* (except for *assistance* and *resistance*.) Later we shall meet words ending in stressed [er] sounds – they all take <ence> as in *confer, conference; concur, concurrence* – but not the stem word *err* which becomes *errant*. We shall also meet words ending <ere> and they all take <ence> – *interfere, interference* – except for one word, *persevere, perseverance*. In Part Four we shall meet the unusual word {*unguent*} which spells [ung-went] because as we shall see in <u> spells [w] in a few rare words e.g., *penguin*. Only *ent* will do, for *unguant* would spell [ung-wont] since [w] muddles <a> to spell [o].

Elegant Patterns. Of course <ance> must follow hard <g> and hard <c>, e.g., *significant* and *elegance* (*elegence* would spell [el-ee-jans]). Note the unusual words {*allegiance*} and *vengeance*. They both go to extra lengths to end on the [ans] sound, as if that sound can be shouted a bit further than [ens]. This makes the words louder and more powerful, to match their emotional meaning.

If the verb ends in <ate> it takes <ant>: *supplicate, supplicant: dominate, dominance*. Only one rebel, *violate,* takes <ence>, {*violence*}. If other forms of the word end in <a> plus a suffix then your choice is likely to be <ance> or <ant>, e.g., *ignoramus, ignorant; vigilante, vigilance*. Verbs we'll meet with unstressed [er] endings take <ance> to form nouns as in *hinder, hindrance* and *utter, utterance*. We shall meet verbs ending -*ear*, -*ure* and -*y* and they also take <ance> to make nouns e.g., *appear, appearance; endure, endurance; defy, defiance*. Return to Reading Rules.

Some words exchange –*ent* for –*ency* [en-see] and others exchange -*ant* for –*ancy* [an-see].
List 2-72/73 continued
AGENCY, CONSISTENCY, CONTINGENCY, COVALENCY, CURRENCY, DECENCY, DELINQUENCY, DEPENDENCY, DESPONDENCY, EXIGENCY, FLUENCY, FREQUENCY, IMPOTENCY, INCOMPETENCY, INCONSISTENCY, INDECENCY, INFREQUENCY,

INSISTENCY, INSOLVENCY, POTENCY, REGENCY, SOLVENCY, STRINGENCY, TENDENCY, VALENCY, ASCENDANCY, BLATANCY, CONSTANCY, CONSULTANCY, DISCREPANCY, FLIPPANCY, HESITANCY, INFANCY, MILITANCY, OCCUPANCY, PETULANCY, PIQUANCY, PREGNANCY, PREOCCUPANCY, REPUGNANCY, TENANCY, VACANCY, VAGRANCY, VIBRANCY.

Rule 2-74 After a consonant, <nce> spells [ns].
Reason as for Rule 2-70.
List 2-74 Words ending with <nce> spells [ns].
CONVINCE, DUNCE*, ENSCONCE, EVINCE, MINCE, ONCE* *f*, PONCE, PRINCE, PROVINCE, QUINCE, SCONCE, SINCE, WINCE.
*Dunce is an eponym. Google John Duns Scotus.
*Once is a Feather Word, as explained in 1-44.
Blending <ed> to Verbs — *boxed, bagged, batted.*
Now we shall add the suffix <ed> on to verbs, to put them in the past. First, we shall hear **why** we do that and then we shall hear **how** we do that.

Long ago, the vowel of a verb changed to show it had happened, as in *we sing,* but *we sang,* and *we have* or *had sung*. Later, <ed> was added to verbs to show they have happened, as in *they melt,* but *they melted,* and *they have melted* or *they had melted*. Many verbs which used to 'ablaut', change their vowels, switched to this modern system. *Melt* used to be *melte, mealt, molten*. A few verbs have kept the <en> ending, in their adjectives, as in *beholden* and *molten*. Two verbs, *do* and *go,* reversed <en>, from *I have doen* or *goen,* to *I have done* or *gone,* (Hewitt, p 150). So many verbs eventually changed to just adding <ed> that those that did not are now called irregular verbs! They used to be the norm.

Why was <ed> added to show a thing was done? Long ago, in Germany, and even today in some languages, a verb was repeated to show it had happened. If we repeat "do" we get "dodo" which in Old English was written *dyde,* which today we write as *did*. To say something is already done, to put it in the past, we could say, "They ask did. You talk did," and so on. The Old English joined *dyde* onto some verbs to show they had happened. Over the years this shortened to [od], [ed] [id] and [uud] as we see in the Lord's Prayer: in the 10th century *hallowed* was *halgod,* 13th century, *halged,* 14th century, *halwid,* see Changes to English Over Time in appendix. In Chaucer's poetry we know *helped* spelt [help-uud] because he rhymed it with *mud,* which spelt [muud] back then. Nearly two hundred years later Shakespeare sometimes wrote *help'd* which shows us that people had begun saying [help-d] instead of [help-uud]. This new way of saying *helped* caught on but the new way of writing it as *help'd* did not. *Helped* was shortened even more, to [helpt]. Linguists tell us this happens when people try to speed up their speech so that they can speak a word as quickly as they can hear it.

Next, *helped* shrank to [helpt] and *sagged* shrunk to [sagd]. President Roosevelt of USA tried to change the spelling of *helped, boxed, capped, cupped, fixed etc.* to match the sounds they spell. In 1906, he gave an executive order to the USA government printers to spell them as *helpt, boxt, capt, cupt, fixt etc.* He was kind. He tried to make reading easier, but, as soon as he left the White House, they stopped doing this because it was only an executive order, not a law.

The suffix <ed> does not shrink quite so much after <d>, in *added,* nor after <t>, in *batted*. If it did, it would sound funny: [bat-t] and [ad-d]. Instead, [e] shrinks to [ə], the little schwa sound, which prevents us saying [tt] and [dd]. So we say [ad-əed] and [bat-əd], very similar to [ad-uud] and [bat-uud].

Even though suffix <ed> spells three different sounds, [t], [d], [əd], we continue to write <ed> each time so that we know all three sounds have sent a verb into the past, the action is done, someone **did** it. Maybe the suffix —*ed* is actually short for the word *did*. Who knows? Maybe we are saying, "Pam bat-did (batted) the ball", "Fred pat-did (patted) the cat," and, "Sam net-did (netted) a crab." Someone wiser than me will know how to solve the cold case spelling puzzle of the origin of suffix —*ed*.

<u>Relevant Writing Rule.</u> There is a rule for writing <ed> onto stem words ending in a consonant: twin that consonant if the preceding vowel is short and stressed, as in *bat, batted*. However, special rules affect words ending in <r> and <l>. We shall meet the rules on doubling <r> at the end of stem later. Rules on doubling <l> are still evolving, and evolving faster in USA than in U.K..

A. After single-syllable words with unigraph (one letter) vowels it is always <ll>.

B. It is always a single <l> within consonant clusters to prevent four or more consonants in a row. Cummings, 1988, gives this sensible advice: <ll> occurs at boundaries in compound words at times and after short unigraph vowels which have not been shortened by other rules. The Prof. adds that "After reduced vowels, the distribution is ambiguous." When adding the suffixes <ing>, <ed>, <est> or <er>, terminal <l> is doubled, whether the preceding unigraph vowel is stressed or not, *travel, travelled; appal, appalled; enthral, enthralled*. However, Americans only double the <l> if the preceding single letter vowel is stressed. So in America these words are correct: *travel, traveling, traveled; appalled, appalling, enthralled, enthralling*.

C. Luckily, we do not have to ask, "Do we twin it?" in words of three or more syllables when adding any suffix to any terminal consonant for primary stress does not occur in the last syllable of words of three or more syllables in English, e.g., *paralleling* is in all English dictionaries, never *parallelling*. (A mnemonic: It's easy to spell *parallels* for it's *all els*.) However, we must remember that when we join words to make compound words they nearly all continue to behave as if they are still on their own. That is why we twin <g> in *waterlogged, overlapped* and *handicapped*.

The letter <y> always acts as a vowel at the end of English words. Some Ab'l words end in <y> spelling [y] but this never happens in English.

<u>Relevant Writing Rule.</u> When adding <ed> to words ending with <y> after a consonant, change the <y> to <i>. This is because <y> is not allowed inside English words, only in Greek words adopted into English. It is also because <y> just replaces <i> at the end of English words because <i> does not end English words. Back when it had no dot on top, a cursive terminal <i> looked like nothing more than a final flourish of the pen. So we write, "Tom <u>defied</u> his mum. His mum <u>cried</u>. Dad <u>allied</u> with Mum and they <u>denied</u> Tom the TV. Tom <u>relied</u> on TV for fun. Mum and Dad were <u>satisfied</u> when Tom <u>replied</u> that he was sorry." {We'll meet <ied> spells [Id] in Part Four. We'll also meet <ied> spells [eed] in *rallied* — {"Tom <u>rallied</u> and <u>sallied</u> forth."}

Another <u>Relevant Writing Rule</u> is, when adding <ed> to words ending with <y> after a vowel, just add <ed>, as in, "He <u>monkeyed</u> about, which <u>delayed</u> their departure." Replacing <y> with <i> would produce three vowels in a row, and four in *buoyed*. <u>Return to Reading Rules.</u>

Rule 2-75 There are three rules for reading words ending <ed> after a consonant, and one rule for reading <ed> after a vowel.

A <ed> spells [t] after unvoiced consonants, but not after [t].

B <ed> spells [d] after voiced consonants but not after [d].

C <ed> spells [əd] after [t] and [d].

D <ed> spells [d] after a vowel.

Reason As we have heard, the suffix <ed> was shortened to [uud] and then shortened further by blending it on to the end of the verb word. In order to blend it onto an unvoiced consonant the mouth changes [d] to [t], but [t] cannot blend smoothly with [t]. The shortened suffix [d] blends straight onto vowels, which are all voiced, and on to voiced consonants, but not onto [d]. Voiced consonants blending with each other is very rare. As we know they only blend with [z] and [d], as in *mugs* and *mugged*.

Let's practise with words from List 1-1, our very first word list. Notice that terminal consonants are twinned when <ed> is added, which keeps the vowel short, stops it spreading out into a long sound. We saw this when <ing> was added to terminal consonants. Once again, we never see twin <x> because it already spells the two consonants [ks] at the end of a word. So <x> acts as 'double gates' when <ed> is added.

We shall look at suffix <ed> after silent [r] in the verbs *bar, bare, err, defer, fire* and *manure* later.

List 2-75

1.<ed> spells [t] after unvoiced [p], [f], [s], [k], [h], [th].
BOXED [bokst], CAPPED, CLUCKED, COPPED, CUPPED, DIPPED, DUCKED, FIXED, FOXED, FROLICKED*, GASSED, HOPPED, LAPPED, LOPPED, MIMICKED*, MIXED, MOPPED, NAPPED, NIPPED, PANICKED*, PICNICKED*, POPPED, RIPPED, SAPPED, SIPPED, SUPPED, TAPPED, TAXED, TIPPED, TRAFFICKED*, UNZIPPED, WAXED, YAPPED, ZAPPED, ZIPPED.
*Note how verbs ending in <c> change to <ck> when adding <ed> just as they did when adding <ing>. {*Arc* (yet to meet) is a rebel and remains *arced*.}

2.<ed> spells [d] after vowels and voiced [b], [v], [z], [g], [j], [l], [m], [n], {[r]}, [dh].
BAGGED, [bagd], BANNED, [band], BEGGED, BINNED, BOBBED, BOGGED, BUMMED, BUSSED, CAGED, CONNED, DABBED, DAMMED, DIMMED, DOGGED, DONNED, DUBBED, FANNED, FIBBED, FOGGED, GAGGED, GUMMED, GUNNED, HEMMED, HUGGED, HUMMED, JABBED, JAGGED, JAMMED, JIGGED, LAGGED, LOGGED, LOVED, LULLED, FILLED, LULLED, MILLED, PULLED, MOBBED, MUGGED, NABBED, NAGGED, {OOZED}, PEGGED, PENNED, PINNED, QUIZZED, RAGGED, RAMMED, RIBBED, RIGGED, RIMMED, ROBBED, RUBBED, SAGGED, SINNED, SOBBED, {SOOTHED}, TABBED, TAGGED, TANNED, TUGGED, WAGGED, {ZOOMED}. Aust. Slang DOBBED, MOBBED.

3.<ed> spells [əd] after [t] and [d].
BATTED [bat-əd], BEDDED, BUDDED, BUTTED, DUBBED, FITTED, GUTTED, JETTED, KIDDED, NETTED, PADDED, PATTED, QUITTED, RIDDED, ROTTED, VETTED.

4. <ed> spells [d] after a vowel.
FREED, {ROWED, PLOUGHED}

Auxiliary Verbs

This book is about spelling, not grammar, but you may want to know why *–ed* is not added to *love* when we say "He did love her." When *did* is added like this to another verb it is called an auxilliary verb and like an auxiliary engine it adds power to the main verb. There are quite a few auxiliary verbs, words like *can, be* {*may, might, should, could, ought* and the old word *durst*}. You can tell when the main verb is getting help from an auxiliary verb because it has no need to change, to add suffixes. There is no suffix on *love* in "He must love her," and no suffix on *sing* in "She can sing," unlike the suffixes on *sing* in "She sings," and "He loves her."

These **auxiliary verbs** do not change at all. We say, *I can run, we can run, you can run, he can run* — not *he cans runs* nor *he cans run* — except for three, which show when something took place, show the tense of a verb. (*Tense* comes from Latin 'tempus', a portion of time. Which tense? — which portion in time?) We will hear about these three exceptions very shortly. They are the three most common auxiliary verbs — *to be, to do* and *to have*.

Let's mark all auxiliary verbs with an auxiliary engine symbol like this §. It looks like an extra pulley driven by an auxiliary engine for added power. So far, we have met the following auxiliary verbs:
CAN§, MUST§, SHALL§ and WILL§. (*Will* can also act as a proper verb, as occurs when we will something to happen.)

Note: The noun *can* has become a verb, as in "He cans the tomatoes". We see it used with the auxiliary verb *can* in "He can can the tomatoes."

The three most common auxiliary verbs are *to be*, *to do* and *to have*. They are used a lot, to show the tense of the main verb: "I am eating; we did eat; he has eaten," and so on. They also help us ask questions, "Did you eat? Have you eaten? Are you hungry? Haven't you been fed? Why weren't you fed?" They also let us say "He was fed. The children have been fed,"
Note how these three auxiliary verbs change endings. They belong to a group of very old verbs, old-fashioned verbs.

Old Fashioned and Worn Down Verbs aka Irregular.
We did not see *digged, eated, hitted* and *winned* in the *boxed, battered* and *bagged* lists. Once upon a time there was another way to show something had already happened. Those British aborigines, the Celts, did it and the Romans did it — they changed the sound inside the verb. In the very olden days, the sound **inside** of the word changed to tell the present from the past.
Now, the present: "It *stings* me. I *feel* sick. I *am* hot. I *win*."
Back then, the past: "It *stung* me. I *felt* sick. I *was* hot. I *won*."
Once upon a time, <u>all</u> verbs changed their inside sounds. Then some did not bother to change and just added *–ed*. At some stage, whenever the English adopted verbs, or made-up new verbs, they added *—ed* to show past tense instead of changing the sound inside the verb. Eventually most verbs added *—ed*. So now the old verbs, which change their inside sounds, seem irregular and abnormal to us. We have to learn them one by one now. Although long ago they were regular, normal, we now call them **irregular verbs.**

That is why little kids say, "We swimmed" instead of, "We swam", until they learn that old version, *swam*. Once upon a time, *swam* would have been called the regular form, back when all the verbs changed their inside sounds. Back then, a lot more verbs belonged to the "Sing-Sang-Sung Gang". However, many of that gang have dropped the [a] vowel sound, so now we hear "*We swum out to the boat yesterday,*" as well as, "*We swam out there yesterday.*" We no longer hear, "*He swang his swag on his back,*" for now we all say *swung* for the past tense. The sound [swu] is easier to say than [swa]. It's a living language. More and more I hear people say, "He come yesterday," instead of "He came yesterday." Did old people like me shake their heads when folk said "swung" instead of "swang"?

Language experts can explain why it was normal to change the inside sound of words. They say it is only natural to use little sounds, which you can only hear close up, for the time which is closest to us, the present, and to use big sounds for far away things like the past. Look at your mouth when you say *swim* and now look when you say *swam*. We open our mouths wider for *swam* and we can shout *swam* louder than we can shout *swim*. The experts say it is only natural to use the bigger mouth, the louder sound for the event that happened furthest away. What do you think? Well, it does not matter now. Words which change their inside sound to show past or present are now in the minority. They are in the minority, but strong enough to be with us still. Some have not given into new ways at all, and remain with us like proud old mountains. Some have given in a bit but are still with us, mountains which have begun eroding. Some have stopped changing their inside sounds but refuse to take an <ed> ending! They are irregular, above the flat landscape of regular verbs, still like mountains but very worn down, e.g., "He *hit* the ball yesterday and he *hit* it today too."

We can think of the next verb as a strong old mountain still showing more than one peak: "I *drove* to my friend yesterday. I *drive* there now and I have *driven* there many times in the past."

Worn Down Mountains
Regardless of how worn down the mountain is, let's use Δ, a picture of a mountain, after all of these old irregular verbs.

We have already met many irregular verbs. Verbs are only irregular in their present and past forms. They are not irregular in their future forms or their present continuous forms.
Future: *He will begin.*
Present Continuous: *He is beginning.*
Present: *I begin, he begins.*
Past: *I began, he began.*
Past Perfect: *I have begun, he has begun.* ('Perfect' means 'I really have'.)
Pluperfect: *I had begun, he had begun.* ('Plu' means 'Plus, more, in the past'.)
If we do not want to say which tense the verb is in, we use the "infinitive" form of the verb, which means we do not define the tense, 'indefined'. When something is not finite it is not completed, not finished.
Infinitive of the verb to begin is: *to begin.*

When we list irregular verbs, we shall list the infinitive form first, the past form and then the past participle form. All the rest are regular and so we do not need to list them.
Q. What is a *participle*? Read on —

Participles participate a lot.

Participles describe a continuous action: *He is <u>beginning</u> a job.* All verbs ending <ing> are present participles of that verb. We just add <ing> to the infinitive form, *begin,* i.e. *beginning.*
Present participles also participate in turning verbs into adjectives: e.g., the *crying* baby; the *bleeding* knees.

Before 2-51B we discussed how <ing> participates in turning verbs into nouns. As we know, these special nouns are called "gerunds". e.g., Pam will quit *smoking.* Fred loves *cooking.* The discussion before 2-15 explains why gerunds do not have to pass the normal test for a noun, which is that if you can put *a* or *the* before a word, then it is a noun.

As you can see, **participles participate** in lots of ways. They also participate in describing a past action: *He has <u>begun</u>* or *He had <u>begun</u>.* We use the past participle of the verb to do this. This one, *begun,* is irregular because, as you can see, we have changed its inside sound. So, when we list irregular verbs, we shall always list the past participle, after the infinitive form and the past form. We shall list it like this: *begin, began, begun.* The infinitive form means the "unfinished" form because it does not have a number or tense. The infinitive form of a verb is usually written *to begin,* not just *begin.*

When we say *to begin* it means the verb which one or more people can do. We could be talking about it being done in the future, present or past. I have dropped the word *to* from the front of the infinitive form. Then it matches the form we use when *I* am doing it in the present. So it will look just like first person present.

By the way, **y**ou may hear the term "a split infinitive". This occurs if we say "to slowly walk" instead of "to walk slowly". It was considered bad English to pop an adverb in between *to* and the verb, but is OK nowadays if it makes the meaning clearer.

Past participles can also participate in turning verbs into adjectives, e.g., the *broken* jug. Adjectives ending in <ed>, or <en>, mean effect or result and those ending in <ing> are used with the person or thing that causes something, brings it about. Hence: "The film is boring and the result is that I am bored". If we change that to "Cooking is boring and the result is that I am bored," or "Hunting is tiring and so I am tired," we can see that participles participate a lot, in verbs, and as nouns and as adjectives.

We have already met a lot of irregular verbs. We shall list them here and mark them with the symbol of a mountain to show they have stayed strong, and stuck to the old ways, changed their inside sound to change tense. In fact, some people call irregular verbs "strong" verbs.

List 2-76
Infinitive, Past, Past Participle
BE ∆, WAS ∆ *, BEEN ∆
BEGET ∆, BEGAT ∆, BEGOTTEN ∆ (*old, not used*)
BEGIN ∆, BEGAN ∆, BEGUN ∆
BEHOLD ∆, BEHELD ∆, BEHELD ∆
BEND ∆, BENT ∆, BENT ∆
BESET ∆, BESET ∆, BESET ∆ (*old, rarely used*)
BET ∆, BET ∆, BET ∆
BID ∆, BID ∆, BID ∆ (in cards)
BID ∆, BADE ∆, BIDDEN ∆ <bade> spells [bad], *fossil <e>, as we know.*
BLESS ∆, BLEST ∆, BLEST ∆
BUST ∆, BUST ∆, BUST ∆
CAST ∆, CAST ∆, CAST ∆ *VS*
CLING ∆, CLUNG ∆, CLUNG ∆
COST ∆, COST ∆, COST ∆
CUT ∆, CUT ∆, CUT ∆
DIG ∆, DUG ∆, DUG ∆
DRINK ∆, DRANK ∆, DRANK ∆ / DRUNK ∆
DWELL ∆, DWELT ∆, DWELT ∆
FALL ∆, FELL ∆, FALLEN ∆ <a>=[or]
FLING ∆, FLUNG ∆, FLUNG ∆
GET ∆, GOT ∆, GOTTEN ∆ / GOT ∆
GO ∆, WENT*∆, GONE ∆
HANG ∆, HUNG ∆, HUNG ∆
Regular Verb HANG, HANGED, HANGED for death by hanging.
HAS ∆, HAD ∆, HAD ∆
HAVE ∆, HAD ∆, HAD ∆
HIT ∆, HIT ∆, HIT ∆
HOLD ∆, HELD ∆, HELD ∆
LEND ∆, LENT ∆, LENT ∆
LET ∆, LET ∆, LET ∆
PUT ∆, PUT ∆, PUT ∆ <u>=[uu]
QUIT ∆, QUIT ∆ / QUITTED, QUIT ∆ / QUITTED
REND ∆, RENT ∆ / RENDED in USA, RENT ∆ / RENDED in USA. To rend is to tear, split apart.
RID ∆, RID ∆ /RIDDED, RID ∆ /RIDDED /RIDDEN ∆
RING ∆, RANG ∆, RUNG ∆
RUN ∆, RAN ∆, RUN ∆
SELL ∆, SOLD ∆, SOLD ∆
SEND ∆, SENT ∆, SENT ∆
SET ∆, SET ∆, SET ∆
SING ∆, SANG ∆, SUNG ∆
SINK ∆, SANK ∆, SUNK ∆
SIT ∆, SAT ∆, SAT ∆
SLIT ∆, SLIT ∆, SLIT ∆
SLING ∆, SLUNG ∆, SLUNG ∆
SLINK ∆, SLUNK ∆, SLUNK ∆

SMELL Δ, SMELT Δ, SMELT Δ
SPELL Δ, SPELT Δ, SPELT Δ
SPILL Δ, SPILT Δ, SPILT Δ
SPIN Δ, SPUN Δ / SPAN in Aust., SPUN Δ
SPRING Δ, SPRANG Δ / SPRUNG Δ in USA, SPRUNG Δ
SPIT Δ, SPAT Δ / SPIT Δ in USA, SPAT Δ / SPIT Δ in USA.
SPLIT Δ, SPLIT Δ, SPLIT Δ
STICK Δ, STUCK Δ, STUCK Δ
STING Δ, STANG Δ / STUNG Δ, STUNG Δ
STINK Δ, STANK Δ / STUNK Δ, STUNK Δ
STRING Δ, STRING Δ, STRUNG Δ
SWELL Δ, SWOLL Δ, SWOLLEN Δ
SWIM Δ, SWAM Δ / SWUM Δ, SWUM Δ
SWING Δ, SWUNG Δ, SWUNG Δ
TELL Δ, TOLD Δ, TOLD Δ
WED Δ, WED Δ, WED Δ
WET Δ, WET Δ, WET Δ / WETTED Δ
WIN Δ, WON Δ *f*, WON Δ *f*
WRING Δ, WRANG Δ / WRUNG Δ, WRUNG Δ

When irregular verbs get prefixes, they do not change – they are still irregular. They copy their stem word exactly. For example, "What *befell* you?" "I *resold* it." "He has *withheld* my bonus pay until next week." Here are some irregular verbs with prefixes.
TO BEFALL Δ
TO INPUT Δ
TO INSET Δ
TO RECAST Δ
TO RESELL Δ
TO RESET Δ
TO UPHOLD Δ
TO UPSET Δ

*Was, like *went*, came from another verb. The verb *to be* is 'an accidental conglomeration from the different Old English dialects. It is the most irregular verb in Modern English and the most common' says Etymonline. It has eight different forms in Modern English: *be, am, is, are, was, were, being, been.* In modern English, only *be* and *go* take their past tenses from entirely different verbs.

*Went evolved from *wended,* the past tense of the verb *to wend.* We do not use it any more unless we say "We wend our way through this shady forest," or "He wends his way without a care in the world." We only use it with "way" nowadays, in the past tenses too — 'I wended my way,' or 'I have wended my way through many marketplaces." *Went* was one form of *wended,* which, after 1066, became the past tense of the verb *to go,* fully replacing *gaed* and *eode* by 1500.

Q. Why don't we list the participles of regular verbs?
Ans. There is no need to list them as they are all the same, made in the regular way — HOP, HOPPED, HOPPED, by adding <ed> for past tense and <ed> for past participle and <ing> for the gerund, HOPPING. The infinitive is always the same as the present tense, HOP, except for third person singular which adds <s>, as in: he, she or it HOPS.

Sometimes, when using a past participle to make an adjective, we disobey all the rules, for then <ed> spells [ed], not [t], after unvoiced consonants, nor [d] after voiced consonants, nor [əd] after [t] or [d]. For instance, listen to the **adjectives** in "Round and round the *rugged* [rug-ed] rocks the *ragged* [rag-ed] rascal ran." And this: "The *wicked* [wik-ed] man hit my *beloved* [bee-luv-ed] Ann. I called on the *blessed* [bles-ed] angels to help me." Note how it is adjectives which let <ed> spell [ed], not verbs, as in "We rugged [rugd] up against the cold." "They ragged [ragd] the new boy mercilessly." "The *aged* [ayj-ed] man had aged [aygd] beyond recognition." Here are more adjectives which end in [ed], in italics: "He crooked his *crooked* finger and jagged a ride over the *jagged* mountain range. We broke the three-*legged* stool and legged it out of there as we cursed those *cursed* crows over and over. The *naked* man snaked his painful way through the slaked lime. We learned he was a *learned* man."

Not all adjectives ending <ed> use it to spell [ed], e.g., the adjective {*slaked*} does not spell [slayk-ed].

List 2-77 Only a few adjectives end with <ed> spelling [ed].
AGED, BELOVED, BLESSED, FATED, DOGGED, ILL-FATED, JAGGED, NAKED, RUGGED, UNREQUITED (LOVE), WICKED, {CROOKED}, {CURSED}, {LEARNED}, {THREE-LEGGED}.

Also, this way of making the adjective different to the past tense verb does not always happen. For instance, we never say a *learned man* as a [lernd man], but we can say a *beloved wife* as [beluvd wIf]. We always say someone is much *loved* as [luvd], never [luved]. Modern words like *jet-lagged* [jet]-[lagd] never did end with [ed].

List 2-77 cont. Some adverbs use <ed> spells [ed] to make them easier to say.
ALLEGEDLY, SUPPOSEDLY, DOGGEDLY.

Verb and adjective *alleged* spells [al-ejd], but adverb *allegedly* spells [al-ej-ed-lee].
Verb and adjective *supposed* spells [sup-ohzd], but adverb *supposedly* spells [sup-ohz-ed-lee]
The verb is *dogged* [dogd], but adjective *dogged* [dog-ed] becomes adverb *doggedly* [dog-ed-lee].

Spelt or spelled?
Spelt, spilt, knelt, blest, bust etc. are old irregular verbs which have 'given in' and become regular *spelled, spilled, kneeled, blessed, busted etc.* in some places, especially America. *Spelt* is the old way. It's in the OED, but many Australian dictionaries give both *spelled* and *spelt*. It's a matter of choice. (The homographs/homonyms *spelt* and *spelt* are written the same and sound the same but one is past tense of verb *to spell* and the other is a type of edible grain.)

The verb *to spell* has a second meaning, 'to relieve someone from work by taking a turn', and although I say, "I spelt the word correctly", I also say, "I spelled him at ditch digging".

One word, which gave in some time ago, is the verb *to pen*, 'to enclose or cage something'. The English used to say, "I pent my sheep yesterday so that we can start shearing early," but now they say, "I penned my sheep yesterday so that we can start shearing early." "The sheep are pent up," has become, "The sheep are penned up." However, we still say, "I feel all pent up," if our feelings are penned up.

We have already listed these worn out old mountains.
BEND Δ, BENT Δ, BENT Δ
BLESS Δ, BLEST Δ, BLEST Δ
DWELL Δ, DWELT Δ, DWELT Δ
LEND Δ, LENT Δ, LENT Δ
REND Δ, RENT Δ, RENT Δ
SEND Δ, SENT Δ, SENT Δ
SMELL Δ, SMELT Δ, SMELT Δ
SPELL Δ, SPELT Δ, SPELT Δ
SPILL Δ, SPILT Δ, SPILT Δ

However, they are not as worn down as others. We could draw some mountains with flat tops, no peaks and very low to the ground for they have been worn down to all sound the same and look the same too. E.g., "I *bet* you that he *bet* $55 on that last week and having *bet* that much I hope he wins."

The following are very worn down mountains, but not yet regular. However, some of these irregular verbs are changing to the regular form in countries like USA: *quitted, rended, ridded, shedded*.
BET Δ, BET Δ, BET Δ
BID Δ, BID Δ, BID Δ (*in cards)
BUST Δ, BUST Δ, BUST Δ
CAST Δ, CAST Δ, CAST Δ [karst]
COST*Δ, COST Δ, COST Δ
CUT Δ, CUT Δ, CUT Δ
HIT Δ, HIT Δ, HIT Δ
LET Δ, LET Δ, LET Δ
PUT Δ, PUT Δ, PUT Δ <u>=[uu]
QUIT Δ, QUIT Δ, QUIT Δ
SET Δ, SET Δ, SET Δ
SLIT Δ, SLIT Δ, SLIT Δ

*This *bid* is used in cards. The old use of *bid* is 'to command or greet', the verb *bid, bade, bidden*. "I bid you good day."

Cost here is intransitive, "be priced at." It *cost* the same today as it *cost* last week but it *has cost* more in the past. Transitive verbs have to be able to have an object, something to act on. The transitive version of the verb *to cost* is, "I *cost* that at $2 now but before I *costed* it at $4, although Fred *had costed* it even earlier at $3."

Adding Ends to Blends — *acceptability, unpredictability*
   Remember the suffixes *–ity, -ety, -it, -id, -ic?* They all put stress on the previous syllable and shorten the one letter vowel in that syllable, even if it was a long vowel before adding a suffix, except for <u> which resists being shortened to [u].
   Remember the little suffix *–al?* It transfers the stress on to the syllable before it if preceded by two consonants.
   Remember, we said:- Some words grow long by adding one suffix **on to another** but we do not change the stress pattern because these suffixes *–ic, -al, -ly* are never stressed themselves and so cannot become stressed. **Ma**gic, **ma**gical, **ma**gically; sat**ir**ic, sat**ir**ical, sat**ir**ically; **par**adox, parad**ox**ical, parad**ox**ically – their stressed syllables (in bold) remain stressed when a second or even third suffix is added. Note the change of stress when the first suffix is added to **par**adox, above.
   You will enjoy the following expanded lists now that you can blend consonants.
List 2-78 Adding <ity> ends to blends.
ACCEPTABILITY, ACRIDITY, ACTIVITY, ADAPTABILITY, ADAPTIVITY, ADJUSTABILITY, ADOPTABILITY, AGGRESSIVITY, ALACRITY, ALKALINITY, AMBIDEXTERITY, APPLICABILITY, ATROCITY, BREVITY, BRUTALITY, CAPTIVITY, CELEBRITY, CLARITY, COLLAPSIBILITY, COMBUSTIBILITY, COMPATIBILITY, COMPLEXITY, COMPLICITY, COMPREHENSIBILITY, COMPRESSIBILITY, CONDUCTIBILITY, CONDUCTIVITY, CONNECTIVITY, CONTEMPTIBILITY, CONTROLLABILITY, CORRUPTIBILITY, CREDIBILITY, CREDULITY, CRIMINALITY, CRUDITY, CULPABILITY, DEFINABILITY, DELECTABILITY, DEMONSTRABILITY, DEPRAVITY, DESTRUCTIVITY, DETECTABILITY, DEXTERITY, DIGESTIBILITY, DEPENDABILITY, DISPENSABILITY, DISPOSABILITY,

DOMESTICITY, DUPLICITY, ECCENTRICITY, EFFECTIVITY, EGOCENTRICITY, ELASTICITY, ELECTRICITY, ELECTRONEGATIVITY, EVENTUALITY, EXCLUSIVITY, EXPANDABILITY, EXTREMITY, FECUNDITY, FESTIVITY, FLAMMABILITY, FLEXIBILITY, FRAGILITY, FRIGIDITY, FRIVOLITY, FRUGALITY, GRAVITY, HOSPITALITY, IDENTITY, IMMENSITY, IMPENETRABILITY, IMPRACTICABILITY, IMPRACTICALITY, IMPROBABILITY, IMPULSIVITY, INACTIVITY, INAPPLICABILITY, INCOMBUSTIBILITY, INCOMPATIBILITY, INCOMPREHENSIBILITY, INCONTESTABILITY, INCORRUPTIBILITY, INCREDULITY, INDEFENSIBILITY, INDEFINABILITY, INDEMNITY, INDESTRUCTIBILITY, INDIGESTIBILITY, INDISPENSABILITY, INDIVISIBILITY, INELASTICITY, INELIGIBILITY, INEQUALITY, INEVITABILITY, INEXPLICABILITY, INFALLIBILITY, INFECTIVITY, INFLAMMABILITY, INFLEXIBILITY, INHOSPITALITY, INSCRUTABILITY, INSENSITIVITY, INSTABILITY, INSTRUMENTALITY, INTANGIBILITY, INTEGRITY, INTENSITY, INTRACTABILITY, INTREPIDITY, INVINCIBILITY, IRREPRESSIBILITY, IRRESISTIBILITY, IRRESPONSIBILITY, MONSTROSITY, MULTIPLICITY, NEGLIGIBILITY, OBJECTIVITY, OBSCURITY, PENETRABILITY, PLASTICITY, PRACTICALITY, PRECOCITY, PREDICTABILITY, PREFERABILITY, PREVENTABILITY, PRIMITIVITY, PRINCIPALITY, PRINTABILITY, PROBABILITY, PROBITY, PROCLIVITY, PRODUCTIVITY, PROFANITY, PROFITABILITY, PROFUNDITY, PROPENSITY, PROPINQUITY, PROSPERITY, PROXIMITY, PUBLICITY, QUANTITY, RESPECTABILITY, RESPONSIBILITY, RUSTICITY, SALUBRITY, SANCTITY, SENTIMENTALITY, SIMPLICITY, SINGULARITY, SOLEMNITY, SOLVABILITY, SPASTICITY, STABILITY, STERILITY, STUPIDITY, SUGGESTIBILITY, SUPPRESSIBILITY, SUSCEPTIBILITY, TANGIBILITY, TRANQUILITY, TRANQUILLITY, TRANSPLANTABILITY, TRINITY, TRUSTABILITY, UNFLAPPABILITY, UNPREDICTABILITY.

Note: in *susceptibility, miscibility, obscenity* and *irascibility* <sc> spells [s] but <sc> spells [sk] in *inscrutability, masculinity, muscularity, obscurity, vascularity* and *viscosity*. Do you see why? Yes, <c> only softens to [s] before <e>, <i> or <y>.

List 2-79 Adding suffix <ic>.
ATAVISTIC, ALTRUISTIC, ANTISEPTIC, ASTRONOMIC, BAROMETRIC, CONCENTRIC, DEMOCRATIC, DRAMATIC, EGOCENTRIC, ELECTRONIC, ENDOSCOPIC, EXOSPHERIC, FATALISTIC, FEMINISTIC, FUTURISTIC, GASTRIC, INFRASONIC, METRONOMIC, PARAMETRIC, PARAPLEGIC, PERISCOPIC, PLANKTONIC, PLATONIC, SIMPLISTIC, STIGMATIC, SPECIFIC, TELEMETRIC, TELESCOPIC, TRAGICOMIC, TRANSGENIC, ULTRASONIC, VOLUMETRIC.

List 2-80 Examples of the suffix <ic> plus the suffix <al>.
ANGELICAL, CANONICAL, COMICAL, LACONICAL, LOGICAL, QUIZZICAL, SATIRICAL, TOPICAL, TROPICAL, WHIMSICAL.

List 2-81 The suffix <al>, and <al> with other suffixes, like <ity> and <ism> and <ly>.
ABDOMINAL, ABDOMINALLY, ACQUITTAL, ANCESTRAL, ANCESTRALLY, ANGELICALLY, ANTENATAL, BAPTISMAL, CLASSICAL, CLASSICALLY, CLASSICISM, COMMITTAL, EQUIVOCAL, EQUIVOCALLY, MUNICIPAL, MUNICIPALITY, OCTAGONAL, OCTAGONALLY, PLACENTAL.

Suffixes affect stem words and each other. For example, *class* changed from spelling [klas] to [klɑrs] in the south of England, but the suffix <ic> always produces a short, stressed vowel behind it and so *classic* spells [klasik]. Also, the suffix <ism> changes [klasik] to [klasi-sizm]. This is because the <c> is followed by <i> of <ism>. As we know, the <s> of <ism> spells its voiced version, [z].

We remember that, inside a syllable, <s> spells [z] between a short vowel and a voiced consonant, if that vowel is stressed. Therefore, *disc* spells [disk] not [dizk]. We remember that in other situations <s> spells [s], for a variety of reasons.

List 2-82 As we know, <sc>, when not followed by <i>, <e> <y> or <h>consonant, spells [sk]. ABSCOND, ABSCONDS, ALFRESCO, ASCARIS, ASCOT, DESCANT, DISC, DISCO, DISCONNECT, DISCONNECTED, DISCONTENT, DISCONTENTED, DISCREDIT, DISCRIMINATING, DISCRIMINATINGLY, DISCS, DISCUS, DISCUSS, ENSCONCE, EPISCOPAL, ESCALATING, ESCALLOP, ESCAPIST, FISCAL, FISCALLY, FRESCO, FRESCOS, HIBISCUS, HIBISCUSES, INDISCRIMINATING, INDISCRIMINATINGLY, INESCAPABLY, KILOPASCAL, KILOPASCALS, MACROSCOPIC, MACROSCOPICALLY, MASCOT, MASCOTS, MENISCUS, MICROSCOPIC, MICROSCOPICAL, MICROSCOPICALLY, MISCALL, MISCARRY, MISCARRYING, MISCAST, MISCASTING, MISCELLANY, MISCLASSIFY, MISCLASSIFYING, MISCONDUCT, MISCONNECT, MISCONNECTED, MISCOPY, MISCOPYING, MOLLUSC, MUSCAT, MUSCATEL, SPECTROSCOPY, TELESCOPIC, TELESCOPICALLY, TELESCOPING, NONDESCRIPT, OBSCURITY, PASCAL, PERISCOPIC, PRESCRIPTIVE, PROBOSCIS, PROSCRIBING, PROSCRIPTIVE, PROSCRIPTIVELY, RASCAL, RASCALLY, RASCALS, REDISCOVERY, SCRIPT, SCROLL, SCULPT.

List 2-83 As we know, <sci> and <sce> both spell [s].
ASCENT, DEHISCE, DEHISCENT, DESCENDANT, DESCENDANTS, DESCENDED, DESCENDENT, DESCENDENTS, DESCENT, EVANESCENT, EXCRESCENCE, FASCINATED, FASCINATING, INCANDESCENT, IRASCIBILITY, IRASCIBLY, IRIDESCENCE, IRIDESCENT, IRIDESCENTLY, ISOSCELES, NASCENT, OSCILLATING, PUBESCENT, PUTRESCENT, REMINISCE, REMINISCING, RENASCENT, RESCIND, RESCINDED, SENESCENT, SUSCEPTIBLY, UNSCENTED, TRANSCEND, TRANSCENDED, TRANSCENDS, VISCERA, VISCERAL, VISCID.

Rebels SCEPTIC spells [skeptik], FASCISM [fash-izm], VFASCIST [fash-ist], CRESCENDO [kre-shen-doh].

Rebels' Reasons — as explained earlier, at 2-3B.

Silent H. — *exhibit, vehicle.*

The letter <h> always spelt [h] in Old English, the language spoken in England before 1066. After that the official language of England was not only French but the French language influenced how people spoke English. H is a silent letter in French. This habit was copied by the English. Some words lost both the sound and the letter: *hit* became *it, hability* became *ability, hable* became *able, rose harbour* became *rose arbour*. A *hostler*, who was someone who hosts horses at an inn, became an *ostler*. Some kept the letter but lost the sound, like *honest.*

So we need to know in which English words <h> is silent. It is silent in digraphs with consonants, as we have seen in *where* and *there,* in *thick* and *thin.* We shall first of all look at <h> next to vowels.

When <h> is added to terminal <a> and <e> in the pseudo words *Ah!* and *Eh?* The vowels spell their long Continental sounds, [ar] and [ay]. Words like *jarrah, cheetah,* and *verandah* also add a silent <h> to ensure the final syllable is important, because they have been adopted from languages which stress syllables evenly. The final<h> of *veranda* has gone missing in USA since 1850, in U.K. since 1950, but not completely in Australia, as seen in this quote: 'Unlike pergolas, verandahs are always attached to the home. The verandah is an iconic feature of an Australian house.'

When silent <h> is added to terminal <o>, in the pseudo word *oh*, it does not spell long Continental [or] but the lifted version, [oh], which lifted in the GVS. The only other words with terminal <oh> are {*ooh*} [oo], {*pooh*} [poo] and {*pharaoh*} [fairoh], to be discussed later.

Some pseudo words end in <h> — *huh, duh* and *uh*. They all sound different — [hu], [der] and [u]. The <h> seems to be there just for emphasis.

Rule 2-84 At the end of a word, or a stressed syllable, <h> is silent. At the beginning of a word, or a stressed syllable, <h> spells [h], except when <h> follows the prefix <ex>, in which case it is silent.

Reason Linguists tell us that because [h] is said with a huff of air through an open mouth, if the mouth is already open saying a vowel sound, there is no way of adding a huffing sound without breaking the syllable. This is why <h> is silent after vowels in the same syllable, as in *hurrah*. Secret Agent H is very useful in the middle of words, between vowels, because he shows where one syllable stops and the next begins. If he comes after a stressed vowel, i.e. at the end of a stressed syllable, he is silent, just the same way he is silent at the end of a word. However, if he comes before a stressed vowel, he acts like he is starting that syllable and speaks out, spells [h], 'huffs and puffs' power into the next syllable. So, he either insulates the two vowels from each other with a silent pause or he separates them by spelling [h]. In English, <h> always spells [h] at the beginning of a word.

Stress is important. We must remember that English words start with stressed syllables, unless they start with prefixes. As we would expect, when <h> ceases to be word initial and instead starts an unstressed syllable, it no longer spells [h], e.g., *harmony* [har-mon-ee] but *philharmonic* [fil-ar-mon-ik], (Cummings, p. 390). Also, the stress in *vehicle* changes in {*vehicular*} and then <h> spells [h] as we shall see in Part Three.

Q. Why is <h> silent after <ex>?

Ans. In Part One we learnt that if <x> is between two vowels, it spells [gz], (Fox, p. 69), **but only** if the second vowel is said stronger than the first, (Cummings, p. 351). In *exhibit*, {*exhale, exhume, exhilarate, exhort, exhaust*} <x> spells [gz] because the second vowel is said stronger than the first. At the same time, <h> should also spell [h] before stressed vowels. Therefore, [eg-zhibit] is impossible because [z] and [h] cannot blend — [z] is a bad blender and will not blend with unvoiced [h]. That is why [h] is silenced and *exhibit* spells [eg-zib-it]. For the same reason, {*exhale*} is pronounced [eg-zayl], *exhume* is [eg-zyoom] or, in USA, [eg-zoom], and so on. **Note**:- In the word {*inhale*}, <h> spells [h] before a stressed vowel, without being extinguished by any preceeding [z]. This often misleads people to pronounce <h> in its partner word, {*exhale*}.

Rebels HONEST {HONOUR/HONOR, HOUR, HEIR}; and {EXHALE} when it spells [eks-hayl].

Rebels' Reasons The reason that initial <h> is silent in these words is historical. It is also silent in the adopted name for a piece of furniture *hautboy*. In USA *herb* spells [erb] and also *humour* spells [yoomer], even [oomer] in some parts of USA. They were all adopted from French words which came from Latin spoken by ordinary Romans who dropped their aitches.

Not needed but nice to know. Ordinary Romans spoke Vulgar Latin, in which *vulgar* means 'common or ordinary', from Latin *vulgaris* which means 'of the common people'. Long ago France was Gaul and the Gauls spoke Gallic. When they were colonized by Rome, the Gauls mixed with the ordinary Roman soldiers and traders, not the lords and ladies, and copied their ordinary Latin words and the way they said them. These ordinary Romans 'dropped their aitches', did not make the effort to say [h].

I learnt about Vulgar Latin from a letter to The Guardian 15.06.07, from Marc Leowenthal, London, U.K: "The form of Latin that people normally study and revere is the classical Latin of the last century BC and the first century AD as written by great authors such as Cicero, Livy, Virgil, Tacitus — the equivalent of the works of the great English writers from the 17th to the 19th centuries. However, like any other language, Latin was a language of the masses and had numerous variations, dialects, argots and genres throughout the classical period and beyond. As such it was subject to change. These forms evolved to become the modern Romance languages. Indeed French is little more than Vulgar Latin that was spoken by the soldiers, settlers and traders in Gaul. For example, the French "tête" (head) comes from Latin "testa", earthenware jar, or, as we might say "jughead'. Now back to things we need to know.

In England, during the Renaissance, scholars of Latin were keen to use Classical Latin pronunciation, not that of Vulgar Latin. So they 'upgraded' some words which come from French by adding <h>. If they thought a word had already been upgraded, but wrongly, they removed <h>. Some words had [h] added by mistake, such as *hermit* and *hostage,* (Cummings, p. 389). It should be *ermit* because Old French *eremite* meant person of the desert, of arid lands, not harid land. They added <h> to *ostage*, but it comes from Latin *obses* means "sit before".

Many people drop [h] from modern words. The word-sound [h] is not part of French or of Australian Ab'l languages, and some Englishmen still drop aitches. Consequently *hand* and *help* are pronounced [and] and [elp] by many people. Then adding [h] occurs through over correction. I have heard people say they '[ad] to [had] water to the stew', or, '[hand] he waved his [and]' and so on. Many more say [eks-hayl] in order to match *exhale* with *inhale*.

List 2-84
Silent H BEHEMOTH*, if pronounced [bee-ə-moth], EXHIBIT, FELLAH, JARRAH*, JIBBAH, GALAH*, GANJAH, HOSANNAH, HURRAH, HUZZAH, MAHARAJAH, MAH-JONG, MULLAH, NULLAH-NULLAH, RAJAH, SAVANNAH, PIRANAH, PUNKAH WALLAH, VEHEMENCE, VEHEMENT, VEHICLE, VERANDAH, {EXHALE}, {EXHORT}, {EXHUME}, {EXHAUST}.
Slang BAH!, BLAH, NAH.
Exclamations OH!, AH!, UH!, EH?, PAH, SIRRAH.
Names ALLAH, AYATOLLAH, DELILAH, DINAH, GRAHAM, HANNAH, JONAH, LILAH, {NORAH}, {SARAH}.
Places CASBAH, YARRAH*.

<h> spells [h], AHA!, ALCOHOL, ABHORRENCE , BEHELD, BEHEMOTH, BEHEST, COHOST, MAHATMA, NIHIL, NIHILISM, NIHILIST, NIHILISTIC, NIHILISTICALLY, Names, MEHEMIA (*Morning Star,* a Maori name.)

<h> spells both [h] and [ ] (Silent H) in BEHEMOTH* if pronounced [bə-hee-məth], HURRAH [hu-rar], MAHARAJAH [mu-har-ru-jar], HALLELUJAH* [hal-lay-loo-yar].
Behemoth can be said either way, (OED) but is very rarely used nowadays.
Jarrah now often spells [ja-rə] but it once had the even stress of Aboriginal languages. George Grey recorded *djar-rail* in 1840 and Moore recorded *djarryl* in 1884, (Blake, p. 95).
Galah was recorded as an Ab'l word in 1890 but Blake p. 93 is not sure which Ab'l language or region it came from. *Galah* spells [gə-<u>lar</u>], stressed at the end, whereas *gala* spells [gar-lə].
Adopted *hallelujah* is so well known that its spelling has not been adapted to English, in that <j> spells [y]. Possibly too sacred to alter — *psalm* was.
Yarrah is recorded by Blake p. 107 as the Wiradjuri Ab'l word in central and southern NSW for common river red gum, *E. Camaldulensis.* These are the trees which line waterways, and even in drought stand out as rivers of green. All over Australia, Ab'l *yarra* means 'river', as does *yallah* and *yardi*.

Secret Agent Aitch aka Helpful Haitch

When letters cluster at syllable boundaries, they spell separate sounds, like <t> and <h>, spelling [t] and [h] in *anthill*. Inside syllables, <t> and <h> form a digraph <th> in which <h> is silent but, as we learnt at rule 1-30, <h> tells its best friend what to spell. We read how letters in digraphs are called 'Best Friends' in some schools and we nicknamed silent <h> in a digraph Secret Agent Aitch and/or Helpful Haitch.

<u>Not needed but nice to know</u>. On the whole, Irish and Roman Catholics say Haitch. Protestants and Anglo-Catholics say Aitch. This shibboleth spread to Australia but intermarriage means parents are no longer as keen to insist on one way or another. English speakers from Singapore, Spain, Portugal and India usually say Haitch and those from Canada and USA say Aitch. The letter's original Latin name began with [h], according to Sue Butler, Macquarie Dictionary. When in digraphs, H is nicknamed Helpful Handy Haitch and/or Secret Agent Aitch. <u>Now back to things we need to know.</u>

Digraph <th> — *this, thin.*

At 1-32 we learnt that it was the Romans who invented the digraph <th> and it actually came to Britain with the Romans but only appears in a few Old English words. Besides, the Romans only used it to replace θ, Theta. They never actually said [th] in adopted Greek words, just used <th> to spell [t]. We know the Anglo-Saxons used [th] in words and that Vikings used [dh] as well as [th], because the Vikings had symbols for each. Edth was written <ð> (a modified form of <d>), and Thorn's symbol was <þ>, one of their runic symbols. Symbol <ð> spelt [dh] and <þ> spelt [th]. So Old English used Thorn and Edth for [th] and [dh], but eventually muddled them up. Then came 1066 and another successful invasion of England. For a long time the writing of English was controlled by French scribes. During that time, Edth and Thorn disappeared from the English alphabet. So *þynne* became *thin* and *fæðm* became *fathom*. If *fæðm* had become *fadhom* we would not need rules to read <th>. My use of [dh] when <th> spells its voiced sound copies the way it is written in Cornish, Albanian and Swahili. Swahili examples are *fadhila* (kindness) and *dhoruba* (storm).

<u>Not needed but nice to know</u>. The Anglo-Saxons brought runes with them to England. A Runic Alphabet was used all the way up until the 12th century in inscriptions in Britain. It was called the Futhark because *f, u,* thorn (*þ*), *a, r,* and *k* were its first six letters— like we call ours the ABC. When Christian missionaries arrived in Old Anglo-Saxon England, they used the Roman Alphabet but added six more letters, including Edth and Thorn, from the Futhark, to spell sounds the Romans did not use. After 1066 they were removed. Edth lasted until 1250. Thorn persisted longer, especially in words like *þat, (that), þe (the),* and *þis (this)*, even as other words were being spelled with <th>. When printing presses arrived in England, without the metal letter <þ> called Thorn, Y was used instead. It looks like a twig with a thorn, like the original letter Thorn. We see <y> spelling [dh] in "Ye Olde Shoppe" signs, which mean 'the old shop', not 'ye old shop'. In the old days a quick way to write *the, that* or *thou* was to write a little <e>, <a> or <o> respectively above Y: Y^e, Y^a, Y^o, but directly above, between the arms of Y, short for *the, that, though*. Eventually both Thorn and Y were replaced by <th>. <u>Now back to things we need to know.</u>

Since we use [dh] much less than [th] we shall first look at rules for reading [dh]. Hard [dh] is usually used in little words like pronouns, like *them,* and prepositions, like *than.* Soft [th] is used in nouns, *moth,* and adjectives, *thin,* and adverbs, *thinly,* and starting verbs, *think.* It's rare for a noun to start with [dh] but common for verbs to end in it. We shall learn later to turn a noun into a verb by changing its soft [th] into a hard one, making *clothe* from *cloth* and *breathe* from *breath.*

<u>Not needed but nice to know</u>. When *through* is a preposition, as in *through the arch* or *through the night,* <th> should spell [dh], but it can only spell [th], according to the next rule. Soft [th] is, however, the norm when it's an adverb, as in *he drove through*; or an adjective, as in *through road* or making a compound noun, as in *breakthrough, throughput.* <u>Now back to things we need to know.</u>

Rule 2-85 The digraph <th> cannot spell [dh] if adjacent to a consonant or is terminal.

Reason This means that <th> spelling [dh], inside a word, must have a vowel on either side of it, and at the end of a word, a silent terminal <e>. We know that Bad Blenders cannot blend with other consonants, not even with each other, except for a following [d] and [z] — in order to express tense, as in *seethed* [seethed], *breathes* [breedhz]. So it is unlikely we would try to read *thrust* as [dhrust] or *sixth* as [siksdh] or [sigzdh]. The problem is that there is no rule to say when <th> cannot spell [th] because <th> can spell [th] anywhere in a word, as in *thin, method, moth, thrash, ethnic, filthy*. Occasionally, terminal [th] changes to [dh] if a vowel is added, as in {*worth* and *worthy* or *north* and *northern*.} It is very rare for a word to start with [dh] unless it is *the* and words like *this, that, these, those, then, than, they, them, their, there, therefore*, prepositions, pronouns etc.

The following rebels include some words we have not listed yet so they have been decoded for you.

Rascals MOUTH verb, BEQUEATH verb. There is no good reason for the verb [mowdh] to be without its silent <e>. *Mouth* has soft [th] for the noun, which in Old English was *muþ,* using Thorn, the symbol for [th]. The verb had the symbol Edth, for [dh], in *muðettan*. When this verb shortened to *muðe* it should have become *mouthe* in Modern English. According to Cummings page 386, *bequeath* and *smooth* were written with a terminal E in the 1600's. In losing its terminal <e> *bequeath* is now often pronounced with [th] instead of [dh], in which case it will not long be a spelling rebel, let alone a rascal. Excuses can be made for *smooth,* so it is just a rebel.

Rebels ALGORITHM, BRETHREN, LOGARITHM, RHYTHM, SMOOTH, WITH.

Rebels' Reasons.

Algorithm [al-gə-ridhem] came from *algorism* in which <s> spells voiced [z] and so <th> spells voiced [dh]. The word links back to the brilliant *al-Khwarizmi* , who introduced Arabic maths to the Western World, including algebra, which is also named after him.}

Brethren [bredhren] seems to have lost its vowel after [dh]. A baby's *pram* used to be a *parambulator* but became *prambulator* and then just *pram*. This shows us that long consonant [r] sometimes flows backwards, silences the preceding vowel, as when *param* became *pram,* to avoid two weak beats side by side. Possibly *bretheren*, as plural of *brother,* became *brethren*, with the [dh] of *brother* retained. (You will remember that plural of *man* was *mannen* and then just *men.*)

Logarithm [log-u-ridh em] comes from *logarithmus*, coined in 1610 by Scottish John Napier. In *arithmetic,* also from *arithmus,* <th> spells [th], as it should, coming before a consonant. However, when Napier removed Latin suffix <us> from *logarithmus*, [m] was stuck without a vowel. As we know, a consonant cannot express itself without a vowel. So [m] in *logarithm* attached itself to [th] as [em] and now rhymed with *fathm,* in which <th> spelt [dh]. Later, *fathm* was respelt as *fathom* but <a> continued to spell a short vowel, as if it was still followed by the two consonants [dh] and [m]. (Compare first vowels in *brethren* and *ether.*)

Smooth [smoodh] had a silent terminal <e> but lost it, Cummings p. 386. Some say the word was all about whether *Smithfield* signified a smooth field or Mr Smith's field. To be clear, a [smooth] field became a [smoodh] and then when the adjective *smooth* became verb there was no need to add silent <e> because it already spelt [smoodh]. A very narrow escape from joining the rascals!

With [widh] could not be followed by <e> because an old word for willow twig already had it: *withe* [withee], which is a willow twig, (Oxford Concise Dictionary), also spelt *withy,* in which <th> spells [dh]. *With* has many meanings. English is not a precise language. Ab'l languages are very precise, like Latin. In English, all the next words in bold can be replaced with the word *with*. Fight **against** him; walk **beside** him; man **carrying** a gun; red-faced **due to** shame; break f**rom** her; **despite** all his talent; write **using** a pen; up **at the same time as** the sun; feel **sympathy for** you; and so on. *With* is used in many words, including THEREWITHAL*, WITHAL*, WHEREWITHAL*, WITHHOLD Δ, WITHIN, WITHSTAND Δ.

Irregular Verbs

WITHHOLD Δ, WITHHELD Δ, WITHHELD Δ.
WITHSTAND Δ, WITHSTOOD Δ, WITHSTOOD Δ.
**Therewithal, withal* and *wherewithal* are the only three words in which terminal <al> spells stressed [orl], because <al> is not a suffix in these words. It is part of the compound word *withal* [widh-orl] which stopped twinning <l> for some reason, possibly thinking the word was long enough and more so when it compounded again to form *therewithal* and *wherewithal*. This is further explained in a Writing Rule after 1-11 under Affixes.

Note in the next list that [dh] words are little ones. They are not nouns, they only stand for nouns, they are pronouns: e.g., *this* is used instead of saying exactly what "this" is. They are for pointing at things, *there*, and they are also adverbs, saying where: *there,* or how: *thus,* or when: *then*, things happen. We have already met some of the words in this list. As we know, *where* is one of only two stem words in which terminal <ere> spells [air]. The other word is *there* [dhair].

List 2-85
THAN, THAT, THE, THEM, THEN, THENCE, THERE, THIS, THUS, THY, THYSELF.
Abbreviations. THO, ALTHO.
The idea that *tho* should spell [dhoh] and *altho* should spell [orl-dhoh] was proposed by USA's Simplified Spelling Board in 1906. President Theodore Roosevelt directed the Government Printer, Mr Charles Arthur Stillings, to use *tho* and *altho* in all Government publications, along with 295 other simplified words. Americans began using these simpler versions of *although* and *though,* until the next president reversed Roosevelt's decision.

Digraph <th> spells [t] in only 2 words and some names.
THYME spells [tIm]
THALER spells [tar-ler].
Thyme is a Greek herb which the Romans called [tIm] because they could not say [th], but they wrote <th> to show it was originally a Greek word. The Romans did not use the Greek's letter *theta* (θ) for soft [th]. *Thaler,* is an old German word. Some Germans pronounced it [darlar] and this became *dollar* in English. Some pronounced it [tarler] which is used in English for a silver coin. No one spells it *thaler* in Germany anymore. It's *taler,* because the Germans stopped saying [th] a long time ago.

Not needed but nice to know. The Romans wrote *Thomas* and *Anthony* with <th>, to show they are Greek names, even though they always said [tomas] and [antonee]. The English copied this way of writing names to show their Greek origins. Sometimes they got it wrong. For instance, the River Thames is not a Greek name. The ancient Brits called it Tamesa and in 51 BC the Romans copied that name, calling it Tamesis. This became just Tames until, centuries later, English scholars thought the Romans had used a Greek name and added the <h> to Thames. (If the English revised their spelling like the Germans do, it would by now be the River Temz.)
Sometimes a word lost its [th] sound, e.g., *nostril* was once *nosthryl* [nos-thril], literally a 'nose-through'! This word *nosthryl* is an Old English word, back when English was a Germanic language, back when Lowland Germans said [th]. Sometimes [t] changed to [th] in English words. For instance, when English scholars found out that *trone* [trohn] was originally a Greek word they added <h> and after that it became *throne* and then people read it as [throhn]. *Author* was *autor* until English scholars learnt that it is a Greek word and popped in an <h>, (Cummings, p. 343).
Thomas and *Thomasina* have never changed, but *Anthony* and *Anthea* and *Theo* can also be said with [th], the Greek way. No words except proper nouns, like *Matthew,* use <tth>. This name is a contraction of a Hebrew compound meaning "gift of God", *mattathyah*. In Hebrew, *mattath* means *gift* and *yah* is short for *Jehovah*. The letters <tth> in the name were copied by the Greeks and the Romans but not the French

who took the name to England as *Mathieu*. However, the disciple *Matthew's* name entered England in the Latin Bible and remained in it after translation into English. Now back to things we need to know.

As we know, Digraph, or 'Best Friends', <th> spells [th] in *thick, thin, thongs* and many other nouns, adjectives and adverbs. Also in verbs, like *think,* but not so much at the end of verbs, where <th> usually spells [dh].

Rule 2-86 One letter vowels, preceding terminal <th> which spells [th] in stem words, spell short vowel sounds, except for <u> which resists shortening.

Reason We can think of terminal <th> as a double gate on single letter vowels, which makes sure they do not spread out into long vowels. So, when a consonant comes between the vowel and <th> it is blocked by a triple gate and also keeps the vowel short, as in *filth* and *depth,* even when <th> is followed by a vowel, as in *filthy*, as we would expect. We'd expect that <u> would resist shortening, as it often resists shortening and previously its excuse has been that it used to be spelt with two letters and the rule only applies to unigraph vowels. This is also the reason this time for *truth* comes from *true*, and *ruthless* from *rue*, an old word for r*egret*. *Bismuth* comes from a German word and *azimuth* comes from French *azimut* which comes from an Arabic word and so <h> may have been added without good reason, without a Greek connection.

Rebels PATH and BATH; BOTH, NINTH.

Rebel's Reasons *Path* and *bath* are only part-time misfits to this rule. They remain [path] and [bath] on many tongues in the north of England and elsewhere too. Down south [a] shifted to [ar]. This vowel shift was probably influenced by the softer French vowel spelt by <a>: [parth] and [barth]. We shall mark them with *VS,* to show that <a> spells [ar], but also [a] in some regions.

Both [bohth] has a long vowel spelt with only one letter before [th]. Why? Many centuries ago people said "*boh*" for *both.* Then they said "*boh the*" (which meant "both the") and then the two words joined up into "*both*" but kept the [oh] sound from *boh.* Then people began all over again for instead of saying, "Both boys like footy," we can also say, "Both the boys like footy." Which do you say? Both are O.K.

Ninth does not belong to the other words ending <inth>. It would be [nin-eth] if we just added <th> to *nine* because [th] follows the rule and makes the preceding <e> spell [e] and so we do not write *nineth,* to prevent [nin-eth]. Instead, we say [nInth], due to *nine* [nIn].

Rule 2-87 One letter vowels, before <th> which terminates a syllable, spell short vowels, unless the word has been built onto a stem word with a long vowel.

Reason We shall learn later that *bathe* spells [baydh] and so *bathing* spells [baydh-ing].

Rebels LETHAL [leeth-əl], BATHOS [bay-thos], ETHOS [ee-thos], PATHOS [pay-thos].

Rebels' Reasons *Lethal* was originally *letal* in Latin, and the <h> was added much later, to show it came from a Greek word, *lethe. Bathos, ethos* and *pathos* are all Greek words. Maybe Rule 2-87 does not apply to Greek words.

List 2-86/87 Soft or unvoiced [th]
ABSINTHE* *silent e,* ANATHEMA, ANESTHETIC USA, ANESTHETICALLY USA, ANESTHETICS USA, ANTHRAX, ANTHOLOGY, ANTHROPOLOGY, ANTIPATHY, ANTITHESIS, ANYTHING, APATHY, ARITHMETIC, ARITHMETICAL, ARITHMETICALLY, AROMATHERAPIST, ASTHMA*, ASTHMATIC, ATHLETIC, ATHLETICALLY, ATHLETICS, AZIMUTH [az-ee-muuth], BANDWIDTH, BATH* *VS,* BETROTHAL*, BISMUTH [biz-muuth]., BOTH <o>=[oh], BROTH, CATHEDRAL*, CATHOLIC, CLOTH, COMETH* *f,* DEPTH*, ELEVENTH, ENTHRAL*, EPITHET, ETHIC, ETHICAL, ETHICS, ETHNIC, ETHNOCENTRICITY, EVERYTHING, FIFTH, FILTH, FILTHY, GOLDSMITH, GOTHIC, HATH*, HELMINTH, HOMOEOPATHY, HUNDREDTH, ISTHMUS*, KITH, LATH, LENGTH, LENGTHY, MAMMOTH, MARATHON, MATH, MATHEMATICS, MATHS, MENTHOL, MISANTHROPY, MISANTHROPIST, MONOLITH,

MONOLITHIC, MONTH ƒ <o>=[u], MOTH, NINTH* <i> =[I], NOTHING* [nuth-iŋ], OSTEOPATH, PARENTHESIS, PARENTHETIC, PARENTHETICAL, PARENTHETICALLY, PATHETIC, PATHOGENIC, PENTATHLON, PATH* VS, PITH, PITHY, PLETHORA, PLINTH*, PROSTHESIS, QUOTH, RUTHLESS [rooth-les], SABBATH, SACKCLOTH, SEVENTH, SIXTH, SLOTH, SMITH, SMITHY, SOMETHING ƒ, STRENGTH, SUNBATH* VS, SWATH <a>= [o], TELEPATH, TELEPATHY, TENTH, THANK, THERAPIST, THESIS, THICK, THICKLY, THICK–WITTED, THICKEN, THICKET, THICKNESS, THICKSET, THIMBLE, THIMBLEFUL, THIN, THINLY, THINNESS, THING, THINGAMAJIG, THINGUMMY, THINGAMABOB, THINK, THINKING CAP, THINK-TANK, THINK UP, THINKING, THISTLE, THONG, THRALL [throrl], THRIFT, THRIFTY, THRILL, THRIPS, THROB, THRONG, THROSTLE [thros-uul], THROTTLE, THRUM (strum), THRUST Δ, THUD, THUG, THUMB, THUMPING, TILTH, TINSMITH, TROTH*, TRUTH [trooth], TWELFTH, TWENTIETH, UNTHINKING (as in thoughtless), UNETHICAL, UNETHICALLY, WIDTH*, WRATH* [roth], ZENITH. <u>Proper Noun</u> CORINTH. <u>Names</u> BETH, BETHAN, CATH, EDITH, ELIZABETH, ETHEL, GARETH, JETHRO, JONATHON, JUDITH, NATHAN, RUTH [rooth], SAMANTHA, SETH, TABITHA, TIMOTHY.

Irregular Verb THRUST Δ, THRUST Δ, THRUST Δ

*In Australia *asthma* and *isthmus* are pronounced how they are written - due to the power of Queen Quill - but in England and USA an old tradition is followed: *asthma* spells [az-mar]. The [az] comes from a word which begins [az] and means 'breathing hard' and <th> was added later to show the link to its Greek origins. The word *isthmus* entered English much later, with the Greek <th>, but was pronounced [is-muus]. So, both words have silent <th>. Why? King Sound dislikes blends of three sounds, (Cummings, p. 391).

Betrothal and *troth* each have <o> spells [oh]. They come from the old verb *to trow* which spelt [troh].

Cathedral spells [kath-ee-dral] due to the lengthening effect of [dr] on <e>, as for [cr] on <a> in *acre*.

Cometh and *hath* are old-fashioned words which we no longer use but which we see in old stories, e.g., in old Bibles.

Enthrall [en-throrl] has become *enthral*, but regains <l> in *enthralling* and *enthralled*.

Nothing seems to have changed [oh] of *no* to [u] when *no thing* became one word, but Etymonline says that this happened way back, in Old English, when it was written *naþing*, from *nan* meaning "not one", today's *none*. Back then, <a> spelt short [u] and long [ar]. In *naþing* we can see the other way that <th> was once written, with <þ>, the letter Thorn.

Plinth and words ending *inth* are very unusual and are extremely old. As our Indo-European speaking ancestors spread west across Europe, they came across such words and adopted them. So, *plinth* and *labyrinth* and *Corinth* and other –*inth* words are survivors of a language even more ancient than Indo-European, (Lerer Part One)

*This way of spelling *thorough/ly* and *through* has been rejected but it was used by USA government printers at Roosevelt's insistence. We shall meet them all later and hear why <th> spells [th] in each.

Wrath is a rebel in that it spells [wroth] even though <r> insulates <a> from <w>. *Wrath* is an old word which means 'tormented and twisted in anger'. It nearly died out but is making a come-back. Words starting <wr> usually involve twisting and turning e.g., *writhing, writing, wrangling, wrestling, wrecking*. By the way, THORO for *thorough*, THOROLY for *thoroughy* and THRU instead of *through* were officially acceptable in USA for a short time, during Roosevelt's time in the White House. He had trouble spelling these words when he was at school and changed them but some senators and many newspaper men believed that since they had had to learn to spell hard words, then everyone else should. The next President was not interested in helping people read and write.

Rule 2-88 When <s> is added to words **ending with <th> which spells [th], then <ths> spell [ths].**

Reason As we know <s> spells [s] after unvoiced sounds, as in *moth, moths, moth's, moths'*. It spells [z] after voiced sounds.

Rebels BATHS and PATHS, but they only rebel when *bath* spells [barth] and *path* spells [parth], then *baths* spell [bardhz] and *paths* spell [pardhz].

Rebels' Reasons This happens when <a> spells [ar] in *bath* and *path* (due to the vowel shift in southern England), for it is easier to say [bardhz] than [barths] and [pardhz] than [parths]. Try it. Conversely, the folk who still say [path] and [bath] say [paths] and [baths] which are easy to say.

More Rebels {MOUTHS, MOUTHS'}

Rebels' Reasons As we know, unvoiced consonants blend with [s], voiced with [z]. So, terminal <s> on verbs which end in <th> spelling [dh], spells [z], as in 'He mouths [mowdhz] his name silently and smooths [smoodhz] his hair.' Also, in the plural noun *mouths*, <s> spells [z]: many [mowdhz] not [mowths], 'We have many mouths to feed.' When <s> shows possession on the singular form, <s> spells [s]: 'His mouth's [mowths] lips were dry.' Showing possession on the plural form, <s> spells [z]: 'Many mouths' [mowdhz] lips were dry.'

List 2-88 Make your own list of words by adding <s> to words ending <th> which spells [th]. Practise reading them. If you can say *months* and *sixths* you are doing well!

Not needed but nice to know. C.M. Matthews, on p. 27, tells us that in the olden days, Old English words usually used <th> to make abstract nouns out of verbs: *steal, stealth; brew, broth; gird, girth; bear, birth; rue, ruth, ruthless; steal, stealth; grow, growth; mow, math, aftermath.* Nouns can become abstract too, by adding <th> as in *moon, month,* but most of all it is added to adjectives to make abstract nouns: *wide, width; strong, strength; true, truth; merry, mirth; slow, sloth; foul, filth; young, youth; hale, health; well, wealth; dry,* became *drouth,* later *drought; dear, dearth* –what was scarce was 'dear, precious'. However, <th> has become an old way to make abstract nouns and people laugh if we say *coolth*. An old suffix with a lot of life in it still is -*ness*. We can add it to any adjectives to make abstract nouns, even to new ones: *posh, poshness!* Now back to things we need to know.

Ugh! Digraph <ugh> — *cough, laugh*.

We have seen that no real words end in <uh>. The pseudo word *uh* has a far stronger friend: *ugh*. This pseudo word ends with [h]'s missing voiced partner, old Yogh. When Yogh's symbol, its English letter, was deleted from the alphabet, it was replaced by <gh>. Then <gh> was either silenced or spelt [f]. The exclamation *Ugh!* echoes the old Yogh sound, now obsolete in English.

After four hundred years of Roman Occupation the Saxons, Angles and Jutes arrived in Britain. They did not speak like Romans or Celts, for they growled deep in their throats, ended their words with such guttural rumbles that you'd have sworn they were choking on their words. And laugh! They laughed so much they coughed. "Ha, ha, ha," they shouted, except it sounded more like "Hla, hla, hla." Sometimes they choked with laughter. One old way of writing *laugh* was *hlahan*, "ha-ha-ing". There were many ways to write it, each way trying to copy the sound of laughter. Nowadays the written word reflects the way we laugh, "la la la", until we choke, "ugh", *la-ugh*. We no longer let <ugh> spell a choking sound, except maybe when we exclaim "Ugh!" at something yucky. Over time, [gh] changed to a polite [f] or ceased altogether. Why don't we write <f> then? Caxton, the first man to start a printing business in England, learnt his trade in Holland. He liked their way of spelling and used it back home in England after 1476. Before printing, everyone spelt as they felt best. Writing was a bit like landscape painting. Everyone tried to paint the scene as true to the look of it as possible and the same with writing. Everyone tried to write a word as close as they could to the sound of it. So, when printing began, the printers spelt it how they thought best. Mind you, the printers often changed spelling to make the words fit on the page! They usually added letters to fill up the lines. They were paid per line so they did not often shorten words.

We can list two words which use <ugh> spells [f]. More will come later, when we shall learn that <ugh> is silent after a long vowel, as in the name *Hugh*. *Cough* first appeared in writing as *coughen*, written by French invaders. In Old English it probably looked more like German *kuchen*. Noah Webster (Webster, 1962 edition, page x) says that, when the French took over English spelling, they wrote <o> before English <u>, to differentiate it from their French <u>. Since then, *cough's* vowel has become [o] rather than [uu]. That is why we can say that <ugh> decodes to [f] in *cough*.

Rule 2-89 Digraph <ugh> after a short vowel spells [f].

Reason This digraph remains to remind us that we used to end these words in a guttural choke, in pre-Norman times. After short vowels it shrivelled to [f]. The name *Hugh* spells [hyoo] and not [hoof] because <gh> only spells [f] after short vowels.

Rebel LAUGH

Rebel's Reason *Laugh* is not a rebel in northern England and anywhere else where it is still pronounced [laf]. However, on most tongues the short [a] has shifted to a long [ar]. Most people say [larf] which means it breaks the rule that <gh> spells [f] only after short vowels.

List 2-89

LAUGH is not a rebel when it spells [laf]
COUGH always spells [kof]

When Noah Webster wrote the first American dictionary, he wanted to write these words *larf* and *coff* but he was told that if he did that only Americans would buy it. He was told no one in England would buy it. "If you want to make a profit you must sell many books, here in America and also in England. And the English will not like your changes to their language." Webster had borrowed money by mortgaging his house. He had spent 27 years writing his dictionary. He needed to sell as many copies as possible to pay his debts and look after his wife and eight children and so he gave in and wrote most words the English way, not his new American way.

Rule 2-90 After short vowels terminal <ughs> spells [fs] and terminal <ughed> spells [ft].

Reason Words in which terminal <gh> spells [f] take the suffix <s> spells [s] and take the suffix <ed> spells [t]. The word-sound [f] is unvoiced and so <s> and <ed> spell unvoiced suffixes so that they are able to blend on to [f].

List 2-90

LAUGHS [larfs] or [lafs], LAUGHED [larft] or laft], COUGHS [kofs], COUGHED [koft].

Chat, chasm, chassis — **busy Secret Agent H.**

Digraph <ch> spells either [k], [ch] or [sh] in the next lists, but first, in one word, <ch> spells [kh], a throaty [k].

Rebel LOCH. This spells [lokh]. The digraph <ch> in *loch* replaces a Gaelic letter which spells [kh] — a sound between [k] and [gh]. The spelling and pronunciation differentiate it from *lock* which means a waterway enclosed by man whereas the Scots use *loch* to mean a lake of fresh or sea water.

In another word, <ch> is silent.

Rascal YACHT. This spells [yot]. It's excuse is flimsy. Caxton, England's first printer, brought the spelling with him from Holland where he trained. Since <j> spells [y] in Dutch he wrote it in English with <y> instead of <j>. Aussies say [yot], Americans say [yart], more like the Dutch word, [yarkht]. England's first yacht was a gift from Holland. A Dutch *jacht* is fast and usually used to hunt enemies at sea, but in 1660 the Dutch gave King Charles 2nd the racing yacht *Mary*. In 1689, they sent another, along with their Prince William and his English princess, Mary, to provide England with a Protestant king and queen. "Keep the yacht, too," they said and since then English royal couples always had a royal yacht, until 1997. The Dutch link is broken but the crazy spelling remains.

We met [sh] in *she*. The sound [ch] starts *cheeky*. The Saxons used <c> to spell [ch]. Italians still use <c> for [ch], as in *cello*. The Saxons did not need <c> for anything else because <k> spelt [k]. However, as we know, the French do not like using <k> for [k]. They needed <c> to spell [k] and due to the many hundreds of years that the French occupied England, the English language changed to suit French ways. So English words changed the way they were written: *dic* became *ditch*, *feccan* became *fetch*, with <t> to make sure the vowel was kept short. Norman [ch] words were added to the English language too.

Secret Agent H does the silent job of making <ch> spell [ch]. Say *chin* with your fingers on your voice box. Do you feel it vibrating? No, because the voice box is not used to say [ch]. So [ch] is an unvoiced sound.

Rule 2-91 Digraph <ch> spells [ch] in many words and shortens the preceding one-letter vowel in the same syllable, even without <t>.

Reason Digraph <ch> spells [ch] due to history, as above. Like digraph <th> it acts as a double gate on vowels in the same syllable, ensuring they do not stretch out into long sounds. Consonants which come between the vowel and the double gate, as in *lunch* and *match,* act as even stronger 'triple gates'. In some words <ch> does not spell [ch], also due to history, as we shall see.

List 2-91 <ch> spells [ch].
ALCHERINGA, ATTACH, ATTACHMENT, BACH*, BACKCHAT, BACKSTITCH, BATCH *collective noun*, BELCH, BENCH, BEWITCH, BITCH, BLENCH, BLOTCH, BOTCH, BRANCH, BRUNCH*, BUNCH, BUNCHY, CATCH, CHAFF [charf] *VS*, CHAMP, CHANCE, CHANGE* [chaynj], CHANNEL, CHAP, CHAPLET, CHARITY, CHASTITY, CHASUBLE, CHAT, CHATTEL, CHATTY, CHECK, CHERRY, CHEST*, CHESTNUT*, CHICK, CHICKEN, CHILD* <i>=[I], CHILDREN, CHILL, CHILLI, CHILLY, CHIMP, CHIN, CHINCHILLA, CHINK, *CHINTZ, CHIP, CHIPMUNK, CHIPOLATA, CHIPPINGS, CHIRRUP, CHISEL, CHIT, CHITCHAT, CHOC, CHOCK, CHOP, CHUB, CHUBBY, CHUCK, CHUCKLE, CHUG, CHUM, CHUMP, CHUTZPAH*, [chuuts-par], CHOP, CHUG CHUG CHUG, CHUNKY, CHUPATTY, CINCH, CLENCH, CLINCH, CLUTCH, CONCH, CROSS-PATCH, CROTCH, CROTCHETY, CRUTCH, DETACH, DETACHMENT, DISENCHANT, DISPATCH*, DITCH, DOGWATCH, DRENCH, DUCHESS, DUCHY, ENRICH, ETCH, EXCHANGE*, FETCH, FILCH, GOLDFINCH, GLITCH, HATCH, HATCHET, HATCHING, HATCHBACK, HATCHET MAN, HEM-STITCH, HENCHMAN, HITCH, HOMESTRETCH, HOTCHPOTCH, HUNCH, HUNCH BACK, HUTCH, INCH, ITCH, KETCH, KETCHUP, KITCHEN, LATCH, LINCHPIN, LUNCH, MATCH, MATCHLESS, MUCH, MUCH OF A MUCHNESS, NOTCH, OSTRICH, PATCH, PATCHY, PENNY PINCHING, PINCH, PITCH, PUNCH, QUENCH, RATCHET, RANCH, RICH, SANDWICH*, SATCHEL, SCRATCH, UP TO SCRATCH, SCRATCHY, SKETCH, SKETCHY, SNATCH, SNITCH, SPINACH, SPLOTCH, SQUELCH, STENCH, STITCH, STRETCH, STRETCHY, SUCH, SWITCH, SWITCHBACK, SWITCHED ON, TENCH (fish), THATCH, TRENCH, TWITCH, UNHITCH, WATCH <a>=[o], WHICH*, WINCH, WITCH, WITCHETTY GRUB*, WITCH-HUNT, WRETCH, WRISTWATCH <a>=[o]. Proper Nouns/Adj. CHAD, CHILE <e>=[ee], FRENCH, DUTCH, MICHIGAN, SCOTCH. <u>Names</u> BUTCH, CHAD, CHARITY, CHERRY, CHASTITY, CHESTY BOND, GRETCHEN, MITCH, MITCHEL, SANCHO.

**Brunch* is a 'portmanteau word'. Bits of sound and meaning from *breakfast* and *lunch* are combined to make a new word, with a new meaning. When Alice asks Humpty Dumpty in *Through the Looking Glass* what *slithy* means he says it means *lithe* and *slimy*, "You see it's like a portmanteau - there are two meanings packed up in one word." Lewis Carroll, who wrote the book, loved inventing words, like *chortle* from *chuckle* and *snort*. Others have invented more, e.g., *pictionary, floordrobe, smog, blog*. (A portmanteau is a big two-sided suitcase.)

*_Change_ and _exchange_ both end in [aynj] since stress is on <ange> in both words, as in _angel_ and _strange_ earlier.

*In _chintz_ and _chutzpah_ <z> spells [s]. We saw the same in _waltz_, all adopted from the German alphabetical code in which <z> spells [ts]. They are all adopted but not adapted on paper. In speech, <t> is silent between consonants in _chintz_ and _waltz_, with longer [n] and [l] flowing over it. Yiddish _chutzpah_ is a mix of Hebrew and German.

*_Chest_ is one of the 4 or 5 words adopted directly from the Romans when they ruled Britain. They spelt it _cista_ and said [kista]. Both the pronunciation and spelling have changed. Most other Latin words were adopted much later, when Latin had become a "dead language" but was still useful for supplying spare parts to make new words.

*_Chestnut_ comes from French _chastaigne_, Latin _castanea_, due to the castanets made from its nutshells, (Fleck 2007).

*_Child_ is another example of the [ld] blend lengthening [i] to [I] as in _mild_. Note that this does not happen in _children_ for the suffix is strong and splits the [ld] blend into [chil-dren].

*_Dispatch_ is also spelt _despatch_ in the OED. Some say that this alternative spelling came about because Samuel Johnson made a mistake in his 1755 dictionary. It is not related to _detach_ and _attach_. Etymonline says it either comes from Spanish _despachar_ or Italian _dispacciare_. Probably because _dispatch_ is easier to say than _despatch_, most people use _dispatch_.

*_Sandwich_ is an eponym — 4th Earl of Sandwich asked his cook to come up with something he could eat as he played cards. He was addicted to gambling.

*_Witchetty_ was adopted from the Ab'l name for the grubs, various large insect larvae, (Blake, p. 105).

Which or that? Use _which_ as a joiner if the phrase is an aside but use _that_ to join a phrase which is the point of the sentence: 'The tree, which had no leaves, was a birch.' 'The tree that had no leaves was a birch.' (Bryson 2004, p198).

Rule 2-92 Terminal <ches> spells [chez] and terminal <ched> spells [cht].
Reason _Riches_ is easier to say than _richs_. We know how word-sounds blend and so we know why _enriched_ spells [en-richt] — suffix <ed> spells [t] after [ch], being an unvoiced consonant.

Rule 2-93 Trigraph <tch> spells [ch].
Reason The [t] in this trigraph is silent unless the word is said very slowly. Also, it is un-necessary. The added <t> is not needed to keep the vowels short, for <ch> acts as a double gate. Sometimes [ch] is spelt with <ch> and sometimes with <tch>. Old English words changed, e.g., _rice_ became _riche_ became _rich_. Then Old French words which used <cch> were adopted into English with <tch> after short vowels, e.g., _hacch_ became English _hatch_. The English did not go back and change <ch> to <tch> in the English words in which <ch> already spelt [ch]. They are the very old words:- _much, rich, enrich, such, which, detach, duchess, duchy, spinach_ and _attach_.

Trigraph <tch> is usually terminal. We almost never see <tch> inside stem words. When we do it's between vowels, after a stressed short vowel and before an unstressed vowel, which only happens in the stem words _satchel, ratchet, ketchup, kitchen, hatchet_, and {_escutcheon, butcher_}. Of course, it also occurs when we add to stem words which end in <tch>, like _patchy, hatchback, matchless, witchetty grub_. _Chitchat_ is a compound word, made of two separate stem words. _Chitchat_ does not spell [chitch-at]. In this case <tch> is a cluster but not a blend because it clusters across syllables, [chit-chat].

<u>Relevant Writing Rule:</u> When <ch> spells [ch] after one-letter vowels, <t> is inserted before <ch>.
<u>Reason</u> This was enforced by the French on the English, as above.
<u>Rebels</u> MUCH, RICH, ENRICH, SUCH, WHICH, DETACH, DUCHESS, DUCHY, SPINACH, OSTRICH and ATTACH, but not _dispatch_. Also SANDWICH and BACH.

Rebels' Reasons *Much etc.* are very old words in which <ch> spelt [ch] after short stressed vowels before <tch> was introduced. The eponym *sandwich* is an old name, spelt the old way. *Bach* is slang, an Australian abbreviation of "bacheloring" or "living as a bachelor and cooking for one's self". Abbreviations do not have to obey rules.

Relevant Writing Rule: When <ch> spells [ch] after a consonant or a vowel spelt with two letters, <t> is never inserted before <ch>.

Reason If another consonant was inserted after the vowel the triple gate would become four doors thick and quite unnecessary. As it is <ch> alone is enough to keep the vowel short. Words like *filch* and *bench* do not need <t>. We shall meet <ch> after vowel digraphs in words like {*church, approach, touch* and *coach*} later. Vowel digraphs rarely shorten. So there is no need for <tch> after vowel digraphs.

Rebel {AITCH} In *Aitch,* the name of letter <h>, <tch> follows a vowel spelt with a digraph!

Rebel's Reason, unknown. In Latin *aitch* was written *ha* but in Old French *aitch* was written *ache* and ended like a Scottish *loch*. Return to Reading Rules.

Digraph <ch> also spells [k], as in *chemist* [kem-ist], and in *Chris* and *Christina.*

Rule 2-94 Digraph <ch> spells [k] in words which have come from Greece and does not act as a double gate on vowels.

Reaso The Greeks used X, *chi,* to spell [kh] and K, *kappa,* to spell [k]. The Romans used <ch> when they adopted Greek words containing Greek X. They did not use Greek X for they already had an X and it made a different sound, the sound at the end of their word for king, *rex*. In English, *Christ* used to be *Cristo* or *Crist* but when scholars discovered that it was originally a Greek word it was changed to *Christ.* Also, [ee] changed in the Great Vowel Shift, lifted and bent into [I].) As we know, the dictionary scholars who produced the OED believed that a word should be written with letters that spell out its history, as well as its sound. (We ordinary folk have taken *Christmas* two steps closer to the Greek, for <X> in *Xmas* spells the original Greek [kh] and we unwittingly add emphasis with a breathy [h] if we feel the excitement of the season.)

List 2-94 <ch> spells [k] in words from Greece or made with Greek word parts.
ARACHNID, TECHNICAL, CHARABANC, CHASM, CHEMISTRY, CHEMIST*, CHIMERA, CHROMATIC, CHRONIC, CHRONICLE, ECHIDNA, EPOCH* [ee-pok], OCHRE [oh-ker], LICHEN [lI-ken], MASOCHISM*, MECHANIC, MECHANISM, MELANCHOLY*, SCHOLASTIC, SCHEMATIC, SEPULCHRE, TECHNICAL, TECHNOLOGY, CHARISMA, CHEMICAL. Proper Nouns CHRIST* <i> =[I], CHRISTMAS*, CHRISSY, NICHOLAS, CHRISTOBEL, CHRISTINE, CHRISTINA, CHRISTOPHER.

Chemist is a "Lemon Rebel" with an excuse. It should be *chemmist,* but was originally *chimista* in which there was no need for twins because the third syllable from the end was short but stressed….referring back to the modifications to Orm's Law we have covered. When shortened to *chemist*, the single <m> remained.

Epoch is now pronounced with a long vowel before the single <p>, but in its original form of *epocha* its first vowel was short but in no need of <pp> because the third syllable from the end was short but stressed.

*In the difficult cluster <stm> in *Christmas* <t> is silenced, for the longer consonant [s] flows right on over short [t] — [kris-mas].

Masochism is an eponym. Google Leopold von Sacher-Masoch.

Melancholy was spelt with just <c> until it was traced to its Greek origin but *colic* kept its simple Latin C even though it was originally Greek with a <k>. The related word *cholera* comes later. BTW, thanks Peter Norman for letting me know I had missed *melancholy* out. I love hearing from my readers.

Rule 2-95 Digraph <ch> spells [sh] in France and in French words that have been adopted into English but not adapted.

Reason At first the French used <ch> for [ch] but then changed their minds and began using <ch> to spell [sh]. We shall meet this in {*chaise-longue, chartreuse, chauffeur, chauvinism, cheroot, chicanery, choux pastry* and *chute*}. They are all late adoptions from French. For instance, the records show that the name Charles came to England long before the name Charlotte, [shar-lot]. These modern French words were adopted but little attempt was made to change their spelling to suit English rules for the foreign spelling gave the words importance, lent a certain 'cachet'. The upper classes took pride in being able to decode the new foreign spelling. Even today, French menus are a bit of a shibboleth. In the Bible story at Judges chapter 12, *shibboleth* was a sort of password which you needed to pronounce correctly to be accepted.

List 2-95 <ch> spells [sh] occasionally, usually in French adoptions.
CACHET [kash-ay], CHAGRIN, CHALET [shal-ay], CHEF*, CHIC [sheek], CHIFFON, CHASSIS* [shas-ee], CHENILLE*, CHEVRON, CHIC [sheek], CHIGNON [sheen-yon], CHIVALRY, CROCHET [kroh-shay], ECHELON, NONCHALANCE, RICOCHET [rik-oh-shay], SACHET [sash-ay]   Names
CHANTRICE, CHANDRA, CHANTAL, MICHELLE, SACHA, SACHI.
*Chassis has a silent terminal <s> and <i> spells a Continental long sound, [shas-ee].
*Chef came into English long after *chief*. French words entered English in two waves. The old Norman chiefs came first and later the French chefs, by which time <ch> spelt [sh] in France. The English enjoyed French cuisine (food) and were proud to use the new term *chef* and spell it the French way.
*In *chenille*, <ille> spells Continental [eel].

There is no way of knowing which words belong to the above list and so we should make a story of them and add new words as we come across them.
Here's an example of a <ch> spells [sh] story, which includes words we have not met yet. The *gauche chef* wore *chiffon* with *nonchalance* much to the *chagrin* of the *chic* upper *echelon*. The guests arrived by *parachute* because the *chassis* of their *machine* had snapped, as planned by the *charlatan* with the black *moustache*. "Superb *cachet*," said *Chantal* to *Michelle* as they sipped *champagne* and flipped through travel *brochures*. They invited *Charlotte* but not Charles to share their holiday." (You'll need chiffon in your dress-up box to act this out, and a moustache, and lemonade, as make-believe champagne!)

Europeans use the same alphabet in a variety of ways. For instance, in the word *Czechoslovakia* <cz> spells [ch] and < ch> spells [k]!

Ship Shape with Secret Agent H
The Saxons arrived in England in ships. They came about 400 years after the Romans arrived in *navis*. That Latin word the Romans used for ships is the ancestor of the word *navy*. If you look in an English to Latin dictionary you will find that, for every word beginning with <sh>, there is a Latin word which sounds quite different: *sheep-ovis, short-brevis, shout-clamour, shepherd-pastor,* because the Romans did not use the [sh] sound in speech. Nor did the Celts, the aborigines of Britain.

The language of the Celts was similar in sounds to Latin and so the Roman alphabet was used to write Celt. When the Saxons and their cousins the Jutes and Angles came a**sh**ore in their **sh**ips, **sh**outing and **sh**owing their strength as they each fla**sh**ed a sax (a sword sharpened on one side with a sharp tip) they not only ba**sh**ed and sma**sh**ed their way across the country side, in a **sh**ocking **sh**indy of violence, they also introduced a new sound to the ears of the Celts and the few remaining Romans. This was the sound [sh].

Skippers on ships. Four hundred years after that, in 800 AD, the Vikings arrived from Denmark in skips! Yes, they pronounced *ships* as [skips]. They excelled in many ways, even winning the throne. Vikings from Denmark became kings of England. England had Danish kings from 991 to 1016 AD. Many Danish sailors became captains. Although English sailors insisted on saying *ships* the captain of each ship insisted that he was the *skipper* of the ship which we say to this day. And we still say *skips*, for little ships.

The English (the Anglo-Saxons) did not use <sh> to spell [sh]. They used <sc> to spell [sh]. So *scip* spelt [ship] for 600 years, until the Normans arrived. The Normans spoke French and in French <sc> spells two sounds, neither of which is [sh]. "You can no longer use <sc> for [sh]", the Norman conquerors said. "Your [sh] sound is rather like our [ch] sound but softer and so we will spell it <sch>." During the next 300 years, people dropped the middle letter and just wrote <sh>. *Englisc* [en-glish] became *English* [in-glish].

However, many other ways of coding [sh] evolved in the English language. We shall meet them all along the 'road to reading'. Make your own decision — with fingers on your voice box, is [sh] voiced or unvoiced? Correct, unvoiced, well done.

Not needed but nice to know. We see fourteen ways of spelling [sh] in English, in s*hip, chef, schnapps, sugar, nation, extension, mission, conscience, social, chaperon, issue, ocean, suspicion* and *sexual*. The Chinese, however, have over 50 ways of writing [sh], with far too many overtones of meaning to express with just 26 letters in our western ABC alphabet. Consequently, Chairman Mao gave up his plan to write Chinese with a western typewriter. The Vietnamese have succeeded in doing so. Vietnamese has more than 26 word-sounds and they write extra sounds by adding marks above and below the letters of the alphabet. They use all the indicator signs - accents, graves, cedillas etc used when writing French, the language of their old colonial masters. (From talks with my nephew William McEwin, Shanghai, 2006.)
Now back to things we need to know.

The digraph <sh> usually comes at the end of words or starts stem words. It is used in words which are old English words. Modern words use other codes for [sh]. The suffixes -*ish* and –*ship* are old but they can join on to new words. There are three words in the following list in which digraph <sh> comes in the middle, marked * and the other three you will meet later, {*marshal, usher,* and *mushroom*}. They are rare, for [sh] is rarely spelt <sh> in the middle of words. {*Goshawk*} has the letters <sh> inside it, but they are not a digraph, as you will learn.
Suffix —*ish*.
Two kinds of suffixes are written with <ish>. The first kind makes adjectives like *fattish, Polish* etc. The second kind makes verbs like *accomplish* and *publish*. As you can see the first kind, which makes adjectives, joins on to stem words which can stand alone: *fat, Pole*. The second, verb-making kind joins on to stems which do not make sense on their own. Maybe they did long ago but nowadays they do not make sense without their suffixes and/or prefixes.
If stem words make sense on their own, they are called **free stems**. If they only make sense when bound to affixes, they are called **bound stems.**

Rule 2-96 Digraph <sh> spells [sh]
Reason Historical reason as above.

Rule 2-97 When the suffix <ish> is added to a stem word to make an adjective it does not change the sound of the stem word, as in *fat, fattish; mode, modish*, (Cummings, p. 121).

Rule 2-98 The "Verbish Rule": When the suffix <ish> comes at the end of a verb it is always preceded by a short, stressed vowel.

Reason This is a pattern observed by Prof Cummings, with double gates as in *publish* or without double gates, as in *punish*. He noticed it only happens in verbs. "We polish [pol-ish] the Polish [poh-lish] statue of Saint Stanislaw."

Rebel IMPOVERISH [im-pov-e-rish], in which [pov] is short and stressed instead of [e].

Rebel's Reason The stress seems wrong in this word as it should be stressed immediately before <ish>. Most people now treat the <e> as silent to make the word conform to the Verbish Rule: [im-pov-rish]. This is an example of words falling into patterns over the years for the brain likes rules, likes words to be sorted into patterns.

List 2-96/97/98

ABOLISH, ACCOMPLISH*, ADMONISH, AMIDSHIPS, ASH, ASHEN, ASHRAM, ASTONISH, BABYISH, BANISH, BASH, BASHFUL <u>=[uu], BATTLESHIP, BISHOP*, BLANDISH, BLEMISH, BLUSH, BOSH *slang*, BOTTLE-BRUSH, BRACKISH, BRANDISH, BRASH, BRUSH, BUSHEL <u>=[uu], CASH, CATFISH, CHERISH, CODFISH, COLDISH, CONCH SHELL, CRASH, CRASH LAND, CRASH HELMET, CRASHING, CRUSH, DASH, DASHING, DEMOLISH, DIMINISH, DISESTABLISH, DISH, DISHCLOTH, DISHY, DONNISH, EMBELLISH, ESTABLISH, FAMISH, FETISH, FINISH, FISH, FISHING ROD, FISHY, FLASH, FLASHBACK, FLASHY, FLESH, FLESHY, FLUSH, FRESH, FLUSH, FRESH, FRESHEN, FRESHNESS, GARISH, GOLDFISH, GUSH, HASH, HASHISH, HELLISH, HOTTISH, IMPISH, JELLYFISH, KITTENISH, LAVISH, LUSH, MANNISH, MAHARASHI, MIDSHIPMAN, MISH-MASH, MUSH, MUSHY, NOSH *slang*, PARISH, PERISH, PASHA, PERISHING, PETTISH, PINKISH, PLUSH, PLUSHY, POLISH, POSH, PACKING SHED, POTTING SHED, PRE-SHRUNK, PUBLISH, PUCKISH <u>=[u], PUNISH, PUNISHMENT, PUSH <u>=[uu], QUASH, RADISH, RAMSHACKLE, RAVISH, RAVISHING, REDDISH, REFRESH, REFRESHING, REFRESHMENT, RELINQUISH, RELISH, REPLENISH, RESHUFFLE, RUBBISH, RUSH, SASH, SCRIMSHRANK SELFISH, SELFISHLY, SELFISHNESS, SHABBY, SHACK, SHADY, SHAFT <a>=[ar], SHAG *bird*, SHAGGINESS, SHAGGY, SHAH, SHALL, SHALLOT, SHALT, SHAM, SHAMBLE, SHAMBLES, SHAMROCK, SHANDY, SHANK, SHAN'T* <a>=[ar], SHANTUNG, SHANTY, SHAVEN <a>=[ay], SHE* <e>=[ee], SHED Δ, SHED *noun*, SHELF, *singular*, SHELVES *plural*, SHELVE *verb*, SHELLAC*, SHELLFISH, SHENANIGANS, SHERIFF, SHERRY, SHIBBOLETH, SHIFT, SHIFTLESS, SHIFTY, SHILLING, SHILLY SHALLY, SHIM, SHIN, SHINDY, SHINGLE, SHINGLES, SHINY, SHUFFLE, SHUTTLE, SHUTTLECOCK, SHIP, SHIPMENT, SHIPPING, SHIPWRECK, SHIVAH *adopted*, SHOCK, SHOCKING, SHOD, SHODDY, SHOP, SHOPPING, SHOT, SHOVEL *f* <o>=[u], SHRANK, SHRAPNEL*, SHRILL, SHRIMP, SHRIMPING, SHRINK Δ, SHRINK - *slang*, SHRINK FIT, SHRINKING, SHRINK WRAP, SHRIVEL, SHRUB, SHRUG, SHRUNK, SHUN, SHUNT, SHUT Δ, SHUT OFF, SHUT UP, SLAP, SLAPDASH, SLASH, SLOSH, SLUGGISH, SLUGGISHLY, SLUSH, SLUSH FUND, SLUTTISH, SMASH, SMASH AND GRAB, SMASH HIT, SMASHING, SNOBBISH, SPLASH, SPLASHBACK, SQUASH <a>=[o], SQUASHY, SQUISHY, STASH, SUNFISH, SWASHBUCKLING <wa>=[wo], SWISH, THICKISH, THRASH, THRESH, THRESHOLD*, THRUSH, UNSELFISH, UNSELFISHLY, UNSELFISHNESS, UPSHOT, USHER*, VANISH, VANQUISH, WAGGISH, WAGGISHNESS, WASH <a>=[o], WASHABLE*, WASHING *noun*, WELSH, WETTISH, WHITISH, WISH, WISHFUL, WISHY-WASHY. Proper Nouns/Adj. BRITISH [british], ENGLISH* [inglish], SHARON, BANGLADESH, FINNISH, FLEMISH [flem-ish], POLISH [poh-lish], SCOTTISH, SHETLAND, SPANGLISH *slang*, SPANISH, WASHINGTON, WELSH, YIDDISH. Names ASHWIN, HAMISH, JOSH, MISHA [mee-sha], NATASHA [nar-tar-shar], SASHA [sar-shar], SHARRON, SHELTON, SHILO [shI-loh], TRISH.

Irregular Verbs

SHED Δ, SHED Δ / SHEDDED, SHED Δ / SHEDDED

SHRINK Δ, SHRANK Δ / SHRUNK Δ (USA), SHRUNK Δ / SHRUNKEN Δ (USA)

SHUT Δ, SHUT Δ, SHUT Δ

Accomplish means 'to complete' and is therefore not a feather word.

Bishop is one of only 6 stem words with <sh> inside it. A Greek *episkopos* (epi-scope) kept an eye on things, shortened to *bishop* in English, but is reflected in *telescope,* (Fleck 2007).

English. As we have read earlier, *England* was named by the Engle. 1 Angle man, 2 Engle men. Their scribes did most of the writing, Saxons preferring the fighting and they all did lots of farming. Anglo-Saxons called their new home *England* — Engle-land, [ayngland]. As we know, <e> spelt the long sound [ay], an extension of short [e], until the Great Vowel Shift 1450-1650. So, this changed to [eengland] in the GVS and then became [ingland] which is easier to say. The short version of [ee] is [i], quicker to say.

Shan't [sharnt] is the abbreviation of *shall not.* As we know vowels change. In pairs like *shall* and *shan't, do* and *don't, will* and *won't, can* and *can't,* vowel change ensures they are not muddled with their opposites.

She used to begin with <h> like *he,* as did *it. He, she* and *it* were once *he, ha* and *hit.* They became much easier to tell apart when *she* spread across England from the east coast in the Midlands and when the <h> in *hit* was dropped.

Shellac comes from shelllac (thin plates or shells of lacquer) but due to the No Triplets Rule it had to discard an <l> from shelllac. It's *shellacking, shellacked* with <k> to prevent <c> softening.

Shrapnel, an eponym, was invented by Henry Shrapnel in the Napoleonic Wars, (Fleck 2007).

Threshold means 'thrash wood'. It is the piece of wood which was beaten or worn away by feet entering the house. It was originally *thresh-wold* which is why we do not hear [h] in it. (Hewitt and Beach, p. 826).

Usher spells [u-sher] with <sh> acting as a double gate on <u> so it spells [u].

*As we know, *washable* takes the suffix <able>, not <ible>, because <able> is grafted onto *wash* which is a free stem.

Shall I or will you?

Both *shall* and *will* are needed to put verbs into the future tense. We say I *shall* and we *shall* do something but you *will,* he *will,* she *will,* it *will* and they *will* do something. That is the tradition when speaking in English about the future.

However, if effort or will-power is required to make something happen we reverse the two little words: "Do you swear the evidence you **will** give (future tense) **shall** (will-power needed) be the truth?" "I **will** try (effort needed) very hard to do that." "You **shall** (effort) clean up your room!" "I will not! I won't." (will-power). Bill Bryson says the tradition is fading and quotes Churchill's, "We shall never surrender", MacArthur's "I shall return" and the song "We Shall Overcome" to prove his point, (Bryson 2004, p. 183), because, although they all refer to will power, they only use *shall,* which just expresses future tense.

Rule 2-99 Terminal <shes> spells [shez] and terminal <shed> spells [sht].

Reason It's easier to say *two wishes* than *two wishs.* And we know that suffix <ed> spells [t] after unvoiced consonants like [sh]. So, it's *fished,* [fisht], *splashed* [splasht], *swished* [swisht], as for *cupped* [kupt], *latched* [lacht], *gassed* [gast].

Meanwhile, back in Paris, French was different to the way the Normans spoke, a bit different to Norman-French. When the Normans conquered England there were twelve different versions of French spoken in France. It depended where you lived how you spoke it, and how the scribes wrote it. The sound <sh> came to be written [ch] in Paris and so new words from Paris were written with <ch> to spell [sh]. {Chief} had arrived around 1280 and used <ch> to spell [ch], the Norman way. *Chef* however arrived in the 1800's. The Normans' [cheef] was [shef] in Paris, chief of the kitchen. English stately homes and big hotels thought it was better to have a *chef* than a {cook} in their kitchens. They spoke of 'French cuisine' and still do, instead of saying 'French cooking'. The English delighted in spelling all the new French words the Parisien French way. So there are words in English, to this day, in which [sh] is spelt <ch> instead of <sh>.

In Germany long ago the language split into Low German in the northern low flat lands and High German in the high mountainous south. Low German words arrived in Britain with the Saxons, Angles and Jutes and developed into Old English, the earliest form of English. Much later on High German words were adopted into the English language but their spelling was not adapted. As you can see, High German [sh] sound was spelt with <sch>. Many of these words were taken to England and America by German Jews who spoke Yiddish, full of [sh] sounds. *Schwa* is pure Hebrew, for 'emptiness'.

Rule 2-100 Digraph <sch> spells [sh] before a consonant.
Reason Author's observation of a strong pattern.
List 2-100 <sch> spells [sh] before a consonant.
SCHMALTZ* <a>=[or], SCHNAPPS, SCHNITZEL, SCHLEP, SCHLIMAZEL, SCHLOCK, SCHMO, SCHMUCK, SCHNOZZLE, SCHWA.   Proper Noun   MR SCHMIDT
*In *schmaltz*, <a> spells [or] in the same way <a> before <l> consonant spells [or] in walk. Also, <z> spells [ts], in German origin words. In *schmaltz*, <t> is silenced, for in the difficult blend [lts] long [l] flows over short [t].

Rule 2-101 Digraph <sch> spells [sk] before a vowel.
Reason It's just an observation of a pattern.
Rebels SCHILLING, SCHEDULE, SCHISM.
Rebels' Reasons for breaking the pattern. The only words to break the pattern are a few in which the following vowel is <i> or <e>. They are also very old words, as compared to the more modern Yiddish words which obey the rule. *Schillings* are Austrian shillings, not in use since the introduction of the euro. Originally pronounced with [k] in German and English. *Schedule* spells [sked-yool] in America and [shed-yool] in Britain, which means it does not always break the pattern. Ditto for *schism*. *Schedule* and *schism* are related to *scissors* and are increasingly pronounced as if <sch> spells [sk], which shows us that words 'like' rules, like to fit a pattern. Australia's shortened version, *sked,* as in the Flying Doctor scheduled roll-call, helps to make [sked-yuul] more acceptable amongst old people, who are usually the last to let old words fit into new patterns.
List 2-101
ESCHSCHOLTZIA*, SCHIZOPHRENIC, SCHISM, SCHOLASTIC, SCHEMATIC, Coming Soon {SCHOLAR}, {SCHOOL}, {SCHEME}, {SCHEDULE}.
**Eschscholtzia* [esh-skolt-zee-ar], the scientific name for *Californian poppy,* is easy to read if we remember that before a vowel <sch> spells [sk] but before a consonant it spells [sh].

Secret Agent H — *alphabet, telegraph*.
Rule 2-102 <ph> spells [f] and vowels before <ph> are short, including vowel plus consonant before <ph> — as in *alphabet* and *pamphlet*.
Reason This digraph is used in words that are considered to have come from the Greek language. The Romans needed another letter when they adopted Greek words which had a very soft [f] sound. Just as <th> spells two sounds today, [th] and [dh], Romans said [f] in two ways. One [f] sound was made with just their lips — not with top teeth on bottom lip — and with more breath than today's [f]. It started as a [p] sound but then got blown away by an [h] sound. So, the Romans used <ph> for this sound and <f> for the [f] sound made with top teeth on bottom lip, like we do today. Eventually everyone got lazy and just said [f] with teeth on lips and not the other puffy soft [f] sound, **except** when saying ***Phew!*** which has a different [f] sound to that in *few*. The <ph> spelling for [f] had nearly died out in England by the 1700's, just as the Renaissance reached England, a time when English academics got interested in the ancient

languages of Italy and Greece, Latin and Ancient Greek. Some words were changed back to <ph> from an <f> spelling to show that they came from Ancient Greek. Some were left with an <f>. The sorting was not perfect. Not all words with Greek origins got <ph> for <f>. For instance, <ph> is in *phantom* but not in the related word, *fantasy*. In the Renaissance, little Latin and Greek word bits were used as 'spare parts' to make big new English words, e.g. *telegraph*. If they had the [f] sound in them and were Greek then they were spelt with <ph>.

Rebels? Some words, like *graph*, spell both [graf] and [grarf] due to vowel shift.

List 2-102 <ph> spells [f]
ALPHABET, ALPHABETIC, AMPHIBIAN, ASPHALT, ATMOSPHERIC, ATMOSPHERICS, ATROPHY, BIOGRAPHY, DELPHINIUM, DIPHTHONG*, ELEPHANT, EPITAPH, GALUMPH, GEOGRAPHY, GRAPH* [ar] or [a], GRAPHIC only [a], GRAPHICAL, GRAPHICALLY, HOMOGRAPH, LEXICOGRAPHY, LITHOGRAPH, LITHOGRAPHIC, MERITOCRACY, NAPHTHA, PAMPHLET, PHALANX, PHALLIC, PHANTASM, PHANTOM, PHARAOH*, PHENOMENAL, PHENOMENON, PHILANTHROPIC, PHILANTHROPIST, PHILANTHROPY, PHILOSOPHICAL, PHILOSOPHY, PHILTRUM, PHLEBOTOMY, PHLEBOTOMIST, PHLEGMATIC, PHLOGISTIC, PHLOX, PHOBIC, PHONETIC, PHONETICS, PHONIC, PHONOGRAPH, PHOSPHORIC, PHOSPHORUS, PHOTOCONDUCTIVITY, PHOTOSENSITIVITY, PHOTOTOXICITY, PHOTOTROPIC, PHOSPHORESCE, PHOSPHORESCENT, PHUT *slang*, PROPHET, PROPHECY* <y>=[ee], PROPHESY* <y> = [I], PARAGRAPH, PROPHET, QUADRAPHONIC, SAXOPHONIST, SERAPH, SERAPHIC, SERAPHICALLY, STENOGRAPHY, SOPHISTRY, SPHAGNUM, SPHERIC, SPHERICAL, SULPHA DRUGS, TELEGRAPH, TELEGRAPHIC, TELEGRAPHIST, TELEGRAPHY, TELEPHONIST, TELEPHONY. <u>Proper Nouns</u> PHILADELPHIA, PHNOM-PENH [nom-pen]. <u>Names</u> ADOLPH, APHRODITE [af-roh-dI-tee], DAPHNE [daf-nee], DELPHINE [del-feen], JOSEPH, OPHRA, PHIL, PHILEMON, PHILIP, PHILIPPA, PHILLIP, PHILLIPA, PHILOMENA, RANDOLPH, STEPHAN*, STEPHANIE*.

Diphthong comes from Greek di- "double" phthongos "sound", Etymonline.

Pharaoh was *pharon* in Old English, *pharaonem* in Latin and *pharao* in Greek. The dictionary committee captured all that history in the current spelling and also added a silent <h> to ensure that *pharaoh* spells [fair-oh] and not [fair-ə].

*The noun *prophecy* comes from French, meaning "the function of a prophet" which is "to speak for another". *Prophet* in Greek is *prophetes*, with *pro* meaning "for" and *phetes* "speaker". The verb, 'to make a prophecy', would end in <fy> spelling [fI] as in defy, except that "profify" or "profefy" are both hard to say. The verb became *prophesy*, with an <s> and spelt [pro-fes-I]. (The [f] in Greek for "speak" flows through to English in *fate* and *fable*, which could be spelt with <ph>.)

We do not list *Stephen* because it spells [stee-ven]. But <ph> in *Stephan* and *Stephanie* always spells [f]. *Stephen* and *Steven* both spell [steev-en], and *Stephan* and *Stefan* both spell [stef-an].

Note: Word initial <phth> can spell just [th] in a few technical words which start with <phth> spelling [th]. For instance, PHTHALIC spells [thal-ik]. This is a chemical which comes from {*naphthalene*} which spells [naf-thal-een], because, as in *diphthong*, <phth> is not at the start of the word, is not word initial.

Rhonda and Secret Agent H

Rule 2-103 Word initial <rh> spells [r].

Reason The Greeks have a letter called *rho*, uppercase **P**, lower-case **ρ**. It looks like a Roman P but is not, for it spells a breathy [r]. The digraph <rh> was used in Latin for Greek *rho* in word-initial position, to start words. It was adopted by the English during the Renaissance for even though the breathiness has gone from <rh> it is used to spell [r] in words which have been adopted from the Greek language. In this way the dictionary writers attempted to trap a word's history in its letters. The Welsh <rh> to spell an unvoiced, "breathy" [r], as in the Welsh names *Rhonda* and *Rhys.*

Rebels? None, they all follow the rule and spell [r]. They start stem words but do not end them, or 'enter' them, even in compound words.

List 2-103 <rh> spells [r]
RHAPSODY, RHESUS, RHEMATIC, RHETORIC, RHINAL, RHINOCEROS*, RHODODENDRON, RHOMBIC. <u>Names</u> RHODA *Greek* , RHONDA *Welsh*, RHYS *Welsh.*
*We can add *rhinoceros* to our little list of words in which terminal <s> spells [s] after an unstressed vowel!
Rh words are all rare words. We shall meet just a few more, including {*rhubarb, rhythm* [ridh-m]}.

Rule 2-104 <rrh> spells [r] and like English <rr> is not word initial, never starts a word.
Reason Greek words with double *rho* have been adopted into English with <rrh>, to show us that they come from Greece.
List 2-104 Trigraph <rrh> spells [r]
CATARRH
You will meet {*diarrhoea* and *gonorrhoea* and *haemorrhage* and *myrrh*}. There are very few <rrh> words.

High and Mighty Secret Agent H.

Rule 2-105 When <igh> comes after a consonant in the same syllable it spells [I], as in *high*.
Reason The word *right* is the most frequently used <igh> word. *Right* comes from long ago when the Romans said *rectus* for 'right', in Latin. In Germany, this became *recht*. In Scotland it became *richt*, in which <ch> spelt [k] followed by old voiced [h]. In Old English, throaty voiced [h] was written with the letter *yogh*, upper-case ꙅ, lower-case ꙅ. The Norman scribes replaced yogh's symbol with <gh>. Old English *riʒt* became *right* and lost its guttural sound. Then its vowel elevated in the Great Vowel Shift, elevated and hit the roof of the mouth and bent a little to become [I]. So then <igh> spelt [I] and the silent <gh> was a handy way to prevent <i> ending words such as *high*, for as we know, teminal <i> is to be avoided.

Another word, *night,* is used a lot. It began as *nacht.* Englishmen stopped its guttural end sound when they began sounding less German and more French under their Norman conquerors. The Scots continued saying it — "Och, it's a braw bricht moonlicht nicht". As we know, the English began copying the French in other ways too. Particularly in the south, they changed [a] in many words to [ar], e.g., *aft, dance* and *chance*. This meant the vowel [ar] in words like Old English *nacht* was moved on to make other sounds, in this case the [I] sound.

Other words changed — Germans no longer say *beraht,* the old word which in English changed long ago to *bright. Right, night, bright,* they all fell into a pattern in which <igh> spelt the long vowel sound [I]. Other words followed, *heg* or *heah* became *high; neah* became *nigh*. In each case <i> follows a consonant, for if it follows a vowel, as in *weigh*, then <igh> does not spell [I]. In each case <igh> is in the same syllable for if <g> split from <h> the letters <igh> do not spell [I], e.g., <igh> in *bighead* [big-hed] does not spell [I].

English has developed other ways to spell [I] but these words have retained <igh> spells [I] to remind us that English was a German language before the Norman Conquest.

List 2-105 After a consonant <igh> spells [I].
ALIGHT, BIGHT, BLIGHT, BRIGHT, DELIGHT, FIGHT* Δ, FLIGHT, FRIGHT, HIGH, KNIGHT* *silent* <k>, LIGHT Δ, MIGHT§, NIGH, NIGHT, PLIGHT, RIGHT, SIGH, SLIGHT, SIGHT, THIGH, TIGHT, WIGHT *obsolete word for human or other being.* SHIPWRIGHT
**Fight* — the present, past and past participle of the irregular verb *to fight* will come later. §

LIGHT Δ, LIT/LIGHTED, LIT/LIGHTED *Lighted* is used more often as an adjective than *lit*.

Not needed but nice to know, about the auxiliary verb MIGHT§: **1** *Might* adds possibility to a verb but less possibility than *may*. **2** *May have* and *might have* have different meanings. *Might have* means that you know something did not happen but might have happened if something else had or had not happened. **3.** Both *may* and *might* can be used to express permission. *Might* has a higher degree of politeness than *may*. For example: "Might I see it?" is a humbler request than "May I see it?" In fact, the latter is almost a command. Now back to things we need to know.

The list continues, to show us all the words we make with these <igh> words. Some are compound words and some have been made by adding prefixes and suffixes.

List 2-105 cont.
AFFRIGHT, ALIGHT, ALL RIGHT*, ARIGHT, BACKLIGHT, BOMBSIGHT, BY RIGHTS, BULLFIGHT, CATFIGHT, COCKFIGHT, COPYRIGHT, DELIGHT, DOGFIGHT, EYESIGHT, FANLIGHT, FIGHT BACK, FIGHTING FIT, FISTFIGHT, FLASHLIGHT, FLIGHT, FLIGHT-DECK, FLIGHTINESS, FLIGHTLESS, FLIGHTY, FRIGHTEN, GASLIGHT, GUNFIGHT, HIGH AND DRY, HIGH AND MIGHTY, HIGH FIDELITY, HIGH JUMP, HIGH LIVING, HIGH SPIRITED, HIGH SPOT, HIGH-CLASS, HIGH-HANDED, HIGHLAND, HIGHLIGHT, HIGHLY, HIGH-MINDED, HIGHNESS, HIGH-PITCHED, HIGH-SPIRITED, HIGH-UP, HINDSIGHT, IN-FIGHT, IN-FLIGHT, INSIGHT, KNIGHT silent <k>, LAMPLIGHT, LIGHTEN, LIGHTING, LIGHTISH, LIGHTNING, LIGHTS, MIDNIGHT, MIGHTINESS, MIGHTN'T, MIGHTY, MILLWRIGHT, NIGHT-CAP, NIGHT-CLUB, NIGHTDRESS, NIGHTFALL, NIGHT-LIGHT, NIGHTLY, NIGHT-SHIFT, PENLIGHT, PUT TO FLIGHT, RIGHT ANGLE, RIGHT-HANDED, RIGHT MINDED, RIGHT-ANGLED, RIGHTFUL, RIGHT-HAND, RIGHT-HANDED, RIGHTLY, SHIPWRIGHT, SIDELIGHT, SIGHTLESS, SIGHTSEEING, SKIN-TIGHT, SKYLIGHT, SLIGHTLY, SPOTLIGHT, SPRIGHTLINESS, SPRIGHTLY, STOPLIGHT, SUNLIGHT, TIGHTEN, TIGHT-LIPPED, TIGHTNESS, TIGHTS, TIGHTWAD, TONIGHT, TOPFLIGHT, TROTH PLIGHT *pledge,* TWILIGHT, ULTRA-LIGHT, UNSIGHTLY, UPRIGHT, UPRIGHTNESS, UPTIGHT. Slang HIGHFALUTIN'. Proper Noun ISLE OF WIGHT. Name DWIGHT.

* There is no such word as *alright*. It is listed in OED as an incorrect form of *all right*. It may be accepted one day. It's interesting that *all ready* began appearing as *already* in 1300. Bryson 2004, p. 11, notes that *almost, altogether* and *alone* were once *all most, all together* and *all one*. Australia may be the first place *alright* is accepted, but it's not all right yet. Correction: it was not all right when I began this book last century, but it is alright now, in the 2020's.

Silent H in initial GH — *aghast, ghost*

Rule 2-106 At the beginning of a syllable <gh> spells [g].
Reason The bad blender [g] is never going to blend with unvoiced [h]. The digraph was used to replace the letter Yogh, which spelt a sound which was then silenced. It does, however, prevent <e> softening <g> to spell [j], as in *ghetto*. It also appears in a few English words in which <g> is not followed by either <e> or <i> or <y>. Why? Caxton liked the look of these words in the Netherlands where he trained as a printer. When he came home and set up his printing press, the first one in England, he printed these words the Dutch way. (No doubt he found their {*gherkins*} were delicious too.} A few newly adopted foreign words use <gh> to spell [g] too.

List 2-106 These are English words which Caxton changed. The vowel after <gh> is long.
AGHAST [agast] or [agarst], originally written as *agast,* but then matched to *ghost*. GHASTLY.
GHOST [gohst], originally written *gast*, but in the Netherlands spelt *gheest*. GHOSTLY.
   {We shall meet the third spelling which Caxton changed when we meet *ghoul*.}

Remember how terminal <st> made <o> spell long [oh] in *most*? It makes *ghost* spell [gohst].
Due to the vowel shift in *ghastly,* and in *aghast,* <a> spells [ar] in the south of England but still spells [a] in the north.

List 2-106 continued: Foreign words in which <gh> spells [g], (Cummings, p. 352).
GHAT [gort], OGHAM [og-əm] , GHETTO [ge-toh], SPAGHETTI [spar-ge-tee]. YATAGHAN [yat-a-gən]. Newer adoptions GHARRY, GHAZI, GHAT. Proper Noun GHANA [garn-ar].

Silent G with M and N — *phlegm, sign.*
Rule 2-107 Terminal <gn> spells [n] and lengthens preceding vowels in the same syllable.
Reason We have seen other nasal blends lengthen vowels, e.g., in *mild.* Well, *sign* follows that pattern. But [gn] is a difficult blend and so the longer, nasal [n] sound flows over the shorter sound and silences it. We find it is easier to say the consonants which do not block much breath, because we need breath to stay alive and do not like to stop breath flowing. When saying [n] and [m] air goes unblocked out the nose. When saying [r] and [l] the mouth is open at all times, and the same goes for vowels, which do not block air at all when we say them. All the others, which are all consonants, are called obstruents because they block a significant amount of our breath. From this we know that, in a cluster which is difficult to say, [l], [r], [m] or [n] will flow over and blot out the other consonant, in order to keep breath flowing.

All words ending <gn> were introduced from France after the Norman Invasion. They belong to the many words we can call Invasion Words. Modern words do not use this method to lengthen vowels. Only a few old terminal <gn> words remain in English.

List 2-107 Terminal cluster <gn> spells [n] and lengthens preceding vowels.
<ign> spells [In] ALIGN, ASSIGN, BENIGN, CONSIGN, CO-SIGN, DESIGN, ENSIGN, MALIGN, RESIGN, SIGN, SIGN OFF, SIGN ON, SIGN UP.
<ugn> spells [yoon] IMPUGN, OPPUGN, REPUGN.
French <agn> spells [ayn] CHAMPAGNE *silent <e>*
French <ogn> spells [ohn] COLOGNE *silent <e>*
French <ign> spells [een] CHIGNON [sheen-yon]

Stem words do not have <gn> inside them in the same syllable, except for SIGNOR and SIGNORITA in which <g> is a silent diacritic and so <gn> is not a blend. The Spanish words *señor* and *señorita* were adopted and adapted, the squiggly diacritic replaced by <g> in a bad attempt to show <n> spells [ŋ].

Rule 2-108 Letters which are silenced in blends can spell sounds when the blend becomes a cluster at syllable boundaries.
Reason Affixes can release letters from blends, as in *signal* and {*acknowledge*} in which the silent <g> of *sign* and the silent <k> of {*knowledge*} is free to spell again. They can spell again, but only if the affix is strong enough to pull into the next syllable. More on this soon, in Soothing Sonorants and Obstructive Obstruents

Rule 2-109 Terminal <gm> spells [m] and terminal <igm> spells [Im].
Reason In the impossible blend [gm], [m] flows back over [g] because [g] blocks more breath than [m]. The only vowel <gm> lengthens is [i] to [I], in *paradigm,* which is the only English word ending <igm>.
List 2-109 <gm> spells [m].
APOTHEGM [ap-oh-them], EPIPHRAGM [ep-ee-gram], PARADIGM [pa-ra-dIm], PHLEGM, [flem], {DIAPHRAGM} [di-a-fram].

Rule 2-110 Word initial <gn> spells [n].

Reason As we have heard, in a difficult blend the consonant which blocks least air wins out, swamps the other. Long ago <gn> spelt [g-n]. Now <gn> spells just [n] at the beginning of words and they are all Old English words.

Rebel GNU

Rebel's Reason *Gnu* spells [gu-noo] because it is not an Old English word. It has been adopted from people who do not find [gn] too hard to say. As we know, it was not always too hard in English.

List 2-110 Word initial <gn> spells [n]

GNASH, GNAT, GNATHIC INDEX, GNOMISH, GNOSIS, GNOSTIC.

Rule 2-111 Initial <kn> spells [n].

Reason Long ago the English pronounced both consonants in <kn>, as [kn]. We have already met some words like *knot* with a silent [k] and heard about Vikings and their *knapsacks* and the Viking hero Knut [ka-nuut] who was king of all England, 1016 - 1035, and a very wise one.

<u>Not needed but nice to know</u>. Lazy people always want their leaders to do everything for them and they like to believe that presidents and kings are powerful enough to fix all their problems. King Knut showed his people that he was just like them, not super-human, when he sat on the beach and ordered the tide not to come in. When the sea began to wash around him, he said to his people "See, I am not all-powerful. You must not rely on me for everything. Everybody has to do their bit." The wrong story got out. Instead of passing on the king's wisdom, they said he was such a big head that he thought he could turn the tide. Never mind. The original sound of this wise king's name has been preserved by changing his written name from Knut to Canute, when people stopped letting <kn> spell [kn]. When they stopped saying this blend, they let the [n] wash backwards over the [k], just like the [n] washes back over the [g] in *sign*, for, as we know, when two consonants are hard to blend the consonant which obstructs less breath flows over the other consonant. Another great leader, (by chance with the same [k-vowel-n] start to his name), John F. Kennedy, repeated King Canute's message when he became President on Jan 20th, 1961: "My fellow Americans: ask not what your country can do for you — ask what you can do for your country." <u>Now back to things we need to know.</u>

List 2-111 We have met some of these words earlier.

KNACK, KNAP, KNELL, KNELT, KNICK-KNACK*, KNIFING, KNIGHT, KNIGHTED, KNIGHTLY, KNIGHTS, KNIT, KNITS, KNITTED, KNITTING, KNOB, KNOBBLY, KNOBBY, KNOCK, KNOCKING, KNOCKOFF, KNOCKS, KNOLL, KNOT, KNOTGRASS, KNOTLESS, KNOTS, KNOTTED, KNOTTILY, KNOTTINESS, KNOTTING, KNOTTY, KNUBBY, KNUCKLE, KNUCKLEBALL, KNUCKLES, KNUCKLING, KNUCKLY.

*The hyphen in *knick-knack* prevents <kk> which is not usually accepted in English. Words like *quokka* and *pukka* are recent adoptions.

Soothing Sonorants and Obstructive Obstruents

The sonorant consonants are special. They are nearly as smooth as vowels because they are not spat out like [t], squeezed out like [z], puffed out like [p], gurgled out like [g] and so on. That's because [l] [r] [w] [y] [m] [n] and [ŋ] block less breath than other consonants, are less obstruent. Later we shall see that [r] prefers to mix with vowels rather than consonants, given the choice, and [l] clings to vowels, too. In some words, e.g., *folk* and *child,* it changes the sound of vowels.

What about [m] and [n]? Yes, they are attracted to vowels too. In *sign,* [n] is so attracted to [I] that it flows back over [g], silencing it. Only when *sign* [sIn] becomes *signal* [sig-nal] is [g] released from silence. It's released because [n] is then attracted to the closer vowel, [a]. In *phlegm* [flem] [g] is also silenced, only heard again in *phlegmatic* [fleg-mat-ik] when [m] is attracted to the closer vowel, [a]. In *damn* air flows continuously after the mouth closes after [a] to say [m] because it flows then through the nose. To add the sound [n] would involve opening the mouth a bit, and blocking air with the tongue behind the top teeth on the gum. It's easier to just say [m]. When some suffixes are added, e.g., in *damnable*, [n] is attracted to [a] in the suffix, changes syllables, and ends its silence. Flexible suffixes cannot change stem words which is why letters remain silent when a flexible suffix is added. For instance, <mb> in *numb* continues to spell [m] in *numbed, numbing, number* and *numbest*. Only some deriving suffixes bring a silenced consonant to life again. For instance, when the suffix starts with <a>, we hear <b> spell [b] again, as in *bombard* [bom-bard] and *damnable* [dam-nable]. This never happens when the deriving suffix <er> is added. For instance, if a chemical creates numbness it could be called a *number* [num-er], and a man who releases bombs is a *bomber* [bom-er]. In both, the <b> remains silent. So it is *signal* [sig-nal] but *signer* [sIn-er]. The deriving suffix —*ing* is used to make nouns, as in 'the *bombing* continued', 'the *signing* took place', and adjectives, as in 'the *damning* evidence', in which <b> remains silent. We shall see the influence of <a> again when we meet {*damnation*}, in which <n> is no longer silent.

Rule 2-112 Consonants which have been silenced in blends of sonorants and obstruents can spell sounds again when blends are split either by prefixes ending in a vowel or deriving suffixes starting with a vowel.

Reason As explained above.

Rebel {SIGNAGE}

Rebel's Reason The suffix -*age* turns a singular noun into a plural collective noun and therefore it serves here as a flexie suffix and as such cannot split a blend, (to my mind).

List 2-112 The first word has an obstruent and a sonorant consonant blend which is split by the affix so that the silenced consonant 'speaks' again.
BOMB and BOMBARD, {BOMBARDIER]; DAMN and DAMNABLE, {DAMNATION}; {DEIGN} [dayn] and DIGNITY; GNOSTIC [nostik] and AGNOSTIC; {DIAPHRAGM} and FRAGMATIC, FRAGMENT; IMPUGN, (bound stem *pugn*) and PUNACITY; REPUGN and REPUGNANT; MALIGN and MALIGNANT; PARADIGM* and PARADIGMATIC; RESIGN and {RESIGNATION};SIGN and SIGNAL, {SIGNATURE}, SIGNET, SIGNIFY; SOLEMN and {SOLEMNIZE}; PHLEGM and PHLEGMATIC; KNOW and ACKNOWLEDGE.

This is the end of Part Two. Isn't that *super-duper*? But why don't we say *duper-super*? In his book *The Language Instinct* Steven Pinker says that we know instinctively how much breath each word-sound blocks. Vowels block air the least, and the Big Blenders — semi-vowels [w] and [y] and the sonorant consonants [n] and [m] and [l] and [r] — hardly block air. As we know, the consonants which do obstruct air flow substantially are called obstruents. Plosives are the most obstructive and they are [b], [d], [g], [k], [p], [t]. Fricatives obstruct much less air and they are [f], [h], [s], [sh], [th], [v], [z], [zh]. Affricates, [ch] and [j], start as plosives and end as fricatives and so they obstruct more air than fricatives but less than plosives. He says we say *super-duper* and *willy-nilly* (not *nilly-willy*) because we instinctively follow the rule that **the word beginning with the less obstruent consonant always comes before the word beginning with the more obstruent consonant.**

So, isn't it nice to know that we know things we never knew we knew? Now you know why *walkie* always comes first in *walkie-talkie*. It explains the order of *wing-ding, wham-bam, razza-matazz, razzle-dazzle, rub-a-dub-dub, roly-poly, loosey-goosey, mumbo-jumbo* and *namby-pamby*. Also *jelly belly, jiggery pokery, hanky panky, hokey pokey, higgledy piggledy, Humpty Dumpty, hickory dickory dock, hunky dory, helter skelter* and *harum scarum*.

Let's bake a Language Layer Cake to celebrate the end of Part Two.
We've met all sorts of words, a few of the original Celt and Latin words, those which arrived with the Anglo-Saxons, some Dutch and Viking words and many of the 10,000 French words which were added

after the Norman Invasion. We've also met lots of prefixes and suffixes and heard how the English people made up new words, using Latin and Greek whole words, or "spare parts" from them.

Linguists see English words in three layers. The bottom layer is full of old or early English words. There is a middle layer of Norman and French 'invasion words' and the top layer is full of invented words which have Latin or Greek stems and lots of prefixes and suffixes, besides all the keenly welcomed foreign words. The bottom layer is squashed by the top layers and plenty of old words have been wiped out or ground down and changed a great deal due to French being England's official language for three hundred years. The layers can be called Old English, Middle English and Modern English.

This gives us ideas for making our Language Layer Cake. What shall we use for each layer? A plain German lardy cake for the bottom layer? A French gateau for the middle layer? What about the top layer? Full of cinnamon and spice, choc bits too, to represent all the affixes. Let's ice it with slang words. Will these icing slang words remain, gain respectability, or lose popularity and drop off? Only time will tell.

That's for the cooks amongst us! Now, for our keen gardeners, here are some writing tips, so that you can grow your own words. We need to know how to join affixes onto stem words if we want to grow or make our own words. Prof Cummings gives really good details on this process in his book, Chapter 10. Here is his advice in brief.

<u>Relevant Writing Rules about affixes.</u>

<u>Prefixes</u> The prefixes which do not change when they are joined on to stem words are *re-* and *un-*. If a prefix ends in the same letter which starts the stem word it does not change e.g., *mis spell* becomes *misspell*. Prefixes change to make speech easier. They follow the blending rules and we already know them: vowels and semi-vowels blend with all consonants; unvoiced consonants blend with everything except Bad Blenders; and Big Blenders (*r, l, m, n, w, y*) blend with everything but not much with themselves. This is why *com* blends on to a word beginning *b, p* or *m*. It drops *m* before *h* and all vowels to avoid closing lips between *o* and *h*, or *o* and a vowel: *cohabitate* not *comhabitate* and *coagulate* not *comagulate*. It changes *m* to *l, n* or *r* before *l, n,* and *r* because *m* does not mix well with other Big Blenders, hence, *collate, connect* and *correct*. When a prefix changes to make matching joining letters like this, we say it "assimilates", becomes similar. When it changes but does not exactly match up, we say it "partially assimilates" which is what *com-* does before all other word starts, for it changes to *con-* as in *confess*. There are rules and some exceptions to the rules for the way all prefixes join on to stem words and they all follow the blending rules. That is why the prefix *ex-* can also be *ef-* or *e-*; *sub-* can be *sur-, sup-, sus-* or *suc-*; *in-* can be *im-* or *ad-* can be *ac,-af-, ag-, al-, an-, ap-, ar-, as-* or *at-*; *dis-* can be *dif-* or *di-*; *ob-* can be *of-, op-, o-* or *os-*; *ab-* can be *abs-* or *a-*; *syn-* can be *syl-, sym-* or *sy-*. The prefix *in-* can mean *not* or *in*. When it means *not* it can be written *im, in* or *ir*. It is *im* before <m> and <p>, as in *immortal* and *impious*; *ir* before <r> as in *irregular* and *in* before all else, as in *insane*. When it means *in* it can also be written *en* or *em*, from the French. It's *em* before <p> and <b> — *empower* and *embolden* — and *en* before all else, e.g., *enfold*. Yes, there are rules and there are reasons for those rules, as the Prof. reassures us.

<u>Suffixes</u> To twin or not to twin when adding suffixes, that is the question. We know twin letters form 'double gates' and so when we add suffixes <ing>, <ed> and all the rest which begin with a vowel — complete list under Affixes in the appendix — we build a double gate to keep the preceding vowel short, by twinning the final consonant, as in *rip — ripping, ripped; wet — wetter, wettest*. We do this before the suffix <le>, too, as in *rip, ripple*. We know why *riffle* rhymes with *ripple* and *rifle* rhymes with *pie full*.

We know that consonant digraphs, e.g., <ph> are never twinned for they look like double gates already. Prof Cummings, (pp. 167 and 176), tells us to twin only if we can say "yes" to the following five questions and then "no" to the sixth:

1st Does the suffix start with a vowel?
2nd Is it to go on a single consonant letter spelling one single sound?
3rd Does that final consonant follow a single vowel letter?

148

4th Does that vowel letter spell a short and stressed vowel sound?
5th Does that vowel sound remain short and stressed after the suffix is added?
6th Is the suffix one of the shortening suffixes, such as *–ic, -ical, -ity, -id, -it, -ism*?
   Let's see if we need to twin in a variety of words.
"No" to 1st knocks out twinning in *droplet* and *hotly,* but *hottest* is a YES
"No" to 2nd knocks out twinning in *foxy* and *oxen* but *hottest* is a YES.
"No" to 3rd knocks out twinning in *swishing* and *bombing,* {*flooding*} and {*deafen*} but *hottest* is a YES.
"No" to 4th knocks out twinning in *finalist, profiting;* and *limited* but *hottest* is a "YES" because all vowels in single-syllable words are considered stressed. Note that even though [i] is stressed in *solidify* it was not stressed before the suffix was added to *solid.*
"No" to 5th for *hottest* means it fulfils all 5 conditions.

Prof Cummings tells us that Twinning Rules do not apply to compound nouns, like *redeye, dropout* and other compound words, like *forever.* The Prof also says that Twinning Rules only apply to free stems. When suffixes are attached to bound stems, stems which cannot stand alone as words, then there is no twinning, e.g., no <tt> in *critic,* no <gg> in *ligament,* no <nn> in *condominium* because *crit, lig* and *domin* cannot stand alone as words, are not free stems.

Complications arise when a word is stressed rather evenly, e.g., *kidnap,* but the Prof. says that words prefer to be regular than irregular – we've seen that with verbs as more and more join the regulars – and so we write *kidnapped, kidnapping* and accept that almost even stress gives "Yes" to 4.

Further complications arise in most two-syllable words ending <l>, like *level, tunnel* or *devil.* OED uses twins when adding suffixes to such words, as in *levelling, tunneller* or *devilled,* but not when adding the suffixes *–ic, -ical, -ity, -id, -it, -ism* because as we know they keep the preceding vowel short without using double gates. So it is *equalled,* but *equality.* We do not twin <l> in *equalize* for, as we shall learn, the suffix *–ize* is a stressed one and so the vowel before it loses stress and it's "No" to Q. 5. Of the words which do not end with <l>, only a few are debatable. OED does not suggest twinning for Cummings' short list of debateable words, *benefit, brevet, facet, focus, gossip, hocus-pocus,* {*worship, chorus*}.

The discussion deepens when Cummings notes that British dictionaries in general choose to twin final <l> and Americans choose not to and some say that it is only the suffixes <ed>, <ing>, <er>, <est> which use twinning after weak vowels. So, we might read *paneller* but *panelist* in American dictionaries. Enjoy growing your own words wherever you live. Return to Reading Rules.

Part Three

In Part Three we'll decode doublets and meet Fairy E and Bossy R and Little Imp. We'll glide vowels on paper planes over syllable boundaries, all of which is to learn new ways to spell long vowels. We'll meet Greek Y too.

In Part One we met box and the plural was boxes;
We learnt the plural of ox should be oxen not oxes.
Now we'll meet goose, and hear two are called geese;
And learn that plural of moose should never be meese.
Just why we shall see, once we've listed *coo-ee*.

We saw in Parts 1 and 2 various ways to spell long sounds. We learnt that terminal vowel letters spell long sounds, as in *ma* and *pa, be* and *she, tie* and *bikini, go* and *do, blue* and *you* and *tutu*. We saw nasal blends "turning" them into long sounds in a few old words, like *yolk, find* and *range,* even when a blended letter is silenced as in *sign*, or a blend has faded all together as in *thigh*. We have used Orm's Law, which follows long, stressed vowels, with a single consonant, as in *legal*.
 In some languages, e.g., Swahili and Dutch, a very simple way of spelling long vowel sounds is used, for the vowel letter is simply written twice. This system is used a little in English too. Adjacent identical consonants are called twins, but identical vowels make a doublet, according to Prof. Cummings.

Doublets — *baa, beet, boot, vacuum.*

The Doublet Rules:
Rule 3-0A Doublets are very stable. They do not change the sounds they spell when suffixes are added or when they are stressed or unstressed.

Rule 3-0B When terminal <s> follows a doublet it spells [z].
Reason As we know, terminal <s> spells [z] after stressed vowels. Terminal doublets spell long sounds and long sounds are stressed sounds, so terminal <s> after doublets always spells [z], whether at the end of plural nouns or at the end of verbs.

Rule 3-0C When terminal <se> follows doublets in nouns and adjectives, it spells [s].
Reason This stops the stem word looking and sounding like a plural word. In the same way *dense* and *dens* differ, this differentiates singular *goose* [goos] and the plural of *goo: goos* [gooz]. Another example is the adjective *loose* and the plural of slang *loo: loos* [looz]. Hear the difference in, 'The moose moos for his mate.'

Rule 3-0D When terminal <se> follows doublets in verbs it spells [z].
Reason This is for the same reason <s> spells [z] at the end of verbs — because verbs are stressed at the end of words. Voiced [z] gives a stronger ending to verbs than its unvoiced partner [s]. "We house (verb) the orphans in our house (noun)." The verb is [howz] and the noun is [hows].
If it wasn't for the Curse of the Dagger — the fear of Zed which is the Sign of the Dagger — we could use <z> and <s> with no need of silent <e>. Even when we do use <z> it is followed by a silent <e>, as in 'We will freeze if he frees us into the snow.' We shall meet exceptions, like the noun *cheese,* but, on the whole, Rule 3-0 helps us differentiate, on paper, the difference between verbs and plurals on the one hand and other words. We shall find in Part Four that this Doublet Rule also works for ordinary digraphs — separates *please* from *pleas* and *tease* from *teas*.

Doublet <aa>

Rule 3-1 Doublet <aa> spells [ar] but is seldom used.

Reason This is an Old English way to spell long vowel sounds – simply write the letter twice! Old English was a Germanic language. Vowel pairs still spell long vowels in German, Dutch and other languages which use Germanic spelling codes. In English, the use of this code reduced under French rule. We only see <ee> and <oo> in our words now. When <aa> is used, it spells [ar], its old (Continental) long sound, not the lifted Anglo long sound [ay].

List 3-1
AADWOLF <o>= [uu], BAA, BAZAAR, KRAAL, SALAAM, {AADVARK}.   Proper Nouns SAATCHI, HAARLEM, in Holland.

Q. What about *Aaron?*
Ans. *Aaron* spells [air-on] and we'll see why when we see what Bossy R does between vowels.

When writing Aboriginal languages, doublets spell long vowels. Hence, in Yinggarda, *thaa* (mouth) spells [thar]; *paabaa* (silly) spells [par-bar] and *nguurru* (horse) spells [ŋoo-roo], with a rolled [r]. Spelling in Yinggarda is easy because it is logical and consistent. The sound [ar] is always written <aa>, never <ar>, for <r> spells [r]. *Kardu* (man) spells [ku-r-doo] and *nyarlu* (woman) spells [nyu-r-loo]. The twin letters <rr> spell a rolled [r] sound which gets very close to a 'trilled' [d]. So [r] in *mara* (hand) vibrates the tongue far less than the rolled [r] in *warralanyi* (sing). It rolls twice in *warrengurru*, (rainbow – literally, "eye-song"). Note: in Ab'l languages, <a> spells Continental short [u] and long [ar].

Doublet <ee>

Rule 3-2 Doublet <ee> spells [ee].

Reason Before the Great Vowel Shift, see appendix, <ee> spelt [ay]. This long sound was elevated to [ee] in the GVS but words continued to use the old spelling, <ee>.

At times, the doublet <ee> is broken up with a hyphen to stop it spelling [ee], e.g., *re-echo, re-edit, re-eject, re-elect, re-emit, re-enlist, re-enroll, re-entry, re-equip, re-erect* and *re-establish* are all hyphenated in OPD 1983. (Also, the doublet is sometimes broken with an apostrophe and then no longer has to spell [ee], e.g., the three old abbreviations E'EN [een] for *even*, E'ER [air] for {*ever*}, NE'ER [nair] for {*never*}.
Rebels FREEST, {FREER} and French adoptions like MATINEE, MELEE, NEGLIGEE, PROTEGEE.
Rebels' Reasons Doublet <ee> does not spell [ee] in {*freer*}, *freest*. Even if we wrote *free, free-er, free-est*, a hyphen is no excuse for triplets, which are forbidden. So, we write *freest*, which spells [free-est] and we shall see later that, in {*freer*}, <eer> spells [ee-er]. Doublets are very stable and suffixes just add on, even if the suffix starts with a vowel, e.g., *kneeing, freeing*. The one exception is when a suffix starting with <e> adds on to a stem ending <ee>, as in *freest, kneed* and *freed*, to avoid <eee>.

Matinee etc. are rebels which can claim 'Diplomatic Immunity' for they are foreign words. In France, <ee> still spells [ay], as it used to in England before the GVS. French words terminating <ee>, sometimes <ée>, have been adopted into English, but still spelt and said the French way. Accent marks are still used on them in some English dictionaries, as in the following, from OPD: *matinée* [mat-in-ay], *mêlée* [mel-ay], *négligée* [neg-li-jay], *protégée* [pro-te-jay]. These accents marks, (diacritics) are usually eliminated in English texts.

Other words, like *absentee*, end in <ee> spells [ee]. Although the French use <ee> as their past participle suffix, it does not always match up in meaning with the English <ed> past participle suffix. An *addressee* is *addressed*, an *examinee* is *examined* but a *referee* is not *referred*, for a *referee* does the referring, *refers* others, and a *lessee* is not leased. On the whole, <ee> does have the meaning of <ed> but it's best to check.
<u>Relevant Writing Rules.</u>

Digraph <ea> ends only six words, *flea, pea, sea, lea, plea* and *tea,* to separate them from *flee, pee, see, lee,* and *tee.* There was no need for *plee* to change its spelling to *plea* — it just happened that way, maybe to match *please.*

Digraph <ee> starts only two words, *eel* and *eerie,* due to the 16th century effort to prevent <ee> from starting words, (Cummings, p. 259).

BTW, doublet <ee> and digraph <ea> spell only 17% of all [ee] sounds in English words, usually just before a terminal consonant, e.g., *beech, been, each.* Return to Reading Rules.

List 3-2 <ee> spells [ee]. *VS* means <a> in these words can spell [a] or [ar], just as *dance* can spell [[dans] or [darns].

ABSENTEE, ADDRESSEE, AGREE, AGREEABLE*, AGREED*, AGREEMENT, AMPUTEE, ANISEED, ANTIFREEZE, ASSIGNEE, ASLEEP, ATTENDEE, BAKSHEESH, BALEEN, BANSHEE, BED-SHEET, BEE, BEECH TREE, BEEF, BEEFY, BEEHIVE, BEEKEEPER, BEELINE, BEEN*, BEEP, BEESWAX, BEET, BEETS, BEETLE, BESEECH Δ, BETWEEN, BETWEEN-TIMES, BLEED Δ, BLEEDING, BLEEP, BLEEPER, BO-PEEP, BREECH, BREECHES, BREED Δ, BREEDING, BREEZE, BREEZILY, BREEZY*, BUCKSHEE, BUCKTEETH, BUMBLE-BEE, BUNGEE, CANTEEN, CAREEN, CHEEK, CHEEKBONE, CHEEKY, CHEEKILY, CHEEKINESS, CHEEP, CHEESE, CHEESECAKE, CHEETAH, CHICKADEE, CHIMPANZEE, COFFEE, COFFEECAKE, COFFEEPOT, COLLEEN, COMMITTEE, CONSIGNEE, CORROBOREE, COTTONSEED, CREED, CREEK, CREEL, CREEP Δ, CREEPY, CREEPINESS, CROSS-BREED PUP, DECREE, DEED, DEEM, DEEP, DEEPEN, DEEP-FRY, DEER, DEGREE, DEVOTEE, DISAGREE, DISCREET, DUNGAREES, ENFEEBLE, ESCAPEE, ESTEEM, EXAMINEE, EXCEED, FEE, FEEBLE, FEEBLEMINDED, FEED Δ, FEEDBACK, FEEDLOT, FEEL Δ, FEELING, FEET, FIFTEEN, FIFTEENTH, FILIGREE, FLEE Δ, FLEECE, FLEECY, FLEET, FLEETINGLY, FRANCHISEE, FREE, FREELY, FREE WHEEL, FREE WHEELING, FREEDOM, FREEHAND, FREEHOLD, FREELANCE *VS*, FREEMAN, FREEMASONRY, FREEWILL, FREEZE Δ, FRISBEE, FRICASSEE, GEESE*, GHEE* *silent* <h>, GENTEEL*, GIDGEE*, GLEE, GRANDEE, GREED, GREEDY, GREEN, GREENNESS, GREEN SALAD, GREENFINCH, GREENS, GREENY, GREET, GREETING, HAREEM, HASHEESH, HEED, HEEL, WELL-HEELED, HEELLESS, HELPMEET, HUMBLE-BEE, HUMVEE*, INDEED, INDISCREET, INTERNEE, IRREDEEMABLE, JAMBOREE, JEEP, JUBILEE, KEDGEREE, KEEL, KEEN, KEEP Δ, KEEP FIT, KEEP UP, KNEE* *silent* <k>, KNEE-CAP, KNEED* *verb*, KNEEL* Δ *silent* <k>, LATEEN, LEE, LEECH, LEEK, LEES, LEGATEE, LESSEE, LEVEE, LICENSEE, LICHEE, LOCK-KEEPER, LORIKEET, LYCHEE, MALLEE*, MANATEE, MANGOSTEEN, MEED, MEEK, MEET Δ, MEETING, MEET UP WITH, NANKEEN, NEED, NEEDLE, NEEDLECRAFT *VS,* NEEDLEWOMAN, NEEDLESS, NEEDFUL, NEEDY, NEEM TREE, NEEP, NOMINEE, OVERWEENING, PARAKEET, PEDIGREE, PEE, PEEK, PEEL, PEELINGS, PEEL OFF, PEEP, PEEP-PEEP, PEERLESS, PEEVE, PEEVISH, PEEWEE, PEEWIT, PHARISEE, PREEN, PRITHEE *obs.,* PROCEED, PUTTEE, QUEEN, QUEENLY, QUEER, QUEERLY, REDEEM, REDEEMABLE, REED, REEDY, REEF*, REEL, REEL, REFEREE, REFUGEE, RUPEE, SCHMEER, SCREE, SCREECH, SCREED, SCREEN, SCREEN PRINTING, SCREEN TEST, SEE Δ, SEE RED, SEE THE BACK OF, SEE, SEE TO, SEED, RUN TO SEED, SEEDBED, SEEDLESS, SEEDLING, SEEDSMAN, SEEDPOD, SEEDY, SEEING THAT, SEEK Δ, SEEKING, SEEL, SEEM, SEEMLY, SEEN*, SEETHE [dh], SEMISWEET, SETTEE, SEVENTEEN, SEVENTEENTH, SHEEN, SHEEP, SHEET, SILKSCREEN, SIXTEEN, SIXTEENTH, SLEEK, SLEEP Δ, SLEEPING PILL, SLEEP ON IT, SLEEPY, SLEEPINESS, SLEET, SLEEVE, SMITHEREENS* [dh], SPEECH, SPEECHLESS, SPEED Δ, SPEEDO, SPEEDY, SPLEEN, SPREE, SQUEEGEE, SQUEEZING, STEED, STEEL, STEELY, STEEP, STEEPEN, STEEPLE, STEEPLEJACK, STREET, SUBCOMMITTEE, SUCCEED,

152

SUNSCREEN, SUTTEE, SWEEP ∆, SWEEPING, SWEEPINGS, SWEET, SWEETNESS, SWEETLY, SWEETEN, SWEETENING, SWEETISH, TEE, TEED*, TEEM, TEEN, TEENS, TEENY, TEEPEE, TEES, TEETH, TEETHE [dh], TEETOTAL, THEE [dh], THREE, THREEFOLD, THREE HANDED, THREE WHEELING, THUGEE, TOFFEE, TRANSFEREE, TREE, TREE TOP, TRUSTEE, TUREEN*, TWEE, TWEEDLE, TWEEN, UNBREECH, UPKEEP, VEE, VELVETEEN, WARRANTEE, WEE, hence *weeny*, WEED, WEEDY, WEEK, WEEKEND, WEEKLY, WEENY, WEEP ∆, WEEPING, WEEPY, WEEVIL, WHEEDLE, WHEEL, WHEEZE, WILDEBEEST. <u>Proper Nouns</u>, GALILEE, GREECE, GREEK adj. <u>Names</u> ASHLEEN, CATHLEEN, COLLEEN, KATHLEEN, Plus CHINCHERINCHEE, a South African flower. <u>Slang</u> GEEK, GEE, GEE-UP, GEE WHIZ!, GREENBACK, UMPTEEN, WEE-WEE, YANKEE, YIPPEE.

∆ These words are irregular verbs from long ago, marked to remind us they are like old mountains, worn down but still with us. Some have changed into regular verbs in one place but not another, like *kneel*, for this can be *kneeled* or *knelt*.

Irregular verbs - present, past and p. participle (*beseech, seek* and *see* will come later)
BLEED ∆, BLED ∆, BLED ∆
BREED ∆, BRED ∆, BRED ∆
CREEP ∆, CREPT ∆, CREPT ∆
FEED ∆, FED ∆, FED ∆
FLEE ∆, FLED ∆, FLED ∆
FREEZE ∆, FROZEN ∆, FROZEN ∆
KEEP ∆, KEPT ∆, KEPT ∆
KNEEL ∆, KNELT ∆ /KNEELED, KNELT ∆ /KNEELED
MEET ∆, MET ∆, MET ∆
SLEEP ∆, SLEPT ∆, SLEPT ∆
SPEED ∆, SPED ∆ /SPEEDED, SPED ∆ /SPEEDED
SWEEP ∆, SWEPT ∆, SWEPT ∆
WEEP ∆, WEPT ∆, WEPT ∆

Agreed and *teed* and *kneed* obey the No Triplets Rule. Hyphens are not used here, as they would be silly inside a syllable, and <eee> is a 'no-no'. *As we know, free stems, like *agree*, take <able>, not <ible>, as a suffix: *agreeable*.

Been and *seen* are past participles of the verbs *to be* and *to see*. As in *given* or *taken*, we add <en> to *be* and get *been*. When we add <en> to *see* we do not write triple <e> because triple letters are not allowed, so it is just *seen*.

Cheese [cheez] and *geese* [gees] look the same now but, long ago, *geese* ended in <s>, *goose* too. In Old English, *cheese* was *cyse*. It was then *cese* in Middle English, with <c> spelling [ch]. Because <s> had a vowel on either side of it, it spelt [z], as in *manganese, these* and *journalese* — more importantly, in a word of that era, *diocese*. I read it, on reddit.com, that Roman Catholics say [dIoh-seez] and Anglo Catholics (Anglicans) say [dIoh-sees]. Since the Church of England did not split from the Church of Rome until 1534, one presumes everyone said [dIoh-seez] and [cheez] in Middle English and carried this on into Modern English. Both words now end with <e> to show they are not plural words, as in 'one chee and two chees,' being two vital Chinese life sources, and as in 'one gee and two gees,' being two exclamations of Gee!

Geese spells [gees] not [jees] because it is a very old word, like the word *get*, [get] not [jet].

Geek [geek] is slang and does not have to obey rules, does not have to spell [jeek].

Genteel is a cousin-word to *gentle*, used when someone is putting on a show of high-born manners, (Burton, p. 76).

Ghee spells [gee] because <h> insulates <g> from the softening affect of <e>.

**Gidgee* is Abl. name of a tree or a spear from that tree in W.Aust. First <g> is hard [g].
**Humvee* is an acronym for "highly mobile multipurpose wheeled vehicle", (Fleck 2007).
**Mallee* is from an Ab'l language in Western Victoria, to describe thicket vegetation. (Blake, p. 98)
The plural of **reef* is *reefs*, not *reeves*.
**Seen* see *been*.
**Smith* spells [smith] but *smithereens* spells [smidhereens] because this comes from the Irish word, *smidirin*, meaning 'little fragments'. The Irish [d] has translated into English as [dh].
Tureen spells [tyureen] and also [chooreen] if its yod fuses with [t], as in *tulip*.
**Knee, kneed* and *kneel* "carry culture." Although <k> in these words and in *knelt*, no longer spells [k], it links us to the history of how our language evolved as described below.

<u>Not needed but nice to know</u>. Long ago some people migrated west across Europe, spreading their Indo-European language over the top of some resident languages and around others. As they walked along, they called their feet "pods" and their knees "genoos" because "genoo" meant bend. When the people went west beyond Greece they split up. Some went north and some went south. The ones who went on through Italy only changed "pod" into "ped", just a vowel change. The ones who went north into Germany and eventually into England made big changes, for they changed consonants.

They changed *pod* into *fot* which became *foot*. They changed *genoo* into *kenee*, [ke-nee]. Then it became just [nee] but the letter <k> remained, like a key to unlock history, to remind us of the past.

When *genoo* reached France, it changed in sound to [jenoo]. When *pod* reached France it became *pas*, went on to England and became *pad* and *path*. So, you can see where *tripod, pedestal, pedal, genuflect* (bend the knee) and even *genuine* came from. In Roman times a new father was given his baby but he did not hold it on his knee, **genu**, until he had examined it. If he decided that it was his baby, that he was the father, he held it close, on his lap. When everyone saw that it was on his knee they said, 'It's **genuine**'. An alternative explanation is that it comes more directly from Latin *genuinus* meaning 'native, natural, innate,' from *gignere* meaning 'to beget, produce'.

Some of the people who spoke the extinct ancestor language, which we call the Indo-European language, migrated east into India. Linguists have worked this out by matching up words like *raj* and *rex*, both meaning "regal leader". Linguists look at the beginnings of words to match them to their relations or cousin-words, not their endings, e.g., *paper - papyrus*.

<u>Relevant Writing Rule.</u> *Exceed, proceed* and *succeed* do not use <cede> to spell [seed] because <cede> means go back, give in, yield as in *cede, concede, accede, recede, precede, secede*. So, we use <ceed> to spell [seed] in these three words because they are all "go forward" words. *Exceed* means "out go" from Latin *ex* for "out", and *cedere* "to go". *Proceed* is *procedere* in Latin meaning "go forward". *Succeed* [suk-seed], comes from *sub*, meaning "under or next below, next after" and "go", *cedere*. Hence "next to go," "next in line," as in "The successor succeeded to the throne." The 'successful' meaning of *to succeed*, i.e., "to turn out well, to have a favourable result," began in the 15th century when folk shortened "he succeeded well," to just "he succeeded." <u>Return to Reading Rules.</u>

Cluster <eer>
Rule 3-3 Cluster <eer> spells [eer], which rhymes with *ear* and *hear*.
Rebel {FREER} in which we shall see <eer> spells [ee-er].
List 3-3
BALLADEER, BANDOLEER, BEER, BEERY, BUCCANEER, CAREER, CAMELEER, CANNONEER, CHEER, CHEER UP, CHEERFUL, CHEERFULLY, CHEERFULNESS, CHEERLESS, COMMANDEER, DEER, DEERSKIN, DOMINEER, ENGINEER, EERILY, EERINESS, FUSILEER, JEER, LEER, LEERY, MEERKAT, MUSKETEER, MUTINEER, ORIENTEER, PAMPHLETEER, PEER, PEERAGE [peer-əj], PEERLESS, PRIVATEER <i>=[I], PROFITEER, PUPPETEER, QUEER,

QUEERLY, RACKETEER, ROCKETEER, SEER*, SCRUTINEER, SHEER, STEER *a beast,* STEER *verb,* STEERING, STEERSMAN, VEER, VENEER, VOLUNTEER.

Seer, one who sees into the future, used to be pronounced [see-er], like *freer* [free-er] still is.

Doublet <ii>

Rule 3-4 The doublet <ii> is illegal in English words, as we already know.

Reason In cursive handwriting <ii> looked like <u>, especially when <i> was without a dot on top.

Rebels We only see <ii> in SKIING and RADII and SHIITAKE. It's [shee-tar-kee] in English, [shee-tar-kay] in Japanese.

Rebels' Reasons *Ski* is a recent adoption and *skiing* is often written *ski-ing* to show [skee-ing]; *radii*, plural of *radius,* spells [rayd-ee-I], from Latin, but *radiuses* is used more now. *Shiitake,* the Japanese mushroom, is adopted but not adapted.

Corporate Rebels: It is a good advertising technique to mis-spell words for they catch the eye. We go on the alert when the unexpected occurs, like <ii>, e.g., the internet server *iinet* [I-I-net] is an eye catcher – no pun intended.

Before proceeding, let me introduce a word which is not trapped in any list because we still spell it and say it however we like! Hooray! for hurrah! and hoorah! in which <oo> spells [oo], [uu] or [u].

Doublet <oo>

Rule 3-5 The doublet <oo> spells [oo] and [uu].

Reason Continental <oo> spells [or], the etension of short [o]. In England this lifted in the GVS to [oh]. Which changed again, in four stages, ranging from wide open mouthed long [oh] to short little [u] right at the back of the mouth. First [oh] changed to [oo] and most <oo> words still spell that sound. However, some shortened that sound, as in *book* and *foot,* to [uu]. Also, words that did not originally use <oo> began to use that doublet to spell [oo]. French *ballon* became *balloon*. English *rum*, in which <u> spelt the short sound in *put, push* and *pull,* extended, lengthened its vowel and is now the word *room*. The question remains, why not use doublet <uu>, to spell this extension? To my mind, *room* is another Cursive Casualty. The doublet <uu> would have looked like <w> when written in cursive and so <oo> replaced <uu>. Besides, <oo> was already being used for all the words with <oo> spelling [or] which lifted that long vowel to [oh] and then [oo], in the GVS.

Rebels BROOCH; FLOOD, BLOOD and six or more scientific words like OOGENESES, OOLITE, OOLITH, OOLITIC, OOLOGIST [oh-ol-oh-jist], OOSPHERE.

Rebels' Reasons *Brooch* is the only word left in which <oo> spells [oh]. When vowels lifted again to [oo], words like {*boat*} used <oa> to spell [oh], to separate them from words like *boot. Brooch,* which means *pin* or *pierce*, was both a noun and a verb, until the written verb changed to {*broach*}. In Holland, <oo> spells [oh], as we see in President Roosevelt's name — his Dutch ancestors arrived in New York back when it was New Amsterdam, some time before 1650.

Then some words shortened from [oo] to [uu], as in *book*. In just two words the sound became even shorter. *Flood* and *blood* changed from [flood] and [blood] to [fluud] and [bluud] (which we still hear in the north of England) and then in the 1600's to [flud] and [blud] but their spelling never changed because their <oo> spelling was already in print in many books.

Note: Doublets are very stable. When we add <ing> or <ed> to *blood* and *flood* we do not twin <d> for there is no need to provide double gates on the short vowel [u] for suffixes are unable to alter the sound a doublet makes in its stem word. Enjoy the following: FLOODING, FLOODED, FLOODLIT, HOTBLOOD, BLOODED, BLOODY, OXBLOOD, UNBLOODED.

In *oogeneses* et cetera, as above, <oo> spells [oh][oh]. Unfortunately, a silent <h>, between the vowels, as in *vehemence,* is missing to separate them. Scientists use the prefix <oo>, short for *oion* (*egg* in Greek), to describe eggs and egg-like things:

Relevant Writing Tip. Doublet <oo> spells [oo] in 40% of all [oo] words, (Cummings, p. 289). The Prof says 75% of <oo> occur just before a final single consonant, as in *aloof* and that <oo> is also fairly common at the end of words, as in *bamboo* but it is quite rare in the first syllable of a word of two or more syllables and such words are often English spellings of foreign words like *boomerang,* or a re-spelling, e.g., *loony,* from *lunatic,* to show a link to *loon,* an old word for a crazy person. The twins <oo> are used inside a word only because <u> spells [yoo] instead of [oo] after consonants like [p] and [h], hence *puny poodle* and *human hoodlum.* Return to Reading Rules.

List 3-5 <oo> spells [oo], but terminal <oor> words come later.
ALOOF, BABOON, BALLOON, BALLOONIST, BALLY-HOO, BAMBOO, BAMBOOZLE, BANDICOOT, BASSOON, BAZOOKA, BEDROOM, BEETROOT, BEHOOVE*, BLOOM, BOO, BOOBY TRAP, BOOGYMAN, BOOM, BOOM!, BOOMERANG, BOON, BOOST, BOOT, BOOTED, BOOTEE, BOOTH, BOOTLEG, BOOTY, BOOZE*, BOOZEROO* *slang,* BOOZY, BROOD, BROODY, BROOM, BROOMSTICK, BUFFOON, BUGABOO, CABOODLE, CABOOSE, CALABOOSE, CESSPOOL, CHOOSE <se>=[z], COCK A SNOOK, COCKATOO, COO, COOEE, COOMB *silent b,* COOT, CROON, CUCKOO, DOGTOOTH, DOODLE, DOOM, DOOMED, DRAGOON, DROOL, DROOLING, DROOP, EYETOOTH, FESTOON, FOOD, FOOL, FOOLISH, FOOLISHLY, FOOLISHNESS, FOOLPROOF, FOOZLE – *slang,* GALOOT, GLOOM, GLOOMILY, GLOOMY, GOBBLEDEGOOK, GOO*, GOOIEST, GOOF, GOOFINESS, GOOFY, GOOGLY, GOOGOL, GOON, GOONS, GOONY, GOOSE, GOOSEFLESH, GOOSENECKED, GOOSEY, GRASSROOT, GREENROOM, GREENWOODS, GRILLROOM, GROOM, GROOMSMAN, GROOVE, GROOVIEST, GROOVY, GUESTROOM, GUMBOOT, GUNROOM, HANDLOOM, HENCOOP, HOOCH, HOODLUM*, HOODOO, HOO-HA, HOOLIGAN, HOOP, HOOP-LA, HOOT, HOOTENANNY, HULLABALOO, IGLOO, JACKBOOT, JIGABOO, KAZOO, KOOKY, LAGOON, LAMPOON, LEGROOM, LOO*, LOOFAH, LOOM, LOON, LOONY, LOOP, LOOP THE LOOP, LOOSE*, LOOSEN, LOOSEN UP, LOOT, MACAROON, MAROON, MIDNOON, MONGOOSE, MONGOOSES* *plural,* MONSOON, MONSOONAL, MOO, MOOCH, MOOCHING, MOOD, MOODILY, MOODINESS, MOODY, MOON, MOONDUST, MOONLESS, MOONLIT, MOONSTRUCK, MOONY, MOOSE, MOOT, MOTHPROOF, MUSHROOM, NINCOMPOOP, NOODLE noun, NOON, NOOSE, OFFSHOOT, OOH*, OOMPAH slang, OOMPH slang, OOPS slang, OOZE, OOZINESS, OOZY, OVENPROOF, PANTALOON, PAPOOSE, PARATROOPS, PEEKABOO, PLATOON, PONTOON, POOCH, POODLE, POOH*, POOL, POOLHALL, POOLROOM, POOP DECK, PRESCHOOL, PROOF, PROOFS, RACCOON/RACOON, RATOON, REBOOT, REPROOF, REROOF, RESTROOM, ROOD*, ROOF, ROOFTOP, ROOM, ROOMFUL, ROOMY, ROOST, ROOT, ROOTHOLD, ROOTLESS, ROOTSTOCK, SALOON, SCHOOL, SCHOOLBAG, SCHOOLCHILD, SCHOOLCHILDREN, SCHOOLROOM, SCOOP, SCOOT, SCROOGE, SHAMPOO, SHELLPROOF, SHOCKPROOF, SHOO, SHOOT Δ, SHOOTING BOX, SICKROOM, SKIDPROOF, SLOOP, SMOOCH, SMOOCHY, SMOOTH* [dh], SMOOTHEST [dh], SNOOD, SNOOP, SNOOTY*, SNOOZE, SOON, SOOTH, SOOTHE, SPITTOON, SPOOF, SPOOK*, SPOOKY*, SPOOL, SPOON, SPOONBILL, SPOON-FED, SPOONFUL, STOOGE, STOOK, STOOP, SUNPROOF, SUNROOF, SUNROOM, SWEET TOOTH, SWOON, SWOOP, TABOO, TAPROOM, TAPROOT, TATTOO, TOLLBOOTH, TOO, TOOL, TOOLBOX, TOOLSHED, TOOT, TOOTH, TOOTHBRUSH, TOOTHLESS, TOOTHPICK, TOOTHY, TROOP, TROOPSHIP, ULTRACOOL, ULTRASMOOTH, UNSCHOOLED, UPROOT, UPSHOOT, VAMOOSE, VINDALOO, VOODOO, WASHROOM, WINDPROOF, WOO, WOOZY, YAHOO, ZOO, ZOOM, ZOOM LENS. Proper Nouns CAMEROON,

COOTAMUNDRA, MOOMBA, TIMBUCTOO. <u>Aussie words</u>. BOOMERANG*, COOLABAH/COOLIBAH*, COOLAMON*, DIDJERIDOO* or, DIDGERIDOO*, JACKAROO, KANGAROO*, NOODLE verb, POTOROO*, RAT KANGAROO, ROCK KANGAROO, SOOL, WAHOO, WALLAROO*, WANDOO TREE*, COOEE*.
SHOOT Δ, SHOT Δ, SHOT Δ, present, past and past participle.
As we know, *mooing, tattooist, voodooism, skidooing, boohooed, etc.* all take suffixes without any risk of altering [oo] due to the great stability of doublets.
**Behoove* is the American way of writing and reading *behove*. It was *behoven* in Middle English. Maybe Americans thought it was a feather word, like *move,* and decided to improve its spelling. Pronounced [bə-hoov] on Australian radio.
**Booze* began as a verb, evolving from an old word *bus* which meant to swell a lot, (until *busting*). The noun came later, but retained a [z] ending due to the Philadelphia distiller E.G., Booze. In 1722 Benjamin Franklin published *boozy* with his 225 synonyms for *drunk*. A **boozeroo* was a N.Z. drinking binge in World War II.
**C*hoose spells [chooz] because it is a verb. The noun {*choice*} ends in soft [s], like nouns *moose* and *goose*.
**Cooee* spells [koo-ee] with extra long vowels and [ee] raised in tone. Tonal change in English is usually reserved for questions. (*Cooee* usually means "Where are you?" i.e. a question.) It's an adoption from an Ab'l language but is also used in the south of the Indian peninsular (Western Ghat), with the same meaning as Australian word *cooee*. Is this coincidence or further evidence that the first Australians travelled through India from Africa?
**Coolabah/coolibah* and *coolamon* have been adopted from the Kamilaroi and other Ab'l languages around Gunnedah, NSW, (Blake, p.91). *Coolibah* was first recorded as *gulubaa.*
**Didgeridoo, didjeridoo, didjeridu* are all used and generally not considered indigenous words, are said to just sound like the drone of the didj, but to my mind these words are very similar to the word *djibolu* used by the Lardil people of Mornington Island in the region where Europeans first experienced the music of the didj, see Wikipedia. After all, many Australian Ab'l words are very onomatopoetic.
**Gooiest* demonstrates the stability of doublets before suffixes.
**Hoodlum* is proof we change words to make them easy to say, (Fleck 2007). In San Francisco gangs surrounded their victims with the cry "huddle them, huddle them" so that by 1877 newspapers called them gangs of "hoodlums".
**Kangaroo* was recorded as 'kanguroo' in Cook's journal, from the Guugu-Timidhir language. The story that Cook's men got it wrong is wrong. Recent work has confirmed that [kaŋ-oo-roo], now pronounced [kan-ga-roo], is indeed the right word in that language for large grey or black macropods, (Blake, p.95).
**Loo* for toilet is said to have begun when situated in the room at the end of the passage in French hotels and always numbered 100 to indicate it was the last room. However, since *cent* (100) sounded the same as *scent* (smell) the numeral 1 was changed to an L, thus reading L00. (Heard by Shane Aylemore, on student-exchange from Carnarvon when in Paris.) This is a better reason than the four possibilities given by Ayto on p. 328 and solves the mystery which he says *loo* presents, in his words "one of the most celebrated puzzles of English etymology". Since then, Etymonline gives us: probably from French *lieux d'aisances,* 'lavatory,' literally 'place of ease,' picked up by British servicemen in France during World War I, or possibly it's an English pun on *Waterloo*, based on *water closet*.
**Loose* spells [loos], as we'd expect, whereas *loos* spells [looz], plural of *loo. Loose* began as an adjective and later it was also used as a verb but [s] did not change to [z] in the verb because then it would sound like {*lose*}, which spells [looz]. The verb *to loose* means 'to untie someone, to loosen something, to let it go'.

*_Mongooses_ are not geese and are not English animals and so they do not use the Old English way of making plurals.

*_Ooh_ is just a pseudo word, with a silent <h> to add emphasis, as in, _Ooh!_ which can express either delight or repugnance.

*_Potoroo_ is from an Ab'l word for kangaroo rats around Port Jackson, (Blake, p.102), and now means all those of the Genus Potorous, in which a Latin 'spare part' has been added to the Ab'l word.

*_Pooh's_ <h> is unnecessary. It is silent. Maybe [h] was once added in speech as if to imitate our reaction to a bad smell, an expulsion of air to prevent breathing it in, as in the exclamation "Pooh-hoo!" See _ooh_.

*_Rood_ is a very old word meaning a wooden cross or a pole.

*Regardless of whether _smooth_ is an adjective or verb we say [dh] in both cases – very unusual. As an adjective it should be [smooth]. The [dh] ending the adjective evolved from OE _smoð_. The verb _smooth_ should be _smoothe_, to obey the general rule that <th> spelling voiced [dh] is always followed by a vowel and verbs end in voiced [dh], not the weaker [th]. The verb evolved from the adjective as OE _smeðan_. Then both adjective and verb became _smooð_ which should have become _smoothe_ but in both cases <e> was not added. One version of the adjective was _smeeth_ as in _smeeth field,_ retained to to this day in numerous Smithfield place names, originally for smooth fields.

*_Snooty_ spells [snootee] or [snuutee]. Is it slang or accepted? _Snoot_ was an old word for _snout_, a nose. Snooty people look down their noses at others.

*_Spook_ and _spooky_ really are spooky, because <ook> usually spells [uuk], as in _book_.

*_Wallaroo_ [wol-u-roo], for mountain kangaroos, has been adopted into English from a Port Jackson Ab'l language.

*_Wandoo_ [won-doo] has not only been adopted into English as the common name for a tree in WA's south west, but, like other Ab'l words used in scientific nomenclature, gets world-wide recognition in _Eucalyptus wandoo,_ (Blake, p. 104).

Now that we can read both _teeth_ and tooth, it's time to say why it's one _foot_ but two _feet_, one _goose_ but two _geese._ Long ago the plural of _foot_ sounded like [foot-eez]. Other plurals were [tooth-eez] and [goos-eez]. Then the vowel inside the stem word changed to be like the ending, (Burbridge, 2002 p. 86), so that the plurals became [feet-eez], [teeth-eez], [gees-eez].

The mouth gets ready to say [eez] too soon and turns the preceding [oo] into [ee] as well. We anticipate something and then put it into action too early, like athletes 'jumping the gun', starting a race early without meaning to.

Once the change was made there was no need to keep the [eez] endings to make plurals. So [feet-eez] became just [feet], [teeth-eez] became just [teeth] and [gees-eez] became just [gees.] Jakob Grimm and his brother travelled Europe collecting folk stories and fairy tales. They heard the old way of saying words and the new way and Jakob worked out that some vowels inside words change, and why, as above. He called this "jumping the gun" vowel change "umlauting" or "sound changing".

Some words umlaut and keep their suffixes, e.g., _old, elder, eldest._ Words can also change back. Modern English speakers have gone back to _old, older, oldest_ except when speaking of people – old people, the elders, get respected with old words. We say _length_ not _longth,_ for the English used to say _long, lenger, lengest. Strength_ grew from _strong, strenger, strengest._ Words changed back to _longest_ and _strongest,_ but _length_ has not gone to _longth,_ nor _strength_ to _strongth._

The word _moose_ has been recently adopted into English and so it would never have been [moos-eez] and then [mees]. However we do not say _two mooses,_ just _two moose._ It seems to be stuck between the old pattern in which _two gooses_ is wrong, but _meese_ would be nothing like its American Indian name, [moos], from the same North American language which gave us _raccoon. Moose_ belongs to a group of words which are written the same, either in singular or in plural form, e.g., *deer, fish, sheep* and *swine.* They are called collective nouns.

Not needed but nice to know. *Moose, deer, fish, sheep* and *swine, buffalo, boar, antelope* and *cattle* are all collective nouns. We can also say *cod, mackerel, trout, salmon,* and mean many fish of that sort. If we wish to speak of just one we put *a* or *the* in front of it. Do you notice that all these animals are useful to humans? They are either hunted or domesticated. Jesperson 1938, p.179: "Most of the words that make their plurals like the singular are old neuters, the *-s* ending belonging to masculines only and having only gradually been extended to the other two genders." So that is why it is two sheep, but not two ewe, nor two ram. The web page rinkworks.com/words/collective.shtml lists animals which are written the same for singular and plural. Take a look. Are they all either friends (useful) or foes (harmful) to humans? Think about some of the nouns in these song lines: "Ride again jackaroo, think I see *kangaroo* up ahead. Oh time is a meddler, Tenterfield Saddler make your bed. Fly away *cockatoo*. Down on the ground *emu* up ahead. Time is a tale teller ...." Other nouns which are the same whether single or plural include *aircraft, cannon, blues* and *fruit*. Maybe you'd like to make a longer list of collective nouns. Now back to things we need to know.

Looking Good, <oo> in Wool

Rule 3-6 The doublet <oo> never spells [uu] at the end of words and only spells [uu] before the five consonants [d], [t], [k], [f] and [l], but only in some words.

Reason Those words which changed their [oo] sound to [uu], the sound we have already met in *put* and *push* and *pull,* are listed below. This change of [oo] to [uu] happened in the south of England. For instance, in Scotland, a *book* is still a [book], not a [buuk]. It only happened in some words, only before [d], [t], [k], [f] and [l]. Even then, not in every <ood>, <oot>, <ook>, <oof> and <ool> word and it is still happening before <l>. For instance, in Sydney a *school pool* was a [skool] [pool] in the 1960's. In Adelaide we said [skuul] [puul]. How do you say *pool* — rhyming with *spool* or *tool?* There is no way of knowing which words changed. All we know is that <oo> never spells [uu] at the end of words and only spells [uu] before the five consonants [d], [t], [k], [f] and [l], but only in some words, e.g., in *foot* but not in *boot*. There is always a reason. In this case, *foot* is an Old English word and *boot* was adopted from French and sounded like [bort] before it became [boot] in the GVS.

Not needed but nice to know. Scottish English uses <oo> to spell just one sound, whether in *good* or *goose* — a short [oo] with forward lips, quite like the sound of the long vowel but using the length of the short vowel. Now back to things we need to know.

List 3-6 <oo> spells [uu]
ADULTHOOD, AFOOT, BABYHOOD*, BENTWOOD, BETOOK, BIGFOOT, BILLHOOK, BOOBOOK, BOOK*, BOOKABLE*, BOOKED, BOOKEND, BOOKING, BOOKISH, BOOKLET, BOOKSHELF, BOOKSHELVES, BROOKLET, BY HOOK AND BY CROOK, CHILDHOOD, CHOOK, COOK, COOKBOOK, COOKTOP, COOL, COOLANT, CROOK, CROOKED, DOGWOOD, DRIFTWOOD, EYEHOOK, FALSEHOOD, FISHHOOK, FLAT-FOOTED, FOOT, FOOT THE BILL, FOOTAGE, FOOTBALL, FOOTBATH, FOOTHILL, FOOTHOLD, FOOTING, FOOTINGS, FOOTMAN, FOOTLOOSE, FOOTPATH, FOOTPRINT, FOOTREST, FOOTSLOG, FOOTSTEP, FOOTSTOOL, FOOTSY, FOOTY, GOOD, GOOD LOOKING, GOOD-GOODY, GOODNESS, GOODS, GOODWILL*, GOODY, GREENWOOD, HANDBOOK, HOOD, HOODED, HOODWINK, HOOF pl HOOVES, HOOK, HOOK UP, HOOKAH, HOOKLET, HOOK-UP, HOTFOOT, IN BAD BOOKS, LOGBOOK, LOOK, LOOK UP, LOOK UP TO, LOOKING, MATCHBOOK, MATCHWOOD, MILKWOOD, MISTOOK, MONKSHOOD, MOOLAH *slang*, MY FOOT!, NOOK, OFF THE HOOK, ON FOOT, ON THE HOOF, PASSBOOK, PLYWOOD, POCKETBOOK, POOF,

POOL, POOP, POTHOOK, PULPWOOD, PUPPYHOOD, PUSSYFOOT, PUSSYFOOTED, ROOK, SHOOK, SOOT, SOOTY, SPOOL, STOOD Δ, STOOL, SWOOSH! TOOK, TOOL, TOOTSY, UNCOOKED, UNHOOK, VROOM *slang,* WHOOPEE! WHOOSH, WILDWOODS, WITHSTOOD, WOMANHOOD, WOOD, WOODBIN, WOOD-BOX, WOODCHUCK, WOODCOCK, WOODCRAFT, WOODCUT, WOODED, WOODEN, WOODEN SPOON, WOODENLY, WOODHEN, WOODLAND, WOODMAN, WOODS, WOODSHED, WOODSMAN, WOODSY, WOODWIND, WOODY, WOOF, WOOL, WOOLLEN, WOOLLENS, WOOLLINESS, WOOLLY, WOOLPACK, WOOLSACK, WOOLSHED, WOOPS, WOOSH. Australian Words BEEFWOOD TREE has red wood, SATIN WOOD TREE, CROOK, GO CROOK, KOOKABURRA, SOOK, WOOLSHED, WOOMERA, WOOP-WOOP imaginary remote place.

Present, past and past participle.
SHOOT Δ, SHOT Δ, SHOT Δ
STAND Δ, STOOD Δ, STOOD Δ

*Babyhood is not Greek but retains <y> because the stress on the third syllable from the end would mean <a> spelt short [a] instead of long [ay], which is exactly what happened to *holy* in *holiday*. See Rule 1-50 and 'Holiday Words.'

*Book comes from the old word *boc* [bohk] for *tree*, or [beek] for beech tree, for they were used for the first message sticks to reach Briton. These first message sticks of [bohk] and [beek] spread the power of writing and reading. We use paper now, not wood, but we still call our books 'message sticks', [buuks].

*As we know, free stems, like *book*, take the suffix <able>, not <ible>, hence *bookable*.

*Goodwill or *good will* but usually *goodwill* in a business meaning, (Bryson, 2004, p.88).

Relevant Writing Rule. Before <k>, [uu] is always spelt <oo>, as in *book*. Only proper nouns break this rule, as in the name Tobruk. Return to Reading Rules.

Not needed but nice to know. Some of the first message sticks were attached to trade items and had numbers on them, a message to a distant customer over the sea, in ancient Britain. Others were inscribed with secret spells and kept hidden by the chiefs. In Australia the same thing happened. Message sticks were used when people were too far away to talk to each other. In my part of Western Australia, some 'rock art' is actually a message, e.g., directing travellers to the next water hole. There are also message sticks, called *pambura*, which means 'for the blind' (blind-for), for people blind to each other due to separation by distance, as explained to me by Maureen Dodd, Acacia Way, Carnarvon. Instances of their use are described in *My Natives and I,* Daisy Bates, 2004. Consequently, the concept of coding messages into symbols was not new to these Aboriginals but symbols on paper were a new thing. They named books after the paper-bark tree, *mirli-mirli* or *mili-mili*, not the wood of their message sticks.

Elders in Australia, as elsewhere, guarded their knowledge. They hid messages in their hair, which they tied up to cover the little plaques they wrote on. Go to our National Museum in Canberra and ask to see number 1985.0065.0101 of the Keith Goddard Collection. It's a flat oval wooden plaque, 175mm long, 90mm wide, 10mm thick, incised with abstract and symbolic geometric lines. These marks are not pictures. They are symbols. They may symbolize whole words, like Chinese writing, or syllables, like Japanese writing, or just consonants, like Hebrew letters, or maybe they symbolized both vowel sounds and consonants, like the Roman alphabet. Maybe they were memory joggers, like the brief notes we use in public speaking to recall whole paragraphs. We do not know, because the skill of reading these Kimberley symbols was and is kept very secret. Other Australian elders kept their secrets, too, thus retaining their power — the power of knowledge. Then again, writing was shared at times, when people were too scattered for words but needed to communicate. Now back to things we need to know.

Cluster <oor>

Rule 3-7 Letters <oor> spells [oor], in which <r> does not spell [r], but instead reduces to /ə/, because English is not a rhotic language.
List 3-7 <oor> spells [oor]
BLACKAMOOR, BOOR, MOOR, MOORHEN, PANDOOR, POOR, SPOOR.
Rebels FLOOR and DOOR are very old rebels.
Rebels' Reasons In Old English *dor* and *flor* spelt [dor] and [flor] due to Bossy R, like *for*, which we met in Part One. In Old English *dor* meant 'gate'. 'Door' was *duru* which meant 'a little gate'. In Dutch one went *door*, meaning 'through', a *dor*. Old English *flor* meant 'floor', (a cousin-word to *flat*), but somehow the English words *floor* and *door* gained an extra <o>. In England the only time <oor> spells [or] is in *floor* and *door*.
Nowadays, in Australia, all words with the <oor> spelling rhyme with *door* and *floor*. Words like *spoor* and *boor* are read more than said. They match the look of the well-known words *door* and *floor*. Queen Quill is our teacher if we do not hear from King Sound. So <oor> spells [or] now in more than two words in Australia.
Two English **Rebels**, *floor* and *door*, and many Aussie followers, loyal subjects of Queen Quill.
BACKDOOR, BLACKAMOOR, BOOR, DOOR, FLOOR, FLOOR-CLOTH, FLOORED, INDOOR, INDOORS, MOOR, MOORHEN, NEXT-DOOR, PANDOOR, POOR, SPOOR, TANDOOR, TANDOORI, TRAPDOOR.
Aussies also pronounce the Indian place names *Pandoor* and *Tandoor* and related dishes *pandoori* and *tandoori* this way — with <oor> spelling [or].

Doublet <uu>

The doublet <uu> looks like <w>, especially in cursive, and so it was not used in the olden days. Even now that doublet <uu> is printed clearly it is still not used as a doublet, except in *muu-muu* and *vacuum*. It's used in Latin words and modern words spelling [yoo-um] and [oo-um], which we will meet later.
Rule 3-8 Doublet <uu> spells [yoo] in only one word and [yoo] in only one word.
Reason *Vacuum* originally spelt [vak-yoo-um], related to *vacant* and descended from Latin *vacere*. *Muu-muu* has been adopted from Hawaii. It is a colourful, waistless, cotton dress, and very cool in hot weather. The words 'Hawaiin muu-muu' show that doublets are welcome in the Hawaiian language, even <ii> and <uu> and three, even four, vowels in a row as well.
List 3-8
MUU-MUU, VACUUM, VACUUM FLASK, VACUUM PUMP.

Fossil E — *are, some.*

We speak a living language. What do you say for *Sunday*? Some of us say *Sundy*, especially amongst friends. Is another little word-ending shrivelling up as we speak? If we say [sun-dee] will we start writing *sunde?* Maybe people will say [sund] one day, and write *sund*.

Many words have lost their old endings. When we see a terminal <e> which does not spell a sound we say it is silent. Such letters are vestiges of old suffixes which shrank back to tiny grunts just like the tiny black dots inside bananas are vestiges of ancient seeds. Bananas no longer need seeds. Silent <e>'s are no longer needed to spell sounds. Unless silent <e>'s were needed for other jobs people dropped them, stopped writing them. Some that should have dropped off long ago have hung on. They are called old fossils, Fossil E's.

There are nine old English words which end in a fossil letter <e>. These fossil <e>'s might have been useful once but now they are as useless as banana seed spots. Teachers can 'fossilize' E by painting it on a stone, as a classroom prop. See the web-site Photo Gallery. BTW, the dress-up box is not just for students. Teachers have been known to dress the part when explaining spelling through history.

List 3-9 Nine old fossils

1. ARE Δ spells [ar], like the vowel in *bar*. It was *aron* in Old English and then shrank to *are*. As part of the verb *to be, are* does not need <e> to obey the Short Word Rule and so it's <e> is a fossil, a vestige of a longer ending.

2. BADE Δ spells [bad]. This is the past tense of *bid*. Many of us now wrongly say [bayd]. The *e* is misleading as well as unnecessary.

3. COME Δ *f* spells [kum] This was *cumin* in Old English, before the Norman Invasion, after which it shrank to *come*. Also in BECOME Δ *f* [bə-kum] and WELCOME Δ *f* [wel-kum].

4. DONE Δ *f* spells [dun]. Many Old English words used <en> in the past particple, instead of <ed>, e.g., *floated* was *floten, melted* was *molten*. The verb *to do* added <en> to say 'It is doen'. Then <en> was reversed. *Doen* became *done* which looked like a feather word so that it came to spell [dun] and <e> joined the other fossil <e>'s. Also UNDONE Δ.

5. GONE Δ spells [gon]. When the verb *to go* added <en> to say *I have gone,* it was at first written *goen.* Then <en> was reversed. The verb *to go* combined with the verb *to wend,* and become "I go, I went, I have gone". See Hewitt, page 150, on *done* and *gone.*

6. NONE *f* spells [nun]. *None* comes from combining *not one*. Long ago *not one* was *ne one* which is why there is no <t> in *none*. We do not say *none* much nowadays, except in old-fashioned phrases like *none other, none the worse*, because when used as an adjective it has reduced down to the word *no*. The silent <e> of *none* shows it was once *'ne one'*. The letter <e> in *one* is not a useless fossil for it's used to obey the Short Word Rule. However, the entire word is a bit of a fossil as we shall soon see.

7 & 8. SHONE Δ and SCONE spell [shon] and [skon]. When things shine, they have a *sheen*, in Germany a [shern], in Holland a [shoon]. Dutch *schoonbroo* is 'fine bread', fine like scones. The vowel shifted and shifted again on the way through Holland to Scotland to England. In some parts of Australia the vowel in *scone* has shifted gain, where folks are led by Queen Quill to say [skohn].

9. SOME *f* spells [sum]. It was *sum*, before the Normans replaced hard-to-read <u> with <o> and added <e> as well.

As we would expect, verbs with Fossil E are old and irregular. They hang on to old ways, as in:
ARE Δ, part of the irregular verb *to be*: *I am* and *he/she/it is*, but *you are, we are, you are,* and *they are.*
BID Δ, BADE Δ, BIDDEN Δ, present, past and past participle.
COME Δ, {CAME Δ}, COME Δ.
SHOE Δ, SHOD Δ, SHOD Δ –as in "He shod the pony. He attached four horseshoes."
DO Δ, DID Δ, DONE Δ *f*
GO Δ, WENT Δ, GONE Δ.
{SHINE Δ }, SHONE Δ, SHONE Δ.

Two old words have a useful terminal <e>. Some say that *one* and *blonde* end with fossil <e>. However, <e> is doing a job in each. So we cannot call <e> a fossil in these words. It is alive and well!
BLONDE [blond] *Blonde* spells [blond] and is the one remaining female **adjective** left in English. We write *blond man* but *blonde woman*.
ONE *f* [wun] The feather word *one* uses silent terminal <e> to obey the Short Word Rule. It evolved as described in 1-12. The [w] sound has remained because it gives emphasis to a word, e.g., *where? what? which?* all start with [w]. When we count, we emphasize each number: 1! 2! 3!

New Fossils.
Terminal <e> in some words has become a fossil <e>, an <e> without a job. Maybe one day we shall stop writing <e>. They are nouns or adjectives. Their first syllables get all the stress and the final syllables have shrunk.
List 3-10

AGATE [ag-at] is a hard rock named after a river in Sicily in which terminal <e> spelt [ee], the Greek way, but the colourfully patterned rock became known as [agat]. That river has since changed its name but now one goes looking for the pretty rock in Queensland's Agate River.
CHEQUE [chek]. *Cheque* is thought to be from *exchequeur*, with a short middle vowel.
DISCIPLINE [dis-i-plən]
DESTINED [destind]
ENGINE [enjin] entered English as *engin* which is French for "clever, ingenious." It retained this spelling in *cotton gin* but gained a silent <e> when just *engine*, to make it look more important, bigger than a *pin* or a *pipkin*
The others are nouns or adjectives, stressed on their first syllable, thus weakening their last syllable down to [at]. When the noun *delegate* becomes a verb, we hear the strong [ayt] ending again.
FAMINE [fam-ən], IMAGINE [im-aj-ən], INTESTINE [in-test-ən], MADAME [mad-əm], MASCULINE [mas-kyoo-lən], MEDICINE [med-is-ən], URINE [yoor-ən].
JASMINE [jazmin] came to England from France as *jasmin*, but being French it looked like it needed an <e>!
TONNE *f* spells [tun] or [tun-ee], (OED.), or [ton], (Radio BBC). My Australian school taught that *tonne* spelt [ton]. The letter <e> does a good job, on paper, in separating a metric *tonne* (1,000 kilograms) from a *ton* (2,240 pounds) but there is little agreement on what *tonne* actually spells, i.e. how to pronounce it.

Terminal E speaks out — *abalone, vigilante*.
We know that terminal <e> does many jobs. In a few rare words it is not silent. We have met *he, be, she, we,* in which <e> spells [ee]. It is not silent at the end of some words from Latin and Greek vocabulary. We must just learn to recognize them – it's a case of "memorize, don't analyse"! Some, like *abalone*, only look Greek, (see Etymonline).
List 3-11 Terminal <e> spells [ee]
ABALONE, ABORIGINE, ACME, ACNE, ANDANTE, ANEMONE, ANTE, CATASTROPHE, {CURARE [kyoo-rar-ree]}, EPITOME, FACSIMILE, MACHETE, [ma-shet-ee], KARATE*, POSSE, RECCE, RECIPE, SIMILE, SYNCOPE, [sin-ko-pee], TSETSE, UKULELE [yook-ə-lay-lee], VIGILANTE, WITHE [widhee], Proper Nouns, CHILE, DAPHNE. Also ACHILLE (of Achille's heel fame), ANDES mountain range
Karate spells [ka- rar-tee], or [kə-rar-tee], with the initial syllable mistakenly treated as an unstressed suffix to mimic its Japanese pronunciation. In Japan it means "empty handed", a fighting style which developed when the peasants of Okinawa were forbidden to carry weapons, (Fleck, 2007).
Notes on Plurals: Words like *antipodes, isosceles, pyrites,* and *faeces* are Greek or Latin plural words now used as singular English words. Long words of two or more syllables ending in <e> pronounced [ee] become plural by gaining <s> and so the last syllable is [eez], as in *aborigines, anemones* and *recipes*. The plural of *apex* is *apices*, *thesis* is *theses*, *basis* is *bases*, and *parenthisis* is *parenthises*, due to their Latin and Greek origins and the <es> endings spell [eez]. However, it's OK to make a plural of any word ending <x> by adding <es> which then spells [ez], as in *appendixes, apexes, matrixes,* and *larynxes*. Also, when we turn compound nouns into plurals, we shall be careful. We are yet to meet: 1 *passer-by*, 2 *passers-by;* 1 *mother-in-law,* 2 *mothers-in law;* 1 *lay-by,* 2 *lay-bys*.

Silent E in *adaptive, accomplice, advantage*.
Silent E has many roles, for instance as **Insulator E.** As we know, terminal <e> prevents <v>, <z> and <u> ending words, e.g., *love, sneeze* and *glue*. It also prevents <l> and <r> ending words after consonants, e.g., *able* and *acre*. We can say <e> insulates these letters from ending words. To dress up as Insulator E, simply strap on a big fluffy (insulating) pillow labelled E.

We see Insulator E ending all words with the suffix –*ive*.

Rule 3-12 Suffix <ive> spells [iv].

Reason We know that <v> is always followed by a silent <e> to prevent words ending in <v>. The suffix -*ive* means *like,* similar to the suffix -*ly* on adjectives. Both suffixes came from the old suffix –*if. Jolly* was *jollif:* "joy-like". Some of these words lost the [f] sound and became "jolli", spelt *jolly,* because, as we know, English words do not end in <i>. However, in most of them the [f] became [v] and so we have a jolly *festive* time, (Prof. Cummings, p. 374). The vowels shortened from those in *joy* and *feast* to those in *jolly* and *festive,* but not all, as we detect in {*plaintiff* and *bailiff*} and other old nouns of the courthouse. Words used in court and in church are the slowest to change their ways. The only adjective left with a long vowel before the suffix –*ive* is {*plaintive*}.

Nouns: *act, feast, mass, rest.* Adjectives: *active, festive, massive, restive.* (A horse was called *restive* when it refused to go forward and just lifted one leg and then another, in other words *resting* all the other legs.) All these nouns end with <s> or <t> and so the suffix <ive> just adds on. We shall learn later on what has happened to words which do not end in <s> and <t> but took on <ive>.

Meanwhile we can read all the words in the next list if we use our decoding rules and remember that English words are usually stressed on the first syllable, as long as it is not a prefix. **Note:** Suffix <ive> always follows [s] or [t] and <ive> is always preceded by unigraph vowels — vowels written with just one letter.

Rebels OLIVE, PLAINTIVE.

Rebels' Reasons The remnant word *plaintive* remains because it's hard to change words written into courtroom rules, even though —*ive* should not follow a vowel digraph. *Olive* has no suffix, it's a stem word from one single Latin word, *oliva,* meaning 'olive tree'. Fruit of the *oliva* is *olivae*.

Q. Is *reflexive* a rebel? No, because —*ive* follows [s], since <x> spells [ks], [ree-flek-siv].

List 3-12 Suffix < ive> spells [iv]

ACTIVE, ADAPTIVE, ADDICTIVE, ADJECTIVE, ADMISSIVE, ADOPTIVE, AFFECTIVE, AGGRESSIVE, APPREHENSIVE, ATTENTIVE, ATTRACTIVE, CAPTIVE, COLLECTIVE, COMBUSTIVE, COMPREHENSIVE, CONDUCTIVE, CONFLICTIVE, CONGESTIVE, CONJUNCTIVE, CONNECTIVE, CONSTRICTIVE, CONSTRUCTIVE, CONSUMPTIVE, CONTRACEPTIVE, CONVULSIVE, CORRECTIVE, DATIVE, DECEPTIVE, DEDUCTIVE, DEFECTIVE, DEFENSIVE, DEFLECTIVE, DEPRESSIVE, DESCRIPTIVE, DESTRUCTIVE, DETECTIVE, DIGESTIVE, DIRECTIVE, DISINCENTIVE, DISMISSIVE, DISRUPTIVE, DISTINCTIVE, DISTRACTIVE, ELECTIVE, ERUPTIVE, EXCESSIVE, EXPANSIVE, EXPENSIVE, EXPRESSIVE, EXTENSIVE, FESTIVE, IMPASSIVE, IMPRESSIVE, IMPULSIVE, INACTIVE, INATTENTIVE, INCENTIVE, INEFFECTIVE, INEXPENSIVE, INFECTIVE, INOFFENSIVE, INSTRUCTIVE, INSTINCTIVE, INVECTIVE, INVENTIVE, IRRESPECTIVE, MASSIVE, MISSIVE, MOTIVE, NATIVE, OBJECTIVE, OBSESSIVE, OBSTRUCTIVE, OFFENSIVE, OPPRESSIVE, PASSIVE, PENSIVE, PLOSIVE, POSSESSIVE, PRESUMPTIVE, PREVENTATIVE, PRODUCTIVE, PROGRESSIVE, PROPULSIVE, PROSCRIPTIVE, PROSPECTIVE, PROTECTIVE, RECEPTIVE, RECESSIVE, REFLECTIVE, REFLEXIVE, REFRACTIVE, REGRESSIVE, REPREHENSIVE, REPRESENTATIVE, REPRESSIVE, REPRODUCTIVE, REPULSIVE, RESISTIVE, RESPECTIVE, RESPONSIVE, RESTIVE, RESTRICTIVE, RETENTIVE, RETROSPECTIVE, SEDUCTIVE, SELECTIVE, SUBJECTIVE, SUBJUNCTIVE, SUBMISSIVE, SUCCESSIVE, SUGGESTIVE, SUSCEPTIVE, UNRESPONSIVE, VINDICTIVE, VOTIVE.

Softener E

As we know, silent <e> softens <g> to [j] as in *cabbage* and <c> to [s] as in *office*.

ADVANTAGE* *VS,* BANDAGE, DISPARAGE, ENVISAGE, FRONTAGE *f,* ACCOMPLICE*, APPRENTICE, AVARICE, BENEFICE and CREVICE and many more are all listed later.

*Accomplice comes from *ad & complex.* Latter means 'twisted or plaited with.' Not related to *company,* therefore it is not a Feather Word.

*Advantage [ad-varn-taj] or [ad-van-taj].

Sometimes silent <e> has to be stopped or blocked from its silent work.

Rule 3-13 <gu> spells [g] before <e>, <i> and <y>.

Reason Sometimes <u> has to protect <g> from <e> softening it! The letter <u> also protects <g> from being softened into [j] by <i> or <y>.

List 3-13
GUESS, GUEST, GUILD, GUILT, GUILTILY, GUILTY, GUY, GUYLINE, ROGUISH, ROGUISHLY, ROGUISHNESS.

I hope you noticed that *guy* is not written like *dye* because it needs <u> to insulate <g> from <y>. This gives *guy* three letters, enough to obey the Short Word Rule, without adding <e>.

French Fossils — *crevasse, rosette.*

There is a silent <e> on many French words. English has adopted French VIGNETTE and invented KITCHENETTE and still uses a few words which end <sse>, due to the now obsolete rule which said that stem words ending [s] spelt <ss> must take a silent <e>.

Reason for this old rule: You already know that words ending with [s] after a single letter vowel must end in <ss>. Well, in the olden days, words ending in <ss> also had an <e> added on. Gradually the <e> was dropped off, as it was not needed, for when we see <ss> we know it is not a plural ending. *Masse* became *mass.* There are only 5 words left showing the old "fossil" <e> after <ss>. Like vowels before terminal <ss>, the vowels before terminal <sse> are all stressed. The opposite is the case for vowels before terminal <s> spells [s], as in *tennis, etc.* because such words have unstressed endings.

Today's rebels are remainders from yesterday.

List 3-14 French Fossils
CREVASSE, FINESSE, FOSSE, IMPASSE, NOBLESSE; CASSETTE, COQUETTE, {CORVETTE}, FLANNELETTE, {LAYETTE}, OMLETTE, PALETTE, PIPETTE, ROSETTE, {ROULETTE}. See more in appendix of French words used in English, under Diplomatic Immunity. Fossil <e> features in names: ANNE, ANNETTE, BABETTE, BELLE, ESTELLE, GISELLE, LUCILLE, NANETTE, NARELLE, NEVILLE.

French words which have <e> on words ending <g> also have <u>, to insulate <g> from <e>'s softening affect. When these words are adopted into English their fossil endings are sometimes removed, but very slowly. The word *tongue* was never French. It was *tunga,* then *tunge* until the Norman scribes changed it to *tonge* to avoid the <u> and <n> combining to look like <w>. They also added <u>, to insulate <g> from <e>, instead of just removing <e>! The dictionary committee thought it looked nice, similar to *langue,* the French word for one's 'tongue, speech or language'.

List 3-14 cont. More French Fossils
ANALOGUE [analog] alternative /ANALOG
CATALOGUE [katalog] or CATALOG
EPILOGUE [epee-log] or EPILOG
HARANGUE [ha-raŋ], no alternative yet.
HOMOLOGUE [hom-o-log] or HOMOLOG
MERINGUE [me-raŋ] *French adoption.*
MONOLOGUE [mon-o-log]

PEDAGOGUE [ped-u-gog], no alternative yet.
PROLOGUE [proh-log] or PROLOG
TONGUE *f* [tuŋ], a Fake French Fossil. As above, it was *tung* in the olden days and then turned into a feather word with a French-looking end, to match *langue* which is 'tongue' in French.
TRAVELOGUE [tra-vel-log]
{LEAGUE, MORGUE, DIALOGUE and SYNAGOGUE} later.

Fairy E — *ape, hope, zone.*

We met little Fairy E in Part One, when we learnt to read *home, came, hope, like, time* and *name*. People tried to obey Orm's Law, to write twins after every short vowel *butt itt iss a bigg jobb ass itt needs a lott off paper annd innk*. Not only did the scribes get tired of twinning, people dropped the ends off words.

Words were longer in the old days. *Hope* was *hopian* and spelt [hohp-ee-an]. We still say [hohp] when we read *hope* because silent Fairy E tells us that it was longer once with just one consonant after <o>, which according to Orm's Law, means <o> spelt a long sound. *Time* was longer once, *tima*, with a long first vowel, because of the single <m>. When it shortened it gained silent Fairy E, to show it was once longer. *Name* also gained a Fairy E when it shortened from two syllables, *nama*, to a single syllable, *name*. *Like* was just *lik*, because it obeyed the rule that vowels followed by a single consonant were long. It needed Fairy E to show it has a long vowel, in case it was read as [lik]. (*Liccian* reduced to *lick*, with <ck> instead of <cc> because English words do not end with <c> unless they have the suffix —*ic*. As we learnt at Rule 1-19, <ck> did not change to just <k>.) *Home* was *ham*, the single <m> showing that <a> spelt a long sound. (Today's word *ham* was written *hamm* back then to show a short vowel.) When old *ham* changed its long vowel sound to another long vowel, [oh], and became *home,* Fairy E was added to make sure we knew that <m> was always single, and followed a long vowel. *Hop* was *hoppian* and then became *hopp* and then just *hop*. *Hopian* shortened too, and we write *hope* to show that it never had <pp> at the end.

Rule 3-15A A one letter vowel followed by a consonant plus terminal <e> spells its long sound.
Reason When scribes got tired of twinning after short stressed vowels in terminal syllables, they added Silent E to consonants which were never twinned. So, because these single consonants marked long vowels, a single consonant followed by a Silent E marks long vowels. In this way we can tell *hope* from *hop.*

The history behind this is more detailed, as follows. Long ago words were longer, e.g., *mop* was *mappe*, *mope* was *mopen. Dot* was *dotte* and *dote* was *doten. Hate* was *hatian* and *hat* was *hæt. Fat* was *fætt* and *fate* was *fatum.* There were no Rebel Lemon words in those days, for they had not yet arrived in England. Words were either 'Regal', with first syllables stressed and long, if single consonants followed vowels, as in *hopian,* or they had double gates after short vowels. So in *hoppian,* <o> spelt [o]. After the Norman Invasion, like the ends of most English words, the end of *hoppian* shrank and fell off for English was neglected under Norman rule, with French as the official language. *Hopian* shrank too, but kept little silent <e> to show that it once had two syllables and so <o>, being in the first syllable and followed by a single consonant, spells [oh].

Although *ham* became home, *hamlet* (a group of homes) did not become *homelet*. When we pronounce the old word *hamlet* we read it like a modern word, so it loses its long vowel in *ham*.

A Magic Reason. Most children are content with the story that Fairy E spreads her magic dust over the previous vowel to make it spell a long vowel sound. Others might like to know that she is all that is left of a longer ending to the word, a word without twin letters after the vowel and so a word with a long vowel.

Rule 3-15B A one letter vowel followed by a consonant plus terminal <e> spells its long sound, in which case <wo> spells [woh] and <wa> spells [way].

Reason In the Great Vowel Shift, long vowels lifted so that long vowels after [w] changed, but short vowels did not. Consequently, words like *woven* and *wane* changed their long vowels from [or] in *wove* and [ar] in *wane* to [oh] and [ay] respectively. It was short vowels which changed in *won* and *wad*, to [u] and [o]. Then, to prevent being muddled with <w>, <u> became <o> in *won,* and so *wad* had to retain <a> but use it to spell [o]. So, because rule 3-15A only refers to long vowels, when <wo> and <wa> are followed by a consonant and Silent E they are neither cursive casualties nor collaterally damaged. For example, *woke* [wohk] is not a Cursive Casualty, and *wake* [wayk] is not collaterally damaged. They suffer no harm when written in cursive, are not Feather Words.

A Magic Reason The 'magic action' of Fairy E stops the muddle you usually get from W! *Wad* spells [wod] but *wade* does not spell [wohd] – it spells [wayd]. *Swath* spells [swoth] but *swathe* spells [swaydh] and although *wan* spells [won], *wane* spells [wayn]. This is because the Magic Action of Fairy E removes the Muddle of W!

<u>Relevant Writing Rhyme.</u> "To make a short vowel long / Just add silent Fairy E on. / As an added attraction / The fairy's magic action / means that W / Can no longer muddle you." <u>Return to Reading Rules.</u>

Any rebels? Many words appear to end with Fairy E but in those words <e> is doing other jobs. For instance, words in which <e> is an insulator, as in *love* or is helping words like *axe* and *one* obey the Short Word Rule. The nine old words end in fossil <e> and some newer words end with fossil <e> too, as we have seen. Silent terminal <e> has no 'magic action' on the vowels in such words.

Silent terminal <e> has no 'magic action' on <i> in the suffix –*ive* nor on the verbs *give* and *live*. All other stem words ending <ive> spell [Iv], e.g., *hive, live* as adjective and the verb *strive*. Note, <ive> in *deprive* [dee-prIv] is not a suffix, nor in *connive* and *contrive,* which is why <ive> does not spell [iv] in these words. Now you can read "*Live* [lIv] ants live [liv] in there."

Rebels LOSE Δ spells [looz], not [lohz]. VASE spells [varz]. WHOSE spells [hooz], as we know.

Rebels' Reasons *Lose* [looz] used to be *losian* and [oh] changed to [oo], in the verb. In the noun *loss* and the adjective *lost* the vowel became [o]. The Irregular Verb *to lose:* LOSE Δ, LOST Δ, LOST Δ. *Vase* spells [vays] in American English, which Etymonline says is the original pronunciation, e.g., Swift rhymed it with *face* and Byron with *place* and *grace*. In Anglo-English this shifted to [varz], during the 1800's. Queen Quill has taken control in parts of Australia, where it often spells [vayz], which is different again.

More Rebels? Two groups of words appear to break the rule that 'Double Gates', either twins or two different consonants, block vowels, keep them short because Fairy E appears to throw her magic dust back over double gates, to lengthen vowels behind 'double gates'. In words like *range* and *strange* it seems that Fairy E is at work but, as we know, this terminal <e> is just there to soften <g> to spell [j]. The vowels lengthen due to an older method of lengthening vowels, the same thing we see in *climb* and *hind* etc. There is only one group of words in which Fairy E succeeds in throwing her magic dust over double gates. We shall meet the Very Powerful Fairy E in {*haste* and *taste*} soon!

    At times, in the following list we shall see silent <e> does **two jobs at once.** For instance,
In *lace* and *face* silent <e> makes <a> spell [ay] and <c> spell [s].
In *mice* and *ice* silent <e> makes <i> spell [I] and <c> spell [s].
In *cage* silent <e> makes <a> spell [ay] and <g> spell [j].
In *clothe* <e> makes <o> spell [oh] and it makes <th> spell [dh].
In *cave* <e> makes <a> spell [ay] and it insulates <v> from coming last.
    At times we shall see <u> preventing <e> doing two jobs.
In *vague* <u> stops <e> softening <g> but <e> still makes <a> spell [ay] with her magic fairy action.

Don't forget that Fairy E can also undo the jobs of others!! Fairy E prevents the muddle you get from W! *Wad* spells [wod] but *wade* does not spell [wohd]. *Wade* spells [wayd] and *wave* spells [wayv] and *wove* spells [wohv].

As expected, <s> spells [z] after stressed vowels and voiced consonants.

We met **The English Yod** just before Rule 1-40. In order to read this list we need to remember that when <u> spells its long sound it spells [yoo]. This is hard to say after [r], [l], and [j] and it has been dropped from words like *rude, lute* and *jute.* Yod has dropped from *chute,* too.

List 3-15 Fairy E at work.

ACE*, ACHE* [ayk], AGE, ALE, APE, ATE, AYE, BAKE, BALE, BANE, BASE, BATE, BATHE [baydh], BIDE Δ, BIKE, BILE, BINE, BITE , BLADE, BLAME, BLAZE, BLOKE, BLUE, BODE Δ, BOLE*, BONE, BRACE, BRIBE, BRINE, BROGUE, BROKE, BRUTE [broot], CACHE [kaysh], CAGE, CAKE, CAME Δ, CANE, CAPE, CASE, CAVE, CEDE*, CHAFE, CHASE, CHIDE Δ, CHIME, CHINE, CHIVES, CHOKE, CHOSE Δ[chohz], CHUTE [shoot], CLONE, CLOSE *verb* [klohz], CLOSE *adj.*[klohs], CLOTHE, CLOTHES [klohdhz], CLOVE, CODE, COKE, CONE, COPE, COVE, CRANE, CRAVE, CRAZE, CRIME, CRUDE [krood], CUBE [yoo], CURE [kyoor], CUTE [kyoot], DATE, DAME, DATE, UP TO DATE, DATE LINE, TO DATE, DICE, DIE, DIKE/DYKE, DIME, DINE, DIVE Δ, DOE, DOGE, DOLE*, DOME, DOPE, DOSE, DOTE, DOVE *verb,* DOZE, DRAKE, DRAPE, DRIVE Δ, DROGUE, DRONE, DROVE, DRUPE, DUDE* [dood], DUKE* [jook], DUNE* [joon], DUPE* [joop], ENGRAVE Δ, EVE, FACE, FADE, FAKE, FATE, FAZE, FIFE, FINE, FIVE, FAKE, FLAME, FLUKE [oo], FLUTE [oo], FRAME, FUGUE [fyoog], FUME [yoo], GALE, GAME, GAPE, GATE, GAVE, GAZE, GENE, GIBE, GLAZE, GLIDE, GLOBE, GRACE, GRADE, GRAPE, GRATE, GRAVE, GRAZE, GREBE, GRIME, GUIDE, GUILE, GUISE [gIz], HAKE, HALE, HATE, HERE, HIDE Δ, HIKE, HIVE, HOLE*, HOLEY, HOME, HOME RULE, HONE, HOPE, HOSE [hohz], HOT PLATE, HOVE, HUGE, ICE, JIVE, JOKE, JUKE BOX [jook], JUTE [joot], KALE, KNAVE* *silent k,* KNIFE* *silent k,* KNIVES *plural,*[z], LACE, LAKE, LAME, LANE, LATE, LATHE, LAZE, LEGUME [le-gyoom], LICE, LIFE, LIVE *adjective,* LIVES *plural,* LIKE, LIME, LINE, LITHE [lIdh]*, LIVE-*adjective,* LOBE, LODE, LONE, LUKE [look], LUTE [loot], MACE, MADE, MAKE Δ, MALE, MANE, MANGE, MATE, MAZE, METE Δ, MICE, MIKE, MILE, MIME, MINE, MISTAKE Δ, MITE, MODE, MOLE*, MOPE, MULE [myool], MUSE [myooz], MUTE [myoot], NAME, NAME-SAKE, NAPE, NAVE, NICE, NICK NAME, NINE, NINE PINS, NODE, NOM DE PLUME, NOSE [nohz], NOTE, NOTE CASE, NUDE, ODE, OPAQUE [oh-payk], PACE, PAGE, PALE, PANE, PATE, PAVE, PEKE, PHASE [fayz], PHONE, PHRASE [frayz], PIKE, PILE, PILES, PINE, PIPE, PLACE, PLAGUE, PLANE, PLATE, PLUME, POKE, POLE*, POSE [pohz], PRICE, PRIDE, PRIME, PRISE [prIz], PRIZE, PROBE, PROLE, PRONE, PROSE [prohz], PROVE, PRUDE, PRUNE, PUCE, PURE [pyoor], QUAKE, QUITE, QUOTE, RACE, RAGE, RAKE, RAPE, RATE, RAVE, RAZE, RHYME, RICE, RIDE Δ, RIFE, RILE, RIME (hoar frost), RIPE, RISE Δ[rIz], ROBE, RODE, ROGUE, ROLE*, ROPE, ROSE [rohz], ROTE, RUCHE [roosh], RUDE [rood], RULE [rool], RUNE [roon], RUSE [rooz], SAFE*, SAGE, SAKE, SALE, SAME, SANE, SAVE, SCALE, SCENE, SCOPE, SCRAPE, SCRIBE, SHADE, SHAKE Δ, SHAME, SHAPE, SHAVE Δ, SHINE Δ, SHINE*, SHONE*, SHRIVE, SHROVE, SIDE, SIDE LINE, ON THE SIDE, BY THE SIDE, SIDE BY SIDE, SIDE EFFECT, SIDE DRUM, SIDE STEP, SIDE STREET, SIDE STROKE, SIDE TRACK, SIDE WIND, SIDE KICK, SINE, SITE, SIZE, SKATE, SKIVE OFF *slang,* SKYDIVE, SLAKE, SLATE, SLAVE, SLICE, SLIDE Δ, SLIME, SLOPE, SMILE, SMITE Δ, SMOTE, SNAKE, SNIPE, SOLE*, SOMETIME* ʃ, SOMETIMES* ʃ, SPACE, SPACE PROBE, SPADE, SPATE, SPICE, SPIKE, SPINE, SPITE, SPLICE, SPOKE, SPRITE, SPRUCE [oo], SPUME [yoo], STAGE, STALE, STATE, STAVE, STILE, STOKE, STOLE, STONE, STOVE, STRAFE, STRANGE, STRIDE Δ, STRIFE, STRIKE Δ, STRIPE, STRIVE Δ, STROBE, STRODE, STROKE, SWATHE [swaydh], SWEDE, SWINE, TAKE Δ, TALE, TAPE, TELL-TALE, THEME,

THESE [dheez], THINE [dhIn], THOSE [dhohz], THRICE, THRIVE ∆, THRONE, THROVE, TIDE, TILE, TIME, TITHE [tIdh], TOGUE, TONE, TOQUE [tohk], TOTE, TRACE, TRADE, TRIBE, TRINE, TRIPE, TRITE, TRUCE, TUBE* [choob], TUNE* [choon], TULE* [chool], TWICE, USE* *verb* [yooz], USE* *noun* [yoos], VAGUE, VALE, VANE, VIBE, VICE, VILE, VINE, VAGUE, VOGUE, VOLE*, VOTE, WADE, WAGE, WAKE ∆, WANE, WASTE, WAVE, WHALE, WHALE BONE, WHILE, WHINE, WHITE, WHOLE* *silent* <w>, WIDE, WIFE, WIVES [wIvz], WINE, WIPE, WISE [wIz], WOVE*, WRITE ∆, WRITHE [wrIdh], WROTE, YOKE, YULE, ZONE. <u>Proper Nouns</u>, JUNE, YULETIDE. <u>Names</u> ABE, BRICE, BRUCE, DALE, DUKE, EVE, IKE, JACE, JADE, JAKE, JAMES, JAMES, JANE, JUDE, JUNE, KATE, LUKE, LUKE, MIKE, MIKE, MILES, PETE*, RHODES [rohdz], ROSE [rohz], SHANE, SPIKE. <u>Compound Words</u> LONESOME: *f* [lohn-sum]and WHOLESOME: *f* [hohl-sum] or [hol-sum] each have a Fairy E and Fossil E.

List 3-15/16's irregular verbs take these present, past and past participle forms.
BIDE ∆, BODE ∆ /BIDED, BODE ∆ /BIDED/BIDDEN
BITE ∆, BIT ∆, BITTEN ∆
BODE ∆, BODED/BODE ∆, BODED/BODEN ∆
CHIDE ∆, CHID ∆ /CHIDED, CHID ∆ /CHIDED ∆ /CHIDDEN ∆
CHOOSE ∆, CHOSE ∆, CHOSEN ∆
COME ∆, CAME ∆, COME ∆
DIVE ∆, DIVED/DOVE ∆ (USA), DIVED/DOVE ∆ (USA)
DRIVE ∆, DROVE ∆, DRIVEN ∆
ENGRAVE ∆, ENGRAVED ∆, ENGRAVEN ∆ /ENGRAVED
GIVE ∆, GAVE ∆, GIVEN ∆
HAVE ∆, HAD ∆, HAD ∆
HIDE ∆, HID ∆, HIDDEN ∆
MAKE ∆, MADE ∆, MADE ∆
METE ∆, METED ∆, METED ∆
MISTAKE ∆, MISTOOK ∆, MISTAKEN ∆
RIDE ∆, RODE ∆, RIDDEN ∆
RISE ∆ [rIz], ROSE ∆ [rohz], RISEN ∆ [ri-zen].
SHALE ∆, SHOOK ∆, SHAKEN ∆
SHAVE ∆, SHAVED/SHOVE ∆, SHAVED/SHAVEN ∆
SHINE ∆, SHONE ∆ /SHINED, SHONE ∆ /SHINED
SLIDE ∆, SLID/SLUD* ∆, SLID ∆
SMITE ∆, SMOTE ∆, SMITTEN ∆
STRIDE ∆, STRIDED/STRODE ∆, STRIDED/STRIDDEN ∆
STRIKE ∆ (hit), STRUCK ∆, STRUCK/STRICKEN ∆
STRIKE ∆ (delete), STRUCK ∆, STRICKEN ∆
STRIVE ∆, STROVE ∆ /STRIVED, STRIVEN ∆ /STRIVED
TAKE ∆, TOOK ∆, TAKEN ∆
THRIVE, THRIVED ∆ /THROVE ∆ (USA), THRIVED ∆ /THROVE ∆ (USA)
WAKE ∆, WOKE ∆ /WAKED, WOKEN ∆ /WAKED
WRITE ∆, WROTE ∆, WRITTEN ∆ /WRIT ∆ - old, as in "writ large".

*Ace [ays] was long ago a small coin in ancient Rome called *as*. It was used to gamble in card games so much that a card was made for it, representing the smallest number, 1, but sometimes given a high value, (Fleck 2007).

Ache spelt [ayk] by a mistake of Sam Johnson who thought it came from Greek for "pain", *akhos*. As we know <ch> spells [k] in words which have come from Greece, but this one is an old English word, and was *atch*. Just as we *bake* a *batch* of cakes, an *atch* used to *ache*. Now an *ache* aches, [ayk] [ayks].

*In *bole, dole, hole, mole, pole, role, sole, stole, vole etc.* <ole> spells [ohl] or just [ol], the latter especially in Australia, because it is easier to say [ol] than [ohl]. When we say that a sock is very *holey* we use [oh] to ensure it does not sound like *holly*. (Holey moley! Now it sounds as though the sock is holy.)

For **duke*, dune* and *dupe*, 'did ya' remember the Special Rule that if <u> spells [yoo] after <d>, then <du> spells [joo]? Have you heard American film stars say [dook] for *duke?* That's because for them <u> spells [oo], not [yoo], after [d]. One film star is called The Duke. How do you say it – [jook] or [dook]?

**Dude* is a rebel, spells [dood], never [jood], because it started out in the 1880's as a slang word in New York. It describes a man who is fastidious about his appearance. The Hebrew name *Jude* means 'the praised one' but, because New Yorkers drop their yods, they thought that immigrant Jews were saying *dude*, I guess.

**Knave* was Old English *cnafa*, meaning 'a boy servant'. Then it came to mean a naughty lad. The word *boy* was not used until after the Norman Invasion, nor was its vowel used in OE. The [k] was then silenced under French influence. OE was Germanic. Maybe the dictionary committee used <k> instead of <c> to show words which were Germanic in origin and not French. The French rarely use <k>. (Although C is a German letter it is only used in digraphs such as Sch, Ch or Ck, not alone. German words which use <c> alone are foreign adoptions.)

**Knife* has a silent <k>, maybe to remind us that the Vikings arrived in England with knives named *knifr*. Today, their descendants in Denmark and Sweden say *knif,* [kənif], and French *canif* spells [kənif] too. The French got their word from the Franks who invaded Gaul as the Romans were leaving. They use it for a penknife. The English stopped saying the [k] sound before all [n] sounds, but they still write it to remind themselves of the Viking invasion and the three Viking kings of England, King Canute — King Knut — and his sons.

**Lithe* spells [lIdh], because in Old English was *liðe* and meant 'soft, gentle, mild'.

**Pete* is short for *Peter,* but "for Pete's sake" means "for pity's sake", (Fleck 2007), and is nothing to do with St. Peter.

**Safe* as a noun came along after the old rule which turns terminal [f] into medial [v] as in *elf, elves.* So, the plural of the noun *safe* is *safes*. The verb ends in the more forceful voiced ending, *I save, he saves.* This pattern was not continued. Nowadays you can *knife* someone with a *knife* and *roof* a hut with a *roof.* We ask *the price* and we *price* our goods. Then again, we *prize* winning a *prize.*

**Shine* is not irregular nowadays when used as a verb to mean polish.

**Shone* is listed with fossil <e> words.

**Slud* is a very old word but still used in some parts. USA radio announcer at Dizzy Dee baseball game: "He slud into third base."

**Sometime* [sum-tIm] is an adjective, 'her sometime friend'; *some time* means 'at some point in time'; *sometimes* is an adverb, 'at/of some times but not all times'.

**Tube, tule* and *tune.* I bet you [bechoo] remembered that if <u> spells [yoo] after <t>, then <tu> spells [choo].

**Use* spells two words: the noun [yoos] and the verb [yooz]. In the olden days if nouns and verbs sounded similar the nouns had soft unvoiced endings and the verbs had harsh, voiced endings. You can hear this when you say a noun and then a verb:— *a life, to live; a calf, to calve; a cloth, to clothe; an excuse, to excuse; a bath, to bathe; the glass, to glaze; the grass, to graze.*

**Whole* received a silent <w> in the 16th century. It originally meant 'good', hence *holy*: 'really good'. *Whole* is related to *hale* in 'hale and hearty'. The English say *Hail!* as a good omen, to wish someone well, good health. The Germans say *Heil!* The Dutch say *Heel!* and the Swedish and Danish say *Hel!* So why add a silent <w>? I surmise that this was added to match <wh> in big things, like *whales. Whopping* meant 'large, big, impressive' by 1620, probably earlier. We can remember the spelling of *whole* by saying, "A whole whale is a whopper, but a half is not. So there is no silent <w> in half." WHOLE is a rebel to Rule 1-27 which states that H is usually silent in Digraph WH.

*Wove is the past tense of the verb {*weave*} which we shall meet in Part Four.

Rule 3-17 Fairy E produces Continental long vowels in Continental adoptions, e.g., <ique> spells [eek] and <ine> spells [een].

Reason When the English adopt a word, they do not adjust its spelling to follow Anglo spelling rules.

List 3 -17 Fairy E at work in Continental Adoptions
AMPHETAMINE, ANTIHISTAMINE, ANTIQUE, AQUAMARINE, BENZINE, CAPRICE [ees], CERISE [ees], CHEMISE [shə-meez],, CLIQUE, COMMUNIQUE, CRITIQUE*, FATIGUE [eeg], FIGURINE, FUSELAGE [arj], GELATINE, INTRIGUE [eeg], LATRINE *VS* [la-treen] or [lar-treen], LOCALE* [arl], MACHINE, MAGAZINE, MELAMINE, MEZZANINE, MORALE* [arl], NECTARINE, NICOTINE, OBLIQUE, PIQUE, PLAQUE [ark], POLICE*, PRESTIGE [eej], PRISTINE, PROMENADE [ard], QUICHE [keesh], RAVINE, TANGERINE, TECHNIQUE, UNIQUE [yoo-neek]. <u>Names</u> ANGELINE, ANGELIQUE, CATHERINE, CHRISTINE [kris-teen], DENISE [de-nees], DOMINIQUE, FRANCINE, IRENE, JAQUELINE, JASMINE, JOSPEHINE, JUSTINE, LUCINE, MARTINE, MAXINE, NADINE, THERESE [te-rayz].

*Locale is a late adoption from French, spelt like that to show it is different to *local* [loh-kəl], an adjective. The noun *locale* is used sometimes when *locality* and *scene* do not provide quite the shade of meaning required. This is how quite a few French words have entered English dictionaries, to provide new shades of meaning, (Etymonline quoting Fowler).

*Morale [mo-rarl], is different in meaning to *moral*.

*Police [pol-ees] means "city" in Greek. *Police* comes from the *policy* of cities keeping law and order with their own forces, the *polisi* [pol-ees-ee] in many countries. In English it shortened to [pol-ees], but never [pol-is]. It's a collective noun and always treated as plural with verbs. "The police are busy", not 'is busy".

Rule 3-18 Fairy E after penultimate vowels on short words ensures they spell Anglo long sounds.

Reason Penultimate means 'second to last'. The use of silent final <e> for spelling long terminal vowel sounds was promoted in spelling books in the 1500 and 1600's, to make quite sure that terminal vowels spelt their long Anglo sounds, so that *brae* spells [bray], because *bra* spells [brar]. And so that *lie* spells [lI], not [lee], as in Mr Li, [mis-ter] [lee]. This works well in short words but not so well in long words. We shall meet long words with penultimate vowels followed by <e> which do not spell long Anglo vowels later, in Part Four. They include adopted Latin and Greek words. In the following short words, Fairy E ensures the word ends in a long Anglo vowel. This silent terminal <e> mulit-tasks when and where neded, e.g., in *true* and *plie*, it insulates <u> and <i> from ending a word. In *due* and *lie* it ensures the words obey the Short Word Rule, have at least three letters.

List 3-18 Fairy E's magic action makes terminal vowels spell their long Anglo sound
ACCRUE, AGUE [ay-gyoo], {ARGUE}, ALOE, AVENUE, BELIE, BLUE, BRAE, BYE, CLUE, CONSTRUE, CUE [kyoo], DIE, DOE, DUE* [joo], DYE, ENDUE* [en-joo], ENSUE, EYE [I], FESCUE, FLOE, FLUE, FOE, GLUE, HOE, HUE, HUE AND CRY, IMBUE, LIE, LYE, OBOE, PIE, PLIE, QUEUE*, RESCUE, RESIDUE*, RETINUE, REVENUE, ROE, RYE, SLOE, STATUE, STYE, SUBDUE* [sub-joo], SUE [soo], TOE, TRUE, UNDUE*, UNTRUE, VALUE, VENUE, VIE, WOE. <u>Names</u> RAE, SUE.

*_Due_ and the other words with <du> follow the Special Rule that if **<u> spells [yoo] after <d>, then <du> spells [joo].**

*In _queue_ [kyoo], <qu> spells just [k], not [kw]. It arrived in England after <u> in <qu> was silenced in France, as in _quiche_. The simplest way to write _queue_ would be _quu_ but <uu> is not allowed nor is terminal <u>. So the French spelling remains. It's best not to pronounce it [kyoo] in France because that means 'backside' (_cul_), see 'Days on the Claise: Fun with French,' on line. In French, _queue_ spells [kay].

Rule 3-19 Most suffixes do not change the sound of stem vowels lengthened by Fairy E, unless the suffix also ends in Fairy E.

Reason We shall discuss suffixes ending in Fairy E later. When words which end in Fairy E get suffixes, the <e> remains if the suffix starts with a consonant, as in _amusement_ and _refinement_. This means <u> in _amusement_ continues to spell [yoo] and <i> in _refinement_ continues to spell [I]. If the suffix starts with a vowel, this replaces Fairy E and the preceding vowel remains long, as in _lining_ from _line_ plus _ing_. We shall meet the suffixes which do change preceding vowels later.

Rebels? WISDOM. _Wise_ does not drop Fairy E in _wisely_ because <i> still spells [I]. Fairy E is dropped in _wisdom_ because <i> spells [i] in _wisdom_. _Wisdom_ is not a reading rebel, but it is a writing rebel. In DULY, TRULY, WHOLLY, NINTH and LINEAGE, dropping <e> makes them writing rebels too but ensures that they are read correctly. If not, _duely_ and _truely_ would rhyme with _cruelly_. _Wholly_ is written like that to avoid _wholely_ which would add an extra syllable, as would _nineth_. As in rule 2-68, <e> spells [e] before [th]. So _nineth_ would spell [nin-eth]. _Lineage_ [lin-ee-uuj] refers to someone's family tree and is not the same as _linage_ [lIn-uuj], which means number of lines of print.

Relevant Writing Rule for dropping Fairy E and other silent <e> endings.

Part One When adding a suffix to a silent <e>, drop that final <e> if the suffix begins with a vowel, _-ed, -ing, -ism –y etc._, but not if it starts with a consonant, _-ment, -ness etc._

Rebels WISDOM, DULY, TRULY, WHOLLY, { ARGUMENT, AWFUL}, NINTH are all rebels because <e> has been dropped from their stems: _wise, due, true, whole, {argue, awe}, nine_. Also, ACREAGE and {LINEAGE}, for <e> is retained on their stems: _acre_ and _line_. No other vowel will substitute for <e> in _acreage_. For instance, the first <a> spells short [a] in _macrophage, acrid_ and _acrobat_. Note that when we speak of the number of lines in print, we use _linage_ [lIn-uuj], which fits the rule, whereas _lineage_ [lin-ee-uuj] refers to someone's family tree. PINEAL and ROSEATE also spell three syllable words, not just _pine_ or _rose_ plus the suffix _-ate_.

MILEAGE can also be written as MILAGE. EYEING can be EYING. The past is always EYED.

Part Two If the silent <e> is softening <g> to spell [j] or <c> to spell [s] then it remains, as in _management_ and _noticeable_, unless the suffix starts with <i> or <y>.

Rebels BINGEING, SINGEING and TINGEING have to differ from _binging, singing_ and _tinging_. CAGEY is the only such word which retains <e>. All others, even _stagy_, are 'ruly', e.g., _lacy, raging_, (Cummings; Lewis 1965). Return to Reading Rules.

Fairy E on Suffixes — _capsule, volume._

Suffixes are usually unstressed, with their unstressed vowels, often reduced to the schwa sound [ə]. However, a suffix ending with Fairy E has a long vowel and long vowels are stressed. This means the vowel before it has to be less stressed, to give the alternate tum-te-tum rhythm of English words. So, the vowel before the suffix is usually a short one to fit the rhythm.

Rule 3-20 Suffixes which end in Fairy E are preceded by a short vowel in the stem word, unless that vowel is spelt with <u>.

Reason This is a pattern Prof Cummings observed in words. He noted that regardless of the sound of the vowel in the stem, be it short or long, it is short when followed by a suffixe ending in Fairy E, a suffix

172

wth a long vowel. We shall start by looking at the suffix —*ule*. The stem word *node* spells [nohd] with a long vowel which shortens in *nodule* [nod-yool]. It's *glode* [glohb], and *global* [gloh-buul] because the suffix does not end in Fairy E. However, in *globule* [glob-yool] the vowel is short [o]. As we would expect, <u> resists being shortened, as in *plume* [ploom] which, with a suffix like —*ule*, becomes *plumule* spelling [ploom-yool], not [plum-yool].

Rebels SPINULE, MINUTE *adj*.

Rebels' Reasons *Spinule* [spIn-yool], keeps its long [I] to show its stem is *spine* not *spin*.

The noun *minute* spells [minet] with a short [i], as in nouns *minimum* and *minuet* and adjectives *mini* and {*miniature*} and the verb *minimize*. The only time <i> spells [I] is in the adjective *minute* [mI-nyoot] and in a collective noun to describe minute things, {*minutiae*}. This stress on both the first and second syllable serves to describe something tinier than the other two adjectives describe. In *tiny* <i> also spells [I]. The adjective *minute* disobeys Rule 3-20, but then again <ute> is probably not a suffix in this word. It is from the Old French word *minut*, from Latin *minuta*. The final <e> in the English noun *minute* [min-ət] does nothing. It does not behave as Fairy E and is therefore a new fossil.

Not needed but nice to know. One meaning of *minute* is that of a small, minute notation or note. Together, these notes or minutes summarize discussion at a meeting, but they are not called [mI-nets], just [min-ets]. 'Minutes' usually means the mini portions of an hour. Each hour is divided into sixty minutes and then a second division results in 360 'seconds', so there are sixty seconds (second division pieces) in a minute. Circles are also divided into minutes. First they are divided into 360 degrees and then each degree is divided into sixty pieces, i.e., minutes. Then each minute is divided again into seconds. The Babylonians counted up to sixty, not one hundred, and then began again. It is hard to draw so many thin slices of a circle but the bigger the circle is, the easier it is to fit in 360 x 60 x 60 slices. Astronomers draw huge circles on their sky-maps. Now back to things we need to know.

List 3-20
CAPSULE, GLOBULE, GRANULE, LEGUME, MINUSCULE, MODULE*, MOLECULE, NODULE*, OVULE, PLUMULE, PUSTULE, RETICULE, RIDICULE, SACCULE, SCHEDULE*, SPICULE, STATUTE, STIPULE, TUBULE, VESTIBULE, VOLUME.
Module, nodule and *schedule* follow the Special Rule that if <u> spells [yoo] after <d>, then <du> spells [joo].

Rule 3-21 Suffixes -*ate* and –*ite* can spell [at] and [it] in words which are not verbs, without altering the preceding vowel.

Reason Just because these suffixes reduce, lose stress, it does not mean that the preceding vowel becomes long. The only vowel which is not short before <ate> and <ite> is that spelt with <u>, as in *fortunate*. Why have some suffixes lost the magic action of terminal <e> on the preceding <i> or <a>? It is because in most adjectives the last syllable is not stressed and so the <i> or <a> shrinks in adjectives. This has produced a new lot of words ending in a fossil <e>, as in these examples in bold type:— my {*favourite*} *Vegemite* — the **opposite** *satellite* — despite her **exquisite** manners. Let's {*appropriate*} some {*appropriate*} equipment. Let's approximate the **approximate** height of the building. The ***fortunate*** lady inherited all of the family fortune.

The words listed below are nouns and adjectives.

Rebels? PIRATE [pI-rət] and PRIVATE [prI-vat] have kept long vowels, because in these words <ate> is not a suffix. It just looks like a suffix. *Pirate* comes from Latin *pirata*; *private* from the Latin *privatus* meaning 'separated or deprived'.

List 3-21

APPROXIMATE [a-prok-si-mət], DEFINITE [def-in- ət], DELICATE [del-ee-cət], DELEGATE [del-e-gat], DESOLATE [dez-oh- lət], DESPERATE [des-pe-rat], DIRECTORATE [dI-rekt-ə-rat], DISPARATE [dis-pa-rat], DOCTORATE [dok-tə-rat], CHOCOLATE [chok-o-lət], EXQUISITE [eks-kwiz-it], FEMININE [fem-in-in], GRANITE [gran-ət], {HYPOCRITE} [hip-oh-krit], IMMACULATE [im-ak-yoo-lat], INDEFINITE [in-def-in-it], INTRICATE [in-tri-kit], LITERATE [lit-e-rat], MINUTE [min-ət] of time., OBDURATE [ob-joo-rat], OPPOSITE [op-o-sit], POMEGRANATE [pom-ee-gran-at], PALATE [pal-at], PREREQUISITE [pree-rek-kwiz-it], SENATE [sen-at], SEPARATE [sep-a-rət].

Not needed but nice to know. The suffix –*ate* came from French as –*at* but then <e> was added to show a long vowel. Originally from Latin, it means *to make, to cause, to act upon, to do something with*. It ends verbs, as in *educate,* makes verbs, *granule* becomes the verb *granulate*, it ends nouns which ended –*atus* and –*atum* in Latin, like *senate*, and it ends adjectives from past participle –*atus* and –*ata* of Latin verbs as in, 'The *desolate* children cried, each in their *separate* rooms.' The suffix –*ite* from French –*ite* which came from Latin –*ita*. It makes adjectives and nouns meaning 'connected with or belonging to', especially useful naming minerals, e.g., *magnetite*. Although Latin is considered a dead language, its donated spare parts have added extra meanings to our words. Now back to things we need to know.

Rule 3-22 On verbs the suffix *-ise* **spells [Iz], not [Is] or [is], and is always stressed.**
Reason The original form, taken from Greek via Latin, is *–ize,* but spelt *–ise* in Britain when <z> was still unpopular. Even Shakespeare berated zed, "Thou unnecessary letter......" he called it in King Lear.
Rebels PREMISE and PROMISE and PRACTISE spell [premis] and [promis] and [prak-tis].
Rebels' Reasons *Premise* is an alternative spelling for noun *premiss,* a statement on which reasoning is based, plural *premisses. Premises* is a different word — a plural noun for building/s and grounds. Although the verb *practise* looks different to the noun *practice* it sounds the same. *Promise* began as a noun, c.1400, from the Latin noun *promissum.* It was used as a verb later on but kept the noun pronunciation. By contrast the verb *compromise* came first, c.1425, from the Latin verb *compromittere*. It was then used as a noun, too. They both spell [kom-prom-Iz], in this case keeping the verb pronunciation because it came first. We can add these three words to the list of new English fossils. Maybe one day we shall write *premis, promis* and *practis*. Note:- *Promise* is "Lemon Rebel", being without <mm> after the short [o]. Its ancestor word *promissum* did not require <mm> because short, stressed [o] was the third syllable from the end of the word. In short, *promise* is an abbreviation and abbreviations do not need to obey rules.

Now we shall read a list of all verbs which have to end <ise>, even though <s> spells [z].
List 3-22A <ise> spells [Iz] if in a verb.
ADVISE, APPRISE, CHASTISE, COMPRISE, COMPROMISE, DEMISE, DESPISE, DEVISE, FRANCHISE, DISFRANCHISE, ENFRANCHISE, EXCISE, IMPROVISE, INCISE, PREMISE, PRISE (up), REVISE, TELEVISE.
Relevant Writing Tips. Here is a full list of all verbs which have to end <ise> even though <s> spells [z] in these words: *advise, apprise, chastise, comprise, compromise, demise, despise, devise, franchise, disfranchise, enfranchise, excise, improvise, incise, premise, prise* (*up*) *revise, televise* and, coming soon, {*advertise, circumcise, enterprise, exercise, supervise, surmise, surprise, disguise, guise*}, (Quinion 2002). Mr. Thompson in 1980, on p. 114, wrote that *ise* is a verb ending and *ice* is a noun ending. This is correct for pairs like verb *practise* and noun *practice*. However, where a noun has become a verb e.g., *sacrifice* and *notice*, the *ice* ending remains. Similarly nouns from verbs, e.g., *enterprise* from *prise*, retain <ise> to spell [Iz]. Thompson's encoding tip is to use the suffix *–ise* at all times to spell [Iz] because *-ise* is always correct and *-ize* only sometimes — which shows we continue to be in fear of Z! Cummings reminds us that it's *finalize* not *finallize* because no twinning is necessary after an unstressed syllable, [fIn-al-Iz]. Return to Reading Rules.

List 3-22B Modern spelling of verbs:
ACCESSORIZE, ACCLIMATIZE, AGGRANDIZE, AGONIZE, ANGLICIZE, ANIMALIZE, ANNUALIZE, ANODIZE, ANTAGONIZE, APOLOGIZE, ATOMIZE, BAPTIZE, BITUMINIZE, BOTANIZE, BRUTALIZE, CANNIBALIZE, CANONIZE, CAPITALIZE, CARAMELIZE, CENTRALIZE, CHARACTERIZE, CIVILIZE, COLONIZE, COMMUNALIZE, CRITICIZE, CUSTOMIZE, DECOLONIZE, DECRIMINALIZE, DEHUMANIZE, DEMAGNETIZE, DEPOLITICIZE, DESENSITIZE, DESTABILIZE, ECONOMIZE, EMPATHIZE, EMPHASIZE, EPITOMIZE, EQUALIZE, EVANGELIZE, FANTASIZE, FEDERALIZE, FEMINIZE, FINALIZE, FOSSILIZE, HOMOGENIZE, HOSPITALIZE, HUMANIZE, IDOLIZE, ITALICIZE, ITEMIZE, LOCALIZE, MAGNETIZE, MAXIMIZE, MECHANIZE, METABOLIZE, MINIMIZE, MOBILIZE, MORALIZE, OPTIMIZE, OSTRACIZE, OXIDIZE, OZONIZE, PAGANIZE, PALLETIZE, PARASITIZE, PARENTHESIZE, PATRONIZE, PENALIZE, POLITICIZE, PRIVATIZE, PUBLICIZE, RANDOMIZE, REVITALIZE, RHAPSODIZE, ROMANTICIZE, SANITIZE, SATIRIZE, SCANDALIZE, SENSITIZE, SKELETONIZE, SOLEMNIZE, STABILIZE, STERILIZE, STIGMATIZE, SUBSIDIZE, TANTALIZE, TRANQUILIZE/ TRANQUILLIZE, UTILIZE, VANDALIZE, VICTIMIZE, VITALIZE, VOCALIZE, VULCANIZE, WOMANIZE.

The verb suffix *–ize* spelling [Iz] (of Greek origin, meaning "cause to be or conform to or resemble"), was intentionally adopted into English by Thomas Nashe (1567-1601) in order to replace lots of little words with one big one. Many technical terms are coined this way, e.g., *oxidize,* as well as verbs of ethnic derivation, e.g., *Americanize* and verbs derived from proper names, e.g., *mesmerize* from Dr Mesmer, the famous Austrian hypnotist. Americans like the suffix *-ize* but the English still seem to fear <z> the 'sign of the dagger', and prefer to write *–ise.*

Almost any noun or adjective can be made into a verb by adding *-ize*, e.g., *hospitalize, finalize,* as long as it is not A) stressed on its last syllable, nor B) back-formed from nouns that have <s> in the stem.
A) Words which are stressed on their last syllable cannot receive the suffix *-ize,* hence *finalize, randomize* but not *corruptize.* The suffix just cannot be used, whether spelt *-ize* or *–ise*. This was pointed out by a wonderful young professor, Hideki Zamma, at the Kobe City University of Foreign Studies in Japan. Hideki's fresh eye on English suffixes was groundbreaking and his death after a car accident in 2016 is a tragedy. It seems the reason for this is that because *–ize* is always stressed, if the last syllable of the stem was stressed there would be two stressed syllables together, which upsets the tum-te-tum rhythm of English. What about *capsize?* Both syllables are stressed, but that's OK because *—ize* has not been added as a suffix. It is not *capsize*. It's a word which sailors probably picked up from Spanish *capuzar,* "to sink by the head", (Online Etymology Dictionary).
B) At the end of Part Two there are conditions for twinning a final consonant before adding a suffix which begins with a vowel. One condition is that the last vowel of the stem word must remain short and stressed after adding the suffix. When the stressed suffix *–ize* or *–ise* is added, the previous syllable loses stress in order to maintain the alternating stress pattern of English. This is why twinning does not occur before these two suffixes. It's why we twin <l> in *equalled* and *equalling* but not in *equalize.*
C) Words which are made by stripping longer words back to stem words with <s> in the stem cannot use *–ize* but can use *–ise* to spell [Iz]. Some words strip back to stems which are free standing words in their own right and some strip back to stems which cannot stand alone, need to be bound to a prefix or a suffix, bound stems, e.g., *television, televise*; *circumcision, circumcise* – (both verbs were made from nouns).
Bryson 2004, p 110 queries *moisturize,* for we already have *moisten,* and says we don't need *finalize* as we have *finish.*

Note that when <i> is in a prefix it spells [i] if the prefix ends in a consonant, e.g., *dis-use,* (because 'double gates' are only needed on stressed vowels) and when the prefix is 'open', ends on the vowel, <i> spells [I], e.g., *di-late*. We have already listed the words in which terminal <ine> spells Continental [een], and also [in] or [ə] if the suffix is unstressed, as in *engine*. In the next list <ine> spells [In] due to the Magic Action of Fairy E.

List 3-23 More 'Magic Action' from Fairy E. Remember, <ise> spells [Iz] in verbs.

ABASE, ABATE, ABLAZE, ABODE, ABRADE, ABSTRUSE, ABUSE, ACCEDE, ACCUSE, ACUTE, ADDUCE, ADORE, ADVICE, ADVISE [Iz], AGAPE, AGILE, ALONE, ALIKE, ALIVE, ALLSPICE, ALLUDE, ALPINE, AMAZE, AMUSE, ANODE, APACE, APPRISE [Iz], AQUILINE [In], ARISE [Iz], ARRIVE, ASIDE, ASININE, ASSUME, ASTRIDE, ASTUTE, ATHLETE, ATONE (from *at one.*), AWAKE* Δ, AWHILE*, BACKDATE, BAGPIPE, BAROQUE, BASEMENT, BECAME Δ, BEEHIVE, BEGUILE, BEHAVE*, BEHOVE, BENZENE, BESIDE, BESTRIDE, BETAKE, BETIDE, BIPLANE, BOLDFACE, BOOTLACE, CANINE, CAPSIZE, CAPSULE [kapsyool], CARAPACE, CHASTISE [Iz], CLOTHES-LINE, CLOTHES-PEG, CLOVEHITCH, COGNATE, COLLATE, COLLIDE, COMBINE, COMMUTE, COMPETE, COMPILE, COMPLINE, COMPOSE [kompohz], COMPRISE, CONCAVE, CONCEDE, CONCISE, CONCLAVE, CONCLUDE, CONCRETE, CONCUBINE, CONDOLE, CONDONE, CONDUCE, CONFIDE, CONFINE, CONFUSE [fyooz], CONFUTE [fyoot], CONNIVE, CONNOTE, CONSOLE, CONSUME, CONTRITE, CONTRIVE, CONVENE, CONVOKE, CORRODE, COSINE, CROCODILE, CRUSADE, CURATE, UP TO DATE, DATE-LINE, DEBATE, DECADE*, DECIDE, DECLINE, DECODE, DECOKE, DEDUCE, DEFACE, DEFAME, DEFILE, DEFLATE, DEFUSE [fyooz], DEGRADE, DE-ICE, DELETE, DELEGATE *verb,* DELUGE [del-yooj], DEMOTE, DENOTE, DENUDE, DEPLETE, DEPOSE [ohz], DEPRAVE, DEPRIVE, DEPUTE, DERATE, DERIDE, DERIVE Δ, DESCRIBE, DESPISE [Iz], DESPITE, DEVICE, DEVISE, DEVOTE, DICTATE, DIFFUSE *adj.*[fyoos], DILATE, DILUTE, DISCLOSE [ohz], DISCRETE, DISGRACE, DISGUISE [dis-gIz], DISINCLINE, DISLIKE, DISPLACE, DISPOSE, DISPUTE, DISREPUTE, DISROBE, DISUSE noun [dis-yoos], DIVIDE [div-Id], DIVINE, DOCILE, DONATE, EFFACE, ELEPHANTINE, ELOPE, ELUDE, EMBRACE, ENCASE, ENCLOSE [ohz], ENCODE, ENGGE, ENRAGE, ENROBE, ENSHRINE, ENSLAVE, ENTHRONE, ENTHUSE [enthooz], ENTICE, ENTWINE, EQUATE, EQUINE, ERASE [e-rayz], ESCAPE, ESTATE, EVADE, EVOKE, EXCISE *verb* [Iz], EXCISE *noun* [Is], EXCITE, EXCLUDE, EXCRETE, EXCUSE v. [yooz], EXCUSE n. [yoos], EXHALE* [eg-zayl], EXHUME* [eg-zyoom], EXILE, EXPLODE, EXPOSE, EXTREME, EXTRUDE, EXUDE, FACILE, FELINE, FEMALE*, FINITE, FISSILE, FLAGSTONE, FOOTNOTE, FRAGILE, FRANCHISE* *n,* FRIGATE, FRUSTRATE, GAMETE, GLANDULE, GLISSADE, GLUCOSE [ohs], GODLIKE, GREENGAGE, GRENADE, HANDSHAKE, HUMANE, IGNITE, IMMUNE, IMPALE, IMPEDE, IMPOSE, IMPUTE, INANE, INCISE [Iz], INCITE, INCLINE, INCLUDE, INDUCE, INFLAME, INFLATE, INFUSE *v,* INMATE, INNATE, INSANE, INSCRIBE, INSIDE, INTAKE, INTONE, INTRUDE, INVADE, INVITE, INVOKE, JEJUNE, JOCOSE, JUJUBE, JUKE-BOX, KEEPSAKE, LICHGATE, LIFE-LIKE, LIFETIME, LOCATE, LUDDITE, LIVE, ENLIVEN, LIVEN UP, MAGNATE, MAKE-UP, MAKE-DO, MAKESHIFT, MANDATE, MANDRAKE, MANHOLE, MEMBRANE, METHANE, MICROBE, MIGRATE, MILESTONE, MINUTE (tiny) [mI-nyoot], MISNAME, MISPLACE, MISPRICE, MISQUOTE, MISRULE, MISSILE*, MISTAKE, MISTIME, MISUSE, MOBILE, MOROSE *adj.* [ohs], MUNDANE, MUTATE, NAPHTHALENE, NARRATE, NECKLACE, NEGATE, NITRATE, NON-WHITE, NUBILE, OBESE, OBLIGE, OBSCENE, OBTRUDE, OBTUSE, OCCLUDE, OCTANE, OCTAVE, OPAQUE, OPINE, OPPOSE, OXIDE, OZONE, PALEFACE, PALMATE, PALPATE, PANCAKE, PANTILE, PARADE, PAROLE, PASTIME *VS,* PERUSE [ooz], PHONE *abbrev.,* PIPELINE, PLENITUDE, POLITE, POST-DATE, POT-HOLE, PRECEDE, PRECISE, PRELATE, PRELUDE, PRESAGE *verb,* PRESCRIBE, PRESIDE,

PRESUME, PRIMROSE, PROBATE, PRODUCE *noun* [pro-joos], PRODUCE *verb* [prə-joos], PROFANE, PROFILE, PROFUSE, PROLAPSE, PROMOTE, PROPOSE, PROSCRIBE, PROSTATE, PROSTRATE, PROTRUDE, PROVIDE, PROVOKE, RACEME, RAMPAGE, REBATE, REBUKE, RECEDE, RECITE, RECLINE, RECLUSE, REDUCE*, REFINE, REFLATE, REFUGE, REFUSE [fyooz], REFUTE, REGALE, REGIME*, REGULATE, RELATE, RELEGATE, REMAKE, REMOTE, RENAME, REPLACE, REPOSE, REPRODUCE, REPUTE, RESIDE [ree-zId], RESOLE, RESUME, RETAKE, RETRACE, REVILE, REVISE [Iz], REVIVE, REVOKE, REVIVE, REWRITE Δ, RHIZOME, RISSOLE [ris-ol] Aust., SACRIFICE, SALINE, SALUTE, SANGUINE <u>=[w], SCHEDULE, SECEDE, SECLUDE, SECRETE, SEDUCE, SEDATE, SENILE, SERENE, SIDELINE, SIDELONG, STATELESS, STATESMAN, STERILE, SUBLIME, SUBSCRIBE, SUBSIDE, SUBSUME, SUCHLIKE, SUFFICE, SUNBATHE, [dh], SUNSHADE, SUNSHINE, SUNSTROKE, SUPINE, SUPPOSE, SUPREME, TACTILE, TEENAGE, TELEPHONE TELEVISE [Iz], TITMICE, TOOTHACHE <ch>=[k], TRADUCE, TRANSLATE, TRANSPOSE, TRAPEZE, TRIBUNE*, TRIBUTE*, TENSILE, UNITE, UNQUOTE, UNWISE [Iz], UPDATE, UPGRADE, VACATE, VACCINE, VIBRATE, VICISSITUDE, WHALEBONE, WISEACRE*, WHOLESALE. Proper Noun/Adj GENTILE*. Names CANUTE, CAROLINE, NICOLE, PRIMROSE, SIMONE.

Irregular Verbs, present, past, past participle.
AWAKE Δ, AWAKED/AWOKE Δ, AWAKENED Δ/AWOKEN Δ.
BECOME Δ, BECAME Δ, BECOME Δ.
DERIVE Δ, DERIVED/DEROVE Δ, DERIVED/DERIVEN Δ
REWRITE Δ, REWROTE Δ, REWRITTEN Δ

*It is not easy to see if a syllable is a suffix or a part of a stem word. *Decade* [dek-ayd] looks like a Rebel Lemon Word, looks as if it should spell [dee-kayd]. However, *dec* is the stem. *Exhume* spells [eg-zyoom] for as we learnt in Part One, if <x> is between two vowels, it spells [gz], (Fox, p. 69), **but only** if the second vowel is said stronger than the first, (Cummings, p. 351). For the same reason **exhale* spells [eg-zayl]. However, many folk now say [eks-hayl] to match *inhale*.

**Franchise* - did you remember that <ise> spells [Is], not [Iz], in nouns?

**Reduce* is a 'duty' word for <du> spells [joo]. There may be others in the list. Can you find them?

**Regime* is adopted from French but not adapted to English spelling. It spells [ray-zheem] because In French <e> spells the long vowel [ay] and <i> softens <g> in French to a sound between [j] and [sh], which we write as [zh]. *Regime* does not rhyme with *retime* because <i> spells [I] in the first syllable of a stem word like *time*, but not in the second syllable of a word like *regime*.

**Tribune* [tri-byoon] and *tribute* [tri-byoot] both have short [i] sounds because they were shortened with the Third Syllable from the End Rule when longer: *tributum, tributus*, in Latin.

Missile* is said [mis**-əl] by some Americans - another new fossil in the making.

Not needed but nice to know. Latin had a word *cedere* for *go*. We spell it *cede*, to mean "go away, go back, withdraw, yield". Hence *concede, accede, recede, precede, secede*. When we mean "go forward" we spell it *ceed*, (think *speed*), hence *proceed, succeed, exceed*. We use *sede* in only one word, *supersede*, because *sede* means *sit*, i.e. to supersede someone is to sit on them. Now back to things we need to know.

No Magic Action in Baggage

We do not expect the "magic action" of Fairy E in *baggage*. We met *baggage* in Part One along with many other words which just use <e> as a softener, to make <g> spell [j]. We can add a few more words to that list now.

Rule 3-24 Suffixes <age> and <ege> spell [uuj] or [əj].

Reason It appears such words began as nouns, with unstressed endings and only later some of them became verbs too. So terminal silent <e> does not make <a> spell [ay] in their verbs. Also, these words

have been both adopted **and** adapted and so the first syllable is stressed, said louder, which weakens the [a] sound before [j] to [uu] and some people say it as a grunt, written [ə]. This only happens when <age> is a suffix, not in *age, cage* nor *engage. Engage* [en-gayj] begins with a prefix and so the stress remains on the second syllable, since most prefixes, as we know, are not stressed. *Teenage* [teen- ayj] and *greengage* [green-gayj] (Gage's green plum), listed in 3-23, are compound nouns, not stems with suffixes.
Rebels RAMPAGE, GARAGE, BARRAGE, COLLAGE, FUSELAGE and MASSAGE. Also RENEGE.
Rebels' Reasons *Rampage* used to spell [ram-pəj] but it rebelled by lengthening its second syllable so that it spells [ram-payj], to match an associated word, *rage,* in which <age> spells [ayj] being a one syllable word.

In *garage, barrage, collage, fuselage* and *massage,* <age> spells [arzh] because they have not been fully adopted from the French. The final syllable is stressed the French way and consequently spells [ar]. When <g> is softened with either <e> or <i> in French it spells a softer sound than [j] but harsher than [sh]. So we write it [zh]. *Garage* [gar-rarzh] can be traced back to *guarde* and *garer,* safe dock for ships, (Ayto). *Barrage* as artillery fire spells [ba-rarzh]. The French pronunciation keeps its meaning separate from *barrage* [ba-rəj] meaning barrier as in a river. *Collage* [ko-larzh]: French pronunciation in artistic matters is not unusual, just as Italian terms and pronunciation are used in music. *Fuselage* is another French word, originally 'spindle-shaped'.

The Prof., (Cummings p. 147), tells us that *renege* [rə-nig] is the only word in which terminal <ge> spells [g], instead of [j]. The Prof. says it is also written *renig.* Maybe the dictionary elders felt spelling it *renig* was 'infradig', too undignified, for a word which comes from Latin's *renegare.*

List 3-24 suffix <age> spells [uuj] or [əj]
ACREAGE*, ADVANTAGE *VS*, BANDAGE, DISADVANTAGE *VS,* DISPARAGE, ENVISAGE, FRONTAGE *f*, LINKAGE, MISMANAGE, PILGRIMAGE, PILOTAGE, PLUMAGE, POSTAGE, PRESAGE* *noun*, PRIVILEGE, SACRILEGE.

*Acreage spells [ayk-ruuj] but, if the <e> was removed, would spell [ak-ruuj]. It's usual to remove <e> when a suffix starting with a vowel is added, but only <cre> will make <a> spell [ay].

*Presage spells [pres-əj] for the noun, ('omen' or 'presentiment'), but it spells [pree-sayj] for the verb ('predict' or 'foreshadow'), which we'd expect, for verbs usually have stronger endings than nouns when using the same word. This noun's sound changed when it became a verb.

No Magic Action in Alice.
In part One we learn that <c> is "Soft in City but not in Kitty' in Part One. We have now met Fairy E. So why doesn't *Alice* spell [alIs]? Why doesn't *Alice* rhyme with *spice?*
Rule 3-25 Fairy E only works her magic action after <c> in single-syllable words.
Reason Fairy E works magic action in words like *ice* and *splice, ace* and *place,* but in words of two or more syllables which end <ice>, or <ace>, terminal <e> just softens <c> to spell [s]. We cannot say that <e> is a fossil, even though it is not Fairy E, for it does a job, softens <c> to [s]. This has been adopted into English as one way of spelling [s] and a very useful way, for if <s> spelt [s] at the end of a singular word it could be mistaken for a plural word.

List 3-25 in which <ice> spells [əs] and <ace> spells [əs]
ACCOMPLICE, APPRENTICE, AVARICE, BENEFICE, CREVICE, EDIFICE, GRIMACE, MALPRACTICE, ORIFICE, POPULACE, PRACTICE, PRECIPICE, PREFACE, PREJUDICE. <u>Names</u> ALICE, JANICE.

As we know, a double gate after a vowel prevents it spreading into a long vowel, as in *dance, sense* and *lunge* for instance. However, we know that the double gate in *range* does not prevent <a> spelling the long sound [ay], in [raynj]. We saw this in other words, like *strange,* but only when <a> was in a stressed syllable, not in *orange*. It is as if <e> is doing two jobs, the job it does softening <g> to spell [j] and its Fairy E job. This also happens in the stressed syllable <aste>, as in *paste*. Due to vowel shift in England, *past* spells [parst], not [payst], and *dance* spells [darns], not to [dayns]. Only the Magic Action of Fairy E can turn [parst] into [payst].

Rule 3-26 The 'Magic Action" of A Very Powerful Fairy E" changes <ast> [ast] to <aste> [ayst].
Reason One old way to lengthen vowels is still used in *hind, comb,* and *strange*. As we know, terminal <e> in words ending <ange> is needed to soften <g> to [j]. However, in *paste* <e> is just a Fairy E and a very powerful fairy at that, for vowels do not normally lengthen behind double gates!! I do not know why Fairy E is needed. Why not write *paist?* Why is *waist* the only word in which <aist> spells [ayst]?
One Rebel CASTE spells [karst]
Rebel's Reason *Caste* is a late adoption from Spanish-Portuguese, (Cummings, p. 103), and so <a> spells the Continental long sound, [ar]. The English word *cast* originally spelt [kast] before vowel shift produced [karst] in the south of England. The two words, *caste* and *cast*, differ in meaning.
List 3-26
BASTE, CHASTE, CHASTEN* [chay-sen], DISTASTE, HASTE, HASTEN* [hay-sen], LAMBASTE*, PASTE, PASTRY*, POST-HASTE, TASTE, TOOTHPASTE, UNCHASTE, WASTE.
Lambaste has even stress on both syllables for it is a compound verb, meaning 'lame and beat', 'lame and thrash'.
Pastry spells [payst-ree] not [payz-tree] or [paz-tree] or [past-ree] due to its origins as *paste* of flour and water.
*When the suffix –en is added to *chaste* and *haste* Fairy E is dropped, but her magic action remains for *chasten* spells [chay-sən] and *hasten* spells [hay-sən]. *Hasten* and *chasten* are old verbs, left over from the days when English verbs had a variety of endings. By the time Chaucer wrote books most of the Old English endings had been dropped but we still see some old endings in his books, e.g., *-en, -est, -eth, -e, -yng, -ynge,* and *-et*.

As we know, <st> spells [s] before suffixes (i.e. unstressed) <le> and <en>. Also <ft> spells [f] before the suffix [ən]. We shall meet {*moisten*} later. Prof. Cummings, on p. 400, explains that when [t] is between [s] or [f], both made at the front of the mouth, and vowels made at the back of the mouth, like [ə], then [t] is bypassed for the tongue takes a shortcut. We notice it does not happen in *sten-gun* and *tungsten* in which <sten> is stressed for [e] is made further forward in the mouth.

When suffixes beginning with a vowel are added to Fairy E, she 'flies away' but her magic remains in the preceding vowel. Some of us sing "When <ing> comes to play, <e> runs away." So it's *haste, hasten*. Also *safe, safest, lace, lacy, devote, devotee*. However, if <ly> comes to play, or any other suffix which starts with a consonant, then <e> remains in place; *safe, safety*.
List 3-27 Magic Action in words of three or more syllables. Twenty words, in which <tu> spells [choo], are in italics. We can nickname them "Tulip Words'.
ABDICATE, ABOMINATE, ABROGATE, ABSOLUTE, ACCELERATE, ACCLIMATIZE, ACCOLADE, ACCOMMODATE, ACCUMULATE, ACCURATE, ACETATE, ACETONE, ACIDULATE*, ACONITE, ACTIVATE, ADEQUATE, ADIPOSE, ADJUDICATE, ADMINISTRATE, ADULATE*, ADULTERATE, ADVOCATE, AGGRAVATE, AGGREGATE, AGITATE, AGONIZE, AGGRANDIZEMENT, AGGRAVATE, AGGREGATE, AGITATE, AGONIZE, ALLOCATE, ALTITUDE, AMALGAMATE, AMERICANIZE, AMMONITE, AMPLITUDE, AMPUTATE, ANECDOTE, ANGLOPHILE, ANIMATE, ANNIHILATE* silent h, ANNOTATE, ANODIZE, ANTAGONIZE, ANTEDATE, ANTELOPE, ANTHOLOGIZE, ANTHRACITE, ANTICIPATE, ANTICLOCKWISE, ANTIDOTE, APOLOGIZE, APPETITE, APPOSITE, APTITUDE, AQUAPLANE, ASSIMILATE, ATOMIZE, ATTITUDE, ATTRIBUTE, CALIBRATE, CAMISOLE,

CAMOMILE, CANDIDATE, CANNIBALIZE, CAPITULATE, CAPTIVATE, CELLULOSE, CENTIGRADE, CENTIPEDE, CENTRALIZE, CENTRIFUGE, COLLABORATE, COLONNADE, COMMUNICATE, COMPLICATE, CONCENTRATE, CONGLOMERATE, CONGRATULATE, CONGREGATE, CONJUGATE, CONSECRATE, CONSIDERATE, CONSOLIDATE, CONSTITUTE, CONSULATE, CONSUMMATE*, CONTAMINATE, CONTRAVENE, CONTRIBUTE, CONTUMELY, CO-OPERATE, CORRELATE, CORRUGATE, CRITICIZE, CROSS-POLLINATE, CULMINATE, CULTIVATE, DECAPITATE, DECENTRALIZE, DECIMALIZE, DECIMATE, DECOMPOSE, DECORATE, DEDICATE, DEFECATE, DEGENERATE, DELIBERATE, DEMOBILIZE, DEMOCRATIZE, DEMONSTRATE, DEMORALIZE, DENIGRATE, DEPOPULATE, DEPRECATE, DESICCATE*, DESIGNATE, DESOLATE, DETONATE, DEVASTATE, DEVOTEE, DICTAPHONE, DISABUSE, DISCONSOLATE, DISENGAGE, DISFRANCHISE, DISINTEGRATE, DISLOCATE, DISSIPATE, DISSOLUTE, DISTRIBUTE, DOGMATIZE, DOMESTICATE, DOMINATE, DUPLICATE*, ECONOMIZE, EDUCATE*, EFFEMINATE, EJACULATE, ELABORATE, ELATED, ELECTROCUTE, ELECTRODE, ELECTROPLATE, ELEVATE, ELIMINATE, ELONGATE, ELUCIDATE, EMANATE, EMANCIPATE, EMASCULATE, EMIGRATE, EMULATE, ENVELOPE* noun, EPISODE, EQUIVOCATE, ERADICATE, ESCALOPE, ESCAPADE, ESTIMATE, EVANGELIZE, EVENTIDE, EVISCERATE, EXACTITUDE, EXAGGERATE, EXASPERATE, EXCAVATE, EXCOMMUNICATE, EXECUTE, EXERCISE, EXHILARATE*, EXPLICATE, EXQUISITE, EXTRADITE, EXTRAPOLATE, EXTRICATE, FABRICATE, FASCINATE, FINALIZE, FLAGELLATE, FUMIGATE, GELIGNITE, GENOCIDE, GESTICULATE, HESITATE, HOMOGENIZE, HOMOPHONE, HUMANIZE, IDOLIZE, ILLEGITIMATE, ILLUMINATE, ILLUSTRATE, IMBECILE, IMITATE, IMMACULATE, IMMIGRATE, IMMOBILE, IMMOBILIZE, IMMUNIZE, INCAPACITATE, INCOMPLETE, INCRIMINATE, INCUBATE, INCULCATE, INCULPATE, INDELICATE, INDICATE, INEXACTITUDE, INFANTICIDE, INFANTILE, INFILTRATE, INFINITE, INFINITUDE, INGRATITUDE, INHUMANE, INNOVATE, INOCULATE, INSECTICIDE, INSEMINATE, INSTIGATE, INSTITUTE, INSULATE, INTEGRATE, INTESTATE, INTIMATE, INTRODUCE*, INUNDATE, INVIGILATE, IRONSTONE [silent r], IRRESOLUTE, IRRIGATE, IRRITATE, ISOLATE, ISOTOPE, ITALICIZE, ITEMIZE, JUVENILE, JUXTAPOSE, KEROSENE, LEGALIZE, LEGISLATE, LEGITIMATE, LEGITIMIZE, LEMONADE, LIQUIDATE, LIQUIDIZE, LOCALIZE, MAGISTRATE, MAGNETIZE, MAGNITUDE, MALACHITE, MANGANESE, MANIPULATE, MARINADE, MARITIME, MASTICATE, MATRICIDE, MATRICULATE, MEDICATE, MEDITATE, METABOLIZE, METRICATE, METRONOME, MICROPHONE, MICROSCOPE, MICROWAVE, MILITATE, MISBEHAVE, MISCALCULATE, MITIGATE, MOBILIZE, MODULATE*, MOLECULE, MONOPOLIZE, MONOTONE, MONOXIDE, MORALIZE, MOTIVATE, MUTILATE, NAVIGATE, NITROBENZENE, NOMINATE, NUMERATE, OBLITERATE, OBSOLETE, OKEY DOKE [slang], OOLITE [oh][oh], ORANGEADE, ORIGINATE, OSCILLATE, OSCILLOSCOPE, OSTRACIZE, OVULATE, OXIDIZE, OXYGENATE, PALISADE, PALPITATE, PANTIHOSE, PANTOMIME, PARACHUTE [shoot], PARADISE, PARAPHRASE, PARASITE, PENALIZE, PENETRATE, PESTICIDE, PHEROMONE, PHILOSOPHIZE, PLATITUDE, POLLINATE, PONTIFICATE, POPULATE, POTENTATE, PRECIPITATE, PREDICATE, PREDISPOSE, PREFABRICATE, PRESSURIZE, PREVARICATE, PROCRASTINATE, PROFLIGATE, PROJECTILE, PROPAGATE, PROSECUTE, PROSTITUTE, PROXIMATE, PUBLICIZE, RECAPITULATE, RECOGNIZE, RECONCILE, RECONDITE, RECONSTITUTE, RECTITUDE, REDUPLICATE*, REHABILITATE, REJUVENATE, RELOCATE, REMONSTRATE, RENUMERATE, REPRODUCE*, RESOLUTE, REUNITE, RUMINATE, SACRIFICE, SACRILEGE, SEPARATE, SERENADE, SIMULATE, SPECULATE, STERILIZE, SUBJUGATE, SUBLIMATE,

TABULATE, TANTALIZE, TELEPHONE, TELESCOPE, TELEVISE, UNDULATE*, UNGRATEFUL, UNTIMELY, URINATE, UTILIZE, VACCINATE, VACILLATE, VANDALIZE, VARICOSE, VEGETATE, VENTILATE, VERISIMILITUDE, VICTIMIZE, VINDICATE, VISUALIZE, VITALIZE, VOLATILE.

Annihilate spells [an-nI-il-ayt] for stress on [nI] means <h> is silent, after a stressed syllable, (with <an> an unstressed prefix). (Note, OPD disagrees and pronounces <hil> as if in *hilarious*, [hil].)

Desiccate was given <cc> to link it to Latin *siccus* "dry", even though it arrived in the French word for dry, *sec*. We remember the single <s> because things dry out or desiccate in the desert. We remember the <cc> because we think of desiCCated Co-Co-nut. For more on this see {*desert* and *dessert*}.

Envelope [**en**-və-lohp] is stressed on the first syllable. It is a noun, formed from the verb *envelop* [en-**vel**-op]. The verb came first and so the prefix had to be stressed in the noun (most unusual) to tell them apart.

Exaggerate is one of the few words in which <gg> is softened to [gj], as in *suggest*. As we know, in other <gg> words it spells [g], e.g., *ragged* spells [rag-ed].

Exhilarate spells [eg-zil-ərayt] because as we know, if <x> is between two vowels, it spells [gz], (Fox, p. 69), **but only** if the second vowel is said stronger than the first, (Cummings, p. 351).

Undulate, acidulate, educate, introduce, reduplicate, reproduce, adulate and *modulate* are all 'duty' words, words in which <du> spells [joo], all 'Soldiers on Duty' words.

Consummate. Please note, <u> spells [u], before double gate <mm>.

We can now read all the words which end in the suffix <able>.
List 3-28 These words use <able>, rather than <ible>, because each stem lacks only its original terminal <e> and in these words <able> has replaced Fairy E.
BRIBABLE bribe, CONSOLABLE console, DATABLE date, DURABLE *bound stem*, DURABILITY, DEFINABLE define, DISPOSABLE dispose, DISPUTABLE dispute, DISREPUTABLE disrepute, EMBRACEABLE embrace, ENDURABLE endure, ENDURABLY, ENGAGEABLE engage, EXCHANGEABLE exchange, EXCITABLE excite, EXCUSABLE excuse, EXTRADITABLE extradite, IMPROVABLE improve, INADVISABLE advise, INAPPLICABLE apply, INCALCULABLE calculate, INCONSOLABLE, INDEFINABLE, INDESCRIBABLE, INDOMITABLE, INDUTABLE duty, INERADICABLE, INESCAPABLE, INEXCUSABLE, INEXPLICABLE, INEXTRICABLE, INFLATABLE inflate, INNUMERABLE numerate, PRESUMABLE presume, QUOTABLE quote, RECOGNIZABLE recognize, REFUTABLE refute, REPUTABLE repute, REUSABLE reuse, TUNABLE tune, UNMISTAKABLE mistake, UNUSABLE, USABLE use.

The next words use <able> because their stems have other suffixes starting with <a>.
ESTIMABLE estimate, INOPERABLE operate, PENETRABLE penetrate, INIMITABLE imitate, INESTIMABLE estimate, EXPLICABLE explicate, IMPREGNABLE impregnate, DEMONSTRABLE demonstrate.

The stem word *flame* has been used to make the following words. The suffix <able>, not <ible>, always replaces Fairy E. In each word *flammable* spells [flam-ə-buul], because <m> has been twinned. However, the four words for just two meanings are very misleading. The prefix <in> does not mean *not* for it is part of the word *inflame*, 'to put a flame in something'.
FLAMMABLE, NON-FLAMMABLE, INFLAMMABLE, NON-INFLAMMABLE.

Ruts in the Road, <sive> and <tive>
The **suffix <ive> makes adjectives and always follows [t] or [s].** It is as if these words are stuck in ruts in the 'road to reading'. They only go along two ruts, the [s] rut and the [t] rut. It's easy when words end in [t], *vegetate, vegetative,* or *relate, relative*. Some words change their ends before adding this suffix,

change them to [t] or [s]. *Expand* becomes *expansive*. Other words change [d] to [s], e.g., *evade* becomes *evasive*. Some change [r] to [s], e.g., *cohere – cohesive*. What if an ending is not easy to change to [t] or [s]? Then words add <at> or <it>, as in *imaginative* and *inquisitive*. The noun form of *abuse* [ə-byoos], not the verb *abuse* [ə-byooz], is used to make *abusive* [ə-byoo-siv], because <ive> cannot join to the terminal [z] of the verb. The verb *accuse* becomes *accusative*, not *accusive* for this reason.

Rule 3-29 Vowels in the stems of words made with suffix –*ive* decode in the usual ways but linking particles <at> and <it> spell [at] and [it], and <s> before <ive> always spells [s].

Reason As we shall see in the following lists, stem words obey all the usual rules. The joiners <at> and <it> are not derived from terminal <ate> or <ite> but are little joiners, like <i> in *handiwork*. Cummings calls little joiners like these "linking particles", (Cummings p. 48). Some words, like *combat* and *legislate*, have no need of a linking particle when taking the suffix <ive>. Others need a link, because, as we know, suffix <ive> only follows [s] or [t]. Suffixes are unstressed (although can get secondary stress, weaker than primary stress on the main syllable) and so <s> before <ive> spells [s], not [z].

List 3-29A Vowels are kept short with double gates before <ive>.
ADDICTIVE, ADJECTIVE, ADAPTIVE, ADOPTIVE, AFFECTIVE, ATTENTIVE, CONDUCTIVE, ERUPTIVE, EXPENSIVE, EXTENSIVE, INEFFECTIVE, INEXPENSIVE, INOFFENSIVE, INSTRUCTIVE, INVECTIVE, INVENTIVE, OPPRESSIVE, RESPONSIVE.

What does <ative> spell when stems ending <ate> add <ive> and drop <e>?
If stress falls on <a> then <ative> spells [ay-tiv].
If stress does not fall on <a> then <ative> spells [ə-tiv].
Stress falls according to the tum-te-tum pattern of English speech. This changes to te-tum-te-if the word starts with a prefix, or seems to start with a prefix. As we know, third or fourth vowel from the end, if stressed, is short, without the need of double gates, unless spelt with <u>.

List 3-29B Stress falls on <a> giving [ay-tiv]
♪te-tum-te-tum-te ADMINISTRATIVE, COMMUNICATIVE, INVESTIGATIVE.
♪tum-te-tum-te CONTEMPLATIVE, IMITATIVE, INNOVATIVE, LEGISLATIVE, PENETRATIVE, QUALITATIVE, QUANTITATIVE, REGULATIVE, REPLICATIVE, SPECULATIVE, STIMULATIVE, VEGETATIVE.

List 3-29C Stress does not fall on <a>, giving [ə -tiv].
♪te-tum-te-tum. ACCUSATIVE, COMPARATIVE, DERIVATIVE, DEROGATIVE, DEMONSTRATIVE, EVOCATIVE*, INDICATIVE, INVOCATIVE*, PROVOCATIVE*, REMONSTRATIVE.
*Note how <k> in *provoke, invoke* and *evoke* is no longer needed in *provocative* etc.
tum-te-tum FRICATIVE, FIXATIVE, LAXATIVE, LUCRATIVE, NARRATIVE, NEGATIVE, RELATIVE, SEDATIVE, TALKATIVE, TENTATIVE.

Do you break IMAGINATIVE and MANIPULATIVE up like this, te-tum—tum-te-tum, in order to keep the beat? I do. *Imag—inative; manip—ulative*. It's a little pause, not a real break. English words do not have breaks in them, except for the interjection "u-oh", or when a Cockney drops the [b] in *bottle,* [bo-el].

List 3-29D Final <itive> spells [i-tiv] when <it> has been added to the stem word, for as we know, <i> spells [I] in the first syllable and [i] after that, unless in a final syllable before Fairy E. As we know, third or fourth vowel from the end, if stressed, is short, without the need of double gates, unless spelt with <u>.
ACQUISITIVE, ADDITIVE, COGNITIVE, COMPETITIVE, ELECTROPOSITIVE, FUGITIVE, GENITIVE, INQUISITIVE, INSENSITIVE, POSITIVE, PRIMITIVE, PUNITIVE, SENSITIVE.

List 3-29 E Those which do not have to add <it> or <at>, spell vowels which match their stem vowels.
ABRASIVE [u-brayd], ABUSIVE [u-byoos], ADHESIVE [ad-hee-siv], COHESIVE [koh-hee-siv], COMBATIVE [kom-bat-iv], CONCLUSIVE [kon-kloo-siv], CONDUCIVE [kon-joo-siv],

CONSECUTIVE, [kon-sek-yoo-tiv], CORROSIVE [kor-roh-siv], DECISIVE [dee-sI-siv], DERISIVE [dee-rI-siv], DIMINUTIVE, [di-min-yoo-tiv], DIVISIVE [di-vI-siv], EFFUSIVE [ef-yoo-siv], ELECTROMOTIVE, [ee-lek-troh-moh-tiv], ELUSIVE [ee-loo-siv], EROSIVE [e-roh-siv], EVASIVE [ee-yay-siv], EXCLUSIVE [eks-kloo-siv], EXECUTIVE [ek-sek-yoo-tiv], EXPLETIVE [eks-plee-tiv], EXPLOSIVE [eks-ploh-siv], ILLUSIVE [i-loo-siv], IMPLOSIVE [im-ploh-siv], INCLUSIVE [in-kloo-siv], INCONCLUSIVE, [in-kon-kloo-siv], INHIBITIVE [in-hib-it-iv], INTRANSITIVE [in-tran-sit-iv], INTRUSIVE [in-troo-siv], INVASIVE [in-vay-siv], LOCOMOTIVE, [loh-koh-moh-tiv], OBTRUSIVE [ob-troo-siv], POLLUTIVE [po-loo-tiv], PROHIBITIVE, [proh-hib-i-tiv], RECLUSIVE [ree-kloo-siv], SECRETIVE [see-kret-iv], TRANSITIVE [tran-sit-iv].

Colourful R and Fairy E — *here, hire, cure.*
The Magic Action of silent terminal <e>, known by the little ones as Fairy E, after the consonant <r>.
As we know, that "Magic Action" lengthens vowels and this happens too when Fairy E follows <r>. Although <r> is not pronounced at the end of words by non-rhotic speakers — rhotics roll their r's — this almost silent letter <r> changes or 'colours' the preceding vowel. Letter <r> is almost silent because, if you listen carefully, you can hear the little Schwa sound, which colours the vowel, makes it sound like a diphthong.

Rule 3-30 Terminal <ere> spells [eer]
Reason Fairy E lengthens vowels, turns short vowels into long ones. Before the Great Vowel Shift, <e> spelt short [e] and long [ay]. Fairy E lengthened [e] to [ay] and when followed by [r] becomes [air] — even though terminal [r] is no longer "rolled", just pronounced in a reduced, non-rhotic form, it makes <ere> spell [air]. This reduced form of [r] is expressed by Schwa as we see when [air] is written in IPA symbols: /eə/. (See sound chart in Introduction)
In French, <ere> still spells [air]: *mère* and *père* spell [mair] and [pair]. In England, in their GVS, [air] lifted to [eer], in all but two words. The GVS only occurred in England, see appendix.
Rebels WHERE and THERE and WERE.
Rebels' Reasons *There* spells [dhair], and *where* spells [wair] because their vowels did not lift. Maybe *here* lifted because it was easier to tell apart then from *there*. Maybe *where* and *there* did not lift because they can be asked or shouted with more emphasis than *here*. Whatever it was, all the other <ere> words lifted too, and now they end in [eer]. *Were* spells [wer] but because [wer] meant *man* it added an <e> to show the difference.
List 3-30 <ere> spells [eer]
HERE, MERE, ADHERE, ATMOSPHERE, CASHMERE, COHERE, ECOSPHERE, HEMISPHERE, INSINCERE, INTERFERE, OOSPHERE [oh-oh-sfeer], PERSEVERE, REVERE, SEVERE, SINCERE, SPHERE*, STRATOSPHERE, TROPOSPHERE, WEREWOLF.
*Since <ph> spells [f] in *sphere* we know this word comes from Greek.

Rule 3-31 Terminal <ire> spells [Ir]
Reason This is expected, for just as *dine* and *fine* spell [dIn] and [fIn], so do *dire* and *fire* spell [dIr] and [fIr]. Fairy E at the end of words, words like *hire,* tell us that they were much once longer words, like today's *irony, iron, irate* and *iris*. As <ir> spells [Ir] in all these words, we would expect words which have shortened to have <ire> spells [Ir]. *Hire* was once *hyrian*. Not all words were longer but they fell into the pattern of <ire> spells [Ir]. For instance, *fire* was written *fyr* and *fier* but then joined the <ire> words. It left behind *fiery*, which never became *firey*. *Sire* is short for Latin *senior*.
Historically, <ire> spelt [eer], before the Great Vowel Shift. Now, ever since the GVS, because the [r] in *fire, hire* etc., is not rolled, (unless the speaker is rhotic), it sounds like a Schwa sound at the end of [I] in

these words which end <ire>. That's why *fire* and *hire* are written in IPA as /faɪə/ and /haɪə/. In this book I say *fire* spells [fIr] and *hire* spells [hIr] because not everyone knows the IPA.

List 3-31

ACQUIRE, ADMIRE, ASPIRE, ATTIRE, CONSPIRE, DESIRE, DIRE, DIRECT, DIRECT ACCESS, DIRECT DEBIT, DIRECTIVE, DIRECTLY, DIRECTNESS, EMPIRE, ENQUIRE*, ENTIRE, FIRE, BACKFIRE, FIREARM, FIREBRAND, FIREDAMP, FIREFLY, FIREMAN, FIREPLACE, FIREPROOF, FIRESIDE, FIREWOOD, FIRING-LINE, HIRE, *INQUIRE, INSPIRE, IRE, LIVE WIRE, MIRE, MISFIRE, PERSPIRE, QUAGMIRE*, RESPIRE, RETIRE, RETIREE, REQUIRE, REWIRE, SAMPHIRE, SAPPHIRE*, SATIRE, SIRE, SPIRE, SQUIRE, TIRE, TRANSPIRE, UMPIRE, VAMPIRE, WIRE. Proper Noun IRELAND.

*OPD says *enquire* is usually used for 'ask' and *inquire* for 'investigate'. So I say an *enquiring mind* and *an inquiry*.

*Don't let W muddle you, *quagmire* spells [kwog-mIr].

*At first the English copied the French spelling of *sapphire*, with one <p> but then they discovered the Romans had used <pp> and so they thought it would make them look smart to use <pp>. The Greeks used <pp> and the Hebrews too but there the story changes because the older Sanskrit word *sanipriya* has a single <p> and means "stone precious to the planet Saturn", i.e. *saturn-precious*.

Long ago there was a noun *ure*. It is obsolete now. It meant 'work, practice, exercise, use.' *Inure* is short for 'put in ure or use'. It now means 'to be used to something, especially hardship' as 'He was inured to failure'.

Rule 3-32 Terminal <ure> spells [yoor] or [oor] in stem words.

Reason In <ure> the silent <e> lengthens the single letter vowel and the almost-silent <r> colours the vowel, turns it into a diphthong, [oo-uh]. This is written /u:ə/ in IPA. In most words <ure> spells [yoor], /ju:ə/ in IPA, because <ure> only spells [oor] after **<r>, <j>, <l> or <s>**. When <u> spells a long sound it's [yoo], unless it follows <r>, <j>, <l> or <s>. Then it's [oo], having 'dropped the yod', the [y] sound. Note:- It is only in English that <u> can spell long [yoo]. We do not hear it in the German word *Uber* and elsewhere on the Continent. More about yods very soon.

List 3-32A <ure> spells [yoor].

CURE, DEMURE, DISFIGURE, FIGURE [fig-u], FIGURE OF FUN, EPICURE, IMMURE, IMPURE, INSECURE, INURE, MANICURE, MANURE*, OBSCURE, PEDICURE, PROCURE, PURE, SECURE*, TENURE.

List 3-32B <ure> spells [oor].

ALLURE, CONJURE, ADJURE, INJURE, LURE.

Epicure is an eponym. It means one who follows Epicurus, a Greek philosopher whose name we spell the Latin way. It now means one who has a refined taste in food and drink, but originally Epicurus taught that pleasure is the highest good and identified virtue as the greatest pleasure. This is similar to the advice to love God and do as you like, because if you love God you will only like doing the right thing. Epicurus taught that virtue is the greatest pleasure and so if you seek pleasure you will do so virtuously.

Manure is [man-yoor] or [mar-nyoor], depending on where you end the first syllable. It originally meant 'to cultivate (land, a garden) by manual labor' 'man-ure' being 'hand-use'. Then it meant to spread dung and then it meant dung and other fertilizer. Until 1700, to manure the mind meant to cultivate one's brain, train one's mental powers.

Secure [sə-kyoor] means 'free from care', *se cura*, literally 'self-care, self-sufficient.'

In List 3-32 words, <ure> ends stem words. Soon, we will meet words which use the suffix <ure>.

Sure, Sugar.

Why isn't SURE listed in 3-32? *Sure* is very unusual. Say *"We miss you"*, over and over, stressing *miss*. Do you hear [wee] [mish-yoo]? This is [sh], spelt <su>.

Rule 3-33 is a Special Rule. Only two words which start with <su>, use <su> to spell [shoo]: *sure* **and** *sugar.*

Reason Back when *sure* used to spell [syoor], it was easier to say [shoor]. Also *sugar* spelt [syoo-gar] but it was easier to say [shoogar]. When [s] combines with [y] we say the two sounds fuse — [s] and [y] combine or fuse and become [sh]. It's called Yod Fusion, (also Yod Coalescence). We shall meet *sugar* again, along with other words in which <ar> spells [ar].

List 3-33 SURE spells [shoor].
SUGAR, SUMAC*, SURE, AS SURE AS, ASSURE, CENSURE, COCKSURE, COMPOSURE, ENSURE (USA), INSURE, SURE-FIRE, FOR SURE!, SURE-FOOTED, SURE THING!, SURE WILL!, SURE DO!, TO BE SURE, TONSURE, UNSURE.

*Sumac is pronounced either [soo-mak] or [shoo-mak], but it is so rare that we do not include it in the rule.

Tulips mature

We already know the Special Rule that if <u> spells its long sound, which is [yoo] in English, then <tu> spells [choo]. This is because [t] and [y] fuse and become [ch]. It is another example of Yod Fusion. We saw this in *tulip*. This means <ture> spells [choor].

Rule 3-34 Terminal <ture> spells [choor].
Reason Yod Fusion.
List 3-34 <ture> spells [choor]
ACUPUNCTURE, ADMIXTURE, ADVENTURE, AGRICULTURE, APICULTURE, AQUACULTURE, AVICULTURE, CANDIDATURE, CAPTURE, CARICATURE, CONJECTURE, CULTURE, DEBENTURE, DENATURE, DENTURE, DISJUNCTURE, DIVESTITURE, ENRAPTURE, EXPENDITURE, FIXTURE, FLORICULTURE, FRACTURE, FUTURE, GESTURE, IMMATURE, INDENTURE, INVESTITURE, JUNCTURE, LECTURE, LEGISLATURE, LIGATURE, MANUFACTURE, MATURE, MINIATURE* *silent <i>,* MISADVENTURE, MIXTURE, MONOCULTURE, MUSCULATURE, NATURE, NOMENCLATURE, PASTURE, PICTURE, POSTURE, PREFECTURE, PREMATURE, PUNCTURE, RAPTURE, RECAPTURE, RUPTURE, SCRIPTURE, SCULPTURE, SIGNATURE, STATURE, STRICTURE, STRUCTURE, SUTURE, TEXTURE, TINCTURE, VENTURE, VESTURE, VINICULTURE, VITICULTURE, VULTURE.

*Miniature has a silent <i> because it began as *miniare* 'to paint or decorate a manuscript in red' with paint from 'red lead', *minium*. This Latin word was used in Italian to describe the very small paintings in manuscripts and then in English came to mean any small painting, because everyone thought it was related to 'mini', but it was really closer to *mineral*. (Ayto, p. 349).

Endure Duty.

We already know the Special Rule that if <u> spells its long sound, [yoo], then <du> spells [joo]. This means <dure> spells [joor].

Rule 3-35 Terminal <dure> spells [joor]
Reason Yod Fusion, in which [d] and [y] fuse and make [j].
List 3-35 <du> spells [joo]
ENDURE, PROCEDURE.

Azure.
Where is AZURE? It also obeys a special rule.
Rule 3-36 is a Special Rule. When <u> spells [yoo] after [z], then <zu> or <su> spells [zhoo].
Reason — Yod Fusion. This began back when <y> had not lost its yod after <z> and [zhoo] was easier to say than [zyoo]. This new consonant, [zh], is very rarely used and it sounds like a voiced [sh]. It is a consonant without a letter or even a digraph of two letters. It is [z] fusing with a yod, the fourth Yod Fusion consonant, after [j], [ch] and [sh]. As we know, <s> spells [z] after a stressed vowel, as in *has*. That is why we hear [zh] in *cl<u>o</u>sure* as well as in *<u>a</u>zure*.
Rebels ZUCCHINI, SHIATZU and other foreign words which never had a yod.
List 3-36
AZURE, COMPOSURE, EMBRASURE ERASURE, CLOSURE, EXPOSURE.

  Not needed but nice to know. The suffix -*ure* forms abstract nouns of action, from the Latin suffix -*ura* which ended female nouns denoting action, e.g., *pressure*, or result, e.g., *creature*. It came into English via the French suffix -*ure*. Also, it denotes a group, like *legislature*. It only appears on words adopted from French and Latin. Now back to things we need to know.

Rule 3-37 Terminal <are> spells [air].
Reason Words ending <are> stopped spelling [ar], in the Great Vowel Shift. This long vowel shifted to [air], which is a lift of frequency. It is also formed slightly higher in the mouth. So, we could call the GVS the Long Vowel Lift. The final <e>, known to children as Fairy E, reminds us that <a> spells a long sound. The <r> is almost silent, just a little schwa sound, which colours [ay] to [air]. In IPA it is /eɪə/. (This almost silent <r> does the same thing to [ay] in *hair*, in which [ay] is spelt <ai> with no need of Fairy E.) At the same time, in the GVS, words ending <ere> changed from spelling [air] to the higher sound of [eer]. As we know, Fairy E is silent, e.g. in *scare*, but when replaced by <y>, as in *scary*, then <ary> spells [air-ee]. The rascal word *scarce*, in which <ar> spells [air], is discussed in 3-67.
Rebels ARE Δ, CURARE, SARI. In these words <ar> spells [ar]. *Curare* and *sari* each end in [ee]. In *are*, terminal <e> is silent.
Rebels' Reasons *Are* took no part in the Great Vowel Shift. It was once *aren* in some parts of England, in others it was *earun* and, up north, *aron* until it just used the first syllable, [ar], and the rest all shrank to a silent <e>. It could have been written *ar* because it is part of the verb *to be* which is allowed to break the Short Word Rule. However, if it used just two letters it could have been mistaken for the word *or*. However, its terminal <e> is actually unnecessary and so it can be called a fossil <e>. The other two rebels are foreign adoptions, from Spanish and Hindi, in which <e> is not silent.
List 3-37 Stem words ending <are> or <ary> and words built on them.
AWARE, ARUM LILY, BARE, BAREBACK, BEWARE, BLARE, CARE, CAREFREE, CAREFUL, CAREFULLY, CAREFULNESS, CARELESS, CARESS, CARETAKER, CAREWORN, CHARY, COMPARE, DARE, DAREDEVIL, DECLARE, ENSNARE, FANFARE, FARE, FAREWELL, FLARE, GARISH, GLARE, GLARY, HARE, HAREBELL, HARELIP, HECTARE, MARE, NECESSARY, PARE*, PARENT*, PARENTAGE [pair....], PARENTHOOD PARINGS, *PREPARE, RARE, RAREFY*, RAREBIT, RARING TO GO, SCARE, SCAREMONGER ƒ [skair-mun-ger], SCARY, SEPARATE* *verb*, SHARE, SHARER, SNARE, SPARE, SQUARE, STARE, TARE, UNAWARE, UNAWARES, UNSPARING, VARY, WARE, WARES, WARY, WELFARE. Proper Nouns
DELAWARE, DELFTWARE, MARY, SARAH, MARYLAND.
Rarefy is one of our 4 rare words ending <efy> spells [efI].
Separate comes from Latin *se* 'without or apart', (Etymonline) and *parare* 'make ready, prepare', i.e. 'prepare apart'. Due to this it can spell [sep-pair-rayt], as well as [sep-a-rayt]. This makes it hard to write

down correctly but one way to remember it is to use a mnemonic, say to yourself, "*separate* is a rat of a word to spell," and make sure you write *a rat* inside *separate*.
The adjectives become adverbs in these words: BARELY, RARELY, SPARELY and SQUARELY.
Rascal SCARCELY uses <ar> to spell [air], with no good excuse. As you will see in 3-67.

Old Fairy E ensures <ore> spells [or].
Rule 3-38 Terminal <ore> spells [or].
Reason Before the Great Vowel Shift, all over Europe, including England, <o> spelt the long sound [or], and its short version [o]. In the GVS, this long vowel [or] lifted to [oh] in many words, but not if written <or>. Normally if <or> is followed by a vowel, as in *sorel,* the <o> spells its short sound but, when <or> is followed by a terminal <e>, the vowel is long. Children say the silent terminal <e> is Fairy E, magically making the preceding vowel long. Using this analogy, let's just say that it must be a very old fairy because right through the GVS, (1450 – 1650), she has steadfastly ensured <o> spells [or] in words ending <ore> and disregarded the fact that elsewhere in words [or] lifted to [oh], and higher still, to [oo]. Before the GVS, everyone was rhotic, everyone rolled their r's. Around 1450 it became fashionable not to do so in London. This fashion spread very slowly. Many English were still rhotic, rolled their Rs until 1800. As we have seen in words like *dare, fire, here* and *pure,* <r> became a little schwa sound. Also, the sound the vowels in <are>, <ere>, <ire> and <ure> spelt changed in the GVS. The first two lifted to [air] and [ee], the next bent a little, to [I] and <u> changed from spelling [oo] to [yoo]. However, there was no change in words ending <ore>, which continued to spell [or].
Old Fairy E stands firm until this day, after nearly every terminal <or>. Those which do not add <e> to terminal <or> are listed below as Writing Rebels, for they do not break spelling rules since both terminal <or> and <ore> spell [or].
Rebels? FOR, OR, NOR and TOR and the suffix —*or* are not rebels. These little words spell [or] without the help of terminal <e>. *Fore, ore* and *tore* are different words and we can see that they are different words, due to the final <e>. When <or> ends a word, we can see it is a suffix, as in *sailor,* because it has no final <e>. If it ended in <e> it would seem more important than a little unstressed suffix. We'd stress it, as in *galore*.
Relevant Writing Tip. There are only four stem words which end in <or>, FOR, OR, NOR and TOR. Other words only end in <or> if they have added the suffix —*or*. *Castor* derives from a name, Greek Kastor, twin brother of Pollux. *Abhor* was *abhorr*. Its stem is now obsolete. Return to Reading Rules.
List 3-38 terminal <ore> spells [or]. **Note:-** When *fore* is used as a prefix it retains silent <e>.
ADORE, AFORE, ANYMORE, ASHORE, BEDSORE, BEFORE*, BEFOREHAND, BOOKSTORE, BORE, CHORE, COMMODORE, CORE, DEPLORE, DRUGSTORE, ENCORE [on-kor], EVERMORE, EXPLORE, EXTEMPORE, EYESORE, FOLKLORE, FOOTSORE, FORE*, FORECAST *VS,* FORECLOSE, FOREFATHERS, FOREFOOT, FOREFRONT, FOREGO (precede), FOREHAND, FORELAND, FORELEG, FORELOCK, FOREMAN, FOREMAST *VS,* FOREMOST, FORENAME, FORERUNNER, FORESEE, FORE-SHEETS, FORESHORE, FORESKIN, FORESTALL, FORESWORE, FORETASTE, FORETELL, FURORE [fyoo-ror], GALORE, GORE, HACKAMORE, HELLEBORE, HERETOFORE, IGNORE, IMPLORE, INSECTIVORE, INSHORE, LAKESHORE, LONG-SHORE, LORE, MEGASPORE, METAPHORE, MICROSPORE, MORE, OFFSHORE, OMNIVORE, ONSHORE, OOSPORE [oh-oh], ORE, PINAFORE, PORE, REBORE, RESCORE, RESTORE, SADDLESORE, SCORE, SEMAPHORE, SHORE, SMOOTHBORE, SNORE, SOPHOMORE, SORE*, SORELY, SPORE, STEVEDORE, STORE, SWORE, THEREFORE, THREESCORE, TORE, WHEREFORE, WHORE*, WORE, YORE, ZOOSPORE [zoh-oh-spor]. Proper Noun SINGAPORE.
**Whore* like *whole* did not always have <w> and has always spelt [hor].

*The prefix *fore-* [for] means *before,* meaning "before in time, place, order or rank," as in *foretell, forerunner, forefather* and *foreman,* or "the front part of", as in {*forehead*}. The prefix *for—* [for] is used chiefly with verbs and grew out of an old Saxon word meaning "away, apart, off" as in *forgo, forbid, forget* and also grew from another word meaning "completely, intensely" as in *forgive.*

Before in time means "before in time past," but *before* also means "in front of me" as in *before me.* Why is the past in front of us? This is best explained in Pisin, PNG pidgin English, in which *before* means 'the past', and *behind* means 'the future'. Why? Because the past is spread out before us, because we can see it. The future is behind us, where we cannot see it. "Lukim yu behain," means "See you later on," and the phrase "gut taim bipo," refers to an era of good times long ago. (*Behain/behind, bipo/before.*)

Sometimes we read in the Bible that someone is *sore afraid.* That *sore* came from Germany where *sehr* means *very,* which may be why when we are 'very afraid', we say we are 'sure afraid', or we 'sure are afraid'.

Suffixes on terminal <re> after single letter vowels.

As we know, suffix <ed> spells [d] after vowels and all voiced consonants, except [d].

So *bore* [bor] becomes *bored* [bord], *hire* [hIr] becomes *hired* [hIrd], *revere* [reveer] becomes *revered* [reveerd], *stare* [stair] becomes *stared* [staird], *cured* [kyoor] becomes *cured* [kyoord].

As we know, suffixes do not change the sound of vowels lengthened by Fairy E. Vowels stay long even if a suffix starts with a different vowel, as in *boring, hiring, revering, staring, curing,* for Fairy E's 'magic action' is carried on by that vowel, or semi-vowel <y> acting as vowel.

We can now read all the following words, and, as we know and would expect, they use the suffix <able>, not <ible> because each has a stem which ends with <e>, in this case with Fairy E.

List 3-39
ADMIRABLE *admire* *[ad-mru-buul]
CURABLE *cure*
COMPARABLE *compare* *[komp-ru-buul]
DESIRABLE *desire*
DURABLE stem is in *endure*
INCOMPARABLE *[in-komp-ru-buul]
INCURABLE *cure*
INSURABLE *sure*
PROCURABLE *procure*

*A syllable fades out of these words to avoid two weak beats in a row, which we shall hear more about soon.

Bossy R, as in *art, fern, bird, torn, urn.*

Whenever <ar> spells [ar], or <or> spells [or] or <er>, <ir> and <ur> all spell [er], it's because R is being bossy, controlling what these vowels spell.

The word-sounds [ar], [or] and [er] are long vowel sounds. Normally <a>, <e>, <i>, <o> and <u> would spell long [ay], [ee], [I], [oh] and [yoo]. Earlier, before the Great Vowel Shift, they spelt long [ar], [ay], [ee], [or] and [oo]. Back then, people rolled their R's. With tongue held high and curled back, [r] was sometimes even trilled! Maybe you have heard [ar] pronounced pirate-style, '*Arrr!*' [ar-r]. Then, when folk stopped rolling R's, instead of saying each [r] separately, like another syllable, the unrolled [r] *attached to the vowel. He became Bossy R. They were said together, the vowel and [r]. However, try saying any of these long sounds with your tongue raised and the tip curled back. All you hear is [ar], [or] or [er]. That is because Bossy R pushes vowels back, further inside the mouth, down into the throat. The tongue actually seems to push sounds back down the throat with its curled-up tip. Say [r] and look at your tongue. The vowels [ar], [or] and [er] are all said at the back of the throat, with the mouth open enough to allow the tongue to curl up and back. Linguists say R controls these vowels and call him Controlling R. Children call him Bossy R. Please note that each vowel is spelt with a single letter. R's effect on digraph vowels, as in, say, *roar,* if any, will be discussed later.

*Not needed but nice to know. Why does [r] "attach" to the vowel? Why is it that [r] is more attracted to vowels than consonants? It is very similar to vowels. When we say [r], breath flows over the tip of our curled-up tongue and over each side of the tongue. So it's produced without blocks or restrictions to air from the lungs, just like a vowel sound. That's why, if a vowel is followed by /r/, it keeps on flowing, stretches into a long sound, as long as [r] does not launch a vowel, come before a vowel, in which case it is equally attracted to the vowel either side of it and has no effect on either, as in *carol* and *coronet,* in which the vowels either side are short, not stretched or controlled by [r]. To ensure this does not happen, [r] needs to be followed by another consonant, as in *Carl* and *corn* in order to stay in control of the preceding vowel. Originally, if AR and OR (also ER, IR, UR and YR) came at the end of a word, another R was added to ensure the long vowel was carried on. This became unnecessary but we still see RR at the end of a few rare words, e.g., *charr, err, birr, dorr, curr* and *myrrh.* Nowadays, if RR occurs inside a stem word, it acts like any other pair of twinned consonants and the preceding vowel is short, as in *borrow* and *horrid.* Now back to things we need to know.

Q. When is R bossy?
Ans. When <a>, <e>, <i>, <o> or <u> is followed by <r> and another consonant, as in *fern, barn, torn, bird* and *hurt,* or nothing at all, as in *bar, her, for, fir* and *fur,* then <r> is bossy and called Bossy R. Originally, Bossy R controlled the vowel behind it only if R was followed by another consonant, as in *fort.* If there was no second consonant, another R was added, as in *err, burr, purr* and *parr,* but most words, like *fur,* have dropped this extra <r>. When R is between vowels, it does not know which vowel to cling to and just hangs between them, does not cling and control them.

The Fussy Sisters.
Before we hear why <er> and <ir> and <ur>, even <yr>, all spell the same sound, [er], you may like to dress up as the Fussy Sisters. You will need quite a few props. Big Sister Roberta, Little Turtle and Virginia the Flirt all look different, <er>, <ir> and <ur>, but they sound the same, [er], [er], [er]. When shopping, they all say, "Er, er, er," because they are fussy and cannot make up their minds.
Big Sister Roberta says "Er, er, er, a fern or a herb? A perm, or some perfume? Er, er, er."
Virginia says, "Er, er, er – a shirt or a dirndl skirt? Shall I be a circus girl or a ladybird? Er, er, er."
Little Turtle murmurs "Er, er, er, which will it be? A turn in the surf or a purple frankfurter? Er, er, er."
Then they all say "Where is Myrtle?". Your teacher will say, "We shall meet Myrtle later, after we have met all the [er] words spelt with <er> and <ir> and <ur>. See website's Photo Gallery

Q. Where in the world does Bossy R control vowels?
Ans. Wherever people have stopped rolling their R's. In Scotland there are many rhotic speakers, people who roll their R's. In most of England, in "The first person returned," <ir> and <er> and <ur> all spell [er], but in Scotland we might hear [i] and then [r] in *first,* [e] and then [r] in *person,* and [u] and then [r] in *returned.*

Q. Does Bossy R obey a rule?
Ans. R is bossy after vowels but not between them.
Reason. R is bossy after vowels, as in *cart, fern, skirt, {myrtle}, fort* and *hurt,* but not between them, as in *hero, era, iris, rural* and *siren* and in the Rebel Lemons *carol, heron, floral, iris* and *{lyric}.* In *hero* and the other 'Regal Words', single letter vowels before single <r> spell their long sounds. In *heron* and

other Rebel Lemons, vowels spell their short sounds, even though they are not followed by the two consonants which are normally required to keep them short. In *car, her, stir, for* and *fur*, R is bossy, because it is not between vowels.

If words ending with <r> get suffixes starting with a vowel, <r> would no longer be bossy because it would be between vowels. If <r> is twinned first and then the suffix added, then <r> will stay bossy. That is why <r> is bossy in *blurred, stirrer, jarring* and *furry*. Can you see that <r> has been added to *blur, stir, jar, fur*? The verb *err* already ends in <rr>, so suffixes pop straight on, as in *erred* [erd] and *erring* [er-ring].

Q. Are there any exceptions to the Bossy R rule?
Ans. Yes. R is bossy after vowels, but not between them, 'cept in words ending ery, ore and ory, 'coz R's bossy then — he's in his glory.
R is bossy, 'in his glory', in *more*. We cannot hear [ar] in *care*. We cannot hear [er] in *here, fire* and *pure*. However, we can hear [or] in *more*. There is no sound change from *fore* to *for*, no change from *ore* to *or*. Listen to these changes: *bar — bare, her — here, fir — fire, purr — pure*. In the first of each pair Bossy R has pushed the vowel to the back of the mouth. The second of each pair have vowels which have not been pushed to the back of the mouth. However, in *fore*, the vowel is already at the back of the mouth. The letters <ore> have been spelling [or] for a very long time, due to Silent or 'Fairy' E. When [or] lifted in many words to [oh] in the Great Vowel Shift, <re> kept it trapped at the back of the mouth as [or]. So we can say that <r> is bossy in *fore*, as well as in *for*. It remains bossy when silent <e> in terminal <ore> is replaced by <y> in terminal <ory>. This occurs in a few stem words, such as *story* and *glory*, and also in complex words, which have been built up from stem words, such as *factory* and *delusory*. We do not see <rr> in *snoring*. Why not? 'When ING comes to play, E runs away' is as true in *snore* as it is in *hope*. The silent <e> which made <ore> spell its old long sound, long ago, only needs replacing by another vowel to keep <o> spelling its old long sound. The [or] of *snore* can still be heard in *snoring* and *snored*.

Verbs are converted to nouns by the addition of the suffix <or>, as in *sailor* and *doctor*. As you will see, in 'Er and Er', coming soon, <or> was originally used to do this, not <er>. It was only later that <er> was also used for making nouns in this way, e.g. to make *baker* from the verb *to bake*. That must be why <r> is bossy in *bakery*, copying Bossy R in *factory*.

Besides those ending in suffix <or>, very few words end in just <or>, not <ore>. We have already met *or, for, nor* and *tor*. The bean and oil called *castor* is named after a Greek healing god called Kastor. The only verb which ends in <or> is *abhor*.

Q. Why isn't R bossy in *marry, ferret, current* and *hurry*? After all, R is meant to be bossy after a single letter vowel and before a consonant, e.g., before <r>.
Ans. A very good question. R used to be bossy in these words, but the words changed. Short vowels take less energy to say than long vowels. *Marry* is short for the old word *marien*, in which [ar] had not yet lifted to [ay]. *Ferret* used to spell [fer-ret], for it was named for its furtive ways. *Merry* used to have the same vowel as *mirth*. *Current* used to share a [ker] stem with *cursive*. *Hurry* [her-ree] and *hurl* and *hurtle* all grew from the same stem, [her], but *hurry* no longer uses the [er] sound. In all these words, <rr> comes at the end of an old word which can no longer stand alone. For instance, the *fer* of *ferret* is not a word on its own. It was the Latin word-part *fur* — check it out on Etymonline as the bound stem for *ferret, cat, thief* and *furtive* in Roman times, in Latin. These old word-parts are now bound stems because they are not words on their own. They are supported by more letters, are bound to these additional letters for support. They all obey Orm's Law now, which says that twin consonants keep vowels short. Nowadays, <rr> is only bossy if its between a free stem, like *star* and the vowel of a suffix, as in *starry, starred,*

starring. Bound stems, like the *ber* of *berry*, cannot stand on their own. The rest of the Bossy R rule is:
Twinned R's only bossy when before a suffix, after a free stem.
When *star* becomes *starry* we revert to the old system of twinning <r> at the end of words, to show it is bossy, as in *err, burr, purr* and *parr,* discussed above. When a suffix starting with a consonant is added there is not need to add another <r>, as in *starlit.*
The stem of *ferry* is *fer,* which cannot stand alone, so it's a bound stem. That is why <rr> — Twinned R — is not bossy in *ferry*. The reason that <rr> is bossy in *furry* is because in this case <rr> is between *fur,* a free stem, and a suffix. In the word *transfer* it is true that the stem is bound but once supported by a prefix it can receive suffixes and needs to twin the terminal <r> to keep it bossy. That is why <er> spells [er] in *transferred, transferring,* and *transferral*. For the same reason, <er> spells [er] in *referral, referrer* and *referring* but not in *referee* and *reference*. The vowel [er] is a long one and, since all long vowels are stressed, we can read each word with correct rhythm. The final two words have no long vowels and their stress pattern is the usual tum-te-tum, to ensure the suffix is unstressed.
In all the following words <rr> is not bossy because it is not between a free stem and a suffix:
BERRY, CARRY, CHERRY, CURRANT, CURRENT, CURRY, DERRY, FERRET, FERRY, FLURRY, GARRET, GHARRY, HARRY, HERRING, HORRID, HURRY, JERRY, LORRY, MARRY, PARRY, PERRY, QUARRY, SCURRY, SHERRY, SKERRY, STIRRUP, SORRY, TORRENT, TURRET, WORRY *f.*
In all the following words <rr> is bossy because it is between a free stem's end and a suffix:
ABHORRED, ERRING, FURRY, STARRY, STIRRED, TRANSFERRED, and many more.

I hope that explains the different vowels in each of the following word pairs: *starry* and *carry*; *erring* and *herring*; *stirred* and *stirrup*; *abhorred* and *horrid*; *furry* and *hurry*.
Due to Twinned R keeping control at the end of a stem word, we can also read the difference between a *scarred* face and feeling *scared* and frightened. Note that <r> is not at the end of the word *scare* and so it cannot be twinned anyway.
This brings us to the full Bossy R Rule. It rhymes a bit, to help you remember it. Add movement and music, and learning will be quick.
Rule 3-40
R is bossy after vowels,
But not between them.
'Cept in words ending ery, ore and ory
'Coz R's bossy then — he's in his glory.
Twinned R's only bossy when
before a suffix, after a free stem.
Bossy R, watch out do, for W will muddle you.
This last line is a warning. We have seen the muddle W makes in *wander* and *wonder* — in which <wa> spells [wo] and <wo> spells [wu]. Well, soon we shall see that <war> spells [wor] instead of [war], and <wor> spells [wer] instead of [wor]. So, 'Watch out Bossy R! W will muddle you'.

Q. How do we read *slurry* and *tarry*?
Ans. Each word has two meanings. In 'Do not tarry by the slurry pit as you may fall in,' <rr> is not bossy because <rr> is only bossy when twinned between a word's end and suffix.
However, when we *slur* our words, say them in a *slurry* way, and describe a *tar* road as very *tarry,* then <rr> is bossy in *slurry* and *tarry* because <rr> is between a word's end and suffix.
The only way we know how to read these two words is to read them in context, with the text, not as words on their own. 'The drunk's words were slurry as he sank into the pond of slurry.' 'The road was so tarry that it made me tarry and I missed my appointment.'

Q. How do we read <s> after Bossy R?
Ans. Use this rule:
Rule 3-40A Terminal <s> after Bossy R always spells [z] and terminal <se> after Bossy R spells [s].
Reason Bossy R follows a long vowel, either [ar], [er] or [or]. Long vowels are stressed vowels. It is this stress which makes a following <s> spell [z], as we also hear in *days, toes, yaws*.
Rebel PARSE
Rebel's Reason *Parse* spells [parz] to separate it from the word *pass*. Sometimes we hear people say [gorz] for *gorse* but they are muddling it with *furze*.

Q. Twinned R seems bossy in CATARRH and {MYRRH], but <rr> is not between a free stem and a suffix.
Answer. In words of Greek origin, <rrh> is the same as <rr>. The dictionary makers wanted to show that these words have been adopted from Greek, in which twin Rho is written <rrh>. Some other Greek adoptions have <rrh> inside words, not at the end. In all cases they obey the rule that 'R is bossy after vowels, but not between them'. For instance, *cirrhosis* spells [si-roh-sis], not [ser-roh-sis]. At the end of words <rrh> is not between vowels and so <rrh> is bossy, as in *catarrh* [kat-ar] and {*myrrh* [mer]}.

Q. Why isn't RR bossy at the other end of a word, between a prefix and the start of a word? Why isn't <rr> bossy in *irresponsible?*
Answer. It so happens that there is no prefix that has a Bossy R. *Inter, super,* and *over* are not prefixes. They form compound words. There is no prefix that spells [er] or [ar] or [or]. Some prefixes look as if they do, e.g., the prefixes in *correct* and *surrogate*, and *irresponsible*. In such cases twinning comes about because, when a prefix is joined onto a stem starting with <r>, the prefix changes, in order to make a smooth join. For instance, instead of *comrec*t we say *correct*. Prefixes *com-, sub-* and *in-* have all changed in order to join smoothly onto the bound stems *rect* and *rogate,* and the word *responsible*.

Q. What do <cer> and <ger> spell when R is bossy?
Answer. When R is bossy, <cer> always spells [ser]. We shall soon see when <ger> spells [ger] and when <ger> spells [jer].

Q. What do <cir> and <gir> spell when R is bossy?
Answer. Letters <cir> spell [ser], and <gir> spells [ger], when R is bossy.

Q. Why isn't R bossy in words ending *ary, iry, ury*?
Ans. We have read that R is bossy in *snore, snored, snoring, story* and *factory* because [or] spelt <o> did not lift to [oh] in the GVS if followed by <r> and another consonant or by <re>. All the other vowels changed in the GVS, even when followed by <re>.
We have read that R is only bossy in <ery> when <ery> is a suffix, as in *bakery,* because it took over from *ory*. *Bakery* was slightly easier to say than *bakory*. We know that when <ery> is not a suffix, it spells [ee-ree], as in *query*. We know that <ary> spells [air-ree] in *vary* and *canary*. As a suffix in {*dictionary*} it also spells [air-ree]. There are no suffixes —*iry* and —*ury*. There are word-endings, as in *wiry* and *jury,* but they are not suffixes. R is not 'bossy' in *wiry* and *jury* — <ir> and <ur> do not spell [er].
In the next collection of rules Bossy R is the star.
They follow on from Rule 3-40, The Bossy R Rule.

Digraph <er> — *berg, verb* and *Motherly Other.*

We can only call <er> a digraph if together they spell a sound different to [e][r]. That sound is [er].

Rule 3-41 When R is bossy, <er> is a digraph spelling [er].

Reason See discussion for Rule 3-40.

Rebels CLERK, SERGEANT.

Rebels' Reasons In both these words <er> spells [ar]. *Clerk* is pronounced [klark] in England, [klerk] in USA and both ways in Australia but s*ergeant* is pronounced [sarjant] by everyone and written *sarje* in short by all. Cummings on page 315 says that <er> spelling [ar] in *sergeant* occurred at the time <ear> began spelling [ar] in *heart.* It came from *sergent,* the Old French word for *servant, (Etymonline).* A *sergeant* was a 'servant at arms' who enforced the law but a *serjeant* (obsolete) was a 'servant at law' who kept order at meetings. *Person* and *parson* began as the same word. Once, all clerks were church clerics, called [klerks]. Possibly this changed to [klarks] later on, to separate them from clerks of the clergy. The Scots use *clerkess* to describe a female clerk and *sergeantess* was in use in England from 1450.

Rebels ERRAND, ERRANT. Reasons soon.

List 3-41 Some words in which <r> comes after vowels but not between them, so <er> spells [er].
AVER [a-ver], BERG, BERM, BLOOMER, BLOOMERS*, CHERT, CONFER, CONQUER*, [kon-ker], DEFER, DETER, EMERGE*, ERR*, FERN, FOSTER, GERM, HER, HERB, HERD, HERS, INFER, INTER, ISOTHERM, ITINERANT, JERK, KERB, LASER*, LATER, LEPER*, LERP*, NERVE*, PANTHER, PANTHER, PER *Latin*, PERK, PERM, PERT, PREFER, REFER, SERF*, SHERBET, SISTER, TERM, TERMS, TERN, TERSE*, THERM, THERMOS, TRANSFER, UNDER, VERB, VERVE*, WERT. Names BERT, BERTRAM, CHER [sher], CHESTER, DENVER, DEXTER, EBENEZER, EGBERT, ERMA, ERN, ERNEST, FERGUS, FERN, FERNANDA, FRASER, GILBERT*, GINGER, HERCULES, HESTER, HOMER, HUBERT, JENNIFER, MERVIN, ROBERT, ROBERTA, RUPERT, SERGE, VERGIL, VERN, VERNON, WALTER, WILBERT, WILMER.

Q. Why do *nerve, verve, emerge* and *terse* need an <e> on the end?

Ans. To insulate <v>, change the [g] to [j] and stop <s> spelling [z] after a vowel.

*Bloomers is an eponym. Google Amelia Jenks Bloomer. (She was not a 'late bloomer'.)

*Err spells [er]. It uses <rr> to obey the Short Word Rule. A silent <e>, *ere*, would produce [eer] as in *adhere.*

*Gilbert must be a very old name for the <i> does not soften the <g>. It must have been as well established before the Norman Invasion as *give, gift etc.*, listed in Part One.

*Conquer spells [kon-ker] but *conquest* spells [kon-kwest]. We hear terminal <quer> spell [ker] in *chequer, exchequer, lacquer, liquor* and *conquer.* Cummings says this only happens before a 'diminutive' suffix. The suffix <est> is a much stronger suffix than <er> — [kon-kə] but [kon-kwest]. The <u> of *conquer* spelt [w] when the word was *conqueren,* according to Peter Shaw on english.stackexchange.com, April 8, 2012.

*Laser [lay-zer], "light amplification by stimulated emission of radiation", is an acronym first used by inventor Gordon Gould, in 1958, (Fleck 2007).

We cannot mark all the Rebel Lemons. *Leper should be <lepper> but like all Rebel Lemons has its (weak) excuse. *Lepra* meant the (peeling) disease of leprosy and was adopted straight from both Greek and Latin. Then it changed into *leprosy* for the disease and the person with the disease was called *leper*, in which the first <e> continued to spell [e]. Old Orm would be turning in his grave! This all happened hundreds of years after he made the rule that [lep-er] should be written *lepper.* Why didn't they follow his rules? Try looking up a word's origin if you want the story behind each Rebel Lemon.

*Lerp has been adopted from the Ab'l language Wemba-Wemba, their word for the manna-like secretions from insects on tree leaves along the River Murray in Australia, (Blake, p. 98).

The plural of *serf is *serfs,* (not *serves.*)

List 3-41 continued in which <r> is twinned at a word's end, as in *err*, or twinned between a word's end and suffix, so <err> spells [er].
AVERRED, AVERRING, ERR, INTERRED, INTERRING, DISINTERRED, DEFERRAL, DETERRED, DETERRING, UNDETERRED, INFERRED, CONFERRER, CONFERRED, TRANSFERRED, REFERRED, REFERRER, REFERRED (put off), DEFERRED (gave in), DEFERRING (giving in), PREFERRED, PREFERRING, REFERRAL.

Relevant Writing Rule. Not all stems ending <er> get twin <r> when adding suffixes, only if <er> spells stressed [er] both before and after the suffix is added. Return to Reading Rules.

In the following words <rr> is not at the end of a free stem before a suffix, so <er> does not spell [er].
BERRY*, CHERRY, DERRY (a song sound), EQUERRY, FERRY, JERRY-CAN, MERRY, PERRY, SHERRY, TERRIFY, TERRIFIC, TERRAPIN and the **Rebels** ERRAND*, ERRANT*,

*Berry. The obsolete stem [ber] is in *berry*, a juicy outer covering of a seed and in *burr*, the dry outer covering of a seed.

*Errand appears to breaks the rule that twinned R's only bossy when before a suffix, after a free stem. In Old English was *ærende* and an angel was an *ærendgast* — 'errand ghost'. So *errand* is not based on *err*.

*Errant is based on two Latin verbs, *iterare* (travel, wander) and *errare* (lose one's way) which were fused by the French into one word and adopted by the English as *aurrent*. Later this word separated into *errant* and *arrant*. Wanderers were suspected of irresponsibility, arrant (very bad) behaviour. Sometimes itinerants are suspected of bad behaviour but the word *itinerant* is no rebel. It grew from the single one root *iterare* and obeys the rule that R is not bossy between vowels.

As we saw in List 3-41, terminal <er> spells [er] because <r> is not between vowels. Likewise, terminal <err> spells [er] because <r> is not between vowels. There is a special rule for when <ther> terminates stem words.

Rule 3-41 At the end of a stem, <ther>, after a vowel, spells [dher].

Reason In Part Two we learnt that the digraph <th> can only spell voiced [dh] if it is followed by a vowel, whereas it can spell unvoiced [th] at any time. Note that if a suffix is added to a stem, e.g., *slithery.* the rule still holds because <ther> is still at the end of a stem.

Any Rebels? No. In *anther, panther, thermos, isotherm etc.* in which <ther> spells [ther] the cluster <ther> is either not at the end of a stem or does not follow a vowel.

List 3-41
ALTOGETHER <a>=[or], BATHER <a>=[ay], BLATHERS, BLETHER, BLITHERING, DITHER, FATHER* <a>=[ar], FATHERHOOD <oo>=[uu], FATHERLAND, GATHER, GATHERING, GRANDFATHER, HITHER, HITHERTO = until now, LATHER, NETHER, RATHER* <a>=[ar], SMOOTHER, SLATHER, SLITHER, SLITHERY, SMITHEREENS, SOOTHER, TETHER, TOGETHER, THITHERTO = until then, WETHER, BELLWETHER, WHETHER, WHITHER, WHITHE/R, ZITHER.

*The only words in which <a> spells [ar] before <th> are *rather* and *father*. Elsewhere <a> spells [a] in *lath* [lath] and *lather* [ladher], and <a> spells [ay] in verbs *bathe* and *lathe*, and in nouns from those verbs, *lathe, bather, bathers* — in adjective *bathing* cap too.

'Utterly Motherly Words'.
There is also a special rule for terminal <other>.

Rule 3-42 At the end of a stem, <other> spells [udher].

Reason Long ago all these words had long vowels, [oh] or [oo] or [or]. *Mother* was [mar-ter] in Latin [mee-ter] in Greek and [moh-dhar] in ancient German. The long vowel crossed to England in [moh-der] and in Ireland is still long in *mathir*. In Germany it shortened in *mutter*, and in England too, to [mu-dher]. Many Old English words shortened long vowels. *Smother* had the same long vowel as in the old word for 'dense, suffocating smoke', *smorthre,* and *brother* was originally [broh-dhar], like today's short form, 'bro', [broh]. We have seen that *rough* spells [ruf]. Later we shall see <ou> in some words from France shortened too, like {*touch, cousin* and *country*}. It seems that, even though the vowel changed, the scribes kept writing *mother, brother, smother etc.* with <o>, instead of <u>. These words are as bad as Rebel Lemons in which the letters did not change when the sounds they spelt changed. Note that if a suffix is added to a stem, as in *brotherly,* the rule still holds because <other> is still at the end of a stem.

Other was 'one of the two', ancient Germanic *anthera,* and then Anglo-Saxon [ardher], later [ohdher], before becoming [udher]. Saying [ardher] or [ohdher] takes more effort than saying [u-dher]. Try it. It's as though energy was transferred to saying stressed[dh] at the front of the mouth, relegating the preceding vowel to the back of the mouth.

Rebels BOTHER, POTHER.

Rebels' Reasons *Pother* spells [podher] not [pudher]. It's thought *bother* grew out of *pother. Pother* is in Irish bibles, in the sense of 'to be grieved or troubled in mind', translated from Greek *potheo,* to regret. A list of all "Utterly Motherly" words is in the appendix under Loose Lists.

Q. Why does <other> only spell [udher] 'at the end of a stem'?

Ans. When the letters <other> appear elsewhere in a word they do not spell [udher]. For example, in *chemotherapy* they spell [oh-thair] and in *endothermy* they spell [oh-ther]. The rule says at the end of a stem because <other> is at the end of a stem in *brotherly*, even though not at the end of a word. There is no such stem as 'chemother' or 'hypnother' or even just 'ther'.

List 3-42.

ANOTHER, BROTHER *f*, BROTHERHOOD *f* <oo>=[uu], FOSTER-BROTHER, FOSTER-, GATHER, GATHERING, GODMOTHER, GRANDFATHER, GRANDMOTHER, MOTHER, 'NOTHER, OTHER, OTHERWISE, SMOTHER, T'OTHER, SMOTHER, STEPBROTHER, STEPMOTHER.

Three terminal ER's.

The first terminal <er> is not a suffix. It may have been long ago but it is now part of a stem word. We see it in *anger, another, number* (1,2,3…) and *limber,* as in 'the acrobat was very limber.'

The next two are suffixes.

In one group, —*er* means more of the same, as in *larger.* In *larger,* —*er* does not change the meaning of the adjective *large.* It adds meaning. *Larger* means 'more large'. *Stranger* means 'more strange.'

In the other group, —*er* changes the meaning of words. Adjectives become nouns, e.g., *strange* becomes the *stranger.* Nouns become new nouns, e.g., the *farm* becomes the *farmer.* Verbs become nouns, e.g., *bake* becomes the *baker.*

Terminal <er> spells [er] whatever kind of <er> it is. If <er> is a suffix, it cannot change the sound of its stem word. *Dumber* still has the silent [b] of *dumb.* In *avenger,* <ge> still spells [j]. *Signer* still has the silent [g] of *sign.* In *singer,* <ng> still spells [ŋ], BUT we do hear [g] in *longer* or *stronger.*

Rule 3-43 Terminal <er> always spells [er]. Suffix <er> does not change the stem word, unless it is an adjective ending <ng>.

Reason This is a very strong pattern which has become a rule.

<u>Not needed but nice to know</u>. Long ago, the suffix which means 'more' was —*era.* When a child says that his drawing is 'bettera' than his brother's, we hear the echoes of Old English, in which *better* was *betera. Best* was *betst* in which the <st> stood for 'highest state', or 'of high standing.' *Good, better, best* was *beet, betera, betst.* <u>Now back to things we need to know.</u>

Rebels? The only two words which are changed by the suffix —*er* are LONGER and STRONGER, but they are not rebels because they are adjectives. *Long* spells [loŋ] but *longer* spells [lon-ger]. *Strong* spells [stroŋ] but *stronger* spells [stron-ger]. These two cases in which the suffix —*er* changes a stem word only happen when —*er* means 'more'. This suffix used to be longer. *Better* was *betera* and so we can assume that *longer* was [lon-gera] and then reduced to [lon-ger]. (I also think [loŋst] would not have expressed the supremacy of 'most long', nor even [lon-gst] — hence [lon-gest].)

Q What about *scandalmonger* and *fishmonger*?
Ans. The suffix —*er* meaning 'more' is only added to adjectives. *Monger* is an Old English noun in which <g> resists the softening French influence of <e> so <g> spells [g], as in *finger*. So <er> is not a suffix of any kind in these old words.

Q. What about *cunninger, knowinger* and *willinger*? Aren't these adjectives ending with <ng>?
Ans. *Cunning, knowing* and *willing* are not stem words and so the addition of —*er* cannot split the Eng blend.

Not needed but nice to know. It is better grammar to say *more cunning, more knowing* and *more willing* than *cunninger etc.* Two-syllable adjectives ending in —*er*, —*le*, or —*ow* take —*er*, as in *cleverer, gentler, hollower*. They also take —*est*, as in *cleverest etc.* However, most two-syllable adjectives use *more* and *most*, as in *more pleasant*, not *pleasanter* and *most pleasant* not *pleasantest*. Now back to things we need to know.

Q, What about *wronger*? *Wrong* is an adjective, ending in <ng> spells [ŋ]. Would *wronger* spell [ron-ger]? Would *wronger* join the adjectives *longer* and *stronger*?
Ans. Yes, it would, if the adjective *wronger* was in use. Some people use the term 'more wrong', and say that 6 as an answer to 22 is more wrong than 5 as an answer. A lawyer might make a case for that, but a mathematician would never agree to it because it is impossible to be wronger than wrong, except humorously. So, in joke, one would say [ron-ger] and [ron-gest]. Some dictionaries list the noun *wronger* [roŋ-er], meaning *wrongdoer*. The Eng blend, [ŋ], is not split, because the only exceptions to the Rule 3-41C. The suffix in the noun *wronger* does not mean 'more wrong'. It is a suffix which makes or derives new words, in this case the noun *wronger,* as in 'the sinful wronger', from the adjective 'wrong' and from the verb 'to wrong'.

The 'more suffix', —*er*, does not change the sound of stem words, except for adjectives ending <ng>. So adjectives like *number* does not spell [num-ber], *larger* does not spell [lar-ger] and *stranger* does not spell [stran-ger].

In Part Two we heard about inflexional or inflected suffixes, which I nickname 'flexible suffixes' because they are like a flexible tail wagging on a dog telling us about the dog — if he is happy, alert or, maybe, afraid. Whatever he is, he is still a dog. The 'more suffix', —*er*, is this type of suffix, a 'flexible' suffix. Whether something is red, redder, or reddest, it is still the colour red. A red dog, no matter how red, is still a red dog.

List 3-43A Adjectives with the flexible suffix —*er*.
BIGGER, BLACKER, BLUER (blue), FITTER, FULLER, GREENER, HOTTER, HUGER (huge), LARGER, LONGER, MADDER, NICER, PALER, PURER, REDDER, RUDER, SAFER, SANER, SMALLER, SMOOTHER, STALER, STIFFER, STRANGER (more strange), STRONGER, SURER, TALLER, THINNER, VAGUER *insulator u,* VILER, WETTER, WIDER, WISER.

Note that the only change that suffix —*er* makes to a stem word is in adjectives ending <ng>. In *stranger* and *huger,* <ge> continues to spell [j]. In order to ensure that stem words do not change, twinning occurs before adding —*er* in adjectives like *red, thin, wet* :- *redder, thinner, wetter*.

The other —*er* suffix was originally —*or*. It began as the Roman suffix in *gladiator*. (A female *gladiator* was a *gladiatrix*.) We still use —*or* in *sailor* and *doctor* but —*or* changed to —*er* in most cases, e.g., *baker, farmer, player* etc. If —*era* and —*or* had not both become —*er*, we'd say, 'He's a bettera farmor than me'. We know that [er] is a very easy sound to make because when we struggle to say other words we just say [er] instead. If the English hadn't become lazy and reduced both suffixes to just —*er*, we would be saying, 'This strangor is strangera than others.'

The —*er* on *larger* belongs to a small group of eleven suffixes which only add to the meaning of a stem word, whereas the —*or* and —*er* suffixes of *sailor* and *farmer* belongs to a group of over one thousand suffixes and prefixes which build words which have different meanings than their stems.

Derivational or 'deriving' suffixes actually drive the word to a new meaning — derail it. Back when river barges did the work of trains, suffixes were said to de-river a word, send it down a different river with a new meaning. The deriving suffix —*or* sends the verb *sail* down a new river of meaning, as the noun *sailor*. The deriving suffix —*er* changes the noun *farm* into another noun, *farmer*. This little deriving suffix can change the meaning of a word but it cannot change the sound of the stem word, it cannot even split the [ŋ] sound at the end of a word. That is why the verb *sing* becomes the noun *singer* [siŋ er]. All other stems remain unchanged too.

List 3-43B Words with deriving suffix—*er*.
AVENGER [jer], BANGER, BATTER, BIDDER, BORER, BRINGER, CLANGER, CLIMBER, COMBER, CUTTER, DIGGER, DIPPER, dinger, DOGGER, FIBBER, GUNNER, HANGER, HITTER, HUGGER, HUMDINGER (a humming dinger), JOBBER, LIMBER, LOGGER, LUNGER [jer], MANAGER [jer], MESSENGER [jer], MONEY *f* CHANGER [jer], PASSENGER [jer], PEGGER, PLUMBER, PLUNGER [jer], RAPPER, RINGER, ROBBER, RUNNER, SCAVENGER [jer], SNORER, SPONGER *f,* [jer], STINGER, STRANGER [jer], STRINGER, SWINGER, WINGER (sporting term), WHINGER [jer], WINNER.

Note 1. When the deriving suffix —*er* is added to stems to make new meanings, twinning is also needed in some cases. To ensure the sound of the stem is not changed, <t> in *bat* is twinned in *batter,* to avoid [bat] becoming [bayt] in '*bater'*.

Note 2. Twin <gg> in *logger* not only keeps [o] short, it prevents <er> softening <g> to [j], for as we know, <gge> does not spell [j].

Note 3. When the suffix <er> is added to terminal <ge>, terminal <e> is replaced by <er> and this means <g> continues to spell [j], and the word ends in [jer]. Words like *avenger* are made when <er> is added to the free stem *avenge*. Some are hard to work out. Some are added to bound stems and some match cousin words. *Messenger* from *message* got its <n> to match the older word *harbinger* and then *passenger* from *passage* added an <n> to match them both.

Not needed but nice to know. Some deriving suffixes (but not —*er*) are strong enough to pull [b] out of silence, in *bombardier* for instance, and in *crumble* and in *dumbo*. We hear [b] in *crumble* and *dumbo* but not in *crumbed* and *dumber* because the flexible suffixes cannot release silenced letters, as in, 'She *crumbed* it and he was *crumbing* it and now chef *crumbs* the fish dish. Tom is *dumb*, Mary is *dumber* but Jo is *dumbest*. This *lamb's* owner fed it but the other *lambs* ran to the *lambs'* mother.' On the other hand, we do not even write some silent letters anymore, in words like *dummy, plummet* and *numskull*. Silent letter <g> is left out of *dunny* made from *dung hill* and <b>'s gone from *plummet* and *numskull*. Now back to things we need to know.

When <er> is terminal, it is not always a suffix on a stem word, because it can be part of a stem word, as in 'number' and 'limber'. So, we hear the [b] in *number one* but not in *number bum* if your bum is number than mine. We hear the [b] in *he's very limber* but not in *he's a tree limber by profession*.

List 3-43C Terminal <er> terminating stem words.
ANGER*, CANCER, CANKER, COSTERMONGER *f* [mun-ger], FINGER, FINGERPRINT, FINGERTIP, FINGER, DANGER, *GINGER, HUNGER*, MANGER [jer], NUMBER *noun*, LAGER [lar-ger], LINGER, MALINGER, TIGER* [tI-ger], NUMBER, LIMBER *adjective*, LUMBER, CHAMBER [chaym-ber].

Ginger is from the old word *gingifer*. Etymonline can tell us the story of each word.

In *anger <a> spells short [a], and is therefore a rebel to Rule 2-53, 'When <ange> is in a stressed syllable it spells [aynj]'. This Old English way to lengthen vowels, as in *danger* and *manger*.

In *anger and *tiger and *hunger <ger> spells [ger], not [jer], because their ancestors all lacked <e> after <g>. Norse *angr* and *hungr* evolved to *angry, anger* and *hungry, hunger* and now *angry* and *hungry* are the only English words to end in <gry>.

*Tiger spells [tI-ger] not [tI-jer] because it arrived from France as *tigre*, in which <g> was insulated from the softening affect of <e> by <r>. This is the very reason that *acre* is not written *acer* and so it should have remained *tigre*. Its female form, *tigress*, was invented by Americans, first seen on paper in 1611.

Not needed but nice to know. Is the word *number* plural or singular? "Always make it 'The number was...' but 'A number were...' The same rule applies to *total*," Bryson 2004, p 149). Now back to things we need to know.

'R is bossy after vowels, **but not between them.**'
List 3-44 R is not Bossy between vowels.
ACCELERATE, ADULTERANT, ADULTERATE, APERIENT, APERITIF, AVERAGE, BALLERINA, BATTERING-RAM, BEVERAGE, BILATERAL, CAMERA, CAMERAMAN, CASSEROLE, CELERITY, CHAPERON <ch>=[sh], CHARACTERISTIC, CHARACTERIZE, CHINCHERINCHEE, CHOLERA <ch>=[k], CLIMACTERIC, COHERENT, CONFERENCE, CROSS-REFERENCE, COLLATERAL, COMMISERATE, COMPUTERIZE CONFEDERATE, CONFEDERATED, CONGLOMERATE, CONSIDERABLE, CONSIDERATE, CONSIDERING, CONSUMERISM, CO-OPERATIVE, COVERAGE*, DEGENERATE, DELIBERATE-*verb*, DELIVERANCE DEXTERITY, DIFFERENCE, DIFFERENT, DOGGEREL, FUNEREAL, EVERY, EVERYBODY, EVERYONE *f*, EVERYTHING, EXAGGERATE <gg>=[gj], EXONERATE, EXUBERANT, EXUBERANTLY, EXUBERANCE, FEDERAL, FEDERATE, FUNERAL, GASTRO-ENTERITIS, GENERA, GENERAL, GENERALISSIMO, GENERALIST, GENERALITY, GENERALIZE, GENERALLY, GENERATE, GENERIC, GENEROSITY, HOMERIC, HUMERUS, HYPERACTIVE, HYSTERECTOMY, ILLITERATE, IMMODERATE, IMPONDERABLE, IMPOVERISH, INCINERATE, INCONSIDERABLE, INCONSIDERATE, INNUMERATE, INOPERABLE, INOPERATIVE, INTOLERABLE, INTOLERANT, INVETERATE, IRREVERENT, KEDGEREE, LEVERAGE, LIBERAL, LIBERATE, LITERACY, LITERAL, LITERALLY, LITERATE, LITERATURE, MACERATE, MANNERISM, MASQUERADE, MAVERICK*, MINERAL, MINERALOGY, MISERABLE, MODERATE, OBLITERATE, OFFERING, OPERA, OPERABLE, OPERATE, OPERATIC, OPERATIVE, OPERETTA, PERIMETER, PERIPHERAL, PERISHER, PEROXIDE, POLYMERIZE, POSTERITY, PREPONDERANT, PREPONDERATE, PROFITEROLE, PROLIFERATE, PROTUBERANT, PULVERIZE, QUADRILATERAL, RECUPERATE, LEVERET, PREFERABLE, PREFERENCE, REFERENCE, REFERENDUM, REGENERATE, RENUMERATE, RENUMERATIVE, REVEREND, REVERENT, REVERENTLY, RUBBERIZE, SCLEROSIS, SELF-CATERING, SEVERAL, SEVERALLY, SEVERANCE, SHERIFF,

SLENDERIZE, SOMBRERO, SPHERICAL, STAGGERING, SUFFERANCE, TEMPERAMENT, TEMPERAMENTAL, TEMPERAMENTALLY, TEMPERANCE, TEMPERATE, TEMPERATURE, TENDERIZE, TOLERATE, TOLERANT, TOLERANCE, TUBEROSE, UTERINE, UTERUS, VENERATE, VETERAN, VOCIFERATE, ULCERATE, UNADULTERATED, REVERENCE, SELF-INTEREST, UNINTERESTED, UNINTERESTING, VARICOSE, VISCERA. Names ASTERIX*, ESPERANTO, CATHERINE, CAMERON, CINDERELLA, ELLERY, FREDERICA, FREDERICK, VERONICA. Proper Adjective LUTHERAN.

Asterix is Celtic for "King of the Stars". The Celts loved making new words. They were the Aborigines of Britain. Can you see king (*rix*) and star (*aster*) in *Asterix*? Australian Aborigines are just as evocative with words, e.g., "Kangaroo-eyes" for Sturt's pea: *malugurru*.

**Maverick*. It's rare a long word retains <ck>. Compare it with *arithmetic*. It's because *maverick* is an eponym. Google Samuel A. Maverick.

'**R is bossy after vowels,** but not between them'. So <er> spells [er], before a consonant and when terminal.

We have already seen shorter words in which <er> spells [er] and also the Rebel *clerk*.

List 3-45
ACCUSER, ACERBITY, ADAPTER, ADDER, ADMINISTER, ADMIRER, ADULTERER, ADVENTURER, ADVERB, ADVERSE, ADVERSITY, ADVERT, ADVERTISE, ADVERTISEMENT, AGGLOMERATE, ALERT, ALERTNESS, ALLERGENIC, ALLERGIC, ALLERGY, ALTIMETER, AMBER, AMMETER, AMPERSAND, ANIMADVERT, ANTECHAMBER [an-tee …], ANTLER, APERTURE, ASSERTIVE, ASTER, ASTERN, ASTROLOGER, ASTRONOMER, ASUNDER, AVER, AVERSE, AVERT, BACKER, BACK-BENCHER, BACKHANDER, BAKER, BALDERDASH, BALUSTER, BANISTER, BANKER, BANNER, BANTER, BATTER, BEGINNER, BERGAMOT, BERK, BERSERK, BERG, BERM, BERTH, BETTER, BETTERMENT, BICKER, BINDER, BITTER, BITTERLY, BITTER-SWEET, BITTERN, BLADDER, BLINDER, BLINKER, BLOCK-BUSTER, BLUBBER, BLUNDER, BLUNDERER, BLUNDERBUSS, BLUSHER, BLUSTER, BOMBER, BONKERS, BOOKSELLER, BOOMERANG, BOOSTER, BOOTLEGGER, BOOZER, BLISTER, BOXER, BRAVER, BREEDER, BROKER, BUFFER, BUGGER, BUMPER, BUNKER, BUSKER, BUTCHER, BUTLER, BUTTER, BUTTERCUP, BUTTERFINGERS, BUTTERFLY*, BUTTERMILK, BUTTERSCOTCH, BUZZER, BYSTANDER, CABER, CALENDER*, CAMBER, CANCER, CANKER, CANTER, CANTILEVER, CAPER, CATCHER, CATER, CATERER, CATHETER, CAVERN, CENSER, CENTER (in USA), CERTIFICATE, CERTIFY, CERTITUDE, CERVICAL, CERVIX, CHAPTER, CHARACTER, CHARACTERLESS, CHATTER, CHATTERBOX, CHEQUER, CHERT, CHERVIL, CHOKER, CHUKKER*, CINDER, CISTERN, CLAPPER, CLERGY, CLERGYMAN, CLEVER, CLEVERLY, CLEVERNESS, CLINKER, CLIPPER, CLIPPERS, CLODHOPPERS, CLOVER, CLUSTER, CLUTTER, COBBER, COBBLER, COFFER, COLANDER*, COMMANDER, COMMONER, COMPUTER, CONCERN, CONCERNING, CONCERT, CONCERTED, CONCERTINA, CONCERTO, CONFER, CONFERMENT, CONFERRABLE, CONIFER, CONJURER* *ƒ* CONQUER*, CONSERVANCY, CONSERVATISM, CONSERVATIVE, CONSERVE, CONSIDER, CONSUMER, CONTROLLER, CONVERGE, CONVERSANT, CONVERSE, CONVERT, CONVERTIBLE, COOKER, COOLER, COOPER, COPPER, COPPERPLATE, CORONER, COVER* *ƒ*, COVER-UP* *ƒ*, COVERT [koh-vert], CRACKER, CROONER, CROSS-FERTILIZE, CULVERT, CUMBERSOME, CUSTOMER, CUTTER, CYBERNETICS, DABSTER, DAGGER, DAMPER, DANDER, DAPPER, DECANTER, DECIDER, DECIPHER, DECODER, DEFENDER, DEFER, DERBY*, DERMATITIS, DERMATOLOGY, DERVISH, DESERT*, DESERTS*, DESERVE*,

DESERVING*, DESSERT*, DESSERT-SPOON, DESSERTSPOONFUL, DETER, DETERGENT, DETERMINABLE, DETERMINANT, DETERMINATE, DETERMINE, DEVELOPER, DIBBER, DICKER, DIFFER, DIGGER, DIMMER, DINER, DINNER, DISCERN, DISCERNING, DISCONCERT, DISCOVER, DISHWASHER, DISMEMBER, DISORDER, DISSERVICE, DISTILLER, DIVERSE, DIVERSIFY, DIVERSITY, DIVERT, DIVERTICULITIS, DIVERTING, DIVIDER, DIVINER, DOCKER, DODDER, DOGGER, DOSSER, DRAPER, DRESSER, DRIFTER, DRILLER, DRINKER, DRIVER, DROVER, DUFFER, DULCIMER, DUSTER, EMBER, EMBITTER, EMERGE, EMERGENCY, ENERGY, ENGRAVER, ENTER, ENTERPRISE, EQUALIZER, ERMINE, ERR*, ESTER, ETCHER, ETERNAL, ETERNITY, EVER, EVERGREEN, EVERLASTING, EWER, EXACERBATE, EXCERPT, EXCHEQUER*, EXERCISE, EXERT, EXPERT, EXPERTISE, EXTENDER, EXTROVERT, EYE-LINER, EYE-OPENER, FACER, FAKER, FANCIER, FEEDER, FEELER, FENDER, FERMENT, FERN, FERTILE, FERTILITY, FERTILE, FERTILITY, FERTILIZE, FERTILIZER, FERVENT, FERVID, FETTER, FEVER, FEVERISH, FEVERISHNESS, FINDER, FINER, FISHERMAN, FITTER, FIVER, FIXER, FIZZER, FLASHER, FLATTER, FLATTERER, FLICKER, FLIPPER, FLIVVER*, FLUSTER, FLUTTER, FLYCATCHER, FLYER, FODDER, FOLDER, FONDER, FOSTER, FOSTER-CHILD, FOSTER-SISTER, FRAMER, FRATERNAL, FRATERNITY, FRATERNIZE, FREER*, FRESHER, FRESHENER, FRITTER, GASHOLDER, GASOMETER, GATHERING, GENDER, GERM, GERMANE, GERMICIDE, GERMICIDAL, GERMINATE, GHERKIN*, GIBBER, GIBBERISH, GLIDER, GLIMMER, GOFFER, GOLFER, GOVERN ƒ, GOVERNANCE ƒ, GOVERNESS ƒ, GOVERNMENT ƒ, GRATER, GRAZER, GREENERY, GRINDER, GRUMBLER, GRUNTER slang (pig), GUN-RUNNER, GUNNER, GUNNERY, GUSHER, GUTTA-PERCHA, GUTTER, GUTTERING, GUTTERSNIPE, GUZZLER, HABERDASHER, HACKER, HAMMER, HAMPER, HAMSTER, HANDLER, HANGOVER, HANKER, HATTER, HAVERSACK, HEDGER, HEELER, HELICOPTER, HELPER, HEMMER, HER, HERB, HERBAL, HERBALIST, HERBICIDE, HERBIVORE, HERD, HERDSMAN, HERS [herz], HERSELF [her-self], HIBERNATE, HIKER, HINDER, HINDERMOST, HIPSTER, HIRER, HOOKER <oo>=[uu], HOOTER, HOOVER*, HOPPER, HOVER [hov-er], HOVERCRAFT, HOWEVER, HUCKSTER, HUGGER-MUGGER, HUNTER, HYGROMETER, HYPERBOLA, HYPERCRITICAL, HYPERSENSITIVE, HYPODERMIC, ICEBERG, IDOLATER, IMMERSE, IMPERFECT, IMPERSONAL, IMPERSONATE, IMPERTINENT, IMPERTINENCE, IMPROPER, INCONTROVERTIBLE, INDETERMINABLE, INDETERMINATE, INERT, INFER, INFERNAL, INFERNO, INFERTILE, INHALER, INNERMOST, INNKEEPER, INSERT, INSURER, INTEGER, INTER, INTERN, INTERNAL, INTERNEE, INTROVERT, INTRUDER, INVERSE, INVERT, INVERTEBRATE INVULNERABLE, IRREVERSIBLE, ISOTHERM, JABBER, JERK, JERKIN, JERKY, JESTER, JIGGER, JIGGERY-POKERY, JITTER, JOBBER, JOKER, JOSSER, JOTTER, JUDDER, JUMPER, KEEPER, KERFUFFLE, KERNEL, KILLER, KILOHERTZ [kiloh-herts], KINDER, KISSER, KNACKER, KNEELER, KNICKERBOCKERS*, KNICKERS, KNITTER, KNOCKER, KNUCKLEDUSTER, KOSHER, LACQUER*, LADDER, LAMASERY, LANCER, LANTERN, LATTERLY, LAVENDER, LECTURER, LETTER, LETTER-BOX, LIBERTINE, LIBERTY, LINER, LISTENER, LITTER, LOCKER, LODGER, LONER, LOOKER-ON, LOVER ƒ, MADDER, MAKER, MANAGER [jer], MANNER, MANNERLY, MANSERVANT, MASTER VS, MARINER, MATER, MATERNAL, MATERNITY, MATTER, MEGAHERTZ PN, MEMBER, MENDER, MERCANTILE, MERCERIZED, MERCHANDISE*, MERCHANT, MERCIFUL, MERCILESS, MERCURIAL, MERCURY, MERCY, MERGE, MERGER, METER, MILER, MILLER, MILLINER*, MINDER, MINER, MINESWEEPER, MINICOMPUTER, MISER, MISTER abbrev. Mr/Mr., MODERN, MODERNISM, MODERNITY, MODERNIZE, MOREOVER, MUMMER, MUSTER, MUTTER, NERVE, NERVELESS, NERVY, NEVER, NEVERTHELESS, NIBBLER,

NIPPER, NUTTER, OBSERVANCE, OBSERVANT, OBSERVE, OBSERVER, OBVERSE, ODOMETER, OFFER, OFFICER, OLD MASTER, OLD-TIMER, OPEN VERDICT, OPENER, OTTER, OVER, OXIDIZER, PACEMAKER, PACHYDERM [pak-i-derm], PAMPER, PANDER, PANTHER, PANZER, PAPER, PAPER-CLIP, PAPER-TIGER, PAPERBACK, PARAMETER, PARATROOPER, PASSER-BY, PASTERN, PATERNAL, PATERNALISM, PATERNITY, PATERNOSTER, PATTER, PATTERN, PAVER, PECKER, PENTAMETER, PEPPER, PEPPERMINT, PERCENT, PERCENTAGE [...əj], PERCH, PERCOLATE, PERFECT, PERFECTLY, PERFIDIOUS, PERFUME, PERFUMERY, PERGOLA, PERHAPS, PERK, PERM, PERMAFROST, PERMANENCY, PERMANENT, PERMANGANATE, PERMEATE, PERMISSIBLE, PERMISSIVE, PERMISSIVENESS, PERMIT, PERMUTE, PERNICKETY, PERPETRATE, PERPETUAL, PERPETUATE, PERPETUITY, PERPLEX, PERPLEXITY, PERQUISITE, PERSECUTE, PERSEVERE, PERSEVERANCE, PERSIFLAGE, PERSIST, PERSISTENT, PERSISTENCE, PERSISTENCY, PERSON, PERSONA, PERSONAL, PERSONABLE, PERSONAGE, PERSONA GRATA, PERSONAL, PERSONALITY, PERSONALIZE, PERSONALLY, PERSONIFY, PERSONNEL, PERSPECTIVE, PERSPICACITY, PERSPICUITY, PERT, PERTINENT, PERVADE, PERVASIVE, PERVERSE, PERVERT, PESTER, PHOTOGRAPHER, PHILANDER, PHILANDERER, PHILOSOPHER, PILFER, PINCERS (plural noun), PINCER (adjective), PIPER, PITCHER, PLANNER, PLANTER, PLASTER, PLATTER, PLOTTER, PLOVER f, PLUMBER (silent b), PLUNDER, POKER, POLISHER, POLLSTER, POLYESTER, POMANDER, PONDER, POSER, POSTER, POSTERN, POTSHERD, POTTER, POVERTY, PREFER, PREFERMENT, PRESERVE, PRETENDER, PRIMMER, PRIMER, PRINTER, PRISONER, PROCURER, PROFFER, PROGRAMMER, PROMPTER, PROPELLER, PROPER, PROPERTY, PROSPER, PROVENDER, PROVERB [pro-verb], PSALTER [sol-ter], PUBLISHER, PUCKER UP, PULLOVER <u>=[uu], PUMPERNICKEL, PUNSTER, PUNTER, PUZZLER, QUAVER, QUICKSILVER, QUITTER, QUIVER, RAMBLER, RASHER, RATTER, RECKONER, RECONSIDER, RECOVER f, REDEEMER, REFER, REFERRAL*, REFINER, REFINERY, REFRESHER, REGISTER, REMEMBER, REMINDER, REMOVER f<o>=[oo], RENDER, RESERVE, RESERVIST, RESISTER, RESPECTER, REVERBERATE, REVERSE, REVERSAL, REVERSE, REVERSIBLE, REVERT, REVOLVER, RIDER, RISER, RIVER [riv-ver], ROBBERY, ROCKER, ROLLER, ROMPERS, ROOSTER, ROSTER, ROTTER, ROVER, RUBBER, RUBBERNECK, RUGGER, RULER, RUNNER, RUNNER-UP, SADDLER, SAFER, SALAMANDER, SALESPERSON, SAMPLER *VS,* SANDER, SANDPAPER, SANDPIPER, SAPPER, SCAMPER, SCANNER, SCATTER, SCHOONER <ch> = [k], SCOOTER, SCRAMBLER, SCRAPPER, SCRAPER, SCRUBBER, SCUPPER, SELF-SERVICE, SELLER, SEMESTER, SENDER, SEQUESTER, SERGE, SERMON, SERMONIZE, SERPENT, SERPENTINE, SERVANT, SERVE, SERVER, SERVICE, SERVICEMAN, SERVILE, SERVING, SERVITUDE, SETTER, SETTLER, SEVER [sev-ver], CHICKEN SEXER, SHAKER, SHAPER, SHARE-CROPPER, SHAREHOLDER, SHAVER, SHELTER, SHEPHERD h, SHEPHERDESS*, SHERBET, SHIFTER, SHIMMER, SHINER, SHIPPER, SHIVER, SHOCKER, SHOOTER, SHOPPER, SHOVELLER f, SHUTTER, SILENCER, SILVER, SILVERSIDE, SILVERSMITH, SIMMER, SIMPER, SINISTER, SINKER, SINNER, SISTER, SISTERHOOD, SITTER, SIXER, SKATER, SKETCHER, SKIPPER, SKULDUGGERY, SKYSCRAPER, SLACKER, SLANDER *VS,* SLATER, SLATTERN, SLATTERNLY, SLAVER, SLEDGE-HAMMER, SLEEPER, SLENDER, SLICER, SLICKER, SLIPPER, SILVER, SILVERWARE, SLOBBER, SLUMBER, SMASHER, SMOKER, SMUGGLER, SNAPPER, SNICKER, SNOOKER, SOBER, SOCCER*, SERVICE, SOFTENER, SOLDER, SONGSTER, SPANNER, SPATTER, SPECTROMETER, SPERM, SPERM WHALE, SPERMATIC, SPERMICIDE, SPHINCTER, SPIDER, SPINNER, SPINSTER, SPLATTER, SPLINTER, SPLUTTER, SPOONERISM, SPOTTER, SPRINKLER, SPRINTER, SPUTTER,

SQUEEZER, STAGER, STAGGER, STAMMER, STEEPLECHASER, STERLING, STERN, STERNUM, STICKLER, STINKER, STOCKBREEDER, STOCKBROKER, STOCKHOLDER, STOCKJOBBER, STOCKRIDER, STOKER, STOPPER, STRANGLER, STRAPPER, STRETCHER, STRIKER, STRIPPER, SUBALTERN, SUBMERGE, SUBMERSIBLE, SUBSCRIBER, SUBTERFUGE, SUBVERSIVE, SUBVERT, SUCKER, SUFFER, SUMMER, SUNDER, SUPER, SUPERB, SUPPER, SUSPENDER, SWAGGER, SWEEPER, SWEEPSTAKE, SWEETER, SWEETENER, SWELTER, SWERVE, TABERNACLE, TAKER, TAMER, TAMPER, TANKER, TANNER, TAPER, TASTER, TATTERS, TAVERN, TAXIDERMY, TAXIDERMIST, TEENAGER, TEETER, TELEPRINTER, TELLER, TEMPER, TENDER, TENDERLY, TENDERNESS, TENDERFOOT, TENTERHOOK, TERM, TERMAGENT, TERMINABLE, TERMINAL, TERMINATE, TERMINOLOGICAL, TERMINOLOGY, TERMINUS, TERMITE, TERN, TERSE, TESTER, THERMODYNAMICS, THERMOELECTRIC, THERMOMETER, THERMOS, THERMOSTAT, THICKER, THINKER, THINNER, THREE-WHEELER, THRILLER, THUNDER, THUNDERBOLT, THUNDERCLAP, TICKER, TIDDLER, TIMBER, TIMEKEEPER, TIMER, TINDER, TIPPER, TIPSTER, TITTER, TODDLER, TONER, TOPER, TOPPER, TOTTER, TRACER, TRACERY, TRACKER, TRADER, TRAFFICKER, TRANQUILLIZER, TRANSCRIBER, TRANSFER, TRANSVERSE, TRAPPER, TRAVELLER, TRAVERSE, TRAVERSAL, TREKKER*, TREMBLER, TRENCHERMAN, TRESPASSER, TRIMMER, TRIPPER, TROOPER, TROTTER, TRUMPETER, TUBER, TUBERCLE, TUBERCULOSIS, TUCKER, TUMBLER, TWEETER, TWEEZERS, TWERP, TWISTER, TWITCHER, TWITTER, UDDER, ULCER, UMBER, UNDER, UNIVERSAL, UNIVERSE, UNIVERSITY, UNNERVE, UNSWERVING, UPPER, USER, USHER, USURER, UTTER, VENTURER, VERB, VERBAL, VERBALIZE, VERBATIM, VERBENA, VERBOSE, VERDANT, VERDICT, VERGE, VERGER, VERMICELLI*, VERMICIDE, VERMIN, VERNAL, VERSATILE, VERSE, VERSICLE, VERSUS, VERTEBRA, VERTEBRATE, VERTEX, VERTICAL, VERTIGO, VERVE, VESPERS, VINTER, WADER, WADERS, WAFER, WAGER, WAGGONER, WELDER, MIG WELDER*, TIG WELDER*, WERT, WESTERING, WESTERLY, WESTERN, WESTERNER, WESTERNIZE, WHALER, WHENEVER, WHEREVER*, WHICHEVER, WHIMPER, WHIPPER, WHISKER, WHISPER, WHITER, WHOPPER, WICKER, WILDER, WINKER, WINNER, WINTER, WIPER, WISER, WONDER *f*, WRITER, WUNDERKIND, YONDER, ZIPPER. Australian words BANKER, BATTLER, BONZER, BOOMER, BUSTER, BUTCHER*, BUTTER-FISH, CHUNDER, COBBER, CRACKER, DAMPER, DIGGER, DOGGER, DUMPER, FETTLER, GIBBER [gib-er], HERD-TESTER, NEVER-NEVER, NOBBLER, NO-HOPER, OCKER, PERVE, POKER, SETTLER, SHICER, SHICKERED, SILVER BEET, SLATER, SPINNER, STONKER, SUPER, TUCKER, TUCKER-BAG, WEEKENDER, YABBER. Proper Nouns/Adj., SEPTEMBER, NOVEMBER, OCTOBER, DECEMBER, SOMERSET *f*, VERMONT, ABERDEEN ANGUS, ALBERTA, BERLIN, BERMUDA, BERNE silent <e>, CAMEMBERT silent <t>, CAPE VERDE, DERBY*, GERMAN, GERMANIC, GERMANY, HERBERT, HOOVER, INTERPOL, LONDONER, PERSPEX, PERTH, QUAKER, RICHTER SCALE <ch>=[k], SHERPA, SHETLANDER, SWITZERLAND, ULSTER, WATERLOO. **Rebel Names** BERKS *abbrev.* [barks], BERKSHIRE [bark-shə].

Butterfly was once a *flutter-bee* and then a *flutter-by* according to Lerer until the mistake 'butterfly' became normal, like *brid* became *bird* by mistake. (Lerer's lecture tapes.)

A *calender* was used in the past to refer to a pressing machine that thinned and changed materials such as cloth, paper, or plastic. It was used in the textile industry.

A *colander* is a perforated utensil for washing or draining food.

Conjurer is pronounced like a Feather Word, [kun-joo-rer], when it means to 'trick, work magic, juggle and muddle'. *Conjure* spells [kon-joor] when people come together (con-join) and swear to do something.

*In *conquer*, <qu> no longer spells [kw]. The [w] disappears when <qu> is followed by the weak suffix <er>. Compare it with *conquest* [kon-kwest] in which the stronger <est> ending attracts [w] into its syllable. Others with a silent <u> *exchequer, lacquer*.

*Cover spells [kuv-er], just like other spells [uth-er], simply because we find it is easier to say [kuv-er] than [kov-er]. *Cover* got its <o> from *colos* which is 'covering' in Old Latin and from which we also get *colour*, in which <o> also spells [u], maybe because we *cover* things with *colour*. Note, *overt* spells [oh-vert], 'open to view', *over* spells [oh-ver] and although it is related to *above* [u-buv] it would sound like *other* if it spelt [uver]. *Hover* spells [hov-er] and began as a term at sea, maybe from *heave-ho!*

*Proper-noun *Derby* and its common-noun eponym *derby* is pronounced both [der-bee] and [dar-bee], depending on who you are and where you are, broadly, it is [dar-bee] in U.K., [der-bee] in USA and parts of Australia.

*The verb *desert* [dez-ert] has a single <s> because it literally means "de-series, undo-series", in other words "sever connection, disconnect, abandon". This verb became the noun *desert*, meaning 'wilderness, place of abandonment and disconnection'. In [dez-ert], the single <s> spells [z] because it is at the end of a stressed syllable, stressed because nouns are stressed on their first syllable. *Desert* was spelt "desart" in the 1700's to avoid confusion with the verb *to desert*. In Latin's "desertum" the prefix <de> means "undo", but in Latin's "deservire" the prefix <de> means "complete", just as *denote* means 'completely mark' or to 'mark completely'. So, the Latin verb *deservire* means *to serve well, serve completely* and from that grew "to deserve" praise or reward and from that one's "just deserts".

*Dessert [də-zert] means 'pudding' or 'sweets'. Everyone cleared the table for it, as it was the last course. They 'de-served' all the other courses, cleared them away. So, it comes from French for "clear the table", remove or take away all other servings. We see another French word, *deshabile*, using this prefix, <des>, to mean 'remove'. This time it means "remove clothing". This prefix is usually <dis>, as in *distanced*, apart or removed, *dismantle etc.* Another word, *dissolve*, has <ss> due to adding a prefix. *Dissolve* and *dessert* are rebels to the rule <ss> spells [s] because they use <ss> to spell [z]. This does not happen in other words, e.g., <ss> spells [s] in *dissatisfied*.

*Err obeys the Short Word Rule with another <r>. If it added <e> it would spell [eer].

*Flivver — did you spot this <vv> writing rebel? It was originally slang, which excuses it from using <vv>, a letter which is not twinned lest it be mistaken for <w>. See Etymonline for *flivver's* origin.

*Freer is said as if it was *free-er* but it has to lose an <e> to obey the No Triplets Rule. *Seer*, which you met earlier, is in *overseer*. It means "over see-er" but it also lost an <e> to obey the No Triplets Rule and now spells [seer].

*Gherkin was a favourite of Caxton who spelt it that way when he set up the first printing press in England. He learnt his trade in the Netherlands where gherkins are today *gurkkjin*, but he would have used an older Dutch spelling.

*Gibber, [gib-er], not [jib-er], is from the Ab'l word *kibber*, 'rock or stone', and used to describe a rock-strewn plain.

*Hoover is an eponym. Google the Hoover Company. Another trade name, Zamboni, is becoming a word for any machine which smooths ice skating rinks and a verb as well, "to zamboni the ice", just as we 'hoover' the carpet. As an eponym, *zamboni* is excused for ending in <i>, which makes it a Rebel with a Reason.

*Lacquer has a silent <u>.

*Merchandise – did you remember that <ise> spells [Is] in nouns?

*Milliner could mean someone who deals in fine cloth from a textile mill, but the word comes from Milano in Italy, from which fine cloth was sent all over Europe and also fine straw bonnets, ribbons etc., and now means "a hatter".

Referral spells [ref-er-ral] because <rr>, twinned R, is bossy only if it's between a word's end and suffix. Here the suffix is —*al*.

Shepherd's silent <h> (and *shepherdess's*) is because <h> comes before an unstressed vowel, [shep-ud] or [shep-əd], as in *vehicle*.

Soccer's <ce> should make it spell [sok-ser]. However, it spells [sok-er] for it 's an abbreviation of *association* in 'Football Association' (as opposed to Rugby football). It was written *socca* in1889, *socker* in 1891, *soccer* in 1895. It's very like the reason *rugby* shortens to *rugger* — to match *soccer*.

Trekker is a rare <kk> word. So is *c*hukker* adopted from India along with polo.

Vermicelli in Italian spells [verm-i-chel-lee], meaning 'little worms', but in English it spells [verm-i-sel-lee].

Welder. *Mig welder, mig* is an acronym from 'metal inert gas' welder. *Tig welder* is a 'tungsten inert gas' welder.

Wherever is a compound word *where ever* with one <e> removed to avoid <ee> in the middle of the word, which might seem to spell [we-reever] or [wair-ee-ver], instead of [wair-ev-er].

List 3-46 Words in which <er> spells [er], before a consonant and when terminal, in which <a> spells [ar], the original long sound spelt by <a>.
AFTER, AFTERLIFE, AFTERMATH, AFTERMOST, AFTERNOON, AFTERSHAVE, ANSWER* silent <w>, CASTER*, DANCER, FASTER, FASTENER, GRASSHOPPER, LAGER [lar-ger], MASTER, MASTERFUL, MASTERLY, MASTER-MIND, PERCHANCE, POSTMASTER, SCHOOLMASTER <ch>=[k], TASKMASTER.

Answer [un-ser] has a silent <w> because [w] is silenced between a consonant and [er] due to the "tendency of [w] to be dropped from a weakly stressed syllable when it comes after a consonant and before a vowel", (Cummings, p. 400). So <w> is a silent letter because it is between a consonant and the weak ending <er>. We still write <w> to remember *answer* was once much longer: "Make your reply *and swear* it's true," shortened to "*and swear*" and then "*an-swer*".

Caster. A sugar caster is used to sprinkle or cast sugar on to food. Finely ground sugar is easier to spread and called caster sugar. The old word *cast* means 'veer about' and now we only hear it when fishing, casting a line, or sailing: Prepare to cast about!"

List 3-47A Words in which <er> spells [er], before a consonant and when terminal, in which <a> spells [or] as in *water*. See Rule 1-14 for the reason.
TALKER, STALKER, WALKER, WALLPAPER, WATER, WATERBRASH, WATERFALL, WATERLESS, WATERMAN, WATERPROOF, WATERSHED, WATERSIDE, WATERY.

List 3-47B in which <er> spells [er], in words in which <a> spells [or] and in some places, like Australia, <a> spells [o] rather than [or]. See reason after Rule 1-15.
ALDERMAN, ALTER, ALTERNATE, ALTERNATIVE, FALTER, HALTER.

List 3-48 Words in which <er> spells [er], before a consonant and when terminal, in which <a> spells [o]. See Rule 1-15.
SQUANDER, SQUATTER, WALTZER, WANDER, WANDERER, WANDERING, WANDERLUST, WASHER, WHATEVER, WHATSOEVER.

As we have learnt earlier, only <ery> is used to spell terminal [er-ree], never <iry> or <ury>.
Rule 3-49 Suffix <ery> spells [er-ree], [ə-ree] or even just [ree].
Reason The suffix has two syllables and being a suffix, both are weak. To avoid two weak beats, we reduce one even more, which means [er] becomes little [ə] or disappears altogether! Do you say [miz-er-

ee] or [miz-ree]? Regardless of how we say it, we must write *misery* not *misry*, and so we must know how to say it correctly, with all syllables.

List 3-49

ADULTERY, BAKERY, BAPTISTERY, BATTERY, BLUSTERY, BRAVERY, BRIBERY, BUGGERY, BUTCHERY, CANNERY, CELERY, CEMETERY, COOKERY, CROCKERY, DELIVERY, DISCOVERY, DRAPERY, DYSENTERY, EMERY, EVERY, FINERY, FISHERY, FLATTERY, FOOLERY, IMAGERY, LOTTERY, MASTERY *VS*, MISERY, MOCKERY, MONASTERY, PAPERY, PEPPERY, PERIPHERY, POTTERY, ROCKERY, ROOKERY, RUBBERY, SCENERY, SHRUBBERY, SLAVERY, SLIPPERY, SNOBBERY, SPIDERY, SPLINTERY, SUMMERY, TRUMPERY, WINERY, WITCHERY. Proper Noun CHANCERY LANE

The words *inter, over, super* and *under* form compound words — they are not suffixes. In compound words <er> spells [er] at the end of the first stem, even if the next stem starts with a vowel. This is because stem words do not change in compound words, except for a few rebels like *breakfast. Interest* is a compound of Latin words *inter* (between) and *est* (is), meaning 'between is'.

Rule 3-50 Terminal <er> spells [er] inside compound words, even if followed by a vowel.

List 3-50

INTEREST, INTERACT, INTERACTIVE, INTERBREED, INTERCEDE, INTERCEPT, INTERCHANGE, INTERCOM, INTERDICT, INTERESTED, INTERESTING, INTERFACE, INTERFACING, INTERFERE, INTERFERENCE, INTERFERON, INTERIM, INTERJECT, INTERLACE, INTERLINE, INTERLOCK, INTERLOPER, INTERLUDE, INTERMARRY, INTERMEZZO, INTERMINABLE, INTERMITTENT, INTERMIX, INTERNECINE, INTERNMENT, INTERPOLATE, INTERPOSE, INTERPRET, INTERPRETER, INTERREGNUM, INTERRELATED, INTERROGATE, INTERRUPT, INTERSECT, INTERSPERSE, INTERSTICE, INTERVAL, INTERVENE, INTERTWINE, OVERACT, OVERBALANCE, OVERBOOK, OVERDO, OVERDOSE, OVERDRIVE, OVERDUE, OVERESTIMATE, OVERFEED, OVERFILL, OVERFISH, OVERFLY, OVERHAND, OVERHANG, OVERKILL, OVERLAND, OVERLAP, OVERLOOK, OVERLY, OVERMAN, OVERMANTEL, OVERMUCH, OVERPRINT, OVERRIDE, OVERRIDER, OVERRIPE, OVERRULE, OVERRUN, OVERSEER*, OVERSHOOT, OVERSHOT, OVER-SIMPLIFY, OVERSLEEP, OVERSPEND, OVERSPILL, OVERSTATE, OVERSTEP, OVERSTRUNG, OVERTAKE, OVERTIME, OVERTOOK, OVERTURE, OVERUSE, OVERWHELM*, SUPERCOOL, SUPER-EGO, SUPERFINE, SUPERIMPOSE, SUPERINTEND, SUPERLATIVE, SUPERSCRIPT, SUPERSEDE*, SUPERSONIC, SUPERTANKER, SUPERVENE, SUPERVISE, UNDERBID, UNDERCUT, UNDERDOG, UNDERDONE, UNDEREXPOSE, UNDERFELT, UNDERFLOOR, UNDERGO, UNDERLINE, UNDERLING, UNDERMANNED, UNDERMINE, UNDERPANTS, UNDERPASS, UNDERPIN, UNDERRATE, UNDERSCORE, UNDERSELL, UNDERSTAND, UNDERSTATE, UNDERTAKE, UNDERTAKER, UNDERTONE, UNDERWENT, UNDERWRITE.

Irregular compound verbs use the same present, past and past participles as their stem verbs. For example, *undertake, undertook, undertaken*.

* In *overwhelm* <wh> is used to mark a superlative situation.

**Supersede* is the only word in which [seed] is spelt <sede>, meaning "super sit, sit on top of or above." Another word, *sedentary,* also comes from Latin for *sit*. We use <cede> for 'yield' in *concede, accede, recede, precede, secede*. Latin *cedere* meant 'go back, yield' and also 'go forward.' We spell it c*ede*, to mean "go away, go back, withdraw, yield". Hence *concede, accede, recede, precede, secede*. When we mean "go forward" we spell it *ceed*, (think *speed*), hence *proceed, succeed, exceed*.

<u>Not needed but nice to know</u>. Try including each way of spelling [seed] in one sentence. For instance: He conceded that his brother's claim to the throne superseded his and so preparations for the coronation proceeded, which included seeding royal flower beds. <u>Now back to things we need to know.</u>

Digraph <ir> — *affirm, zircon.*

We can only call <ir> a digraph if together they spell a sound different to [i][r]. That sound is [er]. As we know, <ger> spells [ger] and [jer]. However, when <ir> spells [er], <gir> always spells [ger]. This is because all such words are very old. The English kept on saying them the same old way regardless of what the French told them about <gi> spells [ji]. So in *gird* and in all other <gir> spells [ger] words, <g> spells [g], i.e., [g] is not softened to [j]. However, when <ir> precedes a vowel, it no longer spells [er] — 'R is bossy after vowels, but not between them' — and <g> is softened by <i> to [j], as in *giraffe* and *giro*.

Rule 3-51 Digraph<ir> spells [er] when R is Bossy.

Reason See Rule 3-40 and discussion.

List 3-51 <ir> spells [er], with [g] to remind us that <gir> spells [ger] when R is bossy.

AFFIRM, AFFIRMATIVE, AFTERBIRTH, ASTIR, BELLBIRD, BIRCH, BIRD, BIRDSEED, BIRTH, BIRTH CERTIFICATE, BIRTH RATE, BIRTH-CONTROL, BIRTHMARK, BIRTHPLACE, BLACKBIRD, CIRCA *abbrev.*, CIRCLE, CIRCLET, CIRCULAR, CIRCULARITY, CIRCULARIZE, CIRCULATE, CIRCULATORY, CIRCUMCISE, CIRCUMFERENCE, CIRCUMFLEX, CIRCUMNAVIGATE, CIRCUMSCRIBE, CIRCUMSPECT, CIRCUMSTANCE, CIRCUMLOCUTORY, CIRCUMVENT, CIRCUS, CONFIRM, DIRGE, DIRK, DIRNDL*, DIRT, DIRTY, EMIR, ENCIRCLE, FAKIR, FIR, FIRM, FIRMAMENT, FIRST, FIRST BASE, FIRST HAND, FIRST-BORN, FIRSTHAND, FIRST-RATE, FLIRT, GIRD* [g], GIRDER [g], GIRDLE [g], GIRL [g], GIRLHOOD [g], GIRLISH [g], GIRLISHLY [g], GIRLISHNESS [g], GIRT [g], GIRTH [g], HUMMING-BIRD, INFIRM, INFIRMARY, INFIRMITY, IRK, IRKSOME, KIRK, KIRSCH, KIRTLE, LADYBIRD, NADIR, NIRVANA, SEMICIRCLE, SHIRK, SHIRR, SHIRRED, SHIRRING, SHIRT, SHIRTING, SHIRTY, SIR, SKIRL, SKIRMISH, SKIRT, SKIRTING, SMIRCH, SMIRK, SONGBIRD, SQUIRM, SQUIRT, STAND FIRM, STIR, STIRRED, STIRRING, BESTIRRED, TERRA FIRMA, THIRD, THIRST, THIRSTILY, THIRSTY, THIRTEEN*, THIRTIES, THIRTIETH, THIRTY, T-SHIRT, UNDERSKIRT, VIRGIN, VIRGIN BIRTH, VIRGINAL, VIRGINITY, VIRTUE, WHIRR*, WHIRRED, WHIRRING, ZIRCON. <u>Names</u> DIRK, VIRGIL, VIRGO, VIRGINIA.

Dirndl is the only word ending <dl>, instead of <dle>. This shows that it's a recent adoption, 1937, not adapted to English spelling rules.

Thirteen is a contraction of Old English *threotine*.

Whirr has no alternative spelling. It always ends <rr> so no-one makes a mistake when adding suffixes: *whirred,* [werd], *whirring* [wer-riŋ], *whirry* [wer-ree]. As we know *wiring* spells [wI-riŋ] and *wiry* spells [wi-ree].

As we know, **'Twinned R's only bossy when before a suffix, after a free stem',** between a word's end and a suffix, as in *whirring* or *stirring*. This means that with his twin inside a stem word he is not bossy, as in *cirrus* and *squirrel*. Note: When <irr> comes at the start of a stem, not at the end, it never spells [er] because words like *irrepressible* and *irregular* are really 'in-repressible' and 'in-regular'. To make a smooth join, suffix <in> changed to <ir>. In fact <rr> is never bossy between a prefix and a word.

List 3-52 in which <irr> does not spell [er]

CIRRHOSIS, CIRRUS, IRREGULAR, IRRELEVANT, IRRESOLUTE, IRRESPECTIVE, IRREPRESSIBLE, IRREVERENT, IRRIGATE, IRRITANT, IRRITATE, MIRROR, SQUIRREL, STIRRUP*.

*One Old English spelling was *stirup*, a compound of old words for *stair* and *rope*. Maybe the dictionary committee felt an <rr> in *stirrup* would better echo the old compound 'stairrope'.

As we know, R is bossy after vowels, but not between them, so when <ir> is followed by a vowel it never spells [er].
Q. What does it spell? **Answer:** It spells [Ir] in the first syllable of a stem word, as in *pirate* and *spire,* and [i-r] in other syllables, as in *aspirin*. As we know, it spells [i-r] in prefixes, as in *irritate* and [i-r] if it is stressed in the third or fourth syllable from the end of a word, as in *con-spi-ra-cy,* or otherwise shortened, as in *spirit* and *satiric*.
Rebels AMIRATE, MIRAGE, ANDIRON.
Rebels' Reasons Adopted *amir* and *amirate* use Continental long sound [ee] and spell [a-meer] and [a-meer-ayt]. *Mirage* [mi-rarj] is a French adoption, the strong French ending reducing the first vowel. An English pronunciation would rhyme it with *mileage*. *Andiron* [and-I-ron] holds logs in a fire place and is made of *iron* [I-on] which helps us remember how to read it. It's possibly an old compound word, 'antlers of iron', for an andiron looks like iron antlers.

List 3-53
<u><i> spells [i]</u> — ASPIRANT, ASPIRIN, EMPIRIC*, JABIRU, SATIRIC*, SATIRIZE*, SPIRIT*.
<u>Stressed 3rd or more syllable from the end, spells a short vowel, [i]</u> — CONSPIRACY, EMPIRICAL, IRIDESCENT, MIRACLE, DIRIGIBLE, SPIRACLE.
<u><i>spells [I] in first syllables</u> — IRATE, IRIS, IRON*, IRONIC [I-ron-ik], IRONMONGER*ƒ*, IRONSTONE, SPIRAL, TIRADE.
*We met *iron* in Part One with some 'Regal Words'. We know <r> is silent but rhotic speakers do say it and then it sounds more like the Swedish cousin-word *järn* [yarn] we mentioned in Part One.
**Satirize* (or *satirise*) ends with secondary stress on the suffix —*ize* and so <i> is unstressed and spells [i].
**Spirit* spells [spi-rit], not [spI-rit] due to the shortening affect of terminal <it>, as in *visit*.
In **empiric* and *satiric,* <i> spells [i], due to the shortening affect of terminal <ic>, as in *epic*.
There are two Bossy R's in the following sentence: "Fir trees burnt in the fiery fire". One is in *fir*, but not in *fire*, because 'R is bossy after vowels, but not between them'.
The second Bossy R is in *fiery*, [fI-er-ree]. As we know, it should be spelt 'firy', like 'wiry', but the extra vowel remained in *fiery,* when old *fier* parted ways with *fire*, Cummings p. 319. (There were two spellings for *fire,* the second matched *brier*. We only use *fier* now when writing *fiery*.) Australian journalists use *firey* for fire-fighters, a slang word which will soon be accepted in dictionaries. The point is, terminal <iry> never spells [er-ree], because it is only 'in suffixes <ery> and <ory>, that Bossy R is in his glory', meaning that he is only bossy in these suffixes, not in the suffixes <ary>, <iry> and <ury>.

Digraph <ur> — *accursed, urn.*

The letters <ur> are only a digraph if and when they spell the single word-sound [er]. In 1500 *fern, furl* and *firm* all had different vowel sounds, when people still rolled their R's, but by 1700 their vowels had all converged to just [er] because R stopped rolling and merged with the vowels which, said with the tongue raised and curled, all sounded like [er]. While they were all converging, moving together in sound, spelling went mad. *Irchon* changed to *urchin*, *chirche* changed to *church*, (but the Scots kept it as *kirk*), *mirke* changed to *murk*, *sirly* changed to *surly,* even though it means "when sir is grumpy."

We will see that at the end of a few words an alternative spelling, <urr>, spells [er], in words like *curr* in some books, possibly to copy *err*. Everyone agrees on *purr* and *burr,* but dictionaries differ on *curr* etc. Because <rr> is not inside a word, *curr* still spells [ker], *purr* still spells [per] and so on.

207

We can read the following list because we know that 'R is bossy after vowels, but not between them' and 'Twinned R's only bossy when before a suffix, after a free stem.'

Rule 3-45 Digraph <ur> spells [er] when R is Bossy.

Reason See Rule 3-40 and discussion.

List 3-54

ACCURSED, BEEFBURGER, BLUR *verb*, BLURRED, BLURRING, BLUR *noun*, BLURRY *adj*, BLURB*, BURDEN, BURDENSOME *f*, BURGER*, BURGLAR, BURLESQUE, BURLY, BURN Δ, BURN *brook*, BURNER, BURNET *plant*, BURNISH, BURNT, BURP, BUR *noun*, BURRED *adj*, BURRY *adj.*, BURR* *noun*, BURSAR, BURSARY, BURST Δ, BURSTING, BURTON slang, CHEESEBURGER, CHURCH, CHURCHMAN, CHURCHWARDEN, CHURCHYARD, CHURLISH, CHURLISHLY, CHURLISHNESS, CHURN, COCKSPUR, CONCUR *verb*, CONCURRED, CONCURRING, CUR/CURR, CURB, CURD, CURDLE, CURFEW, CURL, CURLER, CURLICUE, CURLING a game, CURLY, CURMUDGEON, CURSE, CURSOR, CURSORY, CURT, CURTLY, CURTNESS, CURTSY, CURVE, CURVET, CURVATURE, DEMUR, DURST§, EXPURGATE, EXPURGATOR, FEMUR, FRANKFURTER, FUR *noun*, FURRY *adj.*, FUR *verb*, FURRED, FURFUR, FURBISH, FURL, FURLONG, FURLONG*, FURNACE, FURNISH, FURNISHINGS, FURTHER, FURTHERANCE, FURTHERMORE, FURTHERMOST, FURTHEST, FURTIVE, FURZE, GUTTURAL, GUTTURALLY, HAMBURGER, HURDLE, HURDY-GURDY, HURL, HURLY-BURLY, HURT Δ, HURTFUL, HURTLE, INCUR *verb*, INCURRED, INCURRING, INSURGENT, LANGUR, LEMUR, MANGEL-WURZEL, MASTURBATE, MAZURKA, MURDER, MURMUR, NOCTURNAL, NOCTURNE, NON SEQUITUR, NURSE, NURSERY, NURSERY SLOPES, NURSERYMAN, NURTURE, OCCUR, OVERBURDEN, OVERTURN, PRECURSOR, PURDAH, PURGATIVE, PURGATORY, PURGATORIAL, PURGE, PURL, PURLER, PURPLE, PURPLISH, PURPORT, PURPOSE, ON PURPOSE, PURPOSEFUL, PURPOSEFULLY, PURPOSEFULNESS, PURPOSELESS, PURPOSELY, PURR *noun*, PURR *verb*, PURRED, PURRING, PURSE, PURSER, PURSUANCE, PURSUANT, PURSUE, RECUR, RECURRED, RECURRING, RECURVE, REGURGITATE, RETURN, RETURNING OFFICER, RETURN MATCH, RETURN GAME, RETURN TICKET, SATURNALIA, SCURVY, SLUR *noun*, SLUR *verb*, SLURRED, SLURRING, SLURP, SPLURGE, SPUR *noun*, SPUR *verb*, SPURRED, SPURRING, SPURGE - plant, SPURN, SPURT, SUBURB, SUBURBAN, SUBURBANITE, SULPHUR/SULFUR, SURCHARGE, SURCINGLE, SURD, SURF, SURFACE, SURFER, SURFING, SURGE, SURGEON, SURGERY, SURGICAL, SURLY, SURMISE, SURNAME, SURPASS, SURPASSING, SURPASSINGLY, SURPLICE, SURPLUS, SURPRISE, SURPRISING, SURPRISINGLY, SURVIVAL, SURVIVE*, SURVIVOR, TACITURN, TACITURNITY, TURBAN, TURBID, TURBINE, TURBO-JET, TURBO-PROP, TURBOT, TURBULENT, TURBULENTLY, TURBULENCE, TURD, TURF, TURGID, TURGIDLY, TURGIDITY, TURMERIC, TURN, TURN, TURTLE, TURNER, TURNERY, TURNING, TURNIP, TURNOVER, TURNPIKE, TURNSTILE, TURNTABLE, TURPENTINE, TURPITUDE, TURPS, TURTLE, TURTLE-NECK, URBAN, URBANE, URBANITY, URBANELY, URBANIZE, URCHIN, URGE, URGENT, URN, VIBURNUM. <u>Proper Nouns</u> BURMA, HOMBURG, KURD, KURDISH, LUXEMBURG, PURITAN, TURK, TURKEY, TURKISH, BATTHURST, BATTHURST BURR *a weed*. <u>Names</u> ARTHUR, CURTIS, KURT.

Δ Irregular verbs, present, past, p. participle:
BURN Δ, BURNT Δ /BURNED, BURNT Δ /BURNED
BURST Δ, BURST Δ, BURST Δ
HURT Δ, HURT Δ, HURT Δ

DURST§ is an auxiliary verb. It is very old-fashioned. "I durst not go there," means "I dare not go there". "He durst fight the dragon" means "He dares to fight the dragon."

**Blurb* was coined by American ad-man Gelett Burgess in the twentieth century, (Fleck 2007).
**Burger* probably spells [ber-ger] not [berj-er] because it comes from German not French.
**Furlong* comes from the old word for furrow, *furkh,* down the length of a ten-acre field. Since fields were a bit variable in shape, it was fixed at an eighth of a mile, 220 yards, or 201.168 metres. *Furkh* ('furrow') is probably the origin of an old English verb, which is considered vulgar today and so is not listed with *luck* and other words ending <ck>.
**Burr* describes the rough sound of the sound of <r> by rhotic speakers. It sounds as though the speaker has a bur (a prickly seed) in his mouth, some say.
**S*urvive spells [ser-vIv] because <ive> is not a suffix. In French it was *survivre,* a legal term which meant to live over and beyond someone else, to stay alive.

As we know, 'twinned R's only bossy when before a suffix, after a free stem', i.e., between a word's end and suffix. We know R is not bossy when it is just a smooth link between a prefix and a stem, as in *surrogate*, instead of *subrogate.*

Words in compound words retain a Bossy R. There is a stem word *sur* in French which means 'over', quite the opposite from prefix *sub—*. Pronunciation of *surrender* is [ser-render], 'render over to us your soldiers, your arms, in fact your nation', but more and more we hear [su-render] because the latter is easier to say.

List 3-55 Bossy R is still twinned at the end of CURR and PURR, also BURR. The latter means a Scottish burr, which is speech sounding as if one has a bur in one's throat. Twinned R is bossy in FURRY and PURRING because it is at the end of a free stem, before a suffix. Twinned R is bossy in SURRENDER because it is in a compound word, *sur-render,* as above.

The twins are not bossy in CURRANT, CURRENT, CURRY, FLURRY, HURRY, SCURRY, SLURRY, OCCURRENCE, CURRICULUM, SURROGATE, and {SURROUND} because <rr> does not come at the end of a stemword and before a suffix. These words in 'the twins are not bossy list' look OK to us because they obey Orm's Law, in which twin consonants keep preceding vowels short. Long ago some had the longer [er] vowel, e.g., *current* is related to *cursor* which originally meant "runner" in Latin. They both had the [er] vowel, and so did *curriculum* but now it's said [ku-rik-yoo-luum]. It means a course of study and is related to *cursor,* "runner" in Latin, ancestor word to *course* and *career. Curriculum vitæ* came into use in 1902 meaning "course of one's life" and is shortened to CV. The noun *curry* is from French 'currieier' which means 'to put in order', as in grooming a horse, hence a horse's comb is a curry comb. Another *curry* comes from India, *kari* in Tamil. As for the expression to 'curry favour' see https://horsenetwork.com/2022/04/ and you will learn that *favour* was Fauvel, a powerful horse who was curried, groomed and petted to get on his good side. *Hurry* used to spell [her-ee] and meant to "whirl around, move fast", probably a cousin-word to *hurl. Flurry* meant 'to scatter, fly with a whirring noise', and spelt [fler-ee]. *Slurry* used to be [sler-ee] for *slur* was one English dialect for 'a thin film of mud'. (The rest of England said [slor].) When people "throw mud' they *slur* [sler] a person's reputation. *Currant* comes from "raisin of Corinth" and the <r> of *Corinth* was twinned to the pattern of *berry* and *cherry.*

As we know, R is bossy after vowels, but not between them, so when <ur> is followed by a vowel it never spells [er].
Q. What does it spell? **Ans.** When <ur> is followed by a vowel it spells either [yoor] or [oor], as long as <ur> does not follow a vowel. When it does follow a vowel, as in *amateurish, aural* and *flourish,* <ur> does not spell [yoor] or [yoo]. When single vowel <u> is followed by <r> and another vowel, it obeys Orm's Law and spells its long sounds, because <r> is a single consonant. In words that end in <ure>, the single consonant <r> is followed by Fairy E, e.g., in *cure,* the same way <t> is followed by Fairy E in

cute. So <ure> spells its long sounds due to the action of Fairy E, and other vowels which might replace Fairy E, as in *curable* and *purity*. Other words obey Orm's Law with no need of Fairy E because they have two syllables, like *legal,* in which a single consonant follows a single-letter stressed vowel so the vowel spells its long sound. This happens in <ur> words like *mural, plural, rural* and *fury, jury, urine.*

Q. We already know about long vowel sounds in 'Fairy E' words, and 'Regal Words', but why does <ur> spell two long sounds, [yoor] or just [oor], and how do we know which it spells? Why do we hear just [oor] in *lure, jury* and *rural?*

Ans. Think back. We heard in Part One that people found saying [yoo] after [r], [l] and [j] very difficult. So they dropped yods after [r], [l] and [j]. This explains why *Ruby, Lulu* and *Judy* spell [roobee] not [ryoobee], loo-loo] not [lyoo-lyoo] and [joodee] not [jyoodee]. That is why <u> only spells [oo], not [yoo], in *lure, jury* and *rural*.

Q. We hear [yoor] in *azure, cure, during, fury, mural, puny* and *tureen,* but it sounds more like [zhoor] in *azure,* [joor] in *during* and [choor] in *tureen.* Why?

Ans. It makes it easier to say [y] after these three consonants, [z], [d] and [t], if [y] fuses a little with them. If we pronounce *azure, during* and *tureen* very slowly and clearly we hear [zyoor], [dyoor] and [tyoor], but if we say them less carefully, in everyday speech, we let [z], [d] and [t] fuse with [y], which means we hear [zhoor], [joor] and [choor]. Long ago, when <su> spelt [syoo], the yod fused with [s] and made the Yod Fusion [sh], e.g., in *sure*. In words in which [yoo] is spelt with <ui>, like *suit* the yod eventually dropped, was not fused with [s], so today *suit* spells [soot], not [syoot] nor [shoot]. See appendix on yods for more information.

Rule 3-56 When consonant plus <ur> precedes a vowel, <u> spells its long sounds.

Reason This is because R is not bossy between vowels. There are no exceptions for <ur> before a vowel. Even in words ending <ury>, R is not bossy, unlike in suffixes —*ery* and —*ory*, because <ury> is never a suffix.

So a consonant plus <ur>, before a vowel, spells [yoor], or just [oor] if after <l>, <r> or <j>. People found saying [yoo] after these three very difficult. So they dropped yods after [r], [l] and [j]. This explains why *Ruby, Lulu* and *Judy* spell [roobee] not [ryoobee], loo-loo] not [lyoo-lyoo] and [joodee] not [jyoodee]. Dropped them in *sue* and the name *Sue,* too, but not in *assume* and *pursue*. In parts of USA, yods have dropped after [n], [t] and [d] as well. We hear 'Yod Droppers' in some movies, saying [noo] for *new,* [toon] for *tune* and [doo] for *due.*

Rebel BURY which does not spell [byoo-ree].

Rebels' Reasons We met *bury* [be-ree] in Part One and heard that it used to spell [buu-ree], and also [be-ree], in another part of England. Eventually the two versions of *bury* converged, using one's letter code and the other's sound. (An example, we have already heard, of Mixed Convergence.)

List 3-56A <ur> vowel spells [yoor].
BURETTE, CURE, CURABLE, CURACY, CURATE, CURATIVE, CURATOR, DEMURELY, DEMURENESS, FIGURATIVE, FIGURE OF SPEECH, FURY, IMPURITY, INCURABLE, INCURABLE, MERCURY, OBSCURELY, OBSCURITY, PENURY, PROCURABLE, PROCURATOR, PROCURE, PUREE <ee> =[ay], PURELY, PURIFY, PURIST, PURITY, RECONFIGURABLE, RURAL, SULPHURIC.

List 3-56B <ur> vowel spells [oor].
CONJUROR, INJURY, PERJURE, PERJURY, POLYURETHANE.

Subsets — *ensure, closure, future, endure.*

Certain words are missing from List 3-56A. Where is *insure?* Where is *future?* Where is *endure?* Where is *azure?* In all these words <u> can spell [yoor] but it can also spell [shoor], [choor], [joor] and [zhoor], as in *insure, future, endure* and *azure,* in that order.

Sure is missing because there is no way anyone still says [syoor]. As we know, in *sure* and *sugar,* <y> no longer spells [yoo] because the yod, [y], has merged, or fused, with [s] and produced [sh]. This is Yod Fusion at work.

Long ago, if a word started with <s> which was followed by <u> spelling its long sound, then <u> always spelt [yoo]. We don't hear [y] in *suit* any more, but we do hear it in *pursuit.* We hear it in *insulin* but not in *suet.* That's because <s> must be preceded by a consonant in order to spell [sy] before <u> spelling its long sound. Note:- <u> must spell its long sound. So <su> does not spell [syoo] in *insult*, because <u> spells short [u], but we do hearc [sy] in *insulate* in which <u> spells its long sound.

Rule 3-57A If <u> spells its long sound after <s> spells [s], and <su> follows a consonant, then <su> spells [shoo].

Rebels SUGAR, SURE, TSUNAMI.

Sugar and *sure* are the only remaining stem words in which <su> spells [shoo] when <s> does not follow a consonant. Being word-initial, <su> does not follow a consonant. This also happens in additions to these stems, e.g., SUGARLESS, SUGARY, SURELY, SURENESS, SURER, SUREST, SURETY.

Sure spelt [syoor] about 300 years ago, (Cummings, p. 411), due to <u>, spelling [yoo], instead of just plain [oo]. It became easier to fuse [s] and [y] into [sh] than to blend [s] with [y], in [syoor] and [syoo-gar]. So *sure* became [shoor] and *sugar* became [shuu-gar]. In *suit* the [sy] blend never fused into [sh]. This happened before yods dropped after S starting a word. Since then, yods have dropped from *suit* and *sue,* in which <s> starts a word. I can remember old ladies saying [syoot] but this never became [shoot]. Now the yod has dropped and we say [soot]. We don't call Sue 'syoo' any more either. (Note: the red spice *sumac* [soo-mak] is sometimes pronounced [shumak].)

Tsunami is the only word we use in which <u> spells its long sound and <su> follows a consonant and yet <su> does not spell [shoo]. That is because there never was a yod in *tsunami,* because this word is a foreign adoption in which <u> spells [oo].

List 3-57A
ASSURE, CENSURE, COMMENSURATE, COMMISSURE, ENSURE, FISSURE, INSURE, INSURABLE, LICENSURE, LUXURY*, MENSURATE, PRESSURE, PRESSURIZE, PURSUE, REASSURE, TONSURE, UNINSURABLE, UNSURE.

*In *luxury*, <x> spells [ks]. So *luxury* spells [luk-shoo-ree] — because <u> spells its long sound after [s], and [s] follows a consonant, [k].

Getting [zh] in closure.

In *azure* [ay-zyoor] we hear [zy], and if we speak slowly and clearly we hear [zy] in *closure,* too, [kloh-zyoor]. That's because, as we know, when <s> comes after a stressed vowel and before a vowel it spells [z]. So when <sure> follows a stressed vowel, it spells [zyoor], also pronounced [zhoor] due to Yod Fusion, or just [zhuu] if it is an unstressed suffix. Note: it does not do this after unstressed vowels because <s> after unstressed vowels does not spell [z]. As it is, if [s] follows an unstressed vowel it is spelt <ss> and so the rule is simply:—

Rule 3-57B After a vowel, <sure> spells [zhuu].

Reason Knowing that the vowel followed by <sure> is stressed we know the following syllable will be unstressed, which is why <sure> spells [zhuu] and not [zhoor]. Note: in *assure*, <sure> does not follow any vowel, neither stressed nor unstressed. That is why *assure* spells [u-shoor]. We have discussed Yod Fusion in other words, such as *insure, tulip* and *duty* in which we hear [sh], [ch] and [j]. Now we hear the fourth Yod Fusion, [zh], in *closure*. Yods fuse inside words and also between words. Say 'Asia will amaze ya,' and what do you hear? Do you hear '[ay-zhuu] will [u-may-zhuu]'? We shall hear why there is a yod in *Asia* later on. For now we have a very simple reading rule.

List 3-57B

CLOSURE, COMPOSURE, DISCLOSURE, DISPOSURE, EXPOSURE, FORECLOSURE, USURY

Tulips, naturally.
We know that <tu> spells [choo] in words like *tulip* because it is easier to say [choolip] than [tyoolip]. This is what we call Yod Fusion. The same thing happens in *nature*. It is easier to say [nay-chuu] than [nay-tyoor]. We hear [ch] in all words ending <ture>, e.g., *culture* and *future*. Also, in all words built on words ending in <ture>, like *natural,* because Fairy E makes <u> spell its long sound, in *nature*, for instance, and when another vowel replaces <e> the magic remains.

Rule 3-58 The cluster <ture> spells [chuur] and <ture> plus suffix spells [chuur].

Reason Yod Fusion, as explained above.

Rebels In words in which yods have been dropped after [t], there is no Yod Fusion and therefore no production of [chuur]. Yod dropping after [t] occurs mainly in New York, USA.

List 3-58
ARCHITECTURE <ch>=[k], ARCHITECTURAL, ARCHITECTURALLY, CULTURAL, CULTURALLY, CURVATURE*, FURNITURE*, FUTURISTIC, FUTURITY, GESTURE, HORTICULTURAL, HORTICULTURE, NATURAL, NATURALISM, NATURALISTIC, NATURALIZE, NATURALLY, NATURALNESS, NATURIST, NURTURE*, PASTURE, PASTURAGE, PICTURE POSTCARD, PICTURE-GALLERY, PICTURESQUE, PICTURESQUELY, PICTURESQUENESS, *PITURI, POLYUNSATURATED, SATURATE, SCULPTURAL, SUPERNATURAL, SUPERNATURALLY, SUPERSTRUCTURE, TORTURE, CENTURY, VENTURI, VESTURE.

Curvature, furniture, nurture – look at <ur> in these words. They have <ur> spelling different sounds in the same word! That's because the first <ur> comes before a consonant and the second is after <t> and before a vowel.

Pituri [pichooree] has been adopted from the Ab'l word for the shrub, first written 'pedgery', (Blake, p. 102).

Duty Procedure
As we know, *duty* spells [joo-tee], due to Yod Fusion. It is easier to say [proh-see-juu] than [proh-see-dyoor] and so we let yod, i.e. [y], and [d] fuse which produces Yod Fusion [j] in *procedure.*

Rule 3-59 If <u> spells its long sound in <dure>, or in <dure> plus a suffix, then <dur> spells [juur].

Rebels In words in which yods have been dropped after [d], there is no Yod Fusion and therefore no production of [j]. Yod dropping after [d] occurs mainly in New York, USA.

List 3-59
DURABLE, DURABILITY, DURESS, DURING, ENDURABLE, ENDURANCE, ENDURING, EPIDURAL, OBDURATE, PROCEDURAL, PROCEDURE, UNENDURABLE

Digraph <or> — *abhor, vortex.*

As we know already, <or> spells [or] in *for* and in *fore.*

Rule 3-60 R is bossy after vowels, but not between them, 'cept in words ending ery, ore and ory 'coz R's bossy then — he's in his glory, as in the Bossy R Rule.

Reason See discussion leading up to the Bossy R Rule, Rule 3-40.

Rebel STOREY spells [stor-ree], not [sto-ree]. It is the only word in which <ore> spells [or] inside a stem word. Why does <e> remain?

Rebel's Reason It is not *store* suffix *y,* nor one store above another. Ayto, on p. 505, says that both *story* and *storey* come from Latin *historia* which means 'account of events, narrative, story' and share that ancestor word with *history*. The word *storey* is thought to be used long ago for a pictorial account of events, which could have been a row of statues along one level of a building, or a row of stained-glass windows all along a wall. From this came one storey above another, at different levels on a building. Now we use *storey* for one layer of floor to ceiling in a building, and we call a tall building *multi-storeyed*. After about 1600 *history* has been used for factual stories and *story* for fictional stories.

Rebel ATTORNEY

Rebel's Reasons In *attorney* <or> spells [er], but only in Anglo English. It originally meant "someone to turn to" and *turn* was written *torn* in Old French — possibly <i> or <u> was replaced with <o>? *Attorney* in American English spells [a-torn-ee], and so in America it is not a rebel. It's so like the English to spell it the French way (Old French way in this case) but say it the English way!

List 3-60 Digraph <or> spells [or].

ABHOR, ABHORRED, ABHORRING, ABORT, ABORTIVE, ACCELERATOR, ADAPTOR, ADORN, AFFORD, AGGRESSOR, CHICORY, ALLIGATOR, ALLEGORY, ANCESTOR, ANCHOR, ANTHROPOMORPHIC, ANTHROPOMORPHISM, APPLICATOR, ASSORTED, ASSORTMENT, ATTORNEY*, BACHELOR*, BENEFACTOR, BORDER, BORDERLAND, BORDERLINE, BORN, BORNE*, CALORY, CAMPHOR, CAPACITOR, CAPTOR, CASTOR *oil.*, CATEGORY, CENSOR, CHANCELLOR, CHADOR, CHORD <ch>=[k], COLLABORATOR, COLLECTOR, COLOR*, COMFORT *f*, COMMENTATOR, COMPETITOR, COMPOSITOR, COMPRESSOR, CONCORD, CONCORDANT, CONCORDAT, CONDUCTOR, CONFESSOR, CONFORM, CONFORMIST, CONFORMITY, CONNECTOR, CONSIGNOR*, CONSORT, CONSTRICTOR, CONTRACTOR, CO-ORDINATE, CO-ORDINATOR, CORK, CORKER, CORD, CORM, CORN, CORNER, CORNET, CORNFLAKES, CORNICE [korn-is], CORNY, *CORPS [kor], CORPSE* [korps], CORPULENT, CORPUS*, CORPUSCLE*, CORRIDOR [ko-ri-dor], CORSET, CORTEGE, CORTEX, CORTISONE, DEFORM, DEFORMITY, DENOMINATOR, DEPORT, DEPORTEE, DEPORTMENT, DETECTOR, DIRECTOR, DISCOMFORT *f*, DISCORD, DISCORDANT, DISGORGE, DISORGANIZE, DISPORT, DISTRIBUTOR, DIVORCEE, DOCTOR, DORSAL, DUPLICATOR, EDITOR, ELECTOR, ELEVATOR, EMPEROR, ENORMITY, EQUATOR, EXCAVATOR, EXECUTOR, EXHORT*, EXORBITANT, EXORCIZE, EXORCISM, EXORCIST, EXPLORER*, EXTERMINATOR, EXTORT, EXTRACTOR, FABRICATOR, FACTOR, FASCINATOR, FAVOR*, FOR, FORBID ∆, FORBIDDING, FORBORE, FORCE, FORCE-FEED, FORCEFUL, FORCEPS, FORCIBLE, FORCIBLY, FORD, FORESHORTEN, FOREVER, FORGATHER*, FORGE, FORGER, FORGET ∆, FORGETFUL, FORGIVE ∆, FORGO*, FORK, FORK-LIFT TRUCK, FORLORN, FORLORNLY, FORM, IN GOOD FORM, FORMAL, FORMALITY, FORMALIZE, FORMALDEHYDE [Id], FORMAT, FORMATTER, FORMATIVE, FORMER, FORMIC ACID, FORMLESS, FORMULA, FORMULATE, FORNICATE, FORSAKE ∆, FORT, FORTH, FORTHWITH, FORTIFY, FORTISSIMO, FORTITUDE, FORTRESS, FORTUNATE, FORTUNE, FORTY*, GLORY, GORGE, GORMANDIZER, GORMLESS, GORSE, GORY, HICKORY, HISTORY, HONOR* (USA), *HORDE, HORMONE, HORN, HORNBILL, HORNET, HORNPIPE, HORNY, HORSE*, HORSE-RACE, HORSE-TRADING, HORSE-CHESTNUT, HORSEFLESH, HORSEMAN, HORSE-RADISH, HORSEWHIP, HORSY, HORTICULTURE, HOVERPORT [hov-er-port], IMMORTALITY, IMMORTAL, IMPORT, IMPORTANT, IMPORTUNATE, IMPORTUNE, INBORN, INDICATOR, INFORM, INFORMAL, INFORMALLY, INFORMALITY, INFORMANT, INFORMATIVE, INFORMER, INOPPORTUNE, INORDINATE, INORGANIC, INQUISITOR, INSPECTOR, INSTIGATOR, INSTRUCTOR, INSULATOR, IVORY, JANITOR, LEGHORN, LIQUOR* [lik-or], LORD OF THE MANOR, LORD CHANCELLOR, LORDLY, LORDSHIP, LORGNETTE* [lor-nyet], LUBRICATOR, MAJOR, MAJOR-DOMO, MEMORY, MENORAH, *MENTOR, METAMORPHOSE, METAMORPHOSIS*, METAPHOR, MINOR, MIRROR, MISFORTUNE, MISINFORM, MODERATOR, MONITOR, MORBID, MORDANT, MORGANATIC, MORGUE* *fossil e*,

MORNING, MORPH*, MORPHINE* [mor-feen], MORPHOLOGY, MORSEL, MORTAL, MORTALITY, MORTGAGE* [mor-gej], MORTGAGEE*, MORTGAGER*, MORTIFY [mort-i-fI], MORTISE [əs], MOTOR, MOTOR BIKE, NOR, NORM, NORMAL, NORMALIZE, NORTH [th], NORTHERLY [dh], NORTHERN [dh], NORTHERNER [dh], NORTH-WEST [th], OBJECTOR, OPERATOR, OPPORTUNE, OPPORTUNIST, OPPORTUNISM, OPPORTUNITY, OPPRESSOR, OR, ORATOR [o-ray-tor], ORB, ORBIT, ORBITAL, ORCHESTRA <ch>=[k], ORCHESTRATE [k], ORCHID <ch>=[k], ORDER, IN ORDER TO, ORDER-BOOK, ORDER-FORM, ORDINAL, ORDINAND, ORGAN, ORGANIC, ORGANISM, ORGANIST, ORGANIZE, ORGANZA, ORGASM, ORGY, ORNAMENT, ORNAMENTAL, ORPHANAGE, ORTHODONTICS, ORTHODONTIC, ORTHODONTIST, ORTHODOX, ORTHODOXY, ORTHOGRAPHIC, ORTHOGRAPHICAL, ORTHOGRAPHY*, ORTHOPTICS, ORTOLAN, OVERLORD, PEPPERCORN, PERCOLATOR, PERFORCE, PERFORM, PILLORY, POPCORN, PORCH, PORCUPINE, PORK, PORKER *slang* (pig), PORN *abbrev.*, PORNOGRAPHY, PORPHYRY, PORT*, PORTAL, PORTCULLIS, PORTEND, PORTENT, PORTER, PORTERAGE, PORTHOLE, PORTICO, PORTLY, POST-MORTEM, PRECENTOR, PRECEPTOR, PREDATOR, PREDICTOR, PROCTOR, PROFESSOR, PROGENITOR, PROJECTOR, PROTRACTOR, RACEHORSE, RAPPORT*, RAZOR, RAZOR-BACK, RAZOR-GANG, RAZOR-GRINDER *bird*, RECEPTOR, RECORD *noun/verb*, RECORDER, RECTOR, REFLECTOR, REFORM, REFORMER, REFRIGERATOR*, REMORSE, REMORSELESS, RENOVATOR, REPORT, REPORTAGE, REPORTEDLY, REPORTER, RESISTOR, RESORT, RETORT, RIGOR MORTIS, ROTOR, SANDSTORM, SAVORY *herb*, SAVORY*, SCISSORS*, SCORCH, SCORCHER, SCORCHING, SCULPTOR, SECTOR, SELECTOR, SENATOR, SENOR/SIGNOR [seen-yor], SHORN, SHORT, SHORTAGE, SHORTCAKE, SHORTEN, SHORTENING, SHORTHAND, SHORTHORN, SHORTISH, SHORTLY, SHORTY *slang*, SIMULATOR, SMORGASBORD, SNORKEL, SNORT, SNORTER, SOLICITOR, SORBET, SORBIC, SORCERER, SORCERY, SORDID, SORT, SPECTATOR, SPECULATOR, SPONSOR, SPORT, SPORTING, SPORTIVE, SPORTSMAN, SPORTSMANLIKE, SPORTSWOMEN, SPORTY, STILLBORN, STORK, STORM, STORMY, STORY, STUPOR, SUB-EDITOR, SUBNORMAL, SUBORDINATE, SUBORN, SUCCESSOR, SUPERVISOR, SUPPORT, SUPPRESSOR, SWORD* [sord], SWORDFISH*, TELEPORT, TELERECORDING, TENOR*, TERROR, TERRORIZE, TESTATOR, THENCEFORTH, THUNDERSTORM, TOR, TORAH, TORCH, TORMENT, TORN, TORNADO, TORPEDO, TORPID, TORPIDLY, TORPIDITY, TORPOR, TORQUE, TORSO, TORT, TORTE *silent e*, TORTURE, TOTALIZATOR, *TUTOR [choot-or], TRACTOR, TRANSFORM, TRANSFORMER, TRANSISTOR, TRANSPORT, TRANSPORTER, TEMBLOR*, TREMOR*, UNDERSTORY, UNFORTUNATE, UNHORSE, UNIFORM, *UNSAVORY, UNWORN, VAPORIZE, VECTOR, VENDOR, VENTILATOR, VERMIFORM, VIBRATOR, VICTOR, VICTORY, VISITOR, VORTEX, WARRANTOR*. <u>Proper Nouns</u> BORSTAL, CHANCELLOR OF THE EXCHEQUER, LORD CHANCELLOR, CORNISH, CORNWALL*, CORPUS CHRISTI, DORSET, ECUADOR <u>=[w], FORMICA, GLAMORGAN, LABRADOR, LORD'S SUPPER, MORMON, MORSE CODE, NORDIC, NORMAN, NORSE, NORTHAM [nordhəm] in WA, OLD GLORY, PORTLAND, PORTUGAL, PORTUGUESE, TECHNICOLOR <ch>=[k], TORY, TUDOR*. <u>Names</u> GEORGE, GEORGINA, GORDON, GREGORY, HECTOR, IGOR, JORDAN, LORNA, PANDORA, RORY, VICTOR.

<u>The irregular verbs are as follows:</u>
FORBID Δ, FORBADE Δ [for-bad], FORBIDDEN Δ
FORGET Δ, FORGOT Δ, FORGOTTEN Δ
FORGIVE Δ, FORGAVE Δ, FORGIVEN Δ
FORSAKE Δ, FORSOOK Δ, FORSAKEN Δ

*Bachelor [bach-el-or] breaks the rule that <tch> should follow short vowels. It has been adopted from the Old French word *bacheler* but not adapted to English spelling rules.

*Borne is part of the irregular verb *to bear*, which means *to carry* or *support*.

*Color is an American adaption of *colour* which is why <r> is not doubled before its suffixes: *colored, coloring*. Verbs ending <or>, but not <our>, should twin <r> before a suffix. Anglo dictionaries give *colour, coloured, colouring*.

*The Spanish word c*onsignor, senor/signor* and the French word *lorgnette provide an opportunity to practise the foreign [gn] blend.

The Latin word *corpus,* meaning 'body', entered English on three different occasions.

*Corpse [korps] entered via Old French with a silent <p> which the English began pronouncing when it came to mean "dead body".

*Corps entered English during the 100 Year War against France. It came with silent <p> and silent <s> and it meant a small body of troops. *Corps* spells [kor] and the plural is also *corps,* but then it spells [korz].

*Corpus [kor-puus] came straight from Latin, meaning a collection of facts or things.

*Corpuscle spells [kor-pus-uul] because as we know in <scle> the letter <c> is silenced. This was explained when *muscle* and *crepuscle* were listed.

*Exhort spells [eg-zort] for, as we know, after suffix <ex>, the letter <h> is silent, which is the Special Rule we met when we met *exhibit* in Part Two. Also <x> spells [gz] before stressed syllables.

*Explorer spells [ex-plor-er], not [ex-plo-rer] because as we know, when the deriving suffix <er> is added it does not change the pronunciation of the stem word. (As we know, when deriving suffix <er> is added to *ring* [riŋ] it spells [riŋ-er], unlike adding a flexible suffix to *long* [loŋ], which then spells [lon-ger].)

**Forgather,* also written *foregather,* is no better than *gather,* (Bryson 2004, p. 81), means no more than just 'gather'.

*Forgo is a verb, 'to go without', only used in the present and future, never in the past. There's no such word as *forwent*.

*Forty is an interesting word. It's not like *harbor* from which the Amerians removed <u>. *Forty* is an English word. 'In the 17th century, the Old Bailey (a London court) ruled that *-our* endings were the correct way to spell words with suffixes of Greek and/or Latin origins. Forty, however, has neither Latin nor Greek origins and thus doesn't use the "u," as quoted from https://www.iwriter.com/ website.

*Honor is an alternative spelling for *honour*. When lengthened to *honorific* etc. <u> is dropped by everyone. In all forms it spells [on-er], and rebels against the rule that <h> spells [h] before stressed vowels.

**Horde's* silent <e> separates it from the Old English word for treasure: *hord* (from 'hidden store'). We *hoard* treasure nowadays. 1500 years ago, Mongol hordes were feared. Their camps were called *ordu* in Turkish and a horde of Mongols was a Tatar *orda*. In Polish this became *horda,* in English the end dropped off and was replaced by a silent <e>, (Etymonline and Fleck 2007).

*Horse and all the other words ending *–orse* use the <e> to ensure we say [ors] and not [orz].

*Leghorn (rhymes with *forlorn*) spells [leg-orn] because it is a breed of fowl from Legorno in Italy, now the city of Livorno. Was silent <h> added to describe its horny legs?

*Mentor is an eponym. Mentor was a close friend of Odysseus. While the Greek hero was away fighting the Trojan War, Mentor took on the responsibility of looking after the hero's son.

**Morph,* although a very new word, retains the old Greek <ph> spells [f] in order to show a link to *metamorphosis*.

Silent <t> in *mortgage reflects its French meaning "dead pledge". *Mort* means "dead" and *gage* means "pledge". The English adopted this compound word from their French conquerors but did not adapt its spelling. The French only sound the <t> before a vowel, which explains why we say *mortal* but keep it silent in *mortgage.* By the way, the mortgagor does not die if the loan is not repaid. It is the property, pledged as security, which "dies", is lost or becomes "dead" to the mortgagor, if the loan is not repaid.

*Morphine is an eponym — Morpheus, the god of dreams. Originally German *Morphin* and then French *morphine,* so <ine> spells [een]. (Morphine induces sleep.)

*Port is one of the 4 or 5 Latin words adopted directly from the Romans when they ruled Britain. Most Latin words were adopted later. They called a boat harbour *portus.* Today we say *the port* or *a port* instead of *portus.*

*Rapport spells [ru-por] with a silent <t> and even stress because it is French. Originally only used in English as part of the French phrase *en rapport.* Then it was Anglicized but later pronounced [ru-por] again, as a bit of a shibboleth, a class-marker, proof of good British breeding.

*Refrigerator has no <d> because <i> spells [i] in the fourth stressed syllable from the end without need of help from <d>. However, when abbreviated to one syllable, *fridge,* it needs that <d>.

*Savory and *unsavory* use American spelling in this list, instead of Anglo *savoury.* See **Colour* to learn why there is no <rr> in *savoring* when using American spelling.

A Rascal SCISSORS In **scissors* <ss> spells [z], (which also happens in *dissolve, dessert, hussar, hussy* and the first <ss> of *possess*). They all rebel against the rule that <ss> spells [s]. The <c> in *scissors* was added by the dictionary makers to show where they thought it came from, the Latin word *scindere* which means "to cut" but it actually came from Latin *cisora,* in Old French *cisoires,* in Old English *sisoures.* In the Old English word, the first syllable is diminished, followed by a strong syllable, as in *hussar*. In modern English, the second syllable of *scissors* is weak, but it is still given a zestful [z] start — [si-zəz]. The final <s> also spells [z], presumably because it is not followed by a silent <e> as in *horse,* even though <or> does not spell strong [or], but, instead, weak [ə]. Due to <sc> spelling [s] in *scissors,* <c> was added to the old word 'sythe' so that it became {*scythe*}. In summary, the reason the dictionary committee chose to spell *scissors* like they did is so obscure that it belongs with the rascals.

The [w] was dropped from **sword* but not from *swerve.* This is because [or] is made further back in our mouth than [er]. Try it and see. As we know, another front consonant, [t], is dropped before some back vowels, as in *listen,* [lis-ən]. (Writing the <w> links *sword* to *swipe.*) The only other time <w> is silent after <s> is in *answer,* which is because it's between a consonant and an unstressed vowel. For that same reason **liquor* spells [lik-or] instead of [lik-wor]. Its letters show its link to *liquid* [lik-wid] and anyway the <u> cannot be removed from the <q> even though it does not spell [w] in *liquor.* **Temblor* is only used in USA around volcanoes, for *tremble* lost its [r] in Spanish *temblar* before adoption in USA. *Tremble* gained [b] in the French version of the Latin word, but *tremor* did not.

*Tenor is yet another Rebel Lemon, for it spells [ten-or], not [teen-or]. We can often blame Rebel Lemons on the dictionary makers' knowledge of Latin, for they would have pronounced Latin *tenorum* with the English 'third syllable from the end' rule, even when it was shortened to *tenor.*

*Tutor, Tudor obeys Rule 1-41 in which if <u> spells [yoo] after <t>, then <tu> spells [choo].

**Did you let W muddle you in *warrantor*? It spells [wo-rant-or]. *Warrant* spells [wo-rant], since 'twinned R's only bossy if it's between a word's end and suffix.'

In some words, R is twinned to ensure a prefix makes a smooth join, as in *corrupt,* which sounds smoother than *comrupt.* 'Twinned R's only bossy if it's between a word's end and suffix' and so <rr> is not bossy when making a prefix join on smoothly.

List 3-61 in which <rr> is not bossy, see above.
WORRY* *f*, ABHORRENCE, ABHORRENT, CORRAL* [kə-rarl], CORRECT, CORRELATE, CORRESPOND, CORRIDOR, CORROBORATE , CORRUGATE, CORRUPT, ERROR, HORRID*, HORROR, LORRY, ORRIS, PORRIDGE, SORRY, SPORRAN, TORRENT, TORRID.
*Corral is from Spain, hence pronunciation.

Worry see 3-63.

Horrid changed years ago from spelling [or] to spelling [o]. *Horrid* follows Hewitt's law of ease and also law of economy because in making *horrid* easier to say — quicker in this case — meaning is not lost, so it's a gain without a loss. See Changes to English Over Time in appendix.

As we discussed earlier, some words have <rr> because prefixes have been changed to join on smoothly, e.g., *corrupt* [ko-rupt] was *com-rupt,* 'intensely rupture', but became *corrupt* for ease of pronunciation. So <orr> in *corrupt* never spelt [or].

In Rule 3-60 we are reminded that R is not bossy between vowels. Meet the rebels.

Rebels BORAX, BORON, BORIC, MORON and CHLORINE in which <or> spells [or] before a vowel.

Rebels' Reasons The mineral *borax* used <au> to spell [or] for a long time, but then changed spelling to make its main element, *boron,* look like the word *carbon,* (a similar chemical). *Boric acid* has the same pronunciation as *boron* and *borax,* <or> spells [or]. Normally they would spell [bo-rax] and [bo-ron] and [bo-rik]. *Moron* [mor-ron] was coined in 1910 from a Greek word as the technical definition of an 'adult with a mental age between 8 and 12'. When people began using *moron* as an insult it was dropped from technical use. *Chlorine* was coined in 1810 by Sir Humphry Davy, from Greek *khloros* for "pale green".

More **Rebels** AGORA, DECORUM, MARJORAM, QUORUM.

Rebels' Reasons *Agora* is said to have come from Greek, more often used in *agoraphobia* and *quorum* [kor-um] has kept its Latin pronunciation for <qu>, [k]. Both words might rebel just due to stress patterns. *Majoram* was Latinized from the French name for the common herb, *marjolaine* by combining it with the word *major*. Again, with a weak ending, the second to last syllable ends up stressed, becoming the long vowel [or] not short [o].

Rebels? ANGORA, FEDORA, FLORA and IXORA all began as proper nouns and so do not have to obey spelling rules. *Angora* wool gets its name from Ankara in Turkey. *Fedora* is the center-creased, soft brimmed hat worn by Sarah Bernhardt acting as the Princess Fedora Romanoff. The others come from the Roman goddess Flora of Flowers and the Indian goddess Ishwara. The adjective *floral* is not a rebel, as it spells [flo-ral] not [flor-al].

List 3-62A in which <o> spells [o], when followed by <r> and a vowel.
ABORIGINE*, ABORIGINAL, ALGORISM, ALGORITHM*, ALLEGORICAL, AMORAL, ANORAK, APHORISM, CALORIC, CATAPHORIC, CATEGORICAL, CHLORIC, COMMEMORATE, CORPORAL , CORPORATE, DECORATE, DECORATIVE, DECORATOR, DIRECTORATE, DOCTORATE, EXPECTORANT, EXPECTORATE, EXTEMPORIZE, FLORAL, FOLKLORIC, FORAGE, GLAMORIZE, INCORPORATE, HISTORIC, HISTORICAL, HONORIFIC*, HUMORIST*, INVIGORATE, JAMBOREE, LIQUORICE*, MAJORITY, MEMORANDUM, MEMORIZE, METAPHORIC, METAPHORICAL, MINORITY, MORASS, MOTORIST, ORACLE, ORAL, ORALLY, ORANGE, ORANGES, ORANG-UTAN, ORATE, ORATOR, ORATORICAL, ORATRESS, ORATRIX, ORIFICE, ORIGAMI, ORIGANE [o-rig-ar-nee], ORIGIN, ORIGINAL, ORIGINALITY, ORIGINALLY, ORIGINALS, ORIGINATE, ORIGINATED, ORIGINATOR, OROGENIC*, OROGRAPHY*, OROLOGY*, OROMETER*, OROTUND, PERFORATE, PHOSPHORIC, PLETHORIC, PYLORIC [pI-lo-rik], RESTORATIVE, RHETORIC, RHETORICAL, SONORITY, SOPORIFIC, SORORITY, TEMPORIZE, TERRORISM, THORACIC.

Aborigine, aboriginal, aboriginality match *origin* which spells [o-rij-in], not [or – i-jin]. So *aborigine* spells [ab-o-rij-in-ee] and it means *from the beginning,* because *ab* in Latin mean 'from' and *origine* comes from 'origo', Latin for 'the beginning', the original people. The aborigines of any land are its original inhabitants.

*Algorithm [al-gə-ridh-em] links back to the brilliant *al-Khwarizmi* , who introduced Arabic maths to the Western World, including algebra, which is also named after him. See the rebels under Rule 2-85 for why <th> spells [dh] in this word.

*In *honorific* the first <h> is silent and so it is a rebel to the rule that <h> spells [h] before a stressed syllable.

*Humorist, like *humour*, often has a Silent H in USA.

*Liquorice, or *licorise* in USA, spells [lik-o-rish]. However this is written, in Australia it spells [lik-rish].

**Orogenic, orography, orology* and *orometer* all pertain to 'mountain', which is *oros* in Greek — the making of, the mapping of, the study of and measuring the height of mountains.

When <or> spells unstressed [or] which is followed by an unstressed vowel which is not terminal, [or] shrinks to avoid two weak beats, e.g., *corporal* becomes [kor-pruul]. Further examples are listed below.

List 3-62B in which <or> shrinks, instead of spelling [or] or even [o].
ALLEGORY [al-e-gree], ANCHORAGE [an-krəj], FAVORITE* (USA) [fayv-rit], CORPORAL [kor-pruul], CORROBORATE [kə-rob-ə-rayt], LAVATORY [lav-at-ree], LICORICE/LIQUORICE [lik-rish], MEMORABILITY [mem-ra-bil-it-ee], MEMORABLY [mem-rə-blee], PASTORALIST [parst-ral-ist], PECTORAL [pekt-rəl], TEMPORAL [temp-ə-rəl], Proper nouns, COMOROS [kom-ros], SOROPTIMIST [sə-rop-tə-mist].

*As we know, in most adjectives the suffix <ite> is not stressed and so the [I] shrinks to [i] in *favorite/favourite*.

Don't Let W Muddle You in <wor>!

We warned Bossy R: 'Bossy R, watch out do, for W will muddle you.'

We have seen W muddle the sound of <a> in *won* and *wonder*. Now we shall see what W does to vowels controlled by Bossy R. We have learnt that <er> spells [er], and that <ir> and <ur> spell [er] too. Did you look at the <or> word lists and say "Where is *word*?" Now you will see why <wor> words have their own list.

Rule 3-63 <wor> spells [wer].
Reason Letter (w) muddles <or> into spelling [er] only before a consonant, for terminal <e>, Fairy E, ensures <or> spells [or] in *swore* and *wore* and *whore*. This is because W cannot muddle the magic action of Fairy E. Get out your quills, your feather pens! We know why <o> spells [u] in *won* and *wonder*. The scribes used <o> to stop <un> looking like <m> in these old words but that also did another job, stopped <u> being muddled with <w>. It would have joined on to <w> and looked like Triple U! So, we would expect all old words which once had <wu> in them to have been rewritten <wo>, and also all old words with <wi> to be written <wo>, which, after all, we have already seen in *woman* and *women*. (As we know, <i> did not have a dot in olden times.)

In Latin 'homo' means *human being* and this word travelled through many lands into England where it became two words, *human* and *man*. However, there was another word in Latin which means a male human being, and that was [wer]. This was written *vir*, for in Latin <v> spells [w]. We know <ir> spells [er]. If we ask Etymonline where the word *word* comes from, we see an old German word *wurdun*. We know that <ur> spells [er]. We'd expect *wurdun* to reach England but then lose its ending under Norman domination, when French became the main language of England and English was only used in the lower end of society. We'd expect the old scribes to write <o> for <u> when they recorded the word *word*, in order to prevent <u> and <w> looking like Triple U.

We look at other <wor> words, like *wort*. This was written *wyrt* long ago and we know that <y> was removed from all but Greek words and replaced with <i>. We know that <i> was dotless, back when scribes used feather pens, and that it was replaced when it followed <w> by <o> to improve legibility. What about *whirr,* you ask? Well as we can see, <h> insulates <i> from getting muddled with <w>.

Rebels WORE, SWORE, WORN, and WORRY *f*, WORRISOME *ff*

Rebels' Reasons *Worn* does not spell [wern]. It spells [worn]. It is an adjective made from the past form of the verb *to wear,* as in "He **wore** it a lot and it so it was **worn** a lot and it got very **worn**." *Wore* and *swore* obey the rule that terminal <ore> always spells [or]. *Worry* [wu-ree] would spell [wo-ree] like *sorry* if we did not know that <wor> spells [wer]. In some parts of England people say [wer-ree] for *worry*. The Online Etymology Dictionary tells us that *worry* began as *wyrgan* long before the Normans invaded England. At that time a *wyrt,* a herbal root, was a [wert]. When <i> replaced <y> inside words, *wyrgan* became *wirgan* and *wyrt* became *wirt*. Then *wirgan* shortened to *wirry*. Little <i> was hard to read after <w>, especially as it had no dot, and so the scribes replaced <i> with <o>, as they did in *wimen,* writing *women,* with their feather pens. So *wirry* [wer-ee] became *worry* and *wirt* became *wort* and retained its pronunciation, [wert]. In some parts of England people still pronounce *worry* as [wer-ree] but elsewhere people pronounce it as though <o> replaced <u>, as it did in *son, some, love* etc., Why then do we say it spells [wu-ree]? Possibly, because we expect all Feather Words have used <o> to replace <u> as in *son, some, love* etc., <o> is assumed to have replaced <u>, not <i>. When *worry* was *wyrgan* it meant 'to wrangle, wrestle, strangle, annoy or vex', e.g., dogs harassing sheep, or trying to get meat off a bone, which explains the old phrase "worry a bone". Likewise, when we worry, we wrangle and wrestle with thoughts which annoy and vex our brain. I have marked *worry* with *f* as a feather word, and *worrisome* with *ff*, since both <o>'s in *worrisome* spell [u].

By the way, only two words contain <quor> and, in both, <or> spells [or] after <qu>. They are not 'muddled by W' because in *quorum* [kor-uum] and *liquor* [lik-ə] <qu> spells [k], not [kw].

List 3-63 Don't Let W Muddle You! <wor> spells [wer].
BYWORD, BODYWORK, BOOKWORM, BYWORD, CROSSWORD, FOREWORD, FRAMEWORK, IRONWORK, LUGWORM, MINEWORKER, OVERWORK, PAPERWORK, RAGWORT, REWORD, SILKWORM, STITCHWORT, STONEWORK, TAPEWORM, UNDERWORLD, WATERWORKS, WHORL*, WHORT*, WHORTLEBERRY, WICKERWORK, WORD, WORDILY, WORDINESS, WORDING, WORDLESS, WORDY, WORK, WORK, WORKAHOLIC, WORKER, WORKING, WORKMAN, WORKMANLIKE, WORKMANSHIP, WORKSHEET, WORKSHOP, WORLD*, WORLDLING, WORLDLY, WORM, WORM, WORMWOOD, WORMY, WORSE, WORSEN, WORSHIP, WORSHIPFUL, WORSHIPPER, WORST, WORSTED, WORT*, WORTH, WORTHLESS, WORTHY*.

**Whorl* and *whort* other words with <wh> either gained <h> late or started off as <hw> words and reversed the letters after <wor> spelt [wer]. *Whort* is a plant with whort berries, and *whorl* describes a whirl of flower petals, and was originally *whirl* [wer] which came from *hwyr*. As <y> is not allowed inside stem words it was replaced by <i>, but that produced *hwir* and so <i> was replaced with <o>, to prevent a muddle of <wi> looking like Triple U. Nowadays *whirl* is used as a verb, 'to spin', and also used as a noun, e.g., 'in a whirl', *whirlpool* and *whorl* is just used botanically.

**World* does not mean 'wir-land', i.e., 'man-land', it means the 'age of man', a contraction of *wir ald*. *Ald* meant *old,* and *old* meant *age,* a wonderful time of maturity, as in 'our time has come!' We no longer call men [wer] but we still call them *virile*. Feminine humans, females, are called fertile, not virile. Although *werewolf,* man-wolf, a man who can turn into a wolf, is pronounced [weer-wuulf], *were* is generally assumed to be the same as the long-obsolete Old English noun *wer* 'man', which is a relative of Latin *vir,* 'man', from which English gets *virile,* (Ayto p. 571).

**Word* was Saxon *wurdan* and Latin *verbum*. It ontracted to *wurd* and it was hard to read in cursive. It became a Feather Word, a Cursive Casualty, when <o> replaced <i> for legibility.

Wort [wert] was *wyrt* before <i> replaced <y> inside words. Then dotless <i> was replaced by <o> after <w>. It can now spell [wort] in America, probably due to the U.S. comic strip character "Worry Wart", in which *wart* spells [wort]. Australians say "Cheer up, you old worry wort," in which *wort* spells [wert].
Worthy. As we have heard, occasionally terminal [th] changes to [dh] if a vowel is added, as in *worth* and *worthy* or *north* and *northern*.

Digraph <ar> — *afar, yarn.*
Terrminal <ar> as a suffix is rare. It is only used on two verbs to make nouns — *beg* becomes *beggar; lie* becomes *liar*. The noun *burglar* actually turned into a verb, *burgle,* not the other way around. In *burglar* and other nouns, <ar> is not a suffix. The suffix — *ar* is added to some nouns to make adjectives, like *pole* and *polar*. Both —*ar* and —*ular* are used to mean 'like; resembling, relating or belonging to that noun'.
Terminal <ar> always spells [ar] because <r> is not between vowels at the end of a word: 'R is bossy after vowels, but not between them.'
This same rule, 'R is bossy after vowels, but not between them,' means that <ar> does not spell [ar] in the following words. We have probably met all these words but we shall list them to practise reading words in which <ar> does not spell [ar].
Rebel? LOGARITHM it's only a rebel to this rule if pronounced [log-ar-ridhm] instead of [log-u-ridhm]. It is however a rebel to the rule which says <th> cannot spell [dh] unless followed by a vowel. The excuse for this transgression was given at 2-85.
List 3-64 A in which <ar> does not spell [ar].
AVARICE, CAREEN, CAREER, CAREERIST, CAROTID, CATAMARAN, CELLARET, DUNGAREES, EXHILARATE, HAREM, MAHARAJA, MAHARISHI, MARINA, MARINE, MINARET, NECTARINE, PARANG, PAROLE, POPULARIZE, PARENTHESIS, REGULARIZE, SARONG, SEPARATOR, SUBMARINE, SUMMARIZE, VICARAGE, VULGARISM, VULGARIZE.

As we know, see list 3-37, in *care* and *scare* and *vary*, <ar> does not spell [ar]. We know that [ar] lifted in the Great Vowel Shift to [air], in all except the word *are* and terminal <ar> and when <ar> was followed by a consonant. We know that two more <ar> words break the rule that R is not bossy between vowels — *curare* and *sari*.
Terminal <ary> spells [air-ree] as in *chary, gary, vary, wary* and *Mary*.

Terminal <ary> — *binary, wary.*
Rule 3-65 Terminal <ary> spells [air-ree], but this can reduce to [ree] [e-ree].
Reason Because ends of long words are usually unstressed and two weak beats do not fit the ' tum-te-tum' rhythm of English, terminal [air-ree] often shrinks, to just [ree] in words of four syllables, and to [e-ree] in words of three syllables. This restores the 'tum-te-tum' pattern. This never happens in *canary*, an adopted word for the little birds on the Canary Islands. One island was called Insula Canaria due to its large dogs (canines) which gave the island group and its birds the name Canary.
Rebel CASSOWARY.
Rebels Reason In *cassowary* <ary> spells [ar-ree] — [kas-o-war-ree] — based on the Malay word *kasuari*.
List 3-65 Terminal <ary> spells [air-ree] and to avoid two weak beats together, [air-ree] can shrink, to [ree] or [e-ree].
HONORARY*, ADVERSARY, ANNIVERSARY, APOTHECARY, ARBITRARY, BICENTENARY, BINARY, CANARY, CAPILLARY, CASSOWARY, CHARY, CENTENARY, COMMENTARY, COMMISSARY, COMPLEMENTARY, COMPLIMENTARY, CONTEMPORARY, CONTRARY,

CULINARY, CUSTOMARY, DISPENSARY, DOCUMENTARY, ELEMENTARY, EMISSARY, ESTUARY, EXEMPLARY, GARY, GLOSSARY, GRANARY, IMAGINARY, INTERPLANETARY, ITINERARY, LAPIDARY, LIBRARY, LITERARY, MERCENARY, MILITARY, MOMENTARY, MONETARY, NECTARY, OVARY, PARAMILITARY, *PECCARY, PESSARY, PLENARY, PRIMARY, PULMONARY, QUANDARY, RELICQUARY, ROSEMARY, ROTARY, SALIVARY, SALUTARY, SANITARY, SECRETARY, SEDENTARY, SEDIMENTARY, SOLITARY, SUGARY [sh], SUMMARY, TEMPORARY, TESTAMENTARY, TRIBUTARY, UNDER-SECRETARY, UNITARY, URINARY VARY, VETERINARY, VOLUNTARY, WARY. <u>Proper Noun /Names</u> FEBRUARY, HILARY, HUNGARY, JANUARY, MARY.

*<i>Honorary</i> breaks the rule that <h> spells [h] before stressed vowels, because it stem, <i>honour</i>, also breaks that rule.

*<i>Peccary</i>, tropical America's wild pig, has the unusual <cc> twin.

    Vowel shrinkage occurs according to stress patterns in many words, due to the preferred English stress pattern of alternate weak and strong syllables. For instance, the adjective SEPARATE would end on two weak beats if it wasn't pronounced as [sep-rət]. Verbs end on strongly stressed syllables, so this vowel shrinkage does not occur in the verb SEPARATE, pronounced [sep-air-ayt], but it does occur in the noun SEPARATIST [sep-rat-ist].

In the next list, when it's the first of two weak beats, <ar> spells [ə] before a consonant, e.g., <i>beggarly</i> spells [beg-ə-lee]

List 3-66.
BEGGARLY, IRREGULARLY, JOCULARLY, PARTICULARLY, PERPENDICULARLY, REGULARLY, SCHOLARLY, SIMILARLY, SINGULARLY, UNSCHOLARLY, VULGARLY.

As we know, R is bossy after vowels, but not between them.

Rule 3-67 Digraph <ar> spells [ar] unless followed by a vowel.

Reason As explained when discussing the Bossy R Rule, Rule 3-40.

Rebels ARIA, MASCARA, TIARA; ARE.

Rebels' Reasons <i>Aria, mascara</i> and <i>tiara</i> are Contintental adoptions which use the old <a> spells long vowel [ar], because vowels in Continental words did not change. They did not lift like English vowels in England's Great Vowel Shift. <i>Are</i> also retained its pre-GVS pronunciation, previously having shortened from <i>aren</i>. As we know, <i>are</i> has no need of silent <e> for it is one of the three verbs which can break the Short Word Rule.

Rascals SCARCE, SCARCELY and SCARCITY. <i>Scarce</i> spells [skairs] and no one knows why we do not say [skars]. Maybe we relate <i>scarcity</i> of food or friends to being <i>scared</i>. As we know, <i>scare</i> spells [skair]. Rebels without a reason are 'rascals'. We must be wary of these scary rascals, <i>scarce, scarcely</i> and <i>scarcity</i> — [skairs], [skairs-lee] and [skair-sit-ee].

    The next list includes <i>bar, char, jar, mar, scar, spar, star</i> and <i>tar</i> and words made from these stems by adding suffixes. Note, <r> is twinned at the end of the stem before adding the suffix to retain [ar] in the word, because R not bossy between vowels.

List 3-67A <ar> spells [ar]
AADVARK, AFAR, AJAR, ALARM, ALARMIST, ALTAR, ANGULAR, ANNULAR, APART, APARTMENT, ARBITER, ARBITRATE, ARBITRATOR, ARBORETUM, ARBUSCLE*, ARBUTUS, ARC*, ARCADE, ARCANE, ARCH, ARCH, ARCHANGEL <ch>=[k], ARCHBISHOP, ARCH-ENEMY, ARCHER, ARCHERY, ARDENT, ARGUE, ARGUMENT*, ARGUMENTATIVE, ARGY-BARGY*, ARK, ARM <i>verb/noun,</i> ARMADA, ARMADILLO, ARMAMENT, ARMATURE, ARM-BAND, ARMFUL <u>=[uu], ARMHOLE, ARMISTICE [arm-is-tis], ARMLESS, ARMLET, ARMPIT, ARMS, ARMS RACE, UP IN ARMS, ARMY, ARSE <i>slang,</i> ARSENAL, ARSENIC, ARSON, ART, ART GALLERY, ART <i>old verb,</i> ARTEFACT/ARTIFACT, ARTERY, ARTFUL <u>=[uu],

ARTFULLY, ARTFULNESS, ARTHRITIC [i-tik], ARTHRITIS [I-tis], ARTICHOKE, ARTICLE, ARTICULAR, ARTICULATE, ARTICULATED, ARTIFICE [art-i-fis], ARTISAN, ARTIST, ARTISTIC, ARTISTRY, ARTLESS, ARTY, BAR *noun*, BAR *verb*, BARRED, BARRING, DEBARRED, UNBARRED, BARB, BARBARIC, BARBARITY, BARBECUE, BARBER, BARBITURATE, *BARCOO, BARD, BARDY/BARDI*, BARGE, BARGEE, BARK, BARK, BARKER, BARMAN, BARMY, BARN, BARNACLE, BARNYARD, BARTER, BASTARD* *VS*, BAZAAR, BEGGAR, BEGGARLY, BICARBONATE, BINOCULARS, BIPARTISAN, BIPARTITE, BLACK MARK, BLACK MARKET, BLIZZARD, BODYGUARD, BOLLARD, BOMBARD, BRAGGART, BUDGERIGAR*, BUSBAR, BUZZARD, BY AND LARGE*, CALENDAR, CANARD, CAR, CAR-PARK, CARBIDE, CARBINE, CARBOLIC, CARBON, CARBON DATING, CARBONADE, CARBONATE, CARBONATED, CARBONIZE, CARBORUNDUM, CARBUNCLE, CARBURETTOR, CARCASS, CARCINOGEN, CARCINOMA, CARD, CARD-SHARP, CARDIGAN*, CARDINAL, CARDIOLOGY, CARGO, CARMINATIVE, CARMINE, CARNAL, CARNIVAL, CARNIVORE, CARP, CARPAL, CARPEL, CARPENTER, CARPET, CARPETING, CARPORT, CARSICK, CART, CARTAGE, CARTEL, CARTER, CARTILAGE, CARTOGRAPHY, CARTON, CARTOON, CARTRIDGE, CARTWHEEL, CARVER, CATARRH , CATERPILLAR, CEDAR, CELLAR, CELLULAR, CHADAR, CHAR, CHARRED, CHARRING, CHARLATAN <ch>=[sh], CHARLOCK, CHARD, CHARGE, CHARM, CHARMING, CHART, CHARTER, CIGAR*, COLLAR, COLLARLESS, COMMISSAR, COMPARTMENT, CO-STAR, COVER CHARGE, CUSTARD, DARK, DARKLY, DARKNESS, DARK-ROOM, DARKEN, DARKISH, DARLING, DARN, DARNEL WEED, DASTARDLY*, DART, DEBAR, DEPART, DEPARTMENT, DEPARTMENTAL, DEPARTURE, DISARM, DISARMAMENT, DISCARD, DISCHARGE, DISHARMONY, DOCKYARD, DOLLAR, DOTARD* [dot-əd], DRUNKARD [drun-kəd], DULLARD* [dul-əd], DUSTCART, ENLARGE, ENLARGER, ESPARTO, FAR, INSOFAR, only in USA, FARCE, FARM, FARMER, FARMYARD, FART, FARTHER [dh], FARTHEST [dh], FARTHING [dh], FARTHINGALE [dh], FROG-MARCH, FUNICULAR, GARB, GARBAGE, GARBLE, GARDEN, GARDENER, GARGLE, GARLAND, GARLIC, GARMENT, GARNER, GARNET, GARNISH, GARTER, GLOBULAR, GO-CART, GO-KART, GRANULAR, GUITAR*, HAGGARD, HALLMARK <all>=[orl], *HALYARD, HANDLEBAR, HANGAR, HAPHAZARD, HARD, HARDEN, HARDENER, HARDLY, HARDSHIP, HARDSTAND, HARDWARE, HARDWOOD, HARDY, HARK, HARLEQUIN, HARLOT, HARM, HARMFUL, HARMLESS, HARMLESSLY, HARMLESSNESS, HARMONIC, HARMONICA, HARMONIUM, HARMONIZE, HARMONY, HARNESS, HARP, HARPIST, HARPOON, HARPSICHORD <ch>=[k], HARPY, HARSH, HART, HARVEST, HARVESTER, *HAZARD, HUSSAR*, INARTICULATE, INARTISTIC, INNARDS, INSULAR, INTERLARD, INTERSTELLAR, IRREGULAR, IRREGULARLY, JAR *noun*, JAR *verb*, JARRED, JARRING, JARGON, JOCULAR, JUGULAR, KARMA, LAGGARD*, LANYARD, LARCH, LARD, LARDER, LARDY, LARDY-CAKE, LARGE, LARGELY, LARGENESS, LARGE-SCALE, LARGESSE fossil <e>, AT LARGE, LARGISH, LARK, RISE WITH THE LARK, LARN *slang for learn,* "that'll larn him", LARVA, LETHARGY, LETHARGIC, LETTER-CARD, LIFEGUARD, LODESTAR, LUMBAR, MALLARD DUCK, MANSARD, MAR, MARRED, MARRING, MARBLE, MARCASITE <ite>=[It], MARCH, MARCHER, MARGARINE*, MARGIN, MARGINAL, MARK, MARKSMAN, MARL, MARMALADE, MARMOSET, MARMOT, MARQUEE*, MARQUETRY, MARSH, MARSH-GAS, MARSHAL, MARSHALLING YARD, MARSHLAND, MARSUPIAL, MART, MARTEN, MARTIN, MARTINET, MARVEL, MARZIPAN, MASCARA, MEDLAR, MOLAR, MORTAR, MOTOR CAR, MUDGUARD, MUDLARK, MUSCULAR, MUSTARD, NARCISSUS, NARCOSIS, NARCOTIC, NARDOO*, NARK, NIGGARDLY, OP ART, OPEN ARMS, ORCHARD, OVERARM, PAR, ON A PAR, PARCEL,

PARCH, PARCHMENT, PARDON, PARDONABLY, PARK, PARKA, PARKIN, PARKY, PARLANCE, PARLEY, PARQUET [par-kay] or [par-ket], PARR*, PARSE, PARSEC, PARSLEY, PARSNIP, PARSON, PARSONAGE, PART, PART-TIME, PARTAKE Δ, PARTICIPATE, PARTICIPLE, PARTICLE, PARTICULAR, PARTICULARIZE, PARTING, PARTISAN, PARTLY, PARTNER, PARTRIDGE, PARTY, PARTY LINE, PEDLAR, PENDULAR, PETARD, PHARMACIST, PHARMACY, PILLAR, POLAR, POLARIZE, POLLARD, POPLAR, POPULAR, POSTMARK, PTARMIGAN [pt]=[t], PULSAR, QUASAR, RADAR, RAMPART, REBARBATIVE, RECTANGULAR, REGISTRAR, REGARD, REGARDS, REGARDLESS, REGARDING, REGULAR, REGULARLY, REPARTEE, RETARD, RETARDED, RHUBARB* *silent h,* SAFEGUARD, SAMOVAR, SARCASM, SARCASTIC, SARCOMA, SARCOPHAGUS, SARDINE, SARDONIC, SARGE *slang,* SARSEN, SARSENET, SCAR, SCARRED, SCARRING, SCARF, SCARFS, SCARVES, SCARLET, SCARP, SCHOLAR* <ch>=[k], SCHOLARSHIP, SCIMITAR [sim-i-tar], SECULAR, SEMINAR, SHARD, SHARK, SHARP, SHARPEN, SHARPER, SHARPISH, SHARPSHOOTER, SHIPYARD, SIMILAR, SINGULAR, SITAR, SKYLARK, SLUGGARD, SMARMY, SMART, SMART ARSE slang, SMARTEN, SNARL, SNARL-UP, SOLAR, SONAR, SPAR *verb,* SPARRED, SPARRING, SPAR, SPARK, SPARKLE, SPARKLER, SPARSE, SPARTAN, SPECTACULAR, STANDARD, STANDARDIZE, STAR *verb/noun,* STARRED, STARRING, STARRY* *adjective,* STARCH, STARCHY, STARDOM, STARFISH, STARK, STARLING, STARLIT, STARRY, START, STARTER, STARTLE, STARTLING, STARVE, STARVELING, STELLAR, STREETCAR, STRINGYBARK, SUBSTANDARD, SUGAR* <s>=[sh], SUGAR-BASIN, SUGAR-BEET, SUGAR-CANE, SUPERMARKET, TABARD, TABULAR, TAMMAR*, TAR *verb,* TARRED, TARRING, TAR *noun,* TARDY, TARGET, TARMAC, TARN, TARNISH, TARRY* *adjective,* TARSAL, TARSUS, TART, TARTAN, TARTAR, TARTARIC, TARTLET, TARWHINE fish, TITULAR <i>=[i], TSAR* [zar], TUBERCULAR, UNDERARM, UNDERCHARGE, UNPOPULAR, VANGUARD, VEHICULAR*, VERNACULAR, VICAR, VINEYARD <i>=[i], VULGAR, VULGARLY, WATERMARK, YARD, YARDAGE, YARDSTICK, YARN. Proper nouns ANTARCTIC, ANTARCTICA, AQUARIUS, ARCTIC, ARGENTINA, ARMAGEDDON, ARMENIA, ARMENIAN, BARBUDA, BARBADOS, CARDIFF, CARMELITE, CARNARVON, CHEDDAR, DENMARK, DJAKARTA, FARSI language, HANSARD, MARCH, LASCAR, MADAGASCAR, MAGNA CHARTER <ch>=[k], MARCH, MARSALA, MARS, MARTINI, MARTINMASS, MARXISM, PARMESAN, PARSEE, RASTARFARIAN, SAN MARINO, SPANIARD, SPARKY, STARS AND STRIPES, TARMAC, TARTAR, TEMPLAR, HOBART. Names ARCHIBALD, ARMSTRONG, ARNOLD, BARNABY, BERNARD, CARL, CARLEEN, CARLOS, CARLOTTA, CARMEL, CARMEN, CHARLES, CHARLOTTE [shar-lot], DARCY, DARWIN, FARNHAM, GARVIN, JARVIS, MARCELLE, MARCO, MARGARET, MARGARITA, MARGE, MARK, MARLEEN, MARSHALL, MARTHA, MARTIN, MARTY, MARVIN, NARCISSA, OSCAR, SCARLET, SHARLENE. Words in which <arch> spells [ark] ARCHIPELAGO, ARCHITECT, ARCHITECTURE, ARCHITRAVE, ARCHIVES, ARCHIVIST, MONARCH, MONARCHIST, MONARCHY.

Δ Irregular verb, present, past and past participle:
PARTAKE Δ, PARTOOK Δ, PARTAKEN Δ.

Arbuscle (a plant bigger than a bush but smaller than a tree) spells [ar-bus-uul] because as we know in <scle> the letter <c> is silenced. We discussed this when we met *muscle*.

Arc is the only word in which <k> is not added to <c> when adding <ing> and <ed>, *arcing, arced*.

Argument has lost <e> of *argue* because it is no longer needed to insulate <u> from ending a word.

Argy bargy [arj-ee] [bar-jee] – I hope you remembered <y> softens <g> to [j].

Bastard spells [barst-əd] but also [bast-əd] in parts of England.

*_Barcoo_ is the Ab'l name of a river in Queensland and has been adopted and used in many compound words, such as _barcoo-grass, barcoo-rot,_ (Blake, p. 86).

*A _bardy/bardi_ is the edible wood grub _Bardistus cibarius,_ first named _bardy_ by WA Aborigines. The alternative spelling rebels against the rule against terminal <i>, but is often used to show the name is newly adopted into English.

*_Cardigan_ is an eponym. Google 7th Earl of Cardigan.

*_Cigar_ is a Continental word which has retained its strong ending.

*_Budgerigar,_ an Ab'l word, recorded as 'betshiregah' and 'betcherrygah' and Blake, p. 89, suggests that the first vowel changed from [e] to [uu] to match the vowel in _good,_ both in English and in the old Ab'l word for _good,_ "boojery", which 'once enjoyed currency in colloquial speech', which just means white settlers used it too. Aborigines taught the settlers many words.

*_By and large_ meant sailing 'by the wind and with sails at large'. Sails in a fair wind were "at large", not trimmed to catch fluctuations. Sailing "by the wind" was against the airflow. Now it means 'generally', or 'for the most part', (Fleck 2007).

*_Dastardly, bastard, laggard, halyard_ and _dullard_ all have heavy initial stress and unstressed ends so that <ard> spells [əd].

*_Guitar_ [gee-tar] uses <u> to prevent <g> softening to [j].

*_Hussar_ joins the rebel word _scissors_. In both, <ss> spells [z], instead of [s]. The slang word _Aussie_ [o-zee] also uses <ss> to spell [z].

*_Margarin_e began as [mar-gar-een] but is now said [marj-ar-een]. It should sound like Margaret as it is named after its pearly appearance. Pearls in Greek are margarites. (Similar to naming glycerine by the way it glistens.) However, _marj_, as in Marjorie, sounds more familiar and matches _veg_ [vej].

*_Parr_ is a noun, a young salmon.

*_Vehicular_ spells [vee-hik-yoo-lar] since [hik] is stressed. (In _vehicle,_ <h> is a silent secret agent after stressed [vee].)

*_Marquee_ [mar-kee] is one of the rare times <qu> spells [k]. This usually happens in words recently adopted from French, after they stopped using <qu> for [kw]. Now, in French, <qu> spells [k].

*_Nardoo_ is adopted and adapted from the Ab'l word _ngardu,_ a clover fern with edible seeds, (Blake, p. 101).

*_Rhubarb_ at first sight appears to be Greek, with <rh> for <r>. It grew along River Volga, in ancient times named _Rha. Barbaric_ and _barbarian_ originally meant "foreign, unknown, hard to understand or people from elsewhere with a language which just sounded like _bar-bar,_ or just babble. So _rhabarbaron_ was a foreign food from the River Rha. It entered English as French _rubarbe._ Then during the Renaissance over-enthusiasm for Greek and Latin led to a few mistakes when words were re-spelt. _Rubarbe_ became _rhubarb._ Actors began repeating _rhubarb_ on stage around 1934 to give the impression of a hubbub of conversation, and so they unwittingly renewed the word's old connection with unintelligible babble.

*_Scholar_ [skolar], _scholarship_ follows our rule <sch> spells [sk] before a vowel.

*_Starry_ spells [star-ree]. If written _stary_ it would spell [stair-ree].

*_Sugar_ spells [shuu-gar]. See Special Rule 3-33. About 300 years ago _sugar_ was [syoo-gar], back before yods began dropping, back when <u> spelt [yoo]. What happens when we say "Miss you"? If we say "Miss you" over and over we hear ourselves saying [mish-yuu], for <sy> produces [sh]. That is why we say [sh] in _sugar,_ [shuu-gar].

*_Tammar_ is the Nyungar (SW of WA) name for a type of wallaby, another Ab'l word adopted into English.

*_Tarry_ spells both [tar-ree] and [ta-ree], depending on context. If it is an adjective formed from the noun _tar_ it will spell [tar-ree]. If it is the verb _to tarry_ it will spell [ta-ree]. This is because 'twinned R's only bossy if it's between a word's end and suffix.', as in the adjective _tarry._

*_Tsar, czar_ and _tzar_ all spell [zar]. All are adopted but not well adapted as yet.

Rascal BIZARRE *Bizarre* [bi-zar] breaks Rule 3-67, that 'twinned R's only bossy if it's between a word's end and suffix.' It's like Italian *bizarro* meaning 'angry, fierce, irascible,' and yet said like *bizar,* the Basque word for a beard. Basques are noted for their beards and being irascible. Not really a good enough excuse. Properly adapted to English spelling it should be *bizzar.* It's a rascal word.

List 3-67B Twinned R's only bossy when before a suffix, after a free stem, i.e., if it's between a word's end and suffix. That is why <arr> does not spell [ar] in the following examples.
ARRANT, ARREST, ARRIVE, ARROGANCE, BARRAGE, NARRATIVE, BARRACKS, GARRET, TARRY *verb.*
Arrant began as a variation of *errant* and then came to mean "very errant", (Etymoline). Many words use <rr> after a first vowel which is short, as in *arrive,* because prefixes have been changed to join on smoothly. *Arrive=adrive.* Many came from French words without <rr>, e.g., to *arrest* is *arêter* in French. However, the dictionary makers knew their Latin origins and original prefixes. To ensure that *ad—* would not be lost, they indicated the missing <d> with a smoothly joining substitute letter, <r>, in words like *arrest* and *arrive.*

Collateral Damage — *award, war.*
At rule 1-15, which is "<wa> spells [wo] and <qua> spells [kwo], before a consonant," we met *quad, quaff, wad, wan* and *was*. I said at the time that these words carry collateral damage, caused by cursive casualties. Collateral damage occurs as a result of other damage. The Cursive Casualty words, or Feather Words, which have had <u> and <i> removed and replaced by <o>, e.g., <u> replaced in *won* and *one* and <i> replaced in *women,* have caused further damage. We see more cursive casualties at Rule 3-63, which is <wor> spells [wer]. This means more collateral damage, because we cannot use <wor> to spell [wor]. Due to this collateral damage, we have to keep the old spelling of *war, ward etc.* even though we no longer say them that way.

Don't let W muddle you! R is bossy after vowels, but W muddles [ar] to [or].
Rule 3-68 <ar> after [w] spells [or].
Reason As we know, the old scribes used <wor> to spell [wer], to avoid using <wir> and <wur>, because *wird* or *wurd* would have been illegible in cursive writing. Long ago, *war* was spelt in many ways, including *worre, warre, wearre, war*. It seems there were as many ways to say this word as there were to spell it, including [war] and the less energetic [wor]. The spelling <war> would not be strange in parts of USA where it still sounds like [war]. Some of the Pilgrim Fathers came from parts of England which said [war]. Eventually, most of England changed the vowel to [or] after <w>, because, after saying [w], lips are already in the position to say [or]. Try it. Now say [w] followed by [ar]. Saying [war] takes more energy, lips move.

So *war* became [wor], but could not be written as <wor> because <wor> was already used to spell [er] in *word.* As we have learnt, writing *word* as *wird* or *wurd* was too hard to read in cursive, especially when <i> had no dot on top. So, when the vowel changed, nothing changed on paper, <war> was kept on, to spell [wor]. This is a case of collateral damage, the flow on effect of damage to Feather Words like *word.* The following rule applies when <ar> follows a sound, not a letter. We hear the sound [w] in *quart,* where <u> spells [w].
List 3-68 Don't let W muddle you! When <ar> follows [w] it spells [or].
ATHWART, AWARD, DWARF, FOREWARN, HINDQUARTERS, LUKEWARM, QUARANTINE, QUART, QUARK*, QUARTER, QUARTERDECK, QUARTERLY, QUARTET, QUARTO, *QUARTZ, QUARTZITE, REWARD, REWARDING, STALWART <al>=[orl], SWARD, SWARM, SWARTHY [dh], THWART, TOWARD, TOWARDS, UNTOWARD, WAR, WARRING, WARBLE, WARD, WARDEN, WARDER, WARDROBE, WARDROOM, WARFARE, WARLIKE, WARM,

WARMISH, WARMONGER ƒ, [wor-mun-ger], WARN, WARNING, WARP, WARSHIP, WART, WARTHOG, WARTIME, WHARF*, WHARVES, WHARFINGER.

Quark spells [kwark] or [kwork], take your choice, because it comes from a nonsense word in a book which was not a spoken word. It was first used in physics in 1964 by Murray Gell-Mann who said he took it from James Joyce's "Finnegans Wake".

Quartz [kworts] comes from German in which <z> spells [ts]. The mineral *quartzite* therefore spells [kwort-sIt]. *Wharf* is another example of reversed <hw> for www.etymonline.com gives it in Old English *hwearf* 'shore, bank where ships can tie up'.

<u>Not needed but nice to know</u>. If you are told that *wharf* originates from the 1st letters of 'ware house at river front", just laugh. It's a false acronym. It's like saying that "gentlemen only; ladies forbidden" produced the word *golf*. Sometimes we use a false acronym to help us remember how to spell, e.g., NECESSARY: Never eat chips, eat salad sandwiches and remain young. BECAUSE: Big emus can always understand small emus, or big elephants can add up sums easily. WOULD: Would old uncles like dancing? LAUGH: Laugh and you get happy. SIGNIFICANT: How can I sign if I can't write? DIARROHOEA: Dash in a rush, run on home or else accidents. EIGHT: Eight Indian girls have toys. Partial acronyms also help us spell, as for COMMITTEE: Mutter mutter talk talk eat eat, PAR**ALLELS**: it's all els! <u>Now back to things we need to know.</u>

List 3-69 Words in which <ward> spells [word] but the sound has shrivelled and sounds more like [wəd] because suffixes are unstressed.

BACKWARD, BACKWARDS, FORWARD, FORWARDS, INWARD, INWARDLY, INWARDS, SHOREWARD, WINDWARD.

Rule 3-70 W muddles [a] to [o].

Reason As we know, <wo> spells [wu], in *won,* or [wi] in *women,* and so when <war> no longer spelt [war], but instead spelt [wor] and then short [wo], <wo> could not be used to spell [wo]. The sound changed but the letters <wa> remained, so now <wa> spells [wo] in words like *warrant*. *Warrant* spells [wo-rant] because <rr> is no longer bossy inside a word. Now, twinned R's only bossy when before a suffix, after a free stem, in other words, if it's between a word's end and suffix. *Warrant* comes from *warn* which spelt [warn] and *guard* which spelt [gward] because a warrant warns and guards one from harm. It used to spell [wor-rant], but the first vowel was stressed and shortened by the English, which is why R is no longer bossy with his twin inside this word and others.

List 3-70

WARRANT, WARRANTEE, WARRANTOR, WARRANTY, WARREN, {WARRIOR}.

<u>Relevant Writing Rule.</u> We have learnt how to read words with <rr> after vowels. This book is not about how to write words. It is about how to read words. However, we can help out at times. When writing words down some people say "Ruddy R!" and "L is Hell!", when it comes to adding suffixes. As we know, there is disagreement on whether to twin L. Both *traveller* and *traveler* are correct. My computer is set for Australian spelling and so it chooses <ll>. The good news is that we all follow the same rules when adding suffixes to words ending with a single vowel plus <r>. That is, adding to words ending <ar>, <er>, <ir>, <or> and <ur>. The following rule tells us when to twin R before a suffix.

Adapting Prof. Cummings' general twinning rule, we should twin R before a suffix only if we can say "yes" to all four of these questions:

A. Does the suffix start with a vowel?
B. Is it to go on R following a single vowel letter?
C. Does that vowel with R spell a stressed vowel sound before adding the suffix?
D. Does that vowel sound remain stressed after adding the suffix?

Two-syllable words are usually stressed on the first syllable. However, *aver, inter, deter, confer, refer, defer* and *prefer* are stressed on the second for they each start with a prefix. And so we write <rr> when adding suffixes, if [er] remains stressed, as in *referral*, but not in *referendum*.
AVERRED, AVERRING from AVER ('ad versus', meaning 'agree it is the truth'. We see 'ver' in *verity* aka *truth*).
INTERRED, INTERRING, DISINTERRED from INTER (meaning 'into earth' from Latin in terra.)
DETERRED, DETERRING, UNDETERRED from DETER (meaning 'terrify someone from', i.e., 'frighten off', Etymonline.)
The bound stem 'fer' comes from 'carry' in Latin:
INFERRED, CONFERRER, CONFERRED, TRANSFERRED, **but** *inference, conference,* and *transference.*
REFERRED, REFERRER, REFERRAL, **but** *referendum. Referrer* is often misspelled *referer.* The twin <rr> ensures that [er] is stressed or else the word would become [ref-rer]. However, the misspelling is so common that it has become the standard industry spelling of the world-wide-web for "HTTP referers." *Referral* is mis-spelled less often as it looks 'feral' when mis-spelt 'referal'.
DEFER (to put off) DEFERRED. Also DEFERRENT (noun – that which puts off).
DEFER (to give in) DEFERRED, DEFERRING, **but** *deferent* (adjective), *deferential* (adjective).
PREFERRED, PREFERRING, **but** *preference.*
BAR, BARRED, BARRING, DEBARRED, UNBARRED; CHAR, CHARRED, CHARRING; JAR, JARRED, JARRING; MAR, MARRED, MARRING; SCAR, SCARRED, SCARRING; SPAR, SPARRED, SPARRING; STAR, STARRY, STARRING; TAR, TARRED, TARRING; WAR, WARRING; ABHOR, ABHORRED, ABHORRING; BLURRED, BLURRY; BURRED, BURRY, CONCURRED, CONCURRING; FURRED, FURRY; INCURRED, INCURRING; RECURRED, RECURRING; SLURRED, SLURRING; SPURRED, SPURRING, SPURRY; PURRED, PURRING; FURRED, FURRY; STIRRED, STIRRING, BESTIRRED; SHIRRED, SHIRRING; WHIRRED, WHIRRING. Return to Reading Rules.

We have learnt how to read words with <rr> after vowels — how to know if R is bossy when twinned, or not. For instance, we know that <rr> is bossy in *barred* but not in *barrel.* The rhythm in English words is tum-te-tum, alternately strong and weak beats, alternately stressed and unstressed vowels. As we know, suffixes are usually unstressed. English words start on a strong beat and end on a weak beat. However, when one suffix is added to another suffix, the word gets a double weak beat, as in *miserly*.
Rule 3-71 If <er> spells [er], and is the first of two weak beats, then it can be pronounced [e] or even [ə].
Reason This ensures the usual English rhythm of 'tum-te-tum' in a word and avoids 'tum-te-te'.
List 3-71A avoiding two weak beats
BITTERLY [bi-te-lee], BROTHERLY [bru-dhe-lee], CLEVERLY [kle-ve-lee], ELDERLY [el-de-lee], FATHERLY [far-dhe-lee], GINGERLY [jin-je-lee], GRANDFATHERLY* [grand-far-dhe-lee], GRANDMOTHERLY* [grand-mu-dhe-lee], IMPROPERLY [im-pro-pe-lee], LATTERLY [la-te-lee], LIBERTY [li-be-tee], MASTERLY [mars-te-lee], MISERLY [mI-ze-lee], MOTHERLY [mu-dhe-lee], POVERTY [po-ve-tee], PROPERLY [prop-e-lee], PROPERTY [prop-e-tee], PUBERTY [pyoo-be-tee], SISTERLY [sis-te-lee], SOBERLY [soh-be-lee], SOMBERLY [som-be-lee], SPINSTERLY [spins-te-lee], TENDERLY [ten-de-lee], UTTERLY [u-te-lee], WESTERLY [wes-te-lee].
Grandfatherly can spell [gran-far-dhe-lee] and *grandmotherly* can spell [gran-mu-dhe-lee] because short [d] is lost between the longer consonants [n] and [f] or [m]. In a cluster of three consonants the shortest consonant is usually 'washed over' by the longer ones.

Not needed but nice to know. *Modernity* is not listed because <er> in *modernity* is not unstressed, is not the first of two weak beats for the the suffix <ity> stresses the syllable before it, [mod-ern-i-tee], te-tum-te-tum, as we saw in Part One. Now we can see and hear it again in *eternity, maternity, paternity* and *fraternity*.

Also, *temerity* is not listed. In *temerity* <er> does not spell [er]. *Temerity* spells [tem-e-ri-tee], because a single letter vowel preceding *–ity* is short and stressed even without double gates after it.

Words like *encumbrance, remembrance* and *entrance* have lost the letter <e> as well as the [er] sound, so they are easy to read — but hard to write for we often include the <e> to link them to their verbs: *encumberance, rememberance* and *enterance* are incorrect spellings!

On the other hand, words like *every, delivery, different, misery* and *several* end in two weak beats, tum-te-te. So the penultimate syllable, the second to last syllable, disappears to ensure the rhythm is the normal tum-te of English, *the delivery man*:-tum te-tum-te tum of [dhə] [de-liv-ree] [man]. This means beginner spells write *evry, delivry, difrent, misry, sevral*. We should speak clearly to each other when we learn to read and write. Then we can add the tum-te-tum rhythm of English speech. Now back to things we need to know.

Q. What about two weak beats at the end of *raspberry*?

Answer Words like *cranberry, bilberry* and *raspberry* get a choice, due to <rr>. In these words <er> can spell [e] or [r]. Do you remember that we said *raspberry* spells [rarz-be-ree] or [rarz-pe-ree]? It can also spell [rarz-bree] or [rarz-pree], to avoid ending with two weak beats. *Cranberry* can spell [kran-be-ree] or [kran-bree], *bilberry* can spell [bil-be-ree] or [bil-bree]. {*Strawberry* can spell [stror-be-ree] or [stror-bree].}

Q. What do <er> and <or> and <ar> mean, as deriving suffixes, i.e., when making new words?

Answer. Both <er> and <or>, mean 'one who' or 'that which'. Suffix <ar> means 'of, near, or pertaining to, about something'.

Q. They sound almost the same but how do we know which one to write?

Answer To er or to or — ah, that is a good question. The answer is given in the revelations below.

Relevant Writing Review. We now use <er> for everyday nouns, like *butcher, baker, tinker, writer, grocer, farmer, maker*. Long ago, only <or> was used for this, as in *sailor*. When we use <er> for comparative adjectives it is called a flexible suffix: *big, bigger; rich, richer; poor, poorer*. Long ago, that flexible suffix was <era>. We add deriving <er> to most verbs, especially modern verbs, to make someone or something that performs an activity. That's why a great many words end in <er>.

However, more nouns end <or> than <er>. Modern things and people are named by adding <or>, like *aviator*: "one who flies" and *radiator*: "that which radiates". If in doubt, use **<or>** to make nouns from verbs. By the way, *bettor*: "one who bets" is the noun. "The owner went home a rich man. He was a better bettor than the other punters. He bettered his chances by looking after his animals very well," in which *better* is an adjective and *bettered* is a verb. Also *resistor* and *adaptor* are things, whereas *resister* and *adapter* are people.

Q. What about <ar>? **Ans.** Suffix <ar> is used for adjectives, e.g., *similar, popular*, and a few nouns, *collar, molar, dollar, burglar, cellar, calendar*, all old words, all after <l> except for *calendar*. A *calender* was a "cloth presser" and so <ar> was used to ensure the two words differed. See etymonline for a fascinating link from *calendar* to *calling* the new moon! *Burglar* is an abbreviation of *burgulator*, a fortress-thief from Latin: *burg* (castle, fortress) *latro* (thief), which is possibly linked to *lazy* and *slack*. Return to Reading Rules.

Suffix <ory> — *accessory, valedictory*.
Rule 3-72 Suffix *–ory* spells [or-ree] but it can shrink to [ree].

Reason First, re-read Rule 3-60 to remember why R is bossy in <ory>. The shrinkage in Rule 3-72 happens in order to maintain the tum-te-tum rhythm of English words. This usually happens when <ory> is a suffix, because suffixes are unstressed, and with two unstressed syllables side by side, something has to "give". One of the syllables has to shrink further and the first syllable gives way. In stem words <ory> spells [or-ree], as in *glory* and *category,* because [or] is stressed, is not the first of two weak beats. However, in suffixes, <ory> can spell [ree], to maintain the tum-te-tum rhythm of English. How do we know whether <ory> is part of a stem word or just a suffix, attached to a stem word? Luckily for us, suffix *–ory* has fallen into the same rut in the road which the suffix *–ive* is in. They both join easily on to a stem's terminal [s] or [t]. If there is no terminal [t] nor [s], then the last sound of the stem word changes. Words like *deride* exchange terminal [d] with <s> spells [s] to take suffix *–ory: derisory* [dee-rI-sə-ree] or [dee-rIz-ə-ree]. In some cases, <at>, spelling [at], is added to the stem word e.g., *accuse* [u-kyooz] – *accusatory* [u-kyooz-at-ree]*,* because a stem ending [z] cannot take the suffix <ory>. Other words change their final sound, e.g., final [sh] changes to [t], e.g., *punish – punitory.* Sometimes new ears and eyes notice the way words have fallen into ruts over the years, for example Professor Hideki Zamma of Japan told us a lot about our own language before his early tragic death.

List 3-72 Suffix <sory> can spell [sree] and suffix <tory> can spell [tree], in all these words to avoid two weak beats.

ACCESSORY, ACCUSATORY, ADMONITORY (from admonish), ANTICIPATORY, BENEDICTORY, CELEBRATORY, COMMENDATORY, COMPENSATORY, COMPULSORY, CONDEMNATORY, CONSERVATORY (from conserve), CONSOLATORY, CONTRADICTORY, CONTRIBUTORY, COSIGNATORY, CREMATORY, CURSORY, DECLARATORY (from declare), DEFAMATORY, DELUSORY, DEPOSITORY, DERISORY, DEROGATORY, DESULTORY, DILATORY, DIRECTORY, DISCRIMINATORY, DISSATISFACTORY, DORMITORY, EJACULATORY, ELUSORY, EXCRETORY, EXPLANATORY, EXTRASENSORY, FACTORY, HALLUCINATORY, ILLUSORY, INFLAMMATORY, INTRODUCTORY, INVENTORY, INVESTIGATORY, IVORY [I-vree], *LABORATORY [la-bor-a-tree], LAVATORY [lav-at-ree], MALEDICTORY, MANDATORY, MIGRATORY, NONDISCRIMINATORY, OBLIGATORY, OBSERVATORY, OFFERTORY, OLFACTORY, ORATORY, PEREMPTORY, PERFUNCTORY, PREDATORY, PRE-EMPTORY, PREFATORY, PREHISTORY, PREPARATORY, PROBATORY, PROMISSORY, PROMONTORY, PROVISORY, PUNITORY, PURGATORY, RECTORY, REFECTORY, REFORMATORY, REGULATORY, REPERTORY, REPOSITORY, ROTATORY, SATISFACTORY, SELF-EXPLANATORY, SENSORY, SIGNATORY (signat), SUPERSENSORY, SUPERVISORY, SUPPOSITORY, TERRITORY, TRAJECTORY, TRANSMIGRATORY, UNSATISFACTORY, VALEDICTORY, VIBRATORY, VOMITORY.

Laboratory shrinks to [lab-ra-tree] in some parts of USA!

The Return of —*ible* and —*able* — *convertible, washable*

The 'Can-do' suffixes are back again! Do you remember —*ible* and —*able?* They come from Latin for *have,* "habere", (actually "abere" because ordinary Romans dropped their 'haitches') it means **having a hold** on a situation, having (h)ability, just like, when someone is not coping, Australians say "Get a grip!" (English: 'he has'; French: 'il as'.)

We attach the twins —*ible* and —*able* to verbs to make adjectives to describe someone who is, or something which is, capable of doing that verb. These attachments are in fact suffixes and suffixes are not stressed. We shall list words ending —*able* first and after that let's list all the new —*ible* words we can now read. Since we first met the 'Can Do' suffixes we have learnt to read many more words. We leant after Rule 2-41 that —*able* is used far more than —*ible* and that —*ible* words are all old words modelled on Latin words. Newer words end in -*able*. Writing rules were supplied for when to write —*able* and when to write —*ible*.

Rule 3-73 In stem words <able> spells [ay-buul] but in suffixes it spells [u-buul].

Reason As we know, in the *suffixes* —*ibl*e and —*able* the first syllable is unstressed and the second has secondary stress.

List 3-73

ABOMINABLE, ACCEPTABLE, ADAPTABLE, ADJUSTABLE, *ADMIRABLE, AFFABLE, AMENABLE, AMICABLE, APPLICABLE, ARABLE, ARRESTABLE, BIDDABLE, BRIDGEABLE, CAPABLE, COLLECTABLE, COMMENDABLE, COMMENSURABLE, COMMUNICABLE, COMPARABLE, CONFERRABLE, CONSOLABLE, CONSTABLE, CONTROLABLE, CULPABLE, DAMNABLE, DEFERRABLE DELECTABLE, DEMONSTRABLE, DEPENDABLE, DESIRABLE, DESPICABLE, DETACHABLE, DETESTABLE, DISCREDITABLE, DISENTANGLE, DISPENSABLE, DISPOSABLE, DISPUTABLE, DISREPUTABLE, DURABLE, EMBRACEABLE, ENGAGEABLE, EQUABLE, EQUITABLE, ESTIMABLE, EXCHANGEABLE, EXCITABLE, EXCUSABLE, EXECRABLE, EXPANDABLE, EXPENDABLE, EXPLICABLE, EXTRADITABLE, EXTRICABLE, FAVORABLE (USA), [fayv-rab-uul], HERITABLE, *HONORABLE [on-ra-buul], IMPECCABLE, IMPLACABLE, IMPONDERABLE, IMPRACTICABLE, IMPREGNABLE, IMPROBABLE, IMPROVABLE, INADVISABLE, INAPPLICABLE, INCALCULABLE, INCAPABLE, INCOMPARABLE, INCONSOLABLE, INCONTESTABLE, INCURABLE, INDEFATIGABLE, INDEFINABLE, INDESCRIBABLE, INDICTABLE, INDOMITABLE, INDUTABLE, INEDUCABLE, INEFFABLE, INERADICABLE, INESCAPABLE, INESTIMABLE, INEVITABLE, INEXCUSABLE, INEXORABLE, INEXPLICABLE, INEXTRICABLE, INFERABLE, INFLAMMABLE, INFLATABLE, INHABITABLE, INHOSPITABLE, INIMITABLE, INNUMERABLE, INOPERABLE, INSCRUTABLE, INSOLUBLE, INSURABLE, INTRACTABLE, INEQUITABLE, IRRECONCILABLE, IRRECOVERABLE, IRREDEEMABLE, IRREFUTABLE, IRREMOVABLE, IRREPLACEABLE, IRREVOCABLE, IRRITABLE, MISERABLE [miz-rab-uul], NAVIGABLE, PALATABLE, PALPABLE, PARABLE, PASSABLE, PENETRABLE, PERISHABLE, PICKABLE, POTABLE, PREDICTABLE, PREFERABLE, PRESENTABLE, PRESUMABLE, PREVENTABLE, PROBABLE, PROCURABLE, PROFITABLE, PROGRAMMABLE, PUNISHABLE, QUOTABLE, RECOGNIZABLE, REFUTABLE, REGRETTABLE, RENTABLE, REPUTABLE, RESPECTABLE, RETRACTABLE, RETURNABLE, REUSABLE, SELLABLE, SEPARABLE [sep-rab-uul], SOLVABLE, TAXABLE, TENABLE, TRACTABLE, TUNABLE, UN-GET-AT-ABLE, UNINHABITABLE, UNMISTAKABLE, UNPREDICTABLE, UNSHOCKABLE, UNSHRINKABLE, UNTHINKABLE, UNWARRANTABLE, USABLE, VENTRICLE, VERITABLE, WASHABLE.

*Two weak beats in *admirable* turn it into [admrə-buul]. Can you find any more words with two weak beats? *Demonstrable,* 'demonstrateable', has changed the way it is written to avoid two weak beats.

Honorable, an alternative spelling for *honourable,* is mostly used in USA but also at times in Australia, and has a silent <h>. *Honorable,* and *{honourable},* are rebels to the rule that <h> spells [h] before a stressed syllable, like the rebels *honest, honorific, {heir, honour* and *hour}.* They end in many weak beats and you can see how this is resolved.

We can read more —*ible* words now that we can decode <er> and <or>.

Rule 3-74 In stem words <ible> spells [I-buul] but in suffixes it spells [u-buul].

Reason As we know, in the *suffixes* —*ibl*e and —*able* the first syllable is unstressed and the second has secondary stress.

List 3-74 <ible> spells [u-buul]

CONTROVERTIBLE, CONVERTIBLE, CORRODIBLE, CORRUPTIBLE, DISCERNIBLE, DISPERSIBLE, FORCIBLE, HORRIBLE, IMPERCEPTIBLE, INCONTROVERTIBLE, INCONVERTIBLE, INCORRIGIBLE, INCORRUPTIBLE, INDISCERNIBLE, IRREDUCIBLE, IRREPRESSIBLE, IRRESISTIBLE, IRRESPONSIBLE, IRREVERSIBLE, IRREVERSIBLE, PERMISSIBLE, REVERSIBLE, REVERTIBLE, SUBMERSIBLE, TERRIBLE.

The Greek Suffix –itis — *tonsillitis*.
Rule 3-75 The suffix <itis> spells [I-tis]
Reason In Greek, "arthritis nosos" means "of-joints disease, inflammation, itchiness". English doctors used the adjective "arthritis" to mean "inflamed joints". When it's on the end of a female word, Greek <itis> spells [It-is]. Arthritis and other diseases, being things of nature, were considered female. We can remember it spells [It-is] not [it-is] if we think of that perfect wife and mother, the Greek goddess of nature, Isis.
List 3-75 <itis> spells [I-tis].
APPENDICITIS, ARTHRITIS COLITIS, DERMATITIS DIVERTICULITIS, GASTRITIS, GINGIVITIS, LAMINITIS, MASTITIS, MENINGITIS, NEPHRITIS, TENDONITIS, TONSILLITIS.
<u>Compound Noun</u> POLIOMYELITIS.

Syllables come together. As we know, syllables help us break words up so that we can read them and understand them, but at the same time we do not want to leave our words in pieces. Indeed, the word *syllable* comes from the Greek word *sullabē* for "bring together". When we make a syllabub pudding we bring a lot of delicious things together. When we pronounce our words, we bring the syllables together. This is easy when consonants and vowels alternate, as in *pin-a-fore*. When one syllable ends with a consonant and the next starts with one, as in *pic-nic*, there is no pause between the easy-to-see syllables. But when two vowels meet at the edge of syllables, at the end of one syllable and at the beginning of another, as in *pi-ano*, once we know where the syllable break is, we glide the first vowel over the syllable join, in order to either avoid a break in the word or to avoid a loss of syllables. English does not use glottal stops which are silent gaps inside words, or clicks. So a break is rare between vowels, and only occurs when Secret Agent H steps in, as in *vehicle*. Also when some people, like Cockneys, drop letters, e. g., when they say [bo-el] for *bottle*.
Vowels Glide over Syllable Boundaries
We are going to look at vowels which meet at syllable boundaries.
Let's go looking for them. We have to look **and** listen, for, unless we hear a word spoken, we do not know if the vowels are meeting at the edge of syllables or if they belong to the same syllable. In *boa* the vowels meet at the edge of syllables. However, in *boat* the vowels meet in the same syllable and together they spell a single vowel sound. Just by looking at the letters there is no way of knowing if *boat* is [boh-at] or [boht]. We shall meet *boat* later on but meanwhile we must practise reading all the words we can list in which vowels meet at the edge of syllables, where the first vowel glides into the second.
  Let's look at vowels side by side, in words.
A) We already know a few words in which vowels are side by side inside the same syllable, words like *said, again, against, would, could, should, hoed, toed* and *died,* but they do not have vowels meeting at syllable boundaries, because both vowel letters are in the same syllable.
B) We know <e> is silent in some words, for various reasons, and this can mean we see two vowels meeting at a syllable boundary, but we do not hear two vowels.
List 3-76 seeing but not hearing two vowels at a syllable boundary

ACREAGE*, BINGEING, BURGEON, CURMUDGEON, FLAGEOLET, PAGEANT, PIGEON, PIGEON-CHESTED, PIGEON-HOLE, SERGEANT, SINGEING, STURGEON, SURGEON, TINGEING, VENGEANCE.

C) We see vowels meeting at syllable boundaries in compound words. They spell the same sounds as if they were in separate words. We read the whole word as if it was a separate prefix and a separate stem word; e.g., <a> and <e> meet in *extraordinary* - *extra* still spells [ekstrar], and *ordinary* still spells [ord-in-air-ee]

List 3-77
EXTRAORDINARY
CUNEIFORM* ← *cune & i & form* [kyoon-i-form]
HEREIN ← *here & in* [heer-in]
WHEREIN ← *where & in* [wair-in]
SOMEONE ƒ← *some & one* [sum-wun]
THEREOF ← *there & of* [dhair-ov]
THEREUPON ← *there & upon* [dhair-up-on]
WHEREVER ← *where & (e)ver* [wair-e-ver]
WHEREUPON ←*where & upon* [wair-up-on]
WHOEVER←*who & ever* [hoo-e-ver]
WHOMEVER*← *whom & ever* [hoom-e-ver]

*Sometimes a little particle is added to make two words join up smoothly, as in *cuneiform*.
**Whomever* is seldom used in speech nowadays. Even *whom* is considered old-fashioned.

D) We see and hear vowels meeting at syllable boundaries when a prefix ending with a vowel is added to a stem word which starts with one. We see and hear vowels meeting at syllable boundaries when we add suffix *ing* to stem words.

List 3-78
With prefix COAGULATE, COALESCE, COEDUCATE, COEXIST, COEXISTENCE, COEXISTENT, COEXTENSIVE, COINCIDE, COINCIDENCE, COINCIDENT, COINCIDENTAL, COINCIDENTALLY, DEODORANT, DEODORIZE, EXTRAORDINARY, EXTRAORDINARILY, EXTRAORDINARINESS, PREAMBLE, PREAPPROVE, PREARM, PRE-EDIT, PRE-EMPT, PROACTIVE, REACT, REACTOR, READDRESS, READJUST, REARRANGE, REASSEMBLE, REASSURE <s>=[sh], REIMBURSE, REINCARNATE, REINFORCE, REINFORCEMENT, REINFORCEMENTS, REINSTATE, REISSUE, REITERATE, RETROACTIVE, REUNITE, REUSABLE, REUSE.

List 3-79
With suffix DOING *doing* [doo-ing], FROING *froing* [froh-ing], GOING *going* [goh-ing], TOING *toing* [too-ing].

Whether gliding from prefix to stem, or stem to suffix, the first vowel is long, the second is short as in, for instance, *coagulate*, [oh-a], or *doing* [oo-i]. Now is the time to start making some gliders. Yes, paper planes. This is probably the first time you have been allowed to make paper planes in class. (I am sure your teacher will say that unless you are neat and quick and quiet it will be the last time.) As we know, at the end of a word a vowel sound is long as it has room to stretch e.g., *halo, hero.* But what about the <o> in *koala*? It spells [oh], for whenever two vowels join at a syllable boundary, the first vowel spells its long sound. Why? So that it can stretch over the boundary and join smoothly on to the next syllable.

English is a flowing language, except when Secret Agent H is required to create a small gap between similar vowels. Secret Agent H provides a silent break after a stressed vowel and before an unstressed vowel, as in *annihilate*, *vehicle* but not *vehicular* because [i] is stressed, not [e]. In *vehicular* <h> is not silent, [vee-hik-yoo-lar]. It is not doing a Secret Agent H job, because as we know, <h> spells [h] before a stressed vowel.

We see Secret Agent H in *vehement, vehemence, annihilate* and *vehicle*.

Some languages say each syllable separately, which to an English speaker sounds like a robot speaking. In fact, robots need a speech synthesizer with glide control in order to speak English like a human. One type of synthesizer, US Patent 3816660, advertises it can "control the intensity of an electron beam in such a manner as to smooth the glide portion between adjacent speech sounds." Humans do not need this gadget in order to glide syllables together. However English words do use Glide Rules.

Before we have fun with our gliders, we need to talk about U. In some words <u> does not glide because it is just a silent insulator , insulating <g> from <e> or <i> to prevent <g> spelling [j], as in boundary because <u> guards [g] from being softening by <e>, as in CATALOGUER, GUERILLA, GUERNSEY, GUIDE, GUISE, GUINEA PIG, HARANGUER, INTRIGUER, PLAGUER, VAGUER. To dress-up as Insulator U, simply strap on a big (insulating) pillow labelled U, as in the website's Photo Gallery.

In some words <u> does not glide as one vowel to another because it spells <w>, a consonant, as in *queen* and *equal,* {*languish* and *penguin*}. When <u> spells [w] we call him Penguin U. Find him in the website's Photo Gallery. In Part Four we shall meet more Penguin Words and also Fossil U, as in {*build* and *guard*}.

Glide and Yap — *bias, violin.*

Rule 3-80 The Glide and Yap Rule. When two vowels meet at a syllable boundary, inside a word, the first spells its long sound and the next spells its short sound and the first glides into the next without a gap of silence.

Reason This ensures vowels do not match in sound and by starting with long vowels ensures they can glide smoothly onto the next vowel, to prevent words sounding disjointed and robotic.

Do you have your gliders ready? Practise throwing them so they glide through the air. Name each of the five best paper gliders A, E, I, O, and U. They will glide as [ay], [ee], [I], [oh] and [yoo] or [oo] in the first syllable. Glider I glides as [I] if it is in the first syllable, for, as we know, <i> spells [I] in the first syllable, as in *I* and *die*. (When I glides in a second or third syllable, it glides as the weaker [ee] vowel, as we shall soon hear.) Glider U glides as [yoo], but just [oo] after [l], [r] and [j]. The reason that we do not pronounce [y] after these consonants is that they are difficult to say with ease. Consequently we have dropped yods after these consonants. (In parts of USA, especially in New York, where many people never pronounced <u> as [yoo] in their first language and so just say [oo] in English.)

Set up five targets, each labelled [a], [e], [i], [o] or [u]. Now lie your ruler on the floor as a syllable boundary and glide your gliders over it onto a target. The targets "make", with your help, short sounds of surprise when they are hit. Do you make short little sounds of surprise sometimes? Maybe your dog makes short yaps of surprise. As you glide a glider at a target say the glider's long vowel sound and then the target's short sound — as a short yap of surprise. Do this well and you might be allowed to throw paper planes in class again. Glide and yap! Targets can be drawn on the classroom board.

Rebel KARAOKE, IGUANA

Rebels' Reasons *Karaoke* [kar-ar-oh-kee], glides long [ar] on to long [oh]. In Japanese, *kara* means 'empty' and the rest means 'orchestra'. This is an adopted word, in which syllables do not glide into each other. *Iguana* is another adopted word, from Spanish, in which <a> spells short [u] or long [ar], never [a]. In Australia this word for a large lizard evolved into *goanna* in which [oh] glides into short [a], obvious to the reader because it is followed by twins, <ll>.

As we know, the Great Vowel Shift affected long vowels, not short ones. So our yaps will be [a], [e], [i], [o], [u] or [uu], but our long vowels will depend on whether the word has lifted its long vowel or not.

Also, if it was adopted from Continental Europe after the GVS, it will probably have a Continental long vowel. We hear the Continental long vowels spelt by <a>, <e>, <i>, <o>, and <u> in 'Pa, may we all too?' and the Anglo long vowels in 'Maybe I won't use glue.' In English, <i> also spells long [ee], but not in the first syllable of a word.

List 3-79 Words with Continental long sounds, so <i> glides as [ee] and <a> glides as [ar].
CLIENTELE, CLIENTELE, FIASCO, FIAT, FIORD, FIORD, KIOSK, KIOSK, LIANA, MIASMA, NAÏVE* [nar-eev], PAELLA, PIANIST, PIANO, PIANOLA, PIAZZA, PRION, QUIESCENCE, QUIESCENT, SIENNA, SIERRA, SIESTA, TIARA, TRIO, TRIOLET, VIOLA. Proper Noun/Adj. DION [dee-on], IAN [ee-ən], GIOVANNI [jee-oh-varn-ee], VIENNA, VIENNESE, VIETNAM, VIETNAMESE.

Naïve is adopted from the French who used two dots as a direction to say "native" without the <t>. (Germans call the direction sign ¨ an umlaut and use the two dots differently, to show vowel change: *froh* — 'glad' versus *frölich* —'gay'. Diacritic signs (direction signs) are rarely used in English, and not every dictionary prints them in *naïve*.

Use Anglo long vowels as you "glide and yap" as you read these next words which have vowels meeting at the first syllable boundary. {*Dual, duo* and *duodenum* come later when we glide <u> after <d>.}

List 3-80
ANTLION*, ANTIBIOTIC*, DAIS*, DANDELION*, BEATIFY, BEATITUDE, BIAS, BIENNIAL, BIOCHEMICAL <ch>=[k], BIOCHEMIST, BIOCHEMISTRY, BIODYNAMIC, BIOLOGIC, BIOLOGICAL, BIOLOGICALLY, BIOLOGIST, BIOLOGY, BIOLUMINESCENCE, BIOMASS, BIOMECHANICS <ch>=[k], BIOMEDICAL, BIOMETRY, BIONIC, BIOPIC, BIOPSHERE, BIOPSY, BIOPTIC, BIOTECHNOLOGY <ch>=[k], BIOTIC, BIOTOXIN, COAXIAL, CHAOS* <ch> = [k], CLIENT, COINCIDE, COITUS, COITY, COMPLIANT*, CREOSOTE, CRUEL, CRUELTY, CRUET, DEIFY*, DEITY*, DIABETES [dI-a-bee-teez], DIAGNOSE, DIAGNOSTIC, DIAL, DIALECT, DIALYSIS [dI-al-ee-sis], DIAMETER, DIAMOND*, DIAPER, DIAPHRAGM *silent* <g>, DIARRHETIC, DIARY, DIASPORA, DIATRIBE, DIET, DIETARY [dI-e-tree], DIOCESE, DIODE, DIORAMA, DIOXIDE, DIOXIN, DRUID, FLUID, FLUORESCENT, FLUORIDE, FLUORINE, FRIABLE, FUEL, GEOCENTRIC, GEODESIC, GEODESY, GEOGRAPHER, GEOGRAPHICAL, GEOGRAPHY, GEOLOGICAL, GEOLOGICALLY, GEOLOGIST, GEOLOGY, GEOLOGY, GEOMETRIC, GEOMETRY, GIANT, GOANNA*, HUON PINE, ION, ANION [an-I-on], KAOLIN, KARAOKE*, KOALA*, LAITY*, LEONINE, LEOTARD*, LIABLE, LION, LIONESS, MIOSIS, MIOTIC, MUEZZIN, NEANDERTHAL, NEO-CLASSICAL*, NEOLITHIC*, NEOLOGISM, NEON, NEOPRENE, NUANCE <a> =[o], PEON, OASIS, *PAELLA, PANCREATIC, PHIAL, PIETY [pI-et-ee], also IMPIETY, PIONEER, PLIANT, SUPPLIANT, POEM, POET, POETICAL, POETRY, PRIOR, QUIET, QUIETEN, QUIETLY, QUIETNESS, QUIETUDE, REFUEL, RETRIAL, RIOT, RUIN, SEANCE* [say-ons], SCIENCE, SCIENTIFIC, SCIENTIST, STEATITE, STOIC, STOICAL, STOICISM, SUET, SUICIDAL, SUICIDE, SUNDIAL, THEATRE, THEATRICAL, THEODOLITE, THEOLOGIAN, THEOLOGY, THEOLOGY, THEOSOPHY, TRIAL, TRIANGLE, TRIENNIAL, TRUANCY, TRUANT, TRUISM, TUIT* [choo-it], INTUIT* [in-choo-it], VIABLE, VIADUCT, VIAL, VIANDS *plural noun,* VIOL, VIOLIST, VIOLATE, VIOLENCE, VIOLENT, VIOLET, VIOLIN, VIOLINIST. Proper Nouns/Adj. BRIAN, DIANA, DIANNE *fossil e,* HIAWATHA, IOLANTHE, [I-oh-lan-thee], JESUIT, JOANNE, JOEL, LEAH, LEANNA, LEON, NAOMI, NEAPOLITON, NOAH, NOEL, YAEL [yar-el], ZION.

Antlion is a compound word in which <i> is in the first yllable of *lion*.
Antibiotic is not an outlaw because <i> is in the first syllable of the bound stem *bio*.
Chaos spells [kay-os], not [kay-oz], like *tennis* spells [ten-nis].

*In *compliant* <i> spells [I] because it is in the first syllable of the stem word, *pliant*.
The suffixes *-ity, -ety, -ic, -id* and *–it* stress preceding vowels and without a consonant between the preceding vowel they obey the glide and yap rule, as in **laity*.
**Dais* For centuries in both French and English *dais* has spelt [days]. But that sounds strange because it should have been pronounced [dayz] not [days] because <s> spells [z] after a stressed vowel. So recently another pronunciation has become popular: [day-is] for <s> can spell [s] after an unstressed vowel. This is proof that words eventually conform to patterns – seemingly on their own, but actually this is done by humans in our enjoyment of patterns.
**Dandelion* is a compound word meaning "teeth of lion", (French, *dent de lion*), and so it does not break the rule because <i> is in the first syllable and therefore glides as [I] into [o].
**Deity* [dee-it-ee] and *deify* [dee-i-fI] can also be pronounced with a Continental long [ay], [day-i-tee], [day-i-fI].
**Koala* [koh-ar-lar] was adopted from an Ab'l word in Sydney, by 1798, said to mean, "drinks no water". Note there is no short 'yap', no [a], sound because in this word <oa> spells [oh-ar].
**Leotard* is an eponym. Google Jules Léotard, so <eo> spells [ee-oh].
**Goanna* is named after the similar-looking *iguana* of South America. It is not an Ab'l word. (A goanna is known as a *bungarra* in WA, from the Ab'l Noongar language.)
*The prefix *neo-* [nee-oh] can also be pronounced [ay-oh], the Continental way.
**Seance* [see-ons] is also pronounced [say-ons], the Continental way.
**Tuit* and *intuit* are very new verbs, not yet completely acceptable, created as 'back formations' from *intuition*.

Little Imp, i, — *alias, venial.*

When <i> glides on to <a> in *alias,* it cannot spell a nice long strong [ee], it has to spell a short little unstressed [ee], because it is part of a suffix, but it makes up for it by making the vowel behind it into a long vowel sound. It only lengthens vowels spelt with one letter and only if there is only one consonant between it and the vowel. In this way it is just like its big sister Fairy E. In this situation <i> is called Little Imp. Little Imp works wonders on others, on other vowels. He makes them grow into long vowels, but he cannot work wonders on himself. Unlike Fairy E in *convene* [kon-veen], Little Imp in *convivial* [kon-viv-ee-al] cannot make <viv> spell [vIv] or even [veev]. That is why we say that "Little Imp works wonders on others but not on himself". He cannot make a preceding <i> spell its long sound. Little Imp appears in the website's Dress Up Gallery.

Rule 3-81 Unstressed <i> followed by another unstressed vowel copies the action of Fairy E on all vowels but [i].

Reason We speak of Fairy E to little readers but we know that Fairy E is really a silent remnant of longer "Regal Words" which have lost their ends, but still spell long vowels in the first syllable. We speak of Little Imp, to little readers, but we know that stress in English words follows a 'tum-te-tum' pattern, and we know that suffixes are unstressed, meant to be short and weak. Many words end in two short syllables, words which end in suffixes like *–ia, -ial, -ian, ius* or *–ium*. As we know, two weak beats are unwelcome in English words. They upset the 'tum-te-tum-te-tum' rhythm of English. However, impish little [i] which starts the suffixes *–ia, -ial, -ian, ius* or *–ium* comes to the rescue, for Little Imp makes the preceding vowel long and strong and shrinks himself even littler so that words can end with 'tum-te-tum', even if the last 'tum' is still quite weak, so it's more like 'tum-te-hum'. We say that the syllable after Little Imp has 'secondary stress', which is weaker than primary stress but not as weak as no stress. Little Imp cannot work wonders through double gates, i.e., when preceded by two consonants. So *venial* spells [veen-ee-al] but *bestial* spells [bes-tee-al]. There are many reasons for words to terminate in <ial>, e.g., when suffix

<y> becomes <i> before <al>, for <y> cannot enter an English word, hence *custody* [kus-tod-ee] becomes *custodial* [kus-toh-dee-al].

Rebels We shall meet the rebels {*special, especial, ration* and *national*} later.

List 3-81 Little Imp at work

ALIAS, ALIEN, ALIENATE, ALLUVIAL, AVIONICS, BARONIAL, BINOMIAL, CEREMONIAL, COLLEGIAL, COLLEGIAN, COLLOQUIAL*, COLONIAL, COLONIALISM, CONGENIAL, CONGENIALITY, CONNUBIAL, CONVENIENCE, CONVENIENT, CONVENIENTLY, CRANIAL, CUSTODIAL, DEFOLIANT, DISOBEDIENT, ECCLESIASTIC, ENTHUSIASM, ENTHUSIAST, EPITHELIUM, EXPEDIENCY, EXPEDIENT, FOLIAGE, GENIAL, GLACIAL, GRADIENT, HELION*, INALIENABLE, INEXPEDIENT, INGREDIENT, JOVIAL, JULIENNE fossil <e>, LABIAL, LENIENT, MAGNESIUM, MANIAC, MARSUPIAL, MATRIMONIAL, MEDIAL, MENIAL, PAROCHIAL <ch>=[k], PATRIMONIAL, PECUNIARY, PLAGIARISE, PLAGIARISM, RADIAL, REMEDIAL, SALIENT, TESTIMONIAL, TRINOMIAL, VENIAL. <u>Names</u> FABIAN, JULIETTE.

Colloquial is a rare instance of Little Imp working wonders over double gates, for <qu> spells [kw]. In *toque* Fairy E is only making magic action over a single gate for <qu> in *toque* spells [k]. As we know, when <que> terminates a word, it spells [k].

Helion [heel-ee-on] is the nucleus of a helium atom, not to be muddled with {*hellion*}.

Fairy E, R and Little Imp.

Rule 3-82 Unstressed <i> followed by another unstressed vowel copies the action of Fairy E on all vowels but [i].

Little Imp copies the action of Fairy E on all vowels but [i]. This means that Little Imp copies the result of Fairy E's 'magic action' in that <are> spells [air], <ere> spells [eer], <ore> spells [or] and <ure> spells [yoor]. Because Little Imp works wonders on others but not on himself, he cannot copy the magic action of big sister Fairy E in <ire>, which makes <i> spell [I].

To summarize, when stressed before Little Imp, <ar> spells [air] as in *secretarial* and *herbarium;* <er> spells [eer] as in *ministerial* and *cafeteria,* <or> spells [or] as in *oriel* and *orient* and <ur> spells [yoor], as in *durian* and *mercurial* or [oor], as in *injurious*. By contrast, in *delirium* and *West Irian* the first <i> does not spell [I] because Little Imp cannot work wonders on himself.

The suffixes *-ory, -ery, -ary, -ury,* replace <y> with <i> before gaining *-al,* hence *memory* becomes *memorial.*

Rebels BURIAL, CHARIOT.

Rebels' Reasons *Burial* spells [be-ree-al], (not [byoo-ree-al], because *bury,* as we know, spells [be-ree]. *Chariot* spells [cha-ree-ot], not [chair-ee-ot]. Long ago it had <rr> and spelt [char-ee-ot]. It began just like *car,* from 'carrum' which is what the Romans called the two wheeled Celtic war chariots. Statues and paintings have been made of Queen Boadicea charging the Romans in hers. When *charriote* simplified to *chariot* it lost [ar], its link to its cousin-words *cart* and *car* and *carry.*

List 3- 82 in which Little Imp follows <r>.

<u>Fairy E glides after <r></u> BOREAL, CEREAL, EPICUREAN, ETHEREAL, FUNEREAL, HERCULEAN, SIDEREAL, TOREADOR, VENEREAL. <u>Proper Nouns, & Adjective</u> SALVADOR, SALVADOREAN. <u>Little Imp glides after <r></u> LUXURIANT, LUXURIATE, PERIOD, ADVERSARIAL, AMBASSADORIAL, ANTIBACTERIAL, ANTIMALARIAL, APERIENT, AQUARIUM, ARTERIAL, BACTERIAL, BARIUM, CENSORIAL, CENTURION, CLARION, CONSPIRATORIAL, CRITERION, CURIOSITY, DARIOLE, DELIRIUM*, DICTATORIAL, DISORIENTATE, DURIAN*, EDITORIAL, EQUATORIAL, EXPERIENCE, EXTERIOR, *GERIATRICS, HERBARIUM, HISTORIAN, HONORARIUM*, IMMATERIAL, IMPERIAL, INEXPERIENCE, LARIAT, LEPROSARIUM, MAGISTERIAL, MALARIAL, MANAGERIAL, MATERIAL, MEMORIAL,

MERCURIAL, MINISTERIAL, MORATORIUM, ORIEL (window), ORIENT, ORIENTAL, ORIENTEERING, PICTORIAL, PLANETARIUM, PRURIENCE, PRURIENT, SANITARIUM, SARTORIAL, SECRETARIAL, SENSORIAL, SEPTUAGENARIAN, SERIAL, SOLARIUM, TERRARIUM, TERRITORIAL, TUTORIAL, VALETUDINARIAN, VARIANCE. Proper Nouns & Adjectives DARIEL, DAMARIUS, MIRIAM*, PRESBYTERIAN, WEST IRIAN*, ZACHARIUS <ch>=[k].

*Durian spells [joo-ree-an] due to Yod Fusion.

*Geriatrics spells [je-ree-at-rikc] because <e> spells a stressed vowel in the fourth syllable from the end of the word.

In *honarium <h> is silent, as in the stem word honor/honour.

In *delirium [del-i-ree-um] and *Miriam [mi-ree-am] Little Imp cannot work wonders on himself.

Rule 3-83 When <i> is followed by a vowel in another syllable it glides as [I] when in the first syllable, and as [ee] in all others.

Rebels ANXIETY*, NOTORIETY, PARIETAL, PROPRIETY, SATIETY, SOBRIETY, SOCIETY, VARIETY and all words built on these stems, i.e., IMPROPRIETY, INSOBRIETY, PROPRIETARY, PROPRIETOR, PROPRIETRESS,

Rebels' Reason After <i> the suffix *-ety* is used, instead of *–ity*, to avoid <ii> which is a "no no" in English, e.g., *vary* cannot grow into *variity* because <ii> is not accepted in English. The same goes for *piety* and *anxiety* which share stems with *pious* and *anxious*. In *variety etc.* the gliding vowel, <i>, is stressed and lengthened to [I], even though not in the first syllable, in order to remain separate from the next vowel, [e], as [ee][e] does not mark the syllable boundary clearly.

*Anxiety spells [ang-zI-et-ee] for as you will remember, <x> spells [gz] when it comes after an unstressed vowel and before a stressed vowel as in *exam*.

Also, in *satiety, society* and *variety* <i> is not a 'Little Imp' because it spells [I], not little [i]. Compare this to {foliage} below, in which <i> is a 'little imp' and 'works wonders', making <o> spell [oh].

In the next list Little Imp cannot work wonders on itself and it cannot work wonders through double gates.

List 3-83
ACCORDION, ACQUIESCE, ACQUIESCENT, ACQUIESCENCE, ACROMION, ADVERBIAL, ALLEGIANCE, AMBIENCE, AMBIENT, APHRODISIAC*, AXIAL*, AXIOM*, AXIOMATIC, BASTION, BESTIAL, BESTIALITY, BIAXIAL, BICENTENNIAL, BRANCHIAL <ch>=[k], BRONCHIAL <ch>=[k], CARRION, CAVIARE* [ee-ar], CLARION, CELESTIAL, CENTENNIAL, CHAMPION, CONIDIAL, CONVIVIAL, CONVIVIALITY, DISSENTIENT, EMOLLIENT, ENUNCIATE, EPITHELIAL, ETIOLATE, EXTRATERRESTRIAL, FAMILIAL, FILIAL, FOLIAGE, GANGLION, GENIALITY, HACIENDA*, HISTRIONIC, HOMO SAPIENS, IDIOM, IDIOMATIC, IDIOT, IDIOTIC, INCIPIENT, INDUSTRIAL, INDUSTRIALIST, INSENTIENT, MANIOC*, OBLIVION, OMNISCIENT, PERENNIAL, POTASSIUM, PROVERBIAL, PURSUANCE, PURSUANT, QUADRENNIAL, RADIANT, RECIPIENT, REQUIEM, RESILIENCE, RESILIENT, RESILIENTLY, SCORPION, SENTIENT, SERVIETTE fossil <e>, SPORANGIAL, SUBSERVIENT, TERRESTRIAL, TRANSIENCE, TRANSIENT, TRIVIAL, TWENTIETH, UNCIAL, VESTIGIAL, VESTIGIALLY, VITRIOL. Proper Nouns SANTIAGO. Names GABRIEL/LE *female e*, GILLIAN [jil-ee-an], HARRIET, HENRIETTA, MAXIMILLIAN, SEBASTIAN.

*Aphrodisiac is an eponym. Google Aphrodite.

*Caviare spells [kav-ee-ar] — an adopted Continental word, so [ar] did not lift to [air], like English *are*. In Italian it's *caviale* and Greek *khaviari*. It's a rebel to the rule that <are> spells [air], but not in USA where it's written *caviar*.

In *axial* and *axiom* <x> spells [ks] before an unstressed vowel and forms double gates. So Little Imp has no affect on the preceding vowel, which remains a short [a].

In adopted *manioc* [man-ee-ok] and *hacienda* [ha-see-en-dar], <i> is not unstressed, is not a Little Imp.

List 3-84 More "Glide and Yap" words. Remember that <i> spells [i] or [ee] in all but the first syllable of a word.

ACCRUAL, ALTRUISM, ALTRUIST, ALTRUISTIC, AMBIGUITY, ANNUAL*, ANNUALLY*, ANNUITANT, ANNUITY, ARBOREAL, ARCHAIC <ch>=[k], ARCHEOLOGY [k] (USA), ARGUABLE, *ATRIAL, BILINGUAL, CAVEAT, CHAMELEON [k], COLEUS, CONFLUENCE, CONTIGUITY, CONTINUAL, CONTINUALLY, CONTINUANCE, CONTINUITY, CONTINUUM, CORNEAL, CORPOREAL, DIMINUENDO, DISCONTINUITY, DRUID, EFFLUENT, EGOISM, EPIGEAL, ESCUTCHEON, ESOPHAGEAL (USA), ETHANOIC ACID, FLUID, GARGANTUAN, GENEALOGICAL, GENEALOGIST, GENEALOGY, GENUINE* *fossil* <e>, GRATUITY, GLUTEAL, HABEAS CORPUS, HERCULEAN, HEROIC*, HEROICALLY*, HEROICS*, HEROIN*, HEROINE*, HEROISM*, HIPPEASTRUM, HOMOGENEITY, HOMEOPATHY, IDEOLOGICAL, IDEOLOGY, IDEALIZE, INCHOATE [k], INCONGRUITY, INFLUENCE, INFLUENZA, INGENUITY, INNUENDO, JINGOISM, LINEAGE, LINEAL, LINOLEUM, LUNCHEON, MANUAL*, MANUALLY*, MEANDER, MEDITERRANEAN, MENSTRUAL, MINUET, MISCREANT, MONOTHEISTIC, MOSAIC, MUSEUM, NUCLEUS, PATRIOT*, PATRIOTIC, PATRIOTISM, OLEANDER, OSTEOPATH, PANCREAS*, PERINEAL, PERITONEAL, PERMEABILITY, PERPETUITY, PERSPICUITY, PETROLEUM, PHARYNGEAL, PINEAL, PRE-MENSTRUAL, PROMISCUITY, PROSAIC, SOLOIST, SPELEOLOGY, SPIRITUALITY, SUBTERRANEAN , SUPERFLUITY, TENUITY, TORTUOSITY, TRACHEAL, TRACHEOTOMY, TRUANCY, TRUANT, VACUITY, VALUABLE. Proper Nouns/Adj. ANDEAN, ANTIGUAN, ARAMAIC, CARIBBEAN, COLOSSEUM, CRIMEAN, HADRIAN*, HEBRIDEAN, HINDUISM, ISRAEL, ISRAELITE, MAOISM, MINOAN, NAPOLEONIC, NEAPOLITAN*, SAMOAN, VANUATU*. Names EMMANUEL/LE, ISHMAEL, ISRAEL, JOANNA*, ORPHEUS, PHINEAS, SAMUEL.

In *annual* and *manual* spell [an-yoo-al] and [man-yoo-al] but are usually destressed at the end so that they do not end on two weak beats. This results in [an-yuul] and [man-yuul]. The same thing happens in words ending —*ial,* as we shall see.

Genuine spells [jen-yoo-in] and terminal <e> is a fossil. However, ever since reading became a general skill Queen Quill has overcome King Sound in many words — people follow the written word, instead of copying words they hear. This means some people let *genuine* spell [jen-yoo-In] but we never hear folk say [en-jIn] for *engine* — another word ending in fossil <e>. Long ago <ine> in both words spelt [een] which in the GVS did not lift and bend to become [In] because only stressed long vowels were affected by the GVS. Instead, because [een] ends both words, it shrank to an unstressed [in], turning <e> into a useless fossil.

Hero [heer-roh] switches stress from [eer] to [roh] when [oh] glides onto [ik] in *heroic*. This turns [heer] into the less important sounding [her] or [hə]. This happens in *heroin, heroine* and *heroism* too.

Atrial and *Patriot* spells [pay-tree-ot], not [pat-ree-ot] due to the old lengthening affect of <tr> as we have seen in *mitre,* [mIt-er]. This is seen in *acre* and *ogre* due to the effect of<,cr> and <gr>. Also *Hadrian* spells [hay-dree-an] due to the old lengthening action of <dr>.

Pancreas spells [pan-kree-as], not [pan-kree-az], even though <s> follows a stressed vowel.

Perennial spells [pe-ren-ee-al] but began as two words, *per annus,* Latin for 'through the year', all year round.

Joanna often uses Secret Agent H, *Johanna,* to make sure she does not look like the name of another girl {*Joan*}. *Note: The names *Daniel* and *Eliot* are not listed for they spell [dan-yel] and [el-yot] — more soon on this.

**Vanuatu* spells [van-oo-ar-too], not [van-yoo-u too] because most languages use the Continental alphabetical code, not the way English uses the alphabet.

Glide and Yawn — *apnea, zamia.*

Rule 3-85 The Glide and Yawn Rule. When two vowels meet at the end of a word at a syllable boundary the first spells its long sound which glides into the next which is free to spread out and yawn its long sound.

Rebels MESSIAH and PARIAH each have <i> spells [I] which is normally only allowed in the first syllable. RATAFIA [ra-taf-ee-ar].

Rebels' Reasons *Messiah* [mes-I-ar] is a bad attempt to spell a Hebrew word, and *pariah* [par-rI-ar] is an attempt to spell the Tamil word for a lowly drummer boy on the edge of a parade, a word which came to mean outcaste by high caste Hindi and British people. It also breaks the rule that <ar> before Little Imp spells [air]. The sweet called *ratafia* seems to have adopted the short [a] of another sweet, *taffy*.

In the next list words are marked **i** when Little Imp works wonders. As we know, he can't work wonders on himself, in *tibia etc.*, nor over double gates in *raffia, anorexia* <x>=[ks], *salvia etc.* As we know, after <r>, Little Imp follows the action of Fairy E. So *malaria* spells [mal-air-ree-ar] (as in *hare)*, *Gloria* spells [glor-ree-ar] (as in *gore*), *bacteria* spells [bak-teer-ree-ar] (as in *here*).

List 3-85 Glide and Yawn

ACADEMIA **i**, ADAGIO **i**, AGORAPHOBIA **i**, ALLUVIA **i**, AMBROSIA, AMMONIA **i**, ANOREXIA, [an-o-rek-see-ar], APNEA, ARCHEGONIA <ch>=[k] **i**, AREA, ARIA*, ARPEGGIO, AZALEA, BARATHEA, BEGONIA **i**, BOA, BORONIA, BULIMIA, CAMELIA **i**, CAMEO, CLAUSTROPHOBIA **i**, COCHLEA [k], CONIDIA, CONTAGIA **i**, CORNEA, CORNUCOPIA **i**, DAPHNIA, DIARRHOEA*, DIPSOMANIA **i**, ENCYCLOPAEDIA , ENCYCLOPEDIA in USA, EPITHELIA **i**, ESCALLONIA **i**, ESCHSCHOLTZIA, EVACUEE, EX OFFICIO, FOLIO **i**, FOVEA, GANGLIA, GARDENIA **i**, GONORRHOEA, HAKEA, HEMIPLEGIA **i**, HEMOPHILIA USA, HERNIA, HOMOPHOBIA **i**, IDEA, INSIGNIA, INSOMNIA, INTAGLIO, INTER ALIA **i**, INTELLIGENTSIA, JERBOA, KEA, KLEPTOMANIA **i**, LABIA **i**, LEHUA *tree*, LOBELIA **i**, LOGORRHOEA*, MACADAMIA **i**, MAFIA **i**, MAGNOLIA **i**, MANIA **i**, MEDIA **i**, MEGALOMANIA **i**, MELANCHOLIA **i**, MEMORABILIA, MIA-MIA*, MILLENNIA, MISCELLANEA, MITOCHONDRIA, MONOMANIA **i**, MORPHIA **i**, MULTIMEDIA **i**, MYALGIA, NECROPHILIA, NEPHRIDIA, NOSTALGIA, OBELIA **i**, OLEA, OPHTHALMIA, OSTEO-ARTHRITIS, PANACEA, PARAPHERNALIA **i**, PARAPLEGIA **i**, PATIO, PEDOPHILIA USA, BACTERIA **i**, CAFETERIA **i**, CRITERIA **i**, CURIO **i**, DIPHTHERIA **i**, MALARIA, PHANTASMAGORIA, PHOBIA **i**, PORTFOLIO **i**, PROTEA, PROVISIO, QUADRIPLEGIA **i**, RADIO, RAFFIA, REGALIA **i**, RHEA, RODEO, SALVIA, SANGRIA, SATURNALIA **i**, SCHIZOPHRENIA **i** <ch>=[k];<z> =[ts], SEBORRHEA, SEPIA **i**, SERAGLIO, SKUA, SPORANGIA, STEREO, STEREOPHONIC*, STEREOSCOPIC*, STUDIO **i**, SUBURBIA, TIBIA, TILAPIA **i** [, til-arp-ee-ar], TINEA, TRACHEA [k], TRIVIA, TROCHLEA [k], UREA, WISTERIA **i**, XENOPHOBIA **i**, ZAMIA **i**, ZINNIA. <u>Proper Nouns</u> ALBANIA **i**, ALGERIA **i**, ANTIGUA, ARABIA **i**, ARCADIA **i**, ARMENIA **i**, BOHEMIA **i**, BOLIVIA, BRITANNIA, CAMBODIA **i**, COLUMBIA, CRIMEA, CUMBRIA, CURAÇAO, [kyoor-u-say-oh], CZECHOSLOVAKIA, [chek-oh-slo-var-kee-ar], ETHIOPIA* **i**, GAMBIA, INDIA, INDIANA, LIBERIA **i**, MAFIA, MANTUA*, MONGOLIA **i**, MONROVIA **i**, MONTEVIDEO*, NAMIBIA, NIGERIA **i**, PAPUA, PHILADELPHIA, RASTAFARIAN, RUMANIA **i**, SAMOA, SAO (biscuits), SCANDINAVIA **i**, SOMALIA, [som-arl-ee-ar], TANZANIA, [tan-zarn-ee-ar], TASMANIA **i**,

TUNISIA, UTOPIA **i**, VIA. <u>Names</u> ANASTASIA **i**, ANDREA, ANTONIA **i**, CECELIA **i**, CELIA **i**, CYNTHIA [sin-thee-u], ELIO **i**, LEO*, FELICIA, GLORIA, INDIA, LUCREZIA **i**, MAGNOLIA **i**, MAO, MARCIA, MARIA*, MARIO*, NADIA **i**, JOSHUA, JULIA **i**, JULIO, ROMEO, SERGIO, THEO*, TITANIA* **i**, VICTORIA.

Aria spells the Continental term for an operatic solo song, [ar-ee-ar] because musical terms usually remain in Italian pronunciation.

Diarrhoea and *logorrhoea* have a silent <o>. As <rrho> is <rr> in Greek their spelling links these words to their origins e.g., Latin. *diarrhoea,* came from Greek *diarrhoia* meaning "through-flow". From Greek *logos* for "word", we get "word flow". *Logos* also means speech, discourse and reason, but here it means excessive flow of words. I hope you do not get *logorrhoea* in class! In USA <o> has been dropped from all words ending <rrhoea>.

Leo, Montevideo and *Theo* can all be said the Continental way, <eo> spells [ay-oh], in which case <th> spells its Continental sound [t] in *Theo,* [tay-oh]. In Portuguese *Curaçao*, the cedilla softens <c> to [s].

Mantua spells [man-too-ar] because it is a city in Italy where <u> spells [oo], not [yoo] as in English.

Mia-mia spells [mI-ar-mI-ar] and has been adopted from Ab'l languages. It is an Ab'l word which is in many Ab'l languages, west to east, right across Australia, and sometimes it is just [mI-mI], (Blake, p. 99, Boston p. 98).

Stereophonic and *stereoscopic* follow the rule that words in compound words do not change. So stereo 'glides and yawns' inside these compound words.

Little Imp produces the Continental long vowel [ar] in *Maria, Mario* and *Titania.* In *Ethiopia* there are two Little Imps.

Glide and Roar — *acidifier, vilifier.*

Rule 3-86 The Glide and Roar Rule. When two vowels meet at a syllable boundary and the second vowel is followed by Bossy R, the first spells its long sound which glides into [or], [ar] or [er].

Reason This is just a variation on the Glide and Yap, in which the first vowel is long because the English usually stress beginnings, not ends, and one way to stress a vowel is to say it longer than another. We see and hear vowels meeting at syllable boundaries when we add suffix —*er* to stem words. DOER *doer* [doo-er], GOER *goer* [goh-er]. The stems *do* and *go* retain their unusual long sounds.

Rebels BEHAVIOR [bee-hayv-yə], MISBEHAVIOR and SAVIOR [sayv-yə], are all USA spellings. JUNIOR [joon-yə], SENIOR [seen-yə]; SOLDIER; COPIER, PREMIER.

Rebels' Reasons The first few words do not have <ior> spells [ee-or] because Americans have contracted *behaviour* to *behavior, saviour* to *savior* and so we shall meet and decode them again later. The Romans contracted *juvenior* 'more juvenile' to *junior,* and used *senior* for older, meaning 'more senile'. In *soldier, soldierly,* and *soldiery* we do not hear a glide because here <di> spells [j], which we shall discuss further when we meet *gradual. Copier* and *premier* are rebels — they do not let Little Imp work wonders. They should spell [cohp-ee-er] and [preem-ee-er]. We already know that *copy* is a rebel as it spells [kop-ee] but does not have double gate <pp> to keep [o] short. It is a Rebel Lemon. *Premier* is recorded to spell [prem-ee-er] by the Oxford Dictionary, and yet *premium* spells [pree-mee-um]. In Australia, Rex Text often dictates that *premier* spells [preem-ee-er]. In other words, RexText and Queen Quill overcome King Sound and Queen Speech because people read the written word, the text, and follow the rules. They do not rely on the sound and speech of others.

Some old words adopted from French can be called rebels because we let <i> spell [ee] in the first syllable. They were adopted long ago and instead of changing <ier> to spell [I-er] they merged their "glide and roar" sounds and so <ier> now spells [eer] in these words. *Fierce* originally meant wild beast, a feral animal, unrelated to *fiery*. If we agree that the following rebels have lost their "glide and roar" [ee-er] sound we can let them join the words in Part Four in which <ie> spells [ee].

BIER, FIERCE, TIER, PIER, PIERCE, PIERCING. Also CHIFFONIER, in which terminal <ier> spells [eer] instead of [ee-er] as in *bandolier*.

As we know, first syllables of stem words use <i> and <y> to spell [I].
In the following words <i> has replaced <y> spells [I], either in single-syllable free stem words or in the single-syllable bound stems of words. The words are all verbs which take suffix <er> to form new words meaning someone or something that does that verb. If I *notify*, I am a *notifier*. If I *cry*, I am a *crier*. If you *defy* me, you are a *defier*. If you *occupy* a house, you are the *occupier*.

We met some of the words in the next list in Part One, e.g., *defy*. Knowing how to blend, how to decode <ce> into [s], and with the help of Fairy E and Bossy R we can now read all the following words in which <y> spells [I] and words in which <i> has replaced <y>, simply because <y> is not normally allowed inside English words.

List 3-86A Glide and Roar. <i> glides as [I], having replaced <y> spells [I].
ACIDIFY — ACIDIFIER, AMPLIFY — AMPLIFIER, APPLY — APPLIER, CERTIFY — CERTIFIER, CLARIFY — CLARIFIER, CLASSIFY — CLASSIFIER, CODIFY — CODIFIER, COMPLY — COMPLIER, CRY — CRIER, DECRY — DECRIER, DEFY — DEFIER, DEHUMIDIFY — DEHUMIDIFIER, DEIFY — DEIFIER, DENY — DENIER, DIVERSIFY — DIVERSIFIER, DO — DOER [doo-er], DRY — DRIER, EDIFY — EDIFIER, EMULSIFY — EMULSIFIER, FALSIFY — FALSIFIER, FLY — FLIER/ — FLYER, FRY — FRIER, FORTIFY — FORTIFIER, GENTRIFY — GENTRIFIER, GLORIFY — GLORIFIER, GO — GOER [goh-er], IDENTIFY — IDENTIFIER, INDEMNIFY — INDEMNIFIER, INTENSIFY — INTENSIFIER, JUSTIFY — JUSTIFIER, LIQUEFY — LIQUEFIER, MAGNIFY — MAGNIFIER, MODIFY — MODIFIER, MULTIPLY — MULTIPLIER, NOTIFY — NOTIFIER, NULLIFY — NULLIFIER, OCCUPY — OCCUPIER, OSSIFY — OSSIFIER, PACIFY — PACIFIER, PERSONIFY — PERSONIFIER, PLY — PLIER/PLYER, PRY — PRIER/PRYER, PURIFY — PURIFIER, QUALIFY — QUALIFIER, QUANTIFY — QUANTIFIER, RAREFY — RAREFIER, RATIFY — RATIFIER, RECTIFY — RECTIFIER, SANCTIFY — SANCTIFIER, SCARIFY — SCARIFIER, SIGNIFY — SIGNIFIER, SIMPLIFY — SIMPLIFIER, SPECIFY — SPECIFIER, SUPPLY — SUPPLIER, TESTIFY — TESTIFIER, TRY — TRIER, UNIFY — UNIFIER, VERIFY — VERIFIER, VIE — VIER, VILIFY — VILIFIER.

List 3-86B Glide and Roar, <i> glides as [I], as it's in the first syllable.
BRIAR*, BRIER*, DIARY, FIERY*, LIAR*, HIERARCHY <ch> =[k], HIEROGLYPH, HIEROGLYPHIC, PLIERS, PRIOR *adj.* as in *prior* position. PRIOR TO *adverb*, PRIOR *noun*, head monk. PRIORESS *noun* head nun, PRIORITY, PRIORY.
Brier [brI-er] is unusual, it is a stem word and other stem words ending *ier* are pronounced [eer], like *pier*, which we shall meet in Part Four. *Drier, flier, multiplier* and even *pliers* are not stem words for they have the suffix *–er*. *Brier* can also be spelt *briar*. [brI-ar].
Fiery is the old way of writing *fire* <y>, based on *fier*. It has remained, but *fier* changed to *fire*.
*Note that if I *lie*, tell untruths, I am a *liar*. *Liar* is one of two words in which the suffix —*ar* creates a noun from a verb, along with *beggar*.

List 3-87 Glide and Roar in which <i> glides spelling its Continental long sound [ee], as it's not in first syllable.
AORTA, ANTERIOR, BANDOLIER, BARBECUER, BARRIER, BARRIER CREAM, BARRIER REEF, BOMBARDIER, BRASSIERE* *fossil final* <e>, BRAZIER, BRIGADIER, BULLTERRIER, CARRIER, CARRIER PIGEON, CARRIER-BAG, CASHIER, CAVALIER, CHANDELIER <ch>=[sh],

CHEVALIER <ch>=[sh], CLOTHIER [klohdh-ee-er], COCHLEAR <ch> = [k], COERCE*, COERCIVE, COSTUMIER, CROSIER, DETERIORATE, DOSSIER, EXCELSIOR, EXTERIOR, FARRIER, FINANCIER, FLUORESCENT, FLUORIDE, FOX-TERRIER, FRONTIER, FUSILIER, FURRIER [fu-ree-er] noun, FURRIER [fer-ree-er] adj., GLACIER, GLAZIER, GLUER, GRAZIER, GRENADIER, GONDOLIER, HARRIER [ha-ree-or], HOTELIER, HUMIDIFIER, INFERIOR, INTERIOR, JAGUAR, LINEAR, METEOR, METEORIC, METEORITE, METEOROLOGIST, METEOROLOGY, METEOROLOGICAL, OSIER, PANNIER, PHOTOCOPIER, POSTERIOR, PUERILE, PUERPERAL, PURSUER, QUARRIER, QUEUER, RACKETIER, RAPIER, RECTILINEAR, RESCUER, SANATORIUM, SKI-ER, SUBDUER, SUER, SUPERIOR, TARSIER, TERRIER, THEOREM, THEORETICAL, THEORIST, THEORIZE, THEORY, TUART*, ULTERIOR, VALUER, WARRIOR [wo-ree-or], WORRIER [wu-ree-or]. <u>Proper Nouns</u> FEBRUARY, JANUARY. <u>Names</u> STUART.

Brassiere is pronounced the French way, ending [air], and also with an unstressed English [er], but more often just as the abbreviation *bra* [brar].

Tuart rhymes with *Stuart* for they both obey the Special Rule that if <u> spells [yoo] after <t>, then <tu> spells [choo]. However, since *tuart* was also recorded by the early settlers in WA as *tooart*, it may be that its parent Ab'l language word did not match *Stuart*, probably had no yod. Our pretty student with tulips from Stuart on the website's Photo Gallery reminds us that when <u> spells [yoo] after <t>, then <tu> spells [choo].

As we know, there are two types of suffixes. The 'flexible suffixes' tell us about the word they are attached to — which we can liken to a dog's flexible tail. They do not change their word into another word, with a different meaning. They do not change adjectives into nouns or vice versa. They just tell us about the word they are attached to, **how many**, (plural suffixes *-s, -es*), **when**, (tense markers *–s, -es, -ed;* verb participle suffixes *–ed, -ing*), **whose** (ownership suffixes *-'s, -s'*) or **how much,** (*-er, -est*).

Suffixes which tell us **how much** are added to adjectives very easily if they end in consonants: *fat, fatter, fattest.* If the adjective ends with a vowel, e.g., *sly*, we hear a glide and roar, *slyer*, and then a glide and yap, *slyest*. In some single-syllable adjectives <y> is replaced by <i> inside words where it glides as [I]. In others <y> remains and is allowed inside words because replacing it with an <i> would cause problems. For instance, *spriest* would match *priest* in looks but not in sound. So <y> remains in *spryest*.

List 3-88A
<u><i> and <y> glide as [I].</u>
<u>Glide and Roar</u> in DRIER, SHYER, SLYER, SPRYER, WRYER.
<u>Glide and Yap</u> in DRIEST, SHYEST, SLYEST, SPRYEST, WRYEST.

There is another kind of suffix, which I call a *deriving* suffix. It changes the meaning of a word, often changing a noun into an adjective. A word, travelling down one river, is 'derivered' into another river. It's easier for us to imagine a word de-railed from one railway track to another but this word was made when river travel was common. One word is derived from another by adding a deriving suffix — or prefix. They can be tiny, like the <y> we add to nouns to make them into adjectives, as for *bone, bony* or *mud, muddy*. Then if we want to say **how** bony or muddy we can add a tail, a flexible suffix, like <er> or <est>.

As we know, <y> is not welcome inside English words and so <y> changes to <i> in this case and, as it's never in the first syllable when it's been added as a suffix, <i> always glides as [ee]. We can read them all with the help of Little Imp and everything we have met so far along the 'road to reading'. Enjoy!

List 3-88B
<u>Stem <y>, <y> spells [ee]</u>

ANGRY, ARTY, BALMY, BATTY, BEEFY, BITCHY, BLOODY, BLURRY, BOGGY, BONY, BONNY, BOOZY, BOSSY, BOTCHY, BOXY, BRINY, BRISTLY, BROODY, BUBBLY, BULKY, BUMPY, CATCHY, CATTY, CHALKY, CHANCY, CHATTY, CHEEKY, CHEERY, CHEESY, CHILLY, CHINTZY, CHIPPY, CHIRPY, CHUBBY, CHUNKY, CLASSY, CLINGY, CLOGGY, CLUMSY, COCKY, COMELY *f*, COMFY *f*, CORKY, CORNY, COSY, COSTLY, CRABBY, CRAFTY, CRAGGY, CRANKY, CRAPPY *slang*, CRAZY, CREEPY, CRINKLY, CRISPY, CRUDDY *slang*, CRUMBY, CRUSTY, CUDDLY, CURLY, CURVY, CUSHY, DIRTY, DIZZY, DODGY, DOPY, DORKY *slang*, DOTTY, DRESSY, DRIPPY, DROOPY, DUSKY, DUSTY, EDGY, EERY, EMPTY, FANCY, FATTY, FILTHY, FLABBY, FLAKY, FLASHY, FLIGHTY, FLIMSY, FLINTY, FLIRTY, FLOPPY, FLUFFY, FLUKY, FOGGY, FOLKSY, FOXY, FRILLY, FRISKY, FRIZZY, FROSTY, FROTHY, FRUMPY, FUNKY *slang*, FUNNY, FURRY, FUSSY, FUSTY, FUZZY, GASSY, GEEKY *slang*, GIDDY, GIGGLY, GLARY, GLASSY, GLITZY *slang*, GLOBBY *slang*, GLOOMY, GLOSSY, GODLY, GOOFY *slang*, GOOY *slang*, GORY, GREEDY, GRIMY, GRITTY, GRIZZLY, GROGGY, GROOVY, GROTTY *slang*, GRUBBY, GRUMPY, GUSHY, GUSTY, GUTSY, HANDY, HAPPY, HARDY, HASTY, HAZY, HEFTY, HILLY, HOLY, HUFFY, HUNGRY, HUNKY, HUSKY, ICY, IFFY *slang*, INKY, ITCHY, JAZZY, JOLLY, JUMPY, KINDLY, KINKY, KNOBBY, KNOTTY, KOOKY *slang*, LACY, LANKY, LAZY, LEGGY, LIKELY, LIVELY, LOFTY, LONELY, LOONY, LOOPY, LOVELY, LUCKY, LUMPY, MANGY, MARSHY, MERRY, MESSY, MIGHTY, MISTY, MOODY, MUCKY, MUDDY, MURKY, MUSHY, NASTY, NATTY, NEEDY, NERDY *slang*, NERVY, NIFTY, NIPPY, NOSY, NUTTY, PATCHY, PESKY, PLUCKY, POTTY *slang*, PRETTY, PRICY, PRICKLY, PRISSY, PUDGY, PUSHY, QUIRKY, RATTY, RISKY, RITZY*, ROCKY, ROPY, ROSY, RUSTY, SALTY, SANDY, SCABBY, SCANTY, SCARY, SCRUFFY, SEEDY, SHABBY, SHADY, SHAGGY, SHAKY, SHAPELY, SHIFTY, SHINY, SHODDY, SHRUBBY, SICKLY, SILKY, SILLY, SKETCHY, SKIMPY, SKINNY, SLIMY, SLINKY, SLUSHY, SLUTTY, SMELLY, SMOGGY, SMOKY, SMUTTY, SNAKY, SNAPPY, SNAZZY, SNOBBY, SNOOPY, SNOOTY, SNOTTY, SOGGY, SOOTY, SOPPY, SORRY, SPEEDY, SPICY, SPIFFY, SPINY, SPOOKY, SPORTY, SPOTTY, SPRINGY, SPUNKY, STARRY, STEELY, STICKY, STINGY, STODGY, STONY, STORMY, STURDY, SULKY, SULTRY, SUNNY, SURLY, SWANKY, TACKY, TANGY, TARDY, TASTY, TEENY, TEENSY, THIRSTY, THORNY, THRIFTY, TIDY, TINNY, TINY, TOOTHY, TRASHY, TRENDY, TUBBY, TWISTY, TWITCHY, UGLY, UNHAPPY, UNHOLY, UNLIKELY, WHACKY, WHEEZY, WIRY, WISPY, WITTY, WOBBLY, WONKY, WOOLLY, WOOLY USA, WOOZY, WORDY, WORLDLY, WORTHY, WRIGGLY, WRINKLY, YUCKY, YUMMY, ZANY, ZIPPY.

*Ritzy is an eponym. Lawyers representing the holder of the trade mark name for the luxurious Ritz Hotel ask that *ritzy* be deleted entirely from the dictionary. One can also 'put on the ritz', by acting very posh.

<y> <i> <er> Glide and Roar

ANGRIER, ARTIER, BALMIER, BATTIER, BEEFIER, BITCHIER, BLOODIER, BLUER, BLURRIER, BOGGIER, BONIER, BONNIER, BOOZIER, BOSSIER, BOTCHIER, BOXIER, BRINIER, BRISTLIER, BROODIER, BUBBLIER, BULKIER, BUMPIER, CATCHIER, CATTIER, CHALKIER, CHANCIER, CHATTIER, CHEEKIER, CHEERIER, CHEESIER, CHILLIER, CHINTZIER, CHIPPIER, CHIRPIER, CHUBBIER, CHUNKIER, CLASSIER, CLINGIER, CLOGGIER, CLUMSIER, COCKIER, COMELIER, COMFIER, CORKIER, CORNIER, COSIER, COSTLIER, CRABBIER, CRAFTIER, CRAGGIER, CRANKIER, CRAPPIER *slang*, CRAZIER, CREEPIER, CRINKLIER, CRISPIER, CRUDDIER *slang*, CRUMBIER, CRUSTIER, CUDDLIER, CURLIER, CURVIER, CUSHIER, DIRTIER, DIZZIER, DODGIER, DOPIER, DORKIER *slang*, DOTTIER, DRESSIER, DRIPPIER, DROOPIER, DUSKIER, DUSTIER, EDGIER, EERIER, EMPTIER, FANCIER, FATTIER, FILTHIER, FLABBIER, FLAKIER, FLASHIER, FLIGHTIER, FLIMSIER, FLINTIER, FLIRTIER, FLOPPIER, FLUFFIER, FLUKIER, FOGGIER, FOLKSIER,

FOXIER, FRILLIER, FRISKIER, FRIZZIER, FROSTIER, FROTHIER, FRUMPIER, FUNKIER *slang*, FUNNIER, FURRIER, FUSSIER, FUSTIER, FUZZIER, GASSIER, GEEKIER *slang*, GIDDIER, GIGGLIER, GLARIER, GLASSIER, GLITZIER *slang*, GLOBBIER *slang*, GLOOMIER, GLOSSIER, GODLIER, GOOFIER *slang*, GOOIER *slang*, GORIER, GREEDIER, GRIMIER, GRITTIER, GRIZZLIER, GROGGIER, GROOVIER, GROTTIER *slang*, GRUBBIER, GRUMPIER, GUSHIER, GUSTIER, GUTSIER, HANDIER, HAPPIER, HARDIER, HASTIER, HAZIER, HEFTIER, HILLIER, HOLIER, HUFFIER, HUNGRIER, HUNKIER, HUSKIER, ICIER, IFFIER *slang*, INKIER, ITCHIER, JAZZIER, JOLLIER, JUMPIER, KINDLIER, KINKIER, KNOBBIER, KNOTTIER, KOOKIER, LACIER, LANKIER, LAZIER, LEGGIER, LIKELIER, LIVELIER, LOFTIER, LONELIER, LOONIER, LOOPIER, LOVELIER, LUCKIER, LUMPIER, MANGIER, MARSHIER, MERRIER, MESSIER, MIGHTIER, MISTIER, MOODIER, MUCKIER, MUDDIER, MURKIER, MUSHIER, NASTIER, NATTIER, NEEDIER, NERDIER, NERVIER, NIFTIER, NIPPIER, NOSIER, NUTTIER, PATCHIER, PESKIER, PLUCKIER, POTTIER, PRETTIER, PRICIER, PRICKLIER, PRISSIER, PUDGIER, PUSHIER, QUIRKIER, RATTIER, RISKIER, RITZIER, ROCKIER, ROPIER, ROSIER, RUSTIER, SALTIER, SANDIER, SCABBIER, SCANTIER, SCARIER, SCRUFFIER, SEEDIER, SHABBIER, SHADIER, SHAGGIER, SHAKIER, SHAPELIER, SHIFTIER, SHINIER, SHODDIER, SHRUBBIER, SICKLIER, SILKIER, SILLIER, SKETCHIER, SKIMPIER, SKINNIER, SLIMIER, SLINKIER, SLUSHIER, SLUTTIER, SMELLIER, SMOGGIER, SMOKIER, SMUTTIER, SNAKIER, SNAPPIER, SNAZZIER, SNOBBIER, SNOOPIER, SNOOTIER, SNOTTIER, SOGGIER, SOOTIER, SOPPIER, SORRIER, SPEEDIER, SPICIER, SPIFFIER, SPINIER, SPOOKIER, SPORTIER, SPOTTIER, SPRINGIER, SPUNKIER, STARRIER, STEELIER, STICKIER, STINGIER, STODGIER, STONIER, STORMIER, STURDIER, SULKIER, SULTRIER, SUNNIER, SURLIER, SWANKIER, TACKIER, TANGIER, TARDIER, TASTIER, TEENIER, TEENSIER, THIRSTIER, THORNIER, THRIFTIER, TIDIER, TINNIER, TINIER, TOOTHIER, TRASHIER, TRENDIER, , TRUER, TUBBIER, TWISTIER, TWITCHIER, UGLIER, UNHAPPIER, UNHOLIER, UNLIKELIER, WHACKIER, WHEEZIER, WIRIER, WISPIER, WITTIER, WOBBLIER, WONKIER, WOOLLIER, WOOLIER USA, WOOZIER, WORDIER, WORLDLIER, WORTHIER, WRIGGLIER, WRINKLIER, YUCKIER, YUMMIER, ZANIER, ZIPPIER.

<y> <i><est> Glide and Yap

ANGRIEST, ARTIEST, BALMIEST, BATTIEST, BEEFIEST, BITCHIEST, BLOODIEST, BLURRIEST, BOGGIEST, BONIEST, BONNIEST, BOOZIEST, BOSSIEST, BOTCHIEST, BOXIEST, BRINIEST, BRISTLIEST, BROODIEST, BUBBLIEST, BULKIEST, BUMPIEST, CATCHIEST, CATTIEST, CHALKIEST, CHANCIEST, CHATTIEST, CHEEKIEST, CHEERIEST, CHEESIEST, CHILLIEST, CHINTZIEST, CHIPPIEST, CHIRPIEST, CHUBBIEST, CHUNKIEST, CLASSIEST, CLINGIEST, CLOGGIEST, CLUMSIEST, COCKIEST, COMELIEST, COMFIEST *f*, CORKIEST, CORNIEST, COSIEST, COSTLIEST, CRABBIEST, CRAFTIEST, CRAGGIEST, CRANKIEST, CRAPPIEST *slang*, CRAZIEST, CREEPIEST, CRINKLIEST, CRISPIEST, CRUDDIEST *slang*, CRUMBIEST, CRUSTIEST, CUDDLIEST, CURLIEST, CURVIEST, CUSHIEST, DIRTIEST, DIZZIEST, DODGIEST, DOPIEST, DORKIEST *slang*, DOTTIEST, DRESSIEST, DRIPPIEST, DROOPIEST, DUSKIEST, DUSTIEST, EDGIEST, EERIEST, EMPTIEST, FANCIEST, FATTIEST, FILTHIEST, FLABBIEST, FLAKIEST, FLASHIEST, FLIGHTIEST, FLIMSIEST, FLINTIEST, FLIRTIEST, FLOPPIEST, FLUFFIEST, FLUKIEST, FOGGIEST, FOLKSIEST, FOXIEST, FRILLIEST, FRISKIEST, FRIZZIEST, FROSTIEST, FROTHIEST, FRUMPIEST, FUNKIEST *slang*, FUNNIEST, FURRIEST, FUSSIEST, FUSTIEST, FUZZIEST, GASSIEST, GEEKIEST *slang*, GIDDIEST, GIGGLIEST, GLARIEST, GLASSIEST, GLITZIEST *slang*, GLOBBIEST *slang*, GLOOMIEST, GLOSSIEST, GODLIEST, GOOFIEST *slang*, GOOIEST *slang*, GORIEST, GREEDIEST, GRIMIEST, GRITTIEST, GRIZZLIEST, GROGGIEST, GROOVIEST,

GROTTIEST *slang*, GRUBBIEST, GRUMPIEST, GUSHIEST, GUSTIEST, GUTSIEST, HANDIEST, HAPPIEST, HARDIEST, HASTIEST, HAZIEST, HEFTIEST, HILLIEST, HOLIEST, HUFFIEST, HUNGRIEST, HUNKIEST, HUSKIEST, ICIEST, IFFIEST *slang*, INKIEST, ITCHIEST, JAZZIEST, JOLLIEST, JUMPIEST, KINDLIEST, KINKIEST, KNOBBIEST, KNOTTIEST, KOOKIEST, LACIEST, LANKIEST, LAZIEST, LEGGIEST, LIKELIEST, LIVELIEST, LOFTIEST, LONELIEST, LOONIEST, LOOPIEST, LOVELIEST, LUCKIEST, LUMPIEST, MANGIEST, MARSHIEST, MERRIEST, MESSIEST, MIGHTIER, MISTIEST, MOODIEST, MUCKIEST, MUDDIEST, MURKIEST, MUSHIEST, NASTIEST, NATTIEST, NEEDIEST, NERDIEST, NERVIEST, NIFTIEST, NIPPIEST, NOSIEST, NUTTIEST, PATCHIEST, PESKIEST, PLUCKIEST, POTTIEST PRETTIEST, PRICIEST, PRICKLIEST, PRISSIEST, PUDGIEST, PUSHIEST, QUIRKIEST, RATTIEST, RISKIEST, RITZIEST, ROCKIEST, ROPIEST, ROSIEST, RUSTIEST, SALTIEST, SANDIEST, SCABBIEST, SCANTIEST, SCARIEST, SCRUFFIEST, SEEDIEST, SHABBIEST, SHADIEST, SHAGGIEST, SHAKIEST, SHAPELIEST, SHIFTIEST, SHINIEST, SHODDIEST, SHRUBBIEST, SICKLIEST, SILKIEST, SILLIEST, SKETCHIEST, SKIMPIEST, SKINNIEST, SLIMIEST, SLINKIEST, SLUSHIEST, SLUTTIEST, SMELLIEST, SMOGGIEST, SMOKIEST, SMUTTIEST, SNAKIEST, SNAPPIEST, SNAZZIEST, SNOBBIEST, SNOOPIEST, SNOOTIEST, SNOTTIEST, SOGGIEST, SOOTIEST, SOPPIEST, SORRIEST, SPEEDIEST, SPICIEST, SPIFFIEST, SPINIEST, SPOOKIEST, SPORTIEST, SPOTTIEST, SPRINGIEST, SPUNKIEST, STARRIEST, STEELIEST, STICKIEST, STINGIEST, STODGIEST, STONIEST, STORMIEST, STURDIEST, SULKIEST, SULTRIEST, SUNNIEST, SURLIEST, SWANKIEST, TACKIEST, TANGIEST, TARDIEST, TASTIEST, TEENIEST, TEENSIEST, THIRSTIEST, THORNIEST, THRIFTIEST, TIDIEST, TINNIEST, TINIEST, TOOTHIEST, TRASHIEST, TRENDIEST, TUBBIEST, TWISTIEST, TWITCHIEST, UGLIEST, UNHAPPIEST, UNHOLIEST, UNLIKELIEST, WHACKIEST, WHEEZIEST, WIRIEST, WISPIEST, WITTIEST, WOBBLIEST, WONKIEST, WOOLLIEST, WOOLIEST USA, WOOZIEST, WORDIEST, WORLDLIEST, WORTHIEST, WRIGGLIEST, WRINKLIEST, YUCKIEST, YUMMIEST, ZANIEST, ZIPPIEST.

Glide and Skate — *abbreviate, unevaluated.*

Glide and Yap is modified when long vowels glide across syllable boundaries to vowels which are kept long by the "magic action of Fairy E". For instance, <io> spells [I-o] in *riot* but in *diode* we hear [I-oh]. Thus, we see the Glide and Yap rule give way to the power of Fairy E. In some words [ayt] reduces to [at] to show that it is a noun, not a verb.

Rule 3-89 Glide and Skate Rule: The second vowel in 'Glide and Yap' situations gives way to the power of Fairy E, spells a long vowel sound, as in *skate*.

Reason Due to the power of Fairy E, as explained above.

Rebels MARRIAGE, CARRIAGE, VERBIAGE, FOLIAGE, TRIAGE, plus words in which <ate> spells [at] in nouns.

Rebels' Reasons As we know, there is no magic action from Fairy E in *baggage*, [bag-uuj] or [bag-əj], nor in the <age> suffix on other words. In *marriage* [ma-rəj] and *carriage* [ka-rəj], <i> is silent. It is still written because <y> in *marry* and *carry* is replaced with <i> when the suffix <age> is added. Although silent it remains to link the words with *marry* (not *mar*) and with *carry* (not *car*). The words *verbiage* [ver-bee-əj] and *foliage* [foh-lee-əj] are used less often and so they have not been worn down as much. The newly adopted word *triage* [tree-arj] retains its Continental vowels.

List 3-89

ABBREVIATE, ACCENTUATE [-choo-ayt], ACTUATE [-choo-ayt], AFFILIATE*, ALLEVIATE, *APPROPRIATE, ATTENUATE, ATTENUATED, AVIATOR, BINUCLEATE, COLLEGIATE, CONCILIATE, CREATE, CREATIVE, CREATIVELY, CREATOR, DEFOLIATE, DEFOLIATOR,

DELINEATE, DEVIATE, DIODE, DISSOCIATE, ENUNCIATE, EVACUATE*, EVALUATE, EVENTUATE [-choo-ayt], EXFOLIATE, EXPATRIATE, EXPIATE, EXPROPRIATE, EXTENUATE, FILIATE, FLUCTUATE, GLADIATOR*, GLADIATORIAL, GRADUATE* verb, HUMILIATE, IMMEDIATE, INAPPROPRIATE, INCHOATE <ch>=[k], INEBRIATE, INFURIATE, INSINUATE, INTERCOLLEGIATE, INTERMEDIATE, IRRADIATE, LINEATE, MEDIATE, MEDIATOR, MENSTRUATE, MISAPPROPRIATE, MONONUCLEATE, MULTINUCLEATE, OBVIATE, OPIATE, ORIOLE, PALLIATE, PERMEATE, PETIOLE, PROCREATE, RADIATE, RADIATOR, RECREATE, REPATRIATE, REPUDIATE, RETALIATE*, ROSEATE, RE-CREATE, STRIATED, SUPERANNUATE, TOLUATE, TUATARA/TUATERA, UNATTENUATED, UNEVALUATED.

Affiliate spells [a-fil-ee-ayt], and note how Little Imp works wonders on others but not on himself, not on <fil>.

Appropriate as a verb means to make something one, fit one's personal need. As an adjective, it means fitting, suitable.

Evacuate has only a single <c>, because the third syllable from the end, being stressed, is short without the need of <cc>.

Gladiator spells [glad-ee-ay-tor] because it is built on the Latin noun *gladius* meaning 'sword' (Etymonline) in which the third syllable from the end is stressed and short and therefore does not need double gates.

*{Graduate} as a noun is not listed yet.

Retaliate spells [re-tal-ee-ayt] and therefore should have <ll>. However, the dictionary elders wanted to link it to the Latin word *talio* which meant 'punishment as severe as the wrong done' and combined with *re-* it became the verb *retaliate*, 'to repay in kind,' (Ayto p. 442.) Also, the third syllable from the end is stressed and short without <ll>.

Yod Fusions, [sh], ch], [zh] and [j].

We are now going to examine ways to write [sh], ch], [zh] and [j]. We shall review some spelling codes and meet new ones, for these four consonants.

We learnt to spell [sh] with <sh> at 2-96 and heard why <s> spells [sh] in *sure* at 3-33. Sometimes <sc> spells [sh], we heard, in *fascist* and *crescendo* at 2-83. Consonant [sh] is even spelt <ch>, in *chef,* as we saw at 2-95.

We learnt to spell [ch] with <ch> at 2-91, and with <tu> at 1-41 in *tulip.*

We were introduced to [zh] in *regime* at 3-23 and in some rebels at 3-24, at the end of *massage* for example, and then we read [zh] again, in *azure* at 3-36.

We learnt in the Ground Rules at the start of Part One that <j> spells [j]. Then we found out that <gi> and <ge> can spell [j] at 1-45, as in *gin, cage* and *gem*. Then that <ggi> and <gge> spell [j] between a prefix and a stem, as in *suggest,* but not between a stem and a suffix, as in *tugging* — see 1-45. Also that <du> spells [j] in *duty*, at 1-54, and in *duly*, at 1-58 and at 3-35, we heard [j] in "Endure Duty".

Now we shall meet other letter codes. For example, we shall learn that <t> can spell [sh], if it is in *nation*, for instance. When this happens experts say <t> has been 'palatalized' because fusion with a yod involves the tongue rising towards the palate. They say palatalization has taken place. Other linguists call this 'assibilation', because air hisses through the small gap between tongue and palate. A sibilant sound is a hissing sound. Sounds [s] and [z] are already sibilant sounds, before Yod Fusion turns them into sibilant [sh] and [zh]. Sounds [d] and [j] are not sibilants until Yod Fusion aka palatalization, aka assimilation, has taken place. Cummings p. 407 calls [sh], [ch], [j] and [zh] palatal sibilants. I call them Yod Fusions when they are produced by fusion with a yod. We are now going to focus on decoding Yod Fusions, on how to read, for example, "Occasional detention under dual supervision in a nation of one million lions."

While French was the official language of England many new words arrived from Paris which ended with the suffix —*ion*. The English gave up their own words and copied the French. For instance, they used French *nation* in place of *folc,* gave up *landwaru* (inhabitants of the land) and used *population*, pronouncing it [ee-on] at the end, as they did for *million, billion* and *trillion,* words that had no English equivalent. They said 'in *detention*' instead of 'in *prison*' and made *decisions* in court *sessions*. These words all ended the French way, with [ee-on], until around 1600. As we have heard, when the English revived their language, they made it sound different to French, by raising the pitch of some long vowels, and bending others. This was when *mate* stopped spelling [mart] and began spelling [mayt] and when *I* no longer rhymed with *me* but began spelling [I]. This process took place during the GVS, 1450 – 1650. After that, the English took another step away from French pronunciation by stressing the beginning of French words, saying them the English way. The French give even stress to syllables but, as we know, English syllables alternate in stress, and most suffixes, unless on verbs, are unstressed. However, when the English stressed the start of *million* and de-stressed its suffix, the result was two weak beats at the end of the word: [mil-ee-on]. This became [mil-yon], to fit the English 'tum-te-tum-te' rhythm of speech. As you can see, little unstressed <i> shrank to a yod sound, unstressed [y]. This happened in words in which —*ion* followed <n>, too, as in *minion*. When *nation* was said the English way even more interesting things happened — palatalization! Before we hear how *nation* and many other words were palatized, let's hear the rule for words like *million* and *minion*.

Rule 3-90 In the suffix —*ion*, <i> spells [y] when it follows either <l> or <n> after a short vowel.
Reason This maintains the rhythm of English by preventing two weak beats at the end of a word.
We do not see *antlion* nor *dandelion* here because they are compound words, see 3-80. We do not see *ganglion, helion, perihelion* and *apihelion* here because <lion> does not follow a short vowel, see 3-81.
Rebel UNION [yoon-yon].
Rebel's Reason In this word, the suffix —*ion* spells [yon] after a long vowel. Why? Possibly because a long vowel is the only way to separate it from *onion* which according to Etymonline is actually the same word! 'Union in Latin is *unionem* "oneness, unity, a uniting," also in Latin meaning "a single pearl or onion," from *unus* "one.'
Q. Does this happen in words ending <mion> and <rion>?
Ans. No. Very few words end <mion> and they are rarely used, e.g., *acromion*, which spells [ak-roh-mee-on], (the outer extremity of the shoulder blade). It appears that in none of them does <mion> follows a short vowel. In words ending <rion> it is impossible to say [ryon] as one syllable. Instead, words like *clarion* and *carrion* end with [ree-on]. *Clarion,* for instance, spells [kla-ree-on] with a tum-te-tum beat. As we know, 'R is bossy after vowels, but not between them' and so R does not bond silently with <a> to spell [ar]. Instead <r> spells [r] at the start of the next syllable, [ree]. See 3-83.
List 3-90 in which <ion> spells [yon]
BATTALION, BILLION, BILLIONTH [th], BULLION, BUNION*, COMMUNION, COMPANION, COMPANIONABLE, COMPANIONSHIP, DOMINION, HELLION *slang*, MEDALLION, MILLION, MILLIONTH [th], MINION, MULLION, ONION* *f* [un-yon], OPINION, PAVILION, PILLION, PINION, REBELLION, REUNION, SCULLION, STALLION, TRILLION, VERMILLION, ZILLION, ZILLIONTH [th].
Bunion should be *bunnion* because it originates from *bunny* which was an East Anglian word for 'a little bump', originally a bump was a *bugne,* ancestor word to *bun. Bunny* rabbits — *bunnies* — look like little bumps on the landscape. So add this to the list of Lemon Rebels.
Onion should be *onnion* — another Lemon Rebel.

Rule 3-91 In suffixes —*ia* and —*ial,* <i> can spell [y] after <l> and <m> and <n> if very unstressed.

Reason Suffixes *—ia* and *—ial* are more likely to spell [yuu] and [yuul] at the end of long words, where they are least stressed, as in *petunia* but not in *zinnia*; in *anticolonial,* but not as often in *colonial.* The rule says 'can spell' because *—ia* can also spell [ee-ar]. Some say that *academia* spells [ak-u-deem-ee-ar] and some say it spells [ak-u-deem-yuu], (but in both choices <e> can also spell Continental long [ay] rather than [ee].) We saw *annual* and *manual* spelling [an-yuul] and [man-yuul] in the Glide and Yap list, when they are destressed at the end.

List 3-91

ALLELUIA*, AMIABLE [aym-yə-buul], ANTI-COLONIAL, BEGONIA, BIENNIAL, BINOMIAL, BRILLIANT [bril-ənt], COLONIAL, EGOMANIA, FAMILIAR [fə-mil-yə], FAMILIARITY, FAMILIARIZE, FAMILIARIZATION, INSOMNIA, MACADAMIA, MEMORABILIA [mem-ru-bil-yə], PECULIAR [pe-kyool-yə], PETUNIA, TRINOMIAL, VALIANT [vayl-yuunt], but this is more and more often pronounced [val-yuunt].

*Some Continental languages use <j> to spell [y], so *alleluia* [al-ee-loo-ya] is also *hallelujah* [hal-ay-loo-yar]. The OED lists *halleluja* but in Latin it is both *hallelujah* and *alleluia*.

Names DANIEL and ELLIOT [dan-yuul] and [el-yot].

The DAHLIA plant is pronounced [dayl-yuu] in Australia (but as this flower is named after the botanist Anders Dahl it could also spell evenly stressed Continental [darl-ee-ar].) *Dahlia* is an eponym.

CAMELLIA Australians shorten it to [kam-eel-yuu], but it was originally [kam-el-lee-ar], after botanist Kamel. *Camellia* is an eponym.

Q. Why didn't spelling change when pronunciation changed?

Ans. Two reasons. The dictionary committee liked to spell words in ways which showed where they came from. For instance the suffix *—ion* came from France and respelling it <yon> in words which say it that way would break the link to the French language. The other reason is that writing *milyon* instead of *million* was blocked by the dictionary committee. They decided that <y> was not allowed inside a word unless it was an adopted Greek word. They removed it from words which did not have Greek ancestors and replaced it with <i>. This is why contestants in spelling bees are allowed to ask "Is it of Greek origin?" **Note:** The letter <y> is allowed inside new compound words if it ends a word inside the compound word, e.g., *jerrycan, tommyguns, willywillies.* Four complex words, i.e., stems with suffixes: *babyhood, ladyhood, ladylike* and *ladyship* are rebels with a reason.

Not needed but nice to know. Although <y> was exchanged for <i> inside English words it was never removed from Welsh words. If you go to Wales, you will see <y> inside lots of words. Maybe you will meet Bronwyn and Emlyn, in Caerdydd (Cardiff), 'in a small dining room' – "yr ystafell fwyta fach" – and 'enjoy magnificent views' – "mwynhewch y golygfeydd ysblennydd!" Now back to things we need to know.

When *nation* was said the English way, stressing the first syllable, and ending on a weak suffix, this meant for the suffix *—ion* it would have ended on two weak beats. 'Tum-te-te' is not the rhythm of English. So an interesting thing happened — Yod Fusion!

In English, in some words, in the suffix *—ion,* and also in suffixes *—ia, —ian, —ia, —ience, —ier, —eal, —ean, —eo* and *—ual,* the first weak vowel is reduced to [y], i.e., becomes a yod. This is why we hear <i> spelling [y] in *million* — [mil-yon]. This is easier to say than [mil-ee-on] — shorter, and prevents two weak beats. When <i> spells [y] after [t], [d], [s] or [z] it's even easier to fuse yod with each consonant, which produces Yod Fusions.

Not needed but nice to know. Yod is spelt in other ways, too, e.g., with <u> in *issue.* Also, in some words, yod's fusion is incomplete, for we can still hear yod in some words. For instance, for *issue,* do you say [ishoo] or [ishyoo]? It depends on where you live. In Scotland many people think [ishoo] and even [ishyoo] is a lazy, sloppy way of speaking and they say [is-yoo]. They frown on what they call 'Estuary English'. They call it this because Londoners live on an estuary, the Thames Estuary, and pronounce it [es-choor-ree], but, in a clipped Scots accent, this is [est-yoor-ree]. Now you can see why Scots people dislike being called Scotch. They say that hissing, palatalized word, *Scotch,* is only for things, not for people, not for Scots! Now back to things we need to know.

We shall now see in which words Yod Fusion happens and which sounds are produced.

Yod Fusion [sh] — *action, vivisection.*

Rule 3-92A **Letter <t> spells [sh] after a stressed syllable and before unstressed <i> which is followed by another unstressed vowel, unless preceded by <s>.**

Reason The unstressed <i> spells a little yoddy [y] sound which fuses with [t] in order to avoid two weak beats in the suffix, as in *lotion.* In French, *lotion* ends in [ee-on]. The English shrank the first weak beat, [e], to [y] and let it fuse (or coalesce or merge) with [t]. They shrank the next weak beat [on], to [uun]. To hear which Yod Fusion is produced, say [loh-ty-uun]. Your mouth is open for the stressed vowel and the next sound has your tongue tip just behind your front teeth and then you feel the [y] way back in your throat. If you want to fuse [t] and [y] — in order to eliminate the first of the weak syllables — the only way to do it is to make a sound half way between the front teeth and the back of the throat which means you lift your tongue up near the palate, the roof of the mouth. This results in [sh]. You have palatalized [t]. This does not happen when you start with a closed mouth as in *tune,* or you start with a nearly closed mouth as in [s]. Instead you hear [ch] as in *tune* and {question}.

Rebels EQUATION, PITIABLE [pit-ee-u-buul], DUTIABLE [dyoo-tee- u-buul].

Rebels' Reasons *Equation* is the only word in which <t> spells [zh] after fusing with a yod. It should spell [sh]. All the experts and dictionaries say that *equation* spells [ee-kway-zhuun] but there is no explanation why this word breaks a very firm rule. The other rebels should be Yod Fusion words, like *satiable,* for instance. Cummings says, on page 135, that when a word has a free stem plus a suffix, we are conservative, which means we conserve the sound of the free stem, *pity.* Both *pity* and *duty* replace <y> with <i> when adding the suffix —*able* [ubuul], only because <y> is not welcome inside English words unless they originate in Greece. The other words ending <iable> are *appreciable, differentiable, vitiable, justiciable, satiable* and *sociable.* None of them have free stems.

Rule 3-92B **Single letter vowels preceding single letters spelling [sh] are stressed and long, unless spelt with <i>.**

Reason Why doesn't stressed [i] lengthen to [ee]? Why does *titian* spell [tish-uun] and not [tee-shuun]? It's because, once again, Little Imp works wonders on others but not on himself, as per Rule 3-81. As we know, English words are stressed at the beginning, unless there is a prefix, like *initial,* in which case the second syllable is stressed. Sometimes we can just guess that a start like "in" is a prefix. *Initial* comes from a Latin prefix *in—* plus *itum* from the Latin verb, *ire,* meaning "in go", or "go in, make a start." That's why the first letters of your names are called *initials*. We could re-word the rule by saying 'Single letter vowels preceding single letters spelling [sh] are stressed and long, unless that [sh] is due to fusion with a Little Imp yod.' What do you think? Can you see how some yods are actually Little Imps which have shrunk to [y] to avoid two weak beats?

Rebels DISCRETION, NATIONAL, RATION.

Rebels' Reasons *Discretion* possibly uses short [e] to separate it from *excretion.* Etymonline tells us that *ration* spelt [ray-shuun] and *national* spelt [nay-shuun-əl] until World War I, when the military pronunciation caught on. Also *national* then sounded less like *notional* [noh-shuun-əl].

List 3-92 — in which <t> i before another unstressed vowel spells [sh]

ABORTION, ACTION, ABDUCTION, ABSTENTION, ABSTRACTION, ACTIONABLE, ADDICTION, AFFECTION, AFFECTIONATE, AFFLICTION, APPORTION, ASSERTION, ATTENTION, ATTRACTION, BESTIAL*, BISECTION, BY-ELECTION, CIRCUMSPECTION, CIRCUMSTANTIAL, CIRCUMVENTION, COLLECTION, COLORATION*, COMPACTION,

COMPUNCTION, CONCOCTION, CONDUCTION, CONFECTION, CONFECTIONER, CONFECTIONERY, CONFIDENTIAL, CONFLICTION, CONJUNCTION, CONNECTION, CONSEQUENTIAL, CONSTRICTION, CONSTRUCTION, CONSTRUCTIONAL, CONTENTION CONTORTION, CONTORTIONIST, CONTRACTION, CONTRADICTION, CONVECTION, CONVENTION, CONVICTION, CORRECTION, CREDENTIAL, DECOCTION, DEDUCTION, DEFECTION, DEFERENTIAL, DEJECTION, DEMENTIA, DEPICTION, DERELICTION, DESERTION, DESTRUCTION, DETECTION, DETENTION, DICTION, DICTIONARY, DIETITIAN, DIFFERENTIAL, DIFFERENTIATE, DIFFERENTIATION, DIFFERENTIABLE *mathematical term*, DIFFRACTION DIRECTION, DISAFFECTION, DISCONNECTION, DISINFECTION, DISSATISFACTION, DISSECTION, DISTINCTION, DISTORTION, DISTRACTION, EJECTION, ELECTION, ERECTION, ESSENTIAL, EVICTION, EVIDENTIAL, EXACTION, EXERTION, EXISTENTIAL, EXPATIATE*, EXPEDIENTIAL, EXPONENTIAL, EXTINCTION, EXTRACTION, FACTION, FICTION, FRACTION, FRICTION, FUNCTION, GENUFLECTION, IMPARTIAL, IMPARTIALITIES, IMPARTIALITY, IMPARTIALLY, IMPATIENT, IMPERFECTION, INACTION, INDUCTION, INERTIA, INFECTION, INFLUENTIAL, INFRACTION, INGRATIATE*, INITIAL, INITIALLY, INITIALS, INITIATE*, INITIATIVE, INITIATOR, INJECTION, INJUNCTION, INSATIABLE, INSATIATE* *adjective*, INSERTION, INSPECTION, INSTRUCTION, INSURRECTION, INTENTION, INTERACTION, INTERCONNECTION, INTERJECTION, INTERSECTION, INTERSTITIAL, INVENTION, JUNCTION, JURISDICTION, LILLIPUTIAN, MALFUNCTION, MARTIAL, MARTIAN, MENTION, MILITIA, MILITIAMAN, NEGOTIABILITY, NEGOTIABLE, NEGOTIATE*, NEGOTIATION*, NEGOTIATOR*, NONNEGOTIABLE, NOVITIATE* *noun*, OBJECTION, OBSTRUCTION, OVERCORRECTION, PALATIAL, PARTIAL, PATIENCE, PATIENT, PENITENTIAL, PERFECTION, PORTION, POTENTIAL, PREDICTION, PREFERENTIAL, PRESIDENTIAL, PREVENTION, PRODUCTION, PROJECTION, PROPITIATE*, PROPORTION, PROTECTION, PROVIDENTIAL, PRUDENTIAL, PUTREFACTION, QUOTIENT, REACTION, RECOLLECTION, REDUCTION, REFLECTION, REINFECTION, REJECTION, RESIDENTIAL, RESTRICTION, RESURRECTION, RETENTION, REVERENTIAL, ROTATION, SANCTION, SATIABLE, SATISFACTION, SECTION, SEDUCTION, SELECTION, SEQUENTIAL, SPATIAL, SPECIATION, SUBJECTION, SUBSTANTIAL, SUBSTANTIATE, SUBTRACTION, SUCTION, TANGENTIAL, TERTIARY, TITIAN, TORRENTIAL, TRACTION, TRAJECTION, TRANSACTION, UNMENTIONABLE, VENETIAN, VIVISECTION. <u>Proper Nouns</u> DALMATIA, NASTURTIUM*, NOVA SCOTIA.

Bestial was listed earlier, spelling [bes-tee-uul] (Cambridge Dictionary), but it is also pronounced [bes-chuul] (Merriam-Webster Thesaurus.)

Coloration has dropped <u> in Anglo dictionaries. American dictionaries dropped it earlier, from the stem, *colo~~u~~r*.

Expatiate, initiate, ingratiate, insatiate, negotiate, novitiate and *propitiate*, all end in the unusual suffix <ate> which, unusually for a suffix, is stressed. This is because all these words are verbs and the end of verbs is often stressed. This is only secondary stress, not as strong as the stress before <ti>, but this means that although <i> has fused with <t> to spell [sh] it reappears as unstressed [ee] in order to maintain the tum-te-tum rhythm of English. Whilst we would expect this of verbs, like *negotiate,* and words built on verbs, like *negotiator,* this is also the case in nouns, like *novitiate,* and adjectives, like *insatiate*. This only happens with the suffix —*ate*, e.g, in *negotiate* but not in *negotiable*. Cummings discusses stress and the suffix —*ate* and the way some nouns and adjectives use it, despite lack of a matching verb, on page 151.

Nasturtium means "turned nose" in Latin, because of the plant's strong smell. As Pliny explains, it is literally "nose-twist", from *nasus* "nose" and past participle of *torquere* "to twist", (Etymonline). Gascoyne Aborigines used the same technique when inventing the word *eudamullah* to describe smelly water, literally "tilted nose", (Boston 2004, p. 45). Next time you smell something foul, note the way you twist your head, turning or tilting your nose away from the source.

Rule 3-93A If the word-sound [s] follows a stressed syllable and is before an unstressed <i> or <e> which is followed by another unstressed vowel, it changes to [sh].
Reason When [i] is followed by another weak vowel in a suffix, it shrinks to a yod which fuses with [s] and spells [sh], thus preventing two weak beats in a row, which would interrupt the tum-te-tum rhythmic flow of English. To prove this happens, say *"Miss you"* over and over, with stress on *miss,* and you will find the blend <sy> ends up spelling [sh]. "Miss you" becomes 'Mishya'. There are many ways to spell [s] — with <ss>, or with <sc> before a vowel or with <c> before <i> or <e>. The letter <x> spells [ks] after a stressed vowel, so <x> fits the rule. We heard earlier, if the suffix <al> needs to join on to a terminal [s], the letter <i> is added first: *face, facial.* We'll meet more like this in the next list — *official, provincial, racial, etc.*
N.B. If <s> follows a vowel, being a stressed vowel in this rule, it will spell [z]. It's the [s] sound which is required, and <s> does not always spell [s]. We must look at <s> and if it is single and follows a consonant it will spell [s]. Note well: - when <s> follows <r>, as in *version* for instance, then <r> is part of the digraph <er> which spells the vowel [er] and therefore <s> spells [z] not [s].
Rebels AXIAL, AXIOM.
Rebels' Reasons These words are short enough to accommodate the tum-te-tum rhythm of English speech without reducing [i] to a yod and fusing it with [t] to avoid two weak beats. They are pronounced [ak-see-al] and [ak-see-om] with the tum-te-tum rhythm of English, strongest stress being on the first syllable

Rule 3-93B Single letter vowels preceding single letters spelling [sh] are stressed and long, unless spelt with <i>.
Reason Why doesn't [i] lengthen to [ee]? Why does *titian* spell [tish-uun] and not [tee-shuun]? It's because, once again, Little Imp works wonders on others but not on himself, as per Rule 3-81. We must also remember that Little Imp cannot work wonders through 'double gates' i.e. if preceded by two consonants, as in *apprehension.* This is also true of the 'magic action' of Fairy E.
Rebels SPECIAL spells [speshuul] not [speeshuul], in ESPECIAL too.
Rebels' Reasons *Especial* and *special* mean 'having a specific quality' from Latin *specifus.* It came from French and began in English as *specifical* with <e> spells [e] in the fourth syllable from the end. This obsolete word split into *special* and *specific,* with <e> spells [e] retained in each, which helps separate *special* from {*specious*} [speesh-uus] which means 'pleasing to the sight'. (Special things/people are not necessarily specious!)

List 3-93 In which we see [s], spelt <s>, <ss>, <sc>, <ci>, <ce> and <x> all spelling [sh].
APPRECIABLE, APPRECIATE, APPREHENSION, ASCENSION, ASPHYXIA*, ASSOCIATE* *noun,* CASSIA*, ABSCISSION, ACACIA, ACCESSION, ADMISSION, AGGRESSION, ANCIENT, ANTISOCIAL, APPRECIATE, ARTIFICIAL, ASSOCIATE, BANKSIA, BENEFICIAL, BENEFICIARY, CETACEA*, CETACEAN, COEFFICIENT, COERCION, COMMERCIAL, COMMISSION, COMMISSIONAIRE, COMMISSIONER, COMPASSION, COMPLEXION, COMPREHENSION, COMPRESSION, CONCESSION, CONCUSSION, CONFESSION, CONFESSIONAL, CONSCIENCE*, CONTROVERSIAL, CRUCIAL, CRUCIFIXION, CRUSTACEA, CRUSTACEAN, DECOMMISSION, DECOMPRESSION, DEFICIENCY, DEFICIENT, DEFLEXION, DIMENSION, DEPRECIATE, DEPRESSION, DIGRESSION, DISCUSSION, DISPOSSESSION, DISSOCIATE, ECHINACEA, EFFICIENCY, EFFICIENT, EFFICIENTLY, ELECTRICIAN, EMACIATE, EMISSION, EMULSION, EXCRUCIATINGLY, EXPRESSION, FACIA*, FACIAL, FASCIA*, FINANCIAL, FISSION, FUCHSIA, *GLACIAL, *GLACIATE, GLACIER*, HESSIAN,

IMPRESSION, INEFFICIENT, INGRESSION, INSUFFICIENT, INTERCESSION, INTERGLACIAL, INTERMISSION, INTERRACIAL, JUDICIAL, JUDICIARY, MAGICIAN, MISSION, MULTIRACIAL, OBSESSION, OBSTETRICIAN, OCEAN, OFFICIAL, OFFICIAL/UNOFFICIAL, OFFICIATE, OMISSION, OPPRESSION, OPTICIAN, PASSION, PERCUSSION, PERMISSION, POLITICIAN, POSSESSION, PRECESSION, PREJUDICIAL, PROCESSION, PROFESSION, PROFICIENT, PROGRESSION, PROVINCIAL, RACIAL, RECESSION, REGRESSION, REMISSION, REPERCUSSION, REPOSSESSION, REPRESSION, RETROGRESSION, ROSACEA*, SACRIFICIAL, SECESSION, SESSION, SPECIES*, SOCIABLE, SOCIAL, SPACIAL*, SPECIOUS, SUBMISSION, SUCCESSION, SUFFICIENT, SUPERFICIAL, SUPPRESSION, SUSPICION, TRANSFIXION, TRANSGRESSION, TRANSMISSION, UNSOCIAL. <u>Proper Nouns</u> PRUSSIA, RUSSIA.

Associate as a verb ends so strongly that <c> does not spell [sh]. The noun's weaker ending means that two unstressed vowels follow <c> spells [s] and this means it spells [sh]: [u-soh-shee-ayt].

Asphyxia spells [as-fik-shuu], as with *complexion* [kom-plek-shuun], *crucifixion* [kroo-si-fik-shuun], *deflexion* [dee-flek-shuun] and *transfixion* [trans-fik-shuun].

Cassia — many old people say [kay-shu], stressing the beginning of the word, letting Little Imp lengthen the vowel. Young people now-a-days stress the ending and so the <s> does not become [sh], [kas-ee-ar]. Why <ss>? The <ss> serves as a double gate to keep the preceding one letter vowel short and also means we read it as [s] not [z]. BTW, the flower *ixia* [ik-see-ar] is not a Yod Fusion word because <a> spells [ar], and so <ia> does not spell two weak beats.

Cetacea. Scientific names for animal groups often end in <ea>. For example, *cetacea* for whales and *proboscidea* for elephants. Individual plants often end in <ea> spells [ee-ar] too, e.g., *azalea* and *hakea*. However, plant families end <ae> which can spell [ee] or [I] and we shall learn the rule for that in Part Four.

Conscience is a Yod Fusion word because the first syllable, [kon], is stressed, leaving two weak beats at the end. *Science* is not a Yod Fusion word because in *science*, [sI-ens], <sc> is not followed by two weak beats.

Facia and *fascia* are alternate spellings for the same word. *Facia* is older.

Glacier spells [glay-shee-er] but can also spell [glay-see-er] if the last syllable gets more stress. Ditto *glaciate, glacial*.

Rosacea is a skin condition, not a family of roses. See *cetacea*.

Spacial is an alternative spelling of spatial.

Species spells [spee-sheez]. This Yod Fusion word ends in [z] because <s> spells [z] after stressed vowels and long vowels are stressed vowels. 'The noun *species*, referring especially to a group of organisms sharing common characteristics, can be either singular (e.g., that species is purple) or plural (e.g., these species are yellow)', from www.quora.com.

Note that <ce> spells [s] in *cetacea, cetacean, coercion, crustacea, crustacean, echinacea, ocean, species* and *suspicion* and that [s] changes to [sh] in these words because it is between a stressed syllable and an unstressed <i> or <e> which is followed by another unstressed vowel. However, when [s] does not follow a stressed syllable, in *panacea* [pan-u-see-u] for instance, <ce> does not spell [sh].

Any Rebels? No, *messiah*, which spells [mes-I-ar], is stressed on the last syllable, and so does not produce [sh] — even though in Hebrew it's *mashiah* "anointed" (of the Lord). *Uncial* spells [un-si-al], which conforms to the tum-te-tum beat of English.

Two Misfits: CUSHION [kuush-uun] and FASHION [fash-uun], the only two words to use <sh> before <ion>. *Cushion* arrived in England as *coissin*. *Fashion* arrived as *façon*. They should have adapted to English spelling as *cushen* and *fashen*, but instead were made to match other French adoptions ending

<ion>. Little Imp would like to 'work wonders' on <u> and on <a> but <sh> always follows short vowels, if the vowel is written with one letter.

Q. Why not spell [sh] in all suffixes just one way — instead of <ti>, <si>, <ssi>, <ce>, <ci> or <xi>, as in *nation, expansion, mission, ocean, racial* and *crucifixion*?

Ans. The dictionary committee knew that *nation* comes from Latin *nationem* and that *mission* comes, through French, from Latin *missionem*. Likewise, *expansion* and *crucifixion* come via French from Latin *expansionem* and *crucifixion*. They wanted the appearance of a word to tell its past, just like a rock does, in the hands of a geologist. They also wanted to preserve links between related words. *Nation* is linked to *nativity* (birth). *Nayshen* would lose that link. *Racial* is linked to *race*. *Rashal* looks closer to *rashers of bacon* than *race-related behaviour*. *Ocean* is straight from Latin *oceanus*. Mythological *Oceanus* was the son of Uranus and Gaia and husband of Tethys. The dictionary committee did not want to lose meanings and word connections. They never imagined that everyone would learn to read, especially not busy, working people. The aim of their dictionary was not to make reading easy. It was to decide on just one correct way to spell each word, and they chose a spelling which reflected a word's history. Before that, other dictionaries were lists of English words, with various ways to spell each one. The work of the dictionary committee became the Oxford English Dictionary.

The word-sound [sh] is spelt more often with <t> than any other letter. The following list contains many words ending <tion>, as well as other [sh] words. It's a long list and provides a lot of reading practice. It could be much longer! The website www.morewords.com lists three times as many words ending <tion>.

List 3-94
ABDICATION, ABERRATION, ABLUTION, ABNEGATION, ABOLITION, ABOLITIONIST, ABOMINATION, ABROGATION, ABSOLUTION, ABSORPTION, ACCELERATION, ACCLAMATION, ACCLIMATIZATION, ACCOMMODATION, ACCREDITATION, ACCRETION, ACCUMULATION, ACCUSATION, ACQUISITION, ACTIVATION, ADAPTATION, ADAPTION, ADDITION, ADDITIONAL, ADDITIONALLY, ADJUDICATION, ADJURATION, ADMINISTRATION, ADMIRATION, ADMONITION, ADORATION, ADULATION, ADULTERATION, AFFECTATION, AFFILIATION, AFFIRMATION, AFFORESTATION, AGGLOMERATION, AGGLUTINATION, AGGRAVATION, AGGREGATION, AGITATION, ALIENATION, ALLEGATION, ALLEVIATION, ALLITERATION, ALLOCATION, ALTERATION, ALTERCATION, AMALGAMATION, AMBITION, MELIORATION, AMMUNITION, AMPLIFICATION, AMPUTATION, ANIMATION, ANNEXATION, ANNIHILATION, ANNOTATION, ANNUNCIATION, ANTICIPATION, APPARITION, APPELLATION, APPLICATION, APPORTION, APPOSITION, APPRECIATION, APPROBATION, APPROPRIATION, APPROXIMATION, ARBITRATION, ARGUMENTATION, ARTICULATION, ASPHYXIATION, ASPIRATION, ASSASSINATION, ASSIGNATION, ASSIMILATION, ASSOCIATION, ASSUMPTION, ATOMIZATION, ATTENUATION, ATTESTATION, ATTRIBUTION, ATTRITION, AUTOMATIONS, AVIATION, BOTHERATION, CALCIFICATION, CALIBRATION, CANCELLATION, CANNIBALIZATION, CANONIZATION, CAPITALIZATION, CAPITULATION, CAPTION, CAPTIVATION, CARBONIZATION, CARNATION, CASTIGATION, CASTRATION, CATION, CELEBRATION, CENTRALIZATION, CERTIFICATION, CESSATION, CHARACTERIZATION, CHLORINATION, CIRCULATION, CIRCUMLOCUTION, CIRCUMNAVIGATION, CIRCUMSCRIPTION, CIRCUMVOLUTION, CITATION, CIVILIZATION, CLARIFICATION, CLASSIFICATION, COAGULATION, COALITION, CODIFICATION, COEDUCATION, COEVOLUTION, COHABITATION, COLLABORATION, COLLECTIVIZATION, COLONIZATION, COLORATION*, COMBINATION, COMMEMORATION, COMMENDATION, COMMENSURATION*, COMMERCIALIZATION,

COMMISERATION, COMMOTION, COMMUNICATION, COMPENSATION, COMPETITION, COMPILATION, COMPLETION, COMPLICATION, COMPOSITION, COMPUTATION, COMPUTERIZATION, CONCATENATION, CONCENTRATION, CONCEPTUALIZATION, CONCILIATION, CONCRETION, CONDEMNATION, CONDENSATION, CONDITION, CONDITIONAL, CONFEDERATION, CONFIGURATION, CONFIRMATION, CONFISCATION, CONFLAGRATION, CONFORMATION, CONFRONTATION, CONFUTATION, CONGLOMERATION, CONGRATULATION, CONGREGATION, CONJUGATION, CONNOTATION, CONSECRATION, CONSERVATION, CONSERVATIONIST, CONSIDERATION, CONSOLATION, CONSOLIDATION, CONSTELLATION, CONSTERNATION, CONSTIPATION, CONSTITUTION, CONSTITUTIONAL, CONSULTATION, CONSUMMATION, CONTAMINATION, CONTEMPLATION, CONTINUATION, CONTRIBUTION, CONTRITION, CONVERSATION, CONVOCATION, CONVOLUTION, COOPERATION, COORDINATION, COPULATION, CORONATION, CORPORATION, CORRELATION, CORROBORATION, CORRUGATION, CORRUPTION, CREATION, CREMATION, CRYSTALLIZATION, CULMINATION, CULTIVATION, DAMNATION, DEACTIVATION, DECELERATION, DECIMALIZATION, DECIMATION, DECLAMATION, DECLARATION, DECOMPOSITION, DECORATION, DECRIMINALIZATION, DEDICATION, DEFALCATION, DEFAMATION, DEFECATION, DEFINITION, DEFLATION, DEFORMATION, DEGRADATION, DEHYDRATION, DEIFICATION, DELECTATION, DELEGATION, DELETION, DELIBERATION, DELIMITATION, DELINEATION, DEMARCATION, DEMOLITION, DEMONSTRATION, DEMORALIZATION, DEMOTION, DENIGRATION, DENOMINATION, DENUNCIATION, DEODORIZATION, DEPLETION, DEPOPULATION, DEPORTATION, DEPRECATION, DEPREDATION, DEPRIVATION, DEPUTATION, DERIVATION, DESALINATION, DESECRATION, DESICCATION, DESIGNATION, DESOLATION, DESPERATION, DESTINATION, DESTITUTION, DETERIORATION, DETERMINATION, DETESTATION, DETONATION, DEVALUATION, DEVASTATION, DEVIATION, DEVOLUTION, DEVOTION, DICTATION, DILAPIDATION, DILATION, DILUTION, DIMINUTION, DISCOLORATION, DISCRETION, DISCRIMINATION, DISINTEGRATION, DISLOCATION, DISORIENTATION, DISPENSATION, DISPOSITION, DISPUTATION, DISQUALIFICATION, DISSEMINATION, DISSIPATION, DISSOLUTION, DISTILLATION, DISTRIBUTION, DIVINATION, DOCUMENTATION, DOMESTICATION, DOMINATION, DONATION, DRAMATIZATION, DUPLICATION, DURATION [joor-ay-shuun], EDITION, EDUCATION, EJACULATION, ELABORATION, ELATION, ELECTRIFICATION, ELECTROCUTION, ELEVATION, ELIMINATION, ELOCUTION, ELONGATION, EMACIATION, EMANCIPATION, EMASCULATION, EMBARKATION, EMBROCATION, EMIGRATION, EMOTION, EMULATION, ENCAPSULATION, ENUMERATION, ENUNCIATION, EQUIVOCATION, ERADICATION, ERUDITION, ESCALATION, ESTIMATION, EVACUATION, EVALUATION, EVAPORATION, EVOCATION, EVOLUTION, EXACERBATION, EXAGGERATION, EXALTATION, EXAMINATION, EXASPERATION, EXCAVATION, EXCITATION, EXCLAMATION, EXCOMMUNICATION, EXCRETION, EXECUTION, EXHALATION, EXHIBITION, EXHILARATION, EXHORTATION, EXONERATION, EXPECTATION, EXPEDITION, EXPERIMENTATION, EXPIRATION, EXPLANATION, EXPLORATION, EXPORTATION, EXPOSITION, EXPOSTULATION, EXPROPRIATION, EXPURGATION, EXTENUATION, EXTERMINATION, EXTIRPATION, EXTRICATION, EXUDATION, EXULTATION, FABRICATION, FACILITATION, FALSIFICATION, FASCINATION, FEDERATION, FELICITATION, FERMENTATION, FERTILIZATION, FILTRATION, FINALIZATION, FIXATION, FLIRTATION, FLOTATION, FLUCTUATION, FLUORIDATION FOMENTATION, FORMATION, FORMULATION,

FORNICATION, FORTIFICATION, FOSSILIZATION, FOUNDATION, FRAGMENTATION, FRATERNIZATION, FRUITION, FRUSTRATION, FULMINATION, FUMIGATION, GALVANIZATION, GENERALISATION, GENERALIZATION, GENERATION, GERMINATION, GESTATION, GESTICULATION, GLACIATION, GLOBALIZATION, GLORIFICATION, GRADATION, GRADUATION, GRANULATION, GRATIFICATION, GRAVITATION, GUMPTION, HABITATION, HALLUCINATION, HARMONIZATION, HESITATION, HIBERNATION, HOSPITALIZATION, HUMILIATION, IDEALIZATION, IDENTIFICATION, IDOLIZATION, IGNITION, ILLUMINATION, ILLUSTRATION, IMAGINATION, IMITATION, IMMIGRATION, IMMOBILIZATION, IMMORTALIZATION, IMMUNIZATION, IMPERSONATION, IMPLEMENTATION, IMPLICATION, IMPORTATION, IMPOSITION, IMPROVISATION, INACTIVATION, INCAPACITATION, INCARCERATION, INCARNATION, INCINERATION, INCITATION, INCLINATION, INCONSIDERATION, INCOORDINATION, INCORPORATION, INCRIMINATION, INCUBATION, INDENTATION, INDEXATION, INDICATION, INDIGNATION, INDISCRETION, INDOCTRINATION, INDUSTRIALIZATION, INEBRIATION, INFESTATION, INFILTRATION, INFLAMMATION, INFLATION, INFORMATION, INFURIATION, INHABITATION, INHALATION, INHIBITION, INITIATION, INNOVATION, INQUISITION, INSCRIPTION, INSEMINATION, INSINUATION, INSOLATION, INSPIRATION, INSTALLATION, INSTIGATION, INSTILLATION, INSTITUTION, INSTRUMENTATION, INSUBORDINATION, INSULATION, INTEGRATION, INTENSIFICATION, INTERCEPTION, INTERROGATION, INTIMATION, INTIMIDATION, INTOXICATION, INVESTIGATION, INVITATION, INVOLUTION, IONIZATION, IRRADIATION, IRRIGATION, IRRITATION, ISOLATION, JUBILATION, JUSTICIABLE *legal term*, JUSTIFICATION, LACERATION, LAMENTATION, LEGISLATION, LIBERATION, LIMITATION, LIQUIDATION, LOCATION, LOCOMOTION, LOCUTION, LOTION, LUBRICATION, MACHINATION <ch>=[sh]., MAGNIFICATION, MALNUTRITION, MANIFESTATION, MANIPULATION, MASTURBATION, MATERIALIZATION, MATRICULATION, MATURATION, MAXIMIZATION, MECHANIZATION, MEDIATION, MEDICATION, MEDITATION, MENSTRUATION, MENSURATION, MIGRATION, MINERALIZATION, MINISTRATION, MISINTERPRETATION, MITIGATION, MODERATION, MODERNISATION, MODERNIZATION, MODIFICATION, MODULATION, MOLESTATION, MOLLIFICATION, MOTION, MOTIVATION, MULTIPLICATION, MUNITION, MUTATION, MUTILATION, NARRATION, NATION, NAVIGATION, NECESSITATION, NEGATION, NEGOTIABLE, NEGOTIATION, NEUTRALIZATION, NODULATION, NOMINATION, NORMALIZATION, NOTATION, NOTIFICATION, NOTION, NUMERATION, NUPTIAL, NUTRITION, OBFUSCATION, OBLIGATION, OBLITERATION, OBSERVATION, OCCUPATION, OPERATION, OPPOSITION, ORATION, ORCHESTRATION, ORDINATION, ORGANIZATION, ORIENTATION, OSCILLATION, OSTENTATION, OUTSTATION, OVATION, OVERESTIMATION, OVULATION, OXIDATION, OXYGENATION, PARTICIPATION, PARTITION, PENETRATION, PERFORATION, PERSECUTION, PERSONATION, PERSPIRATION, PERTURBATION, PETITION, PIGMENTATION, PLANTATION, POLLINATION, POLLUTION, POPULATION, POSITION, POTION, PRECIPITATION, PREDATION, PREDESTINATION, PREFABRICATION, PREMONITION, PRENUPTIAL, PREOCCUPATION, PREPARATION, PREPOSITION, PRESENTATION, PRESERVATION, PREVARICATION, PRIVATION, PRIVATIZATION, PROBATION, PROCLAMATION, PROCRASTINATION, PROHIBITION, PROLIFERATION, PROLONGATION, PROMOTION, PRONUNCIATION, PROPAGATION, PROPOSITION, PROSECUTION, PROSTITUTION, PUBLICATION, PULVERIZATION, PURIFICATION, QUALIFICATION, QUOTATION, RADIATION, RAMIFICATION, RATION, RATIONALIZATION,

REALIZATION, REALLOCATION, RECALCULATION, RECALIBRATION, RECERTIFICATION, RECITATION, RECOGNITION, RECOMBINATION, RECONCILIATION, RECONSTITUTION, RECUPERATION, REDISTRIBUTION, REDUPLICATION, REFRIGERATION, REGIMENTATION, REGISTRATION, REGULATION, REGURGITATION, REHABILITATION, REINFESTATION, REJUVENATION, RELATION, RELAXATION, RELOCATION, RENDITION, RENOVATION, REPUTATION, RESERVATION, RESIGNATION, RESOLUTION, RESPIRATION, RESTITUTION, RESTORATION, RETRIBUTION, REVOLUTION, ROTATION, RUINATION, SALIVATION, SALUTATION, SALVATION, SANCTIFICATION, SANITATION, SATIABLE, SATURATION, SECRETION, SEDATION, SEDIMENTATION, SEGREGATION, SENSATION, SEPARATION, SILTATION, SIMPLIFICATION, SIMULATION, SOCIABLE, SOLUTION, SOPHISTICATION, SPECIALIZATION*, SPECIATION*, SPECIFICATION, SPECULATION, STABILIZATION, STAGNATION, STANDARDIZATION, STARVATION, STATION, STATIONARY, STATIONERY, STERILIZATION, STIMULATION, STIPULATION, STRANGULATION, SUBORDINATION, SUBSIDIZATION, SUBSTITUTION, SUFFOCATION, SUPERSTITION, SUPERANNUATION, SUPPLICATION, SUPPOSITION, SUSPICION, TABULATION, TAXATION, TELECOMMUNICATION, TEMPORIZATION, TEMPTATION, TERMINATION, TESSELLATION, TITRATION, TOLERATION, TRADITION, TRANSFORMATION, TRANSITION, TRANSLATION, TRANSPIRATION, TRANSPLANTATION, TRANSPORTATION, TREPIDATION, TRIBULATION, TRIPLICATION, TRIVIALIZATION, ULCERATION, UNDERESTIMATION, UNDERVALUATION, UNIFICATION, VACATION, VACCINATION, VACILLATION, VALUATION, VAPORIZATION, VARIATION, VARIEGATION, VEGETATION, VENERATION, VENTILATION, VERBALIZATION, VERIFICATION, VEXATION, VIBRATION, VILIFICATION, VINDICATION, VIOLATION, VISITATION, VITIABLE *legal term,* VOCALIZATION, VOCATION, VOLUTION, WORKSTATION, ZONATION*.

Commensuration spells [sh] twice, [kom-en-shoor-ay-shuun].

**Specialization.* We heard about the rebel word *special* which disobeys Rule 3-91B, being that single letter vowels preceding single letters spelling [sh] are stressed and long, unless spelt with <i>. In *specialization* we hear [sh] twice, the first spelt with <c> and the second with <t>.

**Speciation* also spells [sh] twice. It's the name of the process for creating a new species.

Rule 3-95 Sound [s] becomes [sh] after a stressed syllable and before <u> spelling its unstressed long sound.

Reason This occurred before yods dropped before [s]. The following listed words with <x> fit this rule because <x> spells [ks]. The stress needs to precede possible [sh] sounds, so *exude* and *disuse* do not fit the rule, because stress is on the second syllable. Letter <u> after [s] needs to spell its long sound, so *exult* and *usurp* do not fit the rule. *Issue* spells [ish-oo] because <s> follows a stressed syllable and precedes <u> spelling an unstressed long word-sound.

Rebels SUGAR and SURE, also SUMAC.

Rebels' Reasons These rebel because [s] does not follow a stressed syllable, <s> being word-initial. There are very few words which start with <su> in which <u> spells its long sound. Before yods dropped after [s], the verb *sue* spelt [syoo]. We still hear [syoo] in *pursue,* made from the stem word *sue*. The stem word *sume* is lost but we can assume that it spelt [shoom] because we hear it in *assume* [a-shoom] in Australia. In the 1950's a man's *suit* spelt [syoot] or [see-oot], before its yod dropped, and some very old folk still say it like that in Australia. One can also hear *suit* as [syoot] and [shyoot] in re-runs of the U.K. TV comedy "Are You Being Served?" *Sumac* is a rare word, pronounced both [soo-mak] and [shoo-mak].

List 3-95

ACUPRESSURE, ASEXUAL, ASSURE, BISEXUAL, FISSUE, HETEROSEXUAL, HOMOSEXUAL, ISSUE, PRESSURE, REASSURE, SEXUAL, SEXUALLY, SEXUALITY, SUSURRANT*, TRANSSEXUAL.

Susurrant [soo-shuu-<u>rant</u>] is a lovely Shhhh! word for it means 'whispering'. The middle syllable is unstressed.

Q. Why can't we just use <sh> to spell [sh]?

Ans. The English adopted many new suffixes from Paris. They were spelt the French way, and, at first, pronounced the French way. The old English words were forgotten. Now only two old English suffixes using <sh> remain, —*ship* and —*ish*. Also, digraph <sh> is very rare inside words, just in *bishop, bushel, marshal, mushroom, pasha, usher*. Then two were added when French *façon* was respelt *fashion* and French *coussin* was respelt *cushion*. Both English words are clumsy hybrids of two ways to spell [sh], using <sh> and also yods, and should spell [fash-yon] and [kuush-yon].

Q. Why were these spelling revisions attempted for only two words?

Ans. The dictionary committee retained French letters to preserve history. They knew that France ruled England and English spelling for hundreds of years. Even now, English is one third French, and another third Latin. Most of the original English words, of Old English, have died out. Even the motto on the Royal Coat of Arms of the United Kingdom is still in French, Old French, 'Honi soit qui mal y pense.' So is the English Monarch's motto, 'Dieu et mon droit.'

The Latin words were not left behind after four centuries of Roman colonization of Britain. Latin words came into English via French. Prof. Lerer estimates maybe as few as five Latin words were adopted by the Celts. Unlike the Gauls, the Celts did not mix and combine their language with that of the Romans. Mind you, the Gauls mainly mixed with lower-class Romans. So they adopted a lot of Vulgar Roman words, as opposed to Classical Latin. For instance, *head* is 'caput' in Latin, but in Roman slang it was 'testa', meaning *jug*. (We still call some people 'jughead'). Vulgar Latin *testa* became French *tête*. Latin and Greek words became highly respected during the Renaissance and many were adopted into English, complete or in part, to make new English words.

Long ago, the En glish used <ce> to spell [ch], as in *cest* but in French <ce> spelt [s]. So *cest* became *chest*. The way of spelling [ch] with <ce> has crept back into English in Italian words like *cello*. However, <t> became the most common way to spell [ch] when the English palatalized it in French words.

Yod Fusion [ch] — *actual, virtually.*

Rule 3-96 When <st> comes after a stressed vowel and before unstressed <i> or <e> followed by another unstressed vowel, then <t> spells [ch].

Reason Suffixes which have two weak beats upset the rhythm of English. If the first is spelt with <i> or <e>, it shrinks to a yod, [y], and fuses with <t> to produce [sh], except that if <t> follows <s> when it fuses with yod it produces [ch]. This is because when [t] follows [s] the mouth is barely open. As in *tune*, in which the mouth is closed before [t], when the mouth is barely open, as in *question*, the fused sound is [ch], not [sh]. Experts say that friction has been added to [sh]. They call it affrication. They show this by adding <t> to the Esh symbol for [sh] so that the IPA symbol for [ch] is [tʃ]. If you look at a word and do not know which syllables are stressed and which are not, remember that most suffixes are unstressed and so the preceding syllable will be stressed, as in *combustion* and since <t> follows <s>, it will spell [ch].

Also, Little Imp cannot work wonders through double doors, through two consonants. So <e> spells short [e] in *question*.

Rebel BESTIAL [bes-ti-uul]

Rebel's Reason This word is short enough to accommodate the tum-te-tum rhythm of English speech without reducing [i] to a yod and fusing it with [t] to avoid two weak beats.

List 3-96
CELESTIAL, COMBUSTION, CONGESTION, CROSS-QUESTION, DIGESTION, INDIGESTION, INGESTION, PREDIGESTION, QUESTION, QUESTIONABLE, SUGGESTION, UNQUESTIONABLE.

We met *tulips* [choo-lips] and *tuna* choon-u] after Rule 1-41: 'If <u> spells a long sound after <t>, then <tu> spells [choo].' We should say <u>can</u> spell [choo] because not everyone speaks like that. Some say [choo-lips] and some say [tyoo-lips].
Merging [t] and [y] together comes in very handy when two weak beats need to be reduced to one in order to keep to the beat of English words, tum-te-tum. Because yods have not dropped after [t], whenever <u> spells its long sound after [t] we hear a little [y], the sound called a yod. We hear [yoo] as the first beat of two weak beats in suffixes after [t], for instance in the French suffix —*ure* which spells [yoor] or, closer to that sound, [yoo-uu], in other words, two weak beats. We hear [yoo] in another suffix after [t] because if suffix —*al* needs to join onto a terminal <t>, the letter <u> is added first: *act, actual; habit, habitual, intellect, intellectual; spirit, spiritual.* This produces the suffix [yoo-uul] with two weak beats. When [y] fuses with [t] the suffix has just one weak beat, as in [ak-shuul].

Rule 3-97 When <t> comes after a stressed syllable and before <u> spelling [yoo], then <t> spells [ch].

Reason As above, but it does not happen all the time, only if the syllable before <tu> is stressed. If we say *picture* slowly, with even stress on each syllable, we hear [pikt-yoor] without the word-sound [sh]. BTW, if the suffix <al> needs to join on to terminal <t> the letter <u> is added first: *act, actual; habit, habitual, intellect, intellectual; spirit, spiritual* and we shall see other examples in the list below.

Rebels VICTUAL, VICTUALLER

Rebels' Reasons *Victual* spells [vit-əl], *victualler* spells [vit-ler] because silent <c> was added later, by scholars, to match Latin *victualis* meaning 'provisions'. So *victuals* is a plural noun but, by back-formation, the verb *to victual* has recently been invented. The original word in English, *vitaylle*, was singular and was a cousin word to *vital*, vital for life. Due to Queen Quill's influence, now that people can read, many people pronounce the silent <c> in *victual*.

List 3-97.
ACCENTUATE, ACCENTUATION, ACTUAL, ACTUALITY, ACTUALLY, ACTUARY, ACTUATE, CONFLICTUAL, CONSTITUENCY, CONSTITUENT, CONTRACTUAL, EFFECTUAL, EVENTUAL, EVENTUALLY, FACTUAL, FACTUALLY, FATUITY, FLUCTUATE, FLUCTUATION, GARGANTUAN, GRATUITY, HABITUAL, HABITUALLY, HABITUATE, HABITUATION, INEFFECTUAL, INFATUATE, INFATUATION, INSTINCTUAL, INTELLECTUAL, INTUITION, INTUITIVE, INTUITIVELY, MUTUAL, OBITUARY, PERPETUATE, PERPETUATION, PERPETUITY, PITUITARY, PUNCTUAL, PUNCTUALLY, PUNCTUATE, PUNCTUATION, RITUAL, SANCTUARY, SITUATE, SITUATION, SPIRITUAL, SPIRITUALISM, SPIRITUALIST, SPIRITUALLY, STATUARY, STATUE, STATUESQUE, STATUETTE, SUBSTITUENT, TUATARA or TUATERA, TUITION, VIRTUAL, VIRTUALLY.

Amazing Asia Words
As we know, when <s> is between vowels it spells [z] after a stressed vowel. There are many occasions when <s> spells [z]. In fact, Prof. Cummings, on p. 394, says <s> is the most common spelling of [z]. We see <s> doing Zed's work, spelling [z] after stressed vowels and voiced consonants, e.g., in *as, has,* (Part 1); *lens, dog's* (Part 2); *divisible, closet, alms, jasmine,* and *nasal* so far, and we shall see it in *raisin* in Part Four.

We know <ss> always spells [s], not [z], (except in *dissolve, dessert, hussar, hussy, possess* and *scissors*). The Yod Fusion Rules show us that <ss> always spells [sh] after a stressed vowel and before a yod, the little unstressed sound spelt by <i> or <e> before another unstressed vowel, as in *fission* or by <u> spelling unstressed [yoo], as in *pressure.*

What does <s>, standing in for [z], spell in the same situation? It spells [zh]. This is the sound of <z> in *azure*. It is the sound we make when we say "Amaze ya" over and over, with unstressed "ya" instead of stressed "you". This is why *Asia* rhymes with 'amaze ya!' Yod Fusion [zh] is the least used word-sound in the English language, says Prof. Cummings on page 407. It was not used in Old English nor in Middle English. It arrived in French words and sayings, like *massage, gigolo* and *joie de vivre*, in which the French use, in order, <ge>, <gi> and <j> to spell what sounds like a soft [j]. which we symbolize with [zh]. Its IPA symbol is /ʒ/, called Ezh. This symbol looks like a stretched lower-case Z. When I went to school, ʒ is how we wrote lower-case Zed in cursive handwriting. The IPA symbol for [sh] is similar. It looks like a stretched lower-case S — /ʃ/ and is called Esh.

Q. Why don't we use <zh> to spell [zh]?

Ans. The dictionary committee kept up the old fear of Z, the sign of the dagger, the zig-zag which is slashed by a zayin, which is an old word for 'dagger'. Instead, we use <s> to spell [z] after stressed vowels, as in *as, has* and *is* etc., but we can't use <sh> to spell [zh] because it already spells [sh]. Instead we have to look at a word. If there is a vowel in the first syllable (first syllables are stressed in English, unless prefixes), and if vowel is followed by a single <s> and then two unstressed vowels, being a suffix, then <s> will spell [zh]. This only happens in English. *Asia* is a Latin proper noun which has spread far and wide but it is only in English that its <s> spells [zh].

Yod Fusion [zh] — *abrasion, vision.*

Rule 3-98 Letters <z> and <s> spell [z] after a stressed vowel and if followed by an unstressed <i> and another unstressed vowel, then [z] becomes [zh], as in *Asia*.

Reason This is how the English reduced two weak beats at the end of French words to an unstressed suffix of just one beat. The first vowel of the suffix reduces to yod, [y], which fuses with [z] to produce [zh]. Then there is only one syllable left in the suffix and the rhythm of English is maintained. This is what happens when we say *abrasion* [u-bray-zhuun], *brazier* [bray-zhuu]. Let's visualize an Amazing Asian vision. Look at the words. Can you see Little Imp at work? He works wonders in *Asia* but not in *vision,* for as we know, Little Imp works wonders on others, on his brother and sister vowels, but not on himself.

List 3-98
ABRASION, ADHESION, ALLUSION, ASPERSION, AVERSION, BRAZIER*, COHESION, COLLISION, COLLUSION, CONCLUSION, CONFUSION*, CONTUSION, CONVERSION, CORROSION, DECISION*, DELUSION, DERISION, DIFFUSION, DISPERSION, DISILLUSION, DIVERSION, DIVISION, EFFUSION, ELISION, ENVISION, , EROSION, EVASION, EXCISION, EXCLUSION, EXCURSION, EXPLOSION, EXTRUSION, FUSION, *GLAZIER, GRAZIER*, HOSIER, HOSIERY, ILLUSION, IMMERSION, IMPLOSION, INCISION*, INCLUSION, INCURSION, INDECISION, INFUSION, INTRUSION, INVASION, INVERSION, LESION, OBTRUSION, OCCASION, OCCLUSION, {PERSUASION*}, PERVERSION, PLOSION, PRECISION, PRECLUSION, PROFUSION, PROTRUSION, PROVISION, RECLUSION, RECURSION, REVISION, SECLUSION, SUBMERSION, SUBVERSION, SUFFUSION, SUPERVISION, TELEVISION, TORSION, TRANSFUSION, VERSION, VISION, Proper Nouns/Adj., ASIAN.

*{*Persuasion* is an example of <u> spelling [w] which we shall discuss in Part Four.}

*Nowadays in Australia the <z> in *grazier, brazier* and *glazier* usually spells [z] because the syllables are evenly stressed.

Rebels? No, *aphrodisiac* [af-roh-dee-zee-ak], *ambrosia* [am-broh-zee-u], *symposia* [sim-poh-zee-u] do not palatize [z] because the vowels after [z] are stressed. Some people say *magnesium* spells [mag-nee-zhee-um], but nobody says *potassium* spells [pot-ash-ee-um].

We met *equation* [ee-kway-zhuun] earlier, at 3-92A, the only word in which <t> spells [zh] after fusing with a yod.

Relevant Writing Rule. If the suffix is <ion>, simply add it to a consonant, *express — expression*, or change a terminal <y> to <i> and add <cation>, *identify — identification, unify — unification*. If the stem word ends <de>, drop the <e> and change <d> to <s> as in *invade — invasion*. Remember that words from the same stem have the same suffixes and so once you sort out how the suffix joins on there is a pattern to follow: *inclusion — conclusion — exclusion*. Return to Reading Rules.

The French suffix —*ure* spells [yoor], and, in *azure,* [z] and [y] fuse to produce [zh]. This also happens wherever <s> spells [z] before <ure> or before another suffix starting with <u> spelling its long sound, [oo] or [yoo].

Rule 3-99 [z] comes after a stressed long vowel and before <u> spelling a long vowel, <s> spells [zh], as in *Asia*.

Reason This fusion of a yod with [z] is for ease of pronunciation, e.g., for *visual*, [vizh-uul] is easier to say than [viz-yuu-uul]. This occurs whether <u> spells [yoo] or [oo], because the fusion with [y] (yod) took place before the yods began dropping after [s] and [z]. Yods occur where <u> spells a long unstressed sound as in *usury* and also where <i> or <e> spell unstressed vowels and are followed by another unstressed vowel, as in *fantasia*.

List 3-99
AZURE, FANTASIA, USURER, USURY, USUAL, USUALLY, USUFRUCTUARY, VISUAL, {LEISURE}, {MEASURE}, Proper Noun ASIA.

Yod Fusion [j] — *contagion, soldier*.

The letter J was the last letter to enter the English alphabet. In Old English, <cg> or just <g> before <i> and <e> was used for [j]. In Middle English and Early Modern English — 1066 to 1500 — <i> and <j> were two different forms of the same letter, each a vowel and a consonant. After 1500, <i> began to be used as a vowel only, <j> a consonant only, but we still write either *hallelujah* or *halleluia,* Cummings p. 417. Prof. Cummings adds that Samuel Johnson was still intermixing <i> and <j> in 1775. As we know, <j> is not used at the end of words to spell [j], but <ge> takes its place after long vowels and <dge> after short vowels, as in *cage* and *cadge*. As explained at 1-45, <gg>, when joining a suffix and followed by <i> or <e>, spells [g], as in *sagging,* but <gg> when joining a prefix and followed by <i> or <e>, spells [j], as in *suggest*.

Rule 3-100 The suffix <gion> spells [juun].

Reason As we would expect, <gi> spells [j] in the suffix <gion> and, as suffixes are unstressed, we'd expect <i> in suffix <gion> to be a Little Imp. Little Imp in suffix <gion> works wonders on others but not on himself, not in *religion*, for instance.

List 3-100
CONTAGION, LEGION, CONTAGION [kon-tay-juun], LEGION, REGION, RELIGION [ree-li-juun]

We normally say *idiot* with a tum-te-tum stress pattern, but if we only stress the first syllable, as we do when saying it in an affectionate manner, it spells [eed-jet], (rhymes with *gadget*). On the other hand, if we say *cordial* with a tum-te-tum stress pattern, <d> no longer spells [j].

When we say "Did you?" with heavy stress on the first word, we hear 'Didja?' and then [dijuu]? If we say "Did you?" with even stress on each word this does not happen. Try it. Now stress 'Did'. This is an example of consonants fusing with yods over word boundaries. We have also heard yods fusing over word boundaries in "Miss-ya", [I mishuu] and in "Amaze you", [u-mayzhuu]. As we know, yods fusing over syllable boundaries, inside words, for ease of speech and to eliminate two weak beats at the end of words.

Rule 3-101 After a stressed vowel and before <i> or <e> and another unstressed vowel the letter <d> spells [j].

Reason When a suffix has adjacent vowels, the first one can reduce further to a yod, if spelt with <i> or <e>, and fuse with [d] in this case, reducing the suffix to just one weak beat. This fits the word to the tum-te-tum rhythm of English. This only occurs in three words.

List 3-101 The three words in which <d> spells [j] without being followed by <u>:-
SOLDIER [sol-juu], CORDIAL [kor-juul], GRANDEUR [gran-juu]

In many words <d> spells [j], when it fuses with a yod from <u> spelling [yoo], as we know in *duly* and *duty* which spell [joo-lee] and [joo-tee] for they obey the special rule that if **<u> spells [yoo] after <d>, then <du> spells [joo]**. So *due* spells [joo] but *doom* spells [doom]. When <oo> spells [oo] the letter <d> does not spell [j], e.g., in *doom, doodle* and *doodads*.

By now we can read many words in which <du> spells [j].

List 3-102
CONDUCIVE, CREDULITY, DUKEDOM, DUPLICATION, DUPLICATOR, DURATION, DURIAN, DURUM *wheat,* DUTIFUL, DUTIFULLY, DUTIFULNESS, EDUCATION, EDUCATIONAL, EDUCATOR, FIDUCIAL, GLANDULAR, INDUBITABLE, INDUBITABLY, INDUCEMENT, MODULAR, MODULATOR, NODULAR, PENDULUM, PENDULA, UNDULATION, UNDULY, UNDUTIFUL, Proper Noun MEDUSA.

We do not hear <d> spell [j] in *exodus* in which <u> spells [uu]. We hear <d> spell [j] in *introduce, produce, conducive* and {*fraudulent*} but not in *introduction, product* and *conduct,* in which <u> spells [u]. We do not hear it when <u> spells [oo] in the foreign word *fondu*.

When <du> spells [joo] is followed by another vowel in the next syllable, the vowels follow the "Glide Rules". Fusion reduces suffixes to one syllable but when another suffix is added then that changes the stress in a word, e.g. when *individual* [in-du-vij-ool] becomes *individually* [in-du-vij-oo-al-i-tee].

List 3-103
ASSIDUITY, DUAL, DUEL, DUELIST, DUET, DUO, DUODENAL, DUODENUM, DUOPOLY, GASTRODUODENAL, INDIVIDUALITY, INDIVIDUALIST, PITUITARY, POSTGRADUATE *noun,* RESIDUUM.

We will finish Book Three by looking at semi-vowel <y> again — half vowel and half consonant. We have seen <y> spell the consonant [y] at the beginning of words, as in *yes* and *yummy*. We know it spells the long Anglo vowel [I] in the first syllable of words, e.g., *my* and *try*, and spells the long Continental vowel [ee] at the end of longer words like *silly* and *funnily*. We have also heard how the letter <y> was removed from inside all words unless they were from the Greek language or in compound words like *crybaby, handyman*.

The Why's and Wherefores of Wye — *acrylic, acolyte.*
Y is called a semi-vowel but it could just as easily be called a semi-consonant.
When acting as a consonant, <y> spells [y]. When acting as a vowel, <y> matches all the functions of <i>. So it can spell [i], [I] and [ee]. It is also used in place of <i> in vowel digraphs, as we shall see in Part Four. When a vowel, it follows all the rules we use to decode <i>. It is only meant to be used inside Greek

words but sometimes the dictionary makers got it wrong, and could have left <y> in a word. Other words are Greek impostors, should not use <y> for <i>. In a spelling bee we are allowed to ask "Is it Greek?" and if the answer is "No," we will not want to use <y>, but just to be sure, because of the impostors, we should then ask, "Was it thought to be Greek?"

Rule 3-104 The letter <y> spells [I] before consonant vowel, but not before consonant plus <ic> or before terminal <sis>.

Reason The dictionary makers let <y> stay inside words which came from Greek words, often adopted by Latin or German on the way into the English language. The letter <y> follows the rules for <i>, and so spells [I] before consonant vowel as in 'Regal Words', as in *hyphen,* and lengthens under the magic action of Fairy E, as in *enzyme,* and glides as [I] from the first syllable onto short vowels, as in *poliomyelitis*. Some are in stems after prefixes, like *analyse*. Just as Bossy R makes <i> spell [er] according to the Bossy R Rule, it also makes <y> spell [er] according to the rule, e.g., in *myrtle*. *Asylum* comes from an ancient Greek word "asylos" which means "what cannot be seized" (cannot be put in a silo) and so <a> in *asylum* is a prefix, meaning "not". Since these are all Greek origin words, or acting like Greek words, <ch> spells [k].

Rebel PHYSIQUE [fiz-eek]

Rebel's Reason *Physique* is pure French. Letter <i> or <y> in French does not spell [I], instead retaining the European vowel values which were lost in England's GVS.

Rebel? No, in *analytic* <y> spells [i] because, as we know, the suffix <ic> shortens the preceding vowel and stresses it, so *analytic* spells [an-a-lit-ik] and obeys the special <ic> rule — remember, special rules take precedence over general rules.

List 3-104A ACRYLIC, ANALYTIC, ANALYTICAL, BIOLYTIC, BUTYRIC (acid), CATALYTIC, CYNIC, DIALYTIC, ELECTROLYTIC, GENOTYPIC, GEOPHYTIC, HIEROGLYPHIC, LYRIC, LYRICAL, MYSTICAL, MYTHIC, PARALYTIC, PATRONYMIC, PHYSICS, PHYSICAL, PHYSICIAN, PHYSICIST, PYRRHIC VICTORY Greek <rrh> = <rr>, SATYRIC, TYPIC, TYPICAL, XEROPHYTIC.

Rebel? No, *analysis* is not a rebel because, as the rule says, <y> does not spell [I] before terminal <sis>. *Lysis* [lI-sis] means "loosening" in Greek and on its own in English means the gradual loosening up of a disease, a gradual recovery from ill health. However, when *lysis* is used as a suffix it spells [lis-is], because suffixes do not use stressed vowels and [I], being long, is a stressed vowel. Instead of spelling it as it sounds, *analisis,* the <y> remains to show that the suffix has a Greek origin. Note that the suffix —*lysis* has two short unstressed vowels and so the main stress falls just before it, with <sis> receiving minor stress to match the tum-te-tum rhythm of English. [an-**al**-i-sis]

List 3-104B. ANALYSIS and all other words ending <lysis>. e.g., DIALYSIS, ELECTROLYSIS, GLYCOLYSIS, HYDROLYSIS, PARALYSIS.

In all the next words <y> is followed by a consonant and then a vowel. Some of these consonants following <y> are spelt with two letters, a digraph, and are still called one consonant. This is because "consonant" refers to a sound, not a letter, e.g., <ch> in *psycho* spells consonant [k]. Also <ps> spells [s], with a silent <p>.

List 3-104C

ACOLYTE, ANALYSE/ANALYZE, ANODYNE, ANTICYCLONE
ASYLUM, ARCHETYPE <ch> = [k], BYRE, BYTE, CYANIDE, CYBERNETICS, CYBERSPACE, CYNOSURE, DEHYDRATE, DYKE*, DYNAMITE, DYNAMO, ECDYSIS, ELECTROLYTE, ENZYME, GYBE, GYRATE, GYRATORY, GYRE, GYRO, GYROCOMPASS, GYROSCOPE, GYROSCOPIC, HYPERBOLE 2nd <e> =[ee], HYPERCRITICAL, HYPERTHERMIA, HYPERMARKET, HYPERVENTILATE, HYPHEN, HYPHENATE, HYPOCHONDRIA <ch>=[k],

HYPOGLYCEMIA cpd. noun, HYPOTHERMIA, IN STYLE, LIFE-STYLE, LYCEUM, LYRE, LYSIN, LYSIS, LYSOL, MYALL*, MYALGIA, MYCELIA, MYNAH (bird), NEOPHYTE, *NYLON, PAPYRUS*, PARALDEHYDE, PARALYSE, POLIOMYELITIS, compound word, PHYLUM, PSYCH UP, PSYCH *verb*, PSYCHE *noun*, PSYCHIATRIST, PSYCHIATRY, PSYCHIC, PSYCHICAL, PSYCHO-, PSYCHOANALYSE, PSYCHOANALYSIS, PSYCHOANALYST, PSYCHOANALYTICAL, PSYCHOLOGICAL, PSYCHOLOGICALLY, PSYCHOLOGIST, PSYCHOLOGY, PSYCHOPATH, PSYCHOSIS, PSYCHOSOMATIC, PSYCHOSOMATICALLY, PSYCHOTHERAPY, PYLON, PYORRHOEA*, PYRE, PYROMANIA, PYTHON, RETYPE, RHYME*, SCYTHE*, STYLE*, STYLISH, STYLISHLY, STYLISHNESS, STYLIST, STYLISTIC, STYLISTICALLY, STYLIZED, STYLUS, SYPHON *also siphon,* SYNE (*auld lang syne*), THYME* <th> =[t], THYMOL, THYMUS, THYROID GLAND, TYCOON*, TYKE, TYPHOON*, TYPHUS, TYPE, TYRANT, TYRE*, TYRO*, VANDYKE *beard,* XYLOPHONE, WRYNECK *bird,* WYND *Scottish alleyway,* ZYGOTE.

Cummings, on p. 87, suggests WHYS, as in "whys and wherefores", could be added to the list. Also, the letter <y> itself, written WYE (occasionally WY), plural WYES.

*Dyke is an alternative English spelling of *dike,* probably to show that [i] in parent-word *ditch* had lengthened.

*Myall has been adopted from an Ab'l language in eastern NSW and means tree and was also used to denote 'wild' aborigines, (Blake, p. 100), in the same way 'bushies' is used for any Australians who live 'in the bush', out of town.

*Nylon was invented in 1938 and named to match other fibres like *cotton* and *rayon.* In an effort to advertise the fact a hole in it did not "run" it began as *no-run* reversed to *nuron* to match *cotton* but as that sounded like a nerve it was changed again to *nilon* and to make sure it was pronounced [nI-lon], (grander sounding than [nil-on]) it was finally changed to *nylon,* (Burbridge, 2004).

*Papyrus. The ancient Greeks wrote with a sharpened stick called a *stylus* on paper, called *papyrus,* made from pressed reeds.

*Pyorrhoea: <rrh> is how <rr> is written in Greek words. The second <o> is silent in this word, which comes from Greek *pythein* 'to cause to rot', i.e. *pyorrhoea* is "pus flow", which happens when gums rot. In USA <o> has been dropped from all words ending <rrhoea>.

Some of the words in 3-104C were re-written during the Renaissance. Sometimes a little knowledge can be a bad thing.

*Rhyme used to be *rime,* until around 1560 it became *rhyme* simply because good rhymes have rhythm. We can say that all <rh> words are Greek originally, except for *rhyme, rhinestones* from the Rhine, and the *rhumba,* which was the *rumba.* The box step is its basic step, called the 'rhumba square', because it is not a perfect right-angled square. Its sides are equal, same sized steps, but not at 90°, and so the rumba, being based on a rhombus, became the rhumba.

*Scythe used to be *sithe*.... until someone decided that it must come from Latin *scindere* — to cut — and not only added the <c> but changed the <i> to <y>, saying the Romans must have got it from the Greeks, and so, because Roman words which came from Greece have <y> instead of <i>, this one must have a <y> in it too! (*Scissors* got its <c> at the same time.) As both verb and noun, *scythe* spells [sIdh].

*Tycoon was originally spelt *taikun,* a Japanese word derived from ancient Chinese for "great prince". Since most words with <y> in the middle of the word are of Greek origin it seems strange to spell a Chinese word as if it was Greek. However, as you will see there are very few words in which <ai> spells [I] and so maybe there was method in this particular madness.

*Typhoon as *tufan* has many sources, Arabic, Persian and Hindi. *Al-tufan* occurs several times in the Koran for 'a flood or storm' and also for Noah's Flood. Chinese (Cantonese) *tai fung* or *daai feng* meant

'a great wind'. Because mythical *Tuphon* was the Greek father of winds, the spelling was changed to *typhoon* to look Greek.

*Style was *stile*, from Latin *stilus* which came from Greek *stulus* meaning *column* or *pillar*. Written in capitals, Greek <u> is <Y>. So, since it came from Greek, the English word was changed from *stile* to *style*. From Latin *stilus* we get "little columns", the origin of the stiletto dagger and the stiletto heel. The English wrote with a little *stylus*, also called a *pen* since it was made from a feather, in Latin, *penna* and in French, *penne*. One's way of handwriting was called one's "style" and then "style" was used for the way one dressed.

*Tyre was also spelt *tire*, probably short for *attire*, because the wheels were clad or attired. Americans still spell it *tire* but the English have reverted to *tyre* ever since wheels were clad in rubber, to tell rubber tyres apart from other wheel cladding, like the metal hoops over wooden cart wheels.

*Tyro was *tiro*. Both spellings are accepted. In Latin a *tiro* is a novice or young soldier, not a tyrant.

*Thyme [tIm] was adopted from the French who got it from the Romans. The Romans copied it from the Greeks, but they could not pronounce the Greek [th] sound. However, they continued to write it with <h> to show that it was a Greek word. The English did the same, letting <y> stay inside a stem word because it's a Greek word.

*Vandyke means a short, pointed beard, as in portraits by Anton Van Dyck (1599-1641); or a type of collar with a deep cut edge, as in his paintings, (Etymonline).

Some words have <y> inside them because they are compound words, like *wryneck*.

Rule 3-105 <y> spells [I] when followed by a vowel, or a consonant either <l> and a vowel or <r> and a vowel.

Reason When followed by a vowel, <y> matches <i>, gliding from first syllable to second, as in *bias*, but it's very rare to see <y> followed by a vowel in this "Glide and Yap" situation. When <y> is followed by a consonant and then either <l> or <r> and then a vowel, it matches <i> in *mitre* and *bible*.

Rebel HYENA spells [hI-een-ar], whereas the others "Yap" on the second vowel, [sI-an-Id], [hI-a-sinth], [mI-el-It-is].

Rebels? No, *myocardia, myopia* and *myosotis* all start with the pefix *myo*— in which [I] glides to a vowel which is long because it is terminal, a 'glide and yawn' scenario.

List 3-105A
CYANIDE, HYACINTH, MYOCARDIA, MYOPIA, MYOSOTIS, POLIOMYELITIS.

List 3-105B
CARBOHYDRATE, CYCLE, CYCLONE, CYCLONIC, CYCLOTRON, DEHYDRATE, ENCYCLOPEDIA USA, HYBRID, HYDRA, HYDRATION, HYDROCHLORIC, HYDROGEN, HYDROLOGIST, HYDROLYTIC, MEGACYCLE, RECYCLE.

Rule 3-106 <y> spells [i] in the third or more syllable from the end of the word.

Reason Many Greek adaptions have <y> spells [i] before a consonant vowel because <y> is in the third syllable from the end of the word, (Cummings, p. 227).

List 3-106A
ASPHYXIATE, CHRYSALIS, CYLINDER, DYSENTERY, GLYCERINE, HYPOCRISY, HYPOCRITE [krit], HYPOCRITICAL, MYRIAD, PHYSIOGNOMY, PHYSIOLOGY, PHYSIOTHERAPIST, PHYSIOTHERAPY, SYBARITE, SYCAMORE, SYCOPHANT, SYCOPHANTIC, TYPICAL, TYPIFY.

List 3-106B Greek Impostors
ACETYLENE [aset-ə-leen], PYJAMAS, PYRAMID [pi-rə-mid].

Impostors' Reasons Pyramids in Greek was *puramis* so the English were wrong to copy the Latin spelling. The Romans thought Greek capital U was Y. *Pyjamas* came into English as *pai jamahs* "loose trousers tied at the waist", worn by Muslims in India, and now a compound noun, from Persian *pai* (foot/leg) and *jamah* (clothing), with no Greek connection. American songwriters, the Gershwins, wrote *pajamas.* The word is pronounced [per-jarm-arz], [pI-jam-az], [par-jəmarz],[pa-ja-maz] or [pee-jarm-arz]. Take your pick. *Acetylene* was made up by the French chemist Berthelot, in 1864, from *acetyl* (coined from acetic in 1839 by German chemist Justus von Liebig) with the chemical ending *–ene,* (Etymonline).

Q. Why did Greeks use Y and Romans use I?
Ans. At first, only the top V of the Greek letter Y was passed on to Rome, and it spelt [uu]. The sound [v] was not used in Rome's language, *Latin, until the tenth century, (Davies p. 104). By the second century AD, Romans were using a lot of Greek words and needed Greek Y because it spelt a sound between the sounds spelt by <i>, short [i] and long [ee], and <v>, short [uu] and long [oo]. When English began as a language, in the fifth century AD, it had a rune called Yogh. Its symbol was later added to the ABC but was then removed and replaced in some words as <ch>, as in *loch* and in some as <gh>. As we know, the sound <gh> spelt was silenced or changed to [f]. In some words, Yogh's sound changed to [y] or [i], written with <y> and <i>. Soon, <y> was used rather than <i> which was almost invisible back then, without a dot on top. That's how Y and I became interchangeable. Fry on page 111 says that <i> almost died out! Printing saved it, because each letter is separate and <i> was easier to read than in cursive. It was also used more when the dictionary committee removed <y> from inside all words which did not come from the Greek language.
*'Latium' was the f-lat region around Rome, and so the people on the flats around Rome spoke 'Latinus'. They actually said *flat* as *plat,* as in *platter.*

Rule 3-107 <yr> spells [er], unless followed by a vowel.
Reason The letter <y> is like <i> and as <ir> spells [er] before a consonant or when terminal, so does <yr>.
List 3-107 <yr> spells [er].
MARTYR, MYRTLE, MYRRH*, SATYR, ZEPHYR
The name *Myrtle* is popular in Australia, for people and plants. The myrtle plant family includes gum trees, bottle brushes and paperbarks. In Greece a myrtle garland is as important as an olive garland, especially to women, as myrtle was the sacred plant of the Greek goddess Aphrodite.

Rule 3-108 <y> spells [i] if followed by <r> and a vowel.
Reason This is so with all vowels, because "R is Bossy after vowels but not between them".
List 3-108
LABYRINTH, SYRINX, SYRINGE*, SYRUP*, TYRANNY, TYRANNICAL, TYRANNIZE. Proper Nouns SYRIA, VALKYRIE
Syringes is one plural form of *syrinx.* It is used as a singular word *syringe* to describe a medical instrument.
Syrup is a Greek Impostor because it comes from Arabia, not Greece, same as *sherbet,* but why do the English use <y> when the French was *sirop* and the Latin was *siropus*?

Rule 3-109 Preceding a terminal consonant, other than <r>, of a prefix or a word, <y> spells [i].
Reason This matches the rule for reading <i> in *bin* and in *bobbin.* As we know, <i> spells [I] in *binary,* and, due to double gates, spells [i] in *singular.* The prefix *syn-* always spells [sin]. It began as a Greek word and was adopted into Latin. It means "with, together, at the same time, like". We also see it in

syllabus for *syn* becomes *syl* before initial <l> to make it join on easier. It also changes to *sym* before the two-lip sounds called bi-labial consonants, <b>, <m>, <p>, <ph>. In Greek, <ph> spelt [p], then [h], and therefore started with lips together. *Syn* sometimes simplifies to *sy-* before <st> and <z> as in *system, systole* and *syzygy.* Otherwise it is always *syn-*, as in *synod.*

List 3-109
GYM, GYM-SLIP, GYP, HYDROXYL, LYCH-GATE, LYMPH, METHYL, MYTH, PTERODACTYL <pt>=[t]. SYMBIOTIC, SYMBOL, SYMBOLOGY, SYMMETRY, SYMMETRICAL, SYMPATHY, SYMPHONY, SYMPTOM, SYNAGOGUE* [sin-u-gog], SYNAPSE, SYNCHROMESH <ch>=[k], SYNCHRONIZE <ch>=[k], SYNCHRONIZER <ch>=[k], SYNCOPATE, SYNCRETIC -*combining beliefs*, SYNDICATE, SYNDROME, SYNERGY, SYNOD, SYNONYM, SYNONYM, SYNOPSIS, SYNOPTIC, SYNTHESIS, SYNTHESIZE, SYNTHETIC, SYNTHETICALLY, SYSTEM, SYSTOLE, SYZGY. Compound Words OXYGEN, PLATYPUS, POLYMATH.

The three compound words obey the rule because <y> originally preceded a terminal consonant: *Oxygen* was two words: *oxys gen*, meaning 'generated by acid'. The <y> in *platypus* is pronounced [i] because it was created (in 1799) from two Greek words, *platys* and *pous,* flat and foot, flat-footed. *Polymath* was made up of *polys* and *manthanein* in 1621. *Polys* means "much" in Greek, and, having a terminal consonant after <y>, is pronounced [polis]. *Manthanein* means "learn" and the whole word *ployymath* means "having learned much." Compound words are almost always pronounced like their parent words. ({*Breakfast*} and *blackguard* are unusual.)

Synod from Greek *synodos,* 'meeting'.

Synagogue can also be *synagog* which matches its pronunciation, [sin-u-gog] and which was the original Greek translation of the Hebrew word. The French added silent terminal <ue> and the English copied the French.

Rule 3-110 Preceding two consonants <y> spells [i].
Reason 'Double gates' keep vowels short, as per Orm's Law. We must remember that <ph> originally, in Greek, spelt two consonants, blended, [ph]. It was later that <ph> was used to spell [f] in words of Greek origin.

Rebel SYPHILIS [sif-il-is]

Rebel's Reason Although <y> does not precede two consonants, since <ph> spells just [f], <y> spells short [i] because it is stressed and three syllables from the end of the word. It's what we call a "Holiday Word". *Syphilis* is not Greek. It's from a Modern Latin 1546 treatise and there is quite a story about this word on Etymonline.

List 3-110
ABYSS, AMETHYST, ANALYST, APOCALYPSE, ASPHYXIATE*, BLASTOCYST, CALYPSO, CATACLYSM, CATALYST, CHLOROPHYLL <ch> =[k], CRYPT, CRYSTAL, CRYSTALLINE, CYMBAL, CYST, DYSFUNCTION, ENCYST, GRYPHON, GYMKHANA, GYMNASIUM, GYMNAST, GYMNASTICS, GYPSOPHILA, GYPSUM, GYPSY*, HYMN* *silent [n]*, HYMNAL, HYPNOTISM, HYSSOP, HYSTERIA, IDIOSYNCRASY, IDYLLIC, LARYNGEAL, LARYNGITIS, LARYNX, LYMPH*, LYMPHATIC, LYNCH*, LYNX, MOLYBDENUM, MYSTERY, MYSTIC, MYSTICAL, MYSTICISM, MYSTIFY, MYSTIFIER, MYSTIQUE, MYSTIQUE, MYTH, MYTHICAL, MYTHOLOGICAL, MYTHOLOGY, NEMATOCYST, NYMPH, NYMPHOMANIA, NYMPHOMANIAC, NYSTAGMUS, OLYMPIC, PHARYNGEAL, PHARYNGITIS, PHARYNX, PHOTOSYNTHESIZE, POLYGLOT, PSYCHOANALYST, PYGMY, RHYTHM <th>=[dh], RHYTHMIC, STRYCHNINE, STYPTIC, SYLLABLE, SYLLOGISM, SYLPH, SYLVAN*, SYMBOL, SYMBOLISM, SYMBOLIZE, SYMMETRICAL, SYMMETRICALLY, SYMMETRY, SYMPATHETIC, SYMPATHETIC, SYMPATHETICALLY, SYMPATHIZE, SYMPATHIZER,

SYMPATHY, SYMPATHIZE, SYMPOSIA, SYMPHONIC, SYMPHONY, SYMPHONY, SYMPOSIUM, SYMPTOM, SYMPTOMATIC, , SYSTEM, SYSTEMIZE, SYSTOLE, SYZYGY, TRYST*.

*In *asphyxiate,* <x> spells the double consonant [ks] and so <y> spells [i].

*ature *Lymph* is not Greek but Latin for 'waters', *lumpæ*. The Romans changed this to *lympha*, influenced by the word *nymph* — a Greek goddess of a fresh water spring.

Lynch is not Greek. This etymon is thought to come from the 1811 Lynch Law, likely named after William Lynch whose vigilance committee kept order in Virginia during the American Revolution. Long ago, an English *lynch* referred to a linking join. When <y> was removed from non-Greek words, it became *linch* but that is now obsolete and we only see it in the compound word *linchpin*.

Gypsy is also spelt *gipsy* because no one knows where they originated. If it was in Greece then <y> is correct but if they set out from another country then medial <i> is correct.

Hymn might spell [hIm] without the silent <n>, since <y> is in the first syllable.

Did you see that *rhythm* has [dh] followed by a consonant? This is very rare and breaks the rule that [dh] is followed by a vowel, except that we **say** a vowel after <th> in *rhythm,* even though we do not write it. It rhymes with *fathom,* as if it was spelt *rhythom* but then it would spell [rIdhom] instead of [ridhom].

Tryst and *sylvan* are non-Greek words which imitate Greek words – see Etymonline.

English Y — *crybaby, yucky, drying, typifying.*

Even before Greek words entered the English language, <y> in the middle of a word was not new to the English language, because, in Old English, <y> and <i> were interchangeable in that position. Then the English settled down to using <i> in the middle and <y> at the end of words. We see this in the words *their* and *they.*

When starting a word, <y> or <i> can be used in English words, because it is only inside a word that <y> has been replaced by <i> in all but words of Greek origin.

When <y> starts a word, it is nearly always followed by a vowel and acts as a consonant, as in *yellow* and *yard,* including *backyard,* in which *yard* is a word in a compound word. In just a few instances, word-initial <y> is followed by consonants and acts as a vowel.

Rule 3-111 Word initial <y> followed by one consonant spells [ee] and followed by two consonants spells []i].

Reason Orm's Law on long and short vowels.

List 3-111

YPERITE, YLANG-YLANG, and the name YVONNE in which <y> spells its long Continental sound [ee].)

YTTERBIUM, and YTTRIA in which <y> spells [i].

As we know, terminal <y> only spells [I] at the end of very short (one syllable) words like *fly* or at the end of —*efy* words, like *liquefy* and —*ify* words, like *magnify*. In all other words, terminal <y> spells [ee], except in the five exceptions *deny, reply, ally, rely, satisfy* which were all discussed earlier.

We see <y> inside English words which are compound words.

Rule 3-112 Initial and terminal <y> of stem words remains inside compound words.

Reason This occurs in compound words like *handyman*, which describes a man who is handy. We never change the <y> of a stem word to <i> when making compound words. *Handiwork* is handiwork with <i> just a "particle" to ease the joining of the stem words into a compound word. Particles do not give meaning. They guide our pronunciation. They make words easier to read out loud and understand. Other examples are the second <o> in *odometer* and the second <t> in *hitter,* (Cummings, p. 33). We see a linking particle in *hydrologist* and *hydrogen*. It is the letter <o>, which makes linking *hydr* with *gen* and with *logist* so much easier to say. The English language always uses <o> as a linking particle in words of Greek origin. It uses <i> as a linking particle in words made from Latin, e.g., *modification*. The Old English word *handgeweorc* copied this Latin link when it became *handiwork,* instead of *handwork* or *handowork*. (The letter <i> is an abbreviation of *in*, not a linking particle, in *handicap*. To do something with your cap in your hand was like doing it with one hand behind your back.)

Rebel HOLIDAY.
Rebel's Reason *Holiday* began as a combination of *holy* and *day* because the first holidays were on holy days. See Rule 1-50 and 'Holiday Words'.
Rascals The plural of *why,* WHYS and plural of the name of the letter <y>, WYES. The plurals *whys* and *wyes,* should drop <y> and add <ies>, so it should be *whies* and *wies* as in *ties*. So they have no excuse, but then again, we hardly ever use these words. See Writing Rule after List 1-57.
More Rebels and their Reasons. BABYHOOD, LADYHOOD, LADYSHIP, LADYLIKE, are not compound words. They are complex words, using suffixes and so <y> should be replaced with <i> but then *lady* and *baby* would lose their long vowels, because stress on the third syllable from the end would shorten it, as has happened for *holy* in *holiday*. *Babihood* might become related to a baby's babbling and *ladihood* would link closer to a *lad* then a *lady*.
List 3-112 examples of <y> inside compound words:
<u><y> spells [y]</u> BACKYARD, BONEYARD.
<u><y> spells [ee]</u> ANYHOW, ANYWHERE, ANYBODY, BABYSITTER, GERRYMANDER. <u><y> spells [I]</u> BYGONE, BYPASSES, BYWORD, MYSELF, THYSELF, CRYBABY, PLYWOOD, SPYGLASS, GOODBYE.

The rule against <y> inside English words refers to stem words, as do all rules, unless affixes, (infixes, prefixes or suffixes) are mentioned.
Rule 3-113 Terminal <y> spelling [ee] continues to do so before suffixes —*ing* and —*ist*.
Reason We cannot replace <y> with <i> for <ii> is forbidden. So *marry* would be *marring* and *copy* would be *copist.* Meaning would be lost.
Rebels are many, e.g., BIOLOGIST, GEOLOGIST.
Rebels' Reasons Meaning is not lost when <y> is removed. A *biologist* has no need to be called a 'biologyist'.
List 3-113
COPYIST, COPYING, ESSAYIST, LOBBYIST, LOBBYING, MARRYING, PARTYING etc.

We also see <y> inside English words with suffixes <ing> or <ist> added to terminal <y> spells [I].
Rule 3-114 Terminal <y> spelling [I] continues to do so before suffixes —*ing* and —*ist* and —*ify* and —*efy*.
Reason Stem words which end in <e> to obey the Short Word Rule no longer need <e> when a suffix is added. However *die* becomes *dying,* to prevent <ii>.
List 3-114
DRYING, DYEING, DYING verb *die*, EYING/EYEING, FLYING, FLYING DOCTOR, FLYING FOX, FRYING, LYING verb *lie*, PRYING, SHYING, TRYING, TYING verb *tie*, TYPING, VYING verb *vie*.
<u>suffix *-efy*</u> LIQUEFYING, PUTREFYING, RAREFYING, STUPEFYING.
<u>suffix *-ify*</u> AMPLIFYING, CERTIFYING, CLARIFYING, CLASSIFYING, CRUCIFYING, DECLASSIFYING, DEIFYING, DEMYSTIFYING, DISQUALIFYING, DIVERSIFYING, ELECTRIFYING, EXEMPLIFYING, FORTIFYING, GLORIFYING, GRATIFYING, IDENTIFYING, INTENSIFYING, MISCLASSIFYING, MISIDENTIFYING, MORTIFYING, MYSTIFYING,

OBJECTIFYING, PERSONIFYING, PETRIFYING, PRETTIFYING, QUANTIFYING, RECERTIFYING, RECLASSIFYING, RECTIFYING, REFORTIFYING, REQUALIFYING, SANCTIFYING, SIMPLIFYING, SPECIFYING, SPEECHIFYING *slang*, STRATIFYING, STULTIFYING, TYPIFY [tip-i-fI], TYPIFYING, TESTIFYING, VITRIFYING.

Very few English words end in [y] before a vowel. *Soya, hoya* and *bunya*, in which <y> spells [y], are all adopted. In all words ending <ye>, as in *dye*, <y> spells [I], except for the word *ye* in which <y> spells [y]. In *embryo* <y> spells [ee] and there is no word ending <yu>.

Names do not have to obey rules but most are quite "ruly". Young Kyle would be a suitable young man to introduce the list of words which obey the rule <y> spells [I] in the first syllable. Rusty could tell us that <y> spells [ee] at the end of most words. Jocelyn could tell us when <y> spells [i]. Yvonne has a rare initial <y> followed by a consonant. She's not listed — maybe busy in the chem. lab. with Ytterbium.

Names in which <y> spells [I] in the first syllable. BRYAN, BRYCE, DRYDEN, KYLE, HYACINTH, HYATT, MYRA, SKYE, SYMON, TYRON, RYAN, TYLER, WYATT, WYOMING, USA. (Rebel, DYLAN).

Names in which <y> spells [i] before a terminal consonant. BERYL, BRONWYN, CAROLYN, CAROLYN, CHERYL, DARYL, GWYN(ETH), JOCELYN, KYM, KYM, LYDIA, LYN, MARILYN, MERYL, ROBYN, SELWYN, WYN.

Names in which <y> spells [i] before "double gates', two consonants. FLYNN, LYNDON, ODYSSEUS, CRYSTAL, DYLLIS, GYPSY, LYNDELL, LYNETTE, PHYLLIS, SYLVESTER, SYLVIA, SYLVIE, ULYSSES.

Names in which <y> before a vowel spells [y]. SONYA, NGUYEN, YASMIN, YOLANDA.

Names in which terminal <y> spells [ee]. AMY, ANTHONY, ANTONY, CLANCY, CROSBY, EMILY, EMORY, HONESTY, IGGY, IVY, JUDY, KATY, LUCY, MELODY, PRUDY, RORY, RUBY, RUDY, RUSTY, SANDY, SELBY, SHELBY, SKIPPY, TIFFANY, TIMOTHY, TRINITY, TRUDY, ZACARY.

Relevant Writing Rules. **1st**. Normally terminal <y> is replaced with <i> if a suffix starts with a vowel: *marry, marriage*. However, when *ing* is added the <y> remains to prevent <ii>, because <ii> is a "no-no". **2nd**. English adjectives remain singular so don't change *silly* to *sillies* for we say *silly man* and *silly men*. We say *funny teddy, funny teddies*. **3rd**. Many verbs end in <y>. If they end in <y> preceded by a vowel we just add <s> when *he, she* or *it* does the verb: *I pray, he prays*. If they end in <y> preceded by a consonant, then we remove the <y> and add <ies>: *I carry, she carries; you rely, he relies*. **4th**. The same rule applies to plural nouns: *bunny, bunnies; monkey, monkeys*. Return to Reading Rules.

Part Four

Part Four takes us right to the end of the reading road with new letter codes for long vowels, including diphthongs, double songs or sounds. Some long vowels have subsequently shortened, as in *break*, which shortens in *breakfast*. English absorbed digraphs from other languages along with their words, which means that they decode in different ways, as in *phaeton* and *faeces*. Also, the controlling nature of Bossy R can change the sound a digraph spells — compare *maelstrom* and *aerodrome*, *neutral* and *amateur*, or *vein* and *heir*. Adding to this the way long vowels lifted in the Great Vowel Shift, but rarely changed their spelling, means that explaining the patterns we shall now admire takes time and patience. Such a variety of patterns adds texture to the rich tapestry of English history visible in English text.

Old and New Vowels — *wound* **noun,** *wound* **verb.**

In the olden days, without radio and good roads, people did not mix much or hear how others spoke. In England the simple word *old* was [ald] up north and [e-arld] down south. *Alderman* is still [al-der-man] up north and [orl-der-man] down south, even though they are both spelt *alderman*. One spelling was chosen, regardless of different pronunciations. There were even *earldormen* once, [erld-er-men], but they became *earls* [erlz].

Original English words are only 20% of today's English words. As we know, the English language is like a vacuum cleaner for it sucks up new words from every corner of the world, from over 350 other languages, (Crytsal p. 144). As we know, many words are adopted into English without their written form adapted to match English words. For example, French *obey* was not changed to *obay*. On other occasions, foreign words are adopted and then read out as if they follow English spelling rules, e.g., as we have seen French *client* [klee-on] has been adopted into English and read out loud as [klI-ent].

Many new words try to enter English with new sounds, sounds that English speakers are not used to making. Each language has its own sounds. There are all together 800 different consonants and 200 different vowels in the world, (Crystal, p. 61). Relax, English did not expand to use 200 vowel sounds!

Languages change, too. Long ago English had three diphthongs, that is, two vowels in the same syllable, and used <æa>, <eo> and <ie> to spell them. These double-sounds dropped out of use. The Old English single vowel letters, (unigraphs, like <e>, <i>, etc.), spelt both short and long vowel sounds, (Miles 2005 p. 81), with short as in 'That dud pen is not good' — [a] [u] [e] [i] [o] [uu]. That was back before English lost the letter Ash, <æ>, which spelt short vowel [a], back when <a> spelt short vowel [u] and <u> spelt short vowel [uu].

Then English gained two new diphthongs, [oi] and [ow]. The diphthong [oi] was not used in Old English words, e.g., *boil* was *byle* [bII], (Cummings, p. 301). This double-sound arrived in 'Invasion Words' in 1066. For instance, the Normans called their male servants 'boy'. We shall see <oy> at the end of words and <oi> inside words, for we know that <y> should not be inside words unless they are Greek. The diphthong [ow] developed from [oo] when it was spelt <ou>. This [oo] lifted in the GVS and hit the roof of the mouth and bent into the double-sound [ow], as in *house*. We shall meet words in which this did not happen, like *you, wound* and *youth*.

Short and Long Vowels *A E I O U and Y*

Before the Norman Invasion, six letters (Ash and A, E, I, O, U) spelt the six short vowel sounds in "That dud pen is not good." When letter Ash was removed, English short vowels became those in 'That pen is not much good' — [a] [e] [i] [o] [u] [uu], with <u> spelling two short vowels, [u] and [uu]. At times <a> spells [u], too, when unstressed, as in *ago,* but now spells the sound Ash once did, [a]. The rest of Europe generally kept on using just five vowel letters to spell the short vowels in "Dud pen is not good."

These short vowels naturally lengthen into the long vowels in "Pa may we all too?" The letters A, E, I, O and U are named on the Continent after their long vowels, [ar], [ay], [ee], [or] and [oo]. However, in English they are known as [ay], [ee], [I], [oh] and [yoo], because in English A, E, I, O and U spell these long sounds, with U spelling either [oo] or [yoo], as in the mnemonic "Maybe I won't use glue." (The mnemonic uses the long vowel sounds in these words.)

We have already heard how U's name gained a yod, because the English could not pronounce [oo] the French way, as in *adieu* [ar-dee-oo], and, instead of [ee-oo], said [yoo]. We have also heard how yods then began dropping in some words, so that now <u> can spell long vowels [yoo] or just [oo].

The vowels in *"Boy!"* and *"Ow!"* are called diphthongs, (literally 'di-song') because they have two sounds, double-song. Say them, [ow] and [oi], and watch each other's lips. Do they move twice? Yes. Lips move whenever there is a change to a different word-sound, even if it is just a change of vowel and does not require lips to close. This makes lip-reading possible. Watch your lips in the mirror as you say all the long vowel sounds. There are three which bend our lips just a little: [ay], [I] and [oh] — see sound chart in the introduction. In upper-class English these sound like single-sounds, monophthongs. Lower class Eliza in the play *Pygmalion* and the film *My Fair Lady* made [I] into a clear double-sound, until Henry Higgins trained her to say [I], not [oi].) My English friend Carol says my Australian *no* sounds like [noh-oo] compared to her short [noh]. The way I speak depends on where I am, and who I am talking to. Although I try 'to be true to myself' I find I cannot help copying others, (Crystal, on p. 55 agrees), or at times over reacting, exaggerating my natural accent. That word *accent* means "add song", add song to speech. Accent involves more than how we say our vowels. It's also how we stress syllables. We linger longer on some syllables, or say them louder, than others. Speakers of English as a second language apply stress in other ways, ways they learnt in their mother-tongues. Welsh syllables are stressed using high and low tones, up and down, like high and low musical notes. The Welsh add this song to English, giving it a Welsh accent. English is now spoken with accents from all over the world.

<u>Not needed but nice to know.</u> Some say that Australian English is influenced by the way convict ancestors spoke during our eighty years of white slavery, but no mention is made of such influence on American English during America's one hundred and sixty years of white slavery. Seeing USA 'in the colonial period as penal settlements and convict establishments move(s) incredulity and indignation in Americans', (Butler 1896 p. 12). As late as 1786 every ship arrived in British America 'with either redemptioners or convicts, in which schoolmasters are not as regularly advertised for sale as weavers, tailors, or any other trade'. Everyone knows that George Washington's family kept slaves, but few hear of the white school master convict bought and kept as a white slave to educate young George Washington, (Butler 1896 p. 27). <u>Now back to things we need to know.</u>

Vowel Best Friends, or Vowel Digraphs.

We've seen that long vowels can be spelt with one vowel letter, with direction from other letters like <lk> in *folk*, <gh> in *high*, Bossy R in *fork* and *for* or Fairy E in *mate*. We've used doublets to spell the long vowels in *soon, been, vacuum,* and *aardvark.* Now we are going to see that they can be written with either two different vowel letters or with one vowel letter and one semi-vowel letter, forming a digraph. "Di" means two and "graph" means carved mark because letters used to be carved in wood or engraved in stone. As we have heard, children call two letters which spell one sound 'Best Friends', instead of 'digraph'. These 'Best Friends' are said to 'go walking' when they are in the same syllable, in other words, forming a digraph. They do not 'go walking' in *aorta,* in *idea,* nor in *pliant.* Children are often taught that when two vowels go walking the first one "does the talking" meaning that the first vowel spells a word-sound and the other one is silent. The first one spells its long sound: "When two vowels go walking the first one does the talking. Very profound, it spells its long sound." Some children say it "talks big". This rule is easy to remember because it is a rhyme but it is not always true. This rule works in *boat* but not in *about*. It works in *bay* but not in *boy*. We shall soon hear a better rule to use when decoding digraphs.

We know that doublets are very stable. No matter what that vowel sound is, a doublet is very stable and will not change when the stem word grows. For instance, <oo> spells [u] in *blood*, and does not change in *bloody* or in the compound word *bloodshot*. What about ordinary digraphs — two vowels which are not identical — are they stable? They do not change the way they are written, e.g., <ea> in *break* [brayk] does not change in the compound word *breakfast* [brek-farst], but the sound it spells changes. Digraph <ea> also spells different sounds in 'we *read* [red] it yesterday but we *read* [reed] it today.' Once again, the dictionary committee wanted the letters to link words to their origins and hence their meanings. We see from its spelling that *breakfast* is the first meal of the day after fasting all night, that we 'break our fast', but it would be easier to read as *brekfast*. *Read* it yesterday would be easier to read as *red* but that would be as mystifying as the riddle: "What is black and white and red all over?" (A newspaper.) We shall meet words which do not decode as they should, in their special lists. For instance, *read* [red] belongs to the Ready Redheads.

The Curse of the Dagger will continue to make trouble for us. Due to the Roman dislike and fear of the Sign of the Dagger, the letter Z, <s> spells both [s] and [z] after vowel digraphs — [s] in *cease, east* and *sausage*, and [z] in *ease, easel* and *cause*, for instance. As we know, <s> never spells [z] at the beginning of words, when word-initial. Inside words, <s> can only spell [s] after a vowel digraph when it is followed by an unvoiced consonant, as in *east*. The rest of the time, <s> after a vowel digraph, followed by a voiced consonant or a vowel (which are all voiced), <s> spells [z], unless the vowel digraph is in a suffix. When word-final, when <s> ends a word, it spells [z] after a stressed vowel digraph. This happens in plurals, like *days, peas, boys, yaws, etc*. When <s> ends a suffix, it follows an unstressed vowel, (suffixes being unstressed) which is why <s> in *wondrous* spells [s], for example. However, when <s> is penultimate (second to last) it can spell either <s> or [z] before a vowel, as in the noun *house* and, from it, the verb *house*, the latter using the stronger, voiced [z] because verbs have strong endings. When verbs become nouns they keep their voiced endings, e.g., *bruise* always spells [brooz] because it was a verb first, before it became a noun as well. Some nouns end with <se> spelling [z] — like *applause, disease, malaise* and *noise* — but others end in [s], like *lease, louse* and *moose*. Since we need to know which nouns have <se> spells [z], list words will be marked. Verbs ending <se> are marked too. We only see <ss> after digraphs inside the French adoptions *reconnaissance* and *renaissance, trousseau* and *caisson* (Cummings p. 403) because English words only use <ss> to spell [s] after short vowels. Even when <ss> spells [z] in the rebel words *dessert* and *dissolve*, <ss> follows a short vowel spelt with one letter.

<u>Relevant Writing Rule</u> Suffixes pop straight on to words ending with vowel digraphs unless it's <e> to <e>. <u>Reason</u>: There is no twinning of terminal stem letters or dropping of <y> for <i> when suffixes are added to vowel digraphs. The only digraph to change is when <e> is dropped from a terminal vowel digraph before a suffix beginning with <e>. This only involves three digraphs, <ee>, <oe> and <ue> and three main suffixes, <ed>, <er> or <est>. For example, we have met *freest*, and shall meet *hoed* and *blued*. (Other suffixes which start <e>, *ery, eal, ence, eer, eur, escent, ent, ee, en, ency, erie, esce, ese, esque, ess, eth, etic* and *ette*, are unlikely to be used.) <u>Note:</u> In *colloquy* and *soliloquy* the <u> is acting as a consonant, not forming a vowel digraph with <y> and so the plurals, *colloquies* and *soliloquies* are not simple pop-ons, not like *buys* and *monkeys* and *buying* and *obeying*. <u>Rebels</u> {LAY, PAY}, SAY. We've already met *said* and we'll see that *lay* and *pay* become *laid* and *paid*, not *payed* and *layed*. <u>Return to Reading Rules</u>.

"When two vowels go walking the first one does the talking. Very profound, it spells its long sound," was introduced under 'Vowel Best Friends or Digraphs'. The semi-vowels <y> and <w> are included, for they act as vowels in vowel digraphs. However, it's a weak rule because it works in *day* and *train* but not in *launch,* nor in *lawn,* nor in *anaemic.* Rule 4-1 is very useful.

Rule 4-1 When two vowels go walking the first one does the talking. Very profound, it spells its long sound. But if the last one is Greek, the first one needn't speak.

Reason The saying "Beware of Greek gifts," explains it all, for when two vowels go walking the first one does the talking, as long as Greek words and Greek letters are not involved. Which letters are Greek? When the Romans took their alphabet to Britain in AD 43 it had only 20 letters, all upper-case: ABCDEFGHIKLMNOPQRSTV. These letters travelled from Greece to today's Tuscany. Once there, around 750 BC, the Etruscans made changes to the letters before they travelled on to Rome. For instance, they flipped letter B, C, D, E, F, K, L, P, R and S from left to right and called them by their sounds instead of using their Greek names. The Romans received these Etruscan letters around 650 BC. Much later, when they adopted some Greek words, they also adopted UWXYZ directly from Greece, so they could spell words like *zephyros*, the Greek word for a west wind. (J was added later.) The letters which came directly from Greece are the ones we call Greek letters. The letter <u> came directly from the Greek language and <w> grew from <u> by doubling it, (Cummings, p. 373). So, it does not work when <au> and <aw> go walking. We write *lawn* but we do not let <a> do the talking, we do not say [layn], or even [larn] with a long Continental vowel. However, as we shall see, <w> lets <o> do the talking in *mow* and *low* and *follow*. This is because <w> came into English twice. It came in from Germany as a runic symbol, which looked like a pointed P, a small triangular flag on a pole. It was called Wynne. After 1066 the Normans replaced Wynne's runic symbol with W, which they used because of their Viking heritage. W has never been a French letter. They changed many Old English word endings to just [oh], spelt <ow>, as in *mow, arrow* and *snow*. In all these Old English words <w> lets <o> do the talking because it did not start out as a Greek letter.

We saw <y> do the talking in <ay> spelling [ay], the long Anglo sound of <a> but we cannot trust it, e.g., it does not let <o> 'do the talking' in *boy* because <y> came from Greece, not Rome. We cannot trust Y, U, or Greek W (excluding W which came from the old English rune Wynne), to let a vowel do the talking because they all originated in the Greek language. The Greeks have given English wonderful words – but we could say their language has been plundered by the English and to get even they have smuggled trouble into the English language inside their words. The Greeks smuggled warriors into Troy by hiding them inside a huge wooden horse which they left outside the city's gates. Their enemies, the Trojans, took it into their city and the rest is history. Can you name the trouble they have smuggled into English in their wonderful words? Yes, Y, U and W, for they do not conform to English decoding rules. There is an old saying, "Beware of Greeks bearing gifts". From Virgil's Aeneid, Book 2, 19 BC, it is "Do not trust the horse, Trojans. Whatever it is, I fear the Greeks even when they bring gifts." However, Sophocles feared the gifts, not the foes, in his play called Ajax - "Foes gifts are no gifts". This fits us better, for we like Greek words, just dislike the letters they carry into English when Y, U and W muck up our decoding rules. That is why we shall find that in vowel digraphs the first one does the talking unless Y, U or W are involved or unless the words themselves came from Greece, like *anaemic*. That is why we are allowed to ask in spelling tests, "Is the word Greek?" as in the movie *Akeelah and the [Spelling] Bee.* Maybe it also explains why we say "It's all Greek to me," when something puzzles us. Check out Floyd with his Trojan Horse in the website's Photo Gallery.

Let's look at all the sounds <a> spells with its best friends.
A Digraphs

Digraph <ay> — *may, always.*
Rule 4-2 <ay> spells [ay].

Reason This digraph is easy for we learnt <say> spells [say] in Part One. This follows the rule "When two vowels go walking, the first one does the talking," and yet one of them is the Greek letter Y. That is because they cannot end in <ai> spells [ay] because English words are not allowed to end in <i>. In the terminal digraph <ay>, the first one does the talking, because the letter <y> has been used in place of <i>. It is OK in French to write *gai* but not in English. The same word in French, *gai*, is *gay* in English. Some words ending <ay> came from Germany with throaty endings, the word *day* was *dæg,* and others ended in the old letter called yogh, used for voiced <h>. Yogh's symbol was <ʒ>. When words lost their guttural [ag] and [a ʒ] endings and just ended in [ay] this word-sound was written <ay> because terminal <ai> is a no-no. In some other words the old yogh became <gh> but *dagh* would have spelt [daf] or [dar], instead of [day]. Instead, <y> replaced old yogh because it looks a bit like that old letter, <ʒ>. By the way, remember that <ays> spells [ayz] because <s> spells [z] after vowel digraphs.

Rebels MAYOR, QUAY, BAYOU, KAYAK, CAYENNE and PRAYER.

Rebels' Reasons *Mayor* spells [mair] and used to be *mair* or *mer* but <y> was used to make it look more like its Latin ancestor *major*. (That was probably to stop people thinking the word came from *mother,* in French, *mère.* For then the town would have a mother to lead and look after it, instead of a sergeant-major.) *Prayer* spells [prair], like its French ancestor *preiere,* and is linked to the word *precarious* for it is risky to obtain things by prayer, very 'precarious'. *Quay* spells [kee] because it was once the Norman French word *key* and later "upgraded" to "pure" French *quai* and then <y> replaced <i> to make it English but the original pronunciation has remained, which means <que> spells [k] even though it is not terminal <que>. This is one of the rare words in which <qu> spells [k] inside a word, because, although <que> is not terminal, it is followed by all vowels, no consonants, which happens in *queue* too. In just three rebels, *bayou, kayak* and *Cayenne,* the capital of French Guiana, <ay> spells [I]. They are all adopted but not adapted. However, Queen Quill and her regal king, Rex Text, have been turning the tables on King Sound and Queen Speech ever since folk began reading, and so Australian cooks read the label on Cayenne pepper tins and call it [kay-en] [pep-er].

Rebels to the Rule against <y> inside English words include the French adoptions LAYETTE, BAYONET, CRAYON, {MAYONNAISE}, and also the old English word MAYHEM.

List 4-2 <ay> spells [ay]

ALLAY, ALWAYS* <al> =[or], ARRAY, ASSAY, ASTRAY, AWAY, AY, AYE, BAY, BAYONET, BIRTHDAY, BRAY, BYWAY, CASTAWAY *VS,* CLAY, CLAYMORE, CRAYFISH, CRAYON, CROSSWAYS, DAY, DAYBOOK, DAYTIME, DEFRAY, DELAY, DISARRAY, DRAY, EDGEWAYS, ENDWAYS, ESSAY, EVERYDAY, EXPRESSWAY, FLAY, FORAY, FRAY, FREEWAY, GANGWAY, GATEWAY, GAY, HAY, HAYMAKING, HAYSTACK, HAYWIRE, HORSEPLAY, INLAY, JAY, JAY-WALKING, LAY Δ, LAY CLAIM TO, LAY HOLD OF, LAY IT ON THE LINE, LAY OPEN, LAY TO REST, LAY WASTE, LAY-BY, LAYER, LAYER CAKE, LAYETTE *fossil* <e>, LAYMAN, LONGWAYS, MAY§, MAYBE*, MAYHEM, MAYN'T, MAYPOLE, MIDDAY, MOTORWAY, PARLAY, PAY Δ, PAYER, PAY FOR, PAYING GUEST, PAY ITS WAY, PAY OFF, PAY-PACKET, PAY UP, PAYABLE, PAYEE, PAYMASTER *VS,* PAYMENT, PAYOLA, PAYROLL, PLAY*, PLAY-BACK, PLAY BALL <all> =[orl], PLAY FOR SAFETY, PLAY FOR TIME, PLAY OFF, PLAY ON, PLAY-PEN, PLAY THE GAME, PLAY THE MARKET, PLAY UP, PLAY WITH, PLAYER, PIANO-PLAYER, PLAYFUL, PLAYING-CARD, PLAYMATE, PLAYTHING, PLAYTIME, PORTRAY, PRAY, RAY, RELAY, REPAY, REPAYABLE, RUNAWAY, RUNWAY, SAY Δ, SAYING, SIDEWAYS, SLAY Δ, SLAYING, SPAY, SPRAY, STAY, STAYER, STAYS, STRAY, SWAY, TODAY [too-day], TRAY, UNDERLAY, WAY, BY THE WAY, BY WAY OF, IN A WAY, IN NO WAY, IN THE WAY, ON THE WAY, UNDER WAY, WAY BACK, WAY-BILL, WAYFARING-TREE, WAYLAY Δ, WAYSIDE, WAYWARD [waywəd]. <u>Proper Nouns</u> FRIDAY, GALLOWAY, MAY, MAYA, MONDAY *f*, SATURDAY, SUNDAY, THURSDAY*

<s>=[z], URUGUAY [er-oo-gway], WEDNESDAY* [wenz-day]. Names FAY, FINLAY, GAY, GAYLORD, GRAYSON, JAY, JAYDEN, KAY, LINDSAY, MAY, RAY, SANJAY.

Always was *all way's* before it contracted and lost the possession apostrophe. "*Always* is an old genitive," says Cummings, p. 252, 'ways of all kinds'.

§*May* is an auxiliary verb. Here are three ways to use it. **1st way.** When adding possibility to a verb, but, the less likely the possibility, the more appropriate it is to use *might*. **2nd way.** *May have* means that you don't yet know whether something has happened – the possibility is still open. *Might have* refers to a past possibility. **3rd way.** Both *may* and *might* can be used to express permission. *Might* has a higher degree of politeness than *may*:— 'Might I help you?' 'May I help you?'

*Maybe is an adverb meaning 'perhaps' and 'possibly', e.g., "Maybe I'll choose you after all." "Do you think maybe we could leave early?" "That looks like a train, or a tram, maybe." It's an adverb, used alongside verbs, but is also used as a stand alone answer to a question, e.g., "Will you marry me?" When we discuss this reply, we turn it into a noun — "It's not a yes but it's a maybe, so at least it's not a no". *May be* is a verb phrase that generally means the same thing as "might be."

*Monday was *Moon Day* but, in Old English, *moon* was written *mona* and so maybe we should say [mohn day], which might end up written as *Moanday*. However, as it looks like a feather word, we readnit and say [mun-day].

*Play is an old English word. We "play tennis" but we do not "play running". Why? Matthews 1979 on p. 125 sees the word as a faithful old servant which discharges its duties to perfection but will not do other things, unlike some words which are easy going and will 'lend a hand' with anything. *Play* originally referred to any activity indulged in for pleasure. We play games, like polo and tennis, but we do not play field sports like running, jumping and the discus, i.e., we do not say "Come and play running with me." Running, riding, swimming and throwing were all practical activities before they became sports. We can only play at things which began as pure fun. We can 'play a part' on stage, and we can 'play music'. However, we do not 'play a picture', nor play a painting, nor a sculpture. Matthews thinks that these activities were chiefly to invoke magic, a serious matter, not play. Despite newer words like *drama, theatre* etc we still go to a *play* and children still *play* games. *Play* is indeed a faithful servant of pure fun.

*In *Thursday* <s> spells [z] because it was *Thor's Day* not 'thurse day' or 'thurst day'. In Old English it was Þurresdæg, in which <es> showed ownership, Thor's day.

*Wednesday was originally "Woden's Day" in which <e> spelt [ə] and then shrank altogether because of the great stress on [woh]. Wodin brought lots of woe for he was a raging, mad, crazy but inspired German god, whom the Romans called Mercury. Back before apostrophes were in use, <es> showed ownership, and so we lose one <e> but one remains, <wodenes> <dæg>, which became <wodnes> <dæg>, and later <wednesday> which we treat as <wedn'sday> because the ownership <e> should have been hooked out when apostrophes came in. This gives us four consonants in a row: [dnsd]. In difficult clusters like this, as we have seen, long consonants flow over short ones, sonorants flow over obstruents. So, [n] flows back over [d] and also <s> spells [z] so that it can blend with voiced [n]. So, we get [wenz-day]. However, Cummings, on page 23, says that many folk now say [wed-nez-day] as they use 'the visual not the aural pronunciation'. In other words, he is saying that Queen Quill and Rex Text are winning the day with this word in America. I am still ruled by King Sound and Queen Speech for the people all around me say [wenz-day].

Relevant Writing Rule. When adding a suffix beginning with a vowel to a word ending in <y> look at the letter behind <y>. If it is a vowel, then do not change <y>, just add the suffix, as in *staying, stayer, stayed, bayish* (colour). If it is a consonant, then change <y> to <i> except before <ing> or <ish> or <ist> as in *envying, babyish* and *copyist*. Return to Reading Rules.

Digraph <ai> — *abstain, wraith.*

Rule 4-3 Inside a stem word <ai> spells [ay].

Reason We'd expect this because <y> is not allowed inside English stem words. As we know, <y> is replaced by <i> inside stem words. We also know that suffixes pop straight onto <ay> and so <y> is allowed inside complex words, words that have grown from stem words into bigger words, words like *stayer* and *paying*.

Rebels DAIS; SAID, UNSAID, AFORESAID, AGAIN, AGAINST; CAPTAIN, CERTAIN, CERTAINLY, CERTAINTY, CHAPLAIN, CHAMBERLAIN; AISLE, ASSEGAI, NAIAD FAIENCE, BANZAI, BONSAI, SAMURAI, TAIPAN, KURDAITCHA; PLAIT, PLAID, DAIQUIRI. Proper Noun: BRITAIN.

Rebels' Reasons *Dais*, a raised platform, first of all rebelled against a terminal <e> even though it has been pronounced [dayz] in both France and England for centuries. However most rebels are brought into line sooner or later, it is just a matter of which will change, the writing or the reading? Nowadays Rex Text usually overrides King Sound which explains why we hear [day-is] more and more. Without the terminal <e> the word looks like a "glide and yap" word, [day-is]. This new pronunciation is actually closer to the word's origins, for in Roman times a raised platform was called a raised *discus.*

We know that *said* [sed] is a shortening of long [sayd]. So *unsaid* spells [un-sed], *aforesaid* spells [a-for-sed]. There are only two other words in which this happens: *again* [agen] and *against*. [agenst]. These are words that are used a lot but are just prepositions, not as important as verbs and adverbs, nouns and adjectives. We like to say unimportant words quickly. *Said* is a verb, but said so often that it, too, shortened, to [sed]. If printing had not been invented, would we have changed them by hand by now? (*Agen* is quicker to write than *again* but that would spell [ajen].) We also shorten the sound of many unstressed word endings containing the digraph <ai>:— *captain* [kap-ten], *certain* [ser-ten], *chaplain* [chap-len], *chamberlain* [chaym-ber-len]. Depending on the stress on syllables, <ai> in complex words like *ascertain* and *certainly* spells either [ay], when stressed, or [e], when unstressed, as in *uncertain, certainly* and *certainty.* Proper Nouns are never rebels because they do not have to obey rules, but *Britain* has been listed because <ai> does not spell [ay]. We say it like the original word *Britton,* named after the Celtic tribe *Brittos.* See Etymonline for more about *Britain.*

Nine Rebels use the German digraph <ai> to spell [I], *aisle, assegai, naiad, faience, banzai, bonsai, samurai, taipan* and *kurdaitcha,* words we rarely use. We see <ai> spells [I] in names like *Cairo, Hawaii* [har-wI-ee], *Kaiser, Nairobi, Taiwan* and *Thailand.* The proper noun *Shanghai* is also a verb, due to the practice of kidnapping to fill crews of ships going to far away places like Shanghai. The past participle, *shanghaied,* gives an unusual three vowels in a row, as does *assegaied. Banzai, bonsai* and *samurai* are Japanese adoptions. *Taipan* was adopted from the Wik-Munkan Ab'l language of Cape York, (Blake, p. 103). *Kurdaitcha* is one of the many Ab'l words adopted into English, a Central Australian term to describe a sorcerer or sorcery mission, probably recorded by Lutheran missionaries.

In three words <ai> spells [a], in *plait, plaid* and *daiquiri. Plait* used to spell [playt]. Its two meanings, "to braid" and "to pleat", then separated into two sounds, [plat] and [pleet]. One got a new spelling, *pleat,* for its new sound and the other, *plait,* kept the old spelling, but got a new sound, [plat]. A *plait* is a *braid* which is "three or more pieces of rope or hair woven together". *Plaid* is Scots for blanket, usually woven in three or more colours to make tartans, the distinctive patterns of each clan. The word *plaid* was written <plad> or <pladd> or <pladde> until 1800. Whatever could have happened to make them change a word's spelling when its pronunciation did not change? Since both *plaits* and *plaids* are woven and since they sounded so similar, [plat] and [plad], it's possible that *plaid* mimicked *plait's* spelling. Shame it wasn't the other way around. Some feel it might have been a case of mixed convergence. As with *busy* and *jury,* this occurs when two earlier separate pronunciations and spellings combine and have the pronunciation of one with the spelling of the other. The verb *ache* and the noun *ache* were once said and written differently.

People *aked* [aykd] an *ache* [aych] (Etymonline), just like we *speak* a *speech* and *bake* a *batch* today, until the words combined, using *ache's* spelling and *ake's* sound. The only other word in which <ai> spells [a] is the Spanish drink *daiquiri* [dak-i-ree], excused as adopted, but not adapted.

List 4-3 <ai> spells [ay] and remember <gh> is silent after long vowels, as in *straight*.

ABSTAIN, ACCLAIM, ACQUAINT, ACQUAINTANCE, AFRAID, AID, AIDE* *fossil e,* AIL, AILERON, AILMENT, AIM, AIMLESS, AIN'T, AITCH*, AITCHBONE*, APPRAISE* <se>=[z], ASCERTAIN, ATTAIN, ATTAINABLE, ATTAINMENT, AVAIL, AVAILABLE, AWAIT, BAIL, BAILIFF, BAIT, BAIZE, BARGAIN, BARMAID, BLACKMAIL, BRAID, BRAILLE*, BRAIN, BRAINLESS, BRAINSTORM, BRAINWASH [wosh], BRAINWAVE, BRAINY, BRAISE* <se>=[z], BRIDESMAID, CAISSON, CAMPAIGN silent <g>, CAPTAIN, CHAIN, CHAIN-LETTER, CHAIN-SMOKE, CHAIN-STITCH, CHAIN STORE, CHAISE* <se>=[z], CHAMBERLAIN, CHAPLAIN, CHILBLAIN, CLAIM, CLAIMANT, COCAINE *fossil <e>,* COCKTAIL, COMPLAIN, COMPLAINT, COMPLAISANT, CONSTRAIN, CONSTRAINT, CONTAIN, CONTAINER, CONTAINERIZE, CONTAINMENT, COXSWAIN, CROSS-GRAINED, CURTAIL, DAILY, DAINTY, DAISY, DECLAIM, DERAIL, DETAIL, DETAIN, DETAINEE, DISCLAIM, DISDAIN, DISTRAIN, DISTRAINT, DOMAIN, DOVETAIL *f*, DRAIN, DRAINAGE, ENTAIL, ENTERTAIN, ENTERTAINMENT, ENTRAILS, EXPLAIN, FAIL, FAILURE, FAIN, FAINT, FAINTLY, FAINTNESS, FAITH, FAITHFUL, FAITHFULLY, FAITHFULNESS, FAITHLESS, FLAIL, FRAIL, FRAILTY, GAIETY*, GAILY, GAIN, GAINFUL, GAINSAY, GAIT, GAITER, GRAIN, GRAINY, HAIL, HANDRAIL, HARE-BRAINED, INGRAINED, JAIL, LACKADAISICAL, LAID, LAIN, LANDRAIL, LEGERDEMAIN, LIAISE [lee-ayz], LIAISON <iai>=[ee-ay], MAID, MAIDEN, MAIDENLY, MAIDEN NAME, MAIDENHOOD, MAIDENHAIR, MAIL, MAIL TRAIN, MAIL, MAIN, MAINLY, IN THE MAIN, MAIN FRAME, MAINLAND, MAINMAST *VS,* MAINSPRING, MAINSTAY, MAINTAIN, MAINTENANCE, MAISONETTE, MAIZE, MALAISE* <se>=[z], MAYONNAISE* <se>=[z], MERMAID, MILKMAID, MONORAIL, MORAINE *fossil e,* NAIL, NURSEMAID, OBTAIN, OBTAINABLE, ORDAIN, OXTAIL, PAID, PAIL, PAID, PAINED, PAINLESS, PAINSTAKING, PAINT, PAINTBOX, PAINTBRUSH, PAINTER, PAINTING, PAINTWORK, PAY-CLAIM, PERTAIN, PLAICE, PLAID, PLAIN, PLAINSONG, PLAINTIFF, PLAINTIVE, PLAINTIVELY, PLAINTIVENESS, PLANTAIN, POLONAISE*, PORCELAIN, PORTRAIT, PORTRAITURE, PRAISE* <se>=[z], PRAISEWORTHY*, <wor>=[wer], PREVAIL, PROCLAIM, PTOMAINE silent <p>, fossil < e>, QUAIL, QUAINT, QUATRAIN*, RAID, RAIL, RAILING, RAILLERY, RAILMAN, RAILWAY, RAILWAYMAN, RAIMENT, RAIN, RAINDROP, RAINFALL, RAINY, RAISE* <se>=[z], RAISIN, RECLAIM, RECONNAISSANCE*, REFRAIN, REGAIN, REMAIN, REMAINDER, REMAINS, RENAISSANCE*, REPAINT, RESTRAIN, RESTRAINT, RETAIL, RETAIN, RETAINER, RETRAIN, SAIL, SAILCLOTH, SAILING-SHIP, SAILOR, SAINT, SAINTLY, SAITHE *fish,* SELF-PORTRAIT, SELF-CONTAINED, SELF-RAISING, SHIRTWAISTER, SLAIN, SNAIL, STAID, STAIN, STAINLESS, STAINLESS STEEL, STAYSAIL, STRAIGHT silent <gh>, STRAIGHTEN, STRAIGHTFORWARD, STRAIGHTFORWARDLY, STRAIN, STRAINER, STRAIT = *restricted,* STRAITENED *adj.,* STRAIT-JACKET, STRAITLACED, SUBMAIN, SUZERAIN, SUZERAINTY, SWAIN, TAFFRAIL, TAIL, TAIL AWAY, TAIL-END, TAIL-GATE, TAIL-LAMP, TAIL OFF, TAILS, TAIL WIND, TAILLESS, TAILOR, TAILORESS, TAILOR-MADE, TAILPIPE, TAILPLANE, TAILSTOCK, TAIPAN, TAINT, TERRAIN*, TRAIL, TRAILER, TRAIN, TRAINABLE, TRAINEE, TRAINER, TRAINSICK, TRAIPSE*, TRAIT optional silent terminal [t], TRAITOR, TWAIN, UNCERTAIN, UNDERPAID, UNGAINLY, UNFAILING, UNFAILINGLY, UNFAITHFUL, UNPAID, UNRESTRAINED, UPBRAID, VAIN, VAINGLORY, VERVAIN, VILLAIN, WAGTAIL, WAIF, WAIL, WAIN, WAINSCOT, WAIST, WAISTED, WAISTBAND, WAISTLINE, WAIT, WAITING GAME, WAITING-LIST, WAITING-ROOM,

WAITER, WAITRESS, WAIVE, WAIVER, WASSAILING, WHITEBAIT, WRAITH. <u>Proper Nouns</u>, BAHRAIN, BAILEY BRIDGE, BAILEY, BRAILLE, CHAROLLAIS <ch>=[sh], FAIR ISLE, GRAIL, HAITI, JAIN, JAMAICA, JAMAICAN, KAITLYN, MAINE, PAISLEY, "to raise CAIN", RENAISSANCE, SPAIN. <u>Names</u> ABIGAIL, AIDAN, AIDEN, AIDEN, AINSLEY, AISHA, BLAISE, <se>=[z], CAIN, CAITLIN, ELAINE, FAISEL [fayzel], GAIL, GERMAINE *fossil e,* HAILEY, JAIDEN, LORRAINE *fossil e,* MADELAINE *fossil e.*

Δ Irregular verbs present, past and past participle.

As we know, SAY, SAID, SAID spells [say] [sed] [sed].

In all the rest <ai> spells [ay]

PAY Δ, PAID Δ, PAID Δ

SLAY Δ, SLEW Δ, SLAIN Δ.

WAYLAY, WAYLAID, WAYLAID.

LAY Δ, LAID Δ, LAID Δ - as in "to put, to place", a transitive verb

Lay is also past tense of the intransitive verb *to lie* which we shall meet later. As we shall hear, intransitives have no object to transfer the action of the verb on to.

*Aide is the person who provides aid. The word *aid* can be a noun or a verb, but *aide* is always a noun, the person who aids someone or provides the aid.

*Aitch is the only word in which <tch> follows a long vowel sound, a rebel to the rule that <tch> follows short vowels.

*Braille is an eponym. Google Louis Braille.

*Chaise spells [shayz], adopted from French, as in *chaise longue,* a long (reclining) chair.

*Gaiety gets the ending *–ety* to avoid adding *–ity* which would produce <ii>, a real "no-no". It is the only word ending with <aiety> and spells the digraph <ai> [ay] before <ety> [et-ee]. {*Moiety*} is the only word ending <oiety> and it also spells a digraph <oi> [oi] before <ety> [et-ee]. All others ending <iety> spell the "glide and yap" [I-et-ee] which we met in Part Three: *anxiety, notoriety, piety, propriety, satiety, sobriety, society* and *variety.*

In **malaise,* *mayonnaise and *raise <s> spells [z].

*Reconnaissance and *renaissance should follow the general rule that when <s> follows a vowel digraph it spells [z], Cummings p. 396. For most people, <ss> spells [s] in this word, myself included, plus the Oxford and Cambridge dictionaries, but some people let <ss> spell [z] in these words, as it does in *scissors.* Twin S, <ss>, only occurs after vowel digraphs in adopted French words.

*Terrain spells [te-rayn] in English, because 'twinned R's only bossy if it's between a word's end and suffix'. In the original French, *terrain* spells [ter-rayn].

In **traipse,* <se> spells [s] because <s> does not follow a voiced sound — <p> spells unvoiced [p]. The <e> ensures that it is not seen as a plural of *traip*...a word which does not exist anyway.

*Don't let W muddle you! *Praiseworthy* spells [prayz-wer-dhee]. *Quatrian* spells [kwot-rayn].

Bossy R and <ai> — *affair, wheelchair.*

Rule 4-4 <air> spells [air]

Reason Bossy R 'colours' <ai> to spell [air]. People used to sing *ayres* at *fayres* long ago when <y> was still allowed inside words. Now the only time we see <ayr> is in names, like Sir Henry Ayres. Also, when the English were rhotic, when they rolled their R's, <air> spelt two distinct word-sounds: [ay- r]. When [r] was reduced to the schwa sound or was silenced altogether, <air> spelt the diphthong [air] which is expressed as /eɪə/ in IPA, which is [ay] followed by little schwa, [ə].

List 4-4 <air> spells [air]

AFFAIR, AIR*, AIRBORNE*, AIRBRUSH, AIRCRAFT, AIRCREW, AIRER, AIRGUN, AIRING, AIRLESS, AIRLIFT, AIRLINE, AIRLINER, AIRLOCK, AIRMAIL, AIRMAN, AIRPORT, AIRSHIP,

AIRSPACE, AIR-STRIP, AIRTIGHT, AIRWAYS, AIRWOMAN, AIRWORTHY, AIRY, BAIRN, CAIRN, CHAIR, CHAIRMAN, CHAIRMANSHIP, CHAIRWOMAN, CORSAIR, DAIRY, DAIRYMAID, DAIRYMAN, DEBONAIR, DESPAIR, DISREPAIR, EASY CHAIR, ÉCLAIR [ay-klair], FAIR, FAIRING, FAIRLY, FAIRWAY, FAIRY, FAIRYLAND, FLAIR, FUN-FAIR, HAIR, HAIRBRUSH, HAIRCUT, HAIRDRESSER, HAIRLESS, HAIRPIN, HAIRSPRING, HAIRY, HORSEHAIR, IMPAIR, IMPAIRMENT, LAIR, LAIRD, MILLIONAIRE, PAIR, PRIAIRIE [pree-air-ee], STAIRWAY, REPAIR, REPAIRABLE, REPAIRER, SECRETAIRE, SOLITAIRE, STAIR, STAIRCASE, STAIR-ROD, STAIRS, UNFAIR, UNFAIRLY, UPSTAIRS, WHEELCHAIR, <u>Proper Nouns</u> AIREDALE, CAIRN TERRIER, NAIRNE *fossil e*.

*The word *air* has many meanings but is spelt just one way. It arrived from Greece as *aer* meaning the air we breathe. It also came into English from Italian as an *aria* and became a song or an *aer*. The Latin word *ager* for field produced *aire* in French when folk laid out their clothes in the fields, aired them, or voiced (aired) their opinions across the field and it came to mean one's manner too, as in a 'mean air', one's outlook across the field. It even came to mean position in the field, e.g., a southerly air. The English adopted all the meanings but use just one way to write [air], *air*.

*Borne [born], is the past participle of "to bear or carry" — very different to "the baby was born".

Digraph <ae>— *brae, Raeleen.*

Rule 4-5 Digraph <ae> spells [ay] except in words of Greek and Latin origin.

Reason Terminal <e> after <a> changes the terminal sound [ar] in *bra* to [ay] in *brae*. It's a case of "when two vowels go walking the first one does the talking, very profound, spells its long sound." In this digraph, <ae>, <e> lets <a> spell its Anglo long sound. This is not always the case, as we shall see, e.g., in *pixie* and *belief*.

List 4-5 <ae> spells [ay]
BRAE, MAELSTROM, PHAETON, TAEL *wt. of silver etc.*, USQUABAE/USQUEBAE, (whiskey/whisky). <u>Proper Adjective</u> GAELIC. Names MAE, RAE, RAELEEN.

Greek and Latin <ae> —*formulae, minutiae.*

Digraph <ae> features in many words which have been adopted but not adapted, words in which <ae> does not spell [ay]. Professor Cummings explains that in the following words, "The *ae* spelling has nothing at all to do with the ash ligature of Old English. It comes, rather, from Greek and Latin," (Cummings, p. 269). Here ligature means the joining of <a> and <e> in the letter Ash, <æ>. The English used <æ> to spell [a] and [ay] because Romans <a> spelt [u] and [ar]. People argue about what sound Roman <ae> spelt. Some say [ee] and some say [I]. However, as it's a dead language, it's hard to be sure, but we have the following rules.

Rule 4-6 In Latin, terminal <ae> preceded by a consonant, spells [I].

Reason Latin words ending consonant <a> gain <e> to become plural. This plural <ae> ending spells [I] because of the rule that <ae> after a consonant spells [I]. Latin adoptions in English can make plurals like this but nowadays they usually use <s>, e.g., *one formula, two formulae* or *formulas*. The suffix <ae> is applied to scientific names of plant families, like *compositae* [kom-poz-it-I], the daisy family, or 'The Daisies'.

List 4-6 FORMULAE, COMPOSITAE.

Rule 4-7 In Latin, terminal <ae> preceded by a vowel, spells [ee].

Reason It's how Latin scholars believe Romans spoke. Families like The Pine Family, *pinaceae*, and The Roses, *rosaceae*, which end <ceae>, are usually pronounced [see] because the first <e> not only softens the <c> but also means <ae> follows a vowel and therefore it spells [ee]. MINUTIAE therefore spells [min-yoo-shi-ee]

List 4-7 MINUTIAE, PINACEAE, ROSACEAE.

Rule 4-8 In words adopted from Greek and Latin, <ae> spells [ee] inside words.
Rebels AESTHETIC, ANAESTHETIC, MAESTRO.

Rebels' Reasons In these rebels <ae> spells [e], [i] and [I]. In *aesthetic,* <ae> spells [i] because the stress shifts from initial [ee] in *aesthete* to the vowel before <ic> in *easthetic,* shortening [ee] spelt <ae> to [i] or [ə]. This also happens in *anaesthetic* but in *anaesthetist* the stress is on <ae> and so it spells [ee]. In *maestro,* <ae> spells [I]. *Maestro* comes from German *meister*, [mI-ster]. It means "master of any art, usually music."

Rascal HAEMORRHAGE It was *emorosogie* in the fifteenth century but then *haemorrhage* took over once the Latin-Greek compound *hæmorrhagia* was known, meaning 'blood burst'. In this word, <ae> should spell [ee], as in *haemoglobin*, 'blood globule (of protein)'.

List 4-8 <ae> spells [ee]
AEGIS, AEON, AESTHETE, AETIOLOGY, ANAEMIA, ANAEMIC, ANAESTHESIA, ANAESTHETIST, ANAESTHETIZE, ATHENAEUM*, CYCLOPAEDIA, ENCYCLOPAEDIA, ENCYCLOPAEDIC, FAECES, GYNAECOLOGIST, GYNAECOLOGY, HAEMATOLOGY, HAEMOGLOBIN, MEDIAEVAL*, MINUTIAE*, NAEVUS, ORTHOPAEDICS, ORTHOPAEDIC, PAEAN, PAEDERAST, PAEDIATRICS, PAEDOPHILIA, SEPTICAEMIA, TOXAEMIA, PALAEOLITHIC. Proper Nouns CAESAR.

Athenaeum is also spelt *atheneum* and when <e> replaces <ae> it continues to spell [ee], [ath-u-nee-um], due to Glide and Yap.

Mediaeval is another word with three vowels in a row. These 3-vowel clusters are unpopular in English but when <e> replaces <ae> in *medieval,* <e> continues to spell long [ee]. This makes a mockery of the Glide and Yap rule and so the classical spelling remains in many dictionaries. (Classical refers to Greek and Latin language and literature. People who study Greek and Latin study "the Classics", also called "reading the Classics".)

Minutiae spells [mIn-**oo**-shee] due to Yod Fusion.

French Aero Club — *aerate, aerospace.*
Rule 4-9 French-adopted <aer> spells [air]
Reason In France in 1783 the Montgolfier brothers were the first in history to leave the earth's surface in a balloon. Aeronautics was born! The next step, Powered Flight! The Aéro-Club de France was founded as the Aéro-Club on 20 October 1898 as a society 'to encourage aerial locomotion'. The Americans followed suit in 1905 by calling their club the Aero Club of America. Since then, all such clubs are *aero clubs,* not *air clubs* nor *airo clubs.* Even without the French <é>, <aero> in English is pronounced the French way, so <aer> spells [air].

List 4-9
AERATE, AERIAL, AEROBATICS, AERODROME, AERODYNAMIC, AEROFOIL, AERONAUTICS, AEROPLANE, AEROSOL, AEROSPACE. Proper Nouns CAERPHILLY *cheese*.

The Single Digraph <ao>.
In only one word <ao> spells [ay] — *gaol*.

Rascal GAOL Americans have totally rejected the weird word *gaol* in which <ao> spells [ay] and <g> spells [j]. This is the only word in the entire English language in which [ay] and [j] are spelt like this. There is a very good word which means exactly the same, *jail.* When asked why *gaol* is still in the dictionary, the English explain that it has been officially on their statutes a long time, since the Norman Invasion. It comes from Old Norman French *gaiole* which became *gayhol* which became *gaol.* The word goes right back to Latin for *caged* in a *cave*. Norman French was considered a bit "infra-dig" by Parisiens but it was the first sort of French to be spoken in England, from 1066. Later, in 1204, England's King John lost control of Normandy but he inherited other French provinces in central and southern France. So new French words arrived in England, amongst them the word *jail,* plus *chattel* instead of Norman *cattle,* and *chase* instead of *catch* and so on. Yes, England got a double dose of French. Nowadays the official word in England is not *gaol* nor is it *jail,* but an even older word, *prison.*

Australians keep it on/in their books too, probably because *gaol* looks scarier than *jail.*

The Old Digraph <aw> — *awe, yawn.*

Prof. Cummings says that digraph <aw> spells [or] in words which do not come from France because there is no <w> in French words. The Stewarts, Scotland's royal stewards, became 'Stuarts' when in exile in France. However, some words from France, like *lau* for 'law', had to swap <u> for <w>, to prevent ending in <u>, a no-no in English. Amongst Words with Diplomatic Immunity, in the appendix, we see <au> ending foreign words, like French *beau* and *gateau,* and German words *hausfrau, landau*. In none of them does <au> spell the sound [or]. As we know, Old English *cwen* became *queen* under the French, to avoid <w>. Also, *ward* and *warranty* were respelt *guard* [gward] and *guaranty* [gwar-un-tee]. Later, the French even took [w] out of words, silenced <u> in *quiche* and so <qu> spells just [k] in recent French adoptions. Letters <u> and <w> were interchangeable in English for a long time and so there is no hard and fast rule about the origins of words with digraphs <aw> and <au>. We can learn to read <aw> words very eaily. Such words were never rhotic, not like <or> words in which [r] used to be pronounced.

The only pitfall is sorting out when <aw> is a digraph and when it isn't. For instance, in *awry* <aw> is not a digraph. It was originally *all wry,* then *a-wry* and hence *awry.* We see <aw> in *await, awake, away, award, aware, awash, awhile, awhirl,* and *awoke*. In these words, <a> is a prefix which does not change the meaning of the stem word but intensifies it, makes it more so. It's officially named an 'intensifying prefix'. We see it also in *afraid* and *astonish*. We also see <aw> in the acronym AWOL, Absent Without Official Leave.

Rule 4-10A Digraph <aw> spells [or].
Rebel AWRY
Rebel's Reason *Awry* is two syllables, prefix *a* plus *wry* which means "distorted, somewhat twisted to one side," from obsolete verb *to wry* "to contort, to twist or turn." *Wrist* is also derived from this old verb.
List 4-10A Digraph <aw> spells [or].
AWE*, AWKWARD, AWL, AWN, BAWL, BRADAWL, BRAWL, BRAWN, BYELAW*, CLAW, COLESLAW, CRAWL, DAWN, DRAW, DRAWL, DRAWN Δ, FAWN, FLAW, GAWK, GAWKY, GAWP* slang, GNAW *silent <g>,* GOSHAWK*, GUFFAW, HAW, HAWK, HEE-HAW, JACKDAW, JAW, JIG-SAW, LAW, LAWN, MACAW, MAW, MAWKISH, PAW, PAWKY, PAWL, PAWN, PAWPAW, PRAWN, RAW, SAW, SAW Δ, SAWN Δ, SCRAWL, SEESAW, SHAWL, SPAWN, SPRAWL, SQUAW, SQUAWK, STRAW, THAW, TOMAHAWK, TRAWL, YAW, YAWL, YAWN.
Irregular verbs in which <aw> spells [or], present, past and p. participle:
DRAW Δ, {DREW Δ}, DRAWN Δ
SEE Δ, SAW Δ, SEEN Δ, as in 'look and see'.
SAW Δ, SAWED Δ, {SAWN Δ} as in 'cut and saw'.
*Did you remember your Short Word Rule which explains the <e> in *awe?*

Byelaw comes from the same root as *build,* for it is a regulation which applies to one particular set of buildings, i.e. neighbourhood. However, dictionaries vary and today both *by-law* and *byelaw* are in print. Also, *bylaw*.

Gawp is slang, probably a combo of *yawn* and *gape*.

*In *goshawk* <sh> is not a digraph. A goshawk is a large type of hawk flown at geese.

List 4-10B in which digraph <aw> spells [or] in many compound words, or complex words grown on stems with terminal <aw> and a few other words too.

AWESOME, AWESTRICKEN, AWESTRUCK, AWFUL*, AWFULLY, AWNING*, BAWDY BRAWNY, BYLAW, BY-LAW, CHAINSAW, CRAWFISH, CRAWLER, DAWDLE*, DRAWBACK, DRAWBRIDGE, DRAWER, DRAWERS, DRAWING-PIN, DRAWING-ROOM, FLAWLESS, FLAWLESSLY, FLAWLESSNESS, FRETSAW, GAWKINESS, HAWTHORN*, HAWSER*, LAW-ABIDING, LAWFUL, LAWLESS, LAWN TENNIS, LAWYER, LOCK JAW, NIGHTHAWK, OVERAWE, PAWNBROKER, PAWN-SHOP, PAWN-TICKET, RAWHIDE, RICKSHAW, SAWDUST, SAWFISH, SAWFLY, SAWMILL, SAWYER, STICKJAW, STRAW POLL, STRAWBERRY*, STRAWBERRY-MARK, TAWDRY*, TAWDRINESS, TAWNY*, TAWSE*, TRAWLER, THE CRAWL a swim-stroke, YAWS*, WITHDRAW.

Awning is not formed on the stem word *awn* but was adopted in the 1600's probably from a seafaring term.

Awful has lost the <e> of *awe* because it is no longer needed to obey the Short Word Rule. It was a Fairy E so it was not needed to 'magically make' a long vowel sound.

Bawdy comes from Old French *baud* meaning 'lively, merry, bold', as on p. 55, Ayto. After 1510's, its meaning changed to 'lewd, obscene, unchaste' and its spelling changed to *bawdy*, influenced by the Welsh word *bawaidd* 'dirty', from Welsh *baw* 'dirt, filth' — see Etymonline.

Dawdle was originally daddle, "to walk unsteadily" but perhaps influenced by the bird *daw* as it was regarded as sluggish and silly.

Hawthorn, a thorny hedge around a *haw,* an obsolete word for 'enclosure, small field, yard'.

Hawser was made from the verb to lift: *hawse,* now obsolete.

Strawberry refers to the way the vines are *strewed* or *strewn* about the plant, not grown on straw, (Fleck, 2007).

Tawdry is an eponym. Rustic and cheap, Tawdry Lace was sold at a country fair to celebrate a saint. The saint was a queen of Northumbria, in the seventh century. Her association with lace necklaces is that she supposedly died of a throat tumor, which, according to Bede, she considered God's punishment for her youthful stylishness: "I deservedly bear the weight of my trouble on my neck, for I remember that, when I was a young maiden, I bore on it the needless weight of necklaces." See Etymonline. Anything cheap and ostentatious, imitating expensive finery, became 'tawdry'.

Tawny. There is no stem word *tawn*. Tawny comes from the French *taune,* but conforms to the <awn> ending as if it were a stem word, because, as we shall see, <au> is not used before <n>, which would be hard to read in cursive.

Tawse is built on an obsolete stem. To *taw* was to scourge leather prior to tanning. A tawse is a school master's leather strap.

Yaws. There is not stem word *yaw*. Yaws is from the Carib word for the disease, ya-ya. Many languages repeat a word to form the plural which is maybe why it is written as a plural in English.

Have a Laff, Quaff and Chaff.

In the next two words <augh> is very new. Originally *laugh* and *draught* used <æh>, in *hlæhhan* and *dræht,* back when <æ> was used to spell [a]. This letter, Ash, was dropped, and the voiced [h] spelt with

<gh>. Then this guttural ending changed to [f], after the short vowel [a]. When that short vowel lengthened to [ar], the French digraph <au> was adopted to spell this longer vowel. Now as we know, <gh> went silent after long vowels, but by now <gh> spelt [f] in *laugh* and *draught* and only the letters <gh> remain, to show us that these words were never French, but, instead, from Old English, a Germanic language. We have already heard how *laugh* once copied the sound we make when we laugh until we choke with laughter: la-la-la-la-la-ugh. *Draught* comes from *draw* (pull) or *drag*, so think of it as drag-drag-drag until you are exhausted, ugh.

Rule 4-11 The letters <augh> can spell [arf] or [af].
Reason Without Ash to spell [a] and with [a] shifting to the long vowel [ar], the <u> was added. Many people still say [laf]. Folk in some parts like nothing better than "a good laff, quaff and chaff." – a laugh, a drink and friendly banter. Many people still say [draft] but they probably do not realize it comes from the words *drag* and *draw*. The north was less influenced by France and French, and more influenced by its Viking past. *Draught* is also spelt *draft*, especially in the military, commercial, and technical world and is almost universal in American English, e.g. *army draft, bank draft, rough draft* and *cold draft*.
List 4-11
DRAUGHT, DRAUGHT BEER, DRAUGHTIER, DRAUGHTIEST, DRAUGHTS, DRAUGHTSMAN, DRAUGHTY, LAUGH, LAUGHABLE, LAUGHABLY, LAUGHED, LAUGHING, LAUGHINGLY, LAUGHINGSTOCK.

Digraph <au> spells [or] — *applaud, vaunt.*

   In French words <au> spells [oh] but long ago the English pronounced <au> as [a], and then [ar] and finally [or]. So now the French digraph <au>, in English, spells [or].
It still spells [oh] in words which are obviously French, like *beau, bureau, {chauffeur}, gateau, plateau, portmanteau* and *tableau* and in three late adoptions which have not been adapted because their meanings would be lost: *aubergine* [oh-ber-jeen], *gauche* [gohsh] and *mauve* [mohv]. However, Australians usually say 'egg-plant', decode *mauve* into [morv] and rarely use the term 'gauche'.
Rule 4-12 In Anglo-English <au> spells [or] but in American English <au> spells [ar].
Reason At the time that the English pilgrims set off to America, <au> in *laugh* was being used to spell [ar] and <au> in American English still spells [ar]. In England, <au> eventually spelt [or]. Yes, English already used <or> to spell [or], but using <au> prevented rhotic speakers pronouncing [r] in [or]. In Australia and most of England [or] has no [r] sound, but in Ireland, Scotland (and USA) it often ends with [r], but not when written with <au>.
Rebels FRAU, GAUSS, KAURI, SAUERKRAUT, CHAUVENIST; also, GAUGE [gayj]; AUNT [arnt]. Also MEERSCHAUM pipe or clay.
Rebels' Reasons In the first four rebels <au> spells [ow] for they have been **adopted** from languages which use <au> to spell [ow], e.g., German. This also occurs in the Proper Nouns *Saudi* and *Nassau*, the *Mau-mau* in Kenya and *Maui* in N.Z.
Chauvenist is an eponym. In Cogniards' 1831 vaudeville "*La Cocarde Tricolore*, Nicholas Chauvin displays exaggerated, blind nationalism.
In one rebel word, *gauge*, <au> spells [ay]. Long ago the French changed the pronunciation of many <au> words and also changed their spelling. They forgot to change *gauge's* spelling when they said it the new way. They remembered to take the <u> out of *save* which was *sauve* and *danger* was *daunger*, *change* was *chaunge*. So, the <u> in *gauge* is a French mistake which the English should correct! The French have changed it and now write it <jauge> and say it [johj] in their language.
Meerschaum is German for 'sea-foam' which describes the soft, white clay. In German <au> spells [u-uu], which in English becomes just [uu].

In some words, <au> was slow to change from spelling [a], as we have heard, in words like *laugh* and *draught*. In parts of USA, *aunt* still spells [ant]. And *sauce* still spells [sas] which is why 'saucey' is often written as *sassy*. Other words were slow to change, too, like *flaunt, gauntlet* and *jaunt*. Even now, Cummings, p. 216, tells us that way up in the Appalachian mountains they still say [hant] for *haunt*. Early settlers brought early pronunciations with them. Later on the English were pronouncing <au> as [ar] when they reached America. Still later, English arriving in Australia pronounced <au> as [or]. Language is a living thing. Although we cannot change letters in words, we can change sounds in words. Australians have changed what <au> spells in some words.

List 4-12A <au> spells [or]; each terminal <ause> spells [orz], because they end verbs, or nouns made from verbs. See next list for Australian pronunciation of some of these words.

APPLAUD, APPLAUSE, ASTRONAUT, ASTRONAUTICS, AUCTION, AUDIBLE, AUDIENCE, AUDIO, AUDIO-VISUAL, AUDIT, AUDITION, AUDITOR, AUDITORIUM, AUGER *noun*, AUGHT*, AUGMENT, AUGUR *verb*, AUGUST*, AUK, AURA, AURAL, AURORA, ASSAULT, AUSTERE, AUSTERITY, AUSTRALITE, AUTHENTIC, AUTHENTICALLY, AUTHENTICITY, AUTHENTICATE, AUTHENTICATION, AUTHOR, AUTHORITARIAN, AUTHORITATIVE, AUTHORITY, AUTHORIZE, AUTHORIZATION, AUTISTIC, AUTISM, AUTOBIOGRAPHY, AUTOCLAVE, AUTOCRACY, AUTOCRAT, AUTOCRATIC, AUTOCROSS, AUTOGRAPH, AUTOMATE, AUTOMATIC, AUTOMATICALLY, AUTOMATON, AUTOMOBILE, AUTOMOTIVE, AUTOPSY, AUTUMN <mn>=[m], AUTUMNAL*, AUXILIARY, BAUBLE, BAUD, BAULK, BAUXITE, BECAUSE*, BRONTOSAURUS, CATERWAUL, CAUCUS, CAUDAL, CAUGHT, CAUL* for kale, CAULI (-FLOWER), CAULK, CAUSAL, CAUSALITY, CAUSATIVE, CAUSE, CAUSTIC, CAUTERIZE, CAUTION, CAUTIONARY, CAUTIOUS, CENTAUR, CLAUSE, CLAUSTROPHOBIA, DAUNT, DAUNTLESS, DEBAUCH, DEBAUCHERY, DEFAULT, DEFAULTER, DEFRAUD, EXHAUST* *silent h*, EXHAUSTIVE *silent h*, FAUCET, FAULT, FAULTLESS, FAULTY, FAUN, FAUNA, FLAUNT, FLAUTIST, FRAUD, FRAUDULENT*, GAUDY, GAUDINESS, GAUNT, GAUNTLET, GAUZE, GLAUCOMA, HAUL, HAULAGE, HAULIER, HAUNCH, HAUNT, HAUNTED, HYDRAULIC, IMPLAUSIBLE, INAUDIBLE, INAUGURAL, INAUGURATE, INEXHAUSTIBLE, JAUNDICE, JAUNT, JAUNTY, JUGGERNAUT, LAUD, LAUDABLE, LAUDANUM, LAUDATORY, LAUNCH, LAUNCHING PAD, LAUNCH PAD, LAUNDER, LAUNDRETTE, LAUNDRY, (POET) LAUREATE, LAUREL, LEPRECHAUN, <ch>=[k], MAUDLIN, MAUL, MAUNDER, MAUSOLEUM, MAUVE, MENOPAUSE, NAUSEA [nor-zee-u], NAUSEATE [nor-zee-ayt], NAUTICAL, OVERHAUL, PAUCITY, PAUNCH, PAUPER, PAUSE, PLAUDITS, PLAUSIBLE, RAUNCHY, SAUSAGE, SAUSAGE ROLL, SAUCE, SAUCEPAN, SAUCER, SAUCY, SAUNA, SAUNTER, SAURIAN lizard-like, SCAUP duck, STAUNCH, TAUNT, TAUT, TAUTEN, TAUTOLOGY, TAUTOLOGICAL, THESAURUS, TRAUMA, TRAUMATIC, VAUDEVILLE, VAULT, VAUNT. <u>Proper Nouns</u> AUGUST, AUSTRALORP, AUSTRALASIA, AUSTRALIA, AUSTRIA, AUTUMN, GAUL, MAUNDY, MAURITANIA, SANTA CLAUS. <u>Names</u> AUBREY, AUDREY, AUGUST, AUGUSTIN, AUGUSTUS, AUSTIN, CLAUDIA, CLAUDIUS, LAURA, MAUD, MAUREEN, PAUL, SAUL, SHAUN.

*The word *because* [bee-coz] was originally *by cause* but it changed to match the words *behind, become* etc. and the first syllable became unstressed, like a prefix, putting stress on the next syllable, and shortening it, too, in most countries. In 1858 the English were being advised to say [bee-corz] not [ba-coz], so it was already changing, (see Anon). The advice was not heeded, certainly not in Australia.

Fraudulent spells [frord-joo-lent]. Due to Yod Fusion, <du> spells [joo].

**August* is an adjective and spells [or-<u>gust</u>], with stress on *gust*, derived from Latin *augustus* meaning noble, magnificent and venerable, probably blessed by 'augurs', priests. As a Proper Noun, (the month of) <u>August</u> has normal English stress, on the first syllable.

*In *autumn,* as we saw in *solemn,* the difficult <mn> blend spells just [m] because <m> is closer to the vowel than is <n>. Both [m] and [n] prefer to blend with vowels than with each other. If <n> spelt [n] on its own, a new syllable would be created, for then we would say [ort-um-ən]. Indeed, as soon as <n> is close to a vowel, it moves into that new syllable, for in *autumnal* it spells [n] again, [ort-um-nal]. This also happens in *solemnize,* [sol-em-nIz], which is often mispronounced as [sol-em-Iz], even in dictionaries.

*It is thought that *caul* is a faulty spelling for *kale*. We'll see it again in {*cauliflower*}, and hear it {*coleslaw*}.

Exhaust spells [eg-zorst], not [eks-hort], because <h> is silent after <ex>, which is the Special Rule we met when we met *exhibit.*

An Aussie Assault on <au>

The Great Vowel Shift was a time of rapid vowel change but vowels change all the time, even today. Some English [or] sounds written <au> can be [o] in Australia, but not all, e.g., initial stress changes *sausage* but not *sauce*. This change occurs mostly before [l] and [r] for they are very attracted to vowels and not to neighbouring consonants. We also see it before [s], because [ost] takes less energy to say than [orst]. Try it!

List 4-12B <au> spells [o] in Oz, Australia.
ASSAULT, AUCTION, AUSTERE, AUSTRALITE, AUSTERITY, BECAUSE*, CAULI {-FLOWER}, CLAUSTROPHOBIA, FAULT, FAULTLESS, FAULTY, HYDRAULIC, LAUREATE, LAUREL, SAUSAGE, SAUSAGE ROLL, VAULT. Proper Nouns AUSSAT *acronym,* AUSSIE <ss>=[z], AUSTRALORP, AUSTRALASIA, AUSTRALIA, AUSTRIA, LAURENCE/LAURIE, POET LAUREATE.

Because is discussed above. Its slang abbreviation, '*cause,* is written *coz* in the "eye dialect" used in recorded conversation.

The Saxons and other Germanic Lowlanders took the guttural sound spelt <gh>, made by vibrating the throat's vellum, to Britain. The English no longer make this throaty sound, except when they exclaim "Ugh!" at something particularly 'cacky'. As we know, [gh] turned into [f] after short vowels and became silent after long vowels.

Naughty Daughters are not French.

Words which have retained <gh> use this digraph to show they did not come from France. They are either Old English words, back when English was a Germanic language, and mimic Germanic spelling. Their vowels changed, as vowels do, and attempts were made to re-spell them with French digraphs, but vowels kept changing. We have already learnt that French scribes added <o> before Old English <u>, e.g., in *cough,* thus mixing French and German spelling in one word. This was meant to separate English <u> from French <u>, but the vowel of *cough* changed anyway.

List 4-12C <aught> spells [ort]
AUGHT, CAUGHT Δ, DAUGHTER, DISTRAUGHT, FRAUGHT Δ, HAUGHTY, NAUGHT, ONSLAUGHT, TAUGHT Δ.

The following information shows us that many of these words originally had [a] sounds or had close relationships with [a] words. We hear Americans in movies saying [tart] for *taught,* and [darter] for *daughter,* because [a] changed to [ar] first, and some time after the Mayflower set out in 1620, [ar] changed to [or] in these words, in England.

Aught arose from a mistake, it was originally *a naught,* then *an aught.* It now means *anything,* 'for aught I know'.

Caught is the past participle of the verb "to catch", [katch] and *daughter* is from Old English (*dohter*).
Distraught is the past participle of the English word *distract* which was invented around 1393, to match *catch, caught*.
Fraught meant *to load, to fill,* but now it is used only as a past participle: "The enterprise was *fraught* with danger." It is related to *freight,* adopted from Dutch *vrecht*. England gained many sea-faring words from Holland when Dutch ships ruled the waves.
Haughty is the Old English word *high* combined with French *haut* (high). The obsolete adjective *haught* meant "above one's self, on a high horse". (By contrast *proud* meant 'brave, out in front of one's men in a battle', using *pro-* as in *pro-active*.)
Naught can be broken into *na-ught,* from Old English *nawhit,* from 'no whit', meaning 'no thing'. (Back then, *whit* was written <wiht>.) *Naughty* meant 'no-thing, needy', having nothing, in other words *bad, lazy, a time-waster*.
Slaughter comes from Old English *slæt* [slat], from Viking *slahtr,* and *onslaught* is from Dutch 'aenslag'.
Taught, past participle of *to teach,* which was *taikjan* in Old English, meaning 'to show' hence *token*, a show of something.

List 4-12C cont. <aught> spells [ort]
DAUGHTERLESS, DAUGHTERS, GODDAUGHTER, GRANDDAUGHTER, HAUGHTIER, HAUGHTIEST, HAUGHTILY, HAUGHTINESS, MANSLAUGHTER, NAUGHTIER, NAUGHTIEST, NAUGHTILY, NAUGHTINESS, NAUGHTS crosses, NAUGHTY, SLAUGHTER, SLAUGHTERED, SLAUGHTERER, STEPDAUGHTER

Irregular verbs – present, past and p. participle.
CATCH Δ, CAUGHT Δ, CAUGHT Δ
none, none, FRAUGHT Δ

Now is a good time to tell you that Prof Cummings noticed a pattern — <aw> is followed by <l>, <n> or <k>, but <au> is not, (Cummings, p. 236). I would not expect to see <auk> because <au> is a French digraph and the French do not use <k> in their words. If <aul> or <aun> is written in cursive legibility might be a problem. In fact we can make a rule which helps us choose <aw> or <au> when writing words.
Relevant Writing Rule. When choosing between <aw> and <au> to spell [or] in stem words, use <aw> when [or] is terminal or when followed by [l], [n] or [k] spelt with <k>.
Rebels. CAUL, CAULIFLOWER, FAUN, FAUNA, HAUL, LEPRECHAUN, MAUL, AUK.
Rebels' Reasons. The only time we see <au> before <k> is in *auk,* a re-spelling of *alka* in which it's possible <l> was mistaken for <u> but this made no difference as both <auk> and <alk> spell [ork]. *Alka* imitated the cry of a water bird.
Seven words use <au> before <l> and <n> to spell [or], in order to show that they came into English via French, not in a Viking, Saxon or other Germanic language. The OED committee left the name of the Roman god of the countryside, *Faunus,* in *faun* (a woodland goat-man-god) to show its non-Germanic origin. His sister, *Fauna,* was goddess of the countryside and her name describes the animal life of a region, its *fauna. Caul* is from French *cale*. In *cauliflower, caulis* is Latin for 'cabbage'. *Haul* was *hale* from Old French *haler,* and *maul* was from an Old French word too. *Leprechaun* is from Latin for 'little body' – *lu* for 'little' and *corpus* for 'body'.
No wonder it took so long to write the OED! The committee spent years researching the origins of each word for their "New English Dictionary on Historical Principles", from 1858 to 1928, by which time it was called the Oxford English Dictionary. Return to Reading Rules.

E Digraphs

We have already seen all the words in which <ee> spells the [ee] sound. Now we shall see all the words in which <ea> spells [ee]. Between them, <ee> and <ea>, they only spell 17% of all [ee] sounds in English words, Cummings p. 260. We shall also meet words in which the digraph <ea> does not spell [ee]. In just one word, <ea> spells [i]. It's in *sheave,* which spells [shiv]. It's the grooved wheel of a pulley. The strange word SHEAVE does not have a list, but the other rebels have their own lists.

Not needed but nice to know. In 40% of words just <e> alone spells [ee], as in *legal, rodeo, area, museum, create, me, aborigine, athlete, adhere, antipodes, cathedral, defrost* and *replant*. Another 40% are spelt with <i> and <y>, as in *anti-aircraft, semi-skilled, insomnia, ruffian, menial, ravine, antique, scorpion, interior, funny, badly, vary* and *vanity*. In 3% [ee] is spelt as in *weird, brief, key* and *donkey, faeces, amoeba, people, quay.* Now back to things we need to know.

The Pleasing Digraph <ea> — *please, zeal.*
Rule 4-13 Digraph <ea> spells [ee] only inside words.
Reason This is because when <ea> is terminal it is not a digraph. It is two separate vowel sounds, long [ee] glides over the syllable boundary on to [ar], "glide and yawn" as in Part Three. It spells [ee-u] as in *idea, azalea, miscellanea*. When a digraph, it follows the general digraph rule: **When two vowels go walking the first one does the talking. Very profound, it spells its long sound. But if the last one is Greek, the first one needn't speak.** So <e> in <ea> 'does the talking', very profound, it spells its long sound, [ee].
Rebels In just six stem words FLEA, PEA, SEA, LEA, PLEA and TEA and their compound words, like *chickpea,* and also in **Rebel** GUINEA, <ea> spells [ee] at the end of a word.
Rebels' Reasons In these words, although terminal, <ea> is a digraph. It separates them from *flee, pee, see, lee,* and *tee*. There is no word *plee* but *plea* just happened that way, maybe to match *please.*
The name *guinea* for a gold coin was adopted from Africa's Gold Coast, most probably with Portuguese spelling, which means it was originally [gin-ee-ar] coast. *Guinea pigs* come from South America. They were bred on ships for meat. Europeans assumed they came from Guinea in Africa, and so they called them guinea pigs.
The word *pea* used to be *pease,* meaning 'one pea', ref. the old rhyme *Pease Porridge Hot,* about pea soup. *Pease* mistakenly sounded plural and so *pea* was invented for just one pea. When making "back-formations", singulars from plurals, we still make mistakes. The singular of *testes* is not *teste.* It's *testis,* just like the singulars of *crises, hypotheses* and *parentheses* are *crisis, hypothesis* and *parenthesis*. Pooh is *feces* or *faeces.* The plural was *faeces* in Latin, the singular was *faex,* but that form didn't make it into English. If you need a singular form of *feces* and don't want to say a *pooh* or a *turd,* back-formation is your best bet, *fece,* as in Urban Dictionary, on the world wide web.
Rebels BEAUTY, BEAUTIFUL and BEAUT.
Rebels' Reasons *Beauty* came into English as *beute,* replacing Old English *wlite* (bright, colourful, pleasing to look at.) We have already seen that <u> spelling [oo] is always preceded by <e> in French which means they say [oo] differently to the rest of Europe, with half-closed, smiling lips. We learnt that when the English aped this pronunciation they ended up with [yoo]. In early English terminal <e> was pronounced and so *beute* spelt [byootee]. Spelling changed, but it is still said [byootee]. Australians have changed *beauty* to {*bewdy*} in eye-dialect. They say [yoo byoodee] when excited or impressed, changing [t] to the stronger voiced [d] sound. They have also shortened the adjective *beautiful* to *beaut* [byoot].
List 4-13 Digraph <ea> spells [ee], and <ear> spells [eer]. Irregular Verbs, marked Δ, will be discussed later. Terminal <se> spells [z] after <ea> unless marked as spelling [s]. If <eas> is followed by an unvoiced consonant, then <s> spells [s].

APPEAR*, APPEARANCE, KEEP UP APPEARANCES, PUT IN AN APPEARANCE, TO ALL APPEARANCES, APPEASE, ARCHDEACON, ARREARS, BEACH, BEACHCOMBER, BEACON, BEAD, BEADING, BEADY, BEADLE*, BEAGLE*, BEAK, BEAKER, BEAM, BEAN, BEANPOLE, BEARD*, BEAST*, BEASTLY*, BEAT Δ, BEAT A RETREAT, BEATEN TRACK, BEAT OFF, BEAT TIME, BEAT UP, BEATER, BEATING, BEATING-UP, BEEFEATER, BELEAGUERED, BENEATH, BEQUEATH, BEREAVE Δ, BESPEAK, BLEACH, BLEAK, BLEARY, BLEAT, BREACH, BREAM, BREATHE, BREATHE AGAIN, BREATHING-SPACE, BREATHER, BUTTER-BEAN, CEASE<se>=[s], CHEAP, CHEAPEN, CHEAPISH, CHEAPJACK, CHEAT, CHICKPEA, CLEAN, CLEANLY, CLEANNESS, CLEAN-CUT, CLEAN-SHAVEN, CLEAN UP, MAKE A CLEAN SWEEP, CLEANER, CLEANERS, TAKEN TO THE CLEANERS, CLEANLY, CLEAR, CLEARLY, CLEARNESS, CLEAR AWAY, CLEAR-CUT, CLEAR OFF, CLEAR THE DECKS, CLEAR UP, IN THE CLEAR, CLEARANCE, CLEARANCE ORDER, CLEARING, CLEARWAY, CLEAT, CLEAVAGE, CLEAVE Δ, CLEAVER, COCHINEAL, CREAK, CREAM, CREAM CHEESE, CREAM OF TARTAR, CREAMERY, CREAMY, CREASE<se>=[s], CREATURE, CREATURE COMFORTS, CREATURE OF HABIT, DAY-DREAM, DEACON, DEAL (timber), DEAL Δ, DEALER, GOOD DEAL, DEAL WITH, DEAN, DEANERY, DEAR, DEARLY, DEARNESS, DECEASE <se>=[s], DECREASE<se>=[s], DEFEAT, DEFEATIST, DEFEATISM, DISAPPEAR, DISEASE, DISEASED, DISPLEASE, DREAM Δ, DREAMER, DREAMLESS, DREAM UP, DREAMY, DREARY, DREARILY, DREARINESS, EACH, EAGER, EAGERLY, EAGERNESS, EAGER BEAVER, EAGLE*, EAGLET*, EAR, BE ALL EARS, EAR-DRUM, EAR-PLUG, EAR-RING, EAR-SPLITTING, EARACHE, EARFUL, EARMARK, EARPHONE, EARSHOT, EARWIG, EASE, AT EASE, EASEL, EASILY, EAST*, EASTERLY*, EASTERN*, EASTWARD*, EASY, EASINESS, EASY CHAIR, EASY GOING, EASY STREET, GO EASY WITH, TAKE IT EASY, EAT Δ, WHAT'S EATING YOU? EATER, EAVES, EAVESDROP, EAVESDROPPER, ENDEARMENT, ENTREAT, FAIRLEAD, FEALTY, FEAR, FOR THE FEAR OF, FEARFUL, FEARFULLY, FEARLESS, FEARLESSNESS, FEARSOME, FEASIBLE, FEASIBLY, FEASIBILITY, FEAST*, FEAST THE EYES ON, FEAT, FEATURE, FEATURELESS, FIG-LEAF, FLEA, FLEA-BAG, FLEA-BITE, FLEA MARKET, A FLEA IN THE EAR, FREAK, FREAKISH, FOOTWEAR, GEAR, IN GEAR, GEARBOX, GEARCASE<se>=[s], GLEAM, GLEAN, GLEANER, GLEANINGS, GREASE<se>=[s], GREASE-GUN<se>=[s], GREASE A PALM<se>=[s], GREASE-PAINT<se>=[s], GREASER<s>=[z], GREASY<s>=[s] or [z], GREASILY<s>=[s] or [z], GREASINESS<s>=[s] or [z], GREAVE, HEAL, HEAP, HEAPS, HEAR Δ, HEARER, HEAR! HEAR!, HEARING, HEARING-AID, HEARSAY, HEAT, HEAT-STROKE, HEAT WAVE, HEATED, HEATEDLY, HEATER, HEATH, HEATHEN, HEAVE Δ, HORNBEAM, IDEAL, IDEALIST, IDEALISTIC, IDEALISM, IDEALIZE, IMPEACH, IMPEACHABLE, IMPEACHMENT, INCREASE <se> = [s], INTERWEAVE, KNEAD silent <k>, LEA, LEACH, LEAD noun, LEAD Δ, LEAD BY THE NOSE, LEAD SOMEONE ON, LEAD UP TO, LEADS, LEADER, LEADERSHIP, LEADING, LEAF, LEAFLESS, LEAFLET, LEAFY, LEAGUE [leeg], LEAK, LEAKAGE, LEAKY, LEAN, LEANNESS, LEAN YEARS, LEAN ON, LEAN-TO, LEANING, LEAP Δ, LEAP YEAR, LEAP-FROG, LEASE<se> = [s], LEASEHOLD, LEASEHOLDER, LEASH, LEAST*, AT LEAST, IN THE LEAST, TO SAY THE LEAST OF IT, LEAVE Δ, LEAVE OFF, LEAVE-TAKING, TAKE LEAVE OF ONE'S SENSES, LEAVINGS, MEAD, MEAGRE, MEAL, MAKE A MEAL OF, MEAL-TICKET, MEALTIME, MEAL, MEALY, MEAN Δ, IN THE MEANTIME, MEAN IT, MEAN WELL, MEANLY, MEANNESS, MEANING, WITH MEANING, MEANINGFUL, MEANINGLESS, MEANS, BY ALL MEANS, BY NO MEANS, MEANS TEST, MEANTIME, MEANWHILE, MEASLES*, MEAT, MEATLESS, MEATY, MINCEMEAT, MISDEAL, MISHEAR, MISLEAD, MOONBEAM, NEAP, NEAP TIDE, NEAR, NEARNESS, NEAR BY, NEAR MISS, NEAR-SIGHTED, NEAR THING, NEARBY, NEARLY, NOT NEARLY, NEAT, NEATEN,

NEATLY, NEATNESS, NORTH-EAST, OVERHEAR, OVERHEAT, PEA, PEA-GREEN, PEA-SHOOTER, PEACE, PEACE-OFFERING, PEACEABLE, PEACEABLY, PEACEFUL, PEACEFULLY, PEACEFULNESS, PEACEMAKER, PEACH, PEACHY, PEACOCK, PEAHEN, PEAK, PEAKY, PEAL, PEANUT, PEANUT BUTTER, PEASE-PUDDING, PEAT, PLEAD Δ, PLEASE, PLEAT, PREACH, QUEASY, REACH, REACHABLE, READ Δ, READ A PERSON'S HAND, READ BETWEEN THE LINES, READ-ONLY, READ PROOFS, READ UP, READABLE, READER, READERSHIP, READING, READING AGE, READING-DESK, READING-LAMP, READING-ROOM, REAL, REAL TIME, REALISM, REALIST, REALISTICALLY, REALITY, REALIZE, REALLY, REAM, REAP, REAR, BRING UP THE REAR, REAR-ADMIRAL, REAR-LAMP, REAR-LIGHT, REARMOST, REASON, REASONABLE, REAVE Δ, RE-HEAT, RELEASE<se> = [s], REPEAL, REPEAT, REPEATABLE, REPEATEDLY, REPEATER, RETREAT, SAUSAGE-MEAT, SCREAM, SCREAMINGLY, SEA, AT SEA, BY SEA, ON THE SEA, SEA ANEMONE *terminal* <e> =[ee], SEA-BIRD, SEA-FISH, SEA FRONT, SEA-GREEN, SEA-HORSE, SEA-KALE, SEA LANE, SEA-LEGS, SEA-LEVEL, SEA-LION, SEA-SALT, SEA SERPENT, SEA SHELL, SEA-SHORE, SEA-URCHIN, SEAFARER, SEAFARING, SEAFOOD, SEAGOING, SEAGULL, SEAL, SEALING-WAX, SEALANT, SEALSKIN, SEAM, SEAMAN, SEAMANSHIP, SEAMY, SEAPLANE, SEAPORT, SEAR, SEASCAPE, SEASICK, SEASIDE, SEASON*, SEASON-TICKET, SEASONABLE, SEASONAL, SEASONING, SEAT, SEAT-BELT, SEATED, SEAWARD, SEAWARDS, SEAWEED, SEAWORTHY, SHEAF *noun, plural* SHEAVES, SHEAR Δ, SHEARER, SHEARS, SHEARWATER, SHEATH *noun,, plural* SHEATHS, SHEATH-KNIFE, SHEATHE *verb*, SLEAZY, SMEAR, SMEARY, SNEAK Δ, SNEAKY, SPEAK* Δ, ON SPEAKING TERMS, NOTHING TO SPEAK OF, SPEAKING-TUBE, SPEAK UP, SPEAKER, SPEAR, SPEARHEAD, SPEARMINT, SQUEAK, SQUEAKER, SQUEAKY, SQUEAL, SQUEAMISH, SQUEAMISHNESS, STEAL Δ, STEAL A MARCH ON, STEAM, STEAM-ENGINE, STEAM IRON, STEAMER, STEAMROLLER, STEAMSHIP, STEAMY, STEAMINESS, STREAK, STREAKER, STREAKY, STREAM, ON STREAM, STREAMER, STREAMLET, STREAMLINE, SWEETMEAL, SWEETMEAT, TEA, TEA-BAG, TEA-CHEST, TEA-CLOTH, TEA-COSY, TEA-LEAF, TEA-PARTY, TEA-PLANT, TEA-ROOM, TEA-ROSE, TEA-SET, TEA-SHOP, TEACAKE, TEACH Δ, TEACH-IN, TEACHABLE, TEACHER, TEACHING, TEACUP, TEAK, TEAL, TEAM, TEAM SPIRIT, TEAM-WORK, TEAPOT, TEAR *noun, liquid,* TEAR-DROP, TEAR-GAS, TEAR-JERKER, TEARFUL, TEASE, TEASEL, TEASER, TEASPOON, TEASPOONFUL, TEAT, THEATRE*, THICK EAR, TREACLE*, TREACLY*, TREASON, TREASONABLE, TREAT, TREATISE, TREATMENT, TREATY, TWEAK, UNBEATABLE, UNBEATEN, UNDERNEATH, UNDERSEAL, UNEATABLE, UNEASY, UNEASILY, UNEASINESS, UNLEASH, UNREADABLE, UNREAL, UNREASON, UNSEAT, UNSPEAKABLE, UPBEAT, UPHEAVAL, UPHEAVE, UPSTREAM, VEAL, WEAK, WEAK-KNEED, WEAK-MINDED, WEAKEN, WEAKLING, WEAKLY, WEAKNESS, WEAL, WEAN, WEARISOME, WEARILY, WEARINESS, WEARY, WEASEL, WEAVE Δ, WEAVER, WEAVER-BIRD, WHEAT, EAR OF WHEAT, WHEATEAR *bird*, WHEATEN, WHEATMEAL, WREAK *silent* <w>, WREATH *silent* <w>, WREATHE *silent* <w>, YEAR, YEAR-BOOK, YEARLING, YEARLY, YEAST*, YEASTY*, ZEAL. <u>Aust. words,</u> BREAM, DREAM-TIME, EAGLE-HAWK, EAR-BASH, EASTERN STATES, OFF THE SHEARS, SUNBEAM, WEANER. <u>Proper Nouns,</u> CHELSEA <s> =[s], EAST END, EASTER, NEAR EAST, PEACH MELBA, SEA LORD. <u>Names</u> BEA, BEAVER, CHELSEA, DEAN, HEATH, JEAN.

Appear was *aperen* in Middle English and no doubt the dictionary committee traced it back through French to Latin *apparere* and used <ea> to spell it. Its shortened form was *peren* and this influenced the spelling of the supposedly unrelated word *peer*, originally *pire*, 'to look closely', probably from the Old Frisian word *piren*. The noun *peer* comes from the Latin for equal, *par*, via Old French *per*. Just to show

how arbitrary spelling was, when *peer* formed the word *umpire* it was spelt with the original spelling of the verb *peer*. *Umpire* means 'without-peer', 'without equal', originally Old French *nonpeer*. The umpire's word is final as no one else is his equal.

*Beard is one of the four words in which <ear> does not spell [er] inside a word, as in *heard* or *early*. The others are {*heart, hearth* and *hearken*}.

*Beadle, beagle, beast, eagle, eaglet, east, easterly, eastern, eastwards, feast, least, measles, treacle, treacly, yeast and *yeasty* are the only words in which <ea> spells [ee] when it is followed by two consonants. These two consonants are mostly <st>. As we saw earlier, <st> never follows <ee> except in the adopted Afrikaans words *hartebeest* and *wildebeest*. Also *freest*. Note: digraphs <sh>, <ch> etc. spell single consonants, as in *leash, teach, heath*.

In the sixteenth century there was quite an effort made to ensure that only <ea> spelt [ee] at the beginning of words and inside words, Cummings p. 259. That's why *eagle* has the unusual <ea> before <gle>. It was *egle*. Many still use single<e> but only one word uses <ee> to start a word, *eel*. (Also *eek!* but that is slang.) The others that have the unusual <ea> before consonant <le>, *beadle, beagle, eagle, measles* and *treacle*, all spelt [ee] with a single letter originally, before the sixteenth push for <ea>. Those with <ea> before <st> were also converted from single letters in the push to use <ea>.

*Season [seez-on] is both a verb and a noun. Fruit which has been through the season is ripe and tasty and we could say it is seasoned, which is why, when we make food tasty with spices, we say we are seasoning it.

Some people say **theatre* spells [thee-tə] and others say it spells [thee-u-ter]/[thee-ə-ter].

*Speak comes from Old English *spæc* [spac]. Remember to write <ea> using the <a> of *talk, crack on. argue, natter, chat*. A *speech*, Old English *specan* [speekan] was more formal, more seemly.

I hope you practised reading the <ee> words at the beginning of Part Three. I hope they are loaded into your automatic detector, for Prof Cummings tells us there is little to distinguish the use of <ea> and <ee> for spelling [ee]. We read both <ee> and <ea> as [ee]. However, in order to write them correctly, we need to search for patterns, with help from the Prof:-

Relevant Writing Tips. As we have seen, only *flea, pea, sea, lea,* and *tea* use <ea> to spell terminal [ee], which separates them from *flee, pee, see, lee,* and *tee* — and *plea* probably ends with <ea> to match *please*. We never see *digraph <ea> spelling [ee] at the end of words of two or more syllables, unless they are compound words, like *chickpea* or rebel *guinea*. On the other hand, only two stem words start with <ee>, *eel* and *eerie*. *The letters <ea> end *area, idea, rhea* and *urea* but they do not form a digraph. They are in adjoining syllables. Also *apnea* and *tinea* but words of six or more letters are very specialized professional terms, created from Latin on the whole.

Both <ee> and <ea> occur most commonly before a final consonant, as in *seem* and *seam, beech* and *beach,* but not often before two consonants. If so, <ee> is only followed by <dl>, <tl> or <pl> (except for *wildebeest* and *hartebeest*, Africaans adoptions, and in *freest*, as in *free, freer, freest*). After <ea>, the two consonants are usually <st>, as in *feast*. The second consonant is only <l> in *beadle, beagle, eagle, measles* and *treacle*.

When the consonant is followed by a vowel, then <ee> is rarely used, only in the stem words *breeze, cheese, fleece, freeze, geese, peeve, seethe, sleeve, sneeze, squeeze* and *wheeze* and their progeny and *squeegee, tweezers, teeter* and *weevil*, plus slang *weeny*. Also in Malay dagger *creese* and *mongeese* from Hindi *mangus* or *mungus*.

Because there is little to choose between <ee> and <ea>, when writing words, we must use reminders. Terminal <ea> rebels are all nouns: 'I wish that flea would flee.' 'Don't pee in the pea garden.' 'That grassy lea is in the lee of the hill'— both nouns. 'The golfers tee off before morning tea.' (I expect you to plea that plea is also a verb and that tee is also a noun.) Reading words with <ee> is easy, with <ea> a bit harder, but writing them correctly is much harder. Use the following list of <ea>/<ee> homophones and put each pair in one sentence, as in *I went to see the sea*. Then try writing a sentence using lots of <ea> words, to link them in your memory, e.g., 'Streaming live, the mean creature screamed at the teacher, unleashing a ream of sleazy insults.' Challenge your partner to continue the story by writing a sentence of <ee> words, e.g., 'We don't need this creep,' said the Queen, 'Sweep him away into the reedbed with the beetles and the weevils.' Continue, taking turns, using the lists below.

EA and EE homophones.
BEECH vs BEACH, BEET vs BEAT, CHEEP vs CHEAP, CREEK vs CREAK, DEER vs DEAR, FEET vs FEAT, FLEE vs FLEA, HEEL vs HEAL, LEE vs LEA, LEAK vs LEEK, MEET vs MEAT, NEED vs KNEAD, PEE vs PEA, PEEK vs PEAK, PEEL vs PEAL, REED vs READ, REEL vs REAL, SEE vs SEA, SEEM vs SEAM, STEEL vs STEAL, TEE vs TEA, TEEM vs TEAM, WEEK vs WEAK.

Words with terminal EA or EE.

Homophones. FLEA, PLEA, LEA, SEA, TEA / FLEE, LEE, SEE, TEE. Other one syllable words:- BEE, FEE, FREE, GEE, GHEE, GLEE, KNEE, SCREE, SPREE, THEE, THREE, TREE, TWEE, VEE, WEE. 2 Syllables GUINEA / AGREE, BANSHEE, BUCKSHEE, BUNGEE, COFFEE, DECREE, DEGREE, FRISBEE, GIDGEE, GRANDEE, HUMVEE, LESSEE, LEVEE, LICHEE, LYCHEE, MALLEE, PEEWEE, WEE-WEE, PUTTEE, RUPEE, SUTTEE, THUGEE, TOFFEE, TRUSTEE, YIPPEE. Proper Noun YANKEE. 3 syllables. ABSENTEE, ADDRESSEE, AMPUTEE, ASSIGNEE, ATTENDEE, CHICKADEE, CHIMPANZEE, COMMITTEE, CONSIGNEE, DEVOTEE, ESCAPEE, EXAMINEE, KEDGEREE, FRANCHISEE, FRICASSEE, GRANDEE, JAMBOREE, JUBILEE, KEDGEREE, LEGATEE, LICENSEE, MANATEE, NOMINEE, PEDIGREE, REFEREE, REFUGEE, TRANSFEREE. Proper Noun GALILEE. 4 syllables. CHINCHERINCHEE (lily), CORROBOREE.

Initial <ea> or <ee>. EAGER, EAGLET, EAGLE, EAR, EASE, EAST, EAVE / EEL and slang EENY and EEK!

EA and EE words with the same endings
—CE:- PEACE / FLEECE, GREECE.
—CH:- EACH, BLEACH   BREACH, EACH, LEACH, PEACH, PREACH, REACH , TEACH / BEECH TREE , BESEECH, BREECH, BREECHES, LEECH, CREECH, SPEECH.
—D:- BEAD, LEAD, PLEAD, MEAD, KNEAD, READ / BLEED, BREED, CREED, DEED, EXCEED, FEED, GREED, HEED, INDEED, MEED, NEED, PROCEED, REED, SCREED, SEED, SPEED, STEED, SUCCEED, WEED.
—F:- LEAF, SHEAF / BEEF, *REEF
—K:- BEAK, BLEAK, FREAK, LEAK, PEAK, SNEAK, SPEAK, SQUEAK, STREAK, TWEAK, WEAK, WREAK / CHEEK, CREEK, GEEK *slang* LEEK, MEEK, PEEK, SLEEK, WEEK. Proper Adj. GREEK
—L:- ANNEAL, APPEAL, COMMONWEAL, CONCEAL, CONGEAL, DEAL, HEAL, IDEAL, MEAL / CREEL , FEEL, GENTEEL, HEEL, KEEL, KNEEL, PEEL, REEL, SEAL, STEEL, WHEEL.
—LE:- BEAGLE, BEADLE, EAGLE, MEASLES, TREACLE / BEETLE, ENFEEBLE, FEEBLE, NEEDLE, STEEPLE, TWEEDLE, WHEEDLE.
—M:- BEAM, BREAM, CREAM, DREAM, FLEAM, GLEAM, REAM, SEAM, SCREAM, STREAM, TEAM / DEEM, ESTEEM, HAREEM, NEEM TREE, REDEEM, SEEM, TEEM.
—N:- BEAN, CLEAN, DEAN, JEANS, LEAN, MEAN, SKEAN dagger, WEAN / BEEN, BETWEEN, GREEN, KEEN, PREEN, SCREEN, SEEN, SHEEN, SPLEEN, TEEN, TWEEN, WEEN, BALEEN, CANTEEN, CAREEN, COLLEEN, FIFTEEN and other teens, MANGOSTEEN, NANKEEN, TUREEN, UMPTEEN *slang*.
—P:- CHEAP, HEAP, LEAP, NEAP, REAP, SLEAP / ASLEEP, BEEP, BLEEP, CHEEP, DEEP, CREEP, JEEP, KEEP, PEEP, PEEP-PEEP, SHEEP, SLEEP, STEEP, SWEEP, WEEP.

—R:- APPEAR, BLEAR, CLEAR, DREAR, DEAR, EAR, FEAR, GEAR, HEAR, NEAR, REAR, SEAR, SMEAR, SPEAR, STEAR, TEAR, YEAR. Name KING LEAR / BEER, CAREER, CHEER, DEER, JEER, LEER, PEER adj./noun. PIONEER, QUEER, SCHMEER, SEER fortune teller, SHEER, SNEER, STEER, VEER, VENEER plus AUCTIONEER, BALLADEER, BANDOLEER, BUCCANEER, CAMELEER… …VOLUNTEER.
—SE:- CEASE, CREASE, EASE, FEASE (feasable), GREASE, LEASE, PEASE, PLEASE, TEASE / CHEESE, GEESE.
—SH:- LEASH / BAKSHEESH tip, bribe noun, CREESH grease verb/noun, SHEESH slang exclamation, SNEESH snuff, take snuff, HASHEESH hemp resin.
—T:- BEAT, BLEAT, CHEAT, CLEAT, DEFEAT, EAT, ENTREAT, FEAT, HEAT, PEAT, PLEAT, MEAT, NEAT, SEAT, TEAT, WHEAT / BEET, DISCREET, FEET, FLEET, GREET, LORIKEET, MEET, PARAKEET, SHEET, SLEET, STREET, SWEET, TWEET.
— TH:- BENEATH, BEQUEATH, HEATH, SHEATH, WREATH / TEETH
—THE:- BREATHE, SHEATHE / SEETHE, TEETHE.
—VE:- BEREAVE, CLEAVE, EAVE, GREAVE, HEAVE, LEAVE, SHEAVES plural sheaf, WEAVE / PEEVE, SHEEVE noun, SLEEVE, STEEVE (stow cargo, *stevedore*.)
—ZE:- FEAZE OUT untangle, SLEAZE / BREEZE, *FREEZE, WHEEZE.
Return to Reading Rules.

Q. Why is [ee] spelt in so many different ways?
Ans. Cummings tells us on page 259 that all long vowels have 'complex family trees'. [ee] had two parents in Middle English, one a little longer than the other. The shorter, 'closed' one —closed mouthed —had five Old English ancestors and the longer, 'open' one — open mouthed — had four OE ancestors. The Middle English parents came through the Great Vowel Shift separately. People tried to spell the closed one with <ee> or <ie>. They tried to use <ea> or <e> for the open one. Then both sounds converged and by 1700 people just said [ee] for both and used <e> to spell both more than any other way.

We saw that when <e> and <a> go walking the first one does the talking: <ea> spells [ee] This works even when Bossy R follows on, for then the [ee] sound ends in [r] as in *ear*. However, <e> does not always do the talking in the digraph <ea>, e.g., in *pear* and *head* which belong to two small rebel gangs. Also, a large gang of forty "ready red-heads" have formed their own gang rules and four rascals have joined their gang. Some irregular verbs have members in other gangs so we shall sort the verbs out at the end of all the words with <ea> digraphs. Also, Bossy R lets three "hearty" rebels use <ear> to spell [ar] and lets 11 "pearly" stem words use <ear> to spell [er]. This just goes to show that, whilst doublets are stable, other vowel digraphs can be so very fickle! *Reed* always spells [reed] but *read* spells [reed] and also [red]. Whilst *hood* always spells [huud], even in *childhood*, *ward* spells [word] but in *backward* spells [wuud]. Digraph <ea> is particularly fickle. It spells many different vowels, as we shall now see.
Let's meet all these rebel groups.

Tear-a-way Rebels, — *tear, bear.*
Rebels In WEAR, BEAR, PEAR, TEAR, SWEAR and words containing these words, <ear> spells [air].
Rebels' Reasons When best friends <ea> went walking, <e> did the talking and together they spelt [ay]. This was before the GVS and [ay] was the long sound spelt by <e>, over most of Europe. Back then, <ear> spelt [ay-r], because the English rolled their R's. When long vowels lifted in England, in the GVS, [ay] lifted to [ee] in most words but not these. Then the English stopped pronouncing <r> as [r], except before a vowel, (as in *rat*). At the end of words it shrank to a little schwa sound. We hear this in *air,* and we see it in the IPA symbol /eɪə/. My symbol is [air]. So *bear* spells [bair]. These words refused to join the words, like *hear*, which lifted their vowels to [eer]. So we call them the 'tear-a-way rebels'. For a memory aid,

search the website's Photo Gallery for a teddy bear. Then you will be able to say, "I **swear** I saw a **bear**, with a **pear**, and a **tear** in his under**wear**".

Rebel List 4-14 In these five tear-a-ways, *wear, swear, bear, pear* and *tear*, and words made with them, <ear> spells [air].
BALL BEARINGS*, BEAR Δ, BEARABLE, BEARER, BEARING, BEARSKIN, BUGBEAR, FORBEAR (cease), FORBEARANCE, FORBEARING, FOREBEAR (ancestor), FORSWEAR Δ, MENSWEAR, PEAR, PEARMAIN, PEAR-SHAPED, SWEAR Δ, SWEARER, SWEAR BY, SWEAR IN, SWEAR OFF, SWEAR-WORD, TEAR Δ, TEARAWAY, TEARING, UNBEARABLE, UNDERWEAR, WEAR, WEARER, WEAR OFF, WEARABLE, WEAR Δ, WEARER, WEAR OFF, WEARABLE.
Ball bearings bear the friction.
The words *tear* and *tear* make it impossible to know how to say them, [teer] or [tair], unless other words surround them. They both have meaning, as a noun and as a verb: "A bear cries *tears* when he *tears* what he wears."
A final problem in decoding <ear> words arises with *wear, wearing* and *weary, wearisome, wearily*. The verb *wear, wearing* has no link to the adjectives *weary, wearisome* and the adverb *wearily*. Although we feel weary when we are worn out, the words have always been separate, ever since the Saxons said *werig* for "tired and weary" and *werian* for "wear garments".

Q. Why do some words use identical letters to spell different sounds? And why do some words use different letters to spell identical sounds?
Ans: Other languages try to keep pure. The spelling of each word is controlled, and new words are 'stopped at the border' and judged on a 'need's only' basis. If the word is needed. it's re-spelt to suit the rules. For instance, *kangaroo* was needed but respelt before allowed entry, into French as *kangourou* and into Italian as *canguru*. Italian spelling is so organized that Italian children learn to read and write in a much shorter time than English speaking children, about two years shorter! If a word changes its sound, then its spelling is adjusted, for instance, there were Dutch spelling reforms in 1954, 1995 and 2005. German even gained a new letter in 2017, Capital ẞ. However, English has not been a pure language ever since 1066, when it only survived by replacing 80% of it words with French ones and then reviving by inventing new words and adopting foreign ones, spelt under foreign rules, and changing others, especially in the GVS, without changing their spelling. Vowels changed most of all. They lengthened under the influence of Bossy R — when people stopped rolling their R's. Long vowels lifted and some bent, in the Great Vowel Shift. Vowels shortened under increased stress, e.g., *know* shortened in *knowledge*. Vowel pronunciation changes all the time and, long ago, spelling used to, but now it is unable to change because it is in print, in dictionaries. The verb 'to tear' was *teran* and the noun was *ter*, until they both changed to *tear*. 'To weep' was *tæherian* and then *tearian* and a 'wept tear' was *teahor* and then *tear*. Words that are spelt the same are called homonyms (same-names) and those that sound the same are called 'homophones' (same-sounds). Their <y> and <ph> label them as Greek words. Greek *homos*, [hom-os], came from an ancestor word meaning 'same' — *somos*. The Greek prefix *homo-* has short vowels, whereas Latin *homo* (man) has long vowels. The word we get from Latin, *Homo,* is only written with a capital and it means any member of the genus Man, which includes extinct and modern man. Even the BBC pronounces *homo* in *homosexual* incorrectly, as [hoh-moh] instead of [homo]. Think 'homogenous' when saying *homosexual:* A homo<u>g</u>enizer blends food to one homo<u>g</u>enous mass, <u>g</u>enerates sameness.

Yea! The Great Steak Break Dancers.

Mostly nowadays <ea> spells [ee] but four words rebel against that. They did not lift their long vowel sounds during the Great Vowel Shift.

Rebels YEA, GREAT, BREAK, STEAK.

Rebels' Reasons In these 4 little rebels <ea> spells [ay], which is the long sound of Continental E, and its name, too. The first vowel in these rebels does the talking, but spells its Continental long sound. *Yea* rhymes with *nay*, so they let it stay. (*Yea* and *nay*, *yes* and *no*.) *Steak* should be written *stake*. The first steak was meat on a stake roasted over a fire. So, *meat* and *stake* are combined in *steak*. We say *great* [grayt], *greater* [grayter], *greatest* [graytest] but long ago some English folk used to say [groot], [gret-er], [gret-est], and others said [grit], [gret-er], [gret-est] or [groht], [gret-er], [gret-est], (Ayto, p. 263). The old words [groot] and [grit] and [groht] all meant 'thick or stout', like today's *gross* and *grotesque*. When these words came to mean *important* and *well-known* and *big* they changed *groot* to a longer, more important sounding [grayt].

Remember this rebel group as "**The Break Dancers**" who "take a **great break** for a **steak, yea!**"

Rebels, List 4- 15 <ea> spells [ay] Yea! The Great Steak Break Dancers.
BEEFSTEAK, BREAK Δ, BREAKABLE, BREAK EVEN, BREAK IN, BREAK IN ON, BREAK OF DAY, BREAK OFF, BREAK THE BANK, BREAK THE ICE, BREAK UP, BREAK WIND, BREAK WITH, BREAKABLE, BREAKAGE, BREAKAWAY, BREAKER, BREAKNECK, BREAKWATER, GREAT, GREATEST, GREATLY, GREATNESS, STEAK, UNBREAKABLE, BREAKWIND, YEA, Proper Nouns, GREAT BRITAIN, GREAT DANE, GREATER LONDON, GREAT LAKES, GREAT SCOTT!, GREAT WAR.

Ready Redheads

Rebel Lemons are the biggest group of English spelling rebels, followed by the Ready Redheads. Pop on a bright red wig as you introduce each of these words or ask students to wear a red wig or head scarf from the dress-up box when they announce these words to the class.

Rebels In 41 words and their extensions and 3 past participles, <ea> spells [e].

Rebels' Reasons In French, the long sound that <e> spells is [ay]. Before the Great Vowel Shift, the long sound <e> spelt was [ay], which changed to [ee] in the GVS. Some then shortened from [ay] to [e]. This usually happened when the vowel sound came before [d], also before [t], [f], [v], [dh], [dh], [z], [zh], and **also** when it came before a cluster of consonants, as in *cleanse, dealt* and *health* but not in *clean, deal* and *heal*. Also before clusters in *cleanliness*, <nl>, and *breakfast*, <kf>. You will notice in the next list that <ea> spells [e] never comes before consonants made with the lips or made right at the back of our mouth and throat?

Rascals TREACHERY, WEAPON, JEALOUS and ZEALOT.

Rascals' Reasons? Being rascals, these four have no good reason to be different. We said <ea> spells [e] usually happens when the vowel sound comes before [d], [t], [f], [v], [dh], [th], [z] or [zh], which is to say it did not **always** happen **but** then again it **never** happens when the vowel comes before other single consonant sounds **except** in these four rascals. (To remember them, beware of the *jealous treachery* of *zealots* with *weapons*.)

Rebels, List 4-16 Forty-nine Ready Redheads in which <ea> spells [e]. These rebels include irregular six past participles, marked **P.P.** Note, the past participle of the verb 'to lead' is *led*, not *lead*. The noun *lead*, a metal, spells [led]. The noun *lead*, a leash, spells [leed].
BREAD, BREADTH, BREAKFAST, BREAST verb/noun, BREATH noun, CLEANSE verb, DEAD, DEAF, **P.P.** DEALT Δ *deal*, DEATH, DREAD verb/noun, **P.P.** DREAMT Δ *dream*, ENDEAVOUR verb/noun, FEATHER, HEAD, HEALTH *heal*, HEATHER *heath*, HEAVEN, HEAVY, LEAD noun, **P.P.** LEAPT Δ, LEATHER, LEAVEN, **P.P.** MEANT Δ, MEADOW, MEASURE*, PEASANT,

PEASANTRY, PHEASANT, PLEASANT, **P.P.** READ Δ, READY, REALM, SEAMSTRESS, **P.P.** SPREAD Δ, SPREAD noun, STEAD, STEALTH *steal*, SWEAT verb/noun, THREAD verb/noun, THREAT, TREAD Δ, TREAD noun, TREASURE* verb/noun, WEALTH *weal*, WEATHER verb/noun.
Measure spells [mezh-oor] and **treasure* spells [trezh-oor] due to Yod Fusion.

Rebels, List 4-16 continued, with compound and complex Ready Redhead words.
DREADFUL, DREADLOCKS, UNDREAMT-OF, BREADCRUMBS, BREADED, BREAD-WINNER, ON THE BREADLINE, ABREAST, BREASTBONE, REDBREAST, IN THE SAME BREATH, SAVE ONE'S BREATH, TAKE ONE'S BREATH AWAY, UNDER ONE'S BREATH, BREATHALYSE, BREATHALYSER, BREATHLESS, BREATHLESSLY, BREATHLESSNESS, BREATHTAKING, BREATHY, WITH BATED BREATH, CLEANLINESS, CLEANSER, CLEANSING, DEAD BEAT, DEAD-BEAT, DEAD DUCK, DEAD END, DEAD END JOB, DEAD FINISH, DEAD HEAT, DEAD LETTER, DEAD MAN'S HANDLE, DEAD MARCH, DEAD MARINE, DEAD-PAN, DEAD RECKONING, DEAD SET, DEADEN, DEADLINE, DEADLOCK, DEADLY, DEADLINESS, SEVEN DEADLY SINS, DEAFNESS, DEAF MUTE, DEAFEN, DEATH ADDER, DEATH-BED, DEATH CERTIFICATE, DEATH DUTY, DEATH PENALTY, DEATH-RATE, DEATH-ROLL, DEATH'S HEAD, DEATH-TRAP, DEATH-WATCH BEETLE, PUT TO DEATH, TO THE DEATH, DEATHLESS, DEATHLY, FEATHER IN ONE'S CAP, FEATHER BED, FEATHER-BED, FEATHER-BRAINED, FEATHER ONE'S NEST, FEATHER STITCH, FEATHERY, AHEAD, FOREHEAD*, HEAD GEAR, HEADACHE, COST PER HEAD, AT THE HEAD OF, HEAD-ON, HEAD OVER HEELS, HEADS WILL ROLL, HEAD WIND, IN ONE'S HEAD, KEEP ONE'S HEAD, LOSE ONE'S HEAD, OFF ONE'S HEAD, OVER ONE'S HEAD, PUT HEADS TOGETHER, TURN A PERSON'S HEAD, HEAD-DRESS, BAREHEADED, BLACKHEAD, BLOCKHEAD, HEADER, HEADING, HEADLAMP, HEADLAND, HEADLESS, HEADLIGHT, HEADLINE, HEADLONG, HEADMASTER, HEADMISTRESS, HEADPHONE, HEADQUARTERS, HEADROOM, HEADSCARF, HEAD-SHRINKER, HEADSTONE, HEADWATER, HEADWATERS, HEADWAY, HEADY, HOGSHEAD, EGGHEAD, LETTERHEAD, LOGGERHEADS, OVER HEAD, SUBHEADING, THICK HEAD, THICK HEADED, HEALTH CENTRE, HEALTH FARM, HEALTH FOODS, HEALTH SERVICE, HEALTH VISITOR, HEALTHFUL, HEALTHY, HEALTHILY, HEALTHINESS, HEAVEN-SENT, HEAVENLY, HEAVILY, HEAVINESS, HEAVY-DUTY, HEAVY GOING, HEAVY-HANDED, HEAVY INDUSTRY, HEAVY METAL, HEAVY MOB, HEAVY WATER, MAKE HEAVY WEATHER OF IT, LEADED, SWING THE LEAD, LEADEN, LEATHER-JACKET, LEATHERY, UNLEAVENED, MEASURABLE, MADE TO MEASURE, MEASURE UP TO, MEASUREMENT, PLEASANTRY, PLEASURE, PLEASURABLE, DISPLEASURE, UNPLEASANT, UNPLEASANTNESS, WELL-READ, ALREADY, READILY, READINESS, AT THE READY, READY-MADE, READY RECKONER, BEDSPREAD, SPREAD-EAGLE, IN A PERSON'S STEAD, INSTEAD, BEDSTEAD, GOOD STEAD, HOMESTEAD, STEADFAST, STEADFASTLY, STEADY, UNSTEADY, UNSTEADILY, STEADILY, STEADINESS, GO STEADY, STEADY ON!, STEALTHY, STEALTHILY, STEALTHINESS, SWEAT-BAND, SWEAT BLOOD, SWEAT-SHIRT, SWEAT-SHOP, SWEATER, SWEATY, THREADBARE, THREADWORM, DRAWN THREAD WORK, THREATEN, TREAD ON AIR, TREAD ON TOES, TREAD WATER, RETREAD, TREADLE, TREADMILL, TREASURER, TREASURE-HUNT, TREASURE-TROVE, TREASURY, COMMONWEALTH, WEALTH TAX, WEALTHY, KEEP A WEATHER EYE OPEN, UNDER THE WEATHER, WEATHER-BEATEN, WEATHER-VANE, WEATHERCOCK, WEATHERMAN, WEATHERPROOF. <u>Proper Nouns</u> THE COMMONWEALTH, DEAD SEA. Names ELEANOR, HEATHER.

*When *forehead* spells [**fo**-red] it has silent <h>, as we'd expect after a stressed vowel and before an unstressed vowel. It can also spell [for-hed] with even stress, (ref. OPD). This is a rare occasion when <ore> in the word *fore* spells [o] — as a part of a compound word. This is similar to *break* in *breakfast,* a long vowel becoming short and stressed.

As you can see, many words in which <ea> spells [e] avoid confusion with words in which <ee> spells [ee]. Can you add to the following list of pairs? They are not homophones because they do not sound the same.

sweat ↔ sweet
head ↔ heed
stead ↔ steed
already ↔ all reedy
dead ↔ deed

M' hearties! — *hearken, heart, hearth.*

In the three **Rebels** HEARKEN HEART HEARTH <ear> spells [ar].
Rebels' Reasons In Middle English, in the time of French domination, the Old English [er] sound changed to [ar], with a roll on the <r>. The sound changed but not necessarily the spelling! That's why we write *clerk* but say [klark] and we write *sergeant* and say [sar-jent]. In some, spelling changed too. *Sterre* changed to *star* and *merk* to *mark*. The following words did not change their letters but they did change their pronunciation e.g., from [hert] to [hart]. *Hearken* did not change but its modern version, *hark,* did, from *heark.* Why did *heark* change to *hark?* Maybe to match the <ar> in *harpy* and *carp* because harpies hark back and carp on about the past.
Hearty [harty] used to be [herty], and Prof Lerer reckons this change was instigated by pirates! We have to admit that "M' Hearties!" sounds far grander than "M' Herties!" England was proud of its pirates. They plundered the dominant fleets of the seventeenth century, the Dutch merchant and navy ships. Some, like William Dampier, received knighthoods. They were top influencers. Pirates call friends, fellow comrades or sailors 'hearties'. When pirates say "me hearties", they're giving due respect to a person for bravery or other admirable qualities. "Hearty" was even another word for "sailor" from the 18th to the early 20th century. I think they copied the Dutch sailors, because *heart* in Dutch was changing from [hert] to [hart] at that time. A pirate's black eye patch and a red head scarf from the dress-up box can be worn when introducing *hearken, heart* and *hearth,* as in website's Photo Gallery.

BTW, *hearken* was a form of the verb *hear* and *hearth* comes from 'heat-place'. *Heart* long ago started with [k], as in 'cardiac arrest' and Italian 'caro mio,' but its [k] became [h] when it spread through Germany and into Germanic languages. English *board* became French *table* but English *heart* never became French *cœur*. It used the same vowel as *Herz*, 'heart' in German, until its [er] changed to [ar].
Rebels, List 4-17 In all these words <ear> spells [ar].
HEARKEN; HEART, AT HEART, BY HEART, CHANGE OF HEART, HAVE A HEART!, HEART ATTACK, HEART FAILURE, HEART-BREAK, HEART-BREAKING, HEART-BROKEN, HEART-LUNG MACHINE, HEART-RENDING, HEART-STRINGS, HEART-THROB, HEART-TO-HEART, HEART-WARMING, SET ONE'S HEART ON, TAKE TO HEART, HEART'S CONTENT, HEARTACHE, HEARTBURN, HEARTBURNING, HEARTEN, HEARTIES**,** HEARTINESS, HEARTFELT, HEARTILY, HEARTLAND, HEARTLESS, HEARTLESSLY, HEARTLESSNESS, HEARTWOOD, HEARTY, SWEET HEART; HEARTH**,** HEARTHRUG.

Eleven Pearls — *pearl, yearn.*

Although three <ear> words changed from spelling [er] to [ar], many words did not change at all. They still have Old English spelling and pronunciation. We say them now without sounding the <r> much but there are parts of England which do them proud, ee-arrr! Down south in England, *old* was *eald* but up north it was *ald*. From them, *earl* and *alderman* grew, as well as *old* and *elder*. What a rich language!

Eleven Rebels In eleven stem words <ear> spells [er] and has done so since way before 1066!

Rebel's Reasons Why not write *derth* and *erl* and *erth* and *herd*? There are only 11 stem words amongst them all…why not change them from <ear> to <er>? At times like these we have to say to ourselves, "Memorize, don't analyse!" However, the dictionary elders must have left the <a> there to give us a clue to the past and so we shall see if they have left us hidden treasure. *Rehearse* means 'rake over' and 're-rake', and *hearse* used to mean 'a rake or frame over a dead body'! *Earth* in Old English was *eorðe*, meaning 'ground, soil, dry land'. *Eorðe* became *eard* which became *earth*. *Early* means 'soon', or the old word *ere*, which in even older times was written *ær*. *Pearl* has a connection with *pear-shaped*, (Etymonline). The old word *earn*, from *earnian*, was 'reward for labour' and the <a> of labour is reflected in the <a> of *earn*. In Old English *learn* was *leornian* and *lærn* meant 'to teach'. We no longer say "She learned me to read," but that old use of the verb is still in use as an adjective for we can 'become learned [lern-ed]', which is different to "I learned [lernd] my work". So the buried treasure is the <a> in *learn*, which connects it to its old meaning *to teach*. Ayto, on p. 464, says there is no connection between *seek* and *search*. The latter is connected to *eager* and *yearn* and *circle*. Do you search in circles, like an eagle circling around? Do you search with eager yearning? *Heard* retains <a> to link it to *hear*. *Dearth* is traced back to *dear th* because when things are scarce they are costly, dear. The adjective *dear* is turned into an abstract noun, meaning scarcity, by adding *th*. (Etymonline).

Rebels, List 4-18 <ear> spells [er] in eleven rebel words, marked *, and their complex words.
DEARTH*, EARL*, EARLY*, EARLY BIRD, EARLINESS, EARLY CLOSING, EARLY ON, EARN*, EARNINGS, EARNEST, EARNESTLY, EARNESTNESS, IN EARNEST, EARTH*, RUN A THING TO EARTH, EARTHEN, EARTHENWARE, EARTHLY, NO EARTHLY USE, EARTHQUAKE, EARTHWORK, EARTHWORM, EARTHY, HEARD* Δ, HEARSE*, LEARN* Δ, LEARNED [lern-ed] *adj.*, LEARNEDLY, LEARNER, PEARL*, PEARL-DIVER, PEARL-FISHER, PEARLING, PEARLY, REHEARSAL, REHEARSE, RESEARCH, RESEARCHER, SEARCH*, SEARCHER, SEARCH-PARTY, SEARCH-WARRANT, SEARCHING, SEARCHLIGHT, UNEARTH, UNEARTHLY, UNHEALTHY, UNHEARD, UNHEARD-OF, YEARN*.

<u>Relevant Writing Rule.</u> Except for *beard*, *heart*, *hearth* and *hearken*, <ear> spells [er] inside words. Note, <ear> never spells [er] at the end of words. <u>Return to Reading Rules.</u>

Can you sing "Pearly shells from the ocean, shining in the sun, covering the shore"? The song and the hand actions are all at http://library.thinkquest.org/J0110077/dance.htm. Try that song and then try this one. Can you see our eleven pearls? *Early birds from the ocean, searching in the earth just behind the shore. / When I heard them, how I yearned, for Earl I loved you, more than all the little pearly shells. / Whenever a hearse goes by, for you I reach, I've got to learn from you, / the love we earned is over, such a dearth of twinkles in the blue,* (Repeat the first four lines again.) See the pearl necklace in the website's Photo Gallery, eleven pearls and an extra for the name *Earl*, as compared to the common noun *earl*.

Irregular Verbs with <ea> — *beaten, dreamt, meant.*

Now we shall examine all the irregular verbs we marked Δ. We know that irregular verbs change the sounds inside them instead of adding <ed> and we know that <ea> can make a range of sounds. Let's see how <ea> changes the sound it spells inside the following irregular verbs.

In the following irregular verbs <ea> spells [ee] in present tense and elsewhere unless indicated.
BEAT Δ, BEAT Δ, BEATEN Δ.
BEREAVE Δ, BEREAVED /BEREFT Δ, BEREAVED/BEREFT Δ.
CLEAVE Δ (split apart), CLOVE Δ, CLOVEN Δ

CLEAVE ∆ (cling to), CLEFT ∆ /CLEAVED, CLEFT ∆ /CLEAVED.
DEAL ∆, DEALT ∆ [delt], DEALT ∆ [delt],
DREAM ∆, DREAMED/DREAMT ∆ [dremt], DREAMED/DREAMT ∆ [dremt]
EAT ∆, ATE ∆, EATEN ∆
HEAR ∆, HEARD ∆ [herd], HEARD ∆ [herd]
HEAVE* ∆, HEAVED /HOVE ∆, HEAVED/HOVE ∆
LEAD ∆, LED ∆, LED ∆.
LEAN ∆, LEANT ∆ [lent] /LEANED, LEANT ∆ [lent] /LEANED
LEAP, LEAPT ∆ [lept]/LEAPED, LEAPT ∆ [lept]/LEAPED
LEAVE ∆, LEFT ∆, LEFT ∆
MEAN ∆, MEANT ∆ [ment], MEANT ∆ [ment]
PLEAD ∆, PLED ∆ /PLEADED, PLED ∆ /PLEADED
READ ∆ **, READ ∆ [red], READ ∆ [red]
REAVE ∆ (to rob), REFT ∆ /ROVE ∆, REFT ∆ /REAVEN ∆. (Out of use, but we are *bereaved* when we are robbed of someone. People who *roved* about moved around *robbing* people. Was the Gypsy Rover in the song of that name a robber?)
SHEAR ∆, SHORE ∆ /SHEARED, SHORN ∆ /SHEARED
SNEAK ∆, SNUCK ∆ /SNEAKED, SNUCK ∆ /SNEAKED
SPEAK ∆, SPOKE ∆, SPOKEN ∆
STEAL ∆, STOLE ∆, STOLEN ∆
TEACH ∆, TAUGHT ∆, TAUGHT ∆.
WEAVE ∆, WOVE ∆, WOVEN ∆

In these irregular verbs <ea> spells [air]
BEAR ∆, BORE ∆, BORN ∆ (give birth) or BORNE ∆ (carried, lifted, borne aloft)
FORSWEAR ∆, FORSWORE ∆, FORSWORN ∆
SWEAR ∆, SWORE ∆, SWORN ∆
TEAR ∆, TORE ∆, TORN ∆
WEAR ∆, WORE ∆, WORN ∆

In this irregular verb <ea> spells [ay]
BREAK ∆, BROKE ∆, BROKEN ∆

In these irregular verbs <ea> spells [e]
SPREAD ∆, SPREAD ∆, SPREAD ∆
SWEAT ∆, SWEAT ∆ /SWEATED, SWEAT ∆ /SWEATED
TREAD ∆, TROD ∆, TRODDEN ∆ /TROD ∆

In this irregular verb <ea> spells [er]
LEARN ∆, LEARNT ∆ /LEARNED, LEARNT ∆ /LEARNED
EARN ∆, EARNT ∆ /EARNED, EARNT ∆ /EARNED

We can see that some irregular verbs are in the process of changing into regular verbs, like old *pled* into modern *pleaded*.

**Many verbs look the same in past and present form, e.g., "I *cut* it today and I *cut* it yesterday", but the verb *to read* is the only one of them to look the same but spell different sounds, [reed] in present tense and [red] in past tense.

*The usage of the verb *heave* is explained in this, "He heaved a sigh as he hove in sight. The boat was hove to and the anchor heaved over board," (Fowlers, p. 242).

Now that you know what each <ea> word spells, you can read the following poem, in which {*suite*} spells [sweet].

Beware of heard, a dreadful word

That looks like beard and sounds like bird,
And dead: it's said like bed not bead —
For goodness sake don't call it deed!
Watch out for meat and great and threat —
They rhyme with suite and straight and debt —
Language? Why, man alive!
I learned to talk it when I was five,
And yet to write it, the more I tried,
I hadn't learnt it by fifty-five. *Anon.*

Continental Digraph <ei> — *abseil, weigh.*

When two vowels go walking, if the first one is <e>, it spells [ee], but in some words it still spells [ay], its long sound before the GVS. In the following words, <ei> spells its long Continental sound and we see that many of these words belong to Old English, which began as a Germanic language, with guttural [gh]. Now we only see <gh>, we do not hear it, because [ay] is a long sound and after long vowels <gh> was silenced. Its presence in these words reminds us that they are very old English words and that they belong to a group which did not lift their shared vowel sound [ay] to [ee] during the GVS.

Rule 4-19 Continental <ei> spells [ay].

Reason Long Continental E is [ay]. In <ei> the first vowel does the talking but it's the Continental long sound we hear. After the French left the throne, the English never got round to replacing <ei> wIth <ai> in the following words. They should be written <ai> but they aren't! Don't forget that <gh> after a long vowel is silent — nor that <g> before <n> in the same syllable is silent.

Rebels FORFEIT, SURFEIT, {COUNTERFEIT}, FORFEITURE, in which <feit> spells [fət]. FOREIGN, SOVEREIGN in which <ei> spells [e].

Rebels' Reasons In such words, French *fait* [fay] was spelt *fet* in Old French. In Middle English it was written *fet,* as expected, due to reduced stress at the end of these words. So terminal *feit* spells unstressed [fət] in *forfeit* and *surfeit* but due to secondary stress in {*counterfeit*} that word is often pronounced [fayt], which is wrong, as it should be [fət]. The tum-te-tum rhythm is maintained enough using [fət]. In *foreign,* stress on the first syllable reduces the second so that <ei> spells [e] in [fo-ren], instead of [ay], and to avoid two weak beats, *sovereign* spells [sov-ren]. The syllable *reign* crept into these words by misconception. *Foreign* means 'on the outside, outsider', and replaced the old word *fremd,* and *sovereign* is related to *soprano,* which is why Milton spelt it *sovran.*

List 4-19 <ei> spells [ay]

ABSEIL, BANTAMWEIGHT, CATCHWEIGHT, DEAD WEIGHT, DEIGN, EIGHT, EIGHTEEN, EIGHTEENTH, EIGHTH, EIGHTSOME, EIGHTY, EIGHTIETH, EIGHTIES, FEATHERWEIGHT, FEIGN*, FEINT, FREIGHT, GEISHA, HEAVYWEIGHT, HEIGH-HO, HUNDREDWEIGHT, INVEIGH, INVEIGLE, LEI*, LIGHTWEIGHT, MEIOSIS, MEIOTIC, MIDDLEWEIGHT, NEIGH, NEIGHBOUR, OBEISANCE, PAPERWEIGHT, PEIN, REIGN, REIN, REINDEER, SHEIK, SKEIN, SEMEIOTIC, SLEIGH, SLEIGHING, SLEIGHT, SLEIGHT OF HAND, SURVEILLANCE, UNDERWEIGHT, VEIL, VEILING, VEIN, WEIGH, WEIGH UP, WEIGHBRIDGE, WEIGHT, WEIGHT-LIFTER, WEIGHTING, WEIGHTLESS, WEIGHTLESSNESS, WEIGHTY. <u>Proper Noun</u> MADELEINE, SINN FEIN.

Note:- <gh> is silent after a long vowel, as expected.

Feign has silent <gn> after a long vowel, as expected.

Lei [lay] is adopted from French Polynesia, but not adapted.

Rule 4-20   <eir> spells [air].

Reason The French long vowel [ay] spelt by <ei> is modified or 'coloured' by Bossy R to [air]. *Heir* is still spelt the French way, in which <h> is silent, so *heir* spells [air]. Heir and all ist progeny join the other words in which initial <h> is silent, like *honest, {honour}, honorary, hour.*

List 4-20 <eir> spells [air]
HEIR *silent <h>,* [air]*,* HEIR APPARENT, HEIR PRESUMPTIVE, HEIRESS, HEIRLOOM, THEIR*.
Proper Noun EIRE.

*Their is spelt like this because it comes from *they.* The <y> was changed to <i> when it was no longer terminal for <y> is not accepted inside English stem words, only Greek words. "**They** love **their** kids" is not allowed to be "**They** love **theyr** kids." It should follow the pattern in "**You** love **your** kids." Then again, if <i> was allowed to end English words, *they* would be *thei.*

German Digraph <ei> — *apartheid, stein.*

Rule 4-21 In words adopted from modern German, <ei> spells [I].

Reason In modern German <ei> spells [I]. The next words did not come with the Saxons to start the English language. In Anglo-Saxon times, *mine* was written *min,* (see Orm's Law). It matched its Germanic cousin, *mein,* in sound, but not in spelling. The following words are modern unadapted adoptions, with a few old ones, like *either*, which have been re-spelt. These words can be nick-named Einstein Words or Heidi Words. A frizzy wig and glasses, from the dress-up box, for Einstein or plaits and a dirndl skirt for Heidi, adds to the fun.

Rebel FRÄULEIN spells [frow-lin] not [frow-lIn].

Rebel's Reason It is adopted but not adapted. As <lein> is not stressed in this German word, it spells [lin]. *Frau=Missus, Fräulein=Miss* for an unmarried woman*.*

List 4-21 <ei> spells [I] in modern German adoptions
APARTHEID <th> spells [t], EIDER DUCK, EISTEDDFOD*, FEISTY, EITHER* [dh], GEIGER, HEIGHT, HEIGHTEN, HEIST*, KALEIDOSCOPE, NEITHER* [dh], POLTERGEIST, SEISMIC, SEISMOGRAPH, SLEIGHT, SLEIGHT OF HAND, STEIN. Proper Nouns BRUNEI, EDELWEISS [ed-el-vIs]. Names EILEEN, EINSTEIN, FAHRENHEIT*, HEIDI, POSEIDON.

**Eisteddford* is a Welsh word and pronounced [I-steth-vod].

Actually, *neither* and *either* can be pronounced <ei> spells [ee], or [I]. It is neither here nor there which you choose, for either will do. They have dual pronunciation, but in this list let <ei> spell [I].

Actually, *either* and *neither* still spelt [aydher] and [naydher] in the seventeenth century, according to 'Encylcopedia Americana' on the topic of spelling. In other words, <e> spelt its long Continental sound, [ay], because <i> let the first vowel do the talking, in places where the long vowel [ay] had not yet lifted to [ee] or [I]. Then came the GVS and [ay] lifted to [ee]. Then some people tried to lift [ee] again, which resulted in [I].

*Fahrenheit [far-en-hIt] or [fa-ren-hIt] is the old way to measure temperature, invented by the German scientist G. D. Fahrenheit.

Heist began as slang, for *hoist* or *lift,* as in 'shoplift' and also in 'hoist another on one's shoulders to help him break in.' It became an accepted noun from 1930, according to Etymonline.

English Digraph <ei> — *ceiling, weird.*

Rule 4-22 In Cursive Casualty words, <ei> spells [ee].

Reason In English words when two vowels go walking the first one does the talking, spells its long sound. It is very unusual for [ee] to be spelt like this. It only happens after <c> and <w>. The digraph <ie> is far more often used to spell [ee]. Digraph <ei> is only used for legibility in cursive. When <i> had no dot on top, <ci> looked like <u> and <wi> looked like Triple U, in cursive handwriting. So words using <ei> after <c> and <w> can be added to our list of Cursive Casualties.

300

Rebels WIELD [weeld], WEINER, [weener], LEISURE [lezh-yoor] and HEIFER [hef-er]
Rebels' Reasons *Wield* was also spelt *weald* which does not join an <i> with <w> in cursive writing. Maybe, once <i> got its dot on top, <ie> prevailed due to 'wielding shields' in mind. There is only one other word in which <ie> follows <w> spelling [w]. It's the recent German arrival, *wiener*, short for *weinerwurst*, Vienna sausage. Take care writing these two rebels lest you create a Triple-U. *Leisure* was originally an old French word but since then the French have changed its sound and spelling but the English spell it the old way and now say it to rhyme with *pleasure*. It is sometimes said [lee-zhar] in America, to rhyme with *easure* made from *ease*. *Heifer* was at first spelt *hægfore*, then *hayfere* and so we can see why it became *heifer* over centuries of French spelling but England speech with its heavy stress on first syllables, shortened that syllable. The many possible origins of this word are given at Etymonline — 'hedge dweller' and 'high-stepper' amongst them, but definitely not 'hay-feeder'. ('Hedge dweller?' Maybe only milking cows are out on the good pasture. 'High stepper?' Because a heifer has not calved, its belly is still high.)

Rebels CAFFEINE, CODEINE, DECAFFEINATED, EITHER [dh], NEITHER [dh], PLEBEIAN PROTEIN, ROTTWEILER, SEIZE, SEIZURE <z> = [zh], SHEIKH *silent h*, SHIEK.
Rebels' Reasons In *neither* and *either* we let <ei> spell [ee] in this list. As we have seen, <ei> can also spell [I] in these words. *Either* and *neither* still spelt [aydher] and [naydher] in the seventeenth century, according to 'Encylcopedia Americana' on the topic of spelling. In other words, <e> spelt its long Continental sound, [ay], because <i> let the first vowel do the talking, in places where the long vowel [ay] had not yet lifted to [ee] or [I]. Then came the GVS and [ay] lifted to [ee]. (Then some people tried to lift [ee] again, which resulted in [I] as in List 4-21 above.) *Sheik* [sheek] is also pronounced [shayk]. *Plebeian* is just *plebian*, in USA, a simplification which is actually a better match to its Latin origin *plebius*, 'of the common people'. However, Anglo-English keeps the second <e> of *plebes*, 'the common people.' In Rome the common people were called *plebes* or *plebs* which came from the Greek word for a crowd or multitude, *plethos*. (Greek *plethos* became English *plethora* and, via Latin, it became English *plenty* and *replenish*.) More reasons are given in the next Writing Rule, including *caffeine's* excuse, but in *decaffeinated*, <ei> spells the reduced vowel [i] so that syllables are alternately stressed.

List 4-22 <ei> spells [ee]
CEILING, CONCEIT, CONCEITED, CONCEITEDLY, CONCEIVABLE, CONCEIVABLY, CONCEIVE, DECEIT, DECEITFUL, DECEIVE, INCONCEIVABLE, INCONCEIVABLY, MISCONCEIVE, PERCEIVE, RECEIPT*, RECEIVE, BE ON THE RECEIVING END, RECEIVING, RECEIVER, UNDECEIVE, WEIR, WEIRD, WEIRDLY, WEIRDNESS.

*Receipt spells [ree-seet]. It lost its Latin [p] sound on the way through France to England but then dictionary scholars wrote <p> back in, to show its connection to Latin *recepta*. *Recepticle* sounds closer to the Latin, with <p> and <t> split into different syllables. The old Romans used to say [pt] but we find that difficult after long vowels and impossible at the start of words which is why *pterodactyl* spells [te-roh-dak-til], with a silent <p>.

Let's try writing the following dictation: ' "Seize that weird heifer," said the foreigner. "Either ride it for leisure, or forfeit it for protein," said his sovereign.' Such words break the well-known writing rule "Use I before E, to spell the sound [ee]". Study the rule below.

<u>Relevant Writing Rule.</u> How do we remember when E comes before I to spell [ee]? "I before E except after C," is a well-known rule, and sometimes we add, "But not when it's "eigh" as in *neighbour* or *weigh*," or "When A or I is the sound, It's the other way round." But this does not accommodate *weir*, *weird* and *seize*, and words ending with –*ein*. Nor plurals like *species* and *policies*, in which <i> <u>does</u> follow <c>.

A. Words ending -*ein*. In c*affeine* and *protein* <ei> did not start out walking together in the same syllable for they come from: caffe in, prote in. *Codeine* comes from French in which <ei> are not in the same syllable – codéine – and probably sounds more like [kohdayeen], but in English it's made to rhyme with *protein*.

B. There are just a few science words straight from Latin like *species* and *facies* which we can now treat as plural, and nouns that end <cy> take <cies> when plural, e.g *policies.*

C. *Seize* comes from Middle English *saisen/seisen* from Old French *saisir/seiser.*

D. *Weird* was once spelt *wyrd* but when <i> replaced <y> in words it was in danger of muddling with <w>, would have made 'Triple U'. So personally, I think <e> was used to insulate <i> from <w>, producing *weird*. This also explains why <e> precedes <i> in *weir.* We will remember that back then <i> had no dot and hence <wi> looked like <uuu>.

Also, we often change Proper Nouns to sound English but keep their original letters as in Madeira Cake, Keith, Neil and Sheila. Only two rare plurals use <ie> after <w>, *newies* and *yowies*.

E. I before E except after C — I expect that was to prevent <ci> being illegible, looking like <u> in cursive, back when <i> had no dot on top. Another Cursive Casualty.

So the correct Encoding Rule is: When deciding whether to use <ei> or <ie> to spell [ee] only use <ei> after <c> and <w> and for words which have two pronunciations, like *neither*. WIELD (kept its old West Saxon spelling and matches *shield*), SEIZE (links us to the modern French word *seiser*), CODEINE, PROTEIN and CAFFEINE and some plural nouns.

Short Rule: Use I before E except after C to spell the sound of EE (but remember that's [ee], not [eer], and remember that "real *sheilas* eat *protein*, drink *caffeine* and *seize* a *codeine*".)

The Real "I before E" Rule
Use I before E
To spell the sound [ee],
But not after C and W please,
Unless making plurals and *wield*
And *codeine, protein* and *seize.*
Please make this poem your shield:
I before E? Not after W, C,
Nor in words of dual sound
Nor when [ay] or [I] can be found
Then it's EI, the other way round.

    Well now, let me explain that in detail:-
Use I before E e.g., *believe, grieve* to spell the sound [ee],
But not after C and W please, e.g., r*e*c*ei*v*e, weird*
Unless making plurals and *wield*, e.g., *species, newies, inconsistencies*
Nor in words of dual sound, e.g., *either, neither* and *leisure*, in which EI spells dual sounds, [ee] or [I], [ee] or [e]. Also *sheik* (or *sheikh*), because they can spell [sheek] or [shayk].
Nor when [ay] or [I] can be found. E.g., [ay] in *neighbour, weight,* and [I] in *height* and *stein.*
Return to Reading Rules.

Digraph <eo>? Old English words used the diphthong <eo> a great deal — *on eorthan, swa swa on heofonum* — 'in earth as also in heaven', see The Lord's Prayer, in 'Changes to English Over Time' in the appendix. Diphthong means 'two songs'. Think of them as bent vowels, vowels with two songs, sounds which seem to bend inside a syllable. The <eo> diphthong has dropped out of English although its echo is heard in the Glide and Yap of *peony*, [pee-o-nee]. *Theof* is now *thief, eorthe* is *earth, freond* is *friend, heom* is *him, sweord* is *sword, heofon* is *heaven, sweorster* is *sister*, (Miles p. 82).

Miles says that most modern words with <eo> did not come from Old English at all, except for *yeoman*. It had the old diphthong, it was [yeeoh-man] but now just [yoh-man]. *People* was written with an <o> to link with French *peuple* and Latin *populum*, (Crytsal p. 121). *Jeopardy* comes from *jeu parti*, French for 'divided play or game'. *Leopard* was believed to be a cross between a lion, *leo*, and a panther way back in Roman times: *leopardus*, which in English became [leepard], then [lepard]. The change to a short vowel also occurred in strong-as-a-lion *Leonard*, "lion hard", and in *Geoffrey*.

People seems to obey the rule 'when two vowels go walking...' which is a fluke, for it was not English to begin with. The letters <eo> in *peony* do not form a digraph. They obey the Glide and Yap Rule across syllables. Proper Nouns like *Geoff* do not have to obey rules.

We are left now with just a few remnant <eo> clusters:-

List 4-23 Development Time-Line
First, <eo> spells [ee-oh] in PEONY. Then, <eo> spells [oh] in YEOMAN. Next, <eo> spells [ee], as a single sound, in PEOPLE. Finally, <eo> spells [e] in LEOPARD, GEOFFREY, JEOPARDY, LEONARD.

Digraph <eu> — *neutral, pleurisy, therapeutic.*
Rule 4-24 The digraph <eu> spells [yoo] or [oo].
Reason We know the rule, 'When two vowels go walking the first one does the talking. Very profound, it spells its long sound. But if the last one is Greek, the first one needn't speak'. We know that <u> is a Greek letter, arriving late in to the Roman Alphabet, directly from Greece. So we would not expect <eu> to spell [ee], but why does it spell [yoo]? This is a French digraph. In French it spells a slightly different [oo] to the [oo] spelt by the French digraph <ou>. The latter spells [oo] with rounded lips. When reading <eu> the French start with rounded lips but then partially close them in a little smile. When the English tried to copy this pronunciation, they found themselves saying [ee-oo] or [i-oo] and then this became [yoo]. Even when French domination waned and English became acceptable amongst the upper classes of England, this way of pronouncing U's long sound, and therefore its name, remained. Mind you, it took concentration. Simple [oo] is so much easier to say. At the beginning of words, [yoo] is no trouble but after certain consonants it was difficult to pronounce the [y], the little sound called a yod. We hear a yod in *eucalypt* and in *euphoria*, but not in *leukaemia* because [y] is hard to say after [l]. Nor do we hear it in *rheumatism* because [y] is hard to say after [r]. So yods have dropped after [l] and [r]. English words don't use <jeu>, but if they did the yod would be dropped, as it has in *juice*. The yod is not pronounced in the verb *sue*, nor in the name, but we hear it in *pursue*. In parts of USA, Yods have dropped after [n], [t] and [d] as well, as in [noo-truul], [toosday] and [doo] — *neutral, Tuesday* and *due*. Elsewhere, the yod can fuse with [t] and [d] to produce Yod Fusions [ch] and [j], as in [chooz-day] and [joo].
Rebels CORDON BLEU, DEUTZIA.
Rebels' Reasons *Cordon bleu* means 'blue ribbon' when judging cookery but the English love using French words in the kitchen, when describing 'cuisine'. They pronounce this one [kordon] [bler]. German *deutzia* spells [doyt-zee-ar] as does <eu> in *Deutschland* (Germany), *deutschmark* (German coinage) and the names *Freud* and *Reuters*.
Rascal LIEUTENANT *Lieutenant* is pronounced [loo-ten-ant] in USA, [le-ten-ant] in the British Navy and [lef-ten-ant] by Britons since before 1400, (Ayto, p. 323). Briefly, I think that [lef-ten-ant] arose because the <v> in old *levetenaunt* was mistaken for <u> when written but, when spoken, because [f] blends with [t] rather than voiced [v], it became [lef-ten-ant]. (The lieutenant's superior had to leave before he could get tenancy of the position, take command, and the lieutenant was left holding command.)
The longer version. It began as a compound of two French words, *lieu tenant*, roughly [loo] [ten-ant], meaning "holds the place of another" (under study) and so the American pronunciation copied the French one. The British Navy's is to be expected because they shorten everything: *boatswain* to *bossun, forecastle* to *fo'c'sle* etc. Website www.takeourword.com suggests it was influenced by the word *leave*, with the

lieutenant's superior having to leave before he could take over command. Website http://iq.lycos.co.uk lists a range of English spelling adaptions from 1375: *lutenand, luf-tenand, leeftenaunt, lutenant, levetenaunt,* all prior to *lieutenant* appearing in print in 1377. Then ten more variations until the current method was settled on in 1610. As we know <u> and <v> were interchangeable, as were <v> and <f> — *elf* and *elves* — and [lef-ten-ant] arose out of the confusion. I hope you agree that this word, LIEUTENANT, is a Rascal.

List 4-24

ADIEU*, EUPHORIA, EUTHANASIA, FEUD, FEUDAL, FEUDALISM, LEUKAEMIA, LEUKEMIA USA, PNEUMONIA *silent* <p>, DEUCE**, DEUTERIUM**, EUCALYPT, EUCALYPTUS*, EUCHARISTIC, EULOGISTIC, EULOGIZE, EULOGY, EUMONG*, EUNUCH [yoo-nuuk], EUPHEMISM, EUPHEMISTIC, EUPHONIUM, EUPHONY, EUPHORIA, EUREKA*, EUCHRED, EURO*, EUTHANASIA, FEU, FEUD, FEUDAL, FEUDAL SYSTEM, FEUDALISTIC, HEURISTICS*, LEUKAEMIA, in LIEU* of [lyoo], MANEUVER*, NEURAL, NEURALGIA, NEURITIS, NEUROLOGY, NEUROLOGICAL, NEUROLOGIST, NEUROSIS, NEURO-SURGERY, NEUROTIC, NEUTER, NEUTRAL, NEUTRALLY, NEUTRALITY, NEUTRAL GEAR, NEUTRALIZE, NEUTRON, PURLIEU, PLEURISY, PNEUMATIC, PNEUMONIA, PSEUDO, PSEUDO-, PSEUDONYM, QUEUE*, RHEUMATIC*, RHEUMATICKY, RHEUMATIC FEVER, RHEUMATICS, RHEUMATISM, THERAPEUTIC. Proper Nouns/Adj. EUCHARIST, EURASIAN, EURO, EUROPE, EUROPEAN, PENTATEUCH, TEUTONIC**. Names EUGENE, EUNICE.

Adieu starts the French farewell: 'To God I commend you,' — 'Ad Dieu vous commant.' The English re-spelt it *adewe* but the dictionary committee wanted to show its origins. The English spelling shows that it is a two-syllable word, whereas *adieu* which could de-code as [a-dee-yoo].

***Deuce, deuterium, Teutonic* are all palatalized. Due to Yod Fusion, <deu> and <teu> spell [joo] and [choo].

**Eucalyptus* is not adopted from an Ab'l word. A French botanist was amazed to see that gum trees have flowers without petals, just little wooden caps, covering the bud until the stamens are ready to open and he joined two Greek words to name such plants "well <eu> covered <kalyptuos>", in 1788.

**Eumong,* is an Ab'l word for *Eucalyptus globulus bicostata,* (Blake, p. 93).

**Eureka* [yoor-ee-kar] lost <h> on the way from Greece to England. Archimedes actually cried out "Heureka! I have found it!" but the modern word **heuristics,* the science of scientific discovery, has retained it, (Fleck, 2007).

**Euro* is the European way of writing an Ab'l word, also recorded as *uro,* and known as rock wallaby or roan wallaroo.

**Euro* is also a new word, a unit of the new European currency, € 1.

**Lieu* is French but used in English in the phrase "in lieu of", and retains French spelling to ensure it spells [[lyoo], not [loo], — [l] usually 'pushes' the yod off [yoo], meaning yod is hard to say after [l], but in this word <i> retains it, [lyoo]. The French word *adieu* [ə-dyoo] or [ə-joo] was once used a lot in English, e.g., "I bid thee adieu."

**Maneuver* is the sensible American spelling of Britsh *manoeuvre/manœuvre*. Americans drop yods after [n] so the word decodes well in American English but in Anglo-English it would be [man-yoover] and maybe that's why it is retained as *manoeuvre,* in wuch the silent <o> seems to prevent <eu> speling [yoo].

**Queue* [kyoo] is actually from Latin via French. *Queue* is one of those rare words in which <qu> spells [k] – a rare moment when "Queen is King" (when <qu> spells [k], not [kw]. Yods are easy to say after [k] which is why we say *queue* spells [kyoo]. Note the final <e> which insulates <u> from coming last. In *cue,* also [kyoo], terminal <e> does that job. Both words come from the same ancestor word for *tail*. As Q is the letter with the tail, it is called *queue.*

Rheumatic Fever means "trouble with rheum" from Greek *rheumatikos.* Greek *rheum*, meaning 'flow' is usually used in English for bodily streams, like pus, but it is also the parent word of *stream*.

Bossy R and <eu> — *amateur, secateurs.*
Rule 4-25 <eur> spells [yer] or [er].
Reason French <eur> spells [er] and words which used this code were adopted from France.
List 4-25
AMATEUR*, AMATEURISHLY, AMATEURISHNESS, ANEURISM, CHAUFFEUR, ENTREPRENEUR, ENTREPRENEURIAL, FLEUR-DE-LIS, GRANDEUR*, MARGUERITE, MASSEUR, MASSEUSE, POSEUR, RACONTEUR, SECATEURS. Names FLEUR, MARGUERITE.
*If the first syllable is stressed in *amateur* Yod Fusion will occur to avoid ending the word with two weak beats.
ardeur spells [grandyoor].

Note: entry 4-26 non-existent.

Digraph <ey> in Stem Words — *convey, they.*
Rule 4-27 In the first syllable of stem words <ey> spells [ay].
Reason As we know, <ay> spells [ay]. However French invasion words used <ey> to spell [ay], because French <e> spells the long Continental sound [ay]. When the English regained control of their language they should have replaced <ey> with <ay> in every word, but by then they were used to <ey> spells [ay]. We shall see some stems which cannot stand alone, bound stems, not free stems, like <vey> in *convey,* and <ey> in *obey.* Remember, when <ey> spells [ay] it is not in a suffix, it's in a stem word.
Rebels KEY, GEYSER, when [gI-zer], EYE.
Rebels' Reasons *Key* is not a French word because the French don't use <k>. *Key* in French is *clef.* It is related to the word *cleaver* and has a cousin *kei* in an old Low German language which was probably respelt with <y> to prevent ending in <i>. Maybe that is why some people say <key> once spelt [kay] but hey, who knows, for now *quay* spells [kee]. We met that little rebel back near the <ay> spells [ay] list. We already know *eye* spells [I], and obeys the Short Word Rule by adding Silent E. In modern German, <ei> spells [I]. One explanation for *eye* is that <eie> would have had <i> replaced by <y> to avoid three vowels in a row, even though *eye* has no Greek ancestor. In fact, the word *eye* was *ege* in Old English, and *egg* was *æg* which became *egge* when Ash was removed from use. Cut a boiled egg in half, and it looks like an eye. In many English words <g> was replaced by <y> at the end of a word, as in *dizzy*, which was *dysig*. The history of *eye* is very muddled. In French it is *oeil* which spells [ay-y]. In English it had many pronunciations and spellings before it settled on [I], spelt *eye*.
There is only one other word in which <ey> spells [I], *geyser,* which is an eponym, from Iceland's *Geysir,* the name of a specific hot spring in the valley of Haukadal, literally "the gusher." *Geyser* is also pronounced [geezer] but then it means a water heater. Cockneys called actors in disguise *geezers.* Maybe a water heater, clad in insulation, is in disguise. Both *eye* and *geyser* break the rule that <y> should not be inside non-Greek words and <ey> spells [I] in only two stem words: *eye* and *geyser*.
Rebel? No, BEYOND is a compound word, made up of *by* and *yond* as in *yonder.* To avoid <yy> the first <y> has become <e>.
Rebel? Proper Nouns do not have to obey the rules. CEYLON [si-lon] is the Portuguese spelling of Sinhala, "place of lions". Now it's Sri Lanka, meaning "a brilliant beautiful jewel of a place".
List 4-27 <ey> spells [ay]
CONVEY, CONVEYANCE, CONVEYANCING, CONVEYOR, DISOBEY, DREY *squirrel's nest,* FEY, FEYNESS, GEYSER, GREY, GREYNESS, GREY AREA, GREY CELLS, GREY MATTER,

305

GREYISH, GREYLAG GOOSE, HEY! LEY, OBEY*, SURVEY, SURVEYOR, THEY, WHEY. Proper Noun REYKJAVIK.

*Obey originally meant 'listen to', "ob audire", in Latin. We see and hear the <d> in *obedience.*

Suffix <ey> — *blimey, valley.*

Rule 4-28 Unstressed <ey> spells [ee].

Reason Some had guttural endings which softened to [ee] and others changed their stressed French [ay] endings to quiet English [ee] endings. When <ey> spells [ee] it is always at the end of a word of two or more syllables and is unstressed. Long ago English had the letter Yogh <ȝ> which spelt guttural voiced [h]. When <ȝ> was dropped from the alphabet <gh> took over its job for a while. As we know, this guttural [gh] sound began dropping out of English after the Norman Invasion. When [eegh] changed to [ee] it was written <ey>. (As we know, <gh> has remained in words like *cough* and *caught*.)

List 4-28 <ey> spells [ee]
ATTORNEY, BLIMEY, CHIMNEY, CHIMNEY-POT, CHIMNEY-SWEEP, CONEY, COVEY, DONKEY*, GALLEY, GOOEY, HIDEY-HOLE, HOCKEY, HOLEY, HONEY ƒ, HONEY-BEE, HONEYCOMB, HONEYMOON, HONEYSUCKLE, HOOKEY *slang*, KIDNEY, KIDNEY BEAN, KIDNEY DISH, LATCHKEY, MEDLEY, MONEY ƒ, MONKEY ƒ, MONKEY NUT MONKEY PUZZLE, MONKEY-WRENCH, MULTI-STOREY, ODYSSEY, OSPREY, STOREY*, TROLLEY, TROLLEY BUS, TURKEY, VALLEY. Proper Nouns MERSEYSIDE. Names ASHLEY, CASEY, COREY, DUDLEY, JEFFREY, JOEY, QUINCEY, RILEY, RIPLEY, TRACEY, ZOEY.

*We met *attorney* and *storey* earlier.

Donkey and *monkey* were invented long after *ass* and *ape*. The suffix —*key* can be an endearment for a little thing — in this case, a little dun coloured animal and a little man. We read *monkey* as a Feather Word, as if it is a Cursive Casuality, [mun-kee]. Maybe *donkey* was written as one but now it is not treated as one, because it spells [don-kee].

Digraph <ew> — *brew, crew.*

E will not do the talking before Greek W, and so <ew> does not spell [ee]. The letter <w> came in to the English alphabet twice, very early as the rune Wynne. It was written as W after some time. Old English used <w> after vowel digraphs <eo> and <ea>. Later on, that simplified to <ew>, as in *sew* [shoh]. Also, *shew* spelt [shoh], but then changed to *show*. Then another W grew out of Double U, back when U and V were interchangeable. This <w> was used to replace <u>, to prevent <u> ending words. Some French words were adopted and their spelling adapted to use <ew>, plus a few Irish ones.

Rule 4-29 <ew> spells [yoo] or [oo].

Reason In this digraph <w> is acting as the vowel <u>, so <ew> spelt [ee-oo] which became [yoo]. After that yods began to drop. We know that yods drop from [yoo] after [l], [r], [s] and [j]. We don't hear a yod in *cashew*, but how do you say *chew*, [chyoo] or [choo]? Does *Jew* spell [jyoo] or [joo]? As we know, some yods do not fuse completely.

Rebel SEW Δ [soh].

Rebel's Reason There was an old word, *shew*, in which <ew> spelt [oh], but that spelling gave way to *show*. Now there is only one word left in which <ew> spells [oh]: *sew* [soh] in which <w> was the original Wynne letter. It was probably not changed when *shew* changed in order to separate it from homophone *sow*. Both *sew* and *sow* involve straight lines, of stitches and of seeds. Remember this for later.

List 4-29A Digraph <ew> spells [oo] in words that have lost yods.
AIRCREW, BESTREW Δ, BREW, BREWERY, CASHEW, CHEW, CHEWY, CLEW, CORKSCREW, CREW, CREW CUT, CREWEL, DREW Δ, ESCHEW, FLEW Δ, GREW Δ, SCREW, LOOSE SCREW, PUT THE SCREW ON, PUT THE SCREWS ON, SCREW-CAP, SCREW-TOP, SCREWBALL,

SCREWDRIVER, SCREWY, SEWAGE, SEWAGE-FARM, SEWAGE-WORKS, SEWER, SEWAGE, SEWERAGE, STREW Δ, THREW Δ, THUMBSCREW, TREWS, UNSCREW. Proper Noun HEBREW. Names ANDREW, DREW.

List 4-29B Digraph <ew> spells [yoo] in words that still have yods.
ASKEW, CHEW, CLERIHEW, CURFEW, DEW, DEW-CLAW, DEWDROP, DEWLAP, DEWY, DEWY-EYED, ESCHEW [esk-yoo], EWE*, EWER, FEW, FEWNESS, A GOOD FEW, QUITE A FEW, FEWER, HEW Δ, HONEY DEW MELON, JEW'S HARP JEWEL, JEWELLER, JEWELLERY, KNEW Δ, LEWD, MEW, MEWS, MILDEW, NEPHEW, NEW, NEWCOMER, NEWEL, NEWFANGLED, NEWISH, NEWLY, NEWLY-WED, NEWS, NEWS-STAND, NEWSAGENT, NEWSCAST, NEWSLETTER, NEWSPAPER, NEWSPRINT, NEWSREEL, NEWSVENDOR, NEWSWORTHY, NEWSY, NEWT*, PEW, PEWTER, PHEW, REAR-VIEW MIRROR, RENEW, RENEWABLE, RENEWAL, SEWER, SINEW, SINEWS, SINEWY, SKEW, ON THE SKEW, SKEWBALD, SKEWER, STEW, STEWARD, STEWARDESS, SPEW, THEWS, VIEW*, ON VIEW, WITH A VIEW TO, VIEWFINDER, REVIEW, PURVIEW, YEW. Australian Words YOU BEWDY *slang.* Proper Nouns/Adj. DEWEY DECIMAL SYSTEM, JEW, JEWESS, JEWISH, JEWRY, NEWTONIAN, NEW ZEALAND. Names BARTHOLOMEW, MATTHEW, STEWART.

*View [vyoo] was adopted as French *veue*. It changed to *vew* in England and then, probably in order to show the link with "see" in Latin, which is *videre*, it gained <i>, long before the dictionary committee was formed. This links it to *vision* and *video* and even *visit*, which means 'to go to see' or to 'come to inspect'. It is the only word in which <i> precedes <ew>.

*Newt [nyoot]. For your interest, this little animal was once *an ewt* but became *a newt*.

*Ewe [yoo]. Interestingly, in Old English, ram and ewe were *eow* and *eowu* but then the Viking word *ramm* (related to *battering ram* and *strong*) was preferred for the male, leaving the milder female with the name *eow* which became just *ew* and had to get a silent <e> to obey the Short Word Rule.

Present, past and p. participles of some irregular <ew> verbs, the rest later.
DRAW Δ, DREW Δ [droo], DRAWN Δ.
STREW Δ [stroo], STREWED, STREWN Δ /STREWED
BESTREW Δ, BESTREWED, BESTREWN Δ /BESTREWED
HEW Δ [hyoo], HEWED, HEWN Δ
SEW Δ [soh], SEWED [sohn], SEWN Δ /SEWED [sohd].

I Digraphs

We have seen <ia> clusters in words. These two letters together do not spell a new single sound for <i> glides on to <a>, like, for instance, [I-a] in *dial*. There is no <ia> digraph.

There is no <ie> digraph in the cluster <ier> which has the digraph <er>, as in <i-er>.
It's not a digraph in *flier*, *brigadier* or *chashier*, for instance. The words end in the suffix <er> so <ier> spells two 'glide and roar' syllables — [I-er} in *multiplier, flier, brier, fiery, hierarchy etc.* and [ee-er] in *brigadier, chashier etc.* In *soldier*, <ier> would spell [ee-er] but <i> becomes a yod which fuses with [d] to produce [sol-jer]. In *soldier*, the suffix means 'one who receives solid, thick coins'.

We already know that, if <i> spells its long sound, it is [I] in the first syllable and [ee] in the rest: *mine* and *machine*. As we know, <i> is rarely terminal in English words. It is insulated by <e>, as in *pie* and *die*, or else <y> is used, as in *cry* and *ply*. As we know, at the end of a single-syllable word, or at the end of a first syllable, <i> and <y> each spell [I]. Consequently <ie> terminating a first syllable spells [I], and continues to spell [I] before suffixes <s> and <d>, as in *dies* and *died*. We also know that <y> is not allowed inside words, unless they have Greek origins and that <i> replaces <y> when suffixed, as in *plies* and *plied*.

As we already know, terminal <i> at the end of two or more syllables, spells [ee], whether it is insulated with <e>, as in *caddie,* or not, as in *taxi*. The same goes for terminal <y>, at the end of two or more syllables, e.g., *baby* and *carry* in which <y> spells [ee]. Terminal <ie> in stem words of more than one syllable spells [ee], as in *caddie*. If <y> is replaced with <ie> when a suffix is added, <ie> spells [ee], as in *babies* and *carried*.

Rule 4-30 When terminal, in <ie>, <i> spells [I] in single-syllable words.
Reason This follows the pattern set by <i> when spelling its long sound, as in *I, mine*. Many words end <ie> in order to obey the Short Word Rule, not just because <i> cannot end a word. If words in the next list have two syllables, then they are compound words which may be so old they are hard to pick. *Pie* began as the name of a bird, a little thief which stole and collected things, from *picus,* Latin for 'woodpecker' (Fleck 2007). A *mag* was a talkative or gossipy woman, Margaret in medieval folk songs, (Fleck 2007). *Pie* was used when a mixture was cooked inside pastry because it looked like a magpie's collection. *Pie* also came to mean "black and white", so a 'pied horse' is a black and white horse.
Rebel? No, PLIÉ is not a rebel unless written *plie,* for it spells [plee-ay] and should be written *plié* for it is a French term used in English ballet corps — bent knees, straight back.
Rebel? No. BRIE is a well-known cheese type in which <ie> spells [ee] at the end of a single-syllable word but as a Proper Noun it does not have to obey rules and as it is a Continental cheese, one would expect <i> to spell its Continental long sound, [ee].
List 4-30
DIE, FIE, LIE, LIE Δ, MAGPIE, PIE, PIEBALD <a> =[or], NECKTIE, TIE, UNTIE, VIE.

Rule 4-31A When terminal, <ies> spells [Iz] in single-syllable stem words.
Reason This occurs when <s> is added to verbs, as in *he lies,* and to make plurals, as in *pies*. Also when <y> spelling [I] at the end of a single-syllable stem is replaced with <ies> to mark a tense in verbs or make plurals. The <s> spells [z] because it follows a stressed vowel, because digraphs spell stressed vowels.
List 4-31A examples only of <ies> spells [Iz].
In Plurals — BUTTERFLIES, *loud* CRIES (cry), FLIES, MAGPIES, LIES, PIES, *coconut* SHIES (shy), SKIES, TIES, pig STIES, *rugby* TRIES (try), *fish and* FRIES (fry).
In Verbs — CRIES, DIES, DRIES (dry), FLIES, FRIES, LIES, PRIES, SHIES, SPIES, TIES, VIES.
We can also use this rule to decode <ies> on sight if we remember in which words <y> spells [I] at the end of some bound stems, in words like *ally, acidify, deny* and *prophecy* and so <ies> spells [Iz] in such verbs.
List 4-31A continued.
ALLIES, ACIDIFIES, APPLIES, CALCIFIES, CLASSIFIES, CODIFIES, DENIES, DESCRIES, DIGNIFIES, DISQUALIFIES <a>=[o], EDIFIES, FALSIFIES, HORRIFIES, HUMIDIFIES, IDENTIFIES, INDEMNIFIES, JOLLIFIES, JUSTIFIES, LIQUEFIES, MAGNIFIES, MODIFIES, MOLLIFIES, MULTIPLIES, MUMMIFIES, NOTIFIES, NULLIFIES, PACIFIES, PROPHESIES, PURIFIES, PUTREFIES, QUALIFIES <a>=[o], RAREFIES, RATIFIES, RELIES, REPLIES, SAPONIFIES, SATISFIES, SIGNIFIES, SOLIDIFIES, SPECIFIES, STUPEFIES <u> =[yoo], TERRIFIES, UNIFIES, VERIFIES, VILIFIES.

Rule 4-31B When terminal, <ied> spells [Id] in single-syllable stem words.

Reason When <ie> spells [I] at the end of a regular verb, the word ends in <ied>, in the past tense, in the past participle and in adjectives made from the verb, as in 'He *fried* the food. He has *fried* the food. We ate *fried* fish. When <i> replaces terminal <y> spelling [I] to change the tense of words then <ied> spells [Id].

List 4-31B examples only.

Verbs — DIED, FRIED, LIED* (*telling untruths*), TIED, VIED. *Adjectives* FRIED, PIED (black and white).

*The verb *lie* also means *lie down* and is irregular, an old verb which has not yet conformed, is sticking to its old ways.

The irregular verb "to lie", LIE Δ, LAY Δ, LAIN Δ [layn].

Pres: The man lies down, or the man is lying down. **Past:** The man lay down yesterday. **P.P:** The man has lain down.

<u>Not needed but nice to know.</u>

To lay is a transitive verb. *She lays an egg. Lay, laid, laid.* Also she's laying an egg, or laying the table.

To lie, as in to tell a lie, is intransitive. You don't lie someone/something. Lie, lied, lied. Also, he's lying, telling untruths.

To lie, as in to lie down, is intransitive. Lie, lay, lain. Also, I am lying, on the floor. <u>Now back to things we need to know.</u>

List 4-31B continued for <ied> in tense change.

ALLIED, ACIDIFIED, APPLIED, CALCIFIED, CLASSIFIED, CODIFIED, CRIED, DENIED, DESCRIED, DIED, DIGNIFIED, DRIED, EDIFIED, FALSIFIED, FRIED, GENTRIFIED, HORRIFIED, HUMIDIFIED, IDENTIFIED, INDEMNIFIED, JOLLIFIED, JUSTIFIED, LIQUEFIED, MAGNIFIED, MODIFIED, MOLLIFIED, MULTIPLIED, MUMMIFIED, NOTIFIED, NULLIFIED, PACIFIED, PLIED, PRIED, PROPHESIED, PURIFIED, PUTREFIED, QUALIFIED <a>=[o], RAREFIED, RATIFIED, RELIED, REPLIED, SAPONIFIED, SATISFIED, SHIED, DIGNIFIED, SOLIDIFIED, SPECIFIED, SPIED, STUPEFIED <u>=[uu], TERRIFIED, TRIED, UNIFIED, UNTIED, UNIDENTIFIED, UNQUALIFIED, UNSPECIFIED, VERIFIED, VILIFIED.

Rule 4-32A When <ie> terminates a stem word of two or more syllables, it spells [ee].

Reason We know that <i> cannot terminate a word, needs insulator <e> and that <i> spells Continental [ee] for its long sound when 'free to stretch out' at the end of words of two or more syllables.

List 4-32A BAILIE, BOGIE, BOOKIE, BUDGIE, CADDIE*, CALORIE, CAMARADERIE, CAPERCAILLIE *bird*, CHAPPIE, COLLIE DOG, COOKIE, COOLIE, COTERIE, DOGGIE, EYRIE [air-ree], GENIE, GILLIE/GHILLIE, GIRLIE, HIPPIE*, JUNKIE, KERCHIEF, KIE-KIE *N.Z. plant*, KOPPIE, LADDIE, LASSIE, LINGERIE, MENAGERIE, MOVIE, OLDIE, ORGANDIE, PRAIRIE, QUICKIE, REVERIE, ROTISSERIE, SOFTIE, SORTIE, SPECIE, WALKIE-TALKIE, WEIRDIE, WHARFIE. <u>Proper Nouns</u> GEORDIE, VALKYRIE. <u>Names</u> ANNIE, ARCHIE, ARNIE, BENNIE, BERNIE, BESSIE, BOBBIE, BRODIE, CECILIE, CONNIE, CORALIE, DARNIE, DEBBIE, DIXIE, DOTTIE, DULCIE, EDDIE, EVIE, FLOSSIE, FONZIE, FRANNIE, FRIEDRICH, GENEVIEVE, GEORGIE, GOLDIE, GRACIE, JAMIE, JEANIE, JESSIE, KIERAN, LASSIE, LEONIE, LORALIE, MAGGIE, MAMIE, MARGIE, MARIE <a>=[ar], MARJORIE, MELANIE, MILLIE, MINNIE, NELLIE, NETTIE, OLLIE, PIXIE, QUEENIE, REGGIE, RICHIE, RICKIE, ROBBIE, RONNIE, ROSALIE, ROSIE, SADIE, SOPHIE, STEPHANIE, STEVIE, SUSIE, SUZIE, TAMMIE, TESSIE, WILLIE, WINNIE.

Caddie is how golfers pronounced French *cadet*. The small tea box is usually spelt *caddy*.

*A *hippy hippie* is a hippie with large hips, (Bryson 2004, p. 95).

Just as <i> and <y> spell [ee] in second syllables, and further along a word, so does <ie>.

Rule 4-32B When <i> in terminal <ies> has replaced <y> spelling terminal [ee], then <ies> spells [eez].

Reason The <s> spells [z] because it follows a stressed vowel, because digraphs spell stressed vowels. Terminal <y> is replaced by <i> when making plurals or when adding <s> to spell verbs.

List 4-32B <ies> spells [eez] in these plurals.

BABIES, DUTIES, FURIES, HOLIES, as in *holy of holies,* IVIES *types of ivy,* JURIES, LADIES, PONIES, QUERIES, RUBIES, TINIES *slang, as in tiny tots.*
BADDIES, BELLIES, BERRIES, BILLIES, BUDDIES, BUGGIES, BULLIES <u>=[uu], CADDIES, CISSIES, CRAWLIES*, CUBBIES, CURRIES, DADDIES, DITTIES, DOGGIES, DOLLIES, DUMMIES, EDDIES, FATTIES, FERRIES, FILLIES, FOLLIES, FUNNIES, TUMMIES, GOLLIES, GULLIES, HILL-BILLIES, HOBBIES, JELLIES, JETTIES, JOLLIES*, KIDDIES, KITTIES, LASSIES, LIPPIES, LOBBIES, LOLLIES, LORRIES, MAMMIES, MIDDIES, MUMMIES, NANNIES, NAPPIES, NAVVIES, PADDIES, PATTIES, PENNIES, PIGGIES, PINNIES, POPPIES, POTTIES, PUPPIES, QUARRIES <a>= [o], RALLIES, SISSIES, SKIVVIES, SUNNIES *sun glasses, slang.,* TABBIES, SULLIES, TALLIES, TEDDIES, TELLIES *slang,* T.V.'s, TINNIES *Ozzie slang, canned beer.,* TODDIES, TUMMIES, WHINNIES, WILLY-WILLIES.

*Crawlies and jollies are Antarctic terms, see www.coolantarctic.com

List 4-32B cont. Terminal <ies> spells [eez] in some words which are written and said as plurals but used as singulars, e.g:-

SERIES — a *series* of things
CARIES — a sickness called *caries*
HUMANITIES — not the plural of *humanity.* It refers to arts subjects, especially the study of the Greek and Latin classics, as opposed to the sciences.
SPECIES — a *species* of bird
RABIES — a disease called *rabies.*
WILLIES — 'He gives me the *willies* and the *heebie-jeebies.*'
HEEBIE-JEEBIES — Slang for nervous anxiety or depression.
PANTIES — an informal word for pants, usually short knickers for women and children.
Proper Nouns:- ARIES, ROCKIES, SCILLIES

List 4-32B cont. <ies> spells [eez] in these verbs.
For example:
BURIES, CARRIES, DALLIES, DIVVIES, MARRIES, MUDDIES, PARRIES, QUERIES, SALLIES, RALLIES, TALLIES, TARRIES, WHINNIES, WORRIES *f*

In the words above, e.g., *flies* and *fillies* and *lied* and *lilies,* <ie> not a digraph because <e> is just insulating <i> from coming last, it is not acting as a 'best friend' which 'goes walking' with <i>.
For digraphs we say, 'When two vowels go walking, the first one does the talking' because long ago, to spell a long vowel, the letter was doubled, as in *peep,* and then, later, scribes just added any vowel to show the first one spelt its long sound. This happened back when all vowel letters, in England and in most of Europe spelt the same long sound. In the case of <i>, it spelt an extension of its short sound, as in *ink.* If [i] is stretched out, said on and on, we hear [ee].

Rule 4-33 When <i> in terminal <ied> has replaced <y> spelling terminal [ee], then <ied> spells [eed].

Reason Letter <i> always spells the same sound as the <y> it replaces.
List 4-33 Past tense ending of verbs with terminal <y> spells [ee]. For example:

CARRIED, DALLIED, DIVVIED, DIVVIED, HURRIED, MARRIED, MUDDIED, PARRIED, RALLIED, SALLIED, RALLIED, TALLIED, TARRIED, WHINNIED, WORRIED *f*.

Digraph <ie> — *achieve, yield.*
Rule 4-34 Digraph <ie> always spells [ee] inside stem words.
Reason The key word here is 'inside'. When a letter or a digraph is inside a syllable, it is not terminal. It is medial. When terminal, or before <s> or <d>, <ie> is not a digraph inside a stem word. As explained above, at the end of words, <ie> is not a digraph. The <e> is actually silent and <i> spells either [ee] or [I]. When a digraph, <ie> spells its long Continental sound, as explained above.
Rebels MISCHIEF, MISCHIEVOUS, SIEVE; FRIEND; HURRIEDLY [hu-rəd-lee].
Rebels' Reasons In *mischief, mischievous* and *sieve* digraph <ie> erroneously spells [i]. Why is it that <ie> spells [ee] in *chief* but [i] in *mischief*? The two "chiefs" are only distant relations. *Mischief* comes from the French word *mischef* which means "happens amiss" which comes from French *meschever*, 'meet with misfortune' i.e. 'misfit' if there was such a verb. Way back in time, French *chever* meant 'come to a head'. The French word *chef* for 'head' was also spelt *chief* by the French. Unfortunately, when the old French word *chief* was adopted for 'headman' in England the spelling carried across into *mischief* but with the French pronunciation, so that *chief* in *mischief* sounds more like French *chef* — head cook — than English *chief*. *Sieve* used to be *sife*. It is related to *sift*. Long ago the word-sounds [f] and [v] swapped around a lot — hence *belief* and *believe*, *safe* and *save*, *elf* and *elves*, *fox* and *vixen*, *sift* and *sieve*. *Hurriedly* is so stressed on the first syllable that the rest of the word shrinks, with [ee] shrinking to [ə]. The 'friendly rebel' *friend* stands alone, for *friend* [frend] is the only stem word in which <ie> spells [e]. Long ago *friend* rhymed with *fiend* [feend]. *Friend* was in *friendly, befriend, friendless* and *friendship* but *fiend* was only in *fiendish*. We know how *break* shortened to [brek] in *breakfast*. *Friend* would have shortened in the longer words and then because [frend] sounded less like *fiend* it stayed short on its own, maybe, says Prof Cummings. I am guessing it would have been muddled with *fremd*, an old word for 'stranger'. *Fremd* was dropped either before that or because of that, because *friend* [frend] caught on. *Fremd* is gone.
Rebels? HYGIENIC, PATIENT etc.? No, some words appear to be rebels with <ie> spelling [e] but *hygienic* is only conforming to the shortening rule imposed when it gained the suffix *–ic* and words like *impatient, proficient, patience, patient* do not contain the <ie> digraph. Instead, Little Imp is followed by another unstressed vowel and to avoid two weak beats, it becomes a yod and fuses with [t] in *patient* and [s] in *proficient*.
List 4-34 <ie> spells [ee] inside stem words and their off shoots.
ACHIEVABLE, ACHIEVE, ACHIEVEMENT, AGGRIEVED, AIRFIELD, APIECE, BAS-RELIEF, BATTLEFIELD, BELIEF, BELIEVABLE, BELIEVABLE, BELIEVE, BELIEVER, BESIEGE, BESIEGER, BIER, BRIEF, BRIEFCASE, BRIEFLY, BRIEFNESS, BRIEFS, CHIEF, CHIEFTAIN, CODPIECE, DIESEL*, DISBELIEVE, FIELD, FIELDER, FIELDFARE *bird*, FIELDSMAN, FIELDWORK, FIELDWORKER, FIEND, FIENDISH, FIENDISHLY, FIERCE, FRIEZE, FRONTISPIECE, GLOCKENSPIEL, GRIEF, GRIEVANCE, GRIEVE, HANDKERCHIEF*, HYGIENE <y> = [I] and silent terminal <e>, IRRETRIEVABLE, LAY SIEGE TO, LIEN, MISCHIEF, MANTLE-PIECE, MASTERPIECE, NIECE, PIECE, PIECEMEAL, PIER, PIERCE, PRIEST, PRIESTESS, PRIESTLY, RELIEF noun, plural RELIEFS, RELIEVE verb, RETRIEVABLE, RETRIEVABLE, RETRIEVAL, RETRIEVE, RETRIEVER, RIESLING, SHIELD, SIEGE, RAISE THE SIEGE, REPRIEVE, RIOT SHIELD, SPIEL, TAILPIECE, THIEF, THIEVE, THIEVERY, THIEVISH, TIER, UNBELIEVABLE, UNBELIEVABLY, UNBELIEVER, UNDERACHIEVE, UNRELIEVED, UNWIELDINESS, UNWIELDY, UNYIELDING, VARIEGATED, WELLIES, WHEELIES, WIELD, WINDSHIELD, YIELD.

Diesel is an eponym. The liquid fuel is named after Rudolf Diesel.

Handkerchief spells [han-ker-cheef] because in the difficult cluster <ndk>, which should spell [ndk], the 'long' sonorant consonant [n] flows over the short obstruent [d] to simplify pronunciation. *Handkerchief* means 'piece of cloth carried in the hand' and not just any cloth. It was originally a 'square piece of fabric folded worn about the head'. *Kerchief* meant 'coverhead', back when a head was called a *chief*. I mention this because the Australian labourer used to tie a knot in each corner of his handkerchief and fit it on his head to prevent sunstroke because a brimmed hat got in the way. Peaked caps were not available back then, when I was little. Thanks to Etymonline I have seen history repeat. Now, handkerchiefs are rare, replaced by throw-away tissues.

O Digraphs,

Digraph <oa> — *coast, toad.*

Rule 4-35 Digraph <oa> spells [oh] except when terminal or before <r>.

Reason When <o> and <a> go walking, the first one does the talking, spells its long sound. A long time ago <oo> spelt [or]. It was the extension of the short sound starting *off.* We still hear <oo> spelling [or] in *floor* and *door*, held fast by Bossy R. As we know, instead of doublets like <oo>, scribes also used two different vowels to spell long sounds, letting the first one spell its long sound, as in *board.* Then the [oo] sound lifted to [oh], as long as it was not held tight by Borry R, as in *floor* and *board.* At this time *boot* and *boat* both spelt [boht],(written <boot>) and *brooch* spelt [brohch]. Then *boot* lifted its vowel from [oh] to [oo], and now <oo> spelt [oo]. There was a real effort in the 16th century to spell all [oh] sounds at the start of words or in the middle of words with <oa>. The verb *brooch* changed to *broach.* It meant 'to pierce a keg or drink barrel', but the jewelry held by a piercing pin, a *broach,* did not change to <oa>. A sailing *boot* was re-written as *boat*. The digraph <oa> did not completely catch on. (Another attempt, to spell initial [ee] and medial [ee] with <ea> had only patchy results.) Digraph <oa> is never used before <s> spelling [z] and so we see *hose,* not *hoas,* and *nose,* not *noas.* This prevents the appearance of a plural, as in one *boa,* two *boas.*

Rebels BROAD, COCOA.

Rebels' Reasons *Broad* is the only stem word in which <oa> spells [or]. This stem has many off-shoots, forms many complex words. The word sound [oh] is longer than [or] and it is thought that [oh] in *broad* shortened to [or] first in these complex words, e.g., in *broadsword* and *broadcast,* just as *break* shortened its vowel in *breakfast,* (Cummings p.240).

Cocoa is the only word in which terminal <oa> spells [oh]. Spanish traders heard the Aztecs say [kar-kar-oh] in Nahuatl, their language, and spelt it *cacao*. The English meant to record it as *cacao* but it was confused with a load of *coconuts,* (Cummings p. 280).

List 4-35 <oa> spells [oh]

APPROACH, APPROACHABLE , APPROACHABILITY, BILLY-GOAT, BOAST, BOASTFUL, BOASTFULLY, BOASTFULNESS, BOAT, BOATER, BOATMAN, BOATING, BOATSWAIN, BROACH, BY-ROAD, CLOAK, CLOAK-AND-DAGGER, CLOAKROOM, COACH, COACHWOOD *tree*, COAST, THE COAST IS CLEAR, COAL*, COASTAL, COASTER, COASTGUARD, COASTLINE, COAT, COAT OF ARMS, COATING, COAX, COCKROACH, COCOA, CROAK, CUT-THROAT, ENCROACH, ENCROACHMENT, FOAL*, FLOAT, FLOATER, FOAM, GLOAMING, GLOAT, GOAD, GOAL*, GOAT, ACT THE GOAT, GET SOMEONE'S GOAT, GOATEE, GOATHERD, GROAN, GROATS, GUNBOAT, HOAX, HOLM-OAK, LIFEBOAT, LOACH FISH, LOAD, LOADED, GET A LOAD OF THIS, LOADED QUESTION, LOAD LINE, LOADS, LOAD LINE, LOADER, LOADSTONE, LOAF, LOAVES, LOAM, LOAN, LOATH, NOTHING LOATH, LOATHE [dh], LOATHING [dh], LOATHSOME [th], MOAN, MOAT, MOATED, OAF, OAK, OAKEN, OAST, OAST-HOUSE, OATCAKE, OATH, ON OATH, UNDER OATH, OATMEAL,

OATS, OVERCOAT, OVERLOAD, PETTICOAT, POACH, RAINCOAT, REFLOAT, REPROACH, REPROACHFUL, ROACH, ROAD, ON THE ROAD, ROAD-BLOCK, ROAD-HOG, ROAD-HOUSE, ROAD-METAL, ROAD SENSE, ROAD TEST n., ROAD-TEST v., ROAD-WORKS *plural noun.*, ROADSIDE, ROADWAY, ROADWORTHY, ROAM, ROAN, ROAST, ROASTING, SCAPEGOAT, SHIPLOAD, SHOAL*, SOAK, SOAP, SOAP-FLAKES, SOAP OPERA, SOAP POWDER, SOAPSTONE, SOAPSUDS, SOAPY, SOAPINESS, THROAT, THROATY, THROES, TOAD, TOADFLAX, TOADSTOOL, TOADY, TOAST, TOASTER, TOASTING-FORK, WAISTCOAT, WOAD, TURNCOAT, UNDERCOAT.

*In Australia, *coal, foal, goal* and *shoal* have changed and sound like [kol], [fol], [gol] and [shol]. We know *fold* spells [fohld] in England but [fold] in Australia and believe this is because it 'reads' like that. Long ago every boundary rider had a book or two in his swag for company in the lonely Outback. Many words were met only in print and so Queen Quill ruled supreme. Lone riders are not the only people who learn new words from books, (not lips), for although English has the largest vocabulary of any language, its average speaker uses very few of them in daily life. Ogden showed that clear communication is possible in English with just 850 words! See Charles Ogden, Wikipedia.

Did you see that <th> spelt [th] in *loath* and *loathsome*, both adjectives, and [dh] in *loathe* (verb) and [dh] in *loathing* (verb). Yes, the voiced sound [dh] is used for verbs — more 'oomph', more energy to say voiced [dh] and verbs need energy! The vowel after <th> tells us the difference between *loath* and *loathe*.

Bossy R Roars — *boar, soar.*

Rule 4-36 <oar> spells [or]

Reason As we have just read, long ago <oo> and <oa> spelt [or], because when <o> spelt its long sound it spelt the Continental long sound. This was before English vowels lifted in the GVS. Then, as we read, [or] lifted to [oh], and later [oo]. However Bossy R made <oa> keep spelling [or]. Try saying [ohr]. It's not easy, is it? It was easier to keep saying [or].

List 4-36

<u>Stem Words</u> BOAR, BOARD, COARSE, HOARD, HOAR, HOARSE, OAR, ROAR, SOAR. <u>Bigger Words</u> ABROAD, BLACKBOARD, BOARD UP, GO BY THE BOARD, ON BOARD, BOARDING, BOARDING-SCHOOL, BOARDROOM, CHIPBOARD, COARSELY, COARSENESS, COARSEN, CUPBOARD, DARTBOARD, DASHBOARD, FIBREBOARD, FLOORBOARD, HARDBOARD, HEADBOARD, HOAR-FROST, HOARY, INBOARD, MATCHBOARD, OVERBOARD, PASTEBOARD, PLASTERBOARD, SAILBOARD, SHIPBOARD, SHOVELBOARD, SHUFFLEBOARD, SIDEBOARD, SIDEBOARDS *slang,* SIGNBOARD, SKATEBOARD, SPRINGBOARD, STARBOARD, SWITCHBOARD, HOARDING, HOARSENESS, OARSMAN, OARSMANSHIP, ROARING, UPROAR.

What does terminal <oe> spell? — *aloe, woe.*

Rule 4-37A Terminal <oe> spells [oh].

Reason We can say it's because when two vowels go walking the first one does the talking, very profound, spells its long sound. We see <oe> at the end of stem words, often to obey the Short Word Rule. However, we also know that <e> was added to terminal <o> to ensure that it spelt [oh] and not [oo] as in *do, to* and *who*. Many of the words also use <e> to pad them up to obey the Short Word Rule, words like *toe* and *foe*. Some do not need padding because they are just little words, like the conjunction *so*.

Three Rascals: words in which <oe> spells [oo]:CANOE, HOOPOE, SHOE.

and extensions of *shoe*: GUMSHOE, BE IN A PERSON'S SHOES, HORSESHOE, ON A SHOE STRING, SHOE-TREE, SHOEHORN, SHOELACE, SHOEMAKER, SHOESHINE.

Rascals' Reasons? Terminal <e> in *canoe* is too modern to be a fossil for *canoe* comes from Spanish *canoa*. *Canoe* which was spelt five different ways by the English until they just copied *shoe's* spelling, maybe because it looks like a floating shoe! *Hoopoe* [hoopoo] is a 1668 English spelling of the Latin name *upupa* which was written to spell the sound of the bird's cry. 'Like the cuckoo, the hoopoe's name is onomatopoeic, as it is named after its soft, far-carrying song poo-poo-poo', quoting Google. No one is sure why the dictionary committee chose *shoe* to spell [shoo]. In Old English, *shoe* was spelt *sho*, actually *sco*, being before 1066, when <sc> spelt [sh]. It was pronounced like *do*. Its plural was *shoen* in the south-west of England, according to the Middle English dictionary at https://quod.lib.umich.edu/m, amongst a variety of other spellings, but then became just *shoes*, with an <e>, because without <e> it would have been *shos* and sounded like [shoz]. After a while everyone wrote *shoe* for the singular and added <s> for the plural. Nowadays we would like to write *one shoo, two shoos* but that might be muddled up with *shoo* as in: '*"Shoo, shoo go away,"* she shouts, as she *shoos* them away'. So, we stick to *one shoe, two shoes*.

List 4-37A <oe> spells [oh]
ALOE, DOE, ICE FLOE, FOE, HOE, JOEY, OBOE, PEKOE, ROE, SLOE, TOE, WOE. BE ON ONE'S TOES, TIPTOE, TOE-CAP, TOE THE LINE, WOEBEGONE, WOEFUL. <u>Names</u> CRUSOE, IVANHOE, JOE, MUNROE, ROSCOE.

Rule 4-37B Terminal <oes> spells [ohz].
Reason Words which end in <o> have to add <es> to become plural or else they would lose their [oh] sound for terminal <os> spells [os], not [ohz]. For instance, the verb *to go* takes <es> in 'he goes'. As we know, <s> spells [z] after a stressed vowel and as *all vowel digraphs are stressed, <oes> spells [ohz]. Words which already end in <oe> take <s> to make plurals and as <oe> already spells [oh], <oes> spells [ohz]. The vowel [oh] is a long vowel and all long vowels are stressed vowels and <s> spells [z] after stressed vowels. (*Except in suffixes, e.g., —*ous*. As we know, not all short vowels are stressed, e.g., they are in *has* and *is*, [haz] and [iz], but not in *tennis* and *omnibus*, [ten-is] and [om-nee-bus].)

Rebels DOES [duz], also DOESN'T [duzənt]
Rebels' Reasons When *do* becomes *does* it changes its vowel sound, to [u], [duz]. The <o> in *does* — like the <o> in *done* — was always pronounced [u]. *Does* was originally *doth* in which <o> spells [u], [duth], as in *other*. Just like *cometh* became *comes*, so *doth* became *does*. Where does the <e> come from? *Doth* was also written *doeth*. Between 1500-1600 the Northumbrian way of writing and saying it, *does* [duz], displaced the other ways and that spelling and pronunciation remains to this day. *Dyde* changed to *did*.

Δ *To do*: present, past, past participle: DO Δ, DID Δ, DONE Δ. Present tense: DOES Δ, as in *I do, you do, he does, she does, it does. We do, you do, they do*. DOESN'T: *I don't* and *it doesn't*.

Rascals CANOES, HOOPOES, LASSOES and SHOES in which <oes> spells [ooz].
Lasso spells [las-oo] as we learnt in Part One. Plural *lassos* would spell [las-oz] and so it copies *shoes* when plural, *lassoes*. *Shoes* is a rascal. Copying a rascal like *shoes* is not a good enough excuse to be a 'Rebel with Reason' and so *lassoes* is a spelling rascal. *Canoe* and
shoe and *hoopoe* were deemed rascals in 4-37A.

List 4-37B terminal <oes> spells [ohz]
AVOCADOES, BANJOES, BUFFALOES, CALICOES, CALYPSOES, CARGOES, COMMANDOES, CONDOES, CRESCENDOES, DADOES, DESPERADOES, DINGOES, DODOES, DOMINOES, ECHOES, EMBARGOES, FARRAGOES, FIASCOES, FLAMINGOES, FRESCOES, GAZEBOES, GECKOES, GHETTOES, GINKGOES, GROTTOES, GOES* Δ, HALLOES, HALOES, HELLOES, HEROES, HOBOES, HULLOES, INDIGOES, INNUENDOES, JINGOES, KIDDOES, LINGOES, MAMBOES, MANGOES, MANIFESTOES, MEMENTOES, MOSQUITOES, MOTTOES, MULATTOES, PECCADILLOES, PINTOES, PLACEBOES, PORTICOES, POTATOES,

PROVISOES, SALVOES, STILETTOES, THROES*, TOMATOES, TORNADOES, TORPEDOES, TUXEDOES, VIRAGOES, VOLCANOES, YOBBOES, ZEROES.

Goes belongs to the present tense of the irregular verb *to* go: GO Δ, WENT Δ, GONE Δ. We met the old fossil *gone* at 3-9. Present tense: *I go, you go, he, she or it goes. We go, you, they go.*

Throes only occurs in the plural form. There is no such word as throe. It is a plural noun. Maybe we could add *noes* and *oes* for more than one *no* and more than one letter O. We also see <oes> at the end of verbs, like *it goes, she vetoes, he hoes.*

Note: We do not see every word which ends in <o> getting <es> for more than one, because some add just <s>. For example, OPD lists one *biro*, two *biros;* two *radios* and two *pianos*. The Macquarie Dictionary gives *dingos, mosquitos, volcanos* and other alternatives, as well.

Digraph <oe> and Ethel — *amoeba, subpoena.*

Digraph <oe> never spells [oh] inside stem words. The Greeks used <oi> to spell [o-ee], a diphthong. The Romans pronounced this more like just [ee] and invented the letter Ethel to spell this sound in the Greek words they adopted. Ethel is a ligature of O and E, Œ œ. When Latin words containing Ethel were adopted by the English, they too adapted the spelling to suit themselves, e.g., *economy, federal, penal, cemetery* all had an Ethel in Latin. In others, < œ> became the two separate letters, <oe>.

In the olden days, words that were adopted into the English language could have been orphans for all the English cared. They just loved new words. They did not stop to ask where they had come from. However, later on, they needed so many new words to describe all the new things and new feelings they were discovering in the period of great learning called the Renaissance that they ran out of words and had to build new ones. They used word-bits from classical Greek and Latin or copied whole words in those ancient languages. Lots of these so-called new things were actually re-discovered from reading old books in Greek and Latin and so it was called a Re-Birth (*Renaissance*) of Learning. The English were so proud of their new knowledge that, instead of adapting Latin and Greek spelling to English spelling, they decided to retain and revive all sorts of Latin and Greek letter arrangements to show where the words came from. Americans have tried to simplify some of these words. They list *fetus, celiac, edema,* in their dictionaries, instead of *foetus, coeliac* and *oedema.*

Not needed but nice to know. The digraph <oe> was once upon a time written <œ> in some words but this ligature letter (made of linked letters), remains only in *manœuvre* [man-oo-ver], and then only in the OED. It's *manoeuvre* in other British dictionaries. In American dictionaries it is *maneuver*, as in List 4-24. This word was originally related to manual labour, in particular the cultivation and manuring of soil. The British army used it for planned movement and manipulation of troops, along with another French term, {*reconnoitre*}. See Etymonline for complaints made by the ordinary 'mob of Great Britain' in 1758 about these unnecessary words. Now back to things we need to know.

Rule 4-38 Medial <oe> spells [ee].
Reason As above, medial <oe> was <œ> in Latin, a special letter for an adopted Greek vowel. This became the digraph <oe> in English words. So, although 'when two vowels go walking the first one does the talking, spells its long sound', as we know 'if the last one is Greek, the first one needn't speak.' In this case the digraph was originally Greek and so the first letter, <o> does not 'speak' its long sound, [oh]. It's hard to decode unless we know that <oe> has Greek origins. It would be easier to spot the Greek link if Ethel, Œ œ, was still in use. It is still used in French, e.g. *un œil, un œuf, l'œvre* — an egg, an eye and a work of art. In French, Ethel spells something like [er].
List 4-38 <oe> spells [ee] in words from Latin and Greek.
AMOEBA, COELACANTH, COELIAC DISEASE, DIARRHOEA, OEDEMA, OESOPHAGUS, OESTROGEN, ONOMATOPOEIA, FOETAL, FOETUS*, GONORRHOEA, ONOMATOPOEIA,

PHARMACOPOEIA, PHOENIX, PYORRHOEA, SUBPOENA.   Proper Nouns PHOENICIA, OEDIPUS COMPLEX.

Foetus arrived in English as *fœtus*. Later it simplified further to *fetus* in American English. Many other American words replaced <œ> or <oe> with <e>.

Rebels STOEP, HORS-D'OEUVRE, MANOEUVRE.   Proper Noun WINDHOEK.

Rebels' Reasons All these words have Diplomatic Immunity. They have been allowed into English without any change to spelling. In other words, they have been adopted, but not adapted to obey English spelling rules. The combination <oe> has a variety of sounds in various countries:

In Afrikaans, <oe> spells [uu] in *stoep*, but in English it spells [oo]. It means 'step' in Dutch and Afrikaans — the broad step outside an entrance, where one can sit and chat. In French *hors-d'oeuvre* [or-derv], <oe> spells [er] as spoken in English. In *manoeuvre* <oe> spells [oo] and shares an ancestor with *manure* for they both mean 'manual labour'. The verb *to manure* came first, before the noun *manure,* which was anything used to manure the soil, whether compost or cow pats. The digraph <oe> spells [uu] in *Windhoek* [vint-hohk], the Capital of Namibia, from Dutch for 'windy corner'. <oe> spells [er] in *hors-d'oeuvre* [or-derv], a French word,

Old English Terminal <ow> — *arrow, yellow.*

In the digraphs <ou>, <ow> and <oy> the letter <o> is not allowed to do the talking because the last letter is Greek, except in some very old English words in which the <w> in <ow> is not Greek and so <ow> spells [oh]. This comes about because the letter W arrived in England twice. It came in first as the old runic symbol Wynn, <ƿ>. The Romans had no <w>. The old scribes of the 600's wrote <uu> for a while but after about 800 they preferred writing <ƿ>. However, after the Invasion of 1066, the Norman scribes insisted on <w> and by 1300 old Wynn, <ƿ>, was gone forever. Old Norman Frenchmen used <w>, as in *ward* but the Central French disliked <w> and insisted on <gu>, as in *guard*. This is why *warden* and *guard* mean the same thing.

Sometimes Norman <w> replaced another Old English letter called Yogh, <ȝ>, which came at the end of *follow, sorrow, etc* in which <ow> spells [oh], not [ow].

Rule 4-39 Digraph <ow> spells [oh] at the end of some very old English words and in them <ows> always spells [ohz].

Reason Long ago the English used lots of word endings. Each ending meant something special, like the word endings in Australian Aboriginal languages. Many old English words ended in *we, rg, lg, rh, u* and ȝ but, when the Norman French arrived, the English language was neglected by the Norman scribes. Old English letters were lost and the only people who kept English alive were the illiterate peasants. They did not bother to use all the fancy word endings and many shrank. Some shrank to [oh] and when English was revived, without the old letter yogh, these endings were spelt <ow>. That is why <ow> spelling [oh] is always at the end of a (stem) word, not in the middle, except for {*bowl, owe* and *own*}, listed soon. When <ow> ends words which are not old English words it spells [ow]. We say they are

Not Really Rebels, just **Rappers** because they are dancing to a new tune. They arrived in England with the French ending <ou> but as <u> must not end an English word it was replaced with <w>. We met them in Part One, and we can add three more words to these rappers:

ALLOW, BOW, BOW-WOW, BROW, CHOW, COW, HOW, NOW, PLOW* USA, PROW, ROW, SOW, VOW, WOW.

If terminal <u> had been insulated with <e> we'd see *houe, noue, etc.* but a cluster of three vowels is not popular in English. To remember when terminal <ow> spells [ow] think of Noah on his ark as he wipes his brow: "How now brown cow. Bow-wow old sow. Don't row. I vow I'll allow you chow in the prow,"- or make up your own and act it out. Remember, Noah did not **row** the ark, so do not include *row* with that meaning!   *In USA a *plough* is a *plow*.

Not needed but nice to know, to prove these 'Rappers' are not old words, not from original Englisc, Old English. We met words like *now* and *how* early in this book because we use them a lot, every day, in fact. However, they are not OE words. They arose arose in the Middle English period, after the Norman Invasion in 1066, or even later, in the Modern English period, which began in 1476 when Caxton returned to England with a printing press. Thus, it is impossible for their <ow> endings to spell [oh], for only Old English words end in <ow> spells [oh]. Prof Cummings, on p. 62, says that *now* was once *hen* — *when*, *hen* and *then* rhymed, like *where*, *here* and *there* used to. Etymonline says that *nu* in Old English was more for emphasis than describing time, like *now* in "Do it and do it now!" Later, after the Norman Invasion, *nou a dayes* only meant "during the day" until *nou* replaced *hen* and was spelt *now*. *Row* as in argue is very new for it began as Cambridge University slang in the 18th century, probably from *rouse*, to stir up, provoke activity. *Prow* was never [proh]. It came from Greek *proira*, front of ship, via Latin and Old French into English as *proue* [prow]. *Sow* was never [soh] but came from old German *sau*, (Ayto, p. 491). *Sow* and *cow* were *cu* and *su* in Old English, and plurals are still *kine* (rarely used) and *swine*. The Indian greeting *How!* is new to English. The questioning word *How?* used to be [kwo] like *quo* in *Quo vadis?* When it changed its sound after 1066 it would have been *hou* if <u> was allowed to end words. *Brow* and *brown* began as the early English words *bru* and *brun* and re-surfaced with new meanings and new spellings after the Norman Invasion, (Ayto, p. 81). *Vow* came from *vou*, an Anglo-Norman word, developed after the Norman Invasion and before the ban on <u> at the end of words. *Chow* is a new word, from Chinese *cha*, for mixed food. *Allow* is another (Norman) Invasion Word, arriving in England as Old French *alouer*. *Plow* is a modern spelling of *plough*. *Bow-wow* was first recorded in 1576, in modern times. (*Woof-woof* was recorded even later, 1804.) Words ending <ou> spelt [oo], before the GVS, during which this long high vowel lifted, could go no higher, bent over, and became the diphthong [ow]. This did not happen in *you* but it did in *thou*. Now back to things we need to know.

List 4-39 <ow> spells [oh] at the end of some very old English words.
ARROW, BARROW, BELLOW, BELOW, BILLOW, BLOW ▲, BORROW, BOW, CALLOW, CROW, ELBOW, FALLOW, FLOW ▲, FARROW, FELLOW, FOLLOW, FURROW, GLOW, GROW ▲, HALLOW, HOLLOW, KNOW ▲, LOW, MALLOW *plant*, MARROW, MEADOW, MELLOW, MORROW, MOW ▲, ROW *noun/verb*, SALLOW, SHADOW, SHALLOW, SHOW ▲, SLOW, SNOW, SORROW, SOW ▲, STOW, SWALLOW, TALLOW, THROW ▲, TOW, WALLOW, WIDOW*, WILLOW, WINDOW, WINNOW, YARROW, YELLOW. <ow> not terminal: BOWL*, OWE*, OWN*.

*In *owe*, **bowl* and **own*, <ow> is not terminal but still spells [oh]. We know that in *owe*, <ow> cannot be at the end due to the Short Word Rule. A *bowl* could not be spelt *bole* because that means something else, a lump on the side of a tree. We cannot write *own* as <one> because we use that to spell *one* [wun].
*In *widow*, <i> spells [i] due to its origin, not through *wife*, but linked to the verb to *winnow*, to separate grain from straw, (Ayto, p. 574).

Many words are made from these stem words, which end <ow> spells [oh]. A few new words, or spellings like *widow*, have copied the ending <ow> spells [oh]. Of course, a lot of stem words ending in <ow> get suffixes, which means that <ow> ends up **inside** words but that's OK because they are still at the end of stem words, e.g., *grown*, *known* and *growth*.

Rebels KNOWLEDGE, KNOWLEDGEABLE and ACKNOWLEDGE; ROWLOCK (and the name ROWLEY, [rol-lee]). In Australia BOWL is a rebel word when it spells [bol].

Rebels' Reasons In these words <owl> spells [ol]. As we know, consonants [l] and [r] blend very closely with vowels and change the way they sound. *Bowl* becomes [bol] on our lips very easily but some folk still say [bohl]. When *know* gains the old suffix *–ledge*, the <l> 'melts' (melds, merges) with the vowel sound [oh] in *know* and we get [nol-ej] instead of [noh-lej]. This is why <ow> spells [o] in *knowledge*, *knowledgeable* and *acknowledge* but not in *knowing*. This also happens in *rowlock* [rol-lok].

List 4-39 cont. Complex words in which <ow> spells [oh] and plural <ows> spells [ohz] because [oh] is stressed.

AGLOW, AIRFLOW, ARROWHEAD, BELLOWS, BESTOW, BLOW-BY-BLOW, BLOW-DRY, BLOWER, BLOWFLY, BLOWLAMP, BLOWN, BLOW-OUT, BLOWPIPE, BLOWY, BEDFELLOW, BORROWER, BOW-LEGGED, BOW-LEGS, BOW-TIE, BOW-WINDOW, BOWLINE, BOWSPRIT, BUNGALOW*, CROSSBOW, EYE-SHADOW, DISOWN, EIDERDOWN, ELBOW-GREASE, ELBOW-ROOM, CROW'S-FEET, CROW'S NEST, CROWBAR, CROWFOOT, FALLOW DEER, FELLOW-FEELING, FELLOW-TRAVELLER, FELLOWSHIP, FLOWN Δ, FOLLOW-ON *n.*, FOLLOW-UP *n.*, FOLLOWING, FURBELOWS, GROWABLE, GROWING PAINS, GROWER, GROWN Δ, GROWN-UP, GROWTH, GROWTH INDUSTRY, HOLLOWLY, INFLOW, INGROWING, KNOWABLE, KNOWING, LANDOWNER, LOWER, LOWER-CASE, LOW-CLASS, LOWER DECK, LOWLAND, LOWLANDER, LOWLY, LOWLINESS, LOW-DOWN, LOW-KEY, LOW-LEVEL, MARSHMALLOW, MARROWBONE, MARROWFAT, MEADOWSWEET *plant*, MOWER, OUTGROWTH, OVERFLOW, OVERGROWN, OVERSHADOW, OVERTHROW, OWING, OWNER, OWNERSHIP, OWNER-DRIVER, OWNER-OCCUPIER, OWNERLESS, PLAYFELLOW, RAINBOW, ROW-BOAT, ROWING-BOAT, ROWING-MACHINE, SALLOW TREE, SHADOWY, SHALLOWLY, SHALLOWNESS, SHOWBIZ, SHOW-CASE, SHOW-DOWN, SHOW-JUMPING, SHOW-OFF, SHOW OF HANDS, SHOW ONE'S SELF, SHOW ONE'S FACE, SHOW-PIECE, SHOW-PLACE, SHOW-ROOM, SHOWING, SHOWMAN, SHOWMANSHIP, SHOWN, SHOWY, SHOWILY, SLOWLY, SLOWNESS, SLOWCOACH, SLOWISH, SLOW-WORM, SNOW-BOUND, SNOW-DRIFT, SNOWED UNDER, SNOWED, SNOW-FIELD, SNOW-GOOSE, SNOW-LINE, SNOW-PLOUGH, SNOW-SHOE, SNOW-WHITE, SNOWBALL, SNOWDROP, SNOWFALL, SNOWFLAKE, SNOWMAN, SNOWSTORM, SNOWY, SORROWFUL, SORROWFULLY, SOWER, SOWN Δ, STOWAGE, STOWAWAY, SWALLOW-DIVE, SWALLOW-TAILED, TOMORROW, TOW-HEADED, TOW-BAR, TOWING-PATH, TOW-PATH, TOWAGE, UNDERGROWTH, UNDERTOW, UNKNOWN, WIDOWED, WIDOWER, WILLOW-HERB, WILLOW-PATTERN, WILLOWY, YELLOWNESS, YELLOW FEVER, YELLOW PAGES, YELLOW STREAK, YELLOWISH. <u>Aust. Words</u> BRIGALOW*, FLY-BLOWN, YELLOW-BELLY, YELLOW-JACKET, YELLOW-TAIL. <u>Names</u> OWEN, ROWAN, ROWLAND.

Irregular verbs in which <ow> spells [oh], present, past and p. participle.
BLOW Δ, BLEW Δ, BLOWN Δ
FLY Δ, FLEW Δ, FLOWN Δ
GROW Δ, GREW Δ, GROWN Δ
KNOW Δ, KNEW Δ, KNOWN Δ
MOW Δ, MOWED, MOWN Δ /MOWED
SHOW Δ, SHOWED, SHOWN Δ /SHOWED
SOW Δ, SOWED, SOWED/SOWN Δ – "sow the seed".
THROW Δ, THREW Δ, THROWN Δ

Brigalow appears to mean 'low boree tree'. The Kamilaroi Aborigines called *Acacia pendula* 'boree'. It is suggested that other acacias, especially low, scrubby ones like brigalow, grew out of that Ab'l word, (Blake, p.89).

Bungalow and *brigalow* are the only adopted words which use <ow> to spell [oh] at the end of a word and the only words of three or more syllables which use <ow> to spell [oh].

Know's <k> was not always silent. We hear it in "*Do you **ken** (know) John Peel at the break of day?*" and in the words *canny* and *cunny* for 'knowing'.

Digraph <ow> only spells [oh] in Old English words, because that <w> evolved in England from yogh and other old word endings. In all other words <ow> spells [ow]. This is because when <o> and <w> go walking, <w> only lets <o> do the talking in Old English words. When <o> goes walking with <w> made from Greek U, it does not do the talking, does not talk big and spell its long sound.

Straight sound [oh] and bent sound [ow].

As we know, *bow* spells [boh] and *row* spells [roh]. They each have two meanings:- a *bow* and arrow and a *bow* tied with ribbon; a *row* of beans and *row* the boat. However, they also spell [bow] and [row], in which <ow> spells the diphthong [ow], a double sound, a bent sound. Homonyms are words which look the same (might even sound the same) but mean different things, like *bow* for arrows and *bow* for hair. Homophones sound the same. '*Bow* down' looks the same as a *bow* tying hair, but does not sound the same.

It is very easy to remember in which homonym <ow> spells the straight sound [oh] because it is used for straight things. It is one straight sound, as straight as a bone, [bohn]. Yes, even in *bow and arrow*, for to make an *arrow* we need a straight stem and to make the *bow* we choose a straight piece of wood too. (A bent piece does not work, has no spring. Try it and see for yourself.) The *bowsprit* [boh-sprit] on a boat is made from a straight piece of wood. A *bow* in the sense of loops in a ribbon was first recorded as the loop at the end of a string attached to a *bow*. It was first recorded as an adjective, *bow-string* and only later became a noun, as in "pretty bow". It is also used as an adjective, meaning 'bow-like' in *bow-legged, bow-tie, bow-window*. They are all *bowed* [bohd] like an archer's *bow* [boh]. The word [boh] is from [bohk]. Long ago a tree was called a *boc* [bohk], even just a piece of tree, like the pieces they scratched messages on to make the first *books*. Please note, even longer ago <o> spelt long [or], an extension of short [o]. That was before the GVS, during which long, straight [o] lifted to long, straight [oh].

When *row* spells [roh] it means a straight line of things. We *sow* [soh] seeds in a *row* [roh]. There is even more proof that [oh] ends straight things for we know an *elbow* [el-boh] means a bone [bohn], which was bent, and that there was an old ancestor (Indo-European) stem word *el* which meant 'bent', (Ayto, p. 196).

Who put the [ow] in bow?

The first *boat* [boht] was a made from a piece of straight wood, a log, a *boc* [bohk]. They developed into rafts or ferries, with a post at the front and back. The front one was called the *stem* for it stopped, i.e. "stemmed", the boat. Nowadays we only use *stem* when stopping the flow of a fluid. We *stammer* when the flow of speech is stopped. The back post on the boat was the *stern* for steering. (Have you heard the expression to "search the boat from stem to stern"?) If the stem of the boat had a central edge which cut the path in the water this was called the *prou* [prow], so-called because it was further forward than the rest of the boat, and *pro* means 'forward', it was 'pro-er' than the rest of the boat. Pro-er became *prou*. Because English words must not end with <u>, that letter was replaced with <w>.

The <ou> in *shoulder* once spelt the bent vowel [ow]. In many languages the prow of the boat is called the 'shoulder' of the boat. Just as we talk about the 'limbs' of trees, some languages call where a branch attaches to the trunk a 'shoulder'. Shoulders are major bends in a body. So 'boc' was given a bent vowel a diphthong, to represent the bend in the tree's various shoulders or branch-joins. This diphthong was <oe> in the new word *boech* [bowk], meaning a 'bent boc [bohk]'. Others wrote it *bough*, to spell [bowgh], to bend the vowel in [bohk]. Later, guttural [gh] was silenced and *bough* spelt [ow]. This bent section of the tree was used to build the *prow* of the boat and pretty soon the pointy bend was also called a [bow].

The straight stick or shaft which pointed beyond the front end to attach sails was still called a [boh-sprit], written *bowsprit,* because it was straight. In some parts of England *bough* was shortened to *bou* and the final <u> needed insulating with <e> but this would have resulted in three vowels in a row. So <u> was doubled, producing <w>, in the same way French *proue* became English *prow*. Consequently, when a *bough* (shoulder) was chosen to construct the bent end of a boat it became the *bow* of the boat. (Picture the boat builders choosing a tree with a strong trunk joined at a shoulder to an equally strong branch at an angle perfect for the front of their boat.) *Bow* is the front of the boat and *prow* refers to the forward-most part of a ship's bow that cuts through the water.

Since *bow* [bow] meant a bend/shoulder in timber, *to bow* [bow] was used to mean 'to bend' — boughs *bow* under the weight of fruit and we *bow* at the waist. A *bower* was originally a simple curved shelter, a humpy. (The Bowery district in New York was once a simple home, a *bowerij*, built by a Dutch settler in New Amsterdam.) Flowering creepers trail over curved *bowers* in some gardens, and so once again *bow* [bow] denotes a curve or bend. As for the word spelt *bough,* we shall meet it again soon.

When <ow> spells [ow], it's a stressed vowel, because long vowels, including diphthongs, are stressed. This means the syllable after [ow] is usually unstressed as in *shower, vowel etc.* even when <ow> is not in the first syllable, e.g., in *disembowel* <ow> spells stressed [ow], with primary stress, heaviest stress.

Rule 4-40 Terminal <ow> spells [ow] in a few rebel words, rather than [oh]. Initial and medial<ow> always spells [ow] in stem words.

Reason This avoids <u> at the end of words, or before <l> nd <n> which would be hard to read in cursive. We have already met terminal <ow> spells [ow] rather than [oh] in ALLOW, BOW* Verb/Noun BOW-WOW, BROW, CHOW, COW, HOW, NOW, PLOW in USA, PROW, ROW* *noisy argument*, SOW* *female pig*, VOW, WOW. These words came into English after 1066 when English spelling was under French control. The Old English <w> in *window* etc. had to compete with the new <w> which was literally a double <u>.

Bow, row and *sow* all have homonyms which look the same but do not sound the same because they are the names ('nyms') of a straight *row* to *sow* seeds, and a straight branch to make a *bow* and arrows, as we already know.

Rebels BOWL, OWE, OWN, as explained earlier, in which medial <ow> spells [oh].
List 4-40B <ow> spells [ow] in these stem words.
AVOWAL, AVOWEDLY, BOWDLERIZE, BOWEL*, BOWER, BROWN, CLOWN, COWARD*, COWER, COWL, COWRIE, CROWD, CROWN, DISEMBOWEL, DOWAGER, DOWEL, DOWER, DOWN, DOWNY, DOWRY, DOWSE <s>=[z], DROWSE <s>=[z], DROWN, FLOWER, FROWN, GOWN, GROWL, HOWL, GROWL, JOWL, NOWT, OWL, POWER, POWWOW, PROW, PROWESS*, PROWL, RENOWN, ROWEL, SCOWL, SHOWER, TOWEL, TOWER, TOWN, TROWEL, VOWEL, WOW!

Bowdlerize is due to the English editor Dr Thomas Bowdler who published his "Family Shakespeare", editing out any words which he thought could not be read out loud to the family. This sort of censoring became a verb in 1836, (Ayto, p. 74).

Bowel comes from Old French *bouel,* in which <u>is not terminal and so does not have to be replaced, but three full vowels in a cluster, as in *bouel,* is usually avoided.

Coward is a combo of Latin *coda* (tail) and the suffix –*ward,* one who goes to the tail of the action or one who "turns tail". In *coward,* the <o> and <w> join up to spell [ow] and the suffix has become –*ard* is in *dullard* and *drunkard,* [əd].

Prowess means advanced or forward skills. "Her prowess as a dressmaker is legendary."

Relevant Writing Rule. Digraph <ow> spells [ow] before vowels, before <l> and before terminal <n>.
Reason. Probably to avoid illegibility in cursive handwriting. Elsewhere <ou> spells [ow].
Rebels: NOWT, COWRIE, DOWRY, HOWDAH, BOWL.

Rebels' Reasons: *Nowt* is a contraction of *not a wit,* (not a bit). *Cowrie* has been badly adapted from the Hindi name for the shell, *kauri*. *Dowry* is a combination of two Latin stem words *donum* "a giving, gift" and *dare* "to give". *Howdah* is adapted from Hindi.

As we know, *bowl* spells [bohl] or [bol], not [bowl].

Relevant Writing Rule. Words derived from stem words with <ow> spells [ow] use [d] and [z] to connect suffixes where needed.

Reason: I think maybe this is because [ow] is always stressed and therefore followed by voiced consonants, not unvoiced, like [t] and [s], when adding suffixes. So *dowdy* not *dowty* is made from *doue,* poorly dressed woman. (The noun *dowd* is a back-formation, Etymonline.) This helps us encode, write, [ow] words. We see that inside words, both stem and derived, <ow> is only followed by <n>, <l>, <d>, <s> or <z>. Otherwise, medial [ow] is spelt <ou> except in *nowt, cowrie, dowry, howdah,* unless it is in a compound word like *cowman*. Return to Reading Rules.

List 4-41 Words built on stem words in which <ow> spells [ow].
ALLOWABLE, ALLOWABLY, ALLOWANCE, AND HOW! *slang,* BLOWZY, BOWER-BIRD, BROWBEAT, BROWN SNAKE, BROWNED OFF, BROWNIE, BROWNING, BROWNISH, BROWSE <s>=[z], CHOW MEIN, COME-DOWN, CORNFLOWER, COWARDICE, COWARDLINESS, COWARDLY, COWBOY, COWLING, COWMAN, COWSHED, COWSLIP, CROWN PRINCE, CROWN PRINCESS, DISAVOW, DOWDILY, DOWDINESS, DOWD, DOWDY, DOWELLING, DOWER HOUSE, DOWN AT HEEL, DOWN BEAT, DOWN ON ONE'S LUCK, DOWN STAGE, DOWN UNDER, DOWN WITH, DOWN-AND-OUT, DOWNCAST, DOWNER, DOWNFALL, DOWNGRADE, DOWN-HEARTED, DOWNHILL, DOWNPOUR, DOWNRIGHT, DOWNS, DOWNSTAIRS, DOWNSTREAM, DOWN-TO-EARTH, DOWNTRODDEN, DOWNTURN, DOWNWARD, DOWNWIND, DOWSER <s>=[z], DROWSY <s>=[z], EMPOWER, ENDOW*, ENDOWMENT, EYEBROW, EYES DOWN, FLOWERLESS, FLOWERPOT, FLOWERY, FROWZY*, GODOWN, GO TO TOWN, GROWLER, GUNPOWDER, HOW ABOUT, HOW COME, HOW DO YOU DO?, HOW MANY, HOW MUCH, HOWDAH, HOWDY *slang,* HOWEVER, HOWITZER*, HOWL DOWN, HOWLER, HOWZAT *slang,* IN A BROWN STUDY, KOWTOW*, MIAOW*, NIGHTGOWN, ON THE PROWL, ON THE TOWN, OVERBLOWN, OVERCROWD, OWLET, OWLISH, POWDER, POWDER BLUE, POWDER-PUFF, POWDER-ROOM, POWDERY, POWER, POWER POINT, POWER POLITICS, POWER-DIVE, POWERFUL, POWERFULLY, POWERHOUSE, POWERLESS, POWWOW*, PROWESS, PROWLER, ROWDIER, ROWDILY, ROWDINESS, ROWDY, ROWDYISM, SUNDOWN, SUNDOWNER, SUNFLOWER, THE DOWNS, THE POWERS THAT BE, TOWELLING, TOWER BLOCK, TOWER OF STRENGTH, TOWERING, TOWN CLERK, TOWN CRIER, TOWN HALL, TOWN HOUSE, TOWN PLANNING, TOWNIE *slang,* TOWNSCAPE, TOWNSFOLK, TOWNSHIP, TOWNSMAN, TOWNSPEOPLE, TOWNSWOMAN, WALLFLOWER, WATERFOWL, WOWSER *slang.* Proper Nouns DOWNING STREET, THE TOWER OF LONDON.

*Miaow [mee-yow] is listed as equivalent to *mew* by the OPD.

*Powwow and *kowtow* are adoptions from North American Indian and Chinese words respectively.

*Howitzer is a German adoption and <z> spells [s] after unvoiced [t].

*Endow is derived from the obsolete stem word *dow,* seen in *dowry*.

*Frowzy is the only <ow> word which uses <z> to spell [z], (Cummings p. 305), and probably came from Old English *frowsty* meaning 'rancid and therefore smelly'. When <s> follows <ow> it always spells [z], even when followed by terminal <e>, as in *browse, drowse*. This does not always happen when <se> follows <ou>, e.g., 'the house [hows] will house [howz] them'.

We have only listed words which contain the digraph <ow>. A digraph occurs when two adjacent letters spell a sound in the same syllable. In words like TOWARDS and TOWARD, <ow> is just a cluster at a syllable boundary, as in NOWADAYS, NOWHERE, NOWISE, TOOWIT and TOWOO. *Toowit and towoo* is the duet between male and female tawny owls.

We have met all the words in which <ow> spells [ow]. All other words which have the diphthong [ow] sound are spelt with <ou>. You will not see [ow] spelt <ou> at the end of a word except in the old word THOU. *Caribou, you, etc.* end [oo].

Digraph <ou> inside words— *about, vouch.*

As we know, because <u> is a Greek letter, <o> 'needn't speak' in the digraph <ou>.
The English language has been adopting French words ever since the Norman Invasion of 1066. A second wave of adoptions occurred of slightly different French words when England waged war with regions of France to the south of Normandy. English soldiers picked up French words and brought them home to England during that war which went on for 100 years. Although there will always be friction between the two neighbouring nations, the English cannot help admiring the sophisticated ways of the French and continue to adopt food and fashion words from France.
In English, the digraph <ou> spells [ow] in old words adopted long ago from French and [oo] in 'more recent' adoptions from French. French <ou> spells [oo]. French scribes were in control of English spelling and so they changed <u> in some Old English words to <ou>. In the GVS the [oo] sound spelt by <ou> was already a high sound and, as it could not lift any further, it bent over into the diphthong [ow], as in *house* and *our*. However, we shall see that if <ou> is followed by <r>, Bossy R can take control, as in *four, colour* and *courage.*
We shall see <ou> in *youth* and *you*, in *shoulder* and *bough* and spelling even more vowels, in many other words. Add to this the way vowels change, but rarely change their letters, means that explaining all the <ou> patterns we shall now admire will take time and patience.
Relevant Writing Rule. Digraph <ou> spells [ow] inside stem words but is not used before <l> and terminal <n> to spell [ow].
Reason As we know, stem words use <ow> to spell [ow] before <l> and terminal <n>. As we know, in *could, would* and *should* <oul> spells [uud]. We shall find that <oul> does not spell [owl] in *moult* and other "Cold Shoulder" words, nor in *soul*.
Rebels NOUN and FOUL.
Rebels' Reasons: Writing *noun,* instead of *nown,* separates it from its cousin *renown. Noun* means "name" and so *re-noun* would mean 're-name' or 'change a name'. However, when someone's name is mentioned repeatedly (*re-*) they become well known, someone of *renown.* Maybe, because in *renown* <ow> matches <ow> in *well known*, it kept the letters <ow> and *noun* became the rebel with <ou> spells [ow]. When <oul> spells [owl] <l> is always followed by another consonant except in *foul,* which in Old English was *ful,* related to *pus* and *ugly* and has kept <u> from ancient times. Cross-check this Writing Rule with the one for <ow> below List 4-40B. Return to Reading Rules.

Rule 4-42 Digraph <ou> spells [ow] inside stem words except before <ld>, <lt>, medial <r>, <gh> and in recent French adoptions.
Reason We have already met the happy rappers *could, should* and *would*. We have also met *our* which spells [owr] but, inside a word, <our> does not always spell [owr] as we shall soon see in words like *court.* Only two words have <oult>, *moult* and *poultry,* and they spell [molt] and [poltry]. Many words use <ould> to spell [old], like *shoulder*. We shall meet these "cold shoulder" words soon. Rules for <ough> come later.
Rebel SOUL

322

Rebel's Reason *Soul* spells [sohl] or even [sol]. It was *sawol*, "seawards", for it was believed that our spirits came in and out of the sea, out at birth and back in at death or onto islands in the sea, like Polynesia's Bali Hai Island or Western Australia's Wadjemup or Place of Spirits, now known as Rottnest Island. Strangely enough, the word *soul* is a double rebel, for it breaks the encoding rule that <ou> should not be followed by <l> and it breaks the decoding rule that says <ou> should spell [ow] not [oh].

List 4-42 <ou> spells [ow], but not before <ld>, <lt> and <r>.

ABOUT, ACCOUNT, ALOUD, AMOUNT, AROUND, AROUSE *verb*, ASTOUND, BOUNCE, ▲BOUND, BOUT, CAROUSE, CLOUD, CLOUT, COUCH, COUNCIL, COUNSEL, COUNT, COUNTY, CROUCH, DENOUNCE, DEVOUT, DOUBT*, DOUSE* *verb*, ENCOUNTER, ESPOUSAL, ESPOUSE *verb*, EXPOUND, FLOUNCE, FLOUNDER, FLOUT, FOUL, ▲FOUND, FOUNT, GOUGE, GOUT, GROUCH, ▲GROUND, GROUND *noun*, GROUSE, GROUT, HOUSE*, JOUST, LOUD, LOUGH, LOUNGE, LOUSE*, LOUT, MOUND, MOUNT, MOUSE*, MOUTH*, NOUN, OUCH, OUNCE, OUST, OUT, POUCH, POUNCE, POUND, POUT, PROFOUND, PRONOUNCE, PROPOUND, PROUD, ROUND, ROUSE *verb*, ROUT, SCOUNDREL, SCOUSE, SCOUT, SCROUNGE, SHOUT, SHROUD, SLOUCH, SNOUT, SOUND, SOUSE* *verb*, SOUTH, SPOUSE, SPOUT, SPROUT, STOUSH, THOUSAND, THOU *obsolete*, [dhow], TOUSLE, TOUT, TROUNCE, TROUSERS, TROUT, VOUCH, WOUND Δ *around*, ROUSE *verb*, STOUSH, VOUCH.

Irregular verb, present, past, p. participle
BIND Δ, BOUND Δ, BOUND Δ
FIND Δ, FOUND Δ, FOUND Δ
GRIND Δ, GROUND Δ, GROUND Δ
WIND Δ, WOUND Δ, WOUND Δ

The <b> in *doubt* is silent. It was *dubitare* in Latin but lost [b] on the way through France to England. Later, overly keen Renaissance scholars wrote <b> back in, to link it with its cousin-word *dubious* and its Latin ancestor *dubitare*.

In verbs *espouse and *house <s> spells [z], as explained earlier. As we'd expect, in nouns *spouse* and *house*, <s> spells [s]. Beware, verb *souse ends [s] for it matches the verb *to sauce* in origin and meaning. The verb *douse, to toss water or drench with water, ends [s], to separate it from *dowse* [dowz], to find water.

*Like *foot* and *feet*, the singular words *mouse* and *louse* undergo the process of umlaut to make their plurals *mice* and *lice*. They were one *mus* [moos] and many *mys* [mees]; and one *lus* [loos] and many *lys* [lees]. When words change their vowel sounds to indicate plurals, we say they undergo "umlaut" which means "change sound about" in German. With French spelling, *mus* became *mous* and *lus* became *lous*. Then, in the Great Vowel Shift, their vowels lifted: [oo] lifted and bent into [ow] and [ee] lifted and bent a little into [I]. Prof. Lerer says the high vowels [oo] amd [ee] lifted, hit the roof of the mouth and bent into the diphthongs [ow] and [I].

House rhymes with *mouse* but we do not say two *hice*. However, when we add <s> to *house*, for many *houses*, they now sound very different — [hows] and [howzez], with <s> following stressed [e] in *houses* and therefore spelling [z]. This does not happen after stressed [ow] in *house* and *louse* because <s> is followed by <e>.

Mouth. We say one [mowth] but many [moudhz] for *mouth* and *mouths*. The verb *to mouth* spells [mowdh] — *I mouth* [mowdh] and *he mouths*, [hee] [mowdhz]. In "my mouth's dry," we hear [mowths] because <s> no longer follows a voiced word-sound.

Thousand [thowz-and] is often shortened to *thou* [thow], retaining the unvoiced [th]. It was once *thuo-hund* "swollen hundred," coined by our ancestors who did not know how to count beyond a hundred when out hunting a herd of more than a hundred, (Fleck 2007). When *thousand* is shortened to *grand*, it is from French for *large*.

List 4-43 Words built on stem words in which <ou> spells [ow].

ABOUT-FACE, ABOUT-TURN, ACCOUNT-BOOK, BY ALL ACCOUNTS, KEEP ACCOUNTS, ON ACCOUNT OF, TAKE INTO ACCOUNT, TURN TO ACCOUNT, ACCOUNTABLE, ACCOUNTABILITY, ACCOUNTANT, ACCOUNTANCY, AGROUND, ALL OUT, ALL-ROUND, ALL-ROUNDER, ABOUND, ANY AMOUNT, BACKGROUND, BAKEHOUSE, BATTLEGROUND, BLOODHOUND, BOUNCER, BOUNCING, BOUNCY, BOUND TO, BOUNDARY, BOUNDEN *adj.*, BOUNDER, BOUNDLESS, BOUNDS, OUT OF BOUNDS, BOUNTIFUL, BOUNTY, CAROUSEL, UNDER A CLOUD, CLOUDBURST, CLOUDLESS, CLOUDY, CLOUDINESS, COME ABOUT, COMPOUND, CONCOURSE, CORNFLOUR, COUNCIL HOUSE, COUNCILLOR, COUNSELLOR, COUNTABLE, COUNTENANCE, COUNTER, COUNTERACT, COUNTER-ATTACK, COUNTERBALANCE, COUNTERCHECK, COUNTERCLAIM, COUNTER-ESPIONAGE, COUNTERFEIT, COUNTER-INTELLIGENCE, COUNTERMAND, COUNTERMEASURE, COUNTER-OFFENSIVE, COUNTERPANE, COUNTERPART, COUNTER-PRODUCTIVE, COUNTERSIGN, COUNTERSINK, COUNTERVAIL, COUNTERWEIGHT, COUNTESS, COUNTLESS, DEVOUTLY, DEVOUTNESS, DISCOUNT, AT A DISCOUNT, DISCOUNT SHOP, DOGHOUSE, DORMOUSE*, DOUBTING THOMAS, NO DOUBT, WITHOUT DOUBT, WITHOUT A DOUBT, DOUBTFUL, DOUBTFULLY, DOUBTLESS, ENSHROUD, ESPOUSAL, FARMHOUSE, FLOURY, FOUL-MOUTHED, FOUL PLAY, FOUNDER, FOUNDRESS, FOUNDER, FOUNDATION, FOUNDATION-GARMENT, FOUNDATION-STONE, FOUNDLING, FOUNDRY, FOUNTAIN, FOUNTAIN-PEN, FOXHOUND, GADABOUT, GLASSHOUSE, GOUGE, GREYHOUND, GROUCHY, GROUND GLASS, GROUND RICE, GROUNDING, GROUNDLESS, GROUNDLESSLY, GROUNDS, GROUNDSEL, GROUNDSHEET, GROUNDSMAN, GROUNDWORK, HIDEBOUND, HOREHOUND *herb*, HOUND, HOUSE-AGENT, HOUSE-BOUND, HOUSE-DOG, HOUSE-FLY, HOUSE OF CARDS, HOUSE PARTY, HOUSE-PROUD, HOUSE-TO HOUSE, HOUSE-TRAINED, HOUSE WARMING, LIKE A HOUSE ON FIRE, IT'S ON THE HOUSE, HOUSE ARREST, HOUSEBOAT, HOUSEBREAKER, HOUSECOAT, HOUSECRAFT, HOUSEFUL, HOUSEHOLD, HOUSEHOLDER, HOUSEKEEPER, HOUSEKEEPING, HOUSEMAID, HOUSEMASTER, HOUSEMISTRESS, HOUSEWIFE, HOUSEWIFERY, HOUSEWORK, HOUSING [how-ziŋ], HOUSING ESTATE, IMPOUND, INSURMOUNTABLE, LAYABOUT, LOUDLY, LOUDNESS, LOUD HAILER, OUT LOAD, LOUDSPEAKER, LOUNGE, LOUNGE SUIT, LOUSY, LOUSE UP, LOUTISH, MADHOUSE, MISCOUNT, MOUNTED, MOUNTAIN, MOUNTAINEER, MOUNTAINOUS, MOUNTEBANK, MOUSER [mow-ser], MOUSETRAP, MOUSING [mow-siŋ], MOUSY [mow-see], MOUTH-WATERING, MOUTHFUL, MOUTH-ORGAN, MOUTHPIECE, MOUTHWASH, NOUS*, OUCH! *slang*, OURSELVES, OUT-AND-OUT, OUTFLOW, OUTGROW, OUT-OF-DATE, OUT OF DOORS, OUT-PATIENT, OUT-TRAY, OUT WITH IT, OUTBID, OUT-TALK, OUTBACK, OUTBOARD, OUTBREAK, OUTBUILDING, OUTBURST, OUTCAST, OUTCLASS, OUTCOME, OUTCROP, OUTCRY, OUTDATED, OUTDISTANCE, OUTDO, OUTDOOR, OUTDOORS, OUTER, OUTER SPACE, OUTERMOST, OUTFACE, OUTFALL, OUTFIELD, OUTFIT, OUTFITTER, OUTFLANK, OUTGOING, OUTHAUL, OUT-HEROD HEROD, OUTHOUSE, OUTING, OUTLANDISH, OUTLAST, OUTLAW, OUTLAY, OUTLET, OUTLINE, OUTLIVE, OUTLOOK, OUTLYING, OUTMODED, OUTMOST, OUTNUMBER, OUTPACE, OUTPOST, OUTPUT, OUTRAGE, OUTRANK, OUTRIDER, OUTRIGGER, OUTRIGHT, OUTRUN, OUTSELL, OUTSET, OUTSHINE, OUTSIDE, OUTSIDER, OUTSIZE, OUTSKIRTS, OUTSMART, OUTSPOKEN, OUTSPREAD, OUTSTANDING, OUTSTANDINGLY, OUTSTAY, OUTSTRIP, OUTVOTE, OUTWARD, OUTWARDLY, OUTWARDS, OUTWEIGH, OUTWIT, OUTWORK, OUTWORN, PARAMOUNT, PENTHOUSE, PLAYGROUND, POUND NOTE, POUNDAGE, PRONOUN, PRONOUNCEABLE, PRONOUNCEMENT, PROUD, PROUDLY, RECOUNT, RE-

COUNT, REDOUBTABLE, REDOUND, REMOUNT, RENDEZVOUS, RENOUNCE, RESOUND, RESOUNDING, IN THE ROUND, ROUND ABOUT, ROUND AND ROUND, ROUND OFF *v.*, ROUND ON *v.*, ROUND ROBIN, ROUND-TABLE CONFERENCE, ROUND THE CLOCK, ROUND TRIP, ROUNDEL, ROUNDERS, ROUNDISH, ROUNDLY, ROUNDSMAN, ROUNDWORM, ROUSING, ROUSTABOUT, ROUTER, SCOUTING *n.*, SCROUNGER, SHOUT DOWN, SOUND *adj. n. v.*, SOUND BARRIER, SOUND EFFECTS, SOUNDING-BOARD, SOUND OFF, SOUND OUT, SOUND-PROOF, SOUND-TRACK, SOUNDING, SOURNESS, SOUR CREAM, SOUR GRAPES, SOURPUSS, SOUSED *slang*, SOUTH-EAST, SOUTH-EASTERLY, SOUTH-EASTERN, SOUTHPAW, SOUTHWARD, SOUTHWARDS, SOUTH-WEST, SOUTH-WESTERLY, SOUTH-WESTERN, SOU'WESTER, STRIKEBOUND, SURMOUNT, SURROUND, TANTAMOUNT, THEREABOUTS, TOUCHABLE, TROUSER-SUIT, OLD TROUT, UNACCOUNTABLE, UNACCOUNTABLY, UNDERGROUND, UNFOUNDED, UNSOUND, OF UNSOUND MIND, VISCOUNT*, VISCOUNTESS*, VOUCHER, VOUCHSAFE, WALKABOUT, WALKING-TOUR, WAREHOUSE, WATERSPOUT, WITHOUT, WOLFHOUND, WOODLOUSE, WORKHOUSE. <u>Australian words</u> OUTBACK, OUTSTATION, ROUSEABOUT, SOURSOB, VOUCHER, VOUCHSAFE, WALKABOUT. <u>Proper Nouns</u> SOUTH AFRICA, SOUTH AUSTRALIA, SOUTH POLE, SOUTH SEA, SCOUTER, NEWFOUNDLAND, MOUNTIE, HOUSE OF COMMONS, HOUSE OF LORDS, GEIGER COUNTER, ROUNDHEAD.

*Dormouse is *dormice* for more than one but they are not mice – the Normans called them *dormeus* meaning *sleepy, dormant,* and the English thought they were saying *dormouse,* (Bryson 2004, p. 62.)

*Nous [nows] is listed as an informal word. In Greek, *nous* means "mind", the means by which we perceive the world. "Use your nous," means use your commonsense as well as your knowledge. Psychologists have a name for this process of cognition or thinking, *noesis,* a formal word, based on Greek *nous,* (Fleck 2007).

*Viscount spells [vI-cownt], *viscountess* spells [vI-cown-tes]. Prof Cummings says long [I] occurred when [s] was dropped, in speech. It began as *visconte,* meaning 'vice count', French for 'deputy earl'. Some folk kept saying [s], some did not, but the dictionary committee chose to keep <s> but only as a silent letter, to show its history and meaning.

Cold Shoulder Words — *boulder, shoulder.*
Rule 4-44 <oul> consonant spells [ohl] or [ol].
Reason We have seen that <o> spells [oh] in *cold* and *folk* — also that we say [fohk] which is easier than [fohlk], and [kold] which is easier than [kohld]. We know that *hole* should spell [hohl] but many of us say [hol]. We know that [l] loves vowels and given the choice, clings to vowels, not consonants. So when <l> is followed by a consonant, it chooses to cling to the preceding vowel. This modifies the vowel sound.
In the following 'cold shoulder' words, <ou> can spell [oh] but usually [o].
Not Really Rebels COULD§ [kuud], SHOULD§ [shuud], WOULD§ [wuud].
Rebels' Reasons They aren't rebels. We met these 'rappers' in Part One, dancing to a tune of their own. Long ago they were quite different, *cuthe, sceolde* and *wolde.* Then the Normans changed the vowel letters to <ou> and a bit later *could* received the letter <l> in order to match its work mates. Then later on, about three hundred years ago, people stopped saying the [l] but kept writing <l> to show they are all mates, three words in which <ould> does not spell [old]. "[shuud] we care? [kuud] we care? Why [wuud] we care?" they said to each other and refused to join the other <ould> words.
These 'rappers' are auxiliary verbs, just like the auxiliary verbs CAN§, SHALL§* and WILL§*.

*You may remember that when it is going to happen anyway, without any effort, we say *I shall, you will, he, she* or *it will.* Also, *we shall, you will, they will.* However, when it requires effort and will power, we say, *I will, you shall, he, she* or *it shall.* Also *we will, you shall, they shall.*

e.g., "We shall eat our dinner soon and you shall eat your greens!"

Note, the transitive verb *to will* is not an auxiliary verb. Its present, past and participle form is WILL, WILLED, WILLED as in "I have willed my estate to you," and so it is a regular verb.

List 4-44 "Cold Shoulder" words
BOULDER, MOULD, MOULDER, MOULDINESS, MOULDING, MOULDY, MOULT, POULTERER, POULTICE, POULTRY, SHOULDER, SHOULDER ARMS, SHOULDER-BAG, SHOULDER-BLADE, SHOULDER-HIGH, SHOULDER-TO-SHOULDER, SMOULDER.

Plus, *soul*, which although has no consonant after <l> and spells [sohl], can also spell [sol], but, as we know, definitely not [sowl]. (The *sole* of a foot also spells [sohl] or [sol], and both *sole* and *soul* rhyme with *bowl* but not with *owl* nor *foul*.)
SOU, SOULFUL, SOULLESS

Bossy R and <ou> — *arbour, court, your.*

Rule 4-45 <our> spells [or] unless followed by a stressed vowel.

Reason Bossy R makes <our> spell [or]. The <u> is now obsolete and in USA it has been removed. It is one of the few reforms which Noah Webster was allowed to make in his dictionary. He was told to remove most of his reformed spellings because his publisher predicted that England would reject them. "You need to sell to the English," he said to Webster, "Unless you want to end up in debtors' prison." The few changes which were allowed meant that, since 1828, *colour* is spelt *color* in USA. Americans also write *favor* and *honor* without the <u>. Anglo English does this a little, in words like *error, terror* and *stupor,* and everyone drops the <u> in words like *vaporize,* from *vapour, honorific* and *honorary* from *honour, coloration* from *colour* and *colourful*. Some use *honorable* too, in place of *honourable*.

Rebels DOUR, FLOUR, SOUR, OUR, HOUR silent <h>, SCOUR, DEVOUR.

Rebels' Reasons If these were pronounced <our> spells [or] they would create homophones with *door, floor, soar, or/ore, whore, score*. *Dour* spells [door], which rhymes with *lure,* and means hard-nosed, hard-hearted, and comes from French *dure* which means 'hard', (Fleck 2007), as in English *durable, enduring*. We would expect *devour* to spell [dee-vor] because it is related to *voracious* [vor-ay-shuus] but as *de* is a prefix the stress is on *vour* and it falls in with the other **Rebels** and lets <our> spells [ow].

More Rebels COURTESY, SCOURGE, and words with cluster <journ>, e.g., JOURNAL, which is [joo-r-nal] in French.

Rebels' Reasons The following rebs are still spelt the way they arrived from France but their sounds have changed, so that now <our> spells [er]:-
ADJOURN, COURTESY, COURTEOUS, COURTEOUSLY, DISCOURTEOUS, DISCOURTEOUSLY, DISCOURTESY, JOURNAL, JOURNALESE, JOURNALISM, JOURNALIST, JOURNEY, JOURNEYMAN, SCOURGE, SOJOURN.

(We see many more leaving the mainstream and following this lot, if <our> is terminal, as in *glamour, colour, favour, humour*.)

More Rebs COURAGE, DISCOURAGE, FLOURISH, NOURISH, NOURISHMENT in which <our> spells [u] when <our> is followed by an unstressed suffix beginning with a vowel.

Rebels' Reasons These words are related to "Utterly Motherly" and can soon be added to {"Mother's Country Cousins".} As we remember, the Old English suffix –*ish* always comes after a short vowel, as in *rubbish* and *bishop* and these words of French origin have taken on English endings and fallen under their "spell", have followed the English pattern.

List 4-45 <our> spells [or]
ARBOUR, ARDOUR, BEHAVIOUR*, BICOLOUR, BOURBON, BOURGEOIS, BOURGEOISIE, CANDOUR, CLAMOUR, CLANGOUR, COURGETTE, COLOUR* *f*[kul-or], COLOURS, COLORANT, COLOURED, COLOURFUL, COLOURING, COLOURLESS, COURSE, OF COURSE,

IN DUE COURSE, COURT, COURT-CARD, COURTESAN, COURTIER, COURTLY, COURTLINESS, COURT-MARTIAL, COURTSHIP, COURTYARD, DISCOLOUR, DISCOURSE, DISHONOURABLE* silent h, DOWNPOUR, ENAMOURED, ENDEAVOUR [en-dev-or], FAVOUR [or, er], FAVOURABLE, FAVOURABLY, FAVOURITE, FAVOURITISM, FERVOUR, FLAVOUR, FLAVOURING, FOUR, FOUR-LETTER WORD, FOUR-POSTER, FOUR-WHEEL, FOURFOLD, FOURSOME, FOURTEEN, FOURTH, GLAMOUR [er, or], HARBOUR, HONOUR* silent h, HONOURABLE* silent h, HUMOUR [er, or], INTERCOURSE, LABOUR, LABOURER, LAW COURT, MISDEMEANOUR, MOURN, MOURNFUL, MOURNFULLY, MOURNFULNESS, MOURNING, NEIGHBOUR, NEIGHBOURHOOD, NEIGHBOURING, NEIGHBOURLY, PARLOUR, PARLOURMAID, POUR, POURER, POUR COLD WATER ON, RACECOURSE, RANCOUR, RECOURSE, HAVE RECOURSE TO, RESOURCE, RESOURCEFUL, RESOURCEFULLY, RESOURCEFULNESS, RIGOUR, SAVIOUR*, SAVOUR, SOURCE, AT SOURCE, SPLENDOUR, TAMBOURINE, TRICOLOUR, TUMOUR* [choomer/or], UNSAVOURY, VALOUR, VAPOUR, VIGOUR, WATERCOURSE, YOUR, YOURS, YOURS TRULY, YOURS EVER, YOURS FAITHFULLY, YOURS SINCERELY, YOURSELF.

*The word *colour* spells [kulor], not [kolor]. So we mark it with the sign of the feather, *f*. *Cover* spells [kuver] and arrived first, from France around 1150. However *colour* was never a feather word and so we should say [kolor] not [kulor]. It was French *colur* when it came into English. The French got it from Latin *colur* which had grown from Old Latin *colos*. Now *colos* means "a covering", "covered in colour". To show off that they knew of this ancient link between the words *cover* and *colour* the dictionary committee wrote *colour* for [kulor] even though there was no need to turn it into a feather word. *Cover* is a feather word, a cursive casualt, as is *colour*.

Where <our> is unstressed the sound is often closer to [er] than [or] but it is also a matter of choice, e.g., for *colour* we can say [kul-or] or [kul-er] but when it is *coloured* most folk say [kul-erd].

*In *honour* and *honourable*, <h> is silent, as discussed in Part Two. In America, the spelling has been simplified to *honor, honorable, honorably*. In Australia, *honourable* is often written *honorable*, also *dishonorable*. They spell [on-ra-buul], [dis-on-ra-buul], to avoid two weak beats.

Note, **saviour* spells [sayv-yor] and **behaviour* spells [bee-hayv-yor], because, to avoid two weak beats in the suffix <iour>, the [i] became a yod, [y].

Queen Elizabeth 1st inadvertently saved the Welsh language by having the Bible translated from Latin into Welsh, to break their allegiance to Rome. Prior to that it was translated into English, which can be said to have saved the English spelling of the day for ever! The book and its words became sacred to English speakers everywhere. It was impossible for dictionary makers to change the spelling of words like *psalm* without upsetting entire congregations and 'to spell *Saviour* as *Savior* would shock the piety of thousands' to quote a quote from Hewitt, p. 594.

Relevant Writing Rule. When adding *ous, ate* or *ite* to terminal *our* drop the <u>, *humour-humorous, labour-elaborate, vapour-evaporate,* **except for** *favour-favourite* [fayv-er-rət], (or just say [fayv-rət] to avoid two weak beats). Return to Reading Rules.

Suffix <ous> — *amorous, wondrous.*

Rule 4-46 Suffix <ous> spells [uus]

Reason Suffixes are unstressed. Many words with suffix <ous> gain additional suffixes as seen below, e.g., —*ously,* —*ousness*. Even then, <ous> spells [uus]. All words ending <ous> are adjectives. Words ending <us>, which also spells [uus], are nouns.

List 4-46 <ous> spells [ows] but when unstressed <ous> spells [uus].
ADVANTAGEOUS, ADVENTUROUS*, ADVENTUROUSLY*, AMOROUS, AMOROUSLY, AMOROUSNESS, AMORPHOUS, ASYNCHRONOUS [ay-sin-kron-uus], AUTONOMOUS,

BARBAROUS, BARBAROUSLY, BITUMINOUS*, BULBOUS, CADAVEROUS, CALLOUS, CANTANKEROUS, CARNIVOROUS, CIRCUITOUS, CIRCUITOUSLY, CLAMOROUS, CONIFEROUS, COURAGEOUS, COVETOUS *f*, CREDULOUS*, DANGEROUS, DECOROUS, DESIROUS, DEXTROUS, DIAPHANOUS, DISASTROUS, DISASTROUSLY, DOLOROUS, ENORMOUS, EROGENOUS, FAMOUS, FABULOUS, FELICITOUS, FERROUS, FIBROUS, FRIVOLOUS, GELATINOUS, GENEROUS, GIBBOUS, GLUTINOUS, GLUTTONOUS, GORGEOUS, GRIEVOUS, HEINOUS* [hay-nuus], HERBIVOROUS, HETEROGENOUS, HUMOROUS, HUMOROUSLY, HYDROUS, IMPIOUS*, INCREDULOUS*, INDIGENOUS, INFAMOUS [in-fə-muus], INIQUITOUS, INTRAVENOUS, JEALOUS, JEALOUSLY, JEALOUSY, LANGUOROUS, LEGUMINOUS, LIMOUSINE*, LUMINOUS, MARVELLOUS, MIRACULOUS, ADVANTAGEOUS, COURAGEOUS, CURVACEOUS, MONOTONOUS, MUCOUS, MULTITUDINOUS, MURDEROUS, MUTINOUS, NECESSITOUS, NERVOUS, NITROUS, OBSTREPEROUS, OMINOUS, OMNIVOROUS, OUTRAGEOUS, OUTRAGEOUSLY, PENDULOUS, PERILOUS, PESTIFEROUS, PIOUS*, POMPOUS, POMPOUSLY, PONDEROUS, POPULOUS, POROUS, POSTHUMOUS*, POSTHUMOUSLY*, PRECIPITOUS, PRECIPITOUSLY, PREPOSTEROUS, PROSPEROUS, PROSPEROUSLY, PUSILLANIMOUS, QUERULOUS, RAMPAGEOUS, RAUCOUS [ror-kuus], RAVENOUS, RAVENOUSLY, RESINOUS, RIDICULOUS, RIGOROUS, SCABROUS, SCANDALOUS, SCRUPULOUS, SCRUPULOUSLY, SCRUPULOUSNESS, SCURRILOUS, SEDULOUS*, SEDULOUSLY*, INCONGRUOUS, SOLICITOUS, SONOROUS, STERTOROUS, STUPENDOUS, SULPHUROUS, SYNCHRONOUS, [sin-kron-uus], THUNDEROUS, TIMOROUS, TREACHEROUS, TREACHEROUSLY, TREMENDOUS, TREMENDOUSLY, TREMULOUS, TUBEROUS, TYRANNOUS, UBIQUITOUS, UNANIMOUS, UNANIMOUSLY, UNSCRUPULOUS, UNSCRUPULOUSLY, VAPOROUS, VENOMOUS, VENOMOUSLY, VERMINOUS, VERMOUTH, VIGOROUS, VIGOROUSLY, VIGOROUSNESS, VILLAINOUS, VISCOUS, VOCIFEROUS, VOLUMINOUS, WONDROUS.

Note that in *advantageous, courageous, gorgeous, outrageous, outrageously* and *rampageous,* the suffix is <ous>, not <eous>, because <e> is in the stem word, softening [g] to [j].

Limousine can spell [lim-uus-een] but usually [lim-uu-zeen], which reduces even further to [lim-ə-zeen], due to the tum-te-tum rhythm of English.

*These are palatalized words due to Yod Fusion.

Heinous spells [hay-nuus], see *weigh*.

*The <h> in *posthumous* and *posthumously* is silent. The original word was *postumus,* from Latin for *coming after,* but then scholars related it to death and burial and added <h> from *humus,* Latin for earth.

Note that *infamous* has a stressed prefix, to stress the fact that "not famous" does not mean "not well known". It means "bad". The Roman goddess Fama was the goddess of rumour, hence *infamous* means 'of bad rumour', 'has a bad reputation'.

In *pious* [pI-uus], <i> spells [I] which is a good example of <i> spells [I] in the first syllable of a stem word. Consequently, in *impious* too.

Suffix <uous> — *ambiguous, vacuous.*

To make adjectives we usually just add <ous>, e.g., *danger, dangerous*. Sometimes <ous> is added to a bound or stripped stem ending <u>, as in *continu ous*. We shall now see words in which the suffix <ous> follows <u> spells [yoo]. It has to spell its long sound in order to glide onto the short vowel in [uus], which is written <ous>, but because it is in a suffix, it spells unstressed [uus], not [ows]. As we know, when <u> spells its long sound, then <tu> spells [choo] and <du> spells [joo]. Also, <su> spells [shoo] in some words. We shall list such Yod Fusion words later.

Rule 4-47 <uous> spells [yoo-uus] but with Yod Fusion it spells [uus].

Reason In the next list we glide <u> spelling [yoo] on to the suffix <ous>. Now, being a suffix, <ous> is already unstressed and quite short but [yoo] glides and lands on <ous> and makes it "yap" and sound therefore even shorter and sharper, so that it sounds like [uus].

Rebels? If the speaker is a Yod Dropper, after [d], [n] or [t], [yoo-us] will be [oo-us], eg., [kon-tin-oo-us] for *continuous*. These words are not rebels, just a branch of a living language.

List 4-47 <uous> spells [yoo-us]

AMBIGUOUS, AMBIGUOUSLY, CONGRUOUS, CONSPICUOUS, CONSPICUOUSLY, CONSPICUOUSNESS, CONTIGUOUS, CONTINUOUS, CONTINUOUSLY, DISINGENUOUS, EXIGUOUS, INCONGRUOUS, INCONGRUOUSLY, INCONGRUITY, INCONSPICUOUS, INGENUOUS, INGENUOUSLY, INGENUOUSNESS, INNOCUOUS, MELLIFLUOUS, PERSPICUOUS, PROMISCUOUS, PROMISCUOUSLY, SINUOUS, STRENUOUS, SUPERFLUOUS, SUPERFLUOUSLY, TENUOUS, TENUOUSLY, TENUOUSNESS, UNAMBIGUOUS, VACUOUS.

Yod Fusion Words

Yod Fusion [sh] Words SENSUOUS [sen-shoo-uus].

Yod Fusion [j] Words in which <duous> spells [joo-uus]: ARDUOUS, ASSIDUOUS, DECIDUOUS, ARDUOUS, ASSIDUOUS, DECIDUOUS.

Yod Fusion [ch] Words in which <tuous> pells [choo-uus]: CONTEMPTUOUS, CONTEMPTUOUSLY, CONTEMPTUOUSNESS, FATUOUS, FATUOUSLY, FATUOUSNESS, FRUCTUOUS, IMPETUOUS, INCESTUOUS, PRESUMPTUOUS, PRESUMPTUOUSLY, PRESUMPTUOUSNESS, SPIRITUOUS, SUMPTUOUS, TEMPESTUOUS, TORTUOUS*, TORTUOUSLY, TUMULTUOUS, UNCTUOUS, VIRTUOUS, VIRTUOUSLY, VIRTUOUSNESS, VOLUPTUOUS, VOLUPTUOUSLY, VOLUPTUOUSNESS.

Suffix <eous> — *crustaceous, herbaceous.*

Suffix <eous> spells [ee-uus] unless <eous> follows [s] or [t] or [j] or [z] and then <eous> spells [uus] after yod fusion.

Rule 4-48 After [s] or [t], Yod Fusion occurs with suffix <eous> which then spells [uus].

Reason We know that Yod Fusioin occurs to prevent two weak beats. The following words are long. We do not get Yod Fusion after [d] in *hideous*. Possibly because the word has only three syllables, tum-te-tum. It was *hideus* in Old French and before that it was *hisdos*, see Etymonline. So in this case <eous> is not a suffix. There is no other word ending <deous>.

List 4-48

BEAUTEOUS, beautiful, BOUNTEOUS* bountiful, CURVACEOUS [kerv-ay-shuus], FARINACEOUS [fa-rin-ay-shuus], LILIACEOUS [lil-ee-ay-shuus], NAUSEOUS* [nor-zhuus], PLENTEOUS* plentiful, RIGHTEOUS [rI-chuus]. Scientific Terms CARBONACEOUS, CETACEOUS, CRUSTACEOUS, DIATOMACEOUS, DRUPACEOUS, ERICACEOUS, FOLIACEOUS, HERBACEOUS, LACTEOUS*, OLIVACEOUS, ORCHIDACEOUS, PAPILIONACEOUS, PECTINACEOUS, PROTEINACEOUS, PUMICEOUS, ROSACEOUS, SAPONACEOUS, SEBACEOUS, SILICEOUS, SOLANACEOUS, VINACEOUS, VIOLACEOUS.

*Beauteous, *bounteous and **plenteous* are rarely spoken, just written for literary impressiveness. So, on paper, there is no Yod Fusion with [t], but I expect fusion could happen if the words are used in speech.

*Nauseous spells [nor-zhuus] because it comes from the verb 'to be sea-sick' which is related to *nautical* and *navy*. Verbs have voiced endings to separate them from their parent nouns, but as we know, if the noun was made from the verb, it retains [z]. Some writers use *nauseated* for stomach sickness and reserve *nauseous* for 'sickening to contemplate' or 'disgusting to look at.'

As we'd expect, the <t> in **righteous* and **lacteous* is palatalized to [ch].

When <eous> follows other sounds, other than [s] and [t], it glides and yaps.

Rule 4-49 Suffix <eous> spells [ee-uus] unless <eous> follows [s] or [t] and then <eous> spells [uus].

Reason It follows gliding rules and so the glider, <e>, spells its long sound. The target, <ous>, spells short yappy [uus], not [ows]. There is no glide and yap when Yod Fusion means <eous> spells just [uus].

List 4-49
AQUEOUS, COURTEOUS, CUTANEOUS, DISCOURTEOUS, ERRONEOUS, EXTEMPORANEOUS, EXTRANEOUS*, GASEOUS, HIDEOUS, HETEROGENEOUS*, HOMOGENEOUS*, INSTANTANEOUS, MISCELLANEOUS, PITEOUS, SIMULTANEOUS, SPONTANEOUS, VITREOUS. <u>Scientific Terms</u> CALCAREOUS, CINEREOUS, CITREOUS, CORNEOUS, CUPREOUS, FERREOUS, IGNEOUS, LIGNEOUS, LUTEOUS, MUCOCUTANEOUS, OCHREOUS, OSSEOUS

Extraneous has the long vowel of *strange,* close cousin-words, meaning the same thing.

Heterogeneous and *homogeneous* are sometimes spelt just <ous>, not <eous> but that is not accepted as correct. Note, the <hom> of *homogeneous* spells [hom], not [hohm].

Suffix <ious> — *amphibious, victorious.*

As we see from the encoding tips, many words end in <ious>. Because suffixes are unstressed, this means <i> is a Little Imp. We know how to read words in which Little Imp works his wonders on others, but not on himself. We also expect that there will be lots of Yod Fusion words, words in which [t] and [s] fuse with yod.

Rule 4-50 Suffix <ious> spells [ee-uus] unless <ious> follows [s] or [t] and then <ious> spells [uus].

Reason If <i> of <ious> is in a first syllable, <ious> spells [I-uus], as in *pious,* as we'd expect, because <i> spells [I] in first syllables of stem words. It should spell little unstressed [i] in <ious> when a suffix, and suffixes are unstressed. However, in order to glide onto [uus] it has to be a bit longer than [i] and becomes [ee]. Unstressed <i> followed by another unstressed vowel, [uu], is a Little Imp, and as we know, he works wonders on the others but not himself, so that <bil> in *bilious* spells [bil] not [bIl] but <o> in *odius* spells [oh]. We have seen [i] resist lengthening before two vowels before, as in *vision.* Of course, the other vowels will not lengthen behind double gates e.g., *atrocious* spells [a-troh-shuus] but *pretentious* spells [pree-ten–chuus]. The second list, B, has Yod Fusion words in which <ious> does not spell [ee-uus]. In list A there is one Yod Fusion [j] word, **dubious* [joo-bee-uus], and one Yod Fusion [ch] word **studious* [schoo-dee-uus] but the Yod Fusion is not in the —*ious* suffix.

List 4-50A Suffix <ious> spells [ee-uus] in these words.
ABSTEMIOUS, ABSTENTIOUS, ACRIMONIOUS, AMPHIBIOUS, BILIOUS* [bil-yuus], CENSORIOUS, CEREMONIOUS, COMMODIOUS, COMPENDIOUS, COPIOUS, CURIOUS, DELETERIOUS, DELIRIOUS, DEVIOUS, DUBIOUS*, EGREGIOUS, ENVIOUS, EUPHONIOUS, FASTIDIOUS, FELONIOUS, FURIOUS, GLORIOUS, GREGARIOUS, HARMONIOUS, HILARIOUS, IGNOMINIOUS, ILLUSTRIOUS, IMPECUNIOUS, IMPERIOUS, IMPERVIOUS, INDUSTRIOUS, INGENIOUS, INGLORIOUS, INJURIOUS, INSIDIOUS, LABORIOUS, LASCIVIOUS, LUGUBRIOUS, MALARIOUS, MELODIOUS, MERETRICIOUS, MERITORIOUS, MULTIFARIOUS, MYSTERIOUS, NEFARIOUS, NOTORIOUS, OBLIVIOUS, OBSEQUIOUS, OBVIOUS, ODIOUS, OMNIFARIOUS, PARSIMONIOUS, PENURIOUS, PERFIDIOUS, PERVIOUS, PRECARIOUS, PREVIOUS, PUNCTILIOUS, REBELLIOUS, SALUBRIOUS, SANCTIMONIOUS, SERIOUS, SPURIOUS, STUDIOUS*, SUPERCILIOUS, SYMPHONIOUS, TEDIOUS, UPROARIOUS, UXORIOUS, VAINGLORIOUS, VARIOUS, VICARIOUS, VICTORIOUS.

*After <n> or <l>, <i> glides as [y] as in *bilious* and *onion.* However, this is happening less as Queen Quill gains power over King Sound. E.g., *alien* [ayl-ee-en] is no longer [ayl-yen] but, then again, we still say *spaniel* spells [span-yel].

List 4-50B Words in which <ious> spells just [uus] due to Yod Fusion.
ADVENTITIOUS, AMBITIOUS, ANXIOUS, ATROCIOUS, AUDACIOUS, AUSPICIOUS, AVARICIOUS, BODACIOUS*, BILIOUS, BODACIOUS, BUMPTIOUS, CALUMNIOUS, CAPACIOUS, CAPRICIOUS, CAUTIOUS, CONSCIENTIOUS, CONSCIOUS, CONTAGIOUS*, CONTENTIOUS, DELICIOUS, DIECIOUS or, DIOECIOUS, DISPUTATIOUS, DISSENTIOUS, EXPEDITIOUS, FACTIOUS, FACTITIOUS, FALLACIOUS, FEROCIOUS, FICTITIOUS, FLIRTATIOUS, FRACTIOUS, GRACIOUS, INAUSPICIOUS, INCAUTIOUS, INFECTIOUS, INJUDICIOUS, JUDICIOUS, LICENTIOUS, LITIGIOUS, LOQUACIOUS, LUSCIOUS, LUXURIOUS, MALICIOUS, MENDACIOUS, NOXIOUS*, NUTRITIOUS, OBNOXIOUS, OFFICIOUS, OSTENTATIOUS, PERNICIOUS, PERSPICACIOUS, PERTINACIOUS, PRECIOUS, PRECOCIOUS, PREDACIOUS, PRESTIGIOUS, PRETENTIOUS, PRODIGIOUS, PROPITIOUS, PUGNACIOUS, RAMBUNCTIOUS, RAPACIOUS, RELIGIOUS, REPETITIOUS, SACRILEGIOUS, SAGACIOUS, SALACIOUS, SCRUMPTIOUS, SEDITIOUS, SEMICONSCIOUS, SEMIPRECIOUS, SENTENTIOUS, SILICIOUS, SPACIOUS, SPECIOUS, SUBCONSCIOUS, SUPERSTITIOUS, SUPPOSITIOUS, SURREPTITIOUS, SUSPICIOUS, TENACIOUS, TORTIOUS, UNAMBITIOUS, UNCONSCIOUS, UNCONTENTIOUS, UNGRACIOUS, UNOSTENTATIOUS, UNPRETENTIOUS, UNSUSPICIOUS, VEXATIOUS, VICIOUS, VIVACIOUS, VORACIOUS.

Bodacious seems very new, but appeared back in 1832, *bold* plus *audacious,* (Fleck 2007).

Noxious is the opposite to *innocuous* which was listed earlier. *Noxious* spells [nok-shuus], but *innocuous* spells [in-nok-yoo-uus]. This is because the stress pattern changes. As we know, Little Imp shrinks to a yod in *noxious* and turns [s] into [sh], the [s] coming from <x> spelling [ks]. Little Imp does not 'work wonders' on <o> because <o> is behind the double gates of [ks] spelt by <x>. However, in *innocuous*, <c> does not spell [s] and cannot therefore be changed to [sh].

Relevant Writing Rule. When **making** adjectives, just add —*ous** (danger, dangerous) **but** if the word

A) ends —*y* this must be removed and replaced with <i>: *fury, furious.*

B) ends with silent *"Fairy E"* this must be removed: *fame, famous.*

C) ends in <e> which softens <g> it must remain: *courage, courageous.* [ku-ray-juus]

D) ends in <e> which softens <c> it must be replaced with <i> *space, spacious* [spay-shuus]; *vice, vicious* [vish-uus].

E) ends in <l> then it must be twinned: *marvel, marvellous.*

F) ends —*our* then remove the <u>: *humour, humorous.*

*Two **Rebels**: *disaster, disastrous; monster, monstrous.*

When writing words which come **ready-made**, based on Greek and Latin stems which are not free stems, not words in their own right, we just have to learn them: e.g., *curious, fabulous, delicious* and *hideous,* which is not based on the word *hide*. It comes from an Old French word *hideus* which meant 'horror and fear' and began as *hisda,* (Etymonline).

When deciding whether to write <ious> or <eous> remember that <eous> is quite rare and it is joined onto materials, like water, *aqueous*. If it is <aceous> it means "belonging to or connected with a family of plants like such and such a plant," e.g., *herbaceous* means a herb-like plant, *liliaceous* means a lily-like plant. It also means "belonging to or connected with a group of animals like such and such an animal," e.g., *cetaceous* means whale-like and *crustaceous* means crab-like, or "in a mineral group containing such and such a mineral", like *carbonaceous,* in a mineral group containing carbon.

The dictionary makers said that if a word came from a Latin word ending <eus> then it would end <eous> in English. Latin words ending <ius> became English <ious> words, but then English got lots of words without direct Latin parents and so they said: "If any English noun ending <ion> can make an adjective, it will end in <ious>, e.g., *caution, cautious.*"

The choice <eous> or <ious> is not clear cut, e.g., *righteous* was once *right-wise* but it was changed to match *beauteous* and *bounteous,* both of which came from Norman English words ending [ee]. *Beauteous* comes from *beaute, bounteous* comes from *bounte* – easier to use *beautiful* and *bountiful*! Return to Reading Rules.

French digraph <ou> — *boulevard, group, you.*

Rule 4-51 Terminal <ou> spells [oo]. Medial <ou> spells [o] in recent French adoptions.

Reason Terminal <ou>, although rare, probably only in *you* and *thou,* never spelt [ow]. It was [oo] spelt by <ou> which lifted to [ow] in the GVS., as we have seen, in *house* etc. As we saw, in Rule 4-42, digraph <ou> spells [ow] inside stem words except before <ld>, as in *could*, <lt> as in *moult* and <rt> as in *court*, and in recent French adoptions such as in list 4-51 below. It is surprising to see that *group* is a 'recent' French adoption, arriving well after the GVS, at the end of the seventeenth century.

After the GVS new French words using <ou> to spell [oo] entered English. Note how <ou> spelling [oo] usually occurs before a consonant plus vowel.

Rebels THOU, BOUQUET.

Rebels' Reasons The only word in which terminal <ou> spells [ow] is *thou*. Long ago it was *thu* (like French *tu*). It was the singular form of *you.* You had many forms, singular and plural, as in: 'Thou see me and I see thee and thy friends, and thine enemies. Ye are all very good to me. I want to thank you all for your help.' Now we just have *you* and *your*. It appears to me that *thou* [dhoo] lifted in the GVS to [dhow] and *you* did not. *Bouquet* spells [boh-kay], instead of the French [boo-kay], maybe to match with *beau* [boh]. Young ladies received *bouquets* from their *beaus*. Now they get flowers from their boyfriends.

List 4-51 In the more recent French adoptions and some newish English words <ou> spells [oo].
ACAJOU*, ACCOUTREMENTS, AMPOULE, BAYOU*, BARRACOUTA, BILLET-DOUX, BIVOUAC, BOUDOIR [boo-dwar], BOULEVARD, BOUTIQUE, BROUGHAM, BROUHAHA, CANTALOUP, CARIBOU*, CHOUX *silent x*, COUCHETTE, COUCH-GRASS, COUGAR, COUPON, COUTURE, CROUP, CROUPIER, CROUTON, DOUCHE <ch> =[sh], GHOUL* *silent h*, GOULASH, GHOULISH*, GROUP, GROUP CAPTAIN, GROUP PRACTICE, GROUP THERAPY, GROUPIE, HOURI, LOUVER or LOUVRE, MARABOU*, MOUSSAKA, MOUSSELINE, MOUSTACHE*, NOUGAT [noo-gar], OUZEL BIRD, PATCHOULI, PIROUETTE, POT-POURRI, POUF/POOF, POUFFE/POOF, RECOUP, REGROUP, RE-ROUTE, ROCOU*, ROUCOU*, ROUGE <ge>=[jsh], ROULETTE *fossil e*, ROUTE, ROUTINE, ROUTINELY, ROUX *silent x*, RUSSIAN ROULETTE, SILHOUETTE*, SOU*, SOUFFLÉ, SOUP, SOUPÇON, SOUVENIR <ir> =[eer], THANK YOU, TOUCAN, TOUCHÉ, TROUBADOUR*, TROUPE, TROUPER, TROUSSEAU, UNCOUTH, WOUND, *noun,* YOU, YOUTH, YOUTH CLUB, YOUTH HOSTEL, YOUTHFUL, YOUTHFULLY, YOUTHFULNESS, YOU'VE. Proper Nouns, GOUDA, KHARTOUM, LOUISIANA, BEDOUIN, BOUGAINVILLAEA. Names DOUGAL, LOU, LOUISE, LOUIS.

*Ghoul was adopted from *ghul*, a translation from the Arabic word. The <gh> remained because *ghoul* seemed right for a "ghastly ghost". *Ghoul, ghoulish, ghoulishly, ghouls. Ghost* was a whim of Caxton, England's first printer. He picked up a liking for the Dutch <gh> combo during his printing apprenticeship. It's the third word Caxton popped <h> into.

*Moustache spells [moo-starsh] if using the modern French pronunciation but it arrived earlier in England as [mos-tarsh] from Italy and Spain, and it usually continues to be said like that, although it uses the French spelling, *moustache*.

*Silhouette is an eponym, from the name of French politician Étienne de Silhouette, who is said to have liked making dark cut-out pictures against white backgrounds. He is also known for his cut-price economies when finance minister in the 1750's, (Ayto, p. 477).

Sou, rocou, roucou, caribou, acajou, bayou are rare words for it is very unusual for a word to end in <u> and they should be labelled "rebel" but they have "diplomatic immunity" for they are foreign words — except for *you*, which made its excuses earlier, in Part One. Note, there is as yet no such word as *thankyou*, for it is two words, *thank you.*

Troubadour [troo-bə-dor] can now be listed. We already know that terminal <our> spells [or].

R is not bossy Touring in Velour — *tour, velour.*

Rule 4-52 <our> spells [oor] in words which came into English later than words in which <our> spells [or].

Reason We are told that originally in England and most of Europe, <o> spelt short [o] and long [or]. Then English [or] rose to [oh] and then [oo] in the GVS. We are told that *more* continues to spell [mor], unlike *mote* [moth], because of Bossy R. So, let's say that *four* spells [for] because of Bossy R, unlike words in which <ou> changed from [oo] to [ow] in the GVS, as in *house.* Then when new words arrived from France, in which <ou> spelt [oo], after the GVS, they continued with their [oo] vowel, the craze for lifting long vowels having ceased.

List 4-52 In these words <our> spells [oor], [oo] with the English, non-rhotic <r>, just a shadow of [r], a little schwa sound. My [oor] is expressed in IPA with /u:ə/, long [oo] followed by schwa.
COURIER, DETOUR, DOUR, GOURD, GOURMET* [goor-may], PARAMOUR, POMPADOUR*, TOUR, TOUR DE FORCE, TOURISM, TOURIST, TOURIST CLASS, TOURIST TRAP, TOURISTY, TOURMALINE, TOURNAMENT, TOURNEDOS, TOURNIQUET <quet>=[kay], VELOUR.

Pompadour is an eponym. Google Jeanne-Antoinette Poisson, Marquise de Pompadour.

Now that we have met *gourmet*, we can make a list of all the words in English which end <et> spells [ay] for we have now met them all.
BALLET, BERET, BOUQUET, BUFFET, CACHET, CROCHET, CROQUET, GOURMET, PARQUET, RICOCHET, SACHET, VALET.

Not needed but nice to know. Try reading this now: "The courier in velour gave the dour tourist a tourmaline bangle from her paramour in tourist class, before eating tournedos at the tournament. He had to detour around the gourmet at the next table — the chap with his hair in a pompadour, eating from a gourd — in order to loosen the bangle which had become a tourniquet on the fat arm of the dour faced dowager." Now back to things we need to know.

We saw in Part Three how *mother, brother, other, smother* etc all have the short vowel [u]. Now we shall see more "Utterly Motherly" words, words whose vowels utter [u] but whose letters are still in fetters – are locked in time, cannot change.

Mother's Country Cousins — *country, youngster.*

Rule 4-53 The digraph <ou> spells [u] in some "Utterly Motherly" words and in "Mother's Country Cousins".

Reason As we know, <ou> is pulled back into the throat to spell [u] in *courage, flourish* and *nourish.* We look for patterns. *South* is [sowth] and *moth* is [moth] but when a vowel follows <th> two things happen. As we learnt in Part Three when <er> starts a syllable after <th>, then <th> spells [dh]. This voiced [dh] pushes the vowel behind it back into the throat to spell [u]. So *southern* spells [su-dhern], like *mother* spells [mu-dher]. We see more patterns. Before <ng> we see <ou> pulled into the throat to spell [u] in *young* from Old English. Also in *rough,* from Old English *ruh* and *rug,* <ou> spells [u]. In words from France, <ou> was dragged down the throat to spell [u] before [nt], [pl], [bl], [ch] and [z], (Cummings, p. 247). For example, in *country, couple, double, touch* and *cousin* <ou> spells [u]. They share a vowel with

333

mother so let's call them her "Country Cousins". Their old French letters spell the new sound [u] but their letters are in fetters, chained to the past, for <ou> has not changed to <u>.

Rebel ROUBLE [roo-buul

Rebel's Reason *Rouble* is a Russian word and is pronounced the Continental way, not like *double*. It is also spelt *ruble,* in which, as expected, <u> spells [oo].

List 4-53 <ou> spells [u] in "Utterly Motherly" and "Country Cousin" words.
COUNTRIFIED, COUNTRY, COUNTRY-&-WESTERN, COUNTRYMAN, COUNTRYSIDE, COUPLE, COUPLET, COUPLING, COURAGE, COURAGEOUS, COUSIN, COUSINLY, CROSS-COUNTRY, DOUBLE, DUGOUT*, AT THE DOUBLE, DOUBLE AGENT, DOUBLE-BREASTED, DOUBLE-CHECK, DOUBLE-CROSS, DOUBLE-DECKER, DOUBLE ENTRY, DOUBLE FIGURES, DOUBLE GLAZING, DOUBLE-DUTCH, DOUBLE-JOINTED, DOUBLE OR QUITS, DOUBLE-PARK, DOUBLE-QUICK, DOUBLE TAKE, DOUBLE-TALK, DOUBLE ENTENDRE, DOUBLER, DOUBLOON*, REDOUBLE, RETOUCH, BE NO TROUBLE, DOUBLE-BANK, DOUBLE-DINK, DOUBLE-GEE, ENOUGH*, FLOURISH, GO TO SOME TROUBLE, IN TOUCH WITH, IN TROUBLE, MAKE TROUBLE, NOURISH, OUT OF TOUCH, *ROUGH <gh>=[f], SLOUGH* *verb*, SOUTHERLY*, SOUTHERN*, SOUTHERNER*, SOUTHERNMOST, TAKE TROUBLE, THERMOCOUPLE, TOUCH, TOUCH BOTTOM, TOUCH DOWN, TOUCH OFF, TOUCH UP, TOUCH WOOD, TOUCHABLE, TOUCH-AND-GO, TOUCHDOWN, TOUCHED, TOUCHER, TOUCHINESS, TOUCHING, TOUCHINGLY, TOUCH-JUDGE - (in rugby), TOUCH-LINE, TOUCH-PAPER, TOUCHSTONE, TOUCH-TYPING, TOUCHWOOD, TOUCHY, TOUGH*, TROUBLE, TROUBLE-MAKER, TROUBLE-SHOOTER, TROUBLESOME, TROUBLE-SPOT, UNCOUPLE, UNTOUCHABLE, YOUNG, YOUNGISH, YOUNGSTER. "Distant Cousin" DOZEN* [duz-en]. Name DOUGLAS.

Doubloon is English from Spain but in English its <ou> spells [u], being worth a double Spanish gold pistole coin.

Dugout was a hollowed log for a boat until it gained a new meaning in trench warfare of World War One. Our soldiers brought home more new words like *oo-roo* from French *au revoir, jeep* from *general purpose vehicle, snafu* from *situation normal, all f-d up.* See Burton, p. 214, for more of these 'war words'.

Southerly [su-dher-ly] means "sunly", towards the sun, which is towards the equator when standing in Europe. *Sunthaz* was prehistoric German for 'sun-side' which is why south in Europe means towards the equator. It's the opposite in Australia.

Dozen comes German *dutzend* and Old French *dozeine,* originally a Latin compound *duo-decim,* two plus ten.

Gruff <ough> — *tough, enough.*

We have just seen *rough* etc. in the list of Utterly Motherly words. Now we can meet the Irish Rebel who stayed put and still spells guttural <gh> in *lough*. *Lough* went to Scotland as *lock* and travelled on to England as *lake*. *Lock,* too, is used in England for the gate and man-made lake in a river. *Hiccup* was *hiccup* until it decided to join *cough*. So, it changed to *hiccough,* but it does not really sound like a cough at all. So, it reverted back to *hiccup* and the word *hiccough* is now obsolete. Do you remember when <gh> spells [f]?

Rule 4-54 After a short vowel, <gh> spells [f], and <ough> spells [uf].

Reason We know that <gh> was used to spell a guttural choking sound which came to England with Saxons and other German speakers. It was written with the old letter yogh, <ȝ>, at first, but the Normans preferred <gh>. It still spells guttural [gh] in Irish *lough*, [logh]. This guttural sound is softer in Scotland, in *loch* [lokh]. In England these Germanic sounds of Old English were dropped after 1066, under French Occupation. Since then, <gh> spells [f] after short vowel sounds and just goes silent after long vowel sounds. We have seen <gh> spelling [f] after another short vowel, in the original pronunciation of *laugh* [laf].

Rebels COUGH, TROUGH; LOUGH, BOROUGH, THOROUGH, with a soft [th]. Also THOROUGHLY, THOROUGHNESS. Place Name YARBOROUGH.

Rebels' Reasons *Cough* [kof] obeys the rule that when <gh> spells [f] the vowel before it is short. However, in *cough* <ou> spells [o], not [u], because of its German start as *kokh*. Maybe French *houper*, 'to cry out', influenced the spelling. *Trough* is the same, with a short vowel before <gh> spelling [f] and yet it too breaks the rule that <ou> spells [u] before <gh> spells [f]. Why? It was Germanic *trog* in Old English (Etymonline) and it seems that French scribes re-wrote it when they took over after 1066.

The Irish word lough [logh] has kept its guttural sound so that <gh> does not spell [f] but spells a sound which has been lost from English, [gh]. Originally, *borough* sounded like [ber-ber]. It's the [er] sound we hear in its cousin word *burgh,* German for *town*. 'Burgh and burgh' (burgh-burgh) make up a region of towns named a 'borough'. Also *thorough* ended in a long vowel sound like *through* for it means "through and through", through every part, [throo] [and] [throo], which became just [thoo-roo]. The more the English stressed the beginning of these words, the shorter the first vowels became and the weaker the endings became. So *borough* became [bu-rə] and *thorough* became [thu-rə] but the old letters <ough> stayed because English words cannot end in <u>, they could not write *buru* and *thuru* and so no one changed the old way of writing *borough* and *thorough*. Place names are proper nouns and do not have to obey rules but Yarborough is listed to show that its ending has a short vowel too. So does South Australia's Peterborough, fondly referred to as 'The Burra'. Coincidentally, *burra* is used in Aboriginal place names, e.g., Queensland's Binna Burra, Ab'l for "where the beeches grow". In many Aust. Ab'l languages it means *great, place* or *big stone,* ref. Cockburn, p. 34, and in Hindustani it means *great,* too.

List 4-54 <ough> spells [uf]

CHOUGH [chuf] bird, ENOUGH [ee-nuf], ROUGH [ruf], SLOUGH* [sluf] *verb*, TOUGH [tuf]; **with suffixes** ROUGHLY, ROUGHNESS, ROUGHAGE, ROUGHEN; **in compound words** ROUGHCAST, ROUGHNECK; **in common usage** 'NOUGH'S ENOUGH, ROUGH-AND-READY, ROUGH-AND-TUMBLE, ROUGH DIAMOND, ROUGH HOUSE, ROUGH IT, ROUGH JUSTICE, ROUGH SHOOTING, ROUGH UP.

*Slough first referred to a snake losing its skin, called a *slug* back then. Later it meant losing any dead or diseased skin.

Silent <gh> — *plough, dough, through.*

General Rule. When terminal <gh> follows long vowels, it is silent.

Reason We know the guttural [gh] sound was scorned by the French conquerors of England and that [gh] changed to [f] after short vowels, as in *tough*. When [gh] went silent after long vowels it could not be dropped from written words, for then <u> would become terminal and English words cannot end in <u>, as we know. Various ways of writing these words were tried out. Some old words had <ough> spells [oo] but they changed to [ow] and some even changed their letters to match, or tried to, like *plow*. In America *plough* is *plow* but in England after changing from *plogr* to *plowghe* to *plow* it fell into a rut with *bough* and the old noun *slough,* as in Bunyan's "Slough of Despond" in Pilgrim's Progress, (not the verb 'to slough [sluf] off skin'.) The end result is that silent <gh> after <ou> spells many different sounds. We see a silent <gh> after other long vowels, too, as in *neigh, weigh* and *high.*

Rule 4-55 After a long vowel, terminal <gh> is silent and <ough> spells either [ow], [oh], or [oo].

Reason Historic, as detailed below. As a memory aid for each word, remember that out [owt]side we *plough* [plow] near the *slough* [slow] and under the shady *bough* [bow], in all of which <ough> spells [ow], even *though* [dhoh] at home [hohm] we take leave of our work, take a *furlough,* [fer-loh] even *although* [orl-dhoh] others are busy in the kitchen kneading *dough,* [doh] we play cards and hope for a *yarborough* [yar-broh], in all of which <ough> spells [oh]. Then we remember that a 'choo-choo' train, goes *through* a tunnel to remind us that in *through*, <ough> spells [oo].

List 4-55A <ough> spells [ow]
BOUGH, PLOUGH, SLOUGH

Reason Onomatopoeia is a big word which means the sound of a word is matched to the sound of the thing it describes, for instance, *cuckoo* sounds like a cuckoo. Some say, digraph <ow> spells the 'bent' sound, double-sound, diphthong [ow], in three words because each is a 'bent stick' rather than a 'straight bone', [bohn].

Digraph <ough> spells bent vowel [ow] in *bough* because a bough bends. As we already know, *boc* [boh] was a piece of straight wood and *boech* was 'bent wood', later written *bough*.

Digraph <ough> spells [ow] in *plough* because the original straight digging stick developed into the "crooked plough" when the Greeks took the Egyptian stick, which was held by hand behind a beast, fitted wheels to it and bent the stick towards the draft animal. This meant the stick no longer scratched the soil but instead, due to its angle, it slid under the soil and ripped it open, see www.ploughman.co.uk. The Americans have spelt it *plow* but the English use *plough*. We have heard that it changed from *plogr* to *plowghe* to *plow* and then fell into a rut with *bough* and now we shall hear why. The Latin word for plough is "arere" hence the English word *arable* which means 'capable of being ploughed'. A plough was also called a *plovus* (<v> spelt [w] in Latin) in the mountains north of Rome and from here it spread across northern Europe. During the 400 years that Britain was a Roman colony there were strict laws that every man, every Celt, had to make his own plough and could not lend it, nor borrow someone else's. For those who could write, it was *plog, ploh* or *plow*. The plough did not improve at all until the Dutch designed a much better one in the 1600's which the English adopted with enthusiasm. The Dutch name for *plough* was a lot like their *plug,* the wooden stick the Dutch stuck in bottles at sea to stop them spilling. Eventually the word *plough* was chosen, for it retains a lot of history in its letters — the consonants make us think of *digging* with a *plug* of wood, but most of all the diphthong [ow] makes us think of the original brainwave to bend a digging stick. Either way, American *plow* or English *plough,* we hear the diphthong [ow] and it takes us right back to the big change from a straight to a bent digging stick.

So, *bough* and *plough* are both bent things with bent sounds, diphthong [ow].

What about *slough?* We know the verb *slough* spells [sluf] with links to an old slug (snake) losing its skin but the noun comes from an old English word *sloh* which spelt [slo-h] with [h] pronounced back in the throat. It was related to the Viking word *slumpe*, 'to fall or sink or slip into a muddy place' and the two words seemed to have combined to produce [slow] written *slough.* Now, it's a long shot to say this represents a bent stick, but we know if we fall into a *slough* we are no longer up-right but very bent over.

List 4-55B <ough> spells [oh].
DOUGH, THOUGH, ALTHOUGH, FURLOUGH, YARBOROUGH.

Except for *yarborough,* these words never did end in a guttural [gh]. A *yarborough* is a hand of thirteen cards in bridge or whist containing no ace and no card higher than a nine. Some people do not like having their names diminished by shortening. Such was the Second Earl of Yarborough. His name, he insisted, ended in [oh], and it was given to this hand of cards, after he bet 1,000 to 1 against its occurrence.

Dough, though and *although* are Old English words and so they could have used terminal <ow> spells [oh]. They do not represent 'bent' things, they are not 'bendy' and so they could have used terminal [ow] spells [oh] but instead they fell in the <gh> rut. None of them ended with old yogh <ʒ>, or <gh>, originally, but some of them had connections to the letter <g>, as we shall see.

Furlough was Dutch *verlof* meaning "permission for leave", and so maybe it was at first in the rut with *cough* and other words in which <gh> spells [f] after short vowels but when its vowel lengthened to [oh] the <gh> went silent.

Dough used to be *duff,* still is, up North in England where dough is made in to delicious plum duff. Down South it changed its short vowel into long [oh] and so the [f] sound went silent. The *dough* spelling came about because long ago men grew the grain and ground it into flour and women kneaded it into dough. They had to *dig* into it to knead it and so it was originally called *dig*. The combination of *dig* and *duff* gives us *dough.*

Though was travelling along really well before it fell in the <ugh> rut. It arrived in England as [dho], written sometimes with Eth and sometimes with Thorn. They may have started out spelling either soft or hard <th>, [th] or [dh]. Nobody knows, for their use was very muddled. Neither Eth <ð> nor Thorn <þ> were amongst the cases of metal letter stamps which arrived in England with the first printing presses and so *Secret Agent H was used, combined with <t>, to spell both [th] and [dh]. *Tho* looked very much like the little word *the,* and might have been mistaken for it. The dictionary makers fixed that by spelling its long [oh] sound with <ough> and so it fell in the rut with *dough* and *furlough.* *Also known as Helpful, Handy Haitch, handy because it was available because the French hardly used <h> in their own language. Still don't, e.g. *has* is *as* in French.

When paper got a tax on it, in the early 1700's, *though* was pulled out of the rut! A tax on paper meant that to save paper they shortened it, using a circumflex to show letters are missing, as in *thô* for *though, thorô* for *thorough*, and *brôt* for *brought*. Then newspapers got around the tax on each page of paper by printing fewer, bigger pages, (which is why sheets of newspaper are so big today) and so there was room for full words again. By the time the tax was dropped, in 1855, *though* had slipped back into the rut, but help was at hand. Benjamin Franklin had written *A Scheme for a New Alphabet and a Reformed Mode of Spelling* in 1779, (see 'childrenofthecode' web site), and another American, Noah Webster, liked his ideas very much. He wanted to use *tho* in his dictionary but his publisher reminded him that he had huge debts, and that such reforms would be unpopular in England, which had the population he needed, to sell books to cover his debts.

So *though* remained in the rut, until pulled out by no less than a president of USA, President Roosevelt! (He is the one nicknamed "Teddy", president from 1901 to 1909, not his fifth cousin "FDR" Roosevelt, president of USA 1933-45.) In 1906 the President ordered the man in charge of printing all government forms and circulars to change the spelling of the 300 words which had been improved by USA's Simplified Spelling Board, amongst them these new spellings: *tho, thoro, thorofare, thoroly, thru,* and *throughout*.

Roosevelt wrote, "There is not the slightest intention to do anything revolutionary or initiate any far-reaching policy. The purpose simply is for the Government, instead of lagging behind popular sentiment, to advance abreast of it … if they meet popular approval, then the changes will become permanent. They are just a slight extension of the unconscious movement which has made agricultural implement makers write "plow" instead of "plough"; which has made most Americans write "honor" without the somewhat absurd, superfluous "u"; and which is even now making people write "program" without the "me"—just as all people who speak English now write "bat," "set," "dim," "sum," and "fish" instead of the Elizabethan "batte," "sette," "dimme," "summe," and "fysshe"; which makes us write "public," "almanac," "era," "fantasy," and "wagon," instead of the "publick," "almanack," "aera," "phantasy," and "waggon" of our great-grandfathers. It is not an attack of the language of Shakespeare and Milton, because it is in some instances a going back to the forms they used, …merely an attempt to…make our spelling a little less foolish and fantastic." (This is only a part of his letter.)

Well, people might have liked this idea but the press went mad. They teased the President for being a notoriously bad speller since childhood and ridiculed, instead of praising him, for trying to help others to read and write. Reporters said it was a plot to give publishers a lot of work and money, re-printing dictionaries and school books. The British papers cunningly hinted USA was not a free democracy. "Here is the language of 80 million people suddenly altered by a mere administrative edict," marvelled an English paper. "Could any other ruler on earth do this thing?"

In the end, the Supreme Court refused to follow the President, as did the House of Representatives, which voted 142-24 to overturn Pres. Roosevelt's order. The President withdrew his spelling edict and admitted defeat in this "undignified contest." (See https://en.wikipedia.org/wiki/English-language_spelling_reform.

List 4-55C THROUGH [throo].

As we have seen in *thorough*, which began as *through and through,* the word *through* was *thuru* until it became wrong to end a word in <u> and so <gh> was added to insulate <u>. It's a shame that <e> was not added as insulation instead. For a long time (300 years until 1700's), *through* was spelt like *to*, as *thro*. Everyone understands *thru* but it is not generally used or accepted. *Through* is the only word in which <ough> spells [oo]. As we know, yods drop after [r], as in *ruby* and *rue,* but there was no need in *through*. *Through* never spelt [thryoo] because <ou> never spelt, nor spells, [yoo], as we learnt when we met the English Yod. There is only one other word in which [oo] precedes <gh>. It's the name *Hugh,* in which <u> spells [yoo] because, unless [oo] is spelt with French <ou> or English <oo>, the long sound is [yoo]. After that's established, when de-coding, let the [y] drop after [r], [l] and [j] or fuse with preceding [d], [t], [s] and [zh] — if you are Australian. Americans drop additional yods, after [d] and [t].

Rule 4-56 Each <ought> spells [ort], and is in past participles of verbs.
Reason Vowels before <ght> are dragged further back in the mouth than vowels before just <gh>. We saw this in *caught* and *taught,* where <aught> spells [ort]. It is the same for words ending <ought>, for <ou> is dragged back further in the mouth than [ow] to [or].
Rebels NOUGHT spells [nort] but is not a past participle; DROUGHT spells [drowt], not [drort].
Rebels' Reasons *Nought's* excuse:- The English used *ne,* like French, for *not*. They did not have the word *not* until later. To say there was "absolutely not anything" they used "ne a whit" — *ne owiht* — which became shortened to *nowt,* which changed to the [nort] pronunciation, and then matched its spelling to <ought> words. Some places in England still say [nowt] but most say [nort].
Drought is a spelling mistake. *Drought* should be *drougth*. A drought is a *long dry* or, in Old English, a *lang drug.* From these old words we got *length* and *drougth.* To cut a long story short, England's French conquerors could not say [th], just [t]. So they reversed <t> and <h> and we are now stuck with a [t] ending instead of a [th] ending.

List 4-56
BOUGHT Δ, BROUGHT Δ, FOUGHT Δ, OUGHT§, SOUGHT Δ, THOUGHT Δ, WROUGHT Δ, BESOUGHT Δ, **plus** FORETHOUGHT, OVERWROUGHT, OUGHTN'T§, SOUGHT AFTER, WROUGHT IRON.

You can see the past participles of verbs in the list of irregular verbs below. They are all old words, as we would expect, for only old verbs are what we now call irregular. Once upon a time all verbs changed their inside sounds to show a change of time. Nowadays we just add <ed>. One of these old verbs has become "regular": Today *I owe* but yesterday *I owed.* We no longer say "Yesterday *I ought."* The old way is in Shakespeare's 1596 play Henry IV: "He said this the other day, you ought him a thousand pound." We now only use *ought* to add power to other verbs.

§ *Ought* is now an auxiliary verb, like an auxiliary engine to other verbs, e.g., "I ought to make my bed." *Ought not* can be abbreviated to *oughtn't* "You oughtn't to light fires."

Irregular verbs – present, past and p. participle.
BUY Δ, BOUGHT Δ, BOUGHT Δ
BRING Δ, BROUGHT Δ, BROUGHT Δ
FIGHT Δ, FOUGHT Δ, FOUGHT Δ
SEEK Δ, SOUGHT Δ, SOUGHT Δ
THINK Δ, THOUGHT Δ, THOUGHT Δ

WORK Δ, WORKED/WROUGHT Δ, WORKED/WROUGHT Δ –*wrought* is very uncommon now, mainly used as an adjective, e.g., *wrought iron*.
BESEECH Δ, BESOUGHT Δ /BESEECHED, BESOUGHT/BESEECHED
　　Congratulations: —
So now you clearly know, of *tough* and *bough* and *cough* and *dough*.
Others may stumble, but not you, on *hiccough, thorough, slough* and t*hrough*.
Read these to me, off you go: *tough* and *bough* and *cough* and *dough*.
As you grow, the more you know.

Digraph <oy> — *annoy, tomboy.*

The Greek letter <y> does not let <o> do the talking in the digraph <oy>. As we know, <y> lets <a> do the talking in *day, may, say etc.* because that <y> replaces the old English letter yogh. The double sound or diphthong [oi] did not exist in Old English words, (Cummings p. 301). It was only used in shouts and cries, pseudo words. For instance, *ahoy* is an old Viking battle cry, (like the Aussie 'battle' cry when barracking at sporting events: "Ozzie, Ozzie, Ozzie, Oy, Oy, Oy). The sound got into English words from Southern Europe. In Old English, *boil* sounded like *bile*. We can write [oi] in two ways. You guessed it. We write <oy> to spell [oi] at the end of words because <i> is not allowed to end words. As <y> is not allowed inside words, (except for the ones adopted from Greek), we use <oi> to spell [oi] in the middle of words.

Rule 4-57　<oy> spells [oi] only at the end of stem words.

Reason We already know why terminal <i> is a 'no-no' but we need to remember that stem words can get suffixes and then <y> appears to be inside words but is actually the end of a stem word, either a free stem, as in *enjoyment*, or a bound stem, like *flamboyant*. So <y> is allowed inside a word when a suffix is added to a stem ending vowel　<y>, e.g., *buoyant, buoyantly* and *buoyancy, enjoyment*. (As we know, when <y> follows a consonant, we do not see this: *merry, merriment*.)

Rebels　DOYEN, DOYENNE, GROYNE, HOYDEN, HOYDENISH, COYPU, HOYA, OYSTER and GARGOYLE in which <oy> spells [oi] inside words.

Rebels' Reasons　*Doyen* (Old French *deien*) was a church leader (dean) of ten men, and only referred to a female leader recently, *doyenne*. *Hoyden* is based on the very old word *heiden*, for 'heathen'. Neither syllable, *doy* nor *hoy*, is a stem word. *Groyne* means a strong, low sea wall, named after *groin*, the obsolete French word for a pig's snout, the nose of a 'grunter'. Land jutting into the water is often named after noses, e.g., "Ningaloo", a point along the Quobba Coast, WA, means 'nose' in the local Ab'l language and many place names in England end in *ness,* from French *nez* for 'nose'. *Coypu* has been adopted from South America but not adapted and has "diplomatic immunity" to break two rules: no <u> at the end of English words and no <y> inside stem words other than Greek words. *Oyster* was spelt correctly, *oister* from French *oistre,* until someone thought it should match the look of the last letters in *youngster* or *gangster,* and changed <i> to <y>, more like <g> in shape. *Gargoyle* inserted <y> inside Old French *gargouille* "throat, waterspout" to draw attention to the second syllable and stress it and separate it from its cousin-word *gargle. Hoya* plants are named after Mr Thomas Hoy, head gardener for an English Duke. Robert Brown, the botanist who named the plants after Hoya, arrived in Australia with Flinders in Dec. 1801 and continued to collect plants all over Australia until May 1805. Science students know of him through his Brownian motion, biology students might know that he was the first to name the HQ in a cell its "nucleus". We have heard a lot of background on words with medial <oy> but no Greek connections. Letter <y> has been wrongly inserted in all but *coypu* and the eponym *hoya*.

List 4-57
ANNOY, AHOY! V*iking battle cry, seaman's attention call*, ALLOY, BLACKBOY, BOY, BOYHOOD, BOY-FRIEND, BOYCOTT*, BOYISH, BOYISHLY, BOYISHNESS, BOYSENBERRY*, BUOY*,

CORDUROY*, COY, DESTROY, DESTROYER, EMPLOY, EMPLOYABLE, EMPLOYEE, EMPLOYER, EMPLOYMENT, ENJOY, ENJOYABLE, ENJOYABLY, FLAMBOYANT, FLAMBOYANTLY, FLAMBOYANCE, JOY, JOYFUL, JOYLESS, JOYOUS, JOY-RIDE, JOY-RIDER, JOY-RIDING, KILLJOY, LOYAL bound stem *loy*, LOYALTY, LOYALIST, PLOY, REDEPLOY, ROYAL, ROYALLY, ROYAL BLUE, ROYAL FLUSH, ROYAL ICING, ROYALIST, ROYALTY, SAVELOY, SAVOY CABBAGE, SELF-EMPLOYED [em-ploid], SONOBUOY*, SOY, SOYA BEAN stem *soy*, TALLBOY, TOMBOY, TOY, TOY WITH, TOYSHOP, TROY WEIGHT, UNALLOYED, UNEMPLOYABLE, UNEMPLOYED, UNEMPLOYMENT, VICEROY, VOYAGE bound stem *voy*, WHIPPING-BOY. *Names ALROY, FLOYD, GILROY, JOY, JOYCE, LLOYD, ROY.

Corduroy spells [kor-joo-roi] due to Yod Fusion.

Noisome has nothing to do with *noisy*. It is related to *annoy*, which spells [an-noi], not [ə-noi].

*There is only one word in which [oi] is spelt <uoy>: *buoy*, as in *life-buoy* [boi]. Prof. Cummings, on page 296, tells us that <u> in *buoy* once spelt [w]. Etymonline suggests that *buoy* is possibly a combination of the old French word *buie* and the Middle Dutch word *boeye*. As in *build*, <u> is silent now.

Sonobuoy is a 'portmanteau' word, which evolved from *sonar buoy*. (Etymonline).

Boycott and *boysenberry* both are eponyms. These 'common nouns' originate in the names of Charles Boycott and Rudolph Boysen. They were once compound words: *boy cott* meaning "cottage boy" and *boy sen* meaning "son of boy". Google these names and learn why they formed eponyms.

*Names are allowed to be unruly, like *Joyce,* but *Floyd* and *Lloyd* are from Wales where <y> goes inside words. *Gilroy* must be a very old name because <gi> spells [gi] not [ji] in *Gilroy*.

Digraph <oi> — *anoint, void.*

Rule 4-58 Digraph <oi> spells [oi] inside words, but not before Bossy R.

Reason Letter <y> is replaced by <i> inside words. Note that although we hear yods in *soya* and *hoya*, [soy-yar] and [hoy-yar], we do not hear them in *paranoia* and *sequoia,* [pa-ra-noy-u] and [sə-kwoy-u], according to the OPD.

Rebels CHAMOIS, PORPOISE, TORTOISE, in which <oi> does not spell [oi], COIF [kwaf], COIFFURE [kwaf-yoor], POI. Proper Noun HANOI.

Rebels' Reasons *Porpoise* [por-puus] means pork fish because it is chubby and has the snout of a pig. Long ago the Romans called it *porculus marinus* which means *sea pig* in Latin. *Fish* is *piscis* in Latin and so the French shortened it to *por-pis* for *pig-fish*. This changed to *porpais* and the English thought it was a French word like *turquoise*. *Tortoise* [tor-tuus] probably comes from Latin *tortus* meaning twisted because the feet of a tortoise look a bit twisted, a bit tortured. It was spelt *tortuse* in 1495 but then it changed to *tortoise,* maybe to mimic *porpoise*. In French *chamois* [sham-war] is a small wild antelope but the English say [sham-ee] for *chamois* and mean "soft leather", not an antelope. It's been adopted and its sound adapted, without adapting the spelling. French fashion words like *coif* and *coiffure* are readily adopted but not adapted. In *poi* ,<oi> spells [oi] at the end of a word, breaking the no terminal <i> rule. *Poi* [poi] is Hawaiian and so it has "diplomatic immunity." As we know, Proper Nouns, like *Hanoi,* do not have to obey rules.

List 4-58 <oi> spells [oi]

ADENOIDS, ADENOIDAL, ADJOIN, ADROIT, ADROITLY, ADROITNESS, ANDROID, ANEROID BAROMETER, ANOINT, ANTHROPOID, APPOINT, APPOINTEE, WELL-APPOINTED, APPOINTMENT, APPOINTMENTS, ASTEROID, AVOID, AVOIDANCE, AVOIDABLE, BOIL, BOILER, BOISTEROUS, BORZOI, BROIL, BROILER, BROILER HOUSE, CASTOR OIL, CELLULOID, CHOICE, CLOISTER, CLOISTERED, COIL, COIN, COINAGE, CONOID, COUNTERFOIL, COUNTERPOISE, DEVOID, DISAPPOINT, DISAPPOINTED, DISAPPOINTMENT, DISJOIN, DOILY*, EMBROIDER, EMBROIL, ENJOIN, EXPLOIT,

EXPLOITATION, FIBROID, FLASHPOINT, FOIBLE, FOIL, FOIST, FUNGOID, GUMBOIL, GOITRE, GROIN*, HAEMORRHOIDS, HOI POLLOI*, HOIST, HOITY-TOITY, HUMANOID, HYDROFOIL, INVOICE, JOIN, JOIN BATTLE, JOIN HANDS, JOIN FORCES, JOIN UP, JOINER, JOINERY, JOINT, JOINT-STOCK COMPANY, OUT OF JOINT, JOINTLY, JOIST, LOIN, LOINCLOTH, LOITER*, LOITERER, MALADROIT, MASTOID, MATCH POINT, METEOROID, MILFOIL, MOIETY, MOIST, MOISTEN* silent <t>, MOISTURE, MOISTURIZE, MOISTURIZER, NEEDLEPOINT, NOISE, NOISELESS, NOISOME, NOISY, NOISINESS, OIL, OIL-COLOUR, OIL-PAINT, OIL-PAINTING, OIL-TANKER, OIL THE WHEELS, OILCAKE, OILCAN, OILCLOTH, OILFIELD, OILSKIN, OILY, OINTMENT, OVOID, PARANOIA, PARANOID, PARBOIL, POIGNANT silent g, POINSETTIA, POINT, POINT-BLANK, POINTED, POINTER, POINTLESS, POISE, POISON, POISONER, POISON PEN, POISONOUS, PURLOIN, RECONNOITRE*, RECOIL, REJOICE, REJOIN, RHEUMATOID, RHOMBOID, ROISTERING, SCHIZOID, SEQUOIA, SIRLOIN*, SOIL, SOLENOID, SPOIL Δ, STANDPOINT, SUBJOIN, SUBSOIL, THYROID, TOIL, TOIL-WORN, TOILET, TOILET-PAPER, TOILET-ROLL, TOILET SOAP, TOILET-TRAINING, TOILET WATER, TOILETRIES, TOILSOME, TOPSOIL, TREFOIL, TURMOIL, TURQUOISE, TYPHOID, UNAVOIDABLE, UNAVOIDABLY, VIEWPOINT, VOICE, VOICE-OVER, VOID, VOILE. Proper Nouns ILLINOIS silent <s>, MONGOLOID, NEGROID, POLAROID.

Irregular Verb *to spoil*, present, past, past participle:
SPOIL Δ, SPOILED/ SPOILT Δ, SPOILED/ SPOILT Δ.

Doily obeys the rule that <y> must not be inside words unless they are Greek, even though they were named after the shop in London's Strand which first sold them, Doyley and Sons.

Groin originally meant 'depression in the ground', and was written *grynde*, said [grInd]. We can see that *groin* is linked to *ground* when we say an animal has 'gone to ground', is hiding unseen in a depression in the ground. It was also used for the groove or depression where each human thigh joins the trunk of the body. The French word *loin*, a region of the body which starts at the *groin*, was adopted by the English and it influenced the old English word *grynde* to change to *groin*, in the 1500's. Two hundred years after that *groin* was also used by architects to mean the 'edge formed by the intersection of two vaults', (Etymonline), but never to mean *groyne*, which we know came from a term for a piggy's nose! (Let's say *piggy*, not just *pig* or *grunter*, to remember which one has <y> inside it!)

Hoi polloi in Greek is 'the many', meaning people, 'the masses'. So, we when say 'the hoi polloi', we are saying *the* twice, 'the the masses', (Bryson 2004, p.97).

Loiter, unlike *goitre*, is spelt the American way, probably to make spelling *loiterer* possible.

*French <oi> spells [war], but not in English *reconnoitre*, which has changed its pronunciation instead of its spelling to become fully adapted as an adopted word.

Moisten spells [moi-sen], for <st> spells [s] before unstressed <en>, as in *hasten, listen* etc.

Sirloin is often said to have been knighted for being such a tasty cut, but actually means "above the loin", (Fleck 2007).

Note: we do not see the Glide and Yap words *coitus* and *coition* listed here with diphthong [oi] words because <oi> is not a digraph in these words, just adjacent letters.

Rule 4-59 Bossy R makes terminal [oir] spell [war].
Reason Terminal [oir] occurs in French words which have been adopted but not adapted.
Rebels CHOIR, CHOIRBOYS, COIR.
Rebels' Reasons *Choir* [kwIr] was spelt *quire* in the first OED. However, to show off that it came from the Latin word *chorus* we **say** it as the French taught us [kwIr] but now **spell** it <choir> to show its origin. *Coir* spells [koi-er].
List 4-59 Bossy R at work.

ABATTOIR [ab-a-twar], BOUDOIR [boo-dwar], MEMOIR [mem-war], RESERVOIR [rez-er-vwar]. As we know, Proper Nouns do not have to obey rules. *Moira* spells [moi-rar], not [mwar-ar].

U Digraphs

Letter <u> is a Greek Gift Letter, and so it's 'not trusted', may not let the first vowel 'do the talking' when two vowels 'go walking,' and it doesn't, not in <au>, <eu>, <iu>, <ou> nor <uy>. However, vowels after <u> in digraphs should let <u> 'do the talking', let <u> 'talk big', very 'profound', spell a long sound. We know <u> spells two long sounds, [yoo], and if yods drop, just [oo]. We know yods drop after [r], [l] and [j]. We know that yods have dropped after [n], [t] and [d] in places like New York — [noo] for *new*, [toon] for *tune* and [doo] for *due*. We know that in other places yods have fused with [t], [r], [s] and [z] to make words easier to say. Consequently, depending on the speaker *tune* spells [tyoon], choon] or [toon]! *Due* likewise: [dyoo], [joo] or [doo].

There is no digraph <uy>. We met <uy> in *buy* in Part One and we learnt that <u> enables it to obey the Short Word Rule, without using a Silent E and looking the same as *bye*. The terminal cluster <uy> also occurs when <u> is a silent insulator between <g> and <y>, as in *guy*, to prevent <gy> spelling [jI] or [jee], as it does in *elegy*.

List 4-60
BUY, GUY [gI], GUY LINE, GUYOT [gee-yot].

Guy meaning a rope, chain or line comes from Old French for "leader or guide", *guie/gui,* [gee]. Since terminal <i> is a 'no-no', it was replaced with <y>. *Guy* is an eponym, meaning stuffed effigy, ever since the Gunpowder Plot in which Guy (Guido) Fawkes was caught trying to blow up the House of Lords and King James I of England on Nov 5th 1605.

Another eponym, *guyot*, began in 1946 when flat topped mountains under the sea were named *guyots*, after the Swiss geologist Arnold Guyot. It has retained the pronunciation of the geologist's name. Proper Nouns like Arnold's surname and *French Guyana, Guyanese,* and *Guy de Maupassant,* the master of the nineteenth-century French short story, are not rebels because as Proper Nouns they do not have to obey rules. In these Proper Nouns <y> spells [ee], the French way.

There is no digraph <ua>. The cluster <ua> is not a digraph. It does not spell a new sound. As we saw in Part Three <ua> forms a Glide and Yap at syllable boundaries in words such as *actual,* or they Glide and Yawn in *mantua* and *skua*. The cluster <ua> is also in words which we shall call Penguin Words, words in which <u> spells the consonant [w] as in *penguin* and *guano*. We shall meet all the words in which <ua> does this, spells [war] or [way], with the other Penguin Words.

There is a digraph <ue> in one word, MUESLI [myooz-lee]. *Muesli* should spell [mooz-lee], according to the OPD, because it is only recently adopted from Swiss-German. However, English speakers have already inserted a yod.

The cluster <ue> forms a Glide and Yap in words like *cruel* and *duet* as we saw in Part Three. We have also met the cluster <ue> in words like *guess* in which <u> insulates <g> from the softening affect of <e>. The <e> is there as Fairy E, but in long words the vowel in the final syllable is no longer a long vowel, e.g., in *analogue* [an-u-log]. By contrast, in single syllable words, terminal <e> lengthens the preceding vowel, as in *vogue* [vohg]. Long words like *analogue* have now no need of the silent Fairy E and therefore no longer need insulator <u>. In USA, such words are spelt *analog, epilog, catalog etc*. How sensible.

List 4-61 <u> as a silent insulator before <e>.
ANALOGUE, BAGUETTE, BROGUE, CATALOGUE, COLLEAGUE, DIALOGUE, DE RIGUEUR*, DROGUE, EPILOGUE, FATIGUE, FUGUE, GUERNSEY, GUERRILLA, GUESS, GUESSER,

GUESSTIMATE, GUESSWORK, GUEST, GUEST-HOUSE, GUEST-NIGHT, GUEST-ROOM, GUEST WORKER, HARANGUE, INTRIGUE, LEAGUE, MARGUERITE, MERINGUE* <i>=[a], MONOLOGUE, MORGUE, PEDAGOGUE, PROLOGUE, RESCUE, ROGUE, ROGUERY, ROGUES' GALLERY, TONGUE* *f*, TONGUE-LASHING, TONGUE-TIED, TONGUE-TWISTER, SHARP TONGUED, TRAVELOGUE, VAGUE, VOGUE. Proper Noun GUERNSEY. Slang GUESTIMATE.

De rigueur is a French phrase. As we learnt earlier, Bossy R makes <eur> spell [er].

Tongue was spelt *tunge* and *tung* originally, but the dictionary committee spelt it to match *langue*, its French equivalent. Tyndale used *tung* in his English bible, along with *heven, erth* and *frute*, His bible was banned and he was hunted, strangled and burnt for expressing the Word of God in the 'language of plough boys'. In other words, for turning it into English and using sensible spelling.

Tongue and *meringue* spell [tuŋ] and [mə-raŋ] for <ng> in the same syllable spells [ŋ].

We shall meet the only word, {*suede*}, in which <u> spells [w] before <e>, with all the other Penguin Words.

The cluster <ue> spells [yoo] or [oo], but as this only ever occurs at the end of a word, we know that <e> is there as Insulator E with no need to act as Fairy E because terminal vowels have room to spread out and spell their long sounds. As Insulator E, <e> insulates <u> from ending a word, a strict no-no in English words.

Rule 4-62 Terminal cluster <ue> spells [yoo] or [oo].

List 4-62A Terminal <ue> spells [oo]

ACCRUE, BARBECUE*, BLUE, BLUENESS, BLUE BABY, BLUE-BLOODED, BLUE-COLLAR WORKER, BLUES, BLUE WHALE, ONCE IN A BLUE MOON, OUT OF THE BLUE, TRUE BLUE, BLUEBELL FLOWER, BLUEBERRY, BLUEBOTTLE FLY, BLUEPRINT, BLUESTOCKING, BLUETIT BIRD, BLUEY or BLUISH, BLUEY-GREEN, CHOP-SUEY, CLUE, CLUELESS, COME TRUE, CONSTRUE, CONTINUE, CUE, CURLICUE, DEVALUE, DISCONTINUE, FESCUE GRASS, GLUE, GRUESOME*, MISCONSTRUE, MISCUE, SUE, TRUE, UNTRUE. Australian words BLUE *slang noun*, BLUEBUSH, BLUE FLYER, (♀ red roo), BLUE GUM, BLUE HEELER DOG, BLUE POINTER SHARK, BLUE-TONGUE LIZARD, BLUEBOTTLE, BLUESTONE, BLUEY, HUMP ONE'S BLUEY. Proper Nouns PRUSSIAN BLUE, BLUE MOUNTAINS.

Gruesome has an obsolete stem word, *grue*, which means "to shiver", written *grrrr* or *brrrr* in "eye dialogue" nowadays.

Barbecue has already been listed because we already know that silent <e> is added to insulate <u> from coming last. This is a case of an adopted word adapting to English spelling rules, unlike the adopted word *emu*. When the buccaneer William Dampier wrote books about his travels, he introduced many new words, e.g., *barbecue, posse, cashew, avocado, chopsticks*. Can you guess where he sailed, from the words he collected?

List 4-62B Terminal <ue> spells [yoo], including words marked * in which [yoo] has fused with [s], [t] and [d].

AGUE=[ay-gyoo], ARGUE, ARGUE THE TOSS, AVENUE, BARBECUE, CUE, DUE*, DUES*, DUE TO, HUE, HUE AND CRY, ISSUE*, QUEUE [kyoo], QUEUING UP, RESCUE, *RESIDUE, RETINUE, REVENUE, STATUE*, STATUESQUE*, STATUETTE*, SUBDUE, TISSUE*, PURSUE*, PURSUER*, UNDUE*, VALUE, VALUE ADDED TAX, VALUES, VALUELESS, VALUER, VENUE, VIRTUE*, BY VIRTUE OF, IN VIRTUE OF, MAKE A VIRTUE OF NECESSITY. Proper Noun TUESDAY*.

*These words have Fused Yods, which, as we know, happens when <u> spells [yoo] after <t> and <d>. Before yods dropped after [s], Yod Fusion with [s] took place in a few words, too.

Old English *Tiwesdæg* was changed to *Tuesday. *Tiwaz* was the old German God of the Sky. As we know, <u> replaced <w> in many English words. Then <iu> spelt [yoo] and was re-written <ue> and pronounced [tyooz-day] or [chooz-day]. In USA, it might 'drop the yod' and spell [tooz-day].

Digraph <ui> — *bruise, suit.*

Rule 4-63 In digraph <ui>, <u> does the talking and spells [yoo] or [oo].

Reason As we know, yods were added to [oo] when the English tried to copy the way the French pronounce [oo] when it is spelt in any way other than <ou>. Yods were added to all words in which <ui> spelt [oo]. We still hear <ui> spelling [yoo] in *nuisance*. Other words in which <ui> spelt [oo] all received yods. We also know that some of these yods were hard to say because they came after [r], [l], [j] and [s]. Yods dropped out of these words. People were slow to drop yods after <s> in *suit*. They said [syoot] and even [shyoot]. I heard [syoot] and [shyoot] as a child, on the lips of the elderly and also in the British TV comedy "Are You Being Served?" Note that *suite* [sweet] is very different to *suit*, [soot].

List 4-63A <ui> spells [oo] when yods have 'dropped'.
BRUISE *verb/noun*, [brooz], CRUISE, CRUISER, FOLLOW SUIT, FRUIT, FRUIT MACHINE, FRUIT SALAD, FRUITERER, FRUITFUL, FRUITFULNESS, FRUITION, FRUITLESS, FRUITLESSLY, FRUITLESSNESS, FRUITY, JUICE, JUICY, JUICINESS, LAWSUIT, PLAYSUIT, RECRUIT, SLUICE, STAR-FRUIT, SUIT, SUITOR, SUITABLE, SUITABLY, SUITABILITY, SUITCASE, SUNSUIT, TRACKSUIT, UNSUITABLE, WETSUIT.

List 4-63B <ui> spells [yoo] where yods 'hang on'.
CONDUIT, CUISINE, PURSUIT.

Yod Fusion takes place in *conduit* — [kon-joot]. In *pursuit* [per-shoot], Yod Fusion can take place because <s> follows a consonant, as in *ensue* but not in *suit* or *sue*. Yods dropped after word-initial [s], but remained and fused after [s] inside words. *Cuisine* spells [kyoo-zeen] in Australia. It is also pronounced [kwə-zeen], using <u> to spell [w] as in *queen*.

Not needed but nice to know. French contribution to the English language continues because, besides being real junkies for new words, Anglos admire and copy French culture, e.g., their cooking, which they call *French cuisine*, pronounced [kwee-zeen] in French but in Australia it is pronounced [kyoo-zeen] more often than not. The French, on the other hand, try to keep their language pure and they have even banned some foreign words, e.g., civil servants cannot say or write "e-mail" and "start-up." Instead, it's "un message electronique" and "une jeune pousse". But France is losing this particular battle. Spoken by 1.6 billion people on the planet, English dominates as the language of business and the Internet. Now back to things we need to know.

Conduit is a rare word. All the folk I know agree with me that this noun spells [kon-joot]. However, I have not been able to find one dictionary which agrees with this, or even gives this pronunciation as an accepted alternative, or even gives [kon-dyoot]. In the OPD *conduit* spells [kon-dit]; The Australian Pocket Oxford 1976 gives [kon-doo-it] or [kun-doo-it] or [kon-dit]; Heinemann Australian Dictionary 1988 gives [kon-dit]; Fowler's Modern English Usage 1927 gives [kun-dit]; Webster's Dictionary gives [kon-dit] or [kon-doo-it]. *Conduit* came into English in 1300, (Etymonline), from French *conduit* [kon-dwee], meaning a pipe with which to lead water, from Latin *ducere* to lead. Since then, it has also come to mean an insulated pipe with which to lead electricity from one place to another. Why do all these dictionaries disagree with each other and with me? The only possibility is that *conduit* fell into disuse and was revived when the conduction of electricity through wires began, after Benjamin Franklin flew his kite in an electrical storm in 1752. Possibly someone matched *electrical conduit* with *electrical circuit,* forcing the stem of *conduit* to rhyme with the (mere) suffix of *circuit*. Fortunately, Australians have restored meaning to the word *conduit* by matching it with *conducive* since both <ui> and <u> spell the long vowel in their ancestor word Latin *ducere* 'to lead'. By contrast, <ui> in *circuit* is not a digraph — <u> is merely insulating <c> from the softening affect of <i>.

The cluster <ui> spells a variety of sounds.
We saw <u> [yoo] glide on to [i] in *vacuity*. We shall meet *penguin* and *suite,* in which <u> spells [w], when we meet the other Penguin Words.

In many words <ui> cluster together simply because <u> is insulating <g> from <i>, to prevent <g> spelling [j]. As we know, in a few old words <gi> spells [gi]. These old words, like *give,* do not need insulation. In the next words <u> is silent and <i> is pronounced according to the rules. Hence *guide* spells [gId] due to the Magic Action of Fairy E, and *guilt* spells [gilt]. Letter <u> also insulates <c> from the softening affect of <i>, as in *biscuit* and *circuit.* We listed some of these words earlier but we can now expand the list of words in which <u> is an insulator.

List 4-64 Silent insulator <u> inside words before <i>.
BISCUIT, CIRCUIT, CIRCUIT-BREAKER, CIRCUITRY, CONTIGUITY, DISGUISE, GUIDANCE, GUIDE, GUIDEBOOK, GUIDED MISSILE, GUIDE-DOG, GUIDE-LINES, GUILD, GUILDER, GUILE, GUILEFUL, GUILELESS, GUILELESSNESS, GUILLEMOT, GUILLOTINE, GUILT, GUILTILY, GUILTINESS, GUILTLESS, GUILTY, GUINEA, GUINEA-FOWL, GUINEA-PIG, GUISE, GUITAR, REBUILD, ROGUISH, ROGUISHLY, ROGUISHNESS. <u>Proper Nouns</u> GIRL GUIDE., GUIDER, GUILDER ROSE, GUILD-HALL, GUINEA-BISSAU, GUINEA, PAPUA NEW GUINEA.

Penguin Words— *anguish, penguin, suede.*
The letter <u> spells [w] in some words. This happens mostly when <u> follows <q>, because, after 1066, foreign scribes replaced <cw> with <qu>. They would not allow <w> after <g> either and to this day we have to use <gu>, never <gw>, to spell [gw]. The foreigners were, of course, French, Norman-French, Norman conquerors. English spelling became very complicated. Simple *cwen* (with single <n> showing that <e> spelt a long vowel sound) became *queen.* Words like *language* and *anguish* replaced the Old English words *tunge* and *angina.* French and other Romance Languages all copied the Roman habit of using <qu> and <gu> to spell [kw] and [gw]. So more words arrived in England in which <u> spelt [w]. Then, some languages dropped [w] after [k], so <u> was silenced after <q> — after <g>, too, in a few words. As we know, letter <u> does not spell [w] after every <q>. It is silent in *quiche* and *queue,* for instance. When the French silenced <u> in *guard* they changed that spelling, but it's still in *guard* in English, bearing silent witness to the past.

Long ago, in Latin, <v> spelt [w]. The Romans adopted Greek U along with Greek words but carved it as V which is why we call Twin V "Double U". Many other languages use <u> or <v> to spell [w]. If their words are adopted into English with unadapted spelling, we have to remember in which <u> and <v> spells [w]. It's a case of 'memorize, don't analyse'. The French write *Suede* for *Swede.* Then again, the Swedes write *Sverige* for *Sweden.* Children enjoy reading these 'Penguin Words' dressed as penguins — see website's Photo Gallery.

List 4-65 pronunciation of some 'Penguin Words', in which <u> spells [w].
<u><ua></u> spells [way] PERSUADABLE, ASSUAGE, DISSUADE, PERSUADE, PERSUADABLE, PERSUASIVE, SUASIVE, URUGUAY.
<u><ua></u> spells [war] GUANO, GUANINE, GUATEMALA, LANGUAGE, LINGUA FRANCA, MARIJUANA [mar-ee-y-war-nar], SUAVE.
<u><ua></u> spells [wə] LANGUAGE [laŋ-wəj], TRILINGUAL.
<u><ui></u> spells [wi] ANGUISH, DISTINGUISH, EXTINGUISH, CONSANGUINITY, LANGUID, LANGUISH, LINGUISTIC, SANGUINE, PENGUIN.

<ui> spells [wee] CUISINE, SUITE French for "each following next in a set", 'to follow' is *suivre* in French. PUISSANCE power or authority, from French.

<ue> spells [way] SUEDE French for *Swede*, Swedish, because Sweden was an early source of untreated, unpolished leather, especially gloves of soft kid skin. PUEBLO, PUERTO RICO, VENEZUELA.

Some examples of old words which continue to be spelt the old way to show where they came from. *Persuade, suasive* — in Latin *suedo* is 'advise or recommend' and *suesco* is 'to accustom or become accustomed', and the adjective, *suavis* means 'sweet, pleasant'. *Suede* — from s*uebi*, one of many Germanic tribes which gave rise to nations like Sweden. Some Proper Nouns are 'Penguin Words': *Uruguay, Ecuador, Venezuela.* Some of the words did not use <u> to spell [w] in Latin, e. g. *languid* comes from Latin *laxus* meaning "relaxed, loose", but there is no such word *laxid.*

Examples of modern adoptions: *guano, iguano* and *jagua* are Spanish and Portuguese renderings of South American languages. The chemical g*uanine* was first isolated from *guano* which means *dung* in the Quechua language of Peru.

List 4-66 Penguin words, listed alphabetically.
ANGUISH, ASSUAGE, CONSANGUINITY, CUIRASS, CUISINE, DISSUADE, DISSUASIVE, DISTINGUISH, DISTINGUISHED, DISUETUDE*, EXTINGUISH, EXTINGUISHER, GUACHARO, GUACAMOLE, GUANINE, GUANO, GUARIBA, GUAVA, GUAYULE, GUIRO, INDISTINGUISHABLE, INDISTINGUISHABLY, IPECACUANHA, JAGUAR*, LANGUAGE, LANGUID, LANGUISH, LANGUISHING, LINGUA FRANCA, LINGUIST, LINGUISTIC, LINGUISTICS, MARIJUANA, MORAL SUASION,, PENGUIN, PERSUADABLE, *PERSUADE, PERSUASION, PERSUASIVELY, PERSUASIVENESS, PUEBLO, SANGUINARY, SANGUINE, SUASION [sway], *SUAVE, SUAVITY, SUEDE*, SUEDE-CLOTH, SUITE*, TRILINGUAL.

Representative <qu> [kw] words: QUACK, QUART, QUEASY, QUEEN, QUELL, QUILL, SQUILLIONS, SQUAT, SQUAW.

Representative <qu> words in which <u> is silent: CHEQUE, CLIQUE, COMMUNIQUE, QUEUE, QUICHE.

Proper Nouns in which <u> spells [w] CHIHUAHUA, ECUADOR, GUATEMALA, GUATEMALAN, KUALA LUMPUR, LUANDA, MANAGUA, NICARAGUA, PARAGUAY, PUEBLO, PUERTO RICAN, PUERTO RICO, URUGUAY, URUGUAYAN, VANUATU, VENEZUELA, VENEZUELAN.

**Jaguar* began as [yag-war] but now we say it as it looks, [jag-yoo-ar]. We say at such times that Rex Text is more powerful than King Sound, that Queen Quill rules it over Queen Speech. The howling monkey g*uariba* [gwar-ee-bar], crying night bird *guacharo* [gwar-char-roh], the rubber shrub *guayule* [gwar-yoo-lee] and *guar gum* are not written and used often enough in English for Rex Text to change the way we say them. As for *guacamole* [gwar-ka-mol-ee], we learn to say it when passing around the avocado dip, long before we see it written.

**Disuetude*, a state of disuse, can be said in two ways: [dis-yoo-i-chood] or [des-wi-chood], as in, "Some customs fall into desuetude."

**Persuade* and all its progeny use <sua> to spell [sway] whereas *suave uses <sua> to spell [swar]. They come from two different Latin words: *suadere* is to advise, urge or sway someone and *suavis* means agreeable or sweet. They both came via France in the middle of the Long Vowel Lift of the GVS but only *persuade* lifted its long vowel [ar] to [ay]. *Suave* kept its long Continental [ar], maybe to sound more 'chic'. Then again, maybe *persuade* only changed because to persuade someone is to sway them.

**Suede* [swayd] has kept its long Continental [ay] vowel, spelt by <e>. Continental long vowels are extensions of their short vowels. Suede, or undressed kid skin, came from *Suède*, French for Sweden.

**Suite* [sweet] is a French adoption and so <ite> spells [eet] even though in the first syllable.

There is no digraph <uo>. We met <uo> clusters in words like *duopoly, duo* and *fluoride,* words in which <u> glides and <o> yaps, yawns and roars.

Fossil U — *buoy, built, guard.*
In five stem words <u> serves no purpose. It does not insulate <g> or <c> from the softening affect of <i>, <e> or <y>, as in *guild*; it does not spell [w] as in *penguin;* it does not glide as in *duopoly*; it is a useless fossil. Some class rooms have a 'Fossil U' sitting on a shelf next to 'Fossil E', as photographed in the website Gallery.

List 4-67 Stem words with Fossil U, and their offspring — complex and compound words.
BUOY [boi], BUILD Δ [bild], GUARD [gard], LANGUOR [langə]. <u>Related Words</u> BLACKGUARD* [blagud], BUOYANT, BUOYANTLY, BUOYANCY, BUILT Δ [bilt], BUILD ON, BUILD UP, BUILDER, BUILDING, BODYGUARD, GUARANTEE, GUARANTOR, GUARDED, GUARDIAN, GUARDSMAN, LANGUOROUS, LIFE-BUOY, UNGUARDED, VANGUARD.
Irregular verb BUILD Δ, BUILT Δ, BUILT Δ

Where did their fossils come from? *Build* has no <g>, no need of <u> to insulate <g> from <i>. *Build* comes from the Old English word *byldan* and as we know <y> is not allowed inside modern English words. Instead of just replacing <y> with <i> it was spelt the French way, <ui>, because the French spelling was favoured in the south of England, where it matched their dialect in which *built* sounded a bit like *bower,* which comes from the same old German word *bu* which starts *burgh,* a dwelling. Now we see why *neighbour* means one who dwells near (nigh), in a 'near building'.

In French, <gu> originally spelt [gw] and so *guard* was [gward] all over France. It travelled to England with the Normans from the north of France and became *ward*. Later on, the [w] sound was dropped in central and south France and *guard* travelled again to England, as [gard]. The silent <u> has remained as a useless fossil, even though the French dropped it, as we see in the French adoption *avant-garde*. The English built a compound word with *guard* and in true English fashion stressed the first sound of it, *blackguard,* so much that it shrank to [bla-guud]!

Some say that *blackguard* is a mock military term for "scullions and kitchen-knaves of noble households, of black-liveried personal guards, and of shoeblacks", which by 1736 had emerged to mean 'one of the criminal class,' (Etymonline). However, as *guard* was originally *ward*, it could be a case of a *drunkard* or *dullard* or a *ward* burning the food *black* in the castle kitchen. Maybe he is just a lazy *laggard* or maybe he's a *black-heart* – unlike *Leonard,* the Lion Heart. Note, King Richard did not have a 'rich heart'. He was a strong king, one who *ruled hard.*

Why is <u> silent in *languor* and *languorous* but not in *languid* and *languish? Languor* was originally Old French *langor,* said and written like that in English. The silent <u> was added later, to show the connection to the Latin verb *languere. Languid* and *languish* arrived later from France, with a <u>, and this <u> spelt [w], and still does in English. BTW, *languor, languid* and *languish* are *langueur, langoureuse/langoureux* and *languir* in Modern French. In none of these French words — the noun, the adjective female/male, nor the verb — does <u> still spell [w]. English words not only carry culture and trap the history of England, but also preserve foreign history, in adopted words which have since changed in their own languages.

Now our journey is over. Congratulations! If someone shows you a word and asks "How do I say this?" you can tell them. If they also ask, "Why is it spelt like that?" you might remember why but if not, you can look it up. You've met the rules — you don't know them by heart, but you know that there are rules, for spelling out words, reading them and also rules for spelling down words, writing them down. They are rules, patterns, codes — whatever you like to call them. Professor Cummings, p. 4, says that spelling is "predictable, consistent, patterned, ruly", and that it includes "misfits and holdouts". The Prof's misfits and holdouts are our rebels. Almost all our rebels have reasons for breaking the rules. Only a very few words, the rascals, lack a good reason. They are listed together after the rebels in 'Loose Lists' in the next section. I have named them after the raskols of Papua New Guinea. PNG has many raskols, law-breakers, but the words of the nation's language, PNG Pisin, are extremely law abiding. There are no Rebels, no Rascals. Each of its twenty-one letters spells one particular consonant or one particular vowel, the latter both long and short. There are only four Best Friends — AI, AU, OI and NG. There are no Cursive Casualties. So there is no Collateral Damage. No wonder our bilingual children found English spelling so extraordinary. Can you see all four PNG Pisin digraphs in the following message? Mi bin r**ai**tim lo**ng** pepa, bin wokim buk. N**au** yu mas ritim ol stori long olgeta b**oi** na gel. Which is to say, I have been writing on paper, been making (working) a book. Now you must read the stories to all the boys and girls.

Appendix

Stress and the Rhythm of Speech

Stressed words are said with strength, pronounced louder and/or longer than other words in a sentence. Stressed syllables are pronounced louder and/or longer than other syllables. When we **stress** a syllable, we give it **strength**. Words which rhyme the best not only end the same, but are stressed the same. That is why *basil* and *frazzle* rhyme better than *basil* and *a drill*. The experts say the strongest syllable has primary stress, the next strongest has secondary stress and so on but it is enough to say a syllable is either stressed or unstressed.

We need to know which syllables to stress in order to read words correctly. In many Asian and Ab'l languages each syllable is given the same time and so it must be strange to have to dwell for a while on one part of an English word and almost skip over another. Since we do not indicate when writing words which syllables are to be stressed, we need to be told or to have a regular pattern to follow.

In English "the main stresses (tums) fall roughly at regular intervals in the stream of speech. It is a 'tum-te-tum-te-tum' way of talking," (Crystal, p. 270). This tum-te-tum rhythm is called "iambic metre" and is very obvious in poetry, as in "Twin-kle twin-kle lit-tle star. How I won-der what you are". English words are usually stressed at the beginning as in *twin-kle*, but affixes can change this. If a prefix is added, the pattern becomes te-tum, as in *unless*. Stress can change a word's meaning too. A prefix may be stressed to show it is a noun, not a verb, as in *com-pact*. Suffixes, like prefixes, are usually unstressed but some can affect the stress pattern, compare *melodic* and *melody*, *masonic* and *mason*. Compound words, like *upset* are usually stressed at the start but, in order to make nouns into verbs, the stress is moved to the last syllable, as in *Don't let this upset upset you*, and, *The collar's overlap will overlap the logo on the jacket*. When we say that a syllable is stressed we mean it is given most stress. Due to the alternate tum-te-tum stress pattern, alternate syllables to the most stressed syllable get a degree of stress called secondary stress. The syllables between stressed syllables are called unstressed syllables.

Why do verb stems get most stress on the final syllable? Cummings explains that because verbs get weak suffixes, e.g., —*ing*, —*ed*, and —*es*, stressing the last syllable of verbs, prior to the suffix, prevents two weak, unstressed syllables side by side. The English tum-te-tum-te alternating stress pattern means verbs get stressed just before their suffixes, on the last syllable of the stem word, also called a base word.

The following list of nouns and their verbs comes from page 70 of *Enquire within upon Everything* by Anon. The book calls stress 'accent' and shows it with a mark after the stressed syllable. Two rebels are listed, as exceptions. Some words are no longer in general use. The book is 155 years old. Quote: "It will be noticed that those in the first column, having the accent on the first syllable, are mostly nouns; and that those in the second column, which have the accent on the second and final syllable, are mostly verbs." Ab'ject—abject', Ab'sent—absent', Ab'stract—abstract', Ac'cent—accent', Affix—affix', As'pect—aspect', At'tribute—attribute', Aug'ment—augment', Au'gust—august', Bom'bard—bombard', Col'league—colleague', Col'lect—collect', Com'ment—comment', Com'pact—compact', Com'plot—complot', Com'port—comport', Com'pound—compound', Com'press—compress', Con fine—confine', Con'cert—concert', Con'crete—concrete', Con'duct—conduct', Con'flict—conflict', Con'serve—conserve', Con'sort—consort', Con'test—contest', Con'text—context', Con'tract—contract', Con'trast—contrast', Con'verse—converse', Con'vert—convert', Con'vict—convict', Con'voy—convoy', De'crease—decrease', Des'cant—descant', Des'ert—desert', De'tail—detail', Di'gest—digest', Dis'cord—discord', Dis'count—discount', Ef'flux—efflux', Es'cort—escort', Es'say—essay', Ex'ile—exile', Ex'port—export', Ex'tract—extract', Fer'ment—ferment', Fore'cast—forecast', Fore'taste—foretaste', Fre'quent—frequent', Im'part—impart', Im'port—import', Im'press—impress', Im'print—imprint', In'cense—incense', In'crease—increase', In'lay—inlay', In'sult—insult', Ob'ject—object', Out'leap—outleap', Per'fect—perfect', Per'fume—perfume', Per'mit—permit', Pre'fix—prefix', Pre'mise—premise', Pre'sage—presage',

Pres'ent—present', Prod'uce—produce', Proj'ect—project', Prot'est—protest', Reb'el—rebel', Rec'ord—record', Ref'use—refuse', Re'tail—retail', Sub'ject—subject', Su'pine supine', Sur'vey—survey', Tor'ment—torment', Tra'ject—traject', Trans'fer transfer', Trans'port transport', Un'dress—undress', Up'cast—upcast', Up'start—upstart'.

Cement and *consols* are exceptions to the above pattern, and should always be accented on the last syllable, says Anon. To these rebels we can add *design* and *report,* which are always accented, or stressed, on the final syllable, even when nouns.

Written English does not use signs to show pronunciation. The word *accent* in Latin means tone, intensity, the song added to speech: literally, "add song". The French use accent signs.

Consonants — Yods, Obstruents and Sonorants

The 'bones of speech' is one name for consonants, because consonants do not change much, unlike vowels, which are called the 'flesh of language'. How do you pronounce *dance*? It's the vowel which varies, not the consonants. Consonants do change, however, from place to place because, as a language spreads, if people cannot say a new consonant, they use a similar one that they can say.

This was noticed by the Grimm Brothers as they travelled Europe, collecting folk stories to write them down before they were forgotten. They noticed that *father, vater* and *pater* all meant the same and sounded the same except for their consonants. They decided that, long ago, as words spread, if people in one place could not say those starting with [f], they used [v], a sound they had grown up with and, in another place, they used [p], a familiar sound to them. Those who could not say [th] or [dh] used [t] or [d]. Consonants [th], [dh], [d] and [t] are all made near each other in the mouth. So are [f], [p] and [v].

One brother, Jakob, worked out how to predict which alternative consonant a particular language group would choose. It's called Grimm's Law, (Hewitt, p. 650). Jakob Grimm also found that Spanish speakers dislike [f] but do not replace it with [v], for they use [l] or [h], sounds they like. Italians like soft sounds and do not like two consonants together, hence they say *piazza* for Latin *platea* and *piano* for Latin *planus.* In English, *jolly* starts with the short, harsh sound in [jol-lee] whereas in French *joli* starts with the long, soft sound in [zholee]. French *chef* spells soft [shef], whereas in English <ch> spells a shorter, harsher sound in *chief.*

Languages which grew from Rome's language, called Latin, include French, Italian, Spanish and Portuguese. They are called Romance Languages. Dutch, English and the other Germanic languages of Europe's western lowlands are called Low German Languages. A third group, High German Languages, are languages of the inland mountain region and include modern German.

Although English began as a Low German language, it has absorbed words from the other two groups plus words from many other languages outside these European groups, words which did not evolve from the ancient ancestor language of these three groups. This ancestor is now extinct. It's called the Proto Indo-European Language, because it is also the ancestor of some Asian languages. It's called Indo-European because it spread east, as well as west, as far east as India, which explains why *bhratar* from India is so very like the same thing in English: *brother*.

Each Voiceless Consonant with its Voiced Counterpart.

Prof. Cummings, on p. 74 of his book sets out consonant pairs. [p] in *pat* with [b] in *bat*; [t] in *tot* with [d] in *dot*; [f] in *fine* with [v] in *vine*; [s] in *sip* with [z] in *zip*; [k] in *cod* with [g] in *god*; [th] in *thin* with [dh] in *then*; [ch] in *chin* with [j] in *gin*; [sh] in *dasher* with [zh] in *azure*; [h] in *hat* but its voiced partner, [gh] is gone from English speech along with its English symbol Yogh. Other English symbols for consonants, like Thorn and Edth, have gone, too.

Silent Consonants.

We never say that a letter is a sound because letters are not sounds, they spell sounds. We do, however say that a letter is a silent letter when they spell no sound. Some of them long ago spelt sounds, e.g., <k> in *know*. Others do a silent job of telling other letters what to spell, e.g., <h> in *phone* tells <p> to spell [f]. A few have been added to words which never had them, e.g., <t> in *subtle*. Vowels are silent on many occasions too, but for now we examine consonants.

Long and Short Consonants

Some consonants sound longer than others. The long ones can go right over the short ones if in a 'difficult' cluster. A difficult cluster occurs when our mouths have too much to do to say a word. In *sword*, [s] is made behind our top teeth in about the middle of the mouth, [w] is made at the front, with our lips, and then [or] is made right at the back, in the throat and [d] is in the middle again. The mouth finds going from middle, to front, to back, to middle too much and misses out the front sound, taking a shortcut to the back of the mouth. That is why [w] is silent in *sword*. This does not happen in *swim* because [i] is not made right at the back of the mouth. It does not always happen, e.g., [w] is in the shorter word *swore,* and also in *swarm*, maybe because [m] takes less energy to say in *swarm* than [d] does in *sword*.

The chart below tells us which consonants – the long ones — have the power to blot out other consonants — short ones— and turn them into silent letters. They do not use that power much.
A consonant is silenced if it blocks so much air that the syllable cannot be said in one breath, as in *gnome, know, sign* and *phlegm*. Then, when another syllable is added, the blockage just marks the end or beginning of that syllable, the consonant is no longer silent, e.g., we hear [g] and [k] in *signal, phlegmatic, acknowledge* and *ignomious*. However, if the second syllable is weak and unstressed, it is not strong enough to pull the consonant out of silence. We do not hear [t] in *whistle,* for instance, nor do we hear [g] in *signed* and *signage*.

Long Consonants: [m], [n], [l], [r], [s], [z], [sh], [zh], [f], [v], [ŋ].
Short Consonants: [b], [t], [p], [d], [t], [k], [g], [ch], [j], [th], [dh], [h], [w], [y].

The sound of each consonant depends on —
where we block air: at our lips, *labial* [p], [b], [w], [m]; or lips plus teeth, *labial-dental* [f], [v]; at our teeth, *dental* [th], [dh]; at the upper gum ridge, *alveolar* [t], [d], [s], [z], [r], [l], [n]; or at the upper gum and hard palate, *alveolar-palatal* [sh], [zh], [ch], [j], [y]; at the soft palate, *velar* [k], [g], [ŋ]; or in the throat, *glottal* [h].
how much air we block, which ranges from completely stopping air flow, *stops*: [p] [t] [k], to *fricatives,* impeding it enough to cause audible friction: [f] [s] [sh] [kh], to *approximants* which barely impede it: [r] [l] [w] [y], to an *affricate,* a stop plus a fricative, which must occur at the same place of articulation: [t] & [sh] = [ch], [d] & [zh] = [j].
whether we use our voice box or not, which depends on the consonant. All vowels use the voice box. Every *voiceless* or *unvoiced* consonant has a *voiced* partner, as listed above, except for [h], because its voiced partner, [gh], a choked guttural sound, fell out of use after the Norman Invasion.
nasalizing. When air travels through our nose we are nasalizing — [m], [n], and [ŋ] are stops, like [b], [d] and [g], but air is only stopped, or partially blocked, through the mouth, for with [m], [n] and [ŋ] we keep it flowing through the nose.
aspiration. When air is released with a noticeable puff we are using aspiration. Sometimes the same sound takes different forms. For instance, English [p] is only aspirated at the beginning of a word.
palatalizing. When the tongue is raised toward the roof of the mouth, the palate, while pronouncing the consonant, we are **palatalizing,** as in [sh], [ch], [zh], [j].

Yod. The English Yod was introduced just before Rule 1-40. It's discussed again here.

The consonant [y] has its own name, Yod. Letters have names but this is the name of a sound. Like the sound Schwa, its name comes from Hebrew. It is spelt with the letter <y> but it can also be spelt with the vowel letter <u>, as in *use* [yooz] and *cute* [kyoot], or with Little Imp, as in *onion* [unyon]. The French use <ou> to spell [oo] and they use <u> to spell an [oo] sound which is a little higher and a little shorter. This first French [oo] is the sound we hear at the end of *kangaroo* and *maribou* and the beginning of *toucan* and *boutique*, in which our lips are round and pushed forward. The second French [oo] starts off the same but then the lips flatten into a little pursed smile. This raises the frequency a little and cuts the vowel off so that it is a bit shorter than the first [oo]. I cannot give any word examples because this higher, shorter [oo] is not used in English. The French use it in *adieu,* and words in which [oo] is spelt with <u> or <eu>, or anything but <ou>. When French was the dominant language in England, people tried to pronounce [oo] the French way, in words like *tune* and *neuter*. All they could manage was [i-oo]. Then they found it was easier to change [i] into [y] because it glided on to [oo] smoothly and so <u> in *tune* and <eu> in *neuter* spelt [yoo]. This happened in words in which [oo] is spelt in other ways, as in *new* and *fruit*, but never when <ou> spelt [oo]. We hear [yoo] in *you* but that is because of the first letter, <y>. If <ou> spelt [yoo] we'd hear *you* spelling [y-yoo].

For some time, only <ou> spelt [oo] and all the rest spelt [yoo], where French influence was greatest, in London, for instance. Then, in most words, <oo> changed from spelling [or] to spelling [oh], as in *brooch,* and then [oo] as in *shoot*, in the GVS. So now both <ou> and <oo> spelt [oo].

Back to [yoo]. People found saying [yoo] after [r], [l] and [j] very difficult. So they dropped [y], i.e., dropped yods, after [r], [l] and [j]. This explains why *Ruby, Lulu* and *Judy* spell [roobee] not [ryoobee], loo-loo] not [lyoo-lyoo] and [joodee] not [jyoodee]. Yods were hard to say after [s] and [z]. Wherever [syoo] was spelt with <su> the yod fused with [s] some time ago. This is why we hear the Yod Fusion [sh], in *sure,* sugar and *fissure*. In words where a single <u> is not used to spell [yoo], yods hung on for centuries until they were dropped, as in *suit*, which only lost its yod mid-twentieth century.

I said that yods 'hung on'. In other words, should we say that yods drop or should we say that they are pushed? When <u> starts a word, spelling its long sound, that sound is always [yoo]. Some say that's because there is nothing behind the yod of [yoo], in *use* or *utility* for example, to push it. We know that, in reality, yods are neither pushed nor do they drop. They are just too hard to say after some consonants.

They take time to say after [d], [t] and [z], as in *dune* [dyoon], *tune* [tyoon] and *azure* [ayzyoor]. Most people solve this by letting [y] push the tongue up to the palate and changing the sound of [d] to [j], [t] to [ch] and [z] to [zh, as in [joon], [choon] and [ayzh-ə]. This is Yod Fusion. It also still happens after [s], as in *mission,* to avoid two weak beats in a suffix. Yod Fusion makes many words easier to say. Consonants [j], [ch] and [sh] have the simple spellings <j>, <ch> and <sh>, but they are also spelt in other ways, due to Yod Fusion, as in *duty, tulip* and *sugar* or *soldier, mission,* and *question.* and *fusion*. The consonant [sh] is spelt with simple <sh> and also thirteen more ways. However, there is no simple spelling for the fourth Yod Fusion, [zh], which we hear in *fusion.*

In parts of USA, especially New York, if people find it hard to say [y] after [d] and [t] they do not fuse yods, they just drop them. These 'Yod Droppers' read *tune* as [toon] instead of [tyoon] or [choon] and read *duke* as [dook], rather than [dyook] or [jook]. To them, *nuclear* is [nook-lee-ar], not [nyook-lee-ar] and the slang verb *to nuke* is [nook]. For even more detail, go to 'Dropping Yods' above Rule 1-60.

Obstruent and Sonorant Consonants
Obstruents: [b], [t], [th], [dh], [p], [d], [t], [k], [g], [ch], [j], [dh], [h], [s], [z], [sh], [zh], [f], [v].
Sonorants: [m], [n], [ŋ], [l], [r], [w], [y].

Obstruent consonants are made, or articulated, by restricting the flow of breath to some degree, on its journey from lungs to atmosphere. They can be spat out like [t], squeezed out like [z], puffed out like [p], gurgled out like [g], or articulated in other ways. Some block more air than others.

Sonorant consonants hardly block any air. They join smoothly with vowels because vowels do not block any air at all. The sonorants are all 'long' except for [w] and [y] which are gliders, glide on to vowels because they end with an open mouth, ready to join on to a vowel, all of which start with open mouths.

Three sonorants, [m], [n] and [ŋ], are called **'Nasals'**, because air keeps flowing, through the nose, though the mouth is shut for [m] and nearly shut for [n] and also the third nasal, Eng, [ŋ]. It is only at the end of a syllable that [n] and [g] merge to create [ŋ]. Eng never starts an English word. So [g] is silenced in *gnarl* and *gnome*. When <ng> starts Ab'l, African, Maori or Vietnamese words which have been adopted into English, the letters spell [n], not [ŋ].

Two sonorants, [r] and [l], are called **'Liquids'**, because breath spills over and flows from the sides of the tongue in their production. The Liquids are very like vowels except that they are shaped by the tongue rather than the lips and the tongue. They blend so well with vowels that the added flow can lengthen vowels. When a vowel keeps on flowing into a Liquid it means <a> and <o> spell their long sounds, the ones they spelt before the GVS, as we hear in *calm, snarl,* and *harm*. Liquid [r] used to make <e>, <i> and <u> spell their old long sounds, too, but these sounds have all ended up as the long sound [er], as in *fern, bird* and *burn*. When <r> follows a vowel and lengthens it, <r> is called 'Controlling R' and nicknamed **'Bossy R'**. The other Liquid, [l], still lengthens vowels in a few words, such as *call, calm, folk-* and *child,* but it's not nearly as 'bossy' as Bossy R. In places I call <l> 'Loving L'. The Nasals lengthen vowels in *kind* and *comb* and *strange*.

In fact, all the sonorants 'love' vowels. They love them more than they love each other. For instance, [mn] or [nm] is impossible in the same syllable and so the nasal nearest the vowel is heard as it flows with the vowel and the other is silenced, as in *mnemonic* and *solemn*.

Liquids, as we have heard, love vowels, open their arms to them, let vowels flow on into them, making vowels longer, especially the Liquid [r] whose love is a controlling love. The situations in which Bossy R controls vowels are set out in spelling rules. Loving L is less active and more random, spelling a pre-GVS vowel with <a> in *calm* and a post-GVS vowel with <i> in *child*. The **Gliders**, [w] and [y], love vowels too, hug them close and bend them, in *cow* and *coy, brown* and *boy,* for instance.

Both Gliders, <w> and <y>, have complex histories. W represents the Old English letter Wynn which spelt [w]. It was removed from the English Alphabet. Other letters were removed too and now <w> represents them at the end of *window,* a word which <w> starts as a consonant and ends as part of a vowel digraph. This use of <w> means that *bow* spells both [boh] and [bow]. As a double <u>, <w> represents <u> when it could otherwise be mistaken for <v>, for instance, in cursive handwriting at the end of a word. Inside words, <u> in cursive is hard to read before <n> and <l>. All this explains why we see <ow> instead of <ou> in *'bow down'* and *owl,* all Cursive Casualty words.

The Greek letter Y is also used as both consonant and a vowel. As a vowel, it shares its role with <i>. This was handy when legibility was a concern, for instance at the end of words. A cursive <i>, back when it had no dot on top, was often seen as amere flourish. They both spelt the long vowel [ee], an extension of their short vowel sound [i], until the GVS. Then stressed [ee] vowels became stressed [I] vowels. So now they both spelt two long vowel sounds. They also acted for each other in digraphs. The only difference between them when spelling vowels is that <y> is not allowed inside words, like *history,* unless they are of Greek origin, like *mystery,* and <i> is not allowed at the end of words, so we read *day train; my smile; obey* and *weigh; oil the toy*. W and Y can be called semi-vowels or semi-consonants.

Vowels and Great Vowel Shift.

Vowels are called the 'flesh of language'. They add flesh to the 'bones of speech'. The rigid consonants are fleshed out with vowels. Flesh changes more than bones. Vowels change more than consonants. Vowels are sorted and described in three ways.

1. How open the mouth is, with open meaning the tongue is low. So, a vowel is open/low or closed/high, with gradations in between, 'mid' in the middle.

2. Where the tongue is, at the front, central or back of the mouth.

3. Whether the lips are rounded, rather than spread or relaxed. A vowel is either rounded or unrounded.

The Great Vowel Shift, GVS.

Vowels change all the time, but great changes took place from 1450, for about two centuries. Some say for longer, because after that some of the seven long straight vowels were lost when they merged with others. English went into the GVS with seven monophthongs and came out with seven, but very different ones, and then they merged and mixed in various words, so that <ea>, which used to spell a word-sound somewhere between [air] and [er], spelt [ee] in *meat* and [ay] in *great*. Since English lost two long vowels after 1650, it is simpler just to explain what happened, in the GVS, to the remaining five.

These are the vowels we hear in "Pa may we all too". Today, in the rest of Europe, these are the long sounds spelt by A, E, I, O and U, [ar], [ay], [ee], [or], [oo], in that order. They spelt those sounds in English too, before the GVS. Now we only hear them spelling these sounds in a few words— *fAther, Eclair, taxI, fOr, Uber.*

As we have heard above, when [oo] was spelt <u>, <eu>, <ew>, <ui>, and anything but <ou>, it was [yoo] on English lips.

By the time the Great Vowel Shift was over, the letters A, E, I, O and U in English words spelt the vowels in "Maybe I won't use glue," with <u> spelling long [oo] and now also long [yoo]. Two sounds, because long [yoo] spread across England and then in some words reverted to just [oo] because people began 'dropping' yods.

In the GVS, stressed vowels rose up, or rose up and bent over. Why was this? It was because upper-class people started 'talking posh' around 1450, in London and the south of England. Before that, they spoke French, which differentiated them. Now that the upper-classes were speaking English again, instead of French, they wanted people to know of their high position in society. So, they raised their long vowels, lifted them. Lifting [ee] and [oo] did not work because they were already made with the tongue high in the mouth. So [ee] and [oo] (if spelt <ou>) hit the roof and bent, into diphthongs, bent sounds, as in *I* and *clout*. The other long vowels rose, too, which is why we call A, E, I, O and U by the names [ay], [ee], [I], [oh] and [yoo]. Feel your jaw move higher as you say [ar] and then [ay]. And say [ay] and then [ee]; [or] and then [oh]. Your lips stay still for these straight vowels, but watch them move a bit for the bent vowel [I] and a lot for the bent vowel [ow].

Straight and bent vowels are officially monophthongs and diphthongs. Another bent vowel, the diphthong [oi], began evolving after 1066, much earlier than the GVS. It seems it began as two vowels — [or-ee] — and then joined up over the syllable boundary, as one vowel sound, albeit a bent vowel, a diphthong, in which the breath keeps flowing but the lips change shape. By the time the GVS was over its evolution was complete, in words such as *soil,* (which evolved from the Old French [sor-ee ..] in verb *soillier*) and *boil* (which has an OE ancestor meaning 'tumour' and a French ancestor meaning 'bubble'). That is to say, [oi], which was never in OE words, evolved in both English and foreign words after 1066.

This made a lot of the words which had sounded similar to French words very different. That would have pleased the English everywhere, because France was not popular. The English had spent over a hundred years fighting for territory in France which they claimed was theirs. In 1453 they lost their last battle. The returning, defeated soldiers had learnt a lot of French words but must have been more than happy to say them a new, English way. Back home in England, the three centuries of French as the official language of England were over. The problem was that English had become half French. Changing the pronunciation of these French words made their language more truly English. The lower classes copied the new way the upper classes said their words, and the wave of change went north, too, all over England.

The reason the Great Vowel Shift helps us understand English spelling is that when the English changed the way they pronounced words they did not alter the way they were spelt. By contrast, when German vowels shifted, their spelling was changed.

Words with short vowels did not change in the GVS. Some short vowels changed due to normal vowel shift, not due to the GVS. For example, we all know that some people say [dans] and some say [darns] when reading *dance* and this short vowel is lengthened in other words too, including *laugh*. This is due to the love-hate relationship England has had with France over time. The longer Continental vowel [ar] was admired by the aristocracy, along with French cuisine and fashion. It seems a lot of French culture was loved but not the French themselves.

I have presented a few of the reasons given for the GVS above. When we meet *hearty* in list 4-17, we hear of the influence of pirate language on English. Others say it all began when London was swamped with Englishmen from elsewhere to fill job vacancies after the Black Death, the first wave of Bubonic Plague. They say Londoners began changing their long vowels to show superiority to their country cousins. Others say the vowel change won English back as the official language of England because changing the vowels turned all the French words which had replaced Old English words into English words. Many causes for the GVS are put forward and argued about, but no one disagrees that it created a big disconnect between writing and reading. English spelling was no longer phonetic. It had been, before 1066, but since then, what with losing six letters and suffering the 'curse of the dagger', casualties from cursive handwriting and consequent collateral damage, as described in this book, and now the GVS, English letters no longer had a one-to-one relationship with the sounds which make our words.

Punctuation and Grammar

The **full stop** or **period** . is used to mark the end of sentences and to show that words have been abbreviated.

The **comma** , from Greek *kómma*, is related to the word *cut* and *chopper*. In English it is used to separate a word or a group of words in a sentence, in order to make the meaning clear.

A row of three dots **...** is an **ellipsis** and shows that words have been left out. In maths an ellipse is an oval shape. Both *ellipsis* and *ellipse* mean "falls short", because a sentence with *ellipsis* falls short of words and an *ellipse* falls short of being a perfect circle.

We use an **apostrophe** ' if we have left out letters, as in *it's, can't, gov't,* for it means *away-turn* in Greek, "turn away, leave out, hook out". We also use it to show possession by all nouns (dog's dinner) and pronouns too (one's happiness), except for these possessive pronouns and adjectives: *yours*, *his*, *hers*, *ours*, *its*, *theirs*, and *whose*. In all other cases add an apostrophe S - *lad's hat, children's bats,* but if it's plural and ends in an S, add an apostrophe without the S – *lads' hats*.

Quotation or **speech marks** " " ' ' If quoting within a speech, change from single marks to double marks or from double to single: "I've been trying to think of a word for two weeks," said a cross-word fanatic. "How about 'fortnight'?" said his pal. Publishers and printers use italics for book titles, plays and films but hand-writers use quotation marks.

A **hyphen** - is used between the words of a compound word or the syllables of a divided word, as at the end of a line or to make meaning clear: re-creation and recreation have different meanings.

The **N-dash** – is used between numbers, dates etc. to mean 'up to and including'. So called because it is the width of n.

The **M-dash** — indicates a sudden break in thought or introduces the unexpected. So called because it is the width of m.

Information inside brackets ( ) is "in parenthesis" (Greek for "put beside"). Extra information or explanation in a sentence can also be put in parenthesis using commas or dashes.

The **colon** [koh-lon]**:** in Greek means 'a limb' and so it marks where the sentence branches. The words prior to the colon are the introduction to the details or the information that the sentence branches into after the colon.

The **semi-colon ;** joins together clauses which are closely related and of equal weight or importance. The semi-colon can be imagined as the pivot of a balanced plank or see-saw, not the beginning of a fresh branch.

The **question mark ?** replaces the full stop, (period), at the end of a direct question. (The beginning of the question is not marked with ¿ as it is in Spanish.) A question mark also indicates missing data. The symbol is generally thought to originate from *quæstio*, Latin for "question", which was abbreviated to *Qo*. The uppercase *Q* was written above the lower-case *o*, and this mark became **?**

The **exclamation mark !** replaces the full stop after an expression of wonder, admiration, fear or other strong emotion, or after a command. The symbol is believed to originate from the Latin word *io*, in capitals, IO, an exclamation of joy, probably written with I above O and the O shrank to a dot.

Punctuation, like spelling, was still a matter of personal choice when William Caxton began printing the first books in English in 1476. He used oblique strokes to group things, a colon for big pauses and used a full stop, not only to end sentences, but also for brief pauses. Early seventeenth century writers used colons, semicolons, and commas interchangeably. Late in that century quotation marks were invented and also precise rules, which tried to force readers to pause twice as long on a semicolon as a comma, and four times as long on a colon. Then people realized that punctuation marks were not just for taking breaths but were essential for giving meaning to sentences. They stopped being so rigid about the length of a pause and instead made sure pauses helped convey meaning. (Ralph Waldo Emersen said that a poor writer lacks 'comma sense'. That's a 'play on words', on 'common sense'.)

The apostrophe is quite recent. Its use has changed since Shakespeare's *go's* for *goes* and Johnson's *grotto's* for *grottoes*. Nowadays we do not put it in plurals except for numbers — *1860's;* abbreviations — *VIP's;* and individual letters — *P's & Q's;* otherwise, how could we write 'Dot the i's and cross the t's.'? We no longer have apostrophes in place names, e.g., *St Pauls* is no longer *St Paul's*. A big London shop started in 1849 as *Harrod's* but changed to *Harrods*. We can apply to local geographical place names boards if we want to keep the apostrophe — like the folk at *Martha's Vineyard*, (Crystal, p. 220).

Basically, the apostrophe indicates missing letters. *Apo* is Greek for *away* or *from* and *strophe* means *turn*. We draw a little hook ' where a letter has been turned away from that word, been hooked out. The letters at the end of words which used to show possession were hooked out long ago and have been missing for centuries. Other letters have been hooked out recently and can be replaced at any time, e.g., *it's* reverts to *it is* or *it has,* depending on the meaning.

In the olden days a noun got the suffix <es> to show it owned something. Why? It is pretty easy to imagine that people got sick of saying "Bob, his dog" in reply to "Whose dog is that?" Maybe they shortened it to "Bob-is dog," and wrote "Bobes dog," in those days. If they shortened it again by leaving out the vowel sound when they said it, they would have put an apostrophe to show that they had left out the <e> in <es>. Can you see why *his* and *its* does not have an apostrophe? Yes, *his* already shows ownership — *his dog* — and *its* already shows ownership, *its flag*.

<u>Words which already show ownership do not have apostrophes.</u>

Adjectives never have apostrophes. The following adjectives show ownership in their spelling: *my, your, her, his, its, our, their*. Note, *you* added <r> to *you* to show ownership which produced *your*. When *they* added <r> it became *theyr* but <y> had to change to <i> because *they* is not a Greek word, and <y> is only allowed inside words of Greek connection. This will help you remember how to write *their*.

356

In footy we say a player has possession when he has the ball. If a noun (person, place or thing) has something we say it is 'in possession' or is 'possessive'.

<u>Possessive pronouns</u> do not need nor do they take apostrophes as they are already showing possession: *Mine* — of me, *yours* — of you, *his* — of him, *hers* — of her, *its* — of it, *ours* — of us, *yours* — of you (plural), *theirs* — of them.

<u>Other pronouns</u>, e.g., *somebody's*, *nobody's*, and nouns, e.g., *men's*, accept the suffix <'s> to show ownership: "Somebody, his dog". "Nobody, his dog". "Men, their dogs". If they are plural and end in <s> they just get the suffix <'>, e.g. *ships'* — "ships, their sails".

A rhyme to summarize.

"Use an apostrophe only when,
A word doesn't show possession.
Then just add apostrophe S.
There is an exception I must confess.
If it's plural and ends in an S,
Add the hook without an S."

Children learn to add [s] to show possession very early. They take a while to remove the second [s] if it's plural and ends in [s]. We see this in the following piece of eye dialect "All the ladzez hats have blowd away", said the little girl, as the lads chased their hats.

Bits on Grammar

The First Person: I, Myself and Me:

I had a little tea party
This afternoon at three.
'Twas very small —
Three guests in all —
Just I, myself and me.
Myself ate all the sandwiches,
While I drank up the tea.
'Twas also I who ate the pie
And passed the cake to me.

I is written in upper-case, even inside a sentence, because <i> had no dot on top long ago and was too small to see clearly. The 'Second Person' is *you* and 'Third Person' is everyone else. Pronouns stand in for nouns. Pronouns are just one of the Nine Parts of Speech, as follows:-

Three little words you often see are ARTICLES: *a*, *an*, and *the*.
A NOUN's the name of anything, as: *school* or *garden*, *toy* or *swing*.
ADJECTIVES tell the kind of noun, as: *great*, *small*, *pretty*, *white* or *brown*.
Instead of nouns the PRONOUNS stand, as: *he* hit *his* head, *your* arm, *my* hand.
VERBS tell of something being done: *to read*, *write*, *count*, *sing*, *jump* or *run*.
How things are done the ADVERBS tell, as: *slowly*, *quickly*, *ill* or *well*.
CONJUNCTIONS join the words together, as: men *and* women, wind *or* weather.
The PREPOSITION stands before the noun, as: *in* or *through* the door.
The INTERJECTION shows surprise, as: *Oh*, how pretty! *Ah*! how wise!
The whole is called NINE PARTS of SPEECH, which reading, writing, speaking teach.

One of my readers saw this poem in my book *The Inside Story on English Spelling* and has been kind enough to alert me to another description of the parts of speech by JC Nesfield in his *Modern English Grammar* (1912-1979). Thank you, Peter Norman, for telling me that Nesfield lists and defines **The Parts of Speech** as:

A **Noun** is a word used for naming some person or thing.

A **Pronoun** is a word used instead of a noun or noun-equivalent.

An **Adjective** is a word used to qualify a noun.

A **Verb** is a word used for saying something about some person or thing.

A **Preposition** is a word placed before a noun or noun-equivalent to show in what relation the person or thing denoted by the noun stands to something else.

A **Conjunction** is a word used to join words or phrases together, or one clause to another clause.

An **Adverb** is a word used to qualify any part of speech except a noun or pronoun.

An **Interjection** is a word or sound thrown *(sic)* into a sentence to express some feeling of the mind.

Nesfield then adds: 'The **Article**s are not a distinct part of speech, but merely adjectives. 'A' or 'an' is an abbreviated form of the adjective 'one'; while 'the' is the root form of 'this', 'that', 'these' and 'those'.'

Pronouns can be further described, as follows. Subject pronouns — they do the action in a sentence — are *I, we, you, he, she, it, they.* Object pronouns — they receive the action — are *me, us, you, him, her, it, them.* Possessive adjectives are not pronouns. They are *my, our, your, his, her, its, their* and come before nouns, as in *my ball.* Possessive pronouns replace nouns, as in *the ball is mine.* They are *mine, ours, yours, his, hers, theirs. Its* is not used in this way.

Grammar, from Greek, means 'the art of letters'. It's an art to use them to convey what we mean. Some more grammatical terms:-

Stem word, also called a **base word**. Since a word starts out as a stem, and then adds on prefixes and suffixes, like a stem grows leaves, I prefer to call a base word a **stem word.** Stem words, like stem cells, can grow and change into new words. Languages are alive, and their words grow and change all the time. There are old suffixes like —*dom* in *kingdom*, and brand-new ones like —*bot,* which refers to any software which performs a task automatically, like a *robot,* hence, *mailbot,* (Crystal, p. 243).

If stem words make sense on their own, they are called **free stems,** e.g., *do* and *use* in *undo* and *useless.* If they only make sense when bound to affixes, they are called **bound stems,** e.g., *ly* and *fy* in *rely* and *defy.*

A compound word is a combination of free stems. Newly formed compound words, like *sun-tan,* have a hyphen and in time they lose it and bond even closer, e.g., OED gives *tea bag* in 1898 edition, *tea-bag* 1936, *teabag* 1977. So, we can use hyphens or remove them. We cannot put them back into words which have lost them. Some words began as two free stems joined but then one stem word shrank. Such shrunken stems are no longer able to stand up, alone. They become **bound stems.**

A complex word is made of a free stem and an affix or affixes, e.g., *unblushingly* is the stem *blush* with three affixes.

Affixes. If a word bit is attached or fixed to the start of a stem it's called a **prefix**, e.g., <un> in *un*do, At the end of stems come **suffixes,** as in magic*al,* magic*ally.*

A common noun is the name of a thing, e.g., *a town,* including abstract things like *happiness.*

A proper noun is the name of a person or place, e.g., *Anne* or *London,* and they all start with capital letters. *Proper* does not mean 'correct' this time, for it means a 'private' name and 'appropriate', a suitable name. Both words stem from Latin *pro privus.* Mr Longbottom might not sound very proper, but it was an appropriate name for the first Mr Longbottom, who, it is surmised, lived at the bottom of a long valley.

Adjectives are "thrown" to nouns like projectiles, adding qualities to nouns, e.g., a *red* sunset.

Verb originally meant 'word' and then became the part of speech that expresses action or being, since even one-word commands can result in action. "Just say the word and it will be done," is a common expression. Verbs include inaction, just *to be* or *to dream*.

An adverb adds information to a verb.

The following are called function words by some people, but not when I went to school. Such people say they help the sentence to function. To my mind all the words in a sentence make it function. However, call them function words if you must. **Pronouns** replace nouns, *pro* means 'stands in for'. **An article** means "a little joint" and joins up the sentence as in 'A dog bit the cat.' (We see *article* in 'articulated' truck, in which the jointed joins, pivot points, are not little.) Nesfield, see above, says that *a, an* and *the* are just adjectives, like *this, that, these* and *those*. In which case they are also articles because they join up words in a sentence in the same way, as in 'This dog bit that cat.'

Pre in **preposition** means *before,* hence prepositioned or "that which is positioned or placed before" and so a preposition must always come before something as in, 'through the arch'. When one just 'drives through', *through* is an adverb. *Con* means *with*. So a **conjunction** 'joins with'. An **interjection** is 'thrown in' or 'injected'.

A syllable is a group of letters gathered together to make a sound which might have enough meaning to be a word or if joined with other syllables makes a meaningful word. Mr. Marmeduke Hewitt, on page 578, tells us the best definition of a syllable is 'a single vowel sound, with or without one or more consonants.'

Cognate words. We shall find many words have been adopted into the English language, or have grown out of adopted words. Others grow out of old English words. Words which grow out of the same parent word are related but, instead of calling them siblings or cousins, they are called **cognates.** There are plenty in English because the English love new words, even if they already have already adopted a related word from another language. They often use a cognate to express a new shade of meaning, e.g., the 'cousin-words' *same* and *similar* do not mean quite the same thing.

Particles are letters which are inserted into words to make them obey rules, like <b> in *robber,* <k> in *panicked* or to spell the sound of the word, like <u> in *gradual, graduate* — for we do not say *grade, gradal, gradate* — or to link stem words, *speedometer,* (Cummings, p.47). A **linking particle,** either <i> or <o>, sometimes links stem words in compound words, as in *speedometer*.

Affixes

There are many **affixes,** word-bits that are fixed or added to simple stem words. We can add just a prefix or just a suffix or add both a prefix and a suffix or even add a prefix to a prefix or a suffix to a suffix. *Inadmissibility* and *inapplicability* are both built on to or grow out of the words *admit* and *apply,* which can be traced back to even shorter words, *mit* and *ply* from other languages. They each have two prefixes and also the suffix *–ity* added on to the suffix *–able*. Cummings, on p. 55, explicates (unfolds) *s*tatistician back to the stem word *state*: (stat)ist)ic)ian) and discusses how each word grew out of the last, noting changes of meaning as this occurred. Affixes change a bit in order to join on smoothly to stem words, as described during this book, which is why *adfix* became *affix*.

There are two kinds of suffixes. The first kind tells us something about the stem, as in *big, bigger, biggest*. That kind is stressed. These **inflexional suffixes** tell us something about the word, the same way a flexing dog's tail — wagging, rigid or droopy — tells us something about the dog. They tell us about the stem word: **how many**, (plural suffixes <s>, <es>, <en>), **when,** (tense markers <s>, <es>, <ed> and verb participle suffixes <ed>, <ing>), **whose** (ownership suffixes <'s> <s'>) and **how much** (<er> <est>), (Cummings p. 34). So there are only 8 inflectional suffixes: <s>, <es>, <en>, <ed>, <ing>, <'s>, <s'>, <er>, <est>. I call all these suffixes '**flexible suffixes.**'

The second kind of suffix changes the meaning of the word, as you can see when the suffix — *or* is added to *act* to make *actor*. They change the meaning of the stem word because these suffixes were derived from other words, e.g., when *hope* changes to *hopeless* or *hopeful*. Words belong to great rivers of language. The word *derived* is like *de-railed,* in that it means diverting a word from one river to another so that it's *de-rivered.* These suffixes are called **derivational suffixes** because they derive one word from another. I call these suffixes 'deriving suffixes'. Prefixes are all 'derivers'. They all change the meaning of a word.

Quinion 2002 shows how 1,250 affixes add a new layer of meaning. He sorts them into 24 groups, as below, with examples of *prefixes-* and *-suffixes* in italics.

Group 1. Drugs and biochemicals: *sero-* serums, *-ergic* neurotransmitters. 2. the living world: *-bacter* a bacterium, *-saur* a reptile. 3. the human body: *cranio-* head part, *-trichous* hairy, has hair. 4. chemicals: *-ium* an element, *thio-* a sulphur compound. 5. colours: *chloro-* green, *-chrome*, colour of some sort. 6. culture and society: *-aholic*, a person excessively fond of something, *demo-* involving people, *step-* relationship through marriage. 7. diminutives: *-een, -en, -ino, -kin, -ling.* 8. direction and movement: *ento-* within, inside, *-petal* centre seeking, moving inwards. 9. food and drink: *glyco-* sugar, *lacto-* milk foods. 10. Gender: *-ess* female, *andro-* male, maleness. 11. communication and language: *-eme* linguistic unit, *grapho-* written images. 12. &13. biological, medical and surgical terms. *–ves, a-, anti-, dis-, dys-, in-, mal-, mis-, nega-, non-, un-.* 14. numbers and multiples *mega-* million, *-teen* thirteen to nineteen. 15. the physical world: *flvio-* river, *irido-* rainbow, *-lith* stone(y). 16. places and people: *afro-, anglo-.* 17. position: *epi-* upon/above, *–wide* extended/throughout. 18. proportions: *-fid* divided, *equi-* equal. 19. qualities: *idio-* personal/own, *-oid* like/representing. 20. religion and spirit: *telo-* ultimate purpose, *–latry* worship of something. 21. sensations: *visco-* sticky, *xero-* dry, *-algia* pain. 22. shapes: *platy-* broad/flat, *-morph* form.

Some suffixes are noun endings, e.g., *-ance, -ation, -ence, -ment, -ness*, as in *entrance, education, existence, freshness.* Some suffixes are usually adjective endings, like *-ful, -ish, -ive, -less, -ous* as in *truthful, selfish, active, harmless, famous.* Some suffixes are usually verb endings such as *-ate* and *-en* as in *hesitate, frighten.* The suffix *-ly* usually ends adverbs, as in *thinly.*

These suffixes all begin with a vowel: *able, ace, acious, acy, ade, adlic, age, aholic, aire, al, alike, amatic, an, ance, ancy, ant, ard, aria, arian, ary, ate, ate, athon, ation, ator, atory, eal, ed, ee, eer, en, ence, ency, ent, er, erie, ery, esce, escent, ese, esque, ess, est, eth, etic, ette, eur, ia, iac, ial, ian, ian, iana, ible, ible, ic, ical, ice, icide, icious, ics, ie, ier, iferous, ify, il, ile, ine, ing, ion, ior, our, ious, ise, ish, ism, ist, isy, itis, ity, ium, ive, ize, ocracy, ode, oholic, oid, ology, omatic, or, ory, ose, osis, othon, ous, ude, ule, ure, ur, ute, y.*

These suffixes all begin with a consonant: *bot, cation, cy, dom, fest, fic, fold, free, ful, fy, gate, gram, hood, le, less, let, like, ling, logia, ly, ment, meter, metry, monger, most, naut, ness, ness, phile, phobe, phobia, rix, ry, s, scape, scope, ship, sion, some, stan, ster, style, sy, tain, teen, teria, th, tude, ty, type, ville, ward, wards, ways, wise, worthy.*

They can each be written on paper 'leaves' and attached to suitable stem words as you meet them. If you cannot think of a word which ends in one of these suffixes try asking www.morewords.com. They can also be sorted in various ways, refer to Quinion above and https://www.learnenglish.de/grammar/suffixtext.html

Aboriginal languages use many suffixes. For instance, Thalanji, an Ab'l language on the west coast of Australia north of Carnarvon, has at least eighty. Some are just one letter, some as long as nine letters. The suffix *—marnu* means 'for' or 'associated with' and so the Thalanji had no trouble naming spectacles: *kurumarnu,* 'for the eyes'. *Kuru,* meaning 'eyes', is well-known to old-timer *wajela,* or 'whitefellers', who use the local name for the Sturt's Desert Pea flower: *Marlukuru,* Kangaroo Eyes. For those who know the flower, or google it, a very apt name. Austin 1992, on Thalanji, lists and explains many Ab'l suffixes.

Here are some English prefixes: *a, an, ab, abs, ac, ad, af, ag, al, an, ant, ante, anti, ap, at, as, auto, be, bi, bio, co, col, com, con, contra, cor, de, dia, di, dis, e, ef, em, en, ex, extra, hemi, hyper, hypo, il, im, in, im, in, infra, intra, im, ir, micro, mis, non, ob, oc, of, op, out, para, peri, post, photo, pre, pro, poly, pro, re, semi, sub, suc, suf, sug, sup, sur, sus, sym, syn, tele, trans, tri, ultra, un.* See www.learnenglish.de/grammar/prefixtext.htm for meanings. *Counter, inter* and *under* are not considered to be prefixes. Instead, they are treated as free stems forming compounds, in *countermand, interlope* and *underhand,* for instance. In compound words, <er> spells [er] at the end of the first stem, even if the next stem starts with a vowel, as in *overact.*

Stress in **complex words** is alternate like all English words but which syllable receives the most or **primary stress** depends on the length of the stem and which affixes have been added. Suffixes are usually unstressed but receive secondary stress at times to match the tum-te-tum rhythm of the English language. For instance, **part**, de**part**, de**part**ment, but de**part**ment**al**. As we meet each suffix and prefix along the 'road to reading' we discuss its affect (action) on the stress of the words it forms. Nowadays one can listen to a word's rhythm on line, how each word sounds, choosing American or Anglo pronunciation. Writing Tip: Affect = Action, Effect = rEsult.

Auxiliary Verbs

Some verbs are auxiliary verbs. They help other verbs, and are also independent verbs, for they can be used by themselves, e.g., *be, have, let, will, dare, need.* Most frequent of all auxiliary verbs are *to be* and *to have – I am going, I have been watching.* Some verbs are pure auxiliaries: *will,* (not the verb *to will*), *would, shall, should, may, might, can, could, must, ought, won't, wouldn't, shan't, shouldn't, mayn't, mightn't, can't, couldn't, mustn't, oughtn't.* They are never independent verbs. Instead, they always precede and help independent verbs. These pure auxiliaries cannot have the word *to* in front of them because they can never be in the infinitive because they are really the past tenses of former strong verbs, which are now known as irregular verbs. We use them as present tense words, but, because they were once past tense verbs, they do not have the suffix <s> for 3rd person singular. So, we do not say *she musts run.* Instead, we say s*he must run.* We never read words and phrases such as *to should, maying* or *he mays* for they are impossible.

The noun *can,* from Old English *canne* for a cup or container, has become a verb since canneries were invented. The tin *can* and the verb it produced is not related to the auxiliary verb *can,* which was originally the past tense of the verb *cunnan,* to know, (Hewitt, p. 191). It originally meant "I know how to do something and I am able to do it too." (The silent <k> in *know,* which was once [k], points back to *cunnan.*)

The noun *will* is from Old English 'determination, purpose; wish, request' and also meant 'joy and delight'.

Could was *cuthe,* another past tense. *Ought* was the past tense of *owe. Must* was *môste,* the past tense of *motan,* to be allowed or permitted. *May* was *mag,* the past of *mowe,* to be able.

Dare is used in the present, and *durst* in the past, when an auxiliary verb. *He (we, you etc.) dare not lie. He (I, they etc.) durst not lie.*

In this book, auxiliary verbs are marked with §, which resembles the pulley of an auxiliary engine. Think of a verb as the engine of a sentence, then an auxiliary verb is an auxiliary engine. Boats which have 'in board' motors, in their hull, often have an extra motor, an 'out board' motor, over the back of the boat, as an auxiliary motor for when extra power is needed.

Rebels and Rascals.

The Rebels and Rascals break reading rules, which make them hard to decode. I have included some which only break writing rules, like *taxi,* which is easy to decode but breaks the rule against ending words with

<i>. *Tabu* breaks a rule by using <u> at the end of a word but also breaks a reading rule because yods do not normally drop after [b]. It should decode as [tab-yoo], like *abuse* [ab-yoos].

Rebel Lemons out-number the other Rebels. They are not listed below with the other rebels. Nor are **Cursive Casualties, Collaterally Damaged Words**, victims of the **Curse of the Dagger**, words with **Diplomatic Immunity** and words ending with **Fossil E,** which include Old and New Fossils and French Fossils. Many such words appear in these groups in the appendix. Words can be ticked off or added to each group as they are met along the 'road to reading'.
The words below are referenced so that you can learn which rules they break and their reasons to do so. For example, 'ACETIC 1-47' is in Part One under Rule 47 and AITCH L4-3' is in Part Four, in List 4-3. Direction to words which stand alone is also given, e.g., 'ACADEMY end of Part One'. Some words are discussed more than once, e.g., 'AGAIN after 1-9, 4-3'.

These are all 'Rebels with a Reason', in alphabetical order. Those without a good excuse follow, in the List of Rascals.
A 1-1 — ACADEMY end of Part One — ACETIC 1-47 — ACKNOWLEDGE 4-39 — ADJOURN 4-45 — AESTHETIC 4-8 — AGAIN after 1-9, 4-3 — AGAINST 4-3 — AGORA 3-60 — AISLE 4-3 — AITCH L4-3 — ALGORITHM 2-85 — ALLOW 1-25B, 4-39 — AMIRATE 3-52 — ANDIRON 3-52 — ANEMIC 1-47 — ANNELID 1-48 — ANXIETY 3-83 — ANY, ANYBODY, ANYONE L1-54 — APPAL 1-14 — ARCED, ARCING 1-44 — ARE 3-37, 3-67 — ARIA 3-67 — ASSEGAI 4-3 — ATTORNEY 3-60 — AUNT 4.12 — AWRY 4-10A — AXIAL, AXIOM 3-98 — AXOLOTL 2-34.

BABYHOOD 3-11 — BANZAI 4-3 — BARRAGE 3-24 — BASS 1-7, 1-10 — BATH 2-86 — BATHOS 2-87 — BATHS 2-88 — BAYOU 4-2 — BEAR 4-14 — BEAUT, BEAUTIFUL, BEAUTY 4-13 — BESTIAL 3-96 — BIER 3-36 — BIOLOGIST 3-112 — BLOOD 3-5 — BONSAI 4-3 — BORAX, BORIC, BORON 3-60 — BOROUGH 4-54 — BOTH 2-86 — BOTHER 3-42 — BOUQUET 4-51 — BOW 1-25B, 4-39 — BOWL 4-39, 4-40 — BOW-BOW 4-39 — BREAD, BREADTH 4-16 — BREAK 4-15 — BREAKFAST, BREAST, BREATH 4-16 — BRETHREN 2-85 — BROAD 4-35 — BROOCH 3-5 — BROW 4-39 — BURIAL 3-82 — BURY after L1-54 — BUS 1-3 — BUSINESS, BUSY L1-54

CAFFEINE 4-22 — CAPTAIN 4-3 — CARRIAGE 3-89 — CASSOWARY 3-65 — CASTE 3-26 — CAYENNE 4-2 — CELLIST, CELLO. CELT 1-44 — CERTAIN, CERTAINLY, CERTAINTY, CHAMBERLAIN 4-3 — CHAMOIS 4-58 — CHAPLAIN 4-3 — CHARIOT 3-82 — CHAUVINIST 4-12 — CHIFFONIER 3-86 — CHLORINE 3-86 — CHOIR, CHOIRBOYS 4-59 —— CHOW 4-39 — CLEANSE 4-16 — CLERK 3-41 — COCOA 4-35 — CODEINE 4-22 — COIF 4-58 — COLLAGE 3-24 — CONEPATL 2-34 — COPY L1-54 — COPIER 3-86 — CORDON-BLUE 4-24 — COUGH 4-54 — COULD 1-26, 4-44 — COUNTERFEIT 4-19 — COURAGE, COURTESY 4-45 — COW 4-39 — COYPU 4-57 — CRESCENDO 1-44, 2-3B — CURARE 3-37

DAIQUIRI, DAIS 4-3 — DEAD, DEAF, DEALT, DEARTH, DEATH 4-16 — DECORUM 3-60 — DESSERT 1-7, L3-45 — DEUTZIA 4-24 — DEVOUR 4-45 — DIRNDL 2-34 — DISCRETION 3-92B — DISSOLVE 1-7, L2-31 — DIV 1-13 — DO 1-24E — DOES, DOESN'T 4-37 —— DOOR 3-7 — DOUR 4-45 — DOYEN 4-57 — DREAD, DREAMT 4-16 — DROUGHT 4-56 — DUCAT 1-40 — DUDE L3-15 — DUTIABLE 3-92A

EARL, EARLY, EARN, EARTH 4-18 — EITHER 4-22 — EMPTY 2-10 — EMU 1-24F — ENDEAVOUR 4-16 — ENDOW 1-25B — ESPECIAL 3-93B — EQUAL 1-39 — EQUATION 3-92A — ETHOS 2-87 — EYE 4-27 —EXEMPT 2-10 —EXHALE 2-84

FAIENCE 4-3 — FASCISM 2-3B — FASCIST 1-44, 2-3B — FEATHER 4-16 — FEDORA 3-60 — FEZ 1-9 — FIERCE 3-86 — FLANGE 2-53 — FLEA 4-13 — FLENSE 2-70 — FLOOD 3-5 — FLOOR 3-7 — FLORA 3-60 — FLOUR 4-45 — FLOURISH 4-45 — FLU 1-24F — FOLIAGE 3-89 — FONDU 1-60, 1-24F — FOREIGN, FORFEIT, FORFEITURE 4-19 — FOSSE 3-14 — FRAU 4-12 — FRAULEIN 4-21 — FREER, FREEST 3-2 — FRIEND 4-34 — FUNGI L1-34 — FUSELAGE 3-24

GAMUT 1-18 — GARAGE 3-24 — GARGOYLE 4-57 — GAS 1-3 — GAUGE 4-12 — GAUSS 4-12 — GEAR, GECKO, GEEK, GEESE, GEEZER, GEISHA, GEL, GELD, GELDING, GEMSBOK 1-45 — GEOLOGIST 3-111 — GESTAPO, GET, GEWGAW 1-45 — GEYSER 1-45, 4-27 — GIBBON, GIDDY, GIDGEE, GIFT, GIG, GIGA-, GIGGLE ,GILD, GILGIE, GILLIE, GILLS, GILT, GIMLET, GINGHAM, GIRL, GIRT, GIRTH, GISMO, GIVE, GIZZARD 1-45 — GNU 1-24F, 1-6, 2-11 — GRAFFITI L2-38 — GREAT 4-15 — GROSS 1-10 — GROYNE 4-57 — GUINEA 4-13 — GULFS L2-33 — GURU 1-24F — GUV 1-13

HEAD, HEALTH 4-16 — HEARD 4-18 — HEARKEN 4-17 — HEARSE 4-18 — HEART, HEARTH 4-17 — HEATHER ,HEAVEN, HEAVY 4-16 — HEIFER 4-22 — HEIR 2-84 — HOMINID 1-48 — HONEST, HONOUR 2-84 — HOLIDAY 3-111 — HONORARY 2-84 — HONORIFIC 2-84 — HOUR 2-84, 4-45 — HOW 1-25B, 4-39 —HOYA, HOYDEN 4-57 — HULA 1-60 — HURRIEDLY 4-34 — HUSSAR 1-7, L3-67A — HUSSIF L1-54 — HUSSY L1-54, 1-7 — HYENA 3-105

1, I'M 1-1 — IMPOVERISH 2-98 — INDICT 2-8 — IXORA 3-60 — IGUANA 3-80

JALOPY 1-61 — JOURNAL, JOURNEY 4-45 — JUJU 1-24F — JUNIOR 3-86

KARAOKE 3-80 — KAURI 4-12 — JAYAK 4-2 — KEY 4-27 — KNEED L3-2 — KNOWLEDGE 4-39 — KURDAITCHA 4-3 — KURU 1-24F

LADYHOOD, LADYLIKE, LADYSHIP 3-111 — LASSO 1-24E — LAUGH 2-89 — LAV 1-13 — LEA 4-13 — LEAD, LEAPT 4-16 — LEARN 4-18 — LEATHER, LEAVEN 4-16 — LEISURE 4-22 — LETHAL 2-87 — LISTEN 2-59 — LLAMA, LLANO 1-16 —— LOCH above 2-91 — LOGARITHM 2-85 — LOSE 3-15B — LOUGH 4-54 —LULU 1-24F

MAESTRO 4-8 —MANIOC L3-83 — MANY L1-54 — MARJORAM 3-60 — MARRIAGE 3-89 — MASCARA 3-67 — MATINEE 3-2 — MAYOR 4-2 — MEADOW, MEANT, MEASURE, 4-16 — MEERSCHAUM 4-12 — MELEE 3-2 — MENU 1-24F — MESSIAH 3-85 — MIRAGE 3-52 — MISCHIEF, MISCHIEVOUS 4-34 — MORON 3-60 — MU 1-24F — MUMU 1-60, 1-24F

NAIAD 4-3 — NATIONAL 3-92B — NEITHER 4-22 — NEGLIGEE 3-2 — NINTH 2-86 — NOTORIETY 3-83 — NOUGHT 4-56 — NOURISH 4-45 — NOW 1-25B, 4-39

O 1-1 — OBESITY 1-59 — OF 1-1 — OFTEN 2-9, 2-59 — ONLY L1-56 cont. — OOGENESES, OOLITE, OOLITH, OOLITIC, OOLOGIST, OOSPHERE 3-5 — OUR 4-45 — OWE, OWN 4-40 — OX 1-6 — OYSTER 4-57

PARIAH 3-85 — PARIETAL 3-83 — PARSE 3-40A — PASS 1-7 — PATH 2-86 — PATHOS 2-87 — PATHS 2-88 — PEA 4-13 — PEAR 4-14 — PEARL 4-18 — PEASANT, PHEASANT 4-16 — PHYSIQUE 3-104 — PIER, PIERCE, PIERCING 3-86 — PITIABLE 3-92A — PLAID 4-3 — PLAIT 4-3 — PLEA 4-13 — PLEBEIAN 4-22 — PLEASANT 4-16 — PLOW 1-25B, 4-39 — POI 4-58 — POLONY 1-61 — PORPOISE 4-58 — POSSE 1-24B — POSSESS 1-7, 1-18 — POTHER 3-42 — PRACTISE 3-22 — PRAYER 4-2 — PREMIER 3-86 — PREMISE, PROMISE 3-22 — PROPRIETY 3-83 — PROTEGEE 3-2 — PROTEIN 4-22 — PROW 4-39 — PUKKA 1-20 — PUS 1-3

QUAY 4-2 — QUIZ 1-9 — QUOKKA 1-20 — QUORUM 3-60

RADII 3-4 — RAMPAGE 3-24 — RASPBERRY 2-11 — RARITY 1-59 — RATAFIA 3-85 — RATION 3-92B — RE 1-24B — READ *past tense*, READY, REALM 4-16 — RECCE 1-24B, 1-44 — RENEGE 1-45 — REV 1-13 — ROTTWEILER 4-22 — ROUBLE 4-53 — ROW 1-25B, 4-39 — ROWLOCK 4-39 — RHYTHM 2-85

SAC 1-19 — SAID after 1-9, 4-3 — SAMURAI 4-3 — SARI 3-37 — SATIETY 3-83 — SAUERKRAUT 4-12 — SAYS after 1-9 — SCEPTIC 2-3B — SCHEDULE, SCHILLING, SCHISM 2-101 — SCOUR 4-45 — SCOURGE 4-45 — SEA 4-13 — SEAMSTRESS 4-16 — SEARCH 4-18 — SEIZE 4-22 — SENIOR 3-86 — SEQUAL, SEQUIN 1-39 — SERGEANT 3-41 — SEW 4-29 — SHALL 1-14 — SHITAKE 3-4 — SHOULD 1-26, 4-44 — SIC 1-19 — SHEIK 4-22 — SIEVE 4-34 — SIGNAGE 2-112 — SIS 1-3 — SKIING 3-4 — SMOOTH 2-85 — SOBRIETY 3-83 — SOCCER 1-44 — SOCIETY 3-83 — SOJOURN 4-45 — SOLDIER 3-86 — SOUL 4-42 — SOUR 4-45 — SOVEREIGN 4-19 — SOW 1-25B, 4-39 — SPECIAL 3-93B — SPIV 1-13 — SPREAD 4-16 — STEAD 4-16 — STEAK 4-15 — STEALTH 4-16 — STOREY 3-60 — STUDY L2-5 — SUGAR, SUMAC, SURE 3-95 — SURFEIT 4-19 — SVELTE 2-1 — SWAG, SWAM, SWANK 1-15 — SWEAR 4-14 — SWEAT 4-16 — SWORE 3-63 — SYPHILIS 3-110

TABU 1-24F, 1-60 — TAIPAN 4-3 — TAXI 1-23A — TEA 4-13 — TEAR 4-14 — THERE 3-30 — THEREWHITHAL 1-14 — THIS 1-3, 1-30 — THOROUH 4-54 — THOU 1-25B, 4-51 — THREAD, THREAT 4-16 — THROUGH 4-54 — THUS 1-3, 1-30 — TIARA 3-67 — TIC 1-19 — TIER 3-86 — TIGER 1-45 — TO 1-24E — TOFU 1-24F — TOPAZ 1-9 — TORTOISE 4-58 — TREAD, TREASURE 4-16 — TREBLE 2-37 — TREK 1-19 — TRIAGE 3-89 — TRIPLE 2-37 — TROUGH 4-54 — TSETSE 2-70 — TUTU 1-41, 1-24, 1-60 — TWO 1-27

US 1-3 — UNION 3-90

VARIETY 3-83 — VASE 3-15B — VERBIAGE 3-89 — VICTUAL 3-97 — VIZ 1-9

VOW 4-39 — WAG, WAGGON/WAGON, WAGON, WALK, WALL, WAX 1-15 — WE'RE 2-40 — WEALTH 4-16 — WEAR 4-14 — WEATHER 4-16 — WERE 3-30 — WHERE 3-30 — WHEREWITHAL 1-14 — WHIZ 1-9 — WHO, WHOM 1-27 — WHOSE 1-27, 3-15B — WHYS 3-111 — WIELD, WIENER 4-22 — WITH 2-85 — WITHAL 1-14 — WOMAN, WOMEN above 1-37 — WORE, WORN, WORRISONE, WORRY 3-63 — WOULD 1-26, 4-44 — WOW 1-25B, 4-39.

YEA 4-15 — YEARN 4-18 — YES 1-3 — YOU 1-24F — YOU'RE 2-40 — ZEBU 1-24F, 1-60.

List of Rascals.
BEQUEATH 2-85 — BIZARRE 3-67 — CANOE, CANOES 4-37 — COLONEL 1-50 — GAOL after 4-9 — HAEMORRHAGE 4-8— HOOPOE, HOOPOES 4-37 — JEALOUS 4-16 — LASSOES 4-37 — LIEUTENANT 4-24 — MANOEUVRE 4-38 — MOUTH *verb* 2-85, L4-42 — SCARCE, SCARCELY 3-67 — SCARCITY 1-59 — SCISSORS 1-7, L3-60 — SHOE, SHOES 4-37 — SMOOTH 2-85 — STOEP 4-38 — TREACHERY 4-16 — WEAPON 4-16 — WHYS 3-111— WYES 3-111 — YACHT above 2-91 — ZEALOT 4-16

Loose Lists
The following lists are 'loose', not sequenced in the way lists are in parts One to Four. Their words have been taken from their home lists in the body of the book and grouped together here as summary lists — incomplete summaries no doubt, so add more yourself. Find them in their lists to learn for about them.

Words in which terminal <s> spells [s], not [z], after a stressed vowel — Rebels, each with a reason.
ALAS, BATHOS, BUS, CHAOS, GAS, KUDOS, MADRAS, OMNIBUS, PANCREAS, PATHOS, PLUS, PUS, SASSAFRAS, THIS, THUS, US, YES.

Words in which terminal <e> on words of two or more syllables is not silent, as in *mate*, and does not grunt, as in *acre*. Words in which terminal <e> spells [ee].
ABORIGINE, ACME, ACNE, ANDANTE, ANEMONE, ANTE, CATASTROPHE, CURARE, EPITOME, FACSIMILE, KARATE, KARAOKE, ORIGANE, POSSE, RECCE, RECIPE, SIMILE, SYNCOPE, TSETSE, UKULELE, VIGILANTE, WITHE. Proper Nouns ACHILLE, ANDES, CHILE, DAPHNE.

The next three lists are old spellings of long vowels using <a> followed by <l>.

In all words <a> spells [or] before <ll> in the same syllable. *Shall* is the only known rebel.
ALL, BALL, BEFALL, BOOKSTALL, CALL, CATCALL, FALL, FALL-SHORT, FORESTALL, GALL, GALL-BLADDER, GALLSTONE, HALL, HALLMARK, INSTALL, MALL, PALL, PALL BEARER, RECALL, SMALL, STALL, TALL, THRALL, WALL.
Including compounds in which one <l> is removed to prevent three consonants in a row: ALMOST, ALREADY, ALSO, ALTHOUGH *adv.*, ALTOGETHER, ALWAYS.

Words in which <a> spells [or] before blends <ld> & <lk> in the same syllable.
ALDER, ALDERMAN, BALD, BALDERDASH, BALK, BALSA, BALSAM, CALK, CHALK, EMERALD, PALSY, PIEBALD, RIBALD, RIBALDRY, SCALD, SKEWBALD, STALK, STANCH, TALK, WALK, WALKIE-TALKIE, WALKWAY, WALKABOUT. Proper Noun BALKAN.

Words in which <a> spells either [or] or [o] before blend <lt> and in terminal <alse>. (Australians say [o].)
ALTERATION, ALTERCATION, ALTERNATE, ALTERNATIVELY, ALTERNATIVE, ALTERNATE, ALTERNATION, ALTERNATOR, COBALT, FALSE, FALSELY, FALSENESS, FALSE ALARM, FALSE PRETENCES, FALSEHOOD, FALSETTO, FALSIFY, FALSIFICATION, FALSITY, FALTER, HALT, HALTER, MALTED MILK, PALTRY, SALT, SALTBUSH, SALT-CELLAR, SALT-LICK, SALT-PAN, SALTS, SALTY. Proper Nouns BALTIC SEA, MALTA, MALTESE CROSS.

<o> spells [oo] in a range of words for various reasons.
APPROVE, DO, IMPROVE, MOVABLE, MOVE, MOVER, ON THE MOVE, GET A MOVE ON, INTO, LASSO, LOSE, LOSE OUT, LOSE GROUND, LOSE HEART, LOSE ONE'S WAY, LOSING BATTLE, MOVE IN, MOVING, ONTO, PROVABLE, PROVE, PROVE ONESELF, PROVEN Δ, NOT PROVEN, REDO, REPROVE, TO, TO-DO, TOMB *silent b*, TWO, UNDO, UNPROVEN, WHO, WHOM, WHOSE, WOMB *silent b*.

In three stem words <one> spells [on]: SHONE, SCONE, GONE and hence in BEGONE, BYGONE, FOREGONE, GONER.

<u> spells [uu] in the next words.
AMBUSH, BUFFET, BULL, BULLDOG, BULLDOZE, BULLET, BULLETIN, BULL, BULLFIGHT, BULLFINCH, BULLION, BULLOCK, BULLRING, BULL'S-EYE, BULL-TERRIER, BULLY, BULLY BEEF, BULRUSH, BULWARK, BUSH, BUSH TELEGRAPH, BUSHEL, BUSHINESS, BUTCH, BUTCHER, BUTCHERY, CUCKOO, CUCKOO-CLOCK, EYEFUL, FULCRUM, FULFIL, FULL, FULLNESS, FULL BACK, FULL-BLOWN, FULL-BLOODED, FULL MARKS, FULL-SCALE, FULL MOON, FULL SPEED, FULL STOP, FULL TIME, FULL-TIME, IN FULL, FULLNESS OF TIME, TO THE FULL, FULMAR BIRD, FULSOME, INPUT, KAPUT, PUDDING, PULL, PULL A FAST ONE, PULLET, PULLEY, PULLOVER, PULPIT, PUSH, PUSHER, AT A PUSH, BE PUSHED FOR, GIVE OR GET THE PUSH, PUSH AROUND, PUSS/ PUSSY CAT, PUSSY WILLOW, PUSSYFOOT, PUT, SUGAR. Australian Words BULL, BULL ANT, BULL-ARTIST, BULL-BAR, BULLDOG, BULLDUST, BULLOCKY, BULN-BULN BIRD, BUSH, BUSH-BAPTIST, BUSH CARPENTER, GO BUSH, BUSHED, BUSHFIRE, BUSHMAN, BUSHRANGER, BUSHY.

<o> spells [uu] in *only three stem words, all Old English words.
1st. BOSOM, BOSOM FRIEND, BOSOMY.
2nd. WOLF, WEREWOLF, WEREWOLVES, WOLF-WHISTLE, WOLFHOUND, WOLVES, WOLVERINE.
3rd. WOMAN, WOMANHOOD, WOMANISH, WOMANIZE, WOMANIZER, WOMANLY, WOMANLINESS, GENTLEWOMAN.
Moslem spells [muuz-lem] but is an old and incorrect way of writing *Muslim*. *Moslem* means 'one who is evil and unjust' and *Muslim* means 'one who gives himself to the God of Abraham.'

Twinned R's only bossy if it's between a word's end and suffix, so Bossy R is not in this list.
ABERRANT, ABHORRENCE, ABHORRENT, ARRANT, ARREST, ARRIVE, ARROGANCE, BARRACKS, BARRAGE, BARREL, BERRY, CHERRY, CIRRHOSIS, CORRECT, CORRELATE, CORRESPOND, CORRIDOR, CORRUGATE, CORRUPT, CURRANT, CURRENT, CURRICULUM, CURRY, DERRY, DETERRENT, DIARRHOEA, ERRAND, ERRANT, ERROR, FERRET, FERRY, FLURRY, GARRET, GONORRHOEA, HAEMORRHOIDS, HORRID, HORROR, HURRY, JERRY-CAN, LOGORRHOEA, LORRY, MERRY, NARRATIVE, ORRIS, PORRIDGE, PYORRHOEA, SCURRY, SHERRY,, SLURRY, SORRY, SPORRAN, SURRENDER, SUSURRANT, TERRAIN, TERRAPIN, TERRIFIC, TERRIFY, TORRENT, TORRID, WARRANT, WORRY *f*

Some vowels lengthen before two, or even three, terminal consonants in the stem and also before <ange> but sometimes the vowel can change depending on the suffix, e.g., [chIld] and [chIldless] but [children], *angel* [aynjel] but *angelic* [anjelik], *wilder* [wIld-er] but *wilderness* [wil-der-nes].

ALIGHT, ALIGN, ALIGNING, ANGEL, ARRANGE, ASSIGN, BEHIND, BENIGN, BIGHT, BIND, BLIGHT, BLIND, BRIGHT, CLIMB, CHAMBER, CHILD, CHILDLESS, CLIMB, CLIMBER, COMB, COMBER, CONSIGN, CO-SIGN, DANGER, DELIGHT(ED), DELIGHTING, DERANGE, DESIGN(ING), ENSIGN, ESTRANGE, FIGHT(ING), FIGHTER, FIND, FLIGHT, FOLK, FRIGHT(FUL), GRANGE, GHOST, GRIND, HIGH, HIGHER, HIND, IMPUGN, KIND, KINDER/EST, KNIGHT, LIGHT(ER/ING), MALIGN(ING), MANGE, MANGER, MIGHT, MILD, MILDER/EST, MILDLY, MIND, MOST, NIGH, NIGHT, OPPUGN, PARADIGM, PINT, PLIGHT, POLK INK, RANGE, RIND, REMIND, REPUGN, RESIGN, RIGHT, SIGH, SIGHT, SIGN, SLIGHT, STRANGE, STRANGER, THIGH, TIGHT, UNBIND, UNKIND, UNWIND, WILD(ER/EST), WILDLY, WIND(ER/ING), WRIGHT, YOLK.

In "Utterly Motherly" words <other> spells [udher].
ANOTHER, BROTHER, BROTHERHOOD, MOTHER, MOTHERHOOD, MOTHER-IN-LAW, MOTHER-OF-PEARL, MOTHER TONGUE, MOTHERCRAFT, MOTHERLESS, MOTHERLAND, MOTHERLY, MOTHERLINESS, MOTHER'S DAY, OTHER, OTHERWISE, SMOTHER.

In "Mother's Country Cousins" <ou> spells [u].
CHOUGH, COUNTRIFIED, COUNTRY, COUNTRYMAN, COUNTRYSIDE, COUNTRY-&-WESTERN, COUPLE, COUPLET, COUPLING, COURAGE, COURAGEOUS, COUSIN, COUSINLY, CROSS-COUNTRY, DOUBLE, AT THE DOUBLE, DOUBLE AGENT, DOUBLE-BREASTED, DOUBLE-CHECK, DOUBLE-CROSS, DOUBLE-DECKER, DOUBLE ENTRY, DOUBLE FIGURES, DOUBLE GLAZING, DOUBLE-DUTCH, DOUBLE-JOINTED, DOUBLE OR QUITS, DOUBLE-PARK, DOUBLE-QUICK, DOUBLE TAKE, DOUBLE-TALK, DOUBLER, DOUBLE-GEE, DOUBLOON, ENOUGH <gh>=[f], FLOURISH, NOURISH, REDOUBLE, RETOUCH, ROUGH <gh>=[f], ROUGHLY, ROUGHNESS, ROUGHAGE, ROUGHEN, ROUGHCAST, ROUGHNECK, OUT OF TOUCH, SOUTHERLY, SOUTHERLY BUSTER, SOUTHERN, SOUTHERNER, SOUTHERNMOST, SLOUGH *verb* <gh>=[f], THERMOCOUPLE, TOUCH, TOUCHED, TOUCHER, TOUCHINESS, TOUCHING, TOUCHINGLY, TOUCHABLE, TOUCHDOWN, TOUCH-AND-GO, TOUCH BOTTOM, TOUCH-JUDGE *in rugby*, TOUCH-LINE, TOUCH OFF, TOUCH-PAPER, TOUCHSTONE, TOUCH-TYPING, TOUCH UP, TOUCH WOOD, TOUCHABLE, TOUCHY, IN TOUCH WITH, TOUGH, TOUGH LOVE, TOUGH GUY, TROUBLE, TROUBLE-MAKER, TROUBLE-SHOOTER, TROUBLESOME, TROUBLE-SPOT, GO TO SOME TROUBLE, IN TROUBLE, MAKE TROUBLE, UNCOUPLE, UNTOUCHABLE, YOUNG, YOUNGISH, YOUNGSTER. "Distant Cousin" DOZEN [duz-en]. Name DOUGLAS.

In "Cold Shoulder" words <oul> spells [ol].
BOULDER, MOULD, MOULDER, MOULDINESS, MOULDING, MOULDY, MOULT, POULTERER, POULTICE, POULTRY, SHOULDER, SHOULDER ARMS, SHOULDER-BAG, SHOULDER-BLADE, SHOULDER-HIGH, SHOULDER-TO-SHOULDER, SMOULDER, SOUL, SOULFUL, SOULLESS.

Cursive Casualties
Cursive Casualty words, which I also nickname Feather Words, were written with feather pens, and then re-spelt to avoid the damage imposed by the cursive style of writing, especially damaging since at that time <i> has no dot on top.
First, look at letter swapping for legibility in cursive handwriting.

In the following words <i> and <e> were reversed in front of <c> and <w>, as otherwise illegible in cursive hand writing. CEILING, CONCEIT, CONCEIVE, DECEIT, DECEIVE, PERCEIVE, RECEIPT, RECEIVE, ROTTWEILER, WEIR, WEIRD.

Secondly, let's look at letter replacement for legibility in cursive handwriting.

In the following words <o> replaces <u> and <o> spells [u], in all but *women*, in which <o> replaces <i> and spells [i]. I call them Feather Words, or Cursive Casualties.

ABOVE, ACCOMPANY, AMOCK/AMUCK, AMONG, AMONGST, BECOME, BECOMINGLY, COLOUR/COLOR USA, COME, COMFORT, COMFORTER, COMFREY, COMFY, COMING, COMELY, COMPASS, COMPANY, however <o> in *companion* is not [u], COSTERMONGER, COVEN, COVENANT, COVER, COVERT, COVET, COVETOUS, COVEY, DISCOMFORT, DISCOVER, DONE, DOVE, DOVETAIL, DOVECOTE, EVERYONE, FISHMONGER, FOREFRONT, FOXGLOVE, FRONT, CONFRONT, IN FRONT, FRONT RUNNER, FRONT-BENCHER, FRONTAGE, FRONTAL, FRONTIER, FRONTISPIECE, GLOVE, GLOVE PUPPET, GLOVES OFF, FIT LIKE A GLOVE, GLOVER, GOVERNANCE, GOVERNESS, GOVERNMENT, GOVERNOR, HONEY, INCOME, INCOME TAX, INCOMING, LOVE, LOVELESS, LOVELORN, LOVELY, LOVELINESS, LOVER, LOVESICK, LOVING, LOVINGLY, MONEY, MONGREL, MONK, MONKEY, MONKEY BUSINESS , MONKEY PUZZLE, MONKEY WRENCH, MONKSHOOD, MONTH, MONTHLY, NONE, NONE THE LESS, ONION, OVEN, OVENWARE, POMMEL, REDONE, SON, SHOVE, SHOVEL, SHOVELBOARD, SHOVELLER, SPONGY, STOMACH, TON, TONGUE, TONNAGE, TONNE, UNDONE, WOMEN* [wimen], WON, WONDER, WONDERFUL, WONDERLAND, WONDERMENT, WONDROUS, WONDROUSLY, WONT, WORRY, WORRISOME. <u>Proper Nouns</u> MIDSOMMER, COVENTRY.

In two words, *one* and *once,* <o> spells [wu]: ONCE [wuns], ONE [wun], ONESELF.

In the following words, <o> replaces <i> or <u> between <w> and <r>, and <wor> spells [wer].

WHORL, WORD, WORK, WORLD, WORM, WORSE, WORSHIP, WORST, WORSTED, WORT, WORTH, WORTHY.

Now let's look at letter addition for legibility in cursive handwriting.

In words like *give* and *blue,* <e> is added to tell round-bottomed cursive <v> and <u> apart, by the different height of links to terminal <e>. These different links are obvious inside a cursive word but not at the end. Examples: GIVE, HAVE, LIVE, SIEVE; BLUE, GLUE, PURSUE, TRUE. The only rebels are some words ending <u>, e.g., YOU, to avoid three vowels in a row; FLU as an abbrev. BUREAU and other French words ending <eau> and foreign adoptions like EMU, MUU-MUU, TU-TU, GURU, TOFU, ZEBU.

Some feather words prior to respelling:
wuurd, wuimen, wuurd, wuurld
cume, wuun, tun, tru, hav.

Did you manage to read *weird, women, word, world, come, won, ton, true* and *have* prior to swapping, replacing or adding letters?

Collaterally Damaged Words

In very few words <wa> spells [wa] not [wo] – WAX, WAG, WAGGLE, WAGGON/WAGON, WACK, SWAM, SWANK. Also, the acronym WAAF = [waf] (Women's Auxiliary Airforce.

In all the rest, Don't Let W Muddle You! <wa> and <qua> spell [wo]. The following words have suffered collateral damage because <o> cannot be used to spell [o] in them as a consequence of <o> replacing <i> or <u> before [w], in cursive casualties, as above. This damage includes when <u> spells [w] after <q>.

BACKWASH, DOGWATCH, EYEWASH, SQUAT, SQUATTER, QUAD, QUADRANT, QUAFF, QUALIFY, QUANTIFY, QUANTITY, QUANTUM, QUARANTINE, QUARREL, QUARRELSOME, QUARRY, QUASH, QUATRAIN, SQUAD, SQUANDER, SQUASH, SQUASHY, SQUASH RACKETS, QUANDARY, SWAP=SWOP, SWAMP, SWAMPY, SWAN, SWAN-SONG, SWAN-UPPING, SWANSDOWN, SWASHBUCKLING, SWATH, SWASTIKA, SWAT, TIGHTWAD, 'TWAS, SWATH, VALSE=WALTZ, WAD, WADDLE, WAFT, WAFTED, WALLABY, WALLET, WALLOP, WALLOPING, WALLOW, WALTZ, WAN, WANNER, WANNEST, WANLY, WANNESS, WAND, WANDER, WANDERER, WANDERLUST, WANT, WANTED, WANTING, WANTON, WAS, WASH, WASH-BASIN, WASHED-OUT, WASH-HOUSE, WASH-OUT, WASH-ROOM, WASH-STAND, WASH-TUB, WASH UP, WASHABLE, WASHER, WASN'T, WASP, WASPISH, WASSAILING, WAST (*thou wast*), WATER*, WATCH, WATCHER, WATCH-DOG, WATCH OUT, WATCH-TOWER, WATCHFUL, WATCHFULLY, WATCHFULNESS, WATCHMAKER, WATCHMAN, WATCHWORD, WATT*, WATTAGE, WATTLE, WHAT, WHAT ABOUT, WHATNOT, WHATEVER, WHATSOEVER, WIGWAM, WRATH, WRISTWATCH. <u>Australian</u> QUANDONG, SQUATTER, SQUATTOCRACY, WADDY, WAGGA RUG, WALLABY, ON THE WALLABY, WALLAROO, WALLOPER, WALNUT, WALRUS, WANDOO TREE, WARATAH, WARRIGAL, WASHER, WATTLE. <u>Proper Nouns</u> WASHINGTON, WAGGAWAGGA.

*Water spells [wo-ter] in Northern England and America, even [wod-er], but in Australia and southern England it spells [wor-ter], as in WATER, WATERCOURSE, WATERCRESS, WATERFALL, WATERFRONT, WATER-MOLE (*platypus*), WATER-SIDER.

*Watt is an eponym and therefore breaks the rule that <tt> is not needed at the end of words after short vowel sounds, and what is more this word already has its required three letters. The word honours Scottish engineer James Watt.

<war> spells [wor] unless followed by a vowel.
AFTERWARDS, ANTIWAR, ATHWART, AWARD, AWKWARD, BACKWARD, BULWARK, COWARD, DOWNWARD, DWARF, FORWARD, INWARD, ONWARD, PRE-WAR, REWARD, STALWART, SEAWARD, STEWARD, SWARD, SWARM, SWART, SWARTHY, THWART, THWART, TOWARD, UPWARD, WAR, -WARD* *suffix*.
*The suffix –*ward* spells [wəd] if unstressed.

The next words have **"Diplomatic Immunity"**.

Many words in English dictionaries have been **adopted but not adapted** from French in that they still have French spelling. In fact, there are about 4,000 words which are written the same way and have the same meaning in French and English, (Jackson 1981 p. 1). Some, like *train, place, table* and *cousin* and loads more are spelt the same and have the same meaning but sound different in French. Some have the same meaning but slight changes in spelling and pronunciation, like *uncle-oncle, object-objet, sign-signe* and so on.

Another lot have been wholly adopted into English, but not at all adapted, for their letters and their sounds are still totally French. As the letters do not spell their English sounds they cannot be sorted into English spelling lists. English speakers have to learn to decode the letters of the words into their French sounds. Some were adopted hundreds of years ago and no longer used in France. For instance, we still write RSVP on invitations, the old French request for a reply, but it is no longer used in France. Here are some examples of French words which are in English dictionaries.

French pronunciation depends on position in sentences, e.g., final consonants are usually silent, unless the next word begins with a vowel and then it is linked onto that word, unless there is a natural pause, e.g., *Comment?* [kom-on]. *Comment allez vous?* [kom -on-tarl-ay-voo]. When word final <s> and <x> are

linked to the next word they spell [z], e.g., *vous enfants* [vooz-on-fon]; <f> when linked is <v>, and <d> when linked spells [d]. In French words all syllables are given equal stress, except the last or last but one, which is stressed, but then usually only in the final word of a sentence or clause, (Jackson 1981 p. 8).
French words used in English:—
ABSINTHE [ab-sinth] (not [ab-sindh]), ABATTOIR [a-bar-twar], ACOUTREMENT [ar-koo-ter-mont], AIDE-DE-CAMP [ay-d-com], À LA CARTE [ar lar cart], APROPOS [ap-roh-poh], ARTISTE [ar-teest], AU GRATIN [oh grar-tun], AU PAIR [oh pair], AVANT-GARDE [avon gard], AVOIRDUPOIS [av-war-dyoo-pwar], BALLET [bal-ay], BEAU [boh], BEAUFORT SCALE [boh-fort], BEAUJOLAIS [boh sho-lay], BÊTE NOIR [bayt nwar], BILLET-DOUX [bil-lay-doo], BIVOUAC [biv –oo-ak], BLANC MANGE [bla-manzh], BLASÉ [blar-say], BI-JOU [bee-zhoo], BIORZOI [bor-jwar], BONHOMIE [bon-o-mee], BOUCLÉ [boo-clay], BORZOI *dog* [bor-zwar], BOUDOIR [boo-dwar], BOUGAINVILLAEA [boo-gun-vil-ee-ar], BOUILLON [boo-yorn], BOUQUET [boo-kay], now [boh-kay], BRODERIE ANGLAISE [brod-er-ee on-glayz], BUREAU [byoo-roh], BUREAUCRACY [byoo-rok-rasee], BUREAUCRAT [byoo-oh-krat], BUREAUCRATIC [byoo-oh-krat-ik], CABARET [kab-er-ay], CACHET [kash-ay], CADRE [kar-drer], CAFÉ [kaf-ay], CARAFE [ka-rarf], CANAPÉ [kan-up-ee], CAVIARE [kav-ee-ar], CHAISE LONGUE [shayz long], CHAMOIS [shamwar] *small wild antelop,* CHAMOIS [sham-ee] *soft leather,* CHAMPAGNE [sham-payn], CHAPERON [shap-er-on], CHAR-A-BANCS [shar-a-barng], plural: CHARS-A-BLANCS [sharz-a-barng], CHARADE [sha-rard], CHARGE D'AFFAIRES [sharj du fairz], CHASSIS [shas-see], CHATEAU [shat-oh], CHATELAINE [shat-e-layn], CHATEAU [shat-oh], CHAUFFEUR [shoh-fer], CHAUTREUSE [shar-trerz], CHEF [shef], CHIC [sheek], CHIGNON [sheen-yon], CLIENTELE [klee-en-tel], COIFFURE [kwar-fyoor], CROISSANT [kwar-sont], COMPOTE [kom-poh], COUP [koo], COUP DE GRACE [koo] [d] [grars], COUP D'ÉTAT [koo] [day-tar], CRÊCHE [kraysh], CRÈME DE MENTHE [kraym du marnth], CRÊPE [krayp], CRÊPE PAPER, CRÊPE SUZETTE, CRI DE COEUR [kree du ker], CULOTTES [kyoo-lts], CORTAGE [kor-tayzh], COUP [koo], COUP DE GRACE [koo d-grar], COUP D'ETAT [koo day-tar], CROQUET [kroh-kay], CUIRASS [kwee-ras], CUISINE [kwee-zeen], CUL-DE-SAC [kul du sak], DAUPHIN [doh-fun], DEBRIS [deb-ree], DEBUT [də-boo], DEBUTANTE [deb-yoo-tont], DÉCOR [day-kor], DÉJÀ VU [day-shar voo], DE LUXE [d lux], DE TROP [d troh], DEMESNE [di-meen], DÉNOUEMENT [day-noo-mon], DEPOT [de-poh], DERRIERE [de-ree-air], DESHABILLE [dayz-u-bee-lay], DESUETUDE [des-wee-tyood], DETOUR [dee-toor], DISCOTHEQUE [dis-koh-tek], DIVAN [dee-van], DUVET [doo-vay], EAU [oh], EAU-DE-COLOGNE [oh-d-k-lohn], ÉCLAT [ay-klar], ÉLITE [ay-leet], ÉLAN [ay-lan], ÉMIGRÉ [em-ee-gray], EN BLOC [on blok], ENCORE [ong-kor], ENCLAVE [on-klarv], ENNUI [ong-wee], EN ROUTE [on root], ENSEMBLE [on-som-buul], EN-TENTE [ong-tongt], ENTRECÔTE [on-tr-koht], ENTRÉE [on-tray], ENTREPRENEUR [on-tr-pren-er], ENTOURAGE [on-toor-arj], EPERGNE [i-pern], ESCARGOT [es-kar-goh], ESPRIT-DE-CORPS [es-pree-d-kor], ESCRITOIRE [es-kree-twar], ETIQUETTE [etee-ket], ÉTUDE [ay-tyood], FAÇADE [far-sard], FAIT ACCOMPLI [fay-tuk-om-plee], FAUX PAS [foh par], FETE [fayt], FIANCÉ [fee-on-say] fiancée (female), FRACAS [frak-ar], GARÇON [gar-son], GATEAU [ga-toh], GAUCHERIE [goh-sheree], GENRE [jon-rer], HABITUÉ [har-bit-yoo-ay], HARICOT [ha-ree-koh], HAUTEUR [hoh –ter], HORS-D'OEUVRE [or-derv], JABOT [sha-boh], JARDINIERE [shar-din-ee-air], JOI-DE-VIVRE [jwar-d-veev-r], LAISSEZ-FAIRE [lay-zay fair], LAMÉ [lar-may], LIEUTENANT [left-en-ant], USA [loo-ten-ant], LINGERIE [lon-jer-ee], MADEMOISELLE [mud-um-war-zel], MANOEUVRE [man-oo-ver], MARQUIS [mar-kee], MARQUISETTE [mar-kee-zet], MEMOIR [mem-war], MÉNAGE [may-narj], MESDEMOISELLES [may-dem-war-zel], MESSIEURS [may-syoo-erz], MILIEU [mee-yer], MIRAGE [mi-rarj], MOIRÉ [mwar-ray], MONSEIGNEUR [mon-say-nyer], MONSIEUR [mon-syoor], MOUSTACHE [mus-tarsh], MOTIF [moh-teef], NAÏVE [nay-eev], NE PLUS ULTRA [n ploo sul-trar], NOUGAT [noo-gar], NOUVEAU [noo-voh], OBJET D'ART [ob-jay dar], OEVRE [oov-rer], PAPIER MÂCHÉ [pap-ee-ay

mash-ay], PARFAIT [par-ay], PÂTÉ [par-tay], PATOIS [pat-war], PEIGNOIR [payn-war], PIECE DE RESISTANCE [pee-es d re-zist-ons], PIED-À-TERRE [pee-ed-u-tair], PINCE-NEZ [parns-nay], PIROUETTE [pee-roh-et], PLATEAU [plat-oh], PLISSÉ [plee-say], PORTMANTEAU [port-mant-oh], PORTMANTEAU WORD, POSTE RESTANTE [pohst restont], PRÉCIS [pray-see], PREMIERE [prem-ee-air], PROTOGEE [proh-toh-zhay], QUI-VIVE [kee-veev], RACONTEUR [ra-kon-ter], RAISON D'ÊTRE [ray-zon-det-rar], RAPPORT [ru-por], RECHERCHE [re-shar-shay], RECONOITRE [rek-on-oy-ter], REGIME [ray-zheem], RENDEZVOUS [ron-day-voo], RESERVOIR [rez-er-vwor], RESTAURANT [res-toh-rong], RETROUSSÉ [re-troo-say], REVEILLE [re-val-i], RISQUÉ [ris-kay], ROSÉ [roh-zay], ROUÉ [roo-ay], ROUGE [roozsh], rouleau [roo-loh], RSVP = respondez s'il vous plait [re-spon-day see-voo-play], 'reply please', now out of date in France. SACHET [sa-shay], SANG-FROID [sung-frwar], SAUTÉ [soh-tay], SAUTERNES [soh-tern], SAVOIR-FAIRE [sav-war-fair], SOBRIQUET [so-bri-kay], SOIRÉE [swar-ray], SOUFFLÉ [soo-flay], SOUPÇON [soo-son], SOUVENIR [soo-ve-neer], SUITE [sweet], TABLEAU [tab-loh], TABLEAUX [tab-loh], TÊTE-À-TÊTE [tayt-u-tayt], TIMBRE [tom-brer], TONNEAU [ton-noh], TOUCHÉ [too-shay], TOUPEE [too-pay], TOURNIQUET [toor-na-kay], TRAIT [tray], TROUSSEAU [troo-soh], VIGNETTE [veen-yet], VINAIGRETTE [vin-ee-gret], VIS-À-VIS [veez-u-vee], VOYEUR [vwar-yer].

We do not always pronounce these words the French way but we continue to spell them the French way. (Australians found it hard to say *au revoir* to the French girls in World War One — [oh re-vwar], Is it true that they changed it to *oo roo*, to say "See you later, until we meet again."?)

English has also **adopted but not adapted** other foreign words. For example —
from **Spain**: SEÑOR [seen-yor] SEÑORA [seen-yor-ar], SEÑORITA [seen-yor-ee-tar], PADRE [par-dray]; COMPADRE [kom-par-dray]; and SUCRE [soo-kray]. (The sucre is the basic monetary unit in Ecuador named after the Venezuelan revolutionary Antonia José de Sucre b.1795 d.1830)
from **Norway**: FJORD [fee-yord];
from **Germany**: DEUTZIA [doyt-zee-u]; HAUSFRAU [hows-frow]; LANDAU [lan-dow]
from the **West Indies**: REGGAE [reg-ay];
from **Italy**: SOTTO VOCE [sot-oh voch-ee], VIVA VOCE [vee-var voch-ee].
from **Persia** CAVIARE [kav-ee-ar]/CAVIAR
from **South Africa** STOEP [stoop]

We use many **Latin words** in our law courts and even in everyday life. The Romans pronounced each letter and <c> was still [k], not yet softened to [ch] by the Italians and to [s] by the French before <e>. The Roman pronunciation of vowels was the basis for southern European vowel sounds.
AD HOC [ad hok], AD LIB [ad lib], AD INFINITUM [ad in-fIn-I-tuum], ALUMNUS, male graduate, ALUMNI, plural [al-um-nee], , ALUMNA, female graduate, ALUMNAE, pl. [al-um-nI], APROPOS* [ap-ru-poh], BONA FIDES [boh-nar fI-deez], CIRCA (c.) [ser-kar], CUI BONO? [kyoo-ee boh-noh], CUM DIV. [kuum deev], EX CATHEDRA [eks kath-ee-drar], HABEUS CORPUS [hay-bee-uus] [kor-puus], IN CAMERA [in-kam-er-ar], MODUS OPERANDI [moh-duud op-er-an-dee], NON COMPOS MENTIS [non kom-pos men-tis], PRIMA FACIE* [pree-mar fay-kee], NON SEQUITER [non sek-wit-er], PERSONA NON GRATA [per-soh-nar non grar-tar], POST MORTEM [pohst-mor-tem], PRO RATA [proh rar-tar], QUID PRO QUO [kwid proh kwoh], QUOD VIDE (q.v.) kwod veed-ay], RIGOR MORTIS [rig-or mor-tis], SINE DIE [see-nay dee-ay], SINE QUA NON [see-nay kwar non], STATUS QUO [star-tuus kwoh], SUB ROSA [sub roh-sar], TERRA FIRMA [te-rar fer-mar], TERRA INCOGNITA [te-rar in-kog-nee-tar], VERSUS (vs.) [ver-suus], VETO [vee-toh].
**Apropos* [ap-ru-poh] is a late addition to this list, thanks Peter Norman for letting me know I missed it. Peter has also said he does not think *apropos of* is correct usage of this word. There's a lot available on

line apropos *of* in this situation. Some say it is inappropriate in all but the phrase, 'Apropos of nothing'. This is said by people who want to change the topic of a conversation their way.

Prima facie is commonly but incorrectly said [prI-ma fay-shee], with Italian modifications.

We also use initials from Latin words and phrases: AD, am, CV, eg, NB, pm, ps, qed, RIP, v *or* vs, all of which can be researched at List of Latin abbreviations - Wikipedia.

Changes to English Over Time

Hewitt and Beach, p. 657, explain that humans instinctively avoid effort. Some call it laziness, some call it economy. It is laziness when it gives up more than it gains. It is economy when it gains more than it abandons. They go on to describe all the old guttural sounds of English which have been changed or abandoned under both the law of laziness and the law of ease, e.g. at the end of *though*. They describe how word-sounds 'initial, medial, and final', have been dropped, added or changed, to avoid effort, but with no effort made to change the letters, as in *hurry*, which once rhymed with *furry*.

English changed a little due to the successful invasion of England by Vikings and then a lot with the successful 1066 invasion by Viking descendants, the Norman French. English was further impacted by Parisien, Central and Southern French, during the three centuries in which French was the official language of England. The switch from Old English to Middle English began in 1066. The transformation to Modern English occurred in the Great Vowel Shift of 1450 to 1650.

Let's use the Lord's Prayer to show how English has changed. It is one of the few bits of the Bible, (Matthew 5, and also Luke 11), expressed in English very early. Bibles were officially in Latin until 1611, with just bits interpreted by priests, who taught this prayer:

Tenth Century. Faeder ure, thu the eart on heofonum (*Father our, thou that art in heaven*) si thin nama ge-halgod. (*by thy name hallowed*)
To-becume thin rice. (*Come thy rule.*) Ge-wurthe thin willa on eorthan, (*Be done thy will in earth,*)
swa swa on heofonum. (*as also in heaven.*) Urme ge-dæghwamlican half gyf us to dæg. (*Our daily loaf give us today.*)
And forgyf us ure gyltas (*and forgive us our guilt*) swa swa we forgyfath urum gyltendum. (*as also we forgive our guilty ones.*)
And neg e-læd thu us on costnunge, (*And not lead thou us in to trial,*) ac a-lysus of yfele. (*but release us from evil.*)
Sothlice. (*Soothly* meaning *truly.*)
In which, 'costnunge' means *costing,* i.e. evaluating or testing; 'swa' means *so*; and 'ge-dæghwamlican' breaks up into 'daeg/hwam/lice' meaning *day/each/like,* i.e. daily.

Thirteenth Century. Fader oure that art in heve, i-halged bee thi nome. I-cume thi kinereiche. Y-worthe thi wylle also is in hevene so be on erthe. Oure ich-days bred gif us to day, & forgif us our gultes, also we forgifet oure gultare, &ne led us nowth into fondingge, auth a-les ows of harme. So be hit.

Fourteenth Century. Oure fadir that art in heuenes, halwid be thi name. Thi kingdom cumme to. Be thi wille don as in heuen and in erthe. Gif to vs this day ouer breed oure other substances, and forgeue to oure detours, and leede vs nat in to temptacioun, but delyuere vs fro yuel. Amen.

Sixteenth Century. O oure father which art in heven, hallowed be thy name. Let thy kingdom come. Thy wyll be fulfiled, as well in erth as hit ys in heven. Geve vs this daye our dayly breade. And forgeve vs oure treaspases, euen as we forgeve them which treaspas vs. Leede vs not into temptation, but delyvre vs from yvell. Amen

Seventeenth Century 1611. Our father which art in heaven, Hallowed be thy name. Thy kingdom come. Thy will be done in earth as it is in heaven. Give us this day our daily bread. And forgive us our trespasses, as we forgive them that trespass against us. And lead us not in to temptation but deliver us from evil. Amen

As you can see, the spelling of the words in the Lord's Prayer has not changed since 1611. One reason for this was that the dictionary committee felt that all the words in the 1611 King James Bible were sacred, including their spelling. The Good News Bible 1976 shows that choice of words has changed since 1611, but not the way each is spelt:— Our Father in heaven; May your holy name be honoured, May your kingdom come; May your will be done on earth as it is in heaven. Give us today the food we need. Forgive us the wrongs we have done, as we forgive the wrongs that others have done to us. Do not bring us to hard testing, But keep us safe from the Evil One.

Some Dates and Developments in English and its spelling.
Very recent developments like texting abbreviations and symbols are excluded.
4,000 BC Neolithic farmers cross the English Channel and settle in what is today called England as well as other parts of the British Isles, language/s unknown.
2,500 BC England is invaded by the Beaker People, who made clay beakers. What did they speak?
500 – 100 BC The Celts invade, from Upper Danube in Europe. Few Celtic words remain today, except in place names, but the language is preserved as the basis of today's Welsh, Cornish, Scots Gaelic and Irish languages.
54 and 55 BC Julius Caesar, general of the Roman army in Gaul, visits Britain and notes in his diary that England's druids wrote their secrets using Greek letters, ref. Dominic Selwood under Websites in appendix. This was possibly due to earlier Greek exploration of British coastline or to connection with Gallic druids. However, there are no Druid written records. I think that these ancient British elders kept the power of spelling a secret, like their Australian Aboriginal counterparts, in order to retain their power in the tribe. Without their rote knowledge, the poems and sagas of the tribe would disappear. While they spent one or two decades teaching younger, emerging elders to memorize them, they, the elders, were well cared for and highly respected. Written knowledge would have been easily passed on and left them old, hungry and disrespected. Besides, written knowledge can be destroyed or fall into the wrong hands. Writing is not needed in a close community. In Ab'l Australia, written messages were only for the blind, those too far away to be seen. Hence our local Ab'l name for message stick: 'pamburu' or 'bamburu'. *Pambu/bambu* means 'blind' (in Yingardda and Wadjari languages) and the suffix *—uru* means 'assistance for'. Some pamburu were passed on in public, others hidden in hair as sacred items. We are not only blind to those far away but also to our dead ancestors, whose messages live on, spelt out in the magic of silent speech, in written symbols. It's not too far a stretch to surmise that British elders kept the secret of spelling to themselves, to records their spells and spiels.
43 AD to **409 AD** Romans return and rule Britain, speaking Latin, which did not mix with Celtic language/s to create 'British', unlike the Latin-Gallic mix which became French. Their alphabet had only twenty letters when they arrived in Britain but gained more during the four centuries they colonized the part of Britain which became England. Romans left behind the ABC but the Brits adopted very few Latin words outside of church matters, (Hewitt, p.475). Romans shared the skill of reading and writing openly, to communicate across their vast empire. Sensitive information was sent by secret codes, e.g., choosing letters a chosen number of steps along the alphabet. The coded message and the number of steps were then sent separately, by messengers unkown to each other.
500 – 600's. Invasions by Saxons, Angles and Jutes, speaking Low German, which developed into English, now called Old English. It had about 50,000 words, including Celtic words, like *crag, dun, brock, combe, torr* and also about 200 Latin words adopted by Anglo-Saxons before moving to Britain. The Anglo-Saxons had their own alphabet, their futhorc. This word echoes the sound values of its first six runes, its letters.
Around **600,** Christian missionaries arrived in England and they put the ABC alphabet to use again. Six runes were added to the ABC in order to spell English word-sounds which the ABC letters did not express,

e.g. the sound at the end of *moth* and the sound beginning *apple*. Also, some letters were written once to spell one sound and twice to spell another, which we still see in *of* and *off: his* and *hiss*; *in baa lamb; bet* and *beet; rod* and *rood*.

700, or maybe as late as **1000**, the heroic epic poem *Beowulf* was written in Old English, all about Vikings, who by then were in England, speaking Norse and adding their words to English. From **793** Vikings from today's Norway, Sweden and Denmark attacked along England's east coast. By **870** Danish Vikings have taken control in the north.

King Alfred reigned in the south from **871 to 899**. He spent a lot of time fighting off Viking invasions from the north but was also very keen on language and literacy. He started schools, translated Latin books into English, and commissioned the Anglo-Ssaxon Chronicle, a history of the English.

886 Danes make truce with King Alfred in the south. North of England is under Danelaw, ruled by the Danes. These Danish Vikings brought new words and new pronunciations, *skirts* for *shirts* and *skips* for *ships*, for instance, but no big changes to spelling. Those who could write, the scribes, matched the symbols (letters and runes) to the sounds as best they could. Just as today there is no one correct way to draw a cat, back then there was no one correct way to spell a word. Besides, each region had its own accent/pronunciation of words.

From **1013**, all England was ruled by Danes, King Canute and his family, until **1042,** when English kings are back in power. Then the English king dies without heirs. The choice is between the dead king's brother-in-law and his cousin William, across the sea in Normandy. Normandy is the 'home of men from the north.' Earlier, when Danish and Norwegian Vikings invaded France, from the north, landing along the French coast, they were allowed to stay as long as they did not come any further south. So they stayed in Normandy and became French but they spoke their own sort of French, with many Viking words, from Germanic languages like Danish and Norwegian. So their French was different to central and southern French. It was Norman French

1066 The English crowned the brother-in-law. This triggered the Norman Invasion of England, in which the new English king was killed. William was crowned King of England but he could not speak English. English was no longer the official language of England. Words changed e.g., *eam* became *uncle, Wolfmonth→ January, Haymonth→ July, Holymonth→ December, waston→ fruit,* and *apple* no longer meant any *fruit*. Not only did King William the First of England speak no English, he was also illiterate. The flowering of the English language was over.

Between **1066 and 1200** Old English was spoken only by illiterate lower classes. Old English was polluted with French words and its spelling changed by French scribes. Then six runic symbols were removed from the English Alphabet and replaced with letters, so that word-sounds had to share letters with others. French phobias were imposed. For instance, when S was used to avoid Z, and CE forced to stand in for S, simple Old English *is* became *ice*.

In approx. **1150** Orm, of East Midlands, researched English spelling, to help priests give sermons in English to the lower classes. He revived an Old English rule, that twinning consonants after vowels keeps the vowel short, wrote it in his book, and wrote his name on the book, Ormulum, meaning 'Of Orm', in Latin. So now we call that Orm's Law.

By **1200** English, what we now call 'Middle English', has ~100,000 words, with 10,000 of them added from Norman French and the majority of Old English words are lost or altered. Its Old English declensions of nouns and conjugations of verbs are in shreds, so much so that whilst in French the verb *aimer,* 'to love', has over twenty possible endings, in English we only use three, as in I, you, we, they *love* — also I etc. will *love:* he, she *loves*; I, you, he, she, we, they *loved* or had *loved* or should have *loved* or will have *loved.* Nouns have lost their gender and many of their 'flexible' suffixes.

1204 England loses Normandy but, through the king, inherits provinces in central and southern France. Central French words are added to Middle English by adoption and adpation. Norman French often retained for one meaning, Central French used for another e.g., *cattle, chattle*. (However, *gaol* is not replaced by *jail*, although they have the same meaning.)

By **1300** the strong Woollen Industry guilds in Northern and Midlands are producing plays in English, called Miracle Plays.

In **1348 – 49** the Black Death halved England's population. Labour short, English-speaking peasants freed from feudal servitude to become yeomen and independent labourers. This took English back into the middle classes and forced the ruling classes to use it, instead of French, so that they could communicate with the middle classes. The plague reduced the number of people who could translate upper class requests made in French to lower class workers in English.

Geoffrey Chaucer **(c. 1343 – 1400)** is writing books in English. In his *Canterbury Tales* we read about an English lady who thought she spoke in good French, but French people could not understand her. She was not the only one. The French openly laughed at England's version of their language and the English found it less humiliating to stop speaking French. The return to English did not stop the flow of French words into English, especially from the central and southern regions of France which were under English rule until in 1429 Joan of Arc led the French towards the freedom which came in 1453 with the final defeat of the English in France.

1362 The Pleading in English Act stipulated that all court cases had to be in English, not French.

1362 was the first year that parliament was in English, not French. Parliamentary proceedings were still recorded in Latin.

1380 First translation of the New Testament into English from Latin, by John Wycliffe who "put the Bible into the hands of the common people." It circulated illegally, in secret, for almost 150 years.

1382 First translation of Old Testament into English from Latin. The complete Wycliffe Bible was handwritten and each Bible copied by hand, secretly.

1385 English is used in schools. **1432** First parliament recorded in English.

1399 – 1413 Henry the Fourth ruled England as the first king, since 1066, to speak English as his first language.

1476 Caxton's return to London as England's first printer, which marks the beginning of Modern English. Availability of books created awareness of the many dialects of English and the need to standardize English. Printing was invented in Europe in 1454, independent of invention of moveable type in China early in eleventh century.

1489 English Law now recorded in English alone. Prior to that in French, translated into English if needed. By **1490** French was understood only by a minority in England, according to Caxton.

It had taken three hundred years for English to once again become the official language of England but it was by now a hybrid mixture of French and English which we now call Middle English.

1450 – 1650 The Great Vowel Shift. This made a huge difference to the way English spelling decodes, simply because spelling did not change with the times. Vowels always change, from place to place and time to time, but in this period huge changes took place, see 'Vowels' in the appendix. When something similar happened earlier in Germany, German spelling was adapted to reflect the change. Not so in England. Although the spelling did not change, the sounds which vowel letters spelt changed a great deal, particularly in words which contained long vowel sounds. Thus, digraphs spell a range of word-sounds, as we see in *heat* and *great* and in *boot* and *floor*, for instance. Although English spelling had already suffered under French rule, this final blow to consistency in English spelling was made by the English themselves.

By **1500** many words were entering English directly from French and Latin origins, due to the Renaissance fervour in England. It changed the people, educated them in Latin and Greek, science and arts. Their inventions and new concepts needed more words, which they made, using Latin and Greek word parts.

Between **1590** and **1610,** 6,000 new words were added every year! By **1610,** English had 200,000 words. Having lost so many words, and indeed nearly dying out, our erstwhile poor and starving language acted like a greedy child in a sweet shop, stuffing itself with words. The collection of new words regardless of need created a huge bank of synonyms. They came from many languages and this meant a lot of words were homophones (sounded identical), which created more spelling confusion.

1536 saw a new Bible translation, which was followed by other translations, despite persecution in most cases. William Tyndale fails to get his printed in England, succeeds in Europe and it is smuggled into England. English Bishops buy up and burn hundreds of copies and then burn Tyndale at the stake. He wanted people to read God's message in their own language, with simple spelling for easy reading. The bishops thought this debased the word of God.

1564 to **1616**, the great writer William Shakespeare added about 10,000 English words to the written record. Spelling continued to vary a lot. For instance, documents show that Shakespeare spelt his name six different ways. At times, if scribes were short of paper, they spelt words the shortest way possible, but if they were paid by the line, they chose the longest spelling possible! England was not the only country which had many ways to spell each word.

There were thousands of handwritten books in Europe but then printing developed, between 1440 and 1450, and by 1500 there were more than nine million books in Europe. Italy was the first to help people read them.

1582 The Accademia della Crusca institution is set up in Florence to preserve linguistic purity of the Italian language. It simplifies spelling and guides the public on how to write and speak Italian, making it a *fixed* language.

From **1600** pirates and explorers began the spread of English around the globe and brought new words back to England. The English language soaked up foreign terms like a sponge, whereas the Italians, and soon the French, stopped them at the border, decided if they were required or superfluous to their needs. Since they had no other word for *kangaroo*, it was allowed in, but not before its spelling was adjusted to *canguro*. Later, *kangaroo* was only permitted to hop over the French border as a law-abiding *kangourou*. By contrast, *zebu* and *emu* were accepted into English, without changing to *zebue* and *emue,* to match English spelling rules.

1604 First English dictionary, with meanings, instead of just word lists in English and Latin. It contained 3,000 "hard words" by Robert Cawdrey, a country school master, who wrote it because he saw the need for it, to explain the meaning of English words.

1611 King James (or Authorized) Bible was published which took seven years and fifty-four translators from Latin, Greek and Hebrew. It used a lot of Tyndale's much-loved New Testament, but not his simple spelling.

1620 Mayflower and other expeditions took English settlers and the English language to America.

1634 Académie Française was set up, to preserve the dignity and integrity of the French language. It decides on the meaning of French words and on the addition of new words, making French a *fixed* language. French spelling was simplified.

1649 King Charles was executed and England became a Protectorate, not a kingdom, until 1659. A great many books and poems were written about revolutionary Oliver Cromwell, both for and against him.

1660 Samuel Pepys began his diary, an excellent record of everyday English.

1775 Samuel Johnson's Dictionary of the English Language describes English words. Neither prescribes nor decides, but records current spelling. This took Johnson and six men six years to produce. It includes vulgar slang, English "as it is".

1800 English speakers were increasing in number, but English was still a minor language compared to French, Russian, Italian, German, and others.

1803 English spreads further when French territory is sold by Napoleon to English-speaking Americans and Canadians.

1828 Noah Webster's American dictionary was published, double the size of Johnson's. After 15 year's work Noah had to remove most of his spelling reforms to ensure it sold enough copies to repay debt and support his wife and 8 children.

1842 The Philological Society was established in England by men who had to be both "learned and leisured". Many on the committee believed that making French spelling and reading easy had brought on the French Revolution. Education was a privilege in England. They were all impressed by a new book, *Principles of Geology*, by Charles Lyall. They said to each other, "We can look at a stone and see its history, see from scratch marks it has come from a glacier, or see from its shape it has rolled in a river bed, or see from its layers it comes from more than one place. Let's make sure that we can look at a word and see from its letters where it comes from."

They agreed it was time to spell each word just one way, instead of many ways. It was time to choose just one way to spell *although*, for instance. From *altho, althô, althagh,* and *although* they chose the one with letters to show its Germanic, Old English, past.

1848 English speaking Americans take over California and New Mexico, ousting Spanish-speaking Mexican colonists.

In **1858** the Philological Society began recording their choice of spelling for each word, in a dictionary called "A New English Dictionary on Historical Principles", NED for short. They took 23 years to produce part one, A to Ant. It was published in 1928 as *The Oxford English Dictionary* (OED). It prescribed English, deciding on just one way to spell each word, to reflect history, but rules and reasons for each spelling were not included.

1880 Konrad Duden produced his famous German dictionary, still in use today. Its written spelling, encoding, is based on southern German and is continually being improved to match up sounds and letters better and better.

1898 Theodor Siebs produced his famous pronunciation rules for decoding written German. German was always spoken way beyond the borders of Germany and in many forms. Pronunciation rules favour northern German.

By **1900**, English was one of the world's major languages, second to French for diplomacy and then first after World War I. The Treaty of Versailles was drafted in English and translated into French. In science publications it shared a prominent role with French and German. English asserted its overwhelming role only in the third quarter of the century, as an important second language in many former British colonies and American dependencies.

In **1950** George Bernard Shaw's will provided prize money for an alphabet with a letter for each word-sound. Mr Kingsley Read's winning entry gave different sounds to upper-case and lower-case letters, a possible 52 sounds. For instance, TiNk spelt think and huNgD spelt hunger. Punctuation marks were the same but there were no initial capitals. Proper nouns began /, e.g., /fred spelt Fred and /rOm spelt Rome. It did not catch on for it was based purely on how words sound. As we learn from Shaw himself in *Pygmalion*, later filmed as *My Fair Lady*, we all pronounce English differently.

By **1980** first spell checkers became available on personal computers.

1996 — latest spelling reforms in Germany, e.g., when to use <s> and <sz> to spell [s] and <ts> and <ß> to spell [z].

There is still no reform system for English spelling, just British vs. American spell check programs. However, by **2000** English was indispensable in prestigious domains such as business, trade, and technology. Five hundred and fifty years after printing on paper was invented, the English computer scientist, Tim Berners-Lee, invented the World Wide Web and Hypertext-Markup-Language.

English, a stew of words from all over the world, continues to spread across that world. Modern English is not a 'pure' language, because Old English declensions and conjugations were neglected and English words replaced with French and other foreign words. It has a huge vocabulary but a very limited use of words in everyday speech. It's said to be easy to learn to speak but hard to read and write. Including non-native speakers, English is used more than any other language. Counting only those whose first language is English, it is the third most used in the world.

Bibliography
Books
Anon. 1858 *Enquire Within Upon Everything, The Great Victorian Domestic Standby.* EBook #10766 online at www.gutenberg.net Release Date: January 21, 2004.
Austin, Peter. 1992 *A Dictionary of Yinggarda, Western Australia.* Linguistics, La Trobe Univ.
Austin, Peter. 1992 *A Dictionary of Payungu, Western Australia.* Linguistics, La Trobe Univ
Austin, Peter. 1992 *A Dictionary of Thalanji, Western Australia.* Linguistics, La Trobe Univ
Austin, Peter. 1992 *A Dictionary of Tharrgari, Western Australia.* Linguistics, La Trobe Univ
Ayto, John. 1990 *Bloomsbury Dictionary of Word Origins. The histories of over 8,000 words explained.* ISBN 0 7475 0971 9.
Bates, Daisy, edited White, Isobel. 1985 *The native tribes of Western Australia.* ISBN 0642993335
Bates, Daisy. 2004 *My Natives and I.* Hesperian Press. ISBN 085905313X.
Barnhart, Robert K. (editor) 2000 Managing Ed. Sol Steinmetz *Chambers Dictionary of Etymology The Origins and Development of Over 25,000 English Words* (previously Barhart Dictionary of Etymology) ISBN 0 550 14230 4.
Blake, Barry J. 1981 *Australian Aboriginal languages, a general introduction.* Angus and Robertson ISBN 0 207 14044 8.
Boston, Paquita. 1990 *A Compendium of Mnemonics, Memory Bridges along the Road to Learning* Unpublished ms.
Boston, Paquita. 2004 *What's in a Name? Place Names of the Gascoyne.* ISBN 0-9756744-0-4 WA Museum Printer.
Boston, Paquita. 2009, 2010, 2014 *Reading with Rules*, first edition, first and second revision. Print to order, Digital Print Australia.
Boston, Paquita. 2014 *The Inside Story on English Spelling* Dr Zed Publishing, ISBN-10 0975674439; ISBN-13 978-0975674437, e-book, paper book, on Amazon etc.
Bryson, Bill. 1990 *Mother Tongue* Penguin Books ISBN 0-140-14305-X.
Bryson, Bill, 2004 *Bryson's Dictionary of Troublesome Words.* Broadway Books, New York ISBN 0-7679-1043-5. (Thank you Chris.)
Burbridge, Kate. 2002 *Blooming English. Observations on the roots, cultivation and hybrids of the English language.* ABC Book Sydney, then 2004 Cambridge University Press ISBN 0521548322.
Burbridge, Kate. 2004 *Weeds in the Garden of Words. Tangled History of the English Language* ISBN 0 7333 14104 Australian Broadcasting Commission.
Burton, Tom. 2004 *Long Words Bother Me.* Sutton Publ. ISBN 07509 3973 7.
Butler, James Davie. Oct 1986 *British Convicts Shipped to American Colonies, American Historical Review* 2, pp 12-33.
Butterworth, John. 2001 *Word Power, The Essential Guide to the History of Words.* The Word Power Series for Children. Illustrated by Nicholls, Lee. Oxford Univ. Press ISBN 0-19-911160-X.
Clendon, Arthur and Vince, J.H. 1931 *The Clarendon Latin Course* publ. Clarendon Press Oxford.
Cockburn, Rodney. 1990 *South Australia. What's in a Name? Historically significant place names.* ISBN 09592519 Axiom Publ.

Crystal, David. 1987 *The Cambridge Encyclopedia of Language*. Cambridge University Press ISBN 0-521-42443-7. (Thank you, Roger Boston.)
Cummings, D. W. 1988 *American English Spelling, An Informal Description.* John Hopkins University Press ISBN 0-8018-3443-0.
Davies, Lyn. 2006 *A is for Ox*. The Folio Society, U.K. (Thank you, Vic and Cecilie Hadlow in N.Z.)
Education Department Western Australia, director Alison Dewsbury 1997 *First Steps Reading Resource Book* Rigby Heinemann ISBN 0 7312 2356 X.
Education Department Western Australia 1997 *First Steps Spelling Resource Book* Rigby Heinemann ISBN 0 7312 2362 4.
Education Department Western Australia 1997 *First Steps Spelling Developmental Continuum* Rigby Heinemann ISBN 0 7312 2361 6.
Education Department Western Australia 2005 *First Steps Writing Map of Development, Addressing Current Literacy Challenges, 2nd Edition.* Rigby Heinemann ISBN 978 0 7312 4101 9.
Encyclopedia Americana International Edition 1829 Grolier Inc. Connecticut.
Fleck, Heather, manager. *The Word Origin Calendar 2007,* Accord Publishing ISBN 1-57939-264-4.
Fowler HW revised by Gowers, Sir Ernest. 1968 *Fowler's Modern English Usage* Oxford at Clarendon Press.
Fox, B.J. and Hull, M.A. 2002 *Phonics for the Teaching of Reading*. 8th Ed. publ. Merrill Prentice Hall 2002 ISBN 0-13-026538-1. (Thank you, Ally.)
Gold, J.S. 1920 *The Australian Progressive Spelling Book* ©Commonwealth and New Zealand. Publ. Adelaide, Hussey and Gillingham.
Halliday, F.E. 1975 *The Excellence of the English Tongue* London ISBN 0 575 02020 2.
Halliday, M.A.K. 1985 *Spoken and written language*. Deakin Univ. ISBN 0 7300 0309 4.
Hewitt, 11. Marmeduke and Beach, George. 1890 *A Manual of Our Mother Tongue*. Morrison and Gibb, Printers, Edinburgh. (Thank you, David Shelton.)
Hince, Bernadette. 2000 *Antarctic Dictionary* CSIRO Publishing.
Hince, B. 2000 ***Antarctic Dictionary.*** CSIRO Publishing.
Jackson, Eugene and Rubio, Antonio. 1981 *French Made Simple*. Heinemann, London.
Jacob, Henry. 1950 *Printed English, consistency in good style*. Publ. Sylvan Press London.
Jespersen, Otto. 1938 *Growth and Structure of the English Language*. Publ. Basil Blackwell ISBN 0 631 12987 1, Pbk.
Konstam, Angus. 2002 *Historical Atlas of the Viking World* ISBN 1902886038.
Lerer, Professor Seth. 1998 *The History of the English Language. Vols 1, 2 and 3 Tape-recorded Course Guidebook,* The Teaching Company www.TEACH12.com, (Thank you, Ally.)
Lewis, Norman 1965 *20 Days to Better Spelling* Hodder and Stoughten Ltd.
Lynch, Adriana. 2004 *How Should Reading Be Taught To Special Needs Children?* Essay for Campbellsville University, towards B. Ed. specializing in Remedial Education. (Thank you, Ally.)
Lonergan, Dymphna, *Ozwords,* Nov.**2002** in www.anu.edu.au/ANDC/ozwords.
Matthews, C. M. 1979 *Words Words Words* ISBN 0 7188 2341 9.
McGuinness, Diane, 1997 *Why Our Children Can't Read and What We Can Do About It.* Publ. Simon and Schuster ISBN 0-684-85356-6. (Thank you, Ally.)
McWhorter, John 2008 *Our Magnificent Bastard Tongue — The Untold History of English* Gotham Books ISBN978-1-592-40395-0.
Mercer Cecil D., Mercer Ann R. 2001 *Teaching Students with Learning Problems.* Merrill Prentice Hall ISBN 0 13 089296 3. (Thank you, Ally.)
Miles, Elaine. 2005 *English words and their Spelling* Publ. Whurr ISBN 1 861564899.

Miles, Elaine. 2005 *English words and Their Spelling, A history of phonological conflicts.* Publ. Whurr ISBN 1 86156 489 9. (Thank you, Ally.)
Moore, Bruce 2008 *Speaking Our Language, The story of Australian English* Oxford University Press Aust and NZ 9780195565782.
Muirden, W. 1913 *The Commonwealth Spelling Book* G Hassell and Son, 104 Currie St, Adelaide.
Nupela Testamen **1969** *The New Testament in New Guinea Pidgin* (*Neo-Melanesian*) The British and Foreign Bible Society, Luther Press, Madang, TPNG.
Hawkins, Joyce H and Turner, George W, compilers 1983 *Oxford Paperback Dictionary, The* (OPD) Melb. Oxford Univ Press, ISBN 019 55 4556 7.
Potter, Simeon. 1966 *Our Language.* Penguin.
Pyles, Thomas and Algeo, John. 1993 *The ORIGINS and DEVELOPMENT of the ENGLISH LANGUAGE 4th Edition* ISBN 0-1550-0168-X. (Thank you, Ally.)
Quinion, Michael. 2002 *Oxford ologie and isms, Word Beginnings and Endings.* Oxford Univ. Press ISBN 0-10-280123-6.
Quirk, Randolph and Wrenn, C.L. 1957 *An Old English Grammar* Publ. Methuen & Co. SBN 416 77240 4.
Ramson W.S. 1966 *Australian English: An Historic Study of Vocabulary 1788-1898* publ. ANU.
Readers Digest 2001 *Wordpower Dictionary* ISBN 0 276 42463 8.
Robinson, Andrew 1995 *Alphabets, Hieroglyphs & Pictograms, The Story of Writing*, Thames and Hudson ISBN 0-500-01665-8.
Samuels M.L. 1975 *Linguistic Evolution with special reference to English* Publ. Cambridge University Press ISBN 0 521 09913 7.
Shaywitz, S. E.; Shaywitz, B.A. 2001 The Neurobiology of Reading and Dyslexia. *Focus on Basics,* Vol. 5, Issue A. August 2001.
Swadesh, Morris. 2006 *The Origin and Diversification of Language.* Ed. Sherzer Joel F ISBN 0-202-30841-3.
The Oxford Paperback Dictionary, Australian Edition, Oxford University Press ISBN 0 19 554556 7
Thompson, Meryl. 1980 *Understanding English Spelling* ISBN 0-9594392-1-8 The Bureau 135 Gilles St., Adelaide.
Twain, Mark. 2006 *The Wayward Tourist* ISBN 978 0 522 85312 4 Melbourne University Press.
Von Brandenstein, C.G. 1998 *Nyungar Anew, Introduction.* Pacific Linguistics, Series C, No. 99. ANU.
Waldman, Niall McLeod. 2004 *Spelling Dearest* Publ. What The Dickens Press. ISBN 1-4184-5330-7 (Thank you, Ally.)
Watson, Don. 2003 *Death Sentence The decay of public language* Publ. Vintage Press ISBN 1-74051-278-2.
Webster, Noah edited McKechnie, Jean. 1962 *Webster's New Twentieth Century Dictionary of the English Language Unabridged* Publ. World Publishing Company N.Y.
Whitaker-Wilson C. 1976 *english pronounced* Sun Books Melbourne ISBN 0 7251 02209.
Winchester, Simon. 1998 *The Surgeon of Crowthorne: A Tale of Murder, Madness and the Oxford English Dictionary.*
Winchester, Simon. 2003 *The Meaning of Everything, The Story of the Oxford English Dictionary.* Oxford University Press ISBN 0-19-860702-4.
Yamaji Language Centre 1997 *Wajarri, The Language of the Murchison.* yamaji@wn.com.au.

Websites
http://spellingexplained.com, book orders, Dress-up Photo Gallery, questions and complaints.

Prof. Don Cummings' website: http://www.dwcummings.com "A site for Spellers, Teachers of Spelling and Reading, and Students of English Words."
http://en.wikipedia.org, Wikipedia, the free encyclopedia, for instance, in Wikipedia, Question_mark covers the origins and uses of punctuation marks and Stress_(linguistics) gives ways to stress syllables.
http://en.wikisource.org/wiki/The_American_Language/Chapter_31 Overview of English-American word differences.
http://www.morewords.com A good site for searching for letter combinations.
http://www.wikihow.com/Pronounce-Latin for Latin pronunciation, for instance.
http://www.etymonline.com Free Etymology Dictionary for the origin of words.
http//www.spellingsociety.org The Simplified Spelling Society's website.
http://www.bartleby.com/211/0202.html Runes in Scandinavian and Old English Literature – some of the secret powers of spelling.
https://en.wikipedia.org/wiki/Pronunciation_of_English_(th)
https://www.bookbrunch.co.uk/page/free-article/the-british-and-reading-a-short-history is Dominic Selwood's short history of British literacy.

www.ingramcontent.com/pod-product-compliance
Lightning Source LLC
Chambersburg PA
CBHW081352070526
44583CB00020B/2532